The Social Foundations Reader

This book is part of the Peter Lang Education list.
Every volume is peer reviewed and meets
the highest quality standards for content and production.

PETER LANG
New York • Bern • Frankfurt • Berlin
Brussels • Vienna • Oxford • Warsaw

The Social Foundations Reader

Critical Essays on Teaching, Learning
and Leading in the 21st Century

Edited by Eleanor Blair and Yolanda Medina

PETER LANG
New York • Bern • Frankfurt • Berlin
Brussels • Vienna • Oxford • Warsaw

Library of Congress Cataloging-in-Publication Data

Names: Blair, Eleanor, editor. | Medina, Yolanda, editor.
Title: The social foundations reader: critical essays on teaching, learning
and leading in the 21st century / edited by Eleanor Blair, Yolanda Medina.
Description: New York: Peter Lang, 2016.
Includes bibliographical references and index.
Identifiers: LCCN 2015029769 | ISBN 978-1-4331-2942-1 (hardcover: alk. paper)
ISBN 978-1-4331-2941-4 (paperback: alk. paper) | ISBN 978-1-4539-15844 (e-book)
Subjects: LCSH: Critical pedagogy. | Education—Social aspects.
Classification: LCC LC196.S628 2016 | DDC 370.11/5—dc23
LC record available at http://lccn.loc.gov/2015029769

Bibliographic information published by **Die Deutsche Nationalbibliothek.**
Die Deutsche Nationalbibliothek lists this publication in the "Deutsche
Nationalbibliografie"; detailed bibliographic data are available
on the Internet at http://dnb.d-nb.de/.

Cover art by Maria Fernanda D'Alessandro, Dominican independent artist.

This book is for our social foundation students; past, present and future. You are the reason that we do what we do. The future of public education and the lives of many children are in your hands. Never doubt the seriousness of your work and remember that the debate is as important as the resolution. EJB/YM

Contents

SECTION II
SOCIAL JUSTICE AND CRITICAL THEORY IN THE SCHOOLHOUSE

SECTION III
TEACHING, LEARNING AND LEADING AGAINST THE GRAIN

SECTION IV
TEACHERS IN 21ST CENTURY SCHOOLS

SECTION V
"SHIFT HAPPENS": CONTEMPORARY ISSUES OF EQUITY AND DIVERSITY

Foreword

Critical Social Foundations in the Corporate Academy

William M. Reynolds

Georgia Southern University

Questioning the ostensibly unquestionable premises of our way of life is arguably the most urgent of services we owe our fellow humans and ourselves. —Bauman (1998, p. 5)

Thus, a life of dissent requires us to expel the "success myths" of capital that pollute the ivy-covered halls of academia and to reject the warped and distorted privileges of power, preserved and doled out to the obedient servants of the empire. And as such, dissident voices reject the incarcerations of our minds and bodies, by the neat and orderly colonizing rationale that conserves the hegemonic order. —Darder (2011, p. 5)

Introduction

In 1994, Rebecca Martusewicz and I edited a book entitled *Inside/Out: Contemporary Critical Perspectives in Education.* We discussed, along with others, how the foundations of education within the context of critical theory and critical pedagogy had the potential of turning people "inside/out" a phrase used by a student in one of our foundations classes. She was describing the experience of her readings and class discussions. The inside surface had been turned to the outside: "Things are no longer seen 'as they usually are'; that some other aspect or new way of looking is brought to our attention; what was once a boundary, frontier, or surface is gone, replaced by another" (Martusewicz & Reynolds, 1994, p. 2). That is the point with critical foundations of education. It can turn "normal" understandings of society, equity, diversity, justice, schooling, curriculum, pedagogy, students, and teachers inside/out. Questions need to be raised about all of it. That was 21 years ago. After teaching educational foundations and curriculum studies for 30 years, I still believe there is the necessity to continually emphasize and reemphasize critical perspectives in both. That is the primary reason *The Social Foundations Reader: Critical Essays on Teaching, Learning and Leading in the 21ˢᵗ Century* by Eleanor J. Blair and Yolanda Medina is crucial for these times. What times, you may ask?

Fast-forward to 2015. Education and schooling have not been turned inside/out but outside/in to a corporate neoliberal nightmare. The neoliberal agenda is to destroy public education and turn it into a race to the bottom—the bottom line that is. The litany of horrors in public schools, meant to educate smart (knowing large quantities of disconnected information), docile consumers, is legendary. The current nightmare includes: standardization, state-developed curriculum, scripted lesson plans, predetermined state objectives, computerized reading tests (constructed by the Accelerated Reading Program Software), i-Ready[1] (computerized instruction), and state-mandated tests (developed by very lucrative textbook/testing corporations such as Pearson) to make sure teachers are compliantly implementing and depositing what they are told to implement and deposit. It is an effort to assure that critical approaches to pedagogy and the effort to produce critical citizens interested in questions concerning social justice are daily thwarted. As Giroux (2013) writes,

> Welcome to the dystopian world of corporate education in which learning how to think, be informed by public values, and become engaged critical citizens are viewed as a failure rather than a mark of success. Instead of producing "a generation of leaders worthy of the challenges,"[2] the dystopian mission of public and higher education is to produce robots, technocrats, and compliant workers. There is more than a backlash at work in these assaults on public and higher education: there is a sustained effort to dismantle education as a pillar of democracy, public values, critical thought, social responsibility, and civic courage. (p. 1)

As Giroux indicates, the public schools were only the first step in the long march of neoliberalism. The destruction of colleges of education is the insidious current move of corporate/neoliberalism. An initial unspoken maneuver is to discourage and ultimately prevent any alternative teaching or content that presents critical perspectives. The foundations of education courses become a target in this agenda as well as critical academics who teach foundations courses within a critical context. The first step on the march to destroy is the takeover of undergraduate teacher education by corporations. It is the move to privatize teacher education. Undergraduate foundations course syllabi are given direction, objectives, and strategies from the state education departments. These, in many cases, can be proactively challenged. The more difficult intrusion to contest is the onslaught of Pearson Corporation into teacher education and teacher certification. Pearson's "sales were up in 2012 to 6.1 billion pounds or $9.21 billon" (Singer, 2013, p. 10). Pearson's edTPA is used as the final step in teacher certification. Currently there are 606 Educator Preparation Programs in 33 states and the District of Columbia participating in edTPA[3] (AACTE, 2015, p. 1). This is the face of teacher education at the present time. Outside corporations are determining whether pre-service teachers become certified. On Pearson's assessment webpage, the process is lauded:

> edTPA includes a review of a teacher candidate's authentic teaching materials. This serves as a culmination of a teaching and learning process that documents and demonstrates each candidate's ability to effectively teach his/her subject matter to all students. (Pearson, 2015, p. 1)

This is what Deleuze warned about concerning education in general. It has turned into a continual assessment factory. It is the businessification of education:

> Even the state education system has been looking at the principle of "getting paid for results": in fact, just as businesses are replacing factories, school is being replaced by continuing education and exams by continuous assessment. It is the surest way of turning education into a business. (Deleuze, 1995, p. 179)

The Dismantling of the Critical Social Foundations of Education

Sadly, the evidence shared in this article suggests that corporate teacher preparation does not support coursework, faculty, or scholarship in educational foundations. In fact, the opposite is present: Corporations maximize profits by preparing school personnel with scripted curricula, by hiring adjunct instructors (many of whom do not hold terminal degrees), by developing online technical coursework and by generating computerized examinations. (Hartlep & Porfilio, 2015, p. 305)

I believe, after 30 years of working to present critical perspectives and critical pedagogy in Social Foundations and Curriculum Studies classes, the ways in which the neoliberal agenda currently works is the dismantling of Colleges of Education and certainly implicit in that dismantling is the expunging of any critical perspectives in any aspect of undergraduate or graduate education. How does the process work? There is, of course, the nuclear option for neoliberals. That is to eliminate Educational Studies or Foundations programs entirely from universities. The rationale is always budget issues. For example, Emory University proposed eliminating its Educational Studies program and The University of Akron "suspended" its Educational Foundations and Social, Philosophical Foundations of Education coursework at the master's level. This is a dangerous trend for critical programs and critical scholars and will, no doubt, continue.

In other cases, critical programs go through a process that calls their existence into question (Reynolds, 2013). This process applies to courses or programs that exhibit critical orientations.[4] The first step in this process is to delegitimize the scholarship that critical scholars and their students produce. The research is characterized as not "real" research. Questions are raised. How is doing research about issues such as social justice, identity formation, popular culture, and so on educational research? There is a need on the part of critical scholars in educational foundations and other areas to constantly defend their scholarly work. It is an attempt to rein in critical work. And, if there is a constant need to defend one's scholarly work, there is less time to actually do the work. The second level in this process is to challenge a program or particular courses. Criticism against critical programs in education starts with the attack on the theoretical nature of the programs and eventually to attacks on the required readings in courses. Of course, the charge of "overly theoretical" programs is illustrative of a fear of theory, and its misunderstanding. It is also a politically regressive, anti-intellectual move to limit the nature of the study of education. There is an underlying fear that theory might, indeed, enable teachers to imagine and think differently about educational issues and their own practice, which could lead to challenging questions about taken-for-granted assumptions in current educational practice.[5] As Giroux (2012) explains,

> Theory is the condition that enables teachers and students to be self-reflexive, develop better forms of knowledge and classroom skills, and gain an understanding of the contexts in which they teach and learn. In fact, these contexts of teaching and learning have already been constituted through struggles over theories that make claim to legitimating what kind of knowledge and practice counts in a classroom. (p. 80)

Another step in this process of dismantling is the attack on individual scholars. The scholars, who challenge the taken-for-granted, find their questioning and critique results in institutional punishment that does not go unnoticed by colleagues who might consider working in critical perspectives. These scholars, particularly in social foundations, suffer under horrendous course loads, denied presentations, funding, or awards. In the corporate university where job intensification is the rule, this treatment is yet another way to discourage and prevent critical perspectives and work in social foundations.

The Failure to Quit

> All of which brings us back again to the preeminence of education experience and to its eminently ethical character, which in its turn leads us to the radical nature of "hope." In other words, though I know that things can get worse, I also know that I am able to intervene to improve them. (Freire, 1998, p. 53)

Despite these dreadful maneuvers by the corporate university with its neoliberal agenda, critical work in the social foundations of education continues. Critical perspectives in the social foundations are more urgent than ever. Howard Zinn described the official charge when he and 550 others were arrested for protesting Reagan's blockade of Nicaragua at the Federal building in Boston. The official charge was

"*Failure to Quit*" (Zinn, 2009, p. 723). The editors and the authors of this volume demonstrate the failure to quit. From the Deweyan perspectives in *My Pedagogic Creed*, to issues of social justice, critical theory, teaching, learning and leading against the grain, 21st century schools, to issues of equity and diversity, these editors and authors demonstrate that critical perspectives need to be read by all involved in education. And, that the social foundations courses and scholarship play an indispensable role in providing a critical education for students who are being trained to be consumer citizens in our public schools and universities. The failure to quit on educating for critical citizens who can work for social justice in the cruel, nightmarish world of the 21st century is a most needed strength.

As critical social foundations educators work with critical theory and critical pedagogy in the 21st century and struggle to have their students understand issues of social justice, equity and diversity, they become more visible and more vulnerable:

> Your challenge now makes you individually more visible and thus more vulnerable. If you are in the opposition instead of safely inside the established consensus (the official curriculum), you risk being fired, or not getting a promotion, or not getting a pay raise, or not getting the courses you want to teach, or the schedule you want, or the leave you apply for or even in some cases you become the target of ultra-conservative groups. (Shor & Freire, 1986, p. 54)

Social foundations texts and courses that are tailored not only to an unquestioning, taken-for-granted point of view, but also support corporate principles and methods are legion. Given that we are experiencing these nightmarish times concerning educational foundations and education in general, a book like *The Social Foundations Reader: Critical Essays on Teaching, Learning and Leading in the 21st Century*, with its stellar lineup of critical chapters, is an absolute necessity for those of who continue to struggle for social justice and a more humane world.

Notes

1.   I-Ready is an individualized computer instruction program where all students and the teachers sit at computers and the interaction in class is on the computer. As the website from *Curriculum Associates,* an independently owned company selling programs to schools, states: "Based on the Diagnostic results, i-Ready automatically provides individualized online and teacher-led instruction targeted to each student's unique needs. In addition, easy-to-read reports provide teachers with a detailed action plan for individual and group instruction and the tools to deliver that instruction in any style learning environment" (Curriculum Associates, 2015).
2.   Giroux (2013) cites David Theo Goldberg, "The University We Are For," Huffington Post (November 28, 2011). Online: http://www.huffingtonpost.com/david-theo-goldberg/university-california-protests_b_1106234.html
3.   The edTPA website breaks down states' participation in their assessments in the following way:
     1. States that use edTPA as the assessment for teacher state licensure: Washington, Oregon, California, Minnesota, Iowa, Illinois, Wisconsin, New York, Georgia, Tennessee, and Hawaii;
     2. States moving toward implementation: Alabama and Ohio;
     3. States participating in edTPA: Idaho, Wyoming, Colorado, Arizona, Texas, Oklahoma, Arkansas, Florida, Michigan, Indiana, South Carolina, North Carolina, Virginia West Virginia, Maryland, Pennsylvania, New Jersey and Connecticut. (AACTE, 2015)
4.   See Reynolds (2013), pp. 233–235.
5.   Reynolds (2013), p. 233.

References

American Association of Colleges for Teacher Education. (2015). *edTPA participation map*. Retrieved from http://edtpa.aacte.org/state-policy

Bauman, Z. (1998). *Globalization: The human consequences*. New York: Columbia University Press.

Curriculum Associates (2015). What is an adaptive diagnostic? Retrieved from http://www.curriculumassociates.com/products/iready/iready-adaptive-diagnostic-assessment.aspx

Darder, A. (2011). *A dissident voice: Essays on culture, pedagogy, and power*. New York: Peter Lang.

Deleuze, G. (1995). *Negotiations: 1972–1990* (M. Joughin, Trans.). New York: Columbia University Press.

Giroux, H. A. (2012*). Education and the crisis of public values: Challenging the assault on teachers, students, & public education.* New York: Peter Lang.

Giroux, H. A. (2013). Beyond dystopian education in a neoliberal society. *Fast Capitalism*, 10.1. Retrieved from http://www.uta.edu/huma/agger/fastcapitalism/10_1/giroux10_1.html

Hartlep, N. D. & Porfilio, B. J. (2015). Revitalizing the field of educational foundations and PK-20 educator's commitment to social justice and issues of equity in the age of neoliberalism. *Educational Studies: A Journal of the American Educational Studies Association, 51*(4), pp. 300–316.

Martusewicz, R. A. & Reynolds, W. M. (1994). *Inside/out: Contemporary critical perspectives in education.* New York: St. Martin's Press.

Pearson (2015). *Assessment.* Retrieved from http://www.pearsonassessments.com/teacherlicensure/edtpa.html

Reynolds, W. M. (2013). "Won't back down": Counter-narratives of visibility and vulnerability in a bleak house. In E. Daniels & B. J. Porfilio (Eds.), *Dangerous counterstories in the corporate academy: Narrating for understanding, solidarity, resistance and community in the age of neoliberalism* (pp. 225–240). Charlotte, NC: Information Age Publishing.

Singer, A. (2013, March 19). Pearson rakes in the profits. The Huffington Post. Retrieved from http://www.huffingtonpost.com/alan-singer/pearson-education-profits_b_2902642.html

Zinn, H. (2009). *The Zinn reader: Writing on disobedience and democracy.* New York: Seven Stories Press.

Introduction

Eleanor J. Blair and Yolanda Medina

The relevance of introductory foundations of education classes to teacher preparation is often debated by those who would like to capture those credit hours for other purposes. And yet, these courses have survived decades of assaults and mutations that reflect efforts to accommodate the needs of competing interests, retaining content related to the historical, social and philosophical foundations of education. If truth is going to be told here, most students have few ideas about what the social foundations represent and many ideas about the lack of importance of these interdisciplinary courses to the practice of teaching in K–12 schools. With this fact in mind, the content of this textbook was selected in an attempt to present the most interesting and compelling ideas of foundations of education scholars within a critical context that promotes a connection between theory and practice. The goal here is to facilitate the development of teachers who actively question taken-for-granted assumptions about how we "do" schooling in the 21st century; teachers who will question not just the context for education, but the content as well.

In social foundations courses, students will often begin the journey from sitting in classrooms as students to leading classrooms of students. Within this context, the study of the social foundations of education has the potential to challenge students to understand the powerful roles and responsibilities of teachers while simultaneously encouraging them to consider how they will negotiate and reconcile the needs of diverse learners. In foundations of education classes, students begin to understand the multiple lenses through which schools can be viewed as both benevolent and malignant institutions, possessing the power to heal and promote or destroy the minds and souls of the children who show up on their doorsteps each year. Like many of my students, as a beginning teacher, I saw schools through the lens of my personal experience; my perspective was limited and seldom challenged by a consideration of the issues and concerns associated with diversity, equity and social justice. In this book, we attempt to introduce teachers to the questions attached to a critical analysis of contemporary schools through the interdisciplinary work of scholars who have significantly impacted our ideas about teaching and learning in the public domain. The discussion and dialogue that emerge from a consideration of these ideas will hopefully be characterized by more questions than answers and a growing certainty that there is no single solution for the problems faced by 21st century schools.

As social foundations professors, we constantly aspire to create courses that contain experiences that are relevant to students' lives, both personally and professionally. However, we are also very aware that many students, both graduate and undergraduate, question the lack of relevance between social foundations courses and issues they are grappling with in 21st century schools. The critical pedagogical beliefs introduced in this text challenge students to consider the roles of privilege, oppression, and marginalization in their own educational experiences, and for many students, this produces discomfort. Students want to believe that they earned their place in the academy through hard work and personal merit; however, considering schools as political spheres where there is a strong correlation between power and privilege and access to knowledge shifts the focus of teaching and learning, and as such, redefines notions of success, achievement and merit. The discussion becomes even more complicated when one considers the tension between the democratic ideals espoused by Dewey (1897) and the private, corporate interests that seek to take over schools using egalitarian mantras that disguise the valuing of profit over ideology. Surprising to most students is the understanding that teaching is always political; there is no such thing as "just teaching"; within their own classrooms, teachers are pedagogical political entrepreneurs, and yet, praxis is often mediated by competing interests (and politics). John Goodlad (2004) was right on target when he suggested that "we must prepare teachers for the schools of tomorrow, not for the schools of today." The students who will use this book are the teachers of tomorrow and preparing them to assume their roles as political actors on the frontlines of schools across American is no easy task. Meaningful reform of 21st century schools will demand that these students participate in creating educational spaces that challenge traditional notions of success and challenge the sources of oppression and marginalization. This textbook is a starting point on that journey, a journey that, by necessity, requires teacher leaders who function as 21st century change agents and participate in a redefinition of teacher roles and responsibilities.

Teachers, Schools and Society

A beginning point for understanding what happens in schools must, by necessity, begin with teachers. Historically, teaching has often been a temporary "blip" in the career paths of individuals on the way to somewhere else. Recently, Ravitch (2010) noted,

> Between 40 percent and 50 percent of new teachers do not survive the first five years. Maybe they couldn't manage the classes; maybe they were disappointed by working conditions; maybe teaching was not for them; maybe they felt that they were unsuccessful; or maybe they decided to enter another profession. For whatever reason, the job is so demanding that nearly half of those who enter teaching choose to leave at an early stage in their career. (p. 177)

This reality is often obscured in discussions of school reform and accountability; the "talk" is all about making education a top priority, but no one is really talking about the fact that schools today still perpetuate myths regarding democratic schools that don't acknowledge the systematic oppression and marginalization that occurs daily for both teachers and students working in these public institutions. Ultimately, and this is the fundamental argument in this book, teachers' work and teachers' voices must be the frontline of any meaningful reform of the schools. Only then will teaching and learning begin to embrace a 21st century ideology that critically examines teaching and learning as political acts embedded in the complexities of bureaucratic agencies operating on behalf of individuals representing corporate/capitalist interests in America. Giroux (2012) argues this point in the following:

> We need to take teachers seriously by giving them the autonomy, dignity, labor conditions, salaries, freedom, time, and support they deserve. The restoration, expansion, and protection of public school

teaching as a public service may be the most important challenge Americans will face in the twenty-first century. (p. 12)

Questions about teacher's work, schools and schooling are related to school reform efforts in profound ways. Thinking about teachers' work within the framework of critical ideologies provides both a challenge and impetus to address the daily assaults on teachers and public education. This book is about thinking about teachers, teaching and schools as revolutionary, transformational phenomena that have the potential of upending previous notions of what schooling and education represent in 21st century schools. Even when teachers get "it" and understand that education is much more than the quantified, minimalist definitions promoted by the accountability measures that have proliferated schools and classrooms, their desires to do more in schools and classrooms are often uninformed by an ideology that might shape and direct their actions with purpose and focus. In effect, teachers have been regularly positioned to enter a semi-profession, attempting to survive and take the road most frequently traveled, supporting the status quo and quickly get tenure.

Foundations of education scholars understand that the problems in public education are deeply engrained in the ideological wars that have dominated the public schools from the very beginning; the problems are resilient and resistant to easy solutions. These problems will require smart teachers doing smart things. Giroux (1988) argues, "In the broadest sense, teachers as intellectuals have to be seen in terms of the ideological and political interests that structure the nature of the discourse, classroom social relations, and values that they legitimate in their teaching ... teachers should become transformative intellectuals if they are to educate students to be active, critical citizens" (p. 127). And herein lies the most important issue, the "problems" that exist in schools today are not just teaching and learning issues that can be solved through political actions and mandates. The "real problems" have a lot to do with teachers who are well-educated, but seldom given the authority to operate as intellectual decision-makers. As transformative intellectuals, teachers would be prepared at every level, both preservice and inservice, to assume roles as researchers and scholars as well as educational practitioners. Teachers would have the tools needed to analyze and design classrooms and schools that facilitate critical thought and action, while recognizing that teaching and learning are endeavors that require these environments to be structured in such a way that they are responsive to a constantly changing milieu. According to Giroux (1988), "central to the category of transformative intellectual is the necessity of making the pedagogical more political and the political more pedagogical" (p. 127). His discussion concludes with the idea that "transformative intellectuals need to develop a discourse that unites the language of critique with the language of possibility, so that social educators recognize they can make changes. In doing so, they must speak out against economic, political and social injustices both within and outside of schools" (p. 128). As teacher educators, we daily confront the chasm between preparing graduate students to teach in traditional school environs and teaching teachers as intellectuals who will enter teaching with a well-defined vision for their roles as teachers, a vision infused with hope and possibilities that will guide the choices and decisions they make as educational leaders. In this way, teacher leadership is redefined and represents a radical repositioning of conversations about teachers' work and teacher leadership.

Teachers' Work

Understanding teachers' work is prerequisite to determining the kinds of changes that are necessary to support the ideological reform of schools through authentic teacher leadership in 21st century schools. In Steve Jobs's commencement address at Stanford University, he spoke about connecting the dots in one's life: "you can't connect the dots looking forward; you can only connect them looking backwards. So you have to trust that the dots will somehow connect in your future. You have to trust in something—your gut, destiny, life, karma, whatever" (Stanford Report, 2005). And so, with this book, we are attempting to connect the dots in public education. If we had not chosen the path that each of us chose in education, we might not understand so clearly the juxtaposition between the "street level" vision of just getting a first teaching job and surviving, and the broader view attained by stepping back to look at the "big picture." When we look back and connect the dots, do we use that knowledge to influence where we go from here? Do we continue to look at the present as merely a continuation of past errors or do we look up and begin to think about formulating a vision of how things can change? Obviously, we are hopeful about the future of public schools. We believe that if we can dream it, we have a chance of making it happen, but there has to be a dream, a vision informed by experience, hope and possibilities. Each teacher is different, but perhaps, the most important quality of a good teacher is simply the courage to act on convictions. Few individuals would dispute the notion that good schools must have extraordinary teachers, and as such, the future of public education my depend upon a critical mass of politically astute teacher leaders who are able to articulate a road map for teachers' work that recognizes the important role of advocacy on behalf of all communities, parents and children. These teachers acting as critical pedagogues will be the foundation of a profession that achieves the levels of status and recognition that are prerequisite for the creation of schools that provide both the context and content of meaningful school reform.

Summary of the Sections of the Book

The authors chosen for this book are renowned scholars who are often cited in the current literature and who teach in the field of social foundations of education. These authors use interdisciplinary approaches that draw on knowledge from one or more of the liberal arts and humanities branches of history, sociology, philosophy, political science, law, anthropology, and cultural studies to critique and analyze societal structures that perpetuate oppression and privilege, and their effects on teaching practices. In this way, social foundations of education scholars have taken on the responsibility to:

- equip pre-service and in-service teachers with the tools needed to advocate for their students and the communities in which they live;

- fight against the narrow views of education where learning is reduced to rote memorization, compliance, and one-size-fits-all curricula;

- create spaces where learning is connected to students' lives and to a sense of justice and equality.

The Committee on Academic Standards and Accreditation, the group responsible for maintaining and updating the principles of the field, released a document in 2013 where they described the role of social foundations of education in the preparation of teachers (Committee on Academic Standards and Accreditation, 2012, p. 111). It states, specifically, through the study of social foundations of education, educators are prepared to:

1. Understand and apply disciplinary knowledge from the humanities and social sciences to interpreting the meanings of education and schooling in diverse cultural context.

2. Understand and apply interpretive, normative, and critical perspectives on education and schooling.

3. Understand how moral principles related to democratic institutions can inform and direct schooling practices, leadership, and governance.

4. Understand the full significance of diversity in a democratic society and how that bears on instruction, leadership, and governance.

5. Understand how philosophical and moral commitments affect the process of evaluation at all levels of schooling practices, leadership, and governance.

6. Critically analyze current educational policies and practices at national, state, and local levels and their impacts on teaching, learning, and the assessment of P–16 students.

With these principles in mind, we developed this book. Our intention is to provide an overview of prominent essays on the social foundations of education that address the aforementioned principles in the most critical manner and give our students a sense of empowerment that will accompany them into their classrooms, schools, and communities.

Divided into five sections, this book covers the interdisciplinary fields of history, philosophy, sociology, cultural studies, political science, and law in Education. Each section has a short introduction where we present an overview of the essays, our reasons for choosing them, and finally, at the end of each section, we offer a few discussion questions to help our readers think more deeply about the issues that we consider important in the study of education. We cannot say that this is an exhaustive project, there are many important scholars whose work is not included here; however, we chose samples of what we consider to be some of the more important contemporary essays written in the social foundations of education field that we agreed all teachers should read.

Section One: *A Foundation for 21st Century Schools* offers a context for viewing the roles and purposes of 21st century schools according to recognized scholars in the field such as Eleanor Blair, Pedro Noguera, Diane Ravitch, Kim Reid and Michelle Knight, John Dewey, Joel Spring, and one classic essay written by John Dewey, whose ideas were the foundation for contemporary thinking regarding the relationship between Democratic and Progressive ideals in Education. The purpose of this section is to highlight the role of schooling in the creation of a democratic society and to draw attention to what is and what should be public educational spheres. These essays address how the current education reforms affect teaching and learning and provide a context for thinking about how, as educators, we can begin to make changes that will benefit all children.

Section Two: *Social Justice and Critical Theory in the Schoolhouse*, gives an overview of the role of Critical Theory and Critical Pedagogy as a way to bring the conversation on Social Justice into the teacher education classroom. Authors such as Paul Carr, Aaron D. Gresson III, Joe Kincheloe, Yolanda Medina, and Ozlem Sensoy and Robin DiAngelos can be found in this section. Each of these authors explores key ideas related to how social justice and critical theory impact the way we view teaching and learning and provide a context for viewing policy, process and product in schools.

Section Three: *Teaching, Learning and Leading Against the Grain* shifts the discussion to a consideration of how the ideals of social justice and critical pedagogy shape educational practice and guide both the questions educators ask, but more importantly, the way they act in schools and classrooms. The authors in this section write from a very personal place: their own subversive experiences as educators, leaders, activists, and parents. Here you will read Mary Cowhey, Julie Gorlewski, Michelle Collay, Bettina Love, Yolanda Medina, and Sandra Liliana Pucci and Gregory Cramer. In these essays, there are multiple examples of how educators as leaders and learners work "against the grain" and use their ideals to inform a view of pedagogical practice as a coordinated, and thoughtful, response to a system that continuously perpetuates social, cultural, and economic inequalities among marginalized groups.

Section Four: *Teachers in 21st Century Schools* acknowledges the essential role that teachers play in the reform of schools for the 21st century. All of the authors in this section agree that, the teaching of particular skills is important, but that the real purpose of teaching is much bigger. Teachers as leaders in the schools is a revolutionary idea that has the potential to transform the profession and place teacher voices on the front-line of meaningful, substantive change in public schools. Gloria Ladson-Billings, Lisa Delpit, Henry Giroux, Patricia H. Hinchey, Barbara Madeloni and Julie Gorlewski provide several different viewpoints on how and why teachers must have an ideological framework and a public forum for their work

The authors in Section Five: *"Shift Happens": Contemporary Issues of Equity and Diversity* hold critical conversations on key issues related to equity and diversity. In addition, they all promote a type of education that is culturally relevant; one that embraces, and utilizes students' cultural experiences as the most important component of the curriculum and in teaching and learning. This sections holds essays by Angela Anselmo and Alma Rubal-Lopez, Sandra A. Butvilofsky, Patrick Finn, James M. Kauffman, Kathleen McGee, and Michele Brigham, Cara Kronen and Doug Risner. While there are myriad issues that impact the provision of equal educational opportunities, many that we don't discuss, these essays provide a context for a continued discussion of how public schools adapt to accommodate the rich backgrounds of the students whom we serve.

All of the chapters in this book have been carefully selected to provide a "different lens" through which future teachers can view teaching, learning and leading in 21st century schools. They were chosen to help teachers consider the important role of critical theory and critical pedagogy in the pursuit of social justice and the creation of school environments that are responsive to issues of equity and diversity. Our hope is that this book will be an important tool for future teachers and teacher educators in the field of the social foundations of education and that these readings will evoke live, critical, reflective discussions of the role of the teacher in the education of all children and in the shaping the future of public education.

References

Committee on Academic Standards and Accreditation (2012). Standards for Academic and Professional Instruction in Foundations of Education, Educational Studies, and Educational Policy Studies (third edition). *Educational Studies: A Journal of the American Educational Studies Association, 49*(2), 107–118.

Dewey, J. (1897). My pedagogic creed. *School Journal, 54,* 77–80.

Giroux, H. (1988). *Teachers as intellectuals: Toward a critical pedagogy of learning.* Westport, CT: Bergin & Garvey.

Giroux, H. (2012). *Education and the crisis of public values: Challenging the assault on teachers, students, and public education.* New York: Peter Lang Publishing.

Goodland, J. (2004). *A place called school* (second edition). New York: McGraw-Hill.

Ravitch, D. (2010). The myth of charter schools. *The New York Review of Books.* Retrieved from http://www.nybooks.com/articles/archives/2010/nov/11/myth-charter-schools/

Standford Report (2005). You've got to find what you love, Jobs says, Stanford University News. Retrieved from http://news.stanford.edu/news/2005/june15/jobs-061505.html

SECTION I
A Foundation for 21st Century Schools

Introduction

Eleanor J. Blair

If I were asked to explain why the foundations of education are a critical part of the education of all teachers, I would argue that their importance lies in establishing a foundation for understanding what, why and how we do public education. In the beginning of my foundations classes, I always offer students a "quick and dirty" view of public education where I trace the evolution of private schools from the seventeenth century—when they served an audience that was almost exclusively affluent, White, and male—to public schools in the nineteenth century—where we find the roots of the idea that a democratic nation where "all men are created equal" demands a school system that recognizes the important roles, both personally and civically, of access to knowledge and equal opportunities. Of course, this discussion goes from simple to complex rather quickly. Public schools have never been sites where equal opportunities thrived; historically, little concern has been shown for issues related to equal access to knowledge or for the needs of ALL children and their families. Of course, intersecting these issues and concerns are important questions about the roles of gender, social class and race in public sites where access to knowledge is negotiated. At this point, students generally find numerous points of interest in the history of American public schools, and the discussion comes alive as preconceived notions about K–12 schooling are challenged and tested. If I am successful, students quickly become engaged in looking at schools from various historical perspective and considering what purposes schools served in previous centuries and what purposes they should be serving today. There are always five questions that guide this discussion:

1. What are the aims and purposes of public education, and how have those changed due to historical, social and political events?

2. What is the relationship between those aims and purposes and the content of the curriculum?

3. How is one's philosophy of education and expectations for teacher and student roles related to the previous two questions?

4. How do the answers to these questions impact the role of assessment in our schools?

5. Which ideological and philosophical beliefs shape and guide the questions we ask about the roles of equity, privilege, oppression and social justice?

The answers to these questions are not simple, and indeed, the answers shift with changes to both the economy and the political orientation of the country; however, the answers are not nearly as important as the discussion that results. Getting students to argue, challenge and discuss taken-for-granted assumptions about how we "do" school is the most important aspect of this discussion—and this section of the book. I frequently resort to my training in educational anthropology to get students to consider the idea that we must "make the familiar strange, and the strange familiar" (Spindler and Spindler, 2000) when we look at public education; we recognize that our "insider" view of schools often obscures our attempts to view schools as an "outsider" and to challenge many of the practices that we take for granted.

Perhaps the hardest part of becoming a teacher is the transition from student to teacher. Everyone thinks they know something about education and schooling because they went to school; we have all been students, therefore it should be easy to be a teacher, right? Nothing is further from the truth; teaching is hard work and it requires both content knowledge and pedagogical skills. Teachers work in environments where they are seldom treated like full-fledged professionals who should have a voice in every decision that is made regarding the content and process of teaching. Teacher attrition is a persistent problem due to the fact that teachers are seldom prepared for the multiple roles and responsibilities that they will be asked to play. According to the Alliance for Excellent Education 2014 report, *On the Path to Equity: Improving the Effectiveness of Beginning Teachers*, each year, approximately half a million teachers move or leave the profession. Add to that mix the fact that teachers today often work in settings where more of the focus is on high-stakes tests than on teaching, and it is obvious why so many teachers leave within the first five years.

The ideas in this book don't change the realities of teaching, but they do provide a foundation for understanding where we have already been, what we have done and where we need to go in the 21st century. In this first section of the book, readers are introduced to six essays by scholars in the field of foundations of education. The essay by Dewey, "My Pedagogic Creed," is a standard in the foundations of education scholarship; no teacher should enter the field without a basic familiarity with the ideas of Dewey. However, the other five essays by Blair, Noguera, Ravitch, Reid and Knight, and Spring are more contemporary writings that explore the issues that dominate our discussions of the changing goals and purposes of public schools and the impact of these issues on the lives of teachers. These essays consider the moral, economic and political agendas that shape the questions we ask and the struggle to find answers that are consistent with a commitment to democratic ideals. A free and public education for all children is a right not an entitlement; understanding that concept and protecting the rights of our most vulnerable children is an important part of the work of all teachers. The essays in this section of the book provide a foundation for thinking about 21st century schools.

References

Alliance for Excellent Education (2014). *On the path to equity: Improving the effectiveness of beginning teachers.* Retrieved from http://all4ed.org/wp-content/uploads/2014/07/PathToEquity.pdf

Spindler, G., and Spindler, L. (2000). *Fifty years of anthropology and education: 1950–2000: A Spindler anthology.* New York: Routledge.

CHAPTER 1

A Pedagogy of Hopelessness

Fear and Loathing in 21ˢᵗ Century American Schools

Eleanor J. Blair

Introduction

In her address to the American Educational Studies Association in November, 2014, Susan Laird, a renowned scholar in the field of philosophy of education, talked about hope, and she asked the question: "How can anyone be an educator without hope?" Perhaps *hope* is a fundamental part of education and the educational process, but my response to her would be that it is entirely possible to be an educator today and be without hope; in fact, schools at every level are full of such individuals. Rather, I would ask the question, "how can anyone be an educator today and not be hopeless?" The November 3, 2014, issue of *Time* magazine is labeled *Rotten Apples* and shows a gavel smashing an apple; the lead article is a sharp and biting critique of the teaching profession generally and tenure specifically. A response by Billy Easton, executive director of the Alliance for Quality Education, was among those that *Time* published online:

> Once again, TIME has chosen to play the teacher bashing blame game with the rotten cover titled "Rotten Apples." TIME is parroting the assault on public schools and teachers being promoted by hedge-fund and Silicon Valley billionaires seeking to privatize our public schools. This latest TIME cover is a head on attack on the profession of teaching. It ignores the real issues impacting quality of students' education, resulting from the systemic inequality and severe underfunding of public schools. (Canedo, 2014, n.p.)

This ongoing assault on teachers and schools steadily chips away at the possibility of one surviving as a hopeful educator. For most educators, at the end of most days, hopelessness is the more reasonable choice based on present circumstances and realities; if you don't hope for much, you won't be disappointed. Hence, the title of this chapter; we live in an era where a pedagogy of hopelessness pervades the schools and has a pernicious effect on every decision made regarding the method, content and practice of teaching, learning and leading. And no one feels this hopelessness more acutely than the teachers, who are daily subjected to assaults on their professional personas, as well as their students and families, who know only too well the outcomes of educational inertia and stagnation.

Public attacks on American teachers and schools represent a malodorous effort to breathe life into the myths of educational incompetence and effectively eliminate the possibility of public schools re-defining the problems of public education in such a way that meaningful public alternatives become a part of the dialogue on school reform. Unfortunately, the products of school reform efforts most often become monikers for shallow and untested educational alternatives that reflect a capitalist bias for neo-liberal school reform efforts that produce "school climates characterized by compliance, conformity, and fear" (Picower & Mayorga, 2015, p. 6). As such, these reforms often obscure the potential for the generation of public, not private, alternatives that would simultaneously reflect a commitment to issues of equity and social justice and a recognition of good teachers as key actors in the process of redefining the roles and responsibilities of public schools in the 21st century.

This chapter is a work in progress; there are no answers or magical solutions, but this is also not a time for cowards to hide behind false optimism and misguided pronouncements of hope and hopeful-ness. Educational concerns regarding equity and social justice demand that there be a public outcry about the future of public schools and the role of hope and hopelessness in the lives of teachers and stu-dents, and yet, the silence is deafening. Public schools and educators are regularly forced to defend the work they do with limited resources and a lack of voice in educational decision-making, but the viabil-ity of these institutions in the 21st century are seldom the subject of serious consideration. Instead, we see evidence of what can only be described as efforts to privatize schools and facilitate a corporate take-over of education under the guise of choice and bottom line economies. All educators—preservice and inservice, higher education and K–12—need to regularly revisit the assumptions, values and beliefs that guide our work and shape the content of our thoughts about teaching, learning and leading because, ultimately, these ideas must be the foundation of meaningful school reform. However, it would be premature to define a solution to our problems without sufficient analysis and an in-depth consider-ation of the many facets of the issue. At a minimum, this chapter is a challenge to consider several key questions: First, is it possible that public schools are educational disasters and no longer relevant to 21st century families and their children? Second, if public schools are characterized by pedagogical hopeless-ness, what are the sources of that hopelessness and how do we begin to rebuild a pedagogy of hope? Will an educational equivalent of Occupy Wall Street—an Occupy Schools Movement/A Social Justice Revolution—be required to protest and call attention to the injustices perpetuated by the public schools? And finally, if public schools were dismantled and/or reformed in another image, what ques-tions (and answers) would guide our efforts? The answers to these questions are important, but the answers are not nearly as important as the argument and discussion.

21st Century Schools on the Front Line of an Educational Disaster

Good teachers and good schools do exist, and occasionally they inspire hopefulness; however, I no lon-ger believe that these isolated examples can support an ideology that is being challenged and dismantled by efforts to demoralize teachers and take away the professional gains of the last 150 years. In 2013, Ellie Herman, an English teacher, embarked upon a yearlong effort to define what a good teacher is. What she found is not surprising; she found that great teachers love their work and demonstrate daily that great teaching is much more than a set of techniques. However, she also confirmed one of the premises of this chapter in the following excerpt:

> I'm scared. If teaching is an art and a science, I'm scared that in our national conversation about educa-tion, we are so intent on demanding accountability for mastering the "science" part that we're creating conditions that seem designed to crush teachers' souls. When our system treats teachers with disdain, creating accountability measures whose underlying premise is that teachers are so incompetent and lazy

that they need to be monitored rigidly, strictly and incessantly, at what point does that myth become corrosive to a teacher's humanity? (Strauss, 2015, n.p.)

The myths about teachers are fundamental to efforts to destroy any remnants of teacher autonomy and replace it with standardized and narrowly defined notions of curriculum and accountability. This process is evident in the preservice education of teachers in colleges of education and extends to the pedagogical decisions being made in schools and classrooms. Today, there is no place for serious, substantive conversations about the myriad definitions of good teaching; instead good teaching is defined for us by outside agencies and constituencies, for example, edTPA, the Common Core State Standards, Charter Schools and Teach for America. As a result of these efforts to minimize and standardize who, what and why we teach, conceptualizations of good teaching as a nuanced, complex and individualistic process are not a welcome part of the conversation within institutionalized public educational places. Thus, it is not really surprising that 21st century schools are increasingly characterized by a lack of vision, purpose and ideology, and the gaps are being filled with answers to all the wrong questions.

Historically, public schools have never been true to democratic ideals; however, there was always the steady progress of reforms that seemed to continually redefine the potential of public schools to respond to changing societal needs and demands. However, today, the vast majority of public schools are stagnant institutions unable to establish their place in 21st century American society. While schools (and teachers) are confronted daily with contradictory attempts to reconcile "old ways" with new demographics and new ways of thinking about teaching and learning, they are simultaneously "handed" top-down mandates that don't facilitate collective action and personal accountability. We regularly fail to meet minimum expectations among our most challenging and diverse students, and the response is often a process of blaming the victim and finding a scapegoat. Our system is broken and empty promises of renewed commitments to innovation and school reform will not fix 21st century schools. Public expressions of optimism and hope are generous, but provide no foundation for meaningful change. Not surprisingly, I am not the only one asking these questions. Twenty years ago, Frank Smith (1995), in a *Phi Delta Kappan* article, speculated that the public schools were no longer a viable option for the delivery of education:

> We should stop worrying about the problems of education, declare it a disaster, and let teachers and students get on with their lives. The trouble with the endless concern over "problems" in education is that many well-meaning but often misguided and sometimes meddlesome people believe that solutions must exist. They waste their own and other people's time and energy trying to find and implement these solutions. Typically, they try harder to do more of something that is already being done (although what is being done is probably one of the problems). (p. 584)

Smith goes on to suggest that public education and the sinking of the *Titanic* have more than a few similarities. Appropriately, his article was accompanied by a drawing of the *Titanic* sinking. I like that comparison because the 21st century reality regarding American public schools is that they are equivalent to an institutional *Titanic*; we have hit the proverbial iceberg and we are sinking. There will be some people who will survive by jumping on lifeboats and quickly paddling away, but for the rest of us, it is a sad picture; we are on the main deck singing and holding hands; we are going down, but we don't know what to do next except continue doing what we do best: carry on with optimism (and hope), and perhaps, talk about the situation a little bit more. Henry Giroux (2012) echoes similar concerns regarding the hopelessness of the current situation:

> As testing becomes an end in itself, it both deadens the possibility of critical thinking and removes teachers from the possibility of exercising critical thought and producing imaginative pedagogical engagements. These modes of bare pedagogy that take their cues from a market-driven business culture treat teachers as fast-food, minimum wage workers and disdain the notion that public schools may

be one of the few remaining places where students can learn how to deal with complicated ideas. As public schools become more business friendly, teachers are rendered more powerless and students more ignorant. (p. 4)

Thus, in this way, rather than schools moving forward and embracing new pedagogies that are infused with "hopeful" visions for 21st century schools, we are on the brink of disaster and rapidly sinking. Our teachers, the people on the frontline of this war, are disenfranchised and their work marginalized. Schools are looking for salvation in all the wrong places.

21st Century Schools, Teachers and edTPA

Like most teachers, I started out my career in education full of hope and excitement; I was going to change the world one child at a time, I was going to make a difference. Forty years later, that hope has diminished and I am daily confronted with schools that are characterized by a pedagogy of hopelessness that is shaped by fear and loathing and a plethora of oppressive practices that deny a place for multiple voices and perspectives in the public schools. All of this occurs, of course, within a context where multicultural education and the language of acceptance and a celebration of diversity are regularly (and fervently) embraced in symbolic, but empty accommodations and recognitions. Critical pedagogical approaches to educational practices that foster equity and social justice are seldom a part of the dialogue of teacher education or school reform, and in fact, teacher education programs are increasingly being usurped by the imposition of hegemonic practices endorsed by teacher performance assessment systems like edTPA.

edTPA and Pearson have rapidly become an integral part of the landscape of teachers' lives, and thus further perpetuate a pedagogy of hopelessness among educators. edTPA is a performance assessment system that requires students in their final semester of teacher training to produce a final product composed of teaching lessons, videos and reflections that are submitted to a "calibrated scorer," whose evaluation reduces student work to a number. While edTPA is the product of the work of professional educators—developed under the leadership of Linda Darling-Hammond and the Stanford Center for Assessment Learning and Equity (SCALE) (Madeloni, 2015, p. 168) and the American Association of Colleges of Teacher Education (AACTE)—its popularity grew quickly and it eventually became necessary to hire Pearson to make it available to a wider educational audience (*About edTPA: Overview,* n.d., n.p.). However, there is no shortage of critics. Barbara Madeloni has the following to say about edTPA:

> As an instrument of neoliberal logic, the edTPA is the teacher education equivalent of Common Core State Standards, high-stakes testing, and value-added teacher evaluations. Each of these imposes a narrowly quantitative narrative of teaching and learning on schools, students, and teachers. Each eliminates understandings of teaching and learning that acknowledge the social-political context in which education takes place and the rich messy complexity of schools. (Madeloni, 2015, as cited in Picower & Mayorga, p. 167).

Pearson Education, Inc., the corporate entity charged with the administration of edTPA, is a part of the problem with how edTPA is perceived by others. Pearson, one of the largest education companies in the world, describes itself in philanthropic terms:

> We believe wherever learning flourishes, so do people. We are the world's leading learning company and we're focused on helping learners of all ages make progress in their lives.

> We provide a range of products and services to institutions, governments, and directly to individual learners that help people everywhere aim higher and fulfill their true potential. The new products and services we are creating are making learning more personal, affordable, and effective. (Pearson, n.d., n.p.)

And yes, "wherever learning flourishes" so does Pearson, financially and politically; they have all the "right" connections. Harvey (2005) highlights the fact that,

> Pearson's obligations, as a publically [sic] traded company, are to stockholders to maximize profit. The hiring of piecemeal workers with no benefits or protections to do the work previously done by faculty is consistent with the neoliberal economic structures being imposed on public entities. (As cited in Madeloni, 2015, p. 124)

Although it is interesting that a corporate testing giant like Pearson (Au, 2013) has managed to make standardization in education synonymous with "progress" and helping people "aim higher and fulfill their true potential" through the products and services they provide, it is simultaneously interesting that they recruit scorers for their tests through Craigslist; for example, an ad appeared for Pearson on Craigslist in Kent, WA, soliciting student assessment scorers full and part-time (*Student Assessment Scorers Full & Part-Time,* n.d., n.p.). The pay was hourly $15.00 day shift/$16.50 night shift plus daily incentives for both shifts. And the lofty requirements for these positions were the following:

- Bachelor's degree required
- Strong attention to detail
- Excellent reading, writing and comprehension skills
- Basic PC skills with the ability to work in a Windows environment
- Ability to follow oral and written instructions
- Proof of degree and eligibility to work in the U.S. required

Within this context, is there any surprise that educators feel a sense of hopelessness? Seemingly important standardized student assessments are now being scored by college graduates with no required background or knowledge of education, curriculum, or developmentally appropriate practices. I am appalled that the scoring of standardized tests for students is viewed as a task requiring few skills and expertise, but I am again reminded that corporate interests will always be focused on the bottom line. Don't be fooled; Pearson is making money on tests, and concerns for progress and helping people achieve their potential are small compared to the need to market these tests and profit from having them mandated for K–12 as well as higher education by as many states as possible. Currently, in many colleges of education, edTPA is "promoted as an answer to the perceived shortcomings of teacher education" (Madeloni & Gorlewski, 2013, n.p.). While teacher education has regularly shifted and changed according to changing social, political and cultural demands, there has never been a formal notification to education faculty that there were serious shortcomings in teacher education, but regardless, an answer to those perceived shortcomings has been provided. According to Madeloni and Gorlewski (2013), "edTPA is the wrong answer to the question of how teacher education should be improved," and yet, it is the answer that became fully operational in 2013 and is now used in some form by institutions in over 35 states and the District of Columbia" (*About edTPA: Overview,* n.d., n.p.). Of course, whenever I mention edTPA at an educational conference or workshop, the response is overwhelmingly negative. Large numbers of teacher educators believe that we have co-opted discussions about good teaching and the training of good teachers, and instead, we now focus all of our efforts on teaching edTPA. Once again, in education, we have looked for quick answers to complex problems and inserted a "one-size-fits-all" mentality into the process of educating teachers. For the vast majority of teacher educators in schools where edTPA is being used, it was implemented through top-down measures of bureaucratic control with a focus on standardization and efficiency; teacher educators had no voice in the creation, design and/or selection of edTPA as a teacher performance assessment system, and serious questions are now being asked regarding the impact of edTPA on resource allocation. According to Wayne Au (2013),

> The edTPA will cost our credential students an additional $300-$350, a price set by Pearson. Cooperating teachers are resisting taking student teachers specifically because the edTPA feels too intrusive and is driving the student teaching experience. Larger universities and teacher credential programs in our region have more resources to devote to preparing their teacher candidates for the edTPA, setting up clear disparities in edTPA scores between program haves and have-nots. (n.p.)

Linda Darling-Hammond and Maria Hyler (2013) concur that there are challenges to the integrity of edTPA as a reliable and valid teacher performance tool, and yet, they argue that edTPA is essential to the establishment of teaching as a real profession:

> We share the concern of edTPA's critics that teacher preparation programs are under attack. At this point, however, we believe that the most effective and ethical response is not to stick our collective heads in the sand and complain that nobody trusts us. Rather, we believe that our collective response should be to embed high-quality performance assessments in high-quality teacher preparation programs, and to ensure that our candidates demonstrate they can meet professionwide standards before being permitted to practice. (Darling-Hammond & Hyler, 2013, n.p.)

Are Darling-Hammond and Hyler really suggesting that teacher educators have only one of two choices: stick our heads in the sand and complain OR accept edTPA as the only method for making "high-quality performance assessments in high-quality teacher preparation programs"? Clearly, that is one way of interpreting their statements, and thus, I am suggesting that all educators, K–12 and higher education, should take offense at the notion that we must acknowledge our incompetence and recognize the only "ethical response" as the acceptance of externally imposed mandates that are inevitable and necessary for the perpetuation of an academic climate of "compliance, conformity, and fear" (Picower & Mayorga, 2015, p. 6) where edTPA can thrive unchallenged by the mundane questions, concerns and issues of practicing educators.

A pedagogy of hopelessness begins within colleges of education and manifests itself in the proliferation of authoritarian policies and practices that guide the work we do in public schools and with practicing teachers; novice teachers often accept this context for their work as non-negotiable, while older, more experienced teachers lament the loss of their autonomy and freedom in the classroom and in their roles as mentors and coaches for new teachers. Yes, the teaching profession has serious issues to address in the areas of status and autonomy, but answers to these concerns will not emerge from a focus on tests and standardization; the teaching profession will change overnight when teachers' voices become front and center to school reform efforts.

Again, programs and initiatives like Teach for America, Common Core State Standards, Charter Schools and edTPA reflect efforts to standardize definitions of good teaching and good schools, and frequently these efforts become the subsidiaries of corporate interests and efforts to privatize schools and/or insert capitalist priorities and profit into the educational enterprise. It is not surprising that the public, as well as many educators, often perceive school reform as new programs or initiatives that are part of a circuitous process where "solutions" are often short-lived and seldom reflect research or best practices. Thus, they are doomed to the same failures of past innovations. Among teacher educators, it is quickly acknowledged that most people believe that edTPA will be around only for few years before it falls victim to a similar fate. Again, Giroux (2012) argues that

> Education has become the new frontier for the investment dollar and very likely the next big bubble to burst. But what do the proposed reforms mean for education on the ground, so to speak, in classrooms across the nation? Educational theory once provided the philosophical principles that guided a vision of

what it means to be a fully functional, educated citizen as well as a vision of the kind of society educated men and women should aspire to build. But educational theory has now been stripped of its critical and emancipatory possibilities. In this latest demand for educational accountability and innovation, pedagogy has been reduced to a managerial and disciplinary process largely driven by market values, a crude empiricism, and the ideology of casino capitalism with its relentless prioritization of economic interests over human needs. (p. 88)

If a pedagogy of hopeless continues to thrive in this environment, are we willing to consider that public schools as we know them today might cease to exist? Smith (1995) has a few ideas in response to these questions,

> We should change the way we talk about schools by talking less about learning and teaching and more about *doing*. ... Instead of talking all the time about what teachers should teach and what students should learn, we should talk about what teachers and students should do. We should talk about experiences that they should be mutually engaged in—experiences involving reading, writing, imagining, creating, calculating, constructing, producing, and performing. ... We must get away from the idea that everything would be fine with our educational institutions if only teachers and students worked harder. That is why we should no longer talk about schools in the language that has made them what they are today. Attempting to "improve" the current rituals of schools or to do them more assiduously will only make matters worse. Education is on the wrong track largely because of "solutions" that have socially isolated teachers and students from one another and from sensible ways of spending their time. (pp. 589–590)

How we define the problems ultimately determines the solutions; however, I want to propose that we begin to think about schools in ways that will produce neither solutions nor answers, but perhaps, public school alternatives to a one-size-fits-all approach to education. More importantly, I believe that the dialogue and the act of dissecting the process and product of public education are far more important than answers and ill-fated, poorly conceptualized, solutions.

The Foundation of Pedagogical Hopelessness

Despite declarations of hope for public education, there seems to be widespread acceptance that the system is flawed, but we keep trying to fix it one broken piece at a time. This reminds me of pictures from my working-class childhood where we couldn't afford to buy new stuff so we kept wrapping things in duct tape and stuffing towels in drafty windows in order to keep things working long past the expiration date. My argument today is that schools have for too long extended the expiration date on their usefulness and we need to consider a new product, a new way of doing things. We have forgotten the lessons of our early psychology classes where we were taught that the whole is greater than the sum of its parts. The goals of public education are still important, but the schools where we seek to accomplish those goals—the "parts" of the larger picture—are problematic.

Cuban and Tyack (1997) refer to the endless "tinkering with utopia" that occurs in American public schools; they juxtapose America's faith in public schools as a panacea with the slow progress of reform efforts. Public schools are "sinking" and the "leaks" are too large to delineate in this chapter, but the failures are regularly documented in the public arena: low achievement among poor children, high dropout rates, a teaching profession that suffers from high attrition and a void of teacher leadership, a lack of healthy debate about teaching and learning, and the widespread use of tests that merely document our inability to teach basic knowledge while excluding concerns related to critical thinking and social justice. We should be pulling out the lifeboats and abandoning the institutional equivalent of a sinking ship, but no, we continue to talk calmly about public schools and the democratic goals of public education as if we could fix these problems. Joel Klein (2011), in the essay "The Failure of American Schools," noted that,

Nearly three decades after *A Nation at Risk*, the groundbreaking report by the National Commission on Excellence in Education, warned of "a rising tide of mediocrity that threatens our very future as a Nation and a people," the gains we made in improving our schools are negligible—even though we have doubled our spending (in inflation-adjusted dollars) on K-12 public education. On America's latest exams (the National Assessment of Educational Progress), one-third or fewer of eighth-grade students were proficient in math, science, or reading. Our high-school graduation rates continues to hover just shy of 70 percent, according to a 2010 report by the Editorial Projects in Education Research Center, and many of those students who do graduate aren't prepared for college. ACT, the respected national organization that administers college-admissions tests, recently found that 76 percent of our high school graduates "were not adequately prepared academically for first-year college courses." (n.p.)

At best, 21st century schools are poor replicas of schools from 50 years ago, and yet, we keep trying to fix them without considering how the needs of contemporary students are dramatically different from those of students 50 years ago. For poor, urban and rural children, most of them representing every imaginable form of diversity, public schools have for too long been the only alternative, the only lifeboat, and we have failed them. We know what works in education; we know how to teach poor children, but we don't do it. We continue to support a model of schooling that perpetuates failure and a pedagogy of hopelessness that extends to both teachers and students. The National Center for Education Statistics provides compelling statistics regarding the inadequacy of public school efforts with low-income students:

> Every year, 1.3 million students drop out of high school in the United States. More than half are students of color, and most are low-income. Low-income students fail to graduate at five times the rate of middle-income families and six times that of higher-income youth, according to a recent study by the National Center for Education Statistics (NCES). (Zhao, 2011, n.p.)

The despair that accompanies this reality is pervasive, and despite the false promises and feigned interests of politicians, legislators, corporate entities, and so-called school leaders, everyone knows the truth; a pedagogy of hopelessness has become a part of the tapestry of most public schools, and as such, it will not be dismissed with one more new innovation or heartfelt, inspiring tale of dedicated teachers or parents and children who are desperate to get a good education and succeed.

Einstein argued that we cannot solve our problems by using the same kind of thinking we've always used; however, I see little evidence that the dialogue about viable educational systems has moved beyond 20th century conceptualizations of public education. Smith (1995) suggested that, "there is not a good term for what education is today—at least, not a euphemistic one. Education is disorganized and disorderly, unplanned and dysfunctional, like assertions of crustaceans on tidal rocks, like a metastasizing growth, or like an accident in progress" (p. 596). And yet, most serious discussions of school reform take for granted the idea that public schools are worthy of reform efforts. I would agree that many of the ideals undergirding the reform of public schools are worthy; however, we ignore fundamental flaws that have always been present. Historically, public schools have successfully served middle class students who attended predominantly white schools taught by white teachers within very traditional bureaucratic organizations; and yet, as previously noted, we regularly ignore statistics showing that we have never served the needs of students who come from diverse backgrounds; whether it is race, ethnicity, sexual orientation, religion and/or economic status, we simply do not see evidence of the kinds of successes with these children that we need from contemporary public schools. Add to this a failure to encourage critical thinking and collective political action among teachers and students, and you have schools that function as factories that value compliance and oppression over thoughtful dialogue and debate regarding the future of public education. As our school populations become increasingly more diverse, we keep doing more of the same. Larry Cuban (1984) suggested in the book, *How Teachers Taught: Constancy and Change in American Education, 1890–1980*, that the only difference between 20th century schools and those of the 1800s was that the desks were no longer bolted to the floor; I would suggest that the same kinds of comparisons are appropriate today. The schools of 2015 are not at all different from the schools that I attended in the 1970s—sure, there is more technology present, but desks are still in straight rows and teachers still stand in the front of rooms, kids are rewarded for compliance and those who aren't compliant go to the office where the principal delivers punishments that range from in-school suspension to expulsion.

In my classes, I challenge students to walk into schools and classrooms committed to not becoming a 2 by 4 teacher; a teacher confined by the 2 covers of the textbook and the 4 walls of the classroom, but their uneasy laughter and shrugging of shoulders confirms to me that for many future teachers, it is hard to imagine what that "new" classroom might look like. Yes, there is more technology and online learning in schools today, but are our notions of innovation and school reform shaped by reconceptualized visions of what teaching and learning might look like if we refused to allow the architecture and legislative mandates of 21st century schools to define the boundaries of education? What would these new notions of education and schooling look like? Is it possible that new institutions and new roles for teachers and students would emerge? As I said earlier in this chapter, I chose education as my career; I thought I could make a difference. The problem is not with notions of change and hopefulness, the problem is with the context for our work as educators; public schools in their current form do not meet 21st century demands for education and the failures become more evident with each decade that passes. Do we continue to waste our time trying to fix what is not fixable or does hope become a viable option only when we leave our comfort zones and begin to break schools down to their essential components and rebuild with no preconceived notion that there will be a one-size-fits-all model for public education.

What Has Hope Got to Do with It?

It would not seem unreasonable to ask questions regarding the relationship between hope and a pedagogy of hopelessness. What has hope got to do with the fear and loathing that dominate schools today? And, more importantly, is there an ideology or a set of questions and answers that are prerequisite to a restoration and rebuilding of public educational spaces that are responsive to the needs of a rapidly changing population of students and their families? Paulo Freire (1994) argued that "without a minimum of hope, we cannot so much as start the struggle. But without the struggle, hope, as an ontological need, dissipates, loses its bearings, and turns into hopelessness. And hopelessness can become tragic despair" (p. 9). The "struggle," as Freire names it, is a "struggle to improve the world" (p. 8). In 21st century public schools, there is a sense of hopelessness that is eerily similar to Freire's description; "hopelessness paralyzes us, immobilizes us. We succumb to fatalism, and then it becomes impossible to muster the strength we absolutely need for a fierce struggle that will re-create the world" (p. 8). I see little evidence of an ongoing struggle in public schools today that is informed by an ideological commitment of social justice; a struggle that by necessity should represent ongoing efforts to re-create the public school arena, not simply succumb to private interests that serve only a few. The most salient struggle engaging most teachers and students is one of survival in an institution that is guided by untenable bottom-line values and beliefs that obscure efforts to define teaching and learning and the climate of schools in anything but minimalistic terms. We are, indeed, paralyzed by the inertia of a behemoth institution that is incapable of meaningful change, and in simpler terms, hope doesn't live here anymore.

Of course, bell hooks (2003) defined the struggle in a different way, a way that names a different set of global, and yet personal, issues that link the pursuit of social justice with teaching and learning. She argued that "struggles of gender equality and ethnic diversity linked issues of ending domination, of social justice with pedagogy" (p. 7). And yet, she acknowledged the failure of hope in light of prevailing contradictory voices: "while the academic world became a place where humanitarian dreams could be realized through education as the practice of freedom via a pedagogy of hope, the world outside was busily teaching people the need to maintain injustice, teaching fear and violence, teaching terrorism" (pp. 8–9). As such, the schools have become a public site for the struggle between a pedagogy of hope and that of hopelessness. hooks (2003) concurs with Freire regarding the important role that despair plays in conceptualizing a hopeful vision for the future:

> Despair is the greatest threat. When despair prevails we cannot create life-sustaining communities of resistance. Paulo Freire reminds us that "without a vision for tomorrow hope is impossible." Our visions for tomorrow are most vital when they emerge from the concrete circumstances of change we are experiencing right now. (p. 12)

Infusing our vision of 21st century schools with hope is task of paramount importance if public schools are to morph into institutions that serve 21st century ideals and don't simply succumb to external forces that seek to characterize them as failures and dismantle the public dream for private interests. Henry Giroux (2013), eloquently suggested in his *Truthout* essay, "Hope in the Age of Looming Authoritarianism," that,

> Hope as a subversive, defiant practice should provide a link, however transient, provisional and contextual, between vision and critique, on the one hand, and engagement and transformation on the other. But for such a notion of hope to be consequential, it has to be grounded in a vision and educational project that has some hold on the present. In opposition to an age of profound pessimism, hope becomes meaningful to the degree that it mobilizes visions, agents, organizations and strategies while reclaiming an ethic of compassion, justice and collective struggle for those institutions in which equality, freedom and justice flourish as part of the ongoing struggle for a global democracy. The greatest threat to social justice and democracy is the disappearance not only of critical discourses that allow us to think outside of and against the demands of official power but also those spaces where politics can even occur, where people can learn and assert a sense of critical agency. (n.p.)

So, where do we go from here? My argument is that new (and different) questions regarding the viability of the public school ideal need to be asked. Recently, I watched Davis Guggenheim's newest contribution to educational documentaries, *Teach*, a film that, at best, is merely an old wine in a new bottle. The viewer is presented with fervent, dedicated young teachers who want to make a difference, poor children of color who are several grades behind, but who want to go to college, and then finally, a dramatic ending where most of the kids make incredible academic progress, and there is a lot of hugging and crying between students and teachers. Beautiful, right? I have to say that I preferred *Waiting for Superman* because, while there was certainly a pro-charter, anti-union bias, the film painfully confronted the realities of many present-day schools where failure and mediocrity are writ large and innovation is a word tossed around at media events, but a phenomenon that is seldom realized in institutions that reward conformity and unquestioning submission to external agents of control. And while Guggenheim is to be commended for putting teachers at the center of this discussion, I am growing cynical and tired of the faux drama and predictable tears at the end of each one of his films. When is Guggenheim going to engage us in the conversation where we acknowledge that we regularly define our problems in shallow ways that have predictably easy solutions? If how we define our problems determine the solutions, when are we going to broach the really unpopular and unsolvable problems of race, poverty and class-bias in American public education? Guggenheim is very comfortable discussing his decision to send his children to a private school, and yet, he continues to profit from multiple films detailing the failings of public schools and the notable successes of the few that he documents in his films. Geoffrey Canada, founder of the Harlem Children's Zone, and a "star" in Guggenheim's *Waiting for Superman*, is eloquent in his discussion of hope for poor children of color, but Canada, like many others fails to ask hard questions about corporate sponsorship of schools that promote white, middle-class ideals or the fraudulent and underhanded practices that routinely impact resource allocation for poor schools and deny public schools the opportunity to promote educational practices that address the needs of ALL children.

The answers to these questions should evoke tears, and even anger, but there is no place in this crisis for another documentary that represents empty inspirational drama. The real drama is the inability of many public schools to do the job they are needed most for: teaching growing numbers of children who come from diverse and rich backgrounds that differ significantly from the norms and values being propagated in the public schools. Guggenheim's films do not inspire purposeful action or dialogue, but rather, they confirm the hopelessness of public schools in their present form and give few reasons to hope that the small successes of individual teachers and/or schools will actually "fix" or change the public schools in meaningful substantive ways. Perhaps it is time for the Michael Moore version of public education docudrama: a serious documentary that evokes passion, even anger, and ultimately action, on the part of major stakeholders, not simply a sense of overwhelming helplessness that is too often a by-product of a pedagogy of hopelessness.

The Emperor's New Clothes

I don't have a single answer to these questions, but I do believe that the most productive action at this time is an acknowledgment that we have lost our way and we need to abandon the road that we are on and seek higher ground. We have pretended for too long that the public schools in their current format represent a viable educational option for the children of America. Is it just another version of the *Emperor's New Clothes* that no one wants to talk about the fact that the public schools are pedagogical failures, and we want to pretend that a different reality exists despite evidence to the contrary? No one wants to believe in a pedagogy of hopelessness because, if this is true, where do we go from here? We want quick answers and cheap fixes—another version of the fast-food, instant gratification mentality that dominates the American mind-set.

Picower and Mayorga (2015) use the Hydra from Greek mythology to discuss school reform efforts:

> The Hydra was an immortal multi-headed creature. Any attempt to slay the Hydra was a struggle in futility and hopelessness, because if one head were removed, the Hydra would grow back two more in its place … the Hydra was only finally able to be slain by Heracles because he worked together with an ally, his nephew, to remove all the heads at once, making it impossible for the decapitated heads to grow back. (p. 4)

They argue that the Hydra metaphor helps "those committed to educational justice to better understand how seemingly individual education 'reforms,' or 'Hydra heads,' are all connected to a broader 'body' that is pushing public education toward privatization" (p. 4). Looking at school reform efforts from this viewpoint, it is easier to understand the pervasive hopelessness that characterizes public schools. Problems are defined in disconnected ways and solutions address one problem at a time while other issues simultaneously proliferate and expand out of control. Jean Anyon (2014) acknowledged that "education is an institution whose basic problems are caused by, and whose basic problems reveal, the other crises in cities" (p. 170). Is it possible that a concerted effort by major stakeholders in public education could successfully (and reflectively) work together to identify the myriad "crises" in schools and within a social justice framework work to address the multiple "heads at once" without co-opting this work to corporate interests?

There are myriad examples of public education that do inspire hope, but there are not enough to serve the needs of the children who need them the most. Charter schools are often maligned in the educational literature (Ravitch, 2010) and frequently representative of another example of the takeover of this country's intellectual capital and privatization of public education. Critics of charter schools cite evidence that "while charter schools were a heterogeneous group in the 1990s, the decades that followed have witnessed homogenizing trends related to the dominance of a market-oriented vision, which includes less and less the pedagogical vision of teachers or the inclusive vision of community groups at the local level" (White, 2015, p. 122). Most often, though, in discussions of charter schools,

I encounter a knee-jerk reaction from many educators that charter schools simply represent the privatization of education and an abandonment of the democratic ideals of public education. Although, if these proponents of public education were honest, they would admit that many, if not most, 21st century public schools do not come close to embracing Dewey's (1916) notions regarding the relationship between democracy and education. And, perhaps, our romantic attachment to the timeless models of public education that we are all familiar with is an impediment to actually engaging in a critical consideration of how these schools might be dismantled and replaced with alternative models that serve the public good and not just the individual needs of special groups. Rather than thinking out of the box about education and attempting to find a nugget of hope in the alternative educational configurations that have emerged, I find instead that we are all locked in the box and accepting of the fact that the ship may be sinking, but we are still on board and not looking particularly hard for a lifeboat. While examples do exist of schools where children from diverse social, cultural and economic backgrounds thrive and experience academic success, the unwillingness of the vast majority of schools to offer the kinds of programs that have proven successful is appalling. Decades of research has shown us what works; we know how to teach all children, and too frequently, we do not do it for a variety of reasons. The failure in this scenario that I find most disturbing is simply the moral morass that allows us to accept widespread failure for some as inevitable despite a commitment to the democratic ideals that supposedly inform our commitment to public education and equal educational opportunities for all. Within the context of these beliefs, there is no expectation for a public response, there is no place for hope, there is no place for a different vision; we are all simultaneously helpless and victimized.

Is there a place for change in the landscape of public education? I contend that it is only in acknowledging public schools as an "educational disaster" that we can begin to sort out the most salient aspects of education and schooling. Only then can we imagine the different ways that we might be able to create public spaces that embrace and celebrate the tenets of a more hopeful pedagogy, the kind of critical pedagogical educational movement articulated by Paulo Freire, "guided by both passion and principle to help students develop a consciousness of freedom, recognize authoritarian tendencies, empower the imagination, connect knowledge and truth to power, and learn how to read both the word and the world as part of a broader struggle for agency, justice, and democracy" (as cited in Giroux, 2012, p. 116). As Eldridge Cleaver once said, "If you are not a part of the solution, you are a part of the problem." As educational leaders, we have a moral obligation to be a part of the solution, to initiate the dialogue and discussion about change and meaningful school reform, and not simply the reform of existing institutions, but the reforming of educational alternatives, places where relevant teaching and learning experiences can be negotiated and the needs and the desires of diverse learners can be met; to do otherwise would be immoral. Madeloni and Gorlewski (2013) provide a similar admonition:

> These are treacherous times for public education. Schools and colleges are under unprecedented attack by those who seek to undermine public education. While we try to defend ourselves, we must also work to create education that is challenging, creative, joyful, deeply engaging, and liberatory. *How* we resist is as critical as that we resist, for within our resistance we create new spaces for imagination. We do not need more technocratic efficiency, simulated objectivity, or corporate incursions. The troubles of teacher education are human troubles, requiring human answers: conversations, time, space for conflict, space for appreciation and love, space for humor and uncertainty. Teacher educators, like all teachers, must be free to disagree and develop questions that are not standardized. Teacher education can create possibilities for radical imagination in which we rehumanize the classroom and develop the theory and heart to practice education as freedom. Let's make our voices heard. Let's reclaim the conversation. (Madeloni & Gorlewski, 2013, n.p.)

It is imperative that we stand up and defend what is good and important in public schools, and actively challenge the pundits who are undermining our efforts and moving education from a public arena to a private domain. I often tell students that this is not pretty, polite work, but rather, a revolution in the making; the stakes are high, our children are at-risk and the democratic ideals that Dewey espoused are being tested. Defeat is not an option. It is a dismal thought to consider that public education is a hopeless affair, and it definitely makes teacher recruitment a difficult chore, but are we better off to confront the reality and attempt to fix it or simply pretend that everything is fine with a few exceptions and if we stay the course, small pockets of success will be our consolation? For me, the answer is obvious. I find the thought of an educational equivalent of Occupy Wall Street/NYC Protest for World Revolution to be both exciting and energizing; perhaps an Occupy Schools Movement/A Social Justice Revolution would give people a "tipping point" for irrefutable change. While my sentiments may reflect those of a small, but enthusiastic group, I believe that our voices are important and we are ready to walk in solidarity toward taking back our schools and replacing hopelessness with a renewed hopefulness that has an ideological commitment to educational equity in all forms, for all people. It is only in this way that a pedagogy of hopelessness can be replaced with a vision that creates and sustains 21st century alternative educational initiatives that are dynamic and evolving institutions that serve all teachers and all learners regardless of race, ethnicity, social class, gender, sexual orientation and/or race.

References

About edTPA: Overview. Retrieved from http://edtpa.aacte.org/about-edtpa

Anyon, J. (2014). *Radical possibilities: Public policy, urban education, and a new social movement* (Critical Social Thought) (2nd ed.). New York: Routledge.

Au, W. (2013). What's a nice test like you doing in a place like this? The edTPA and corporate education "reform." *Rethinking Schools, 27,* 4. Retrieved from http://www.rethinkingschools.org/archive/27_04/27_04_au.shtml

Canedo, N. (2014). Teachers petition for Time Magazine to apologize for "Rotten Apples" cover. Retrieved from http://www.syracuse.com/news/index.ssf/2014/10/time_magazine_teachers_tenure_cover_rotten_apples.html

Cuban, L. (1984). *How teachers taught: Constancy and change in American classrooms, 1890–1980* (Research on Teaching Monograph Series). London: Longman Group United Kingdom.

Cuban, L. & Tyack, D. (1997). *Tinkering toward utopia: A century of public school reform.* Boston, MA: Harvard University Press.

Darling-Hammond, L. & Hyler, M. E. (2013). The role of performance assessment in developing teaching as a profession. *Rethinking Schools, 27,* 4. Retrieved from http://www.rethinkingschools.org/archive/27_04/27_04_darling-hammond_hyler.shtml

Dewey, J. (1916). Democracy and education: An introduction to the philosophy of education. University of California Libraries.

Edwards, H. S. (2014). Taking on teacher tenure. *Time, 184,* 17, 34–39.

Freire, P. (1994). *Pedagogy of hope: Reliving "Pedagogy of the Oppressed."* New York: Continuum.

Giroux, H. (2012). *Education and the crisis of public values: Challenging the assault on teachers, students, and public education.* New York: Peter Lang Publishing.

Giroux, H. (2013). Hope in the age of looming authoritarianism. Retrieved from http://www.truth-out.org/opinion/item/20307-hope-in-the-age-of-looming-authoritarianism

Guggenheim, D. (Director). (2010). *Waiting for Superman* (Motion Picture). United States: Paramount Vantage.

Guggenheim, D. (Director). (2013). *Teach* (Motion Picture). United States: Participant Media.

Harvey, D. (2005). *A brief history of neoliberalism.* New York: Oxford University Press.

hooks, b. (2003). *Teaching community: A pedagogy of hope.* New York: Routledge.

Klein, J. (2011). The failure of American schools. *The Atlantic.* Retrieved from www.theatlantic.com/magazine/archive/2011/06/the…/308497/

Madeloni, B. (2015). edTPA: Doubling down on Whiteness in teacher education. In B. Picower & E. Mayorga (Eds.), *What's race got to do with it: How current school reform policy maintains racial and economic inequality* (pp. 121–145). New York: Peter Lang Publishing.

Madeloni, B. & Gorlewski, J. (2013). Wrong answer to the wrong question: Why we need critical teacher education, not standardization. *Rethinking Schools, 27,* 4. Retrieved from http://www.rethinkingschools.org/archive/27_04/27_04_madeloni-gorlewski.shtml

Pearson (2015). Retrieved from http://www.pearsoned.com/

Picower, B. & Mayorga, E. (2015). *What's race got to do with it: How current school reform policy maintains racial and economic inequality.* New York: Peter Lang Publishing.

Ravitch, D. (2010). The myth of charter schools. *The New York Review of Books.* Retrieved from http://www.nybooks.com/articles/archives/2010/nov/11/myth-charter-schools/

Smith, F. (1995). Let's declare education a disaster and get on with our lives. *Phi Delta Kappan, 76,* 8, 584–590.

Strauss, V. (2015). What makes a great teacher. Retrieved from www.washingtonpost.com/blogs/answer-sheet/wp/2015/02/02/what-makes-a-great-teacher/

Student Assessment Scorers Full & Part-Time (n.d.). Retrieved from http://seattle.craigslist.org/skc/edu/4898387624.html

White. T. (2015). Charter schools: Demystifying Whiteness in a market of "No Excuses" corporate-styled charter schools. In B. Picower & E. Mayorga (Eds.), *What's race got to do with it: How current school reform policy maintains racial and economic inequality* (pp. 121–145). New York: Peter Lang Publishing.

Zhao, E. (2011). High school dropout rates for poor and minority students disproportionately high. *The Huffington Post.* Retrieved from http://www.huffingtonpost.com/2011/10/20/high-school-dropout-rates_n_1022221.html

CHAPTER 2

My Pedagogic Creed

John Dewey

Article One. What Education Is

I believe that all education proceeds by the participation of the individual in the social consciousness of the race. This process begins unconsciously almost at birth, and is continually shaping the individual's powers, saturating his consciousness, forming his habits, training his ideas, and arousing his feelings and emotions. Through this unconscious education the individual gradually comes to share in the intellectual and moral resources which humanity has succeeded in getting together. He becomes an inheritor of the funded capital of civilization. The most formal and technical education in the world cannot safely depart from this general process. It can only organize it; or differentiate it in some particular direction.

I believe that the only true education comes through the stimulation of the child's powers by the demands of the social situations in which he finds himself. Through these demands he is stimulated to act as a member of a unity, to emerge from his original narrowness of action and feeling and to conceive of himself from the standpoint of the welfare of the group to which he belongs. Through the responses which others make to his own activities he comes to know what these mean in social terms. The value which they have is reflected back into them. For instance, through the response which is made to the child's instinctive babblings the child comes to know what those babblings mean; they are transformed into articulate language and thus the child is introduced into the consolidated wealth of ideas and emotions which are now summed up in language. *from babbling — articulate language*

I believe that this educational process has two sides—one psychological and one sociological; and that neither can be subordinated to the other or neglected without evil results following. Of these two sides, the psychological is the basis. The child's own instincts and powers furnish the material and give the starting point for all education. Save as the efforts of the educator connect with some activity which the child is carrying on of his own initiative independent of the educator, education becomes reduced to a pressure from without. It may, indeed, give certain external results but cannot truly be called educative. Without insight into the psychological structure and activities of the individual, the educative process will, therefore, be haphazard and arbitrary. If it chances to coincide with the child's activity it will get a leverage; if it does not, it will result in friction, or disintegration, or arrest of the child nature.

I believe that knowledge of social conditions, of the present state of civilization, is necessary in order properly to interpret the child's powers. The child has his own instincts and tendencies, but we do not know what these mean until we can translate them into their social equivalents. We must be able to carry them back into a social past and see them as the inheritance of previous race activities. We must also be able to project them into the future to see what their outcome and end will be. In the illustration just used, it is the ability to see in the child's babblings the promise and potency of a future social intercourse and conversation which enables one to deal in the proper way with that instinct.

I believe that the psychological and social sides are organically related and that education cannot be regarded as a compromise between the two, or a superimposition of one upon the other. We are told that the psychological definition of education is barren and formal—that it gives us only the idea of a development of all the mental powers without giving us any idea of the use to which these powers are put. On the other hand, it is urged that the social definition of education, as getting adjusted to civilization, makes of it a forced and external process, and results in subordinating the freedom of the individual to a preconceived social and political status.

I believe each of these objections is true when urged against one side isolated from the other. In order to know what a power really is we must know what its end, use, or function is; and this we cannot know save as we conceive of the individual as active in social relationships. But, on the other hand, the only possible adjustment which we can give to the child under existing conditions, is that which arises through putting him in complete possession of all his powers. With the advent of democracy and modern industrial conditions, it is impossible to foretell definitely just what civilization will be twenty years from now. Hence it is impossible to prepare the child for any precise set of conditions. To prepare him for the future life means to give him command of himself; it means so to train him that he will have the full and ready use of all his capacities; that his eye and ear and hand may be tools ready to command, that his judgment may be capable of grasping the conditions under which it has to work, and the executive forces be trained to act economically and efficiently. It is impossible to reach this sort of adjustment save as constant regard is had to the individual's own powers, tastes, and interests—say, that is, as education is continually converted into psychological terms. In sum, I believe that the individual who is to be educated is a social individual and that society is an organic union of individuals. If we eliminate the social factor from the child we are left only with an abstraction; if we eliminate the individual factor from society, we are left only with an inert and lifeless mass. Education, therefore, must begin with a psychological insight into the child's capacities, interests, and habits. It must be controlled at every point by reference to these same considerations. These powers, interests, and habits must be continually interpreted—we must know what they mean. They must be translated into terms of their social equivalents—into terms of what they are capable of in the way of social service.

Article Two. What the School Is

I believe that the school is primarily a social institution. Education being a social process, the school is simply that form of community life in which all those agencies are concentrated that will be most effective in bringing the child to share in the inherited resources of the race, and to use his own powers for social ends.

I believe that education, therefore, is a process of living and not a preparation for future living.

I believe that the school must represent present life—life as real and vital to the child as that which he carries on in the home, in the neighborhood, or on the playground.

I believe that education which does not occur through forms of life, forms that are worth living for their own sake, is always a poor substitute for the genuine reality and tends to cramp and to deaden.

I believe that the school, as an institution, should simplify existing social life; should reduce it, as it were, to an embryonic form. Existing life is so complex that the child cannot be brought into contact with it without either confusion or distraction; he is either overwhelmed by multiplicity of activities which are going on, so that he loses his own power of orderly reaction, or he is so stimulated by these various activities that his powers are prematurely called into play and he becomes either unduly specialized or else disintegrated.

I believe that, as such simplified social life, the school life should grow gradually out of the home life; that it should take up and continue the activities with which the child is already familiar in the home.

I believe that it should exhibit these activities to the child, and reproduce them in such ways that the child will gradually learn the meaning of them, and be capable of playing his own part in relation to them.

I believe that this is a psychological necessity, because it is the only way of securing continuity in the child's growth, the only way of giving a background of past experience to the new ideas given in school.

I believe it is also a social necessity because the home is the form of social life in which the child has been nurtured and in connection with which he has had his moral training. It is the business of the school to deepen and extend his sense of the values bound up in his home life.

I believe that much of present education fails because it neglects this fundamental principle of the school as a form of community life. It conceives the school as a place where certain information is to be given, where certain lessons are to be learned, or where certain habits are to be formed. The value of these is conceived as lying largely in the remote future; the child must do these things for the sake of something else he is to do; they are mere preparation. As a result they do not become a part of the life experience of the child and so are not truly educative.

I believe that moral education centres about this conception of the school as a mode of social life, that the best and deepest moral training is precisely that which one gets through having to enter into proper relations with others in a unity of work and thought. The present educational systems, so far as they destroy or neglect this unity, render it difficult or impossible to get any genuine, regular moral training.

I believe that the child should be stimulated and controlled in his work through the life of the community.

I believe that under existing conditions far too much of the stimulus and control proceeds from the teacher, because of neglect of the idea of the school as a form of social life.

I believe that the teacher's place and work in the school is to be interpreted from this same basis. The teacher is not in the school to impose certain ideas or to form certain habits in the child, but is there as a member of the community to select the influences which shall affect the child and to assist him in properly responding to these influences.

I believe that the discipline of the school should proceed from the life of the school as a whole and not directly from the teacher.

I believe that the teacher's business is simply to determine on the basis of larger experience and riper wisdom, how the discipline of life shall come to the child.

I believe that all questions of the grading of the child and his promotion should be determined by reference to the same standard. Examinations are of use only so far as they test the child's fitness for social life and reveal the place in which he can be of most service and where he can receive the most help.

Article Three. The Subject-Matter of Education

I believe that the social life of the child is the basis of concentration, or correlation, in all his training or growth. The social life gives the unconscious unity and the background of all his efforts and of all his attainments.

I believe that the subject-matter of the school curriculum should mark a gradual differentiation out of the primitive unconscious unity of social life.

I believe that we violate the child's nature and render difficult the best ethical results, by introducing the child too abruptly to a number of special studies, of reading, writing, geography, etc., out of relation to this social life.

I believe, therefore, that the true centre of correlation of the school subjects is not science, nor literature, nor history, nor geography, but the child's own social activities.

I believe that education cannot be unified in the study of science, or so-called nature study, because apart from human activity, nature itself is not a unity; nature in itself is a number of diverse objects in space and time, and to attempt to make it the centre of work by itself, is to introduce a principle of radiation rather than one of concentration.

I believe that literature is the reflex expression and interpretation of social experience; that hence it must follow upon and not precede such experience. It, therefore, cannot be made the basis, although it may be made the summary of unification.

I believe once more that history is of educative value in so far as it presents phases of social life and growth. It must be controlled by reference to social life. When taken simply as history it is thrown into the distant past and becomes dead and inert. Taken as the record of man's social life and progress it becomes full of meaning. I believe, however, that it cannot be so taken excepting as the child is also introduced directly into social life.

I believe accordingly that the primary basis of education is in the child's powers at work along the same general constructive lines as those which have brought civilization into being.

I believe that the only way to make the child conscious of his social heritage is to enable him to perform those fundamental types of activity which makes civilization what it is.

I believe, therefore, in the so-called expressive or constructive activities as the centre of correlation.

I believe that this gives the standard for the place of cooking, sewing, manual training, etc., in the school.

I believe that they are not special studies which are to be introduced over and above a lot of others in the way of relaxation or relief, or as additional accomplishments. I believe rather that they represent, as types, fundamental forms of social activity; and that it is possible and desirable that the child's introduction into the more formal subjects of the curriculum be through the medium of these activities.

I believe that the study of science is educational in so far as it brings out the materials and processes which make social life what it is.

I believe that one of the greatest difficulties in the present teaching of science is that the material is presented in purely objective form, or is treated as a new peculiar kind of experience which the child can add to that which he has already had. In reality, science is of value because it gives the ability to interpret and control the experience already had. It should be introduced, not as so much new subject-matter, but as showing the factors already involved in previous experience and as furnishing tools by which that experience can be more easily and effectively regulated.

I believe that at present we lose much of the value of literature and language studies because of our elimination of the social element. Language is almost always treated in the books of pedagogy simply as the expression of thought. It is true that language is a logical instrument, but it is fundamentally and primarily a social instrument. Language is the device for communication; it is the tool through which one individual comes to share the ideas and feelings of others. When treated simply as a way of getting individual information, or as a means of showing off what one has learned, it loses its social motive and end.

I believe that there is, therefore, no succession of studies in the ideal school curriculum. If education is life, all life has, from the outset, a scientific aspect; an aspect of art and culture and an aspect of communication. It cannot, therefore, be true that the proper studies for one grade are mere reading and writing, and that at a later grade, reading, or literature, or science, may be introduced. The progress is not in the succession of studies but in the development of new attitudes towards, and new interests in, experience.

I believe finally, that education must be conceived as a continuing reconstruction of experience; that the process and the goal of education are one and the same thing.

I believe that to set up any end outside of education, as furnishing its goal and standard, is to deprive the educational process of much of its meaning and tends to make us rely upon false and external stimuli in dealing with the child.

Article Four. The Nature of Method

I believe that the question of method is ultimately reducible to the question of the order of development of the child's powers and interests. The law for presenting and treating material is the law implicit within the child's own nature. Because this is so I believe the following statements are of supreme importance as determining the spirit in which education is carried on:

1. I believe that the active side precedes the passive in the development of the child nature; that expression comes before conscious impression; that the muscular development precedes the sensory; that movements come before conscious sensations; I believe that consciousness is essentially motor or impulsive; that conscious states tend to project themselves in action.

    I believe that the neglect of this principle is the cause of a large part of the waste of time and strength in school work. The child is thrown into a passive, receptive or absorbing attitude. The conditions are such that he is not permitted to follow the law of his nature; the result is friction and waste.

    I believe that ideas (intellectual and rational processes) also result from action and devolve for the sake of the better control of action. What we term reason is primarily the law of orderly or effective action. To attempt to develop the reasoning powers, the powers of judgment, without reference to the selection and arrangement of means in action, is the fundamental fallacy in our present methods of dealing with this matter. As a result we present the child with arbitrary symbols. Symbols are a necessity in mental development, but they have their place as tools for economizing effort; presented by themselves they are a mass of meaningless and arbitrary ideas imposed from without.

2. I believe that the image is the great instrument of instruction. What a child gets out of any subject presented to him is simply the images which he himself forms with regard to it.

    I believe that if nine-tenths of the energy at present directed towards making the child learn certain things, were spent in seeing to it that the child was forming proper images, the work of instruction would be indefinitely facilitated.

    I believe that much of the time and attention now given to the preparation and presentation of lessons might be more wisely and profitably expended in training the child's power of imagery and in seeing to it that he was continually forming definite, vivid, and growing images of the various subjects with which he comes in contact in his experience.

3. I believe that interests are the signs and symptoms of growing power. I believe that they represent dawning capacities. Accordingly the constant and careful observation of interests is of the utmost importance for the educator.

    I believe that these interests are to be observed as showing the state of development which the child has reached.

I believe that they prophesy the stage upon which he is about to enter.

I believe that only through the continual and sympathetic observation of childhood's interests can the adult enter into the child's life and see what it is ready for, and upon what material it could work most readily and fruitfully.

I believe that these interests are neither to be humored nor repressed. To repress interest is to substitute the adult for the child, and so to weaken intellectual curiosity and alertness, to suppress initiative, and to deaden interest. To humor the interests is to substitute the transient for the permanent. The interest is always the sign of some power below; the important thing is to discover this power. To humor the interest is to fail to penetrate below the surface and its sure result is to substitute caprice and whim for genuine interest.

4. I believe that the emotions are the reflex of actions.

I believe that to endeavor to stimulate or arouse the emotions apart from their corresponding activities, is to introduce an unhealthy and morbid state of mind.

I believe that if we can only secure right habits of action and thought, with reference to the good, the true, and the beautiful, the emotions will for the most part take care of themselves.

I believe that next to deadness and dullness, formalism and routine, our education is threatened with no greater evil than sentimentalism.

I believe that this sentimentalism is the necessary result of the attempt to divorce feeling from action.

Article Five. The School and Social Progress

I believe that education is the fundamental method of social progress and reform.

I believe that all reforms which rest simply upon the enactment of law, or the threatening of certain penalties, or upon changes in mechanical or outward arrangements, are transitory and futile.

I believe that education is a regulation of the process of coming to share in the social consciousness; and that the adjustment of individual activity on the basis of this social consciousness is the only sure method of social reconstruction.

I believe that this conception has due regard for both the individualistic and socialistic ideals. It is duly individual because it recognizes the formation of a certain character as the only genuine basis of right living. It is socialistic because it recognizes that this right character is not to be formed by merely individual precept, example, or exhortation, but rather by the influence of a certain form of institutional or community life upon the individual, and that the social organism through the school, as its organ, may determine ethical results.

I believe that in the ideal school we have the reconciliation of the individualistic and the institutional ideals.

I believe that the community's duty to education is, therefore, its paramount moral duty. By law and punishment, by social agitation and discussion, society can regulate and form itself in a more or less haphazard and chance way. But through education society can formulate its own purposes, can organize its own means and resources, and thus shape itself with definiteness and economy in the direction in which it wishes to move.

I believe that when society once recognizes the possibilities in this direction, and the obligations which these possibilities impose, it is impossible to conceive of the resources of time, attention, and money which will be put at the disposal of the educator.

I believe it is the business of every one interested in education to insist upon the school as the primary and most effective instrument of social progress and reform in order that society may be awakened to realize what the school stands for, and aroused to the necessity of endowing the educator with sufficient equipment properly to perform his task.

I believe that education thus conceived marks the most perfect and intimate union of science and art conceivable in human experience.

I believe that the art of thus giving shape to human powers and adapting them to social service, is the supreme art; one calling into its service the best of artists; that no insight, sympathy, tact, executive power is too great for such service.

I believe that with the growth of psychological science, giving added insight into individual structure and laws of growth; and with growth of social science, adding to our knowledge of the right organization of individuals, all scientific resources can be utilized for the purposes of education.

I believe that when science and art thus join hands the most commanding motive for human action will be reached; the most genuine springs of human conduct aroused and the best service that human nature is capable of guaranteed.

I believe, finally, that the teacher is engaged, not simply in the training of individuals, but in the formation of the proper social life.

I believe that every teacher should realize the dignity of his calling; that he is a social servant set apart for the maintenance of proper social order and the securing of the right social growth.

I believe that in this way the teacher always is the prophet of the true God and the usherer in of the true kingdom of God.

CHAPTER 3

Finding Hope Among the Hopeless

Pedro A. Noguera

It was an overcast, Thursday afternoon. The fog was rolling in across the Bay and the temperature was dropping. It was the kind of day that is more typical of summer than fall in the Bay Area.

It was late in the day and I was feeling particularly uninspired about my job. When I first started working as the Executive Assistant to Mayor Loni Hancock, I thought I had the best job in the city. I was at the center of power in local government, and I thought I was in a position to make things happen. From the very first day the job had been demanding, but in a good way. Every day I was presented with new challenges and new issues to work on. At first I thought that I was in a position to have an impact on issues I cared about—homelessness, drug abuse, and the plight of the city's youth. About 3 months into the job, my optimism had given way to the grim reality that change comes slowly in municipal government.

I soon realized that the Mayor's office was not a place where sweeping reforms would be launched and fundamental changes would be initiated. Even more depressing for me was the realization that rather than power, what I had was responsibility. I was responsible for figuring out what the city should do about the homeless who were camping out in the park behind City Hall. I was responsible for explaining to frightened residents why the police couldn't stop the drug dealers who were terrorizing their neighborhood. I was responsible for meeting with protesters who wanted to make Peoples Park into a national shrine, and old ladies who wanted their neighbors to trim their trees so that their view of the Bay would not be obstructed.

I was growing tired of Berkeley politics, and for the first time in my life I felt discouraged, despondent, and downright depressed about my work. Perhaps I had been too naive. Why should I have thought that crime and poverty could be solved by one city, even as they plagued communities throughout the United States?

The year was 1988 and crack cocaine and the violence that accompanied it were devastating the Black community in Berkeley. As the Mayor's representative, I was frequently the person who had to respond to community complaints about drive-by shootings and crack houses that operated like open markets. I quickly learned that city government lacked the resources to solve any of the major problems facing residents. As the person most likely to hear the pain and anguish of the community and to be blamed for the city's failures, I had grown extremely frustrated after just 2 years on the job.

Feeling beleaguered and burdened by the responsibilities of the job, I was miraculously drawn back into education by the principal of a local high school who came to my office that foggy afternoon accompanied by one of his students. My friend George Perry recently had been assigned to serve as principal of the local continuation school, East Campus (a school for students who had been removed from the traditional high school due to poor behavior and/or grades). It turned out that he had been assigned to his new job as punishment for the trouble he had caused in the district. However, instead of scaring him into retirement as the higher-ups had hoped, the assignment renewed George's sense of purpose about his work in education.

He came to see me because I once had served as the student body president at UC Berkeley, and he wanted me to convince his student, John Peters, to run for student body president of his school. As George sang the praises of his student leader, I took a good look at John and immediately surmised that he was probably a street-level drug dealer. With gold teeth in his mouth, a thick gold chain around his neck, and a beeper at his waist, John fit a profile I had come to know well. I looked at John and then back at George, and my look revealed my confusion about what he had in mind. But instead of voicing my doubts, I listened as George told me why he wanted John to run for student body president and I listened closely as John told me about himself. Within minutes I understood what George was thinking. John was intelligent, articulate, and extremely charismatic. George knew that if he could co-opt John by convincing him to play a positive role at his school, he might be able to find a way to get other students to begin to take their education more seriously. John was a natural leader and George understood that he needed John on his side. He needed John to be a force for good at the school.

East Campus once had served as an alternative school for kids who did not fit in at the large, impersonal environment at Berkeley High School. Over time, it had become a dumping ground for troubled kids like John. Tucked away at the margins of the school district, East Campus was a school in name only. The first time I visited the school there were more kids in the parking lot blasting their car radios and smoking pot, than there were in the classrooms. In a city that took great pride in its commitment to racial integration, the school was over 90% Black. Hardly any students attended class, and those that did seemed to be there in body only.

Despite the sorrowful state of the school, I was so taken by John and by what my friend George Perry was trying to accomplish, that I immediately was convinced that working at the school was where I should be, given my desire to make a difference. I saw the potential to transform this small forgotten school into a place that could become a genuine alternative for kids who were being killed and imprisoned each day because of the drug trade on the streets. Shortly after my visit, I left my job with the Mayor to join George as a teacher at East Campus.

Confronting the "Crisis" in Urban Public Schools

I begin this chapter with this story about my entry into the field of education because it is reflective of how I have come to understand the promise and the potential of urban public schools in the United States. Like East Campus, many other urban schools have been written off as failures. Failure is the word used most frequently to describe urban public schools in the United States, because the list of problems confronting these institutions is so long and daunting. Low test scores, low grades, high dropout rates, poor attendance, and generally unmotivated students usually top the list of failings. Burned-out and ineffective teachers, who care more about protecting their jobs than helping students, typically follow complaints about students. Those more intimately familiar with conditions in urban districts point to dilapidated and unsafe buildings, administrations hopelessly mired in politicized and inefficient bureaucracies, and an endless series of reforms that never seem to lead to genuine improvement (F. Hess, 1999).

If these characterizations were limited to a handful of urban schools or districts, the "problem" might not seem so daunting, but this is not the case. Urban school failure is pervasive. It is endemic in the nation's largest cities—New York, Chicago, Los Angeles, and Philadelphia, and not uncommon in small towns such as East St. Louis, Poughkeepsie, Camden, and Compton. In fact, wherever poor people are concentrated and employment is scarce, public schools are almost always very bad. In many parts of the country, the problems present within urban schools are perceived as so numerous and intractable that the term "crisis" frequently is applied to describe the situation; and this is how it is described by those who haven't given up hope completely.

Yet, although the problems and issues confronting urban public schools in the United States are profound and deeply discouraging, characterizing their plight as either one of crisis or utter hopelessness is inaccurate. Nor do such grim portrayals serve as a genuine diagnosis of the problems or shed light on what should be done to address them. Such descriptions do, however, play an important role in influencing popular conceptions of urban schools, and ultimately they influence how policy makers approach the task of "fixing" the schools.

Were the situation in urban schools truly a "crisis," one might expect to see urgent responses from leaders at the local, state, and federal levels. After all, the education and welfare of millions of children are at stake, and if a crisis were genuinely perceived, would not drastic measures be taken to alleviate the suffering, not unlike the actions taken following an earthquake or a hurricane? However, even during a period in which educational issues are receiving more media coverage and more attention from policy makers than ever before,[1] there is a stunning lack of urgency associated with official responses to the issues confronting urban public schools.

Moreover, in everyday parlance, the term *crisis* typically is thought of as a temporary condition, a temporary although serious deviation from the status quo. Injured individuals and beleaguered communities affected by a storm or fire generally are not thought of as being in a permanent state of crisis. Even if the problems have devastating long-term consequences, over time the condition ceases to be described as a crisis. Eventually, there is a recovery and a return to a state of normalcy. Crises that persist or become more severe, like illnesses that take a turn for the worse and are deemed incurable, generally are characterized as chronic and debilitating conditions, unfortunate but permanent states for which solutions may never be found.

Similarly, while the term *crisis* may not appropriately characterize the situation in urban schools, those who describe them as doomed and hopelessly unfixable are also off the mark. There is no question that the problems of urban schools are entrenched and intractable. However, compelling evidence suggests that despite their failings and weaknesses, urban public schools are in fact indispensable to those they serve. Without any viable alternative available, urban public schools cannot be written off as rotten structures in need of demolition.

The Indispensable Institution

Despite the severity of the conditions present in many urban schools, and despite the intractability of the problems they face, these deeply flawed institutions continue to serve millions of children throughout the United States. In fact, the largest school districts in the nation are classified as "urban" and they serve nearly one-third of school-aged children (Council of the Great City Schools, 2001). In a profound demonstration of faith, millions of parents voluntarily take their children each day to the very schools that have been described as "desperate hell holes" (McGroarty, 1996). Certainly, many do so with reluctance and considerable consternation. In many cases, parents enroll their children only because they lack options or access to schools they regard as better or safer. However, many others do so willingly, hoping against the odds that for their child, or at the particular school their child attends, something good will happen, and a better future through education will be possible.[2] At a minimum, they may enroll their sons and daughters because they know that even at a failing public school their children will have access to a warm meal and adult supervision while they are there.

I was reminded of the difficult choices facing poor parents during conversations with Salvadoran refugees in a run-down neighborhood of inner-city Los Angeles. I was meeting with a group of parents at the Central American Refugee Center shortly after the Rodney King uprising of 1991. We met in an area of downtown LA called Pico Union, one of the most densely populated neighborhoods in the United States and home to thousands of undocumented war refugees from Central America. Although it did not receive much media attention, it had been one of the epicenters of violence and looting during the riot. The parents I met with described the riot as the product of rising frustrations, and while others debated whether the outburst should be called a riot or a rebellion, these refugees of brutal civil wars termed it *"un explosion social"* (a social explosion).

As they described the perils they faced raising children in this crime-ridden, drug-infested neighborhood, they made me aware of how important the public schools were to them. They did not complain about the overcrowded classrooms, the absence of certified teachers, or the dismal state of the facilities. Instead, they spoke with genuine appreciation about how happy they were to have a safe place to send their children. The fact that their children were fed, and in at least one school provided health care, added to their sense of gratitude. *"Somos probes, sin poder o derechos. Por los menos nuestro hijos teinen una educacion. Si, hay problemas en las escuelas, pero tenemos esperanza que el futuro de los hijos va estar mejor."* (We are poor, without power or rights. At least our children have an education. Yes, there are problems in the schools, but we have hope that the future for our children will be better.)

In economically depressed inner-city communities like Pico Union, public schools play a vital role in supporting low-income families. Even when other neighborhood services, including banks, retail stores, libraries, and other public services, do not exist, are shut down, or are abandoned, public schools remain (Noguera, 1995b). They are neighborhood constants, not because they succeed in carrying out their mission or because they satisfy the needs of those they serve, but because they have a relatively stable source of funding ensured by the legal mandate to educate children.

Urban public schools frequently serve as important social welfare institutions.[3] With meager resources, they attempt to address at least some of the nutritional and health needs of poor children. They do so because those charged with educating poor children generally recognize that it is impossible to serve their academic needs without simultaneously addressing their basic need for health and safety. For many poor children, schools provide a source of stability that often is lacking in other parts of their lives, and while many urban public schools are plagued by the threat of violence and intimidation, most are far safer than the communities in which they are located (Casella, 2001). The bottom line is that even when there is little evidence of educational efficacy, urban public schools still provide services that are desperately needed by poor families, and federal and state policies offer few alternatives.

In the absence of genuine alternatives, even failing public schools retain a dependent although disgruntled constituency base because they are typically the only social institution that provides a consistent source of stability and support to impoverished families. For this reason, those who castigate and disparage urban public schools without offering viable solutions for improving or replacing them jeopardize the interests of those who depend on them. Politicians who often lead the chorus of criticismshave largely failed to devise policies to address the deplorable conditions present in many inner-city schools and communities. Even in the few cases where drastic measures, such as state takeovers of troubled districts (most often, urban school systems), have been taken, the results achieved generally have failed to live up to the expectations or promises. Most of the popular educational reforms enacted by states and the federal government (e.g., standards and accountability through high-stakes testing, charter schools, phonics-based reading programs, etc.) fail to address the severe social and economic conditions in urban areas that invariably affect the quality and character of public schools.

The central argument of this chapter is that until there is a genuine commitment to address the social context of schooling—to confront the "urban" condition—it will be impossible to bring about significant and sustainable improvements in urban public schools. The complex and seemingly intractable array of social and economic problems in urban areas must be addressed and school-based policies that respond to these problems must be devised; otherwise, pervasive school failure in cities across the United States will continue to be the norm.

Public schools are the only institutions in this country charged with providing for the educational needs of poor children. Given the role they play, it would be a mistake to allow them to deteriorate further or to become unsalvageable. Undeniably, they often carry out their mission poorly, without adequately serving the educational needs of the children under their charge. However, public schools in the United States are the only social institutions that cannot by law turn a child away regardless of race, religion, immigration status, or any other trait or designation (Kirp, 1982). Access to public education in the United States is complete, universal, and compulsory (Tyack, 1980), and, as such, it is also the only public service that functions as a form of social entitlement: a "positive right"[4] and social good provided to citizens and noncitizens alike (Carnoy & Levin, 1985). For all of these reasons, public education, even in the poorest sections of the inner city, constitutes a vital public resource. Rather than being regarded as hopelessly unfixable, urban public schools, particularly those that serve poor children, must be seen for what they are: the last and most enduring remnant of the social safety net for poor children in the United States.

Seen in this light, the problems confronting urban public schools must be approached from a different perspective. Instead of castigating and decrying their failures, and inadvertently joining the chorus clamoring for their total demolition, those who recognize the value and the importance of the services schools provide must instead adopt a position of critical support. In the same way that it would be unwise for criticisms of overcrowded buses or trains to prompt calls to abandon mass transportation, those who deplore conditions in urban public schools must recognize that, despite their weaknesses, urban public schools are desperately needed by those they serve. Just as complaints about long lines and poor service should not be used to justify the elimination of public hospitals and clinics that provide health services to the poor and elderly, the failures of urban public schools should not be used as a rationale for their elimination. At least until a genuine, superior alternative for all children is available, public education, with all its faults and weaknesses, remains "the one best system," or at least the only system we have (Tyack, 1980).

However, critical support should not be confused with unquestioning loyalty to public education. Parents, especially those whose children are forced to attend the worst schools, generally have very little loyalty to the "system," and for good reason. The parents I spoke with in Pico Union appreciated the support their children received from struggling schools in their neighborhood, but in all likelihood would jump at the opportunity to enroll their children in better schools if it were possible. Few parents are willing to sacrifice the needs of their children because they wish to show support for the democratic principles underlying the existence of public schools. Given the opportunity, most parents actively seek schools they think have the greatest potential to meet the needs of their children. Whether this occurs in a public, private, or charter school is generally less relevant than whether the school is accessible, affordable, safe, and educationally viable. Defenders of public education who refuse to recognize this reality of parenting undoubtedly will feel betrayed when those who were once their most reliable consumers, namely, poor parents, abandon public schools when provided with options they perceive as superior.

Critical supporters of public education must recognize that it is the rights of children and their families to a good education, and not a failed system, that must be supported. Critical supporters must not be afraid to honestly identify and call attention to the failures of the system, whether these are related to unresponsive leadership or the poor quality of teaching. Critical supporters must demonstrate active support for change and improvement, and, given the sorrowful plight of many schools, they must be open to considering a variety of strategies for innovation. This should not be interpreted as a naive willingness to embrace every new fad in educational reform that comes along. Rather, critical supporters should recognize that all reforms should be evaluated and assessed by the academic and social outcomes obtained by children. With calls for privatization gaining support and momentum, the only way to save public education is to radically alter it. Ensuring that the needs of students and their parents are treated as the highest priority, may be the most radical reform of all.

Pragmatic Optimism as a Guide

This chapter was written to show how urban schools are affected by the social environment in which they are located and to put forward a set of strategies to transform, improve, and fundamentally restructure them. The ideas presented are the product of years of research, teaching, and service in urban schools throughout the United States. These years of experience have provided me with a strong sense of the grim reality present in many urban public schools, and also insights into what I believe it will take to make change possible. I characterize my perspective on the issues and problems confronting urban public schools as one of critical support and pragmatic optimism.

My pragmatism comes from personal and direct experience grappling with the problems facing urban public schools; and so does my optimism. As a middle and high school teacher in Providence, Rhode Island, and in Oakland and Berkeley, California, I have seen firsthand how hard it can be to work within schools and districts where the academic failure of large numbers of students has been the norm for a very long time. In such places, patterns of failure for certain kinds of students are so commonplace and so deeply entrenched that failure tends to be accepted as inevitable and unavoidable. Through research carried out at numerous urban schools, I have seen how easy it is for teachers and administrators to rationalize and therefore accept failure. Given the abundance of unmotivated and underprepared students, dysfunctional and distressed families, unresponsive and incompetent administrators and teachers, and, most of all, misguided and foolhardy politicians, there is no shortage of compelling excuses for persistent failure. Yet, ultimately even this litany of charges just provides the person espousing them with a justification for the inability to make a difference with the children he or she serves. The tendency for some educators to cast blame elsewhere, while accepting responsibility for very little, provides me with a strong sense of pragmatism as I consider what it will take to bring about change.

Additionally, having served as an elected Director and President of the School Board in Berkeley, California, I also realize how difficult it is to reverse negative trends and change things for the better. Serving from 1990 to 1994, a period during which many schools faced severe financial hardships, I realized that my job was to manage what I came to regard as a miserable status quo. My responsibility as a board member required me to eliminate vital programs in order to balance the district budget. I was forced to take the heat for strained relations with our labor unions because we were unable to satisfy their legitimate demands for higher wages. Worst of all, I was forced to vote to expel some of our neediest students, setting them loose on the streets without adequate provision for their education or welfare, because they engaged in violent or dangerous behavior.

If I had not become a pragmatist from such experiences, I undoubtedly would have abandoned my interest in working for the betterment of urban public schools long ago. Pragmatism makes it possible for one to act even in difficult circumstances when one must accept and recognize the limitations of what may be possible. Pragmatism also makes it possible to avoid demonizing beleaguered administrators, angry parents, and frustrated teachers, because it allows one to understand the legitimate source of their resentment, even if it does not provide a way to adequately respond to it.

However, my pragmatism has not given way to cynicism or disillusionment. I remain profoundly aware of the unique potential inherent in education; it alone has the ability to transform and improve the lives of even the neediest and most downtrodden individuals. At the most basic level, I know that all children, regardless of their race or class background, can learn and grow in positive and productive ways when provided the opportunity, and that even in the poorest communities it is possible to create schools that serve children well. I know these things not because of blind faith but largely from direct experience. I have taught in schools that were dumping grounds for "at-risk" adolescents, and I have worked with students who had been written off as incorrigible and unteachable. I have seen these same students learn, grow confident in their abilities, and aspire to achieve goals that previously seemed impossible.

— love this

Gaining a Perspective on Success and Failure

My faith in the possibility that education can serve as a vehicle of individual transformation, and even social change, is rooted in an understanding that human beings have the ability to rise above even the most difficult obstacles, to become more than just victims of circumstance. I have seen education open doors for those who lacked opportunity, and open the minds of those who could not imagine alternative ways of being and living. Like Brazilian educator Paulo Freire (1970), I have seen education enable students to "perceive critically the way they exist in the world; to see the world not as a static reality, but as a reality in process, in transformation" (p. 71).

My optimism is rooted in my faith in people. It is a faith affirmed by teachers like Timiza Wagner, who, unlike me, spent nearly 20 years teaching at East Campus, tirelessly working to instill a sense of hope among young people who had been written off as hopeless by the schools that served them. It is a faith that is renewed by finding schools like Henshaw Middle School in Modesto, California, where most of the children are recent immigrants, speak Spanish as their first language, and have parents who work at the dirty jobs that most Americans refuse to take. Yet, this is a school whose students consistently achieve at high levels (Carnegie Foundation, 1994/1995), and a school where parents are respected as genuine partners despite all the things they do not have. I have worked with other schools that provide an oasis of hope to children who live in neighborhoods and housing projects that seem unfit for human habitation, whose lives are so difficult and arduous that coming to know them well can be a painful experience. I also have had the privilege of working with schools that gradually have been transformed from dumping grounds for bad kids and poor teachers, into model schools that provide students with genuine alternatives from the uncaring, impersonal environments present in many urban public schools. Finally, I have observed teachers who consistently create educational magic in their classrooms, who incite and motivate their students to want to learn, who set high standards for themselves and their students and make it clear that not learning simply is not an option.

Experiences such as these enabled me to overcome the pessimism I felt while working in the Mayor's office: a pessimism that so often overwhelms those who work in urban schools in the United States. As a university professor, of course, I have the luxury to visit both good and bad schools, but unlike those I observe and work with, I get to leave the despair and return to the comfort of the university. I work with and speak to thousands of teachers, students, and parents, and I hear them express their frustrations about politicians who either do not understand or do not care about the conditions in inner-city schools. I also serve on national committees that are charged with studying the problems confronting urban education, and occasionally I am asked to testify before policy makers about what should be done. I use these opportunities to voice the concerns of those who are never heard because their plight and suffering simply are not seen as important.

Yet despite my extensive involvement, I still get to leave the schools whenever I want. I get to return to my office at the university where I can escape the daily grind and the mind-numbing routine of so many schools. I can escape the loud hallways and the tedious faculty meetings that drive even idealistic and committed teachers to cynicism or out of teaching altogether. I get to see the big picture, to keep one foot in and one foot out of urban public schools, and I am allowed time to reflect on what I have seen. I have time to review the data I have collected, to reflect on the stories I have heard, and the opportunity to write and speak about my experiences at some distance from the places where the drama of school plays itself out. I am mindful of the many privileges I enjoy in relation to this work, and I feel compelled to use my position to speak on behalf of those who do not possess similar opportunities and advantages. I do not take this responsibility lightly. My experience leaves me compelled to be accountable for my words and deeds.

When I compare my situation with the reality of most teachers, counselors, and administrators who work within urban public schools, or with the lives of the children who attend them, I am forced to reflect on my own life and the privileges I enjoy. As a former student in New York City's public schools, I am keenly aware that things could have turned out differently for me. Most of my closest friends did not go to college, much less an Ivy League university. The fortunate found dead-end jobs that provide them and their families with a degree of stability. The less fortunate are either dead or wasting away their lives in prison. The long list of those who met such a fate suggests their demise was more than the result of poor choices made or a lack of self-discipline.

My personal fortune does not lead me to the conclusion that if I, a working-class kid from Brooklyn, can find success through education, then so can anyone else who makes the effort. Unlike individuals such as John McWhorter (2000) and Shelby Steele (1990), who use their personal success as a basis for castigating others, especially Black people, for laziness and anti-intellectualism,[5] my experience has taught me that there is more to achieving academic and personal success than effort alone. Children don't get to choose their parents, the neighborhood they'll grow up in, the school they'll attend, or the teachers to whom they'll be assigned. While growing up, I knew many kids who tried hard to do well in school, whose parents supported them and who valued education as strongly as did mine. Yet, most of them were not as fortunate. Due largely to circumstances beyond their control, their dreams and those of their parents were never realized, not because of a lack of effort, but because of a lack of luck and opportunity.

As the second of six children from working-class Caribbean immigrant parents, neither of whom graduated from high school or attended college, I benefited from having learned at an early age to understand the importance of education. Even though neither of my parents had the time or knowledge to navigate the school system, they still managed to convey the importance of academic success to their children, and succeeded in sending all six to some of the most highly regarded universities in the nation. We didn't attend elite private or suburban schools. There was no money for private tutors, computers, or expensive vacations. Yet, education worked for us, even though, for the most part, we succeeded in spite of the system, not because of it. As new immigrants, my parents rejected the idea that the skin color and culture made us racially inferior. We were taught that character and hard work mattered more than race, and that none of the White children we went to school with were inherently superior. Ours is an old success story, one of immigrants who are able to reap the rewards of American opportunity through hard work and determination. Yet, such stories do not negate the fact that, without a Herculean effort, the vast majority of those who are born poor, stay poor.

Now, as the parent of four children, all of whom have attended urban public schools, I continue to enjoy a position of privilege. Unlike me, my children have access to the resources available to most middle-class families—summer enrichment programs, music lessons, and foreign travel. They attend public schools but we have the know-how to make the system work for them and the resources to make up for what they do not receive in school. I know how to advocate for my children and I know how to help them navigate schools that consistently fail large numbers of students. My education grants me class privileges, and generally I am treated with courtesy and respect when I visit my children's schools. Unlike many other parents, I am treated like a valued customer: a client who has the ability and where-withal to exit the system if I feel unsatisfied with the quality of service.

My experience as a parent and student in urban public schools has taught me that while effort is a key ingredient for individual success, for those who are born poor it is not a guarantee. My understanding of the broad patterns of failure and success in American society leads me to conclude that under the present conditions, academic failure for large numbers of poor and working-class children is inevitable. Although we may be in a "new economy" in which many jobs require advanced skills and education (Murnane & Levy, 1996), there is still a need for people who are willing to accept low-status, low-wage work. As long as some schools (suburban and private) are able to generate a sufficient number of academically qualified students for high-skill, high-wage labor, or as long as such labor can be imported, the failure of low-performing schools does not pose a problem for the economy.

Politically, the quality of schools corresponds closely to the strength of electoral constituencies (a point that I have developed further in other writings, where I examined the effects of poverty and racial segregation on local control over schools). Since the end of World War II, political power has shifted in most states from the cities to the suburbs (Clark, 1985; Gratz & Mintz, 1998). Moreover, in high-poverty urban areas, voter participation tends to be low, and ties to political parties are often weak (Schorr, 1997). Cities increasingly lack the political clout needed to obtain muchneeded resources from state government. In some cases, cities still serve as important centers of economic and cultural activity. But even when they retain a degree of viability, they are more likely to employ those who reside elsewhere than those who live within city limits.[6]

Throughout the United States, failing schools are treated as local matters, and responsibility for improving them is delegated to those who reside in the communities they serve. This continues to be the case whether or not communities can generate the resources to address the needs of poor students. From afar, state governments have established academic standards and systems for holding schools accountable (Blasi, 2001; Elmore, 1996), even though it is widely recognized that there are many schools where basic "opportunity to learn standards" have not been met (Oakes, 2002). Of course, state governments do find ways to commit resources to an ever-expanding penal system that stands ready to absorb those who have encountered failure elsewhere.

The consistency of patterns of success and failure, both academic and ultimately economic, and the predictability of these patterns—their correlation with the racial and socioeconomic backgrounds of children—explain why the problems of America's urban public schools are written off as inevitable. Although academic failure in urban schools may be lamented by politicians and deplored by the media, and although those seen as responsible may be viciously castigated, such posturing should not be confused with a serious response to the problem. Ultimately, the lack of a concerted and sustained effort to respond to failing urban public schools can be explained only by understanding that America simply does not care that large numbers of children from inner-city schools and neighborhoods are not properly educated.

This is not a conspiracy theory. For me, it is simply a starting point for my pragmatism. The plight of inner-city schools and many rural schools that serve poor children throughout the United States is not a secret or unknown fact. It is widely recognized that many urban public schools are places that should be avoided because they are dangerous, chaotic, and potentially damaging to those who go there. Yet, it also is understood that certain children—the poorest and neediest—will end up there. For this reason, the possibility that low-performing schools will be forced to close and that other schools will be required to educate their students, as called for in a new policy from the Bush administration, seems implausible. Just as it was true during the bitter and bloody conflicts over busing, it continues to be true today: There aren't many schools in affluent areas that want to serve poor children, especially those who are not White. For this reason it is highly unlikely that the new policy—various forms of school choice or even vouchers—will provide the least powerful children access to schools that are as good as those that serve affluent children.[7]

Urban schools and the children who attend them languish under third world–like conditions, even as President George W. Bush boldly promises to "leave no child behind." Millions of dollars from private and public sources are spent in the name of reform and restructuring, and an entire industry of education experts has been created to go about the work of improving America's schools, but the situation in inner-city schools remains largely unchanged.

In my travels across the United States, I frequently encounter a small number of effective schools that cater to poor children. However, I realize that their scarcity is not an accident.[8] In the San Francisco Bay Area, elementary schools such as Washington in Richmond, Emerson in Berkeley, and Hawthorn in San Francisco serve as living proof that it is possible to create schools that serve poor children well. Their existence, like the 4,000 high-performing, high-poverty schools throughout the nation identified by the Education Trust, reminds us that the problem is not the children but the schools they attend (Education Trust, 2002). Still, knowing that such schools exist forces me to ask why we continue to allow them to be exceptions amid a sea of miserable inadequacy.

The extreme disparities in wealth that pervade U.S. society are largely responsible for the plight of young people and the state of education in urban areas. However, the dearth of good schools is also the inevitable byproduct of a system that is almost completely unaccountable to those it serves. Public education is one of few enterprises where the quality of service provided has no bearing whatsoever on the ability of the system to function. Even when there is little evidence that schools are able to fulfill their basic mission—educating children—the system continues to chug along and all employees get paid (some quite well). This is why I believe that the high-stakes exams that have been adopted in states such as Massachusetts and California are fundamentally flawed and morally irresponsible. The exams are used to hold students accountable for their achievement even though the authorities who have imposed the exams know that they cannot guarantee the quality of the education students receive.

As long as we are able to convince ourselves that simply providing access to education is equivalent to providing equal opportunity, we will continue to treat failing schools as a nonissue. We also will continue to delude ourselves with the notion that the United States is a democracy based on genuine meritocratic principles: a society where social mobility is determined by individual talent and effort. We hold on to this fantasy even as a quarter of the nation's children are denied adequate educational opportunity.

Ultimately, this denial relegates the problems and issues confronting urban public schools to the margins of public life in American society. The media frequently carries stories about deplorable conditions in urban public schools, but typically it does so as if they occurred far away in some third world nation. Occasionally, the media will report on the triumphant stories of poor children like Cedric Jennings, the lead character in *A Hope in the Unseen* (Suskind, 1999). Cedric manages to overcome tremendous obstacles while going to school in southeast DC, and he manages to succeed against great odds. Yet, even in telling his story, the idea that individual effort rather than structural change is the solution is reinforced. As a society we are generally far more comfortable extolling the virtues of individual responsibility and merit, even as the structural nature of the problems affecting poor kids and schools in poor neighborhoods go unexplored and unaddressed in policy.

The fact that the United States tolerates the failure of so many of its urban schools suggests that there is either a pervasive belief that poor children are not entitled to anything better, or an active conspiracy to ensure that the majority of children who are born poor, stay poor. Whether we accept either of these explanations is ultimately less important than what critical supporters actually do to ensure that present and future generations of children are provided with the opportunity to attend better schools.

Limits and Possibilities of Changing Urban Public Schools

One of the goals of this chapter is to put forward a framework that can be used to guide the improvement of urban public schools, one that takes the social context—or what I have termed the urban condition—into account. Drawing on my research and teaching experience, and from a perspective based on pragmatic optimism, my starting point for such a framework is to recognize the limits and possibilities of what can be changed in the current circumstances.

My own thinking about limits and possibilities is influenced by the work of Brazilian educator Paulo Freire (1972). Freire uses the concept of a "limit situation" in theorizing about his work in adult literacy. For Freire, illiteracy is much more than a failure to master the mechanics of reading and writing. It is rather a symptom of a larger condition of oppression and powerlessness and therefore cannot be fixed through traditional approaches to adult education. Instead, through dialogue and communication based on mutual respect and reciprocity, Freire calls upon educators to teach students to "read the world." This entails helping students to acquire an understanding of the forces that maintain imbalances in wealth and power so that the students can see their "situation as an historical reality susceptible to transformation" (p. 73). It also involves a move away from fatalistic perspectives that lead individuals to accept and adapt to oppressive circumstances, and calls for the adoption of a critical stance toward relations of power.

Freire recognized that a critical perspective (he uses the term *critical consciousness*) is not enough to transform social conditions, so he calls on teachers to treat conditions of oppression as "limit situations": problems that require critical reflection, engagement, and praxis. By this he meant that in any historical period, the possibilities for change must constantly be assessed and reflected upon so that strategies for countering these conditions can be devised. Freire conceived of human liberation and social justice as states of being that people must aspire to and devise courses of action to realize. By viewing the constraints on their freedom and dignity as limited situations, Freire believed the oppressed would be less inclined to see their situation as having been ordained by God. He hoped that such a shift in perspective would open the possibility that the oppressed would consider ways to act on these constraints and gradually expand possibilities for a greater degree of freedom. Freire (1970) writes:

> As they separate themselves from the world and locate the seat of their decisions in themselves and in their relations in the world and with others, men overcome the situations which limit them: the "limit situations." Once perceived as fetters, as obstacles to their liberation, these situations stand out in relief from the background, revealing their true nature as concrete historical dimensions of a given reality. ... As critical perception is embodied in action, a climate of hope and confidence develops which leads men to attempt to overcome the limit situations. (p. 89)

If we apply Freire's approach to understanding the limit situations that confront urban schools, there is a greater likelihood that we can devise creative approaches that make it possible to move beyond the dismal status quo. In the case of urban public schools, the constraints that stand in the way of change are both internal and external to school systems. Externally, the constraints are related primarily to the effects of poverty and social isolation on families in economically depressed inner-city neighborhoods. External conditions related to poverty invariably affect schools and have an impact on teaching and learning (Anyon, 1996; Maeroff, 1988; Schorr, 1997). Many inner-city communities have been in a constant state of economic depression for a very long time, and in many areas even the prosperity of the 1990s failed to significantly lower unemployment or bring about significant improvements in the quality of life (Phillips, 2002). The absence of well-paying jobs and a vibrant retail sector has converted many of these communities into what some economists refer to as "no zones"—no banks, no stores, no pharmacies, no community services. In the absence of a functioning formal economy, many residents generate income through the informal economy where many of the transactions and economic activities are illegal (e.g., drug trafficking, prostitution, gambling, "off-the-books" labor). Consistently, research has shown that when poverty is concentrated and poor people are socially isolated, the health and welfare of children and families suffer (Greenberg & Schneider, 1994; Massey & Denton, 1993; Wilson, 1987).

The role that local and state politicians play vis-à-vis urban schools and communities is another important external factor that influences the operation of schools. In many cities, the public school system is the leading employer, and the jobs available within the school system often offer higher pay than similar jobs in the private sector. The officials who manage schools are often quite powerful. The contracts that officials grant for construction, food services, and maintenance constitute a significant source of revenue for external suppliers. When those responsible for schools treat the economic activities of the school system as a cash cow and source of patronage, educational issues often become a low priority. In such cases, it is not uncommon for resources that should be directed to support schools, to be redirected into questionable activities. Political corruption, instability in leadership, institutional indifference, and administrative interference and/or ineptness can all have a profound effect on the ability of schools to function (Anyon, 1996; Henig et al., 1999). Finally, when battles for political control of schools take on greater importance than fulfilling their educational mission, key players and constituencies can become too distracted to focus on the critical educational work that needs to be done.

A broad array of demographic and socioeconomic factors, including the arrival of new immigrants (Suarez-Orozco & Suarez-Orozco, 2001) and neighborhood instability, also exert powerful influences over schools and the children who attend them. For example, as middle-class families have moved out of rust-belt cities like Buffalo, Detroit, Cleveland, and Hartford since the 1960s, the quality of schools has declined precipitously. Schools decline partially because there is less money available as the tax base is eroded, but also because when household income goes down and the percentage of low-income, single-parent families goes up, the challenges facing schools increase significantly. Likewise, other trends, such as housing affordability and stability, the accessibility of health care, and the impact of welfare reform, profoundly affect schools and the quality of children's lives.

These external constraints cannot be ignored or treated as factors that are beyond the reach of schools and therefore impossible to address. The tendency to ignore the environmental context is commonplace, even though a vast body of research has shown that external factors such as poverty play highly significant roles in influencing the quality of schooling provided to children (Anyon, 1996; Coleman et al., 1966; Jencks, 1972; Noguera, 1995a). Despite widespread recognition of the dire social problems confronting urban public schools, it is rare for politicians to devise policies that take social context into account. Instead, there are numerous examples of policies that treat schools uniformly and subject both rich and poor to the same laws and regulations.

Internal constraints also limit and hinder the possibilities for schools to improve. High turnover among superintendents, principals, and teachers adds to the sense of instability present in some schools and results in inexperienced professionals being assigned the most difficult and complex educational jobs (Darling-Hammond, 1997). Even when turnover is not as great a problem, urban districts often have large numbers of teachers who are demoralized and/or burned-out as a result of poor working conditions and low salaries. The morale of school personnel and the culture and organizational climate within schools and administrative offices have a tremendous bearing on the capacity of schools to change and improve. Genuine reform and improvement are impossible to achieve in schools where disorder and chaos are prevalent (Payne, 1984, 2001).

Similarly, inadequate facilities, which in many urban areas may include broken windows, poor heating and ventilation, and a wide array of cosmetic and structural deficiencies, as well as a shortage of instructional materials such as computers and textbooks, also constitute important internal constraints on schools. Finally, the common tendency to pursue costly reforms without a commitment to evaluate the effectiveness of new measures adds to the sense of demoralization experienced by school personnel and contributes to a profound cynicism among them about the possibility of reform itself.

Commenting on the tendency of policy makers to issue new recommendations for reform without evaluating or learning from past failures, Sarason (1971) writes:

> When you read the myriad of recommendations these commission reports contain, it becomes clear that they are not informed by any conception of a system. This is a charitable assessment. It deserves emphasis that none of these reports confronts the question of why these recommendations for changing this or that part of the system have been ineffective. More upsetting is the question of why so many people think the situation has not remained the same but deteriorated. Why, in the quiet of night, do so many people think that the situation is hopeless? (p. 15)

Many of the conditions described above are not unique to urban schools, but are present to varying degrees within schools throughout the United States (Cuban & Tyack, 1995; Wagner, 1994). However, they are more likely to be present and to be particularly severe in urban public schools that are located in economically depressed neighborhoods.

Yet, despite the real obstacles created by internal and external constraints, there are realistic possibilities for improvement and reform. The most compelling evidence that such openings exist in spite of these constraints is the existence of what are now recognized widely as "effective schools" that serve poor children and operate in low-income urban areas. Isolated and few in number though they may be, a significant number of schools that serve poor children manage to demonstrate that it is possible for students to achieve at high levels. Research on such schools has shown that they succeed both because they find ways to develop the internal capacity of schools to support good teaching and learning, and because they face the external constraints head-on (Haycock, 2002). They do this by explicitly devising strategies that enable them to cope with, and in some cases overcome, the obstacles present within the external environment. Such schools find ways to provide coats to children in the winter and additional food to children who don't eat regularly at home. By finding ways to mitigate the impact of external constraints, such schools provide a reasonable basis for pragmatic optimism.

Furthermore, possibilities for change and improvement are enhanced when capable and committed educators are organized to serve the needs of children. Programs such as the Omega Boys Club in San Francisco, Young Black Scholars in Los Angeles, and the Paul Robeson Institute in New York have been highly effective in furthering academic achievement of poor minority students.[9] Of course, the success of such programs is contingent on the availability of competent and committed personnel, a fact that often makes replication difficult. However, this fact should not negate the possibility that similar programs can be adopted to help schools to improve. Rather, it should underscore the importance of the most critical ingredient of school success—the availability of highly skilled and dedicated professionals without whom success simply is not possible. Furthermore, the success of certain interventions, as well as even the temporary success of certain schools, serves as proof that the possibility for transforming urban public schools is real.

Finally, and most important, the possibility for better education exists because children are fundamentally educable and capable of learning at high levels. This fact must be articulated repeatedly because in too many cases it is not the premise on which reforms are based. When the adults who serve children do not believe their students are capable of learning and achieving at high levels, they are less likely to provide students with an education that challenges them to fully realize their intellectual potential. Invariably, adults who question the ability of students to learn set lower standards and hold lower expectations (Ladson-Billings, 1994). Most disturbing of all is the fact that such educators provide an education to their students that they would regard as unacceptable for their own children.

Working with an awareness of the limits and possibilities for school improvement, we are compelled to revisit the issue of commitment, effort, and will. While such subjective characteristics may not suffice as explanations for student achievement, they are indispensable features of any school change process. Put most simply, schools improve when people work harder and smarter (Elmore, 1996).

When they invest greater time and energy into improving their practice and coordinating the services they provide to children and their families in a more coherent manner, increased achievement is more likely. This is not to suggest that hard work alone is all that is needed to improve urban schools. However, even if all of the key ingredients are in place and optimal conditions have been created to support teaching and learning, success will still require hard work.

The work required to improve schools that serve poor children entails much more than a mechanistic adherence to a set of prescribed reforms or the adoption of a new curriculum. One consistent feature of schools that succeed at educating poor children is that they are guided by a coherent mission: one that is embraced enthusiastically by teachers, students, and parents (Edmonds, 1979; Meier, 1995; Sizemore, 1988). Such schools almost always are led by dedicated and exemplary principals who motivate and inspire their staff while simultaneously generating a sense of accountability to those they serve. Successful schools, especially those that succeed over a long period of time, often have an intangible quality about them that produces high morale, and an *esprit de corps* that compels those who teach or learn there to approach their work with a sense of purpose and commitment.

I was reminded of this characteristic of effective schools when I went to see an old friend from college. I sought out my college roommate, Amateka Morgan, after nearly 20 years without contact, hoping that he might have some wisdom to share with my 17-year-old son Joaquin, who was about to enroll in college in New York City. We found Amateka working in a private Islamic primary school in the Williamsburgh section of Brooklyn. Two weeks before school was to begin, he was hard at work waxing floors, painting walls, and moving furniture. He explained that he recently had resigned from Girls and Boys High School (a large comprehensive public school in Brooklyn) where he had been employed for over 10 years as a science teacher and track coach. He told us that although he enjoyed working at the school, he had grown tired of hearing people say that if he could save one or two children, he would have accomplished something. Smiling broadly, he informed us, "At this school, we know we can save all of our children. The only thing limiting us is the size of the building. Even though we don't have facilities like the public schools we can do a better job because we love the children, and it shows in what they can do" (personal communication, September 2, 2000).

Without the kinds of qualities demonstrated by my old friend—commitment, enthusiasm, compassion, solidarity, and love—it is doubtful that public schools can be reformed. Individuals possessing such qualities also need support derived from structural changes aimed at easing the effects of poverty. However, without such individuals change may not be possible at all. The nature of work in urban schools is simply too difficult, the working conditions too harsh, and the external obstacles too numerous. Without the extra boost provided by an emotional or philosophical motivation for doing the work, success cannot be achieved. Unfortunately, such traits cannot be invoked by policy makers, or mandated by superintendents or school boards; if they are not rooted within an individual's value system, often they cannot be cultivated. In some cases, individuals can be inspired to manifest these qualities, but they cannot be coerced to do so. Hence, to a large degree, the possibility for transforming urban public schools is contingent on our ability to find ways either to attract highly motivated and competent professionals to work in them, or to inspire and support those who are already there. Assessing the situation in urban schools with a healthy dose of pragmatism forces us to recognize that neither task is easy.

Improving the Quality of Public Education in the San Francisco Bay Area

For nearly 20 years I taught and conducted research in several schools in the San Francisco Bay Area. These experiences provide the empirical basis for my analysis of the limits and possibilities of improving urban schools. Widely regarded as one of the most prosperous regions in the United States due to its proximity to Silicon Valley, the national center of the "new economy," the Bay Area would seem to have every ingredient needed to make the probability for success in public education high. Yet, like urban schools throughout the rest of the nation, public schools in the Bay Area exhibit most of the familiar signs of failure and distress, despite their location in this affluent region.

In the forthcoming chapters I will explain why public education in the Bay Area has largely failed to live up to its promise and potential. Through a series of case studies, I will show how several schools have been affected by and have attempted to respond to the challenges of the urban environment. I will do this by drawing attention to both the reasons for failure and the factors that have enabled some schools to produce a degree of success.

It is my hope that this book will not only inform readers about the peculiarities of this region, but also provide insights that can help us to understand what it will take to reverse trends in urban education generally. It is my hope that by grounding this analysis in the experience of real schools and communities, I will make a credible and realistic case for radically improving urban public schools. Drawing on my position of critical support and pragmatic optimism, I will describe how schools can respond to the forces of social inequality and fulfill the promise of American education. That promise is rooted in Horace Mann's belief that schools should function as the great "equalizer" of opportunity: an arena where inherited privileges do not determine one's opportunities (Tyack, 1980). Improving the state of America's urban schools necessarily will be a central element of any effort to realize that promise.

Notes

1. Several public opinion polls have shown that education is regarded as the number one domestic policy issue. Even after September 11, education follows closely behind concerns about security and terrorism. For an analysis of public opinion and the response of policy makers, see "The 29th Annual Phi Delta Kappa/Gallup Poll of the Public's Attitudes Toward Public Schools" in *Phi Delta Kappan*, September 1997, pp. 41–56.
2. Polls of parents reveal that while many are critical of public education in general, they tend to hold more positive views toward the particular schools their children attend. For a discussion of the polling data, see "31st Annual Phi Delta Kappa/Gallup Poll of the Public's Attitudes Toward Public School" by L. C. Rose and A. M. Gallup in *Phi Delta Kappan*, September 1999, pp. 41–56.
3. In addition to education, a growing number of schools serving poor children frequently provide a variety of other services to children, including free lunch, health centers, immunizations, etc. See "Rising to the Challenge: Emerging Strategies for Educating Youth at Risk" by N. Legters and E. McGill in *Schools and Students at Risk* edited by R. Rossi (New York: Teachers College Press, 1994).
4. In a public lecture at a conference entitled Human Rights in the Americas (May 1993), the former Dean of Boalt Law School at UC Berkeley, Jesse Choper, used the terms *positive* and *negative rights* to distinguish between rights that constitute a social entitlement (e.g., housing, health care, etc.) and rights that are intended to prevent individuals from exercising certain "freedoms" (i.e., religious beliefs, gun ownership, speech, etc.).
5. Shelby Steele and John McWhorter are two of the better-known Black scholars who have argued that the failure of African Americans is explained largely by what McWhorter refers to as "self sabotage" and Steele describes as embracing "victim focused identity." See *Losing the Race* by J. McWhorter (New York: Free Press, 2000) and *The Content of Our Character* by S. Steele (New York: St. Martin's Press, 1990).
6. It is not uncommon for the best-paying jobs available in cities to be held by individuals who live outside of the city limits. For a discussion of the role cities play within regional economies, see "Cities and Uneven Economic Development" by M. Savage and A. Warde in *The City Reader* edited by R. Legates and F. Stout (New York: Routledge, 1996).
7. Part of the problem with most voucher and choice plans is that they fail to address the fact that most of the better suburban and private schools lack the space to accommodate significant numbers of poor children from the inner city. For an analysis of choice plans and access to schools, see *Who Chooses? Who Loses?* by B. Fuller and R. Elmore (New York: Teachers College Press, 1996).
8. The Education Trust and the Heritage Foundation have identified a number of high-performing schools that serve minority children. Several of these are located in high-poverty, inner-city communities. However, these schools are relatively isolated, and their existence generally has been difficult to replicate. See *No Excuses, Lessons from 21 High Performing, High Poverty Schools* by S. C. Carter (Washington, DC: Heritage Foundation, 2000) and "New Frontiers for a New Century" in *Thinking K–12*, 5(2), Spring 2001.
9. For an analysis and discussion of academic programs that have proven effective in serving low-income minority students, see "Promising Programs for Elementary and Middle Schools: Evidence of Effectiveness and Replicability" by O. Fashola and R. Slavin in *Journal of Education for Students Placed at Risk*, 2(3), 1997, pp. 251–307.

References

Anyon, J. (1996). *Ghetto schooling: A political economy of urban educational reform*. New York: Teachers College Press.

Blasi, G. (2001). *Reforming educational accountability*. Unpublished conference paper, Los Angeles.

Carnegie Foundation. (1994/1995). *Quarterly report*. New York: Author.

Carnoy, M., & Levin, H. (1985). *Schooling and work in the democratic state*. Stanford: Stanford University Press.

Carter, S. C. (2000). *No excuses: Lessons from 21 high performing, high poverty schools*. Washington, DC: Heritage Foundation.

Casella, R. (2001). *Being down*. New York: Teachers College Press.

Clark, D. (1985). *Post-industrial America*. New York: Methuen.

Coleman, J., Campbell, E., Hobson, C., McPartland, J., Mood, A., Weinfeld, F., & Yonk, R. (1966). *Equality of educational opportunity*. Washington, DC: U.S. Department of Health, Education and Welfare, Office of Education.

Council of the Great City Schools. (2001). *Foundations for success*. Prepared by the Manpower Research and Development Corporation, Washington, DC.

Cuban, L., & Tyack, D. (1995). *Tinkering toward Utopia*. Cambridge, MA: Harvard University Press.

Darling-Hammond, L. (1997). *The right to learn: A blueprint for creating schools that work*. San Francisco: Jossey-Bass.

Edmonds, R. (1979). Effective schools for the urban poor. *Educational Leadership, 37*(1), 15–27.

Education Trust. (2002). *Dispelling the myth revisited: Preliminary findings from a nationwide analysis of high-flying schools*. Washington, DC: Author.

Elmore, R. (1996). The new accountability in state educational policy. In H. Ladd (Ed.), *Performance based strategies for improving schools*. Washington, DC: Brookings Institution.

Fashola, 0., & Slavin, R. (1997). Promising programs for elementary and middle schools: Evidence of effectiveness and replicability. *Journal of Education for Students Placed at Risk, 2*(3), 251–307.

Freire, P. (1970). *Education for critical consciousness*. New York: Continuum.

Freire, P. (1972). *Pedagogy of the oppressed*. New York: Continuum.

Fuller, B., & Elmore, R. (1996). *Who chooses? Who loses?* New York: Teachers College Press.

Gratz, R., & Mintz, N. (1998). *Cities back from the edge*. New York: Wiley.

Greenberg, M., & Schneider, D. (1994). Violence in American cities: Young black males is the answer, but what was the question? *Social Science Medicine, 39*(2), 179–187.

Haycock, K. (2002). Thinking K–16. In P. Barth (Ed.), *New frontiers for a new century: A national overview* (Vol. 5). Washington, DC: Education Trust.

Henig, J. R., Hula, R. C., Orr, M., & Pedescleaux, D. S. (1999). *The color of school reform: Race, politics, and the challenge of urban education*. Princeton, NJ: Princeton University Press.

Hess, F. (1999). *Spinning wheels: The unpolitics of urban school reform*. Washington, DC: Brookings Institution.

Jencks, C. (1972). *Inequality*. New York: Harper Books.

Kirp, D. (1982). *Just schools*. Berkeley: University of California Press.

Ladson-Billings, G. (1994). *The dreamkeepers*. San Francisco: Jossey-Bass.

Legters, N., & McGill, E. L. (1994). Rising to the challenge: Emerging strategies for educating youth at risk. In R. Rossi (Ed.), *Schools and students at risk* (pp. 23–47). New York: Teachers College Press.

Maeroff, G. (1988). Whithered hopes and stillborn dreams: The dismal panorama of urban schools. *Phi Delta Kappan, 69*(9), 632–638.

Massey, D., & Denton, N. (1993). *American apartheid*. Cambridge, MA: Harvard University Press.

McGroarty, D. (1996). *Break these chains*. Rocklin, CA: Prima.

McWhorter, J. (2000). *Losing the race*. New York: Free Press.

Meier, D. (1995). *The power of their ideas*. Boston: Beacon Press.

Murnane, R., & Levy, F. (1996). *Teaching the new basic skills*. New York: Free Press.

New frontiers for a new century. (2001, Spring). *Thinking K–12, 5*(2).

Noguera, P. (1995a). A tale of two cities: School desegregation and racialized discourse in Berkeley and Kansas City. *International Journal of Comparative Race and Ethnic Studies, 2*(2), 48–62.

Noguera, P. (1995b). Preventing and producing violence in schools: A critical analysis of responses to school violence. *Harvard Educational Review, 65*(2), 189–212.

Oakes, J. (2002). Adequate and equitable access to education's basic tools in a standards-based educational system. *Teachers College Record* [special issue].

Payne, C. (2001). *So much reform, so little change*. Unpublished conference paper, Boston.

Payne, C. M. (1984). *Getting what we ask for: The ambiguity of success and failure of urban education*. Westport, CT: Greenwood Press.

Phillips, K. (2002). *Wealth and democracy*. New York: Broadway Books.

Rose, L. C., & Gallup, A. M. (1999, September). 31st annual Phi Delta Kappa/Gallup poll of the public's attitudes toward public school. *Phi Delta Kappan*, pp. 41–56.

Sarason, S. (1971). *The culture of the school and the problem of change*. Boston: Allyn & Bacon.

Savage, M., & Warde, A. (1996). Cities and uneven economic development. In R. Legates & F. Stout (Eds.), *The city reader*. New York: Routledge.

Schorr, L. (1997). *Common purpose: Strengthening families and neighborhoods to rebuild America*. New York: Anchor Books.

Sizemore, B. (1988). The Madison Elementary School: A turnaround case. *Journal of Negro Education, 57*(3), 243–266.

Steele, S. (1990). *The content of our character.* New York: St. Martin's Press.

Suarez-Orozco, C., & Suarez-Orozco, M. (2001). *Children of immigration.* Cambridge, MA: Harvard University Press.

Suskind, R. (1999). *A hope in the unseen.* New York: Broadway Books.

29th annual Phi Delta Kappa/Gallup poll of the public's attitudes toward public school. (1997, September). *Phi Delta Kappan,*
    pp. 41–56.

Tyack, D. (1980). *The one best system.* Cambridge, MA: Harvard University Press.

Wagner, T. (1994). *How schools change.* Boston: Beacon Press.

Wilson, W. (1987). *The truly disadvantaged.* Chicago: University of Chicago Press.

CHAPTER 4

What I Learned About School Reform

Diane Ravitch

In the fall of 2007, I reluctantly decided to have my office repainted. It was inconvenient. I work at home, on the top floor of a nineteenth-century brownstone in Brooklyn. Not only did I have to stop working for three weeks, but I had the additional burden of packing up and removing everything in my office. I had to relocate fifty boxes of books and files to other rooms in the house until the painting job was complete.

After the patching, plastering, and painting was done, I began unpacking twenty years of papers and books, discarding those I no longer wanted, and placing articles into scrapbooks. You may wonder what all this mundane stuff has to do with my life in the education field. I found that the chore of reorganizing the artifacts of my professional life was pleasantly ruminative. It had a tonic effect, because it allowed me to reflect on the changes in my views over the years.

At the very time that I was packing up my books and belongings, I was going through an intellectual crisis. I was aware that I had undergone a wrenching transformation in my perspective on school reform. Where once I had been hopeful, even enthusiastic, about the potential benefits of testing, accountability, choice, and markets, I now found myself experiencing profound doubts about these same ideas. I was trying to sort through the evidence about what was working and what was not. I was trying to understand why I was increasingly skeptical about these reforms, reforms that I had supported enthusiastically. I was trying to see my way through the blinding assumptions of ideology and politics, including my own.

I kept asking myself why I was losing confidence in these reforms. My answer: I have a right to change my mind. Fair enough. But why, I kept wondering, why had I changed my mind? What was the compelling evidence that prompted me to reevaluate the policies I had endorsed many times over the previous decade? Why did I now doubt ideas I once had advocated?

The short answer is that my views changed as I saw how these ideas were working out in reality. A part of the long answer is what will follow in the rest of this chapter. When someone chastised John Maynard Keynes for reversing himself about a particular economic policy he had previously endorsed, he replied, "When the facts change, I change my mind. What do you do, sir?"[1] This comment may or may not be apocryphal, but I admire the thought behind it. It is the mark of a sentient human being to learn from experience, to pay close attention to how theories work out when put into practice.

What should we think of someone who never admits error, never entertains doubt but adheres unflinchingly to the same ideas all his life, regardless of new evidence? Doubt and skepticism are signs of rationality. When we are too certain of our opinions, we run the risk of ignoring any evidence that conflicts with our views. It is doubt that shows we are still thinking, still willing to reexamine hardened beliefs when confronted with new facts and new evidence.

The task of sorting my articles gave me the opportunity to review what I had written at different times, beginning in the mid-1960s. As I flipped from article to article, I kept asking myself, how far had I strayed from where I started? Was it like me to shuffle off ideas like an ill-fitting coat? As I read and skimmed and remembered, I began to see two themes at the center of what I have been writing for more than four decades. One constant has been my skepticism about pedagogical fads, enthusiasms, and movements. The other has been a deep belief in the value of a rich, coherent school curriculum, especially in history and literature, both of which are so frequently ignored, trivialized, or politicized.[2]

Over the years, I have consistently warned against the lure of "the royal road to learning," the notion that some savant or organization has found an easy solution to the problems of American education. As a historian of education, I have often studied the rise and fall of grand ideas that were promoted as the sure cure for whatever ills were afflicting our schools and students. In 1907, William Chandler Bagley complained about the "fads and reforms that sweep through the educational system at periodic intervals." A few years later, William Henry Maxwell, the esteemed superintendent of schools in New York City, heaped scorn on educational theorists who promoted their panaceas to gullible teachers; one, he said, insisted that "vertical penmanship" was the answer to all problems; another maintained that recess was a "relic of barbarism." Still others wanted to ban spelling and grammar to make school more fun.[3] I have tried to show in my work the persistence of our national infatuation with fads, movements, and reforms, which invariably distract us from the steadiness of purpose needed to improve our schools.

In our own day, policymakers and business leaders have eagerly enlisted in a movement launched by free-market advocates, with the support of major foundations. Many educators have their doubts about the slogans and cure-alls of our time, but they are required to follow the mandates of federal law (such as No Child Left Behind) despite their doubts.

School reformers sometimes resemble the characters in Dr. Seuss's *Solla Sollew*, who are always searching for that mythical land "where they never have troubles, at least very few." Or like Dumbo, they are convinced they could fly if only they had a magic feather. In my writings, I have consistently warned that, in education, there are no shortcuts, no utopias, and no silver bullets. For certain, there are no magic feathers that enable elephants to fly.

As I flipped through the yellowing pages in my scrapbooks, I started to understand the recent redirection of my thinking, my growing doubt regarding popular proposals for choice and accountability. Once again, I realized, I was turning skeptical in response to panaceas and miracle cures. The only difference was that in this case, I too had fallen for the latest panaceas and miracle cures; I too had drunk deeply of the elixir that promised a quick fix to intractable problems. I too had jumped aboard a bandwagon, one festooned with banners celebrating the power of accountability, incentives, and markets. I too was captivated by these ideas. They promised to end bureaucracy, to ensure that poor children were not neglected, to empower poor parents, to enable poor children to escape failing schools, and to close the achievement gap between rich and poor, black and white. Testing would shine a spotlight on low-performing schools, and choice would create opportunities for poor kids to leave for better schools. All of this seemed to make sense, but there was little empirical evidence, just promise and hope. I wanted to share the promise and the hope. I wanted to believe that choice and accountability would produce great results. But over time, I was persuaded by accumulating evidence that the latest reforms were not likely to live up to their promise. The more I saw, the more I lost the faith.

It seemed, therefore, that it would be instructive to take a fresh look at the reform strategies that are now so prominent in American education and to review the evidence of their effectiveness. This chapter is my opportunity to explain some of what I have learned about school reform and also to suggest, with (I hope) a certain degree of modesty and full acknowledgment of my own frailties and errors, what is needed to move American education in the right direction.

The first article I ever wrote about education was published in a small (and now defunct) education journal called the *Urban Review* in 1968. Its title—"Programs, Placebos, Panaceas"—signaled what turned out to be a constant preoccupation for me, the conflict between promise and reality, between utopian hopes and knotty problems. I reviewed short-term compensatory education programs—that is, short-term interventions to help kids who were far behind—and concluded that "only sustained quality education makes a difference." My second article, titled "Foundations: Playing God in the Ghetto" (1969), discussed the Ford Foundation's role in the protracted controversy over decentralization and community control that led to months of turmoil in the public schools of New York City.[4] This question—the extent to which it is appropriate for a mega-rich foundation to take charge of reforming public schools, even though it is accountable to no one and elected by no one—has been treated elsewhere in my writings. The issue is especially important today, because some of the nation's largest foundations are promoting school reforms based on principles drawn from the corporate sector, without considering whether they are appropriate for educational institutions.

In the late 1960s, the issue of decentralization versus centralization turned into a heated battle. Newspapers featured daily stories about community groups demanding decentralization of the schools and blaming teachers and administrators for the school system's lack of success with minority children. Many school reformers then assumed that African American and Hispanic parents and local community leaders, not professional educators, knew best what their children needed.

As the clamor to decentralize the school system grew, I became curious about why the system had been centralized in the first place. I spent many days in the New-York Historical Society library studying the history of the city's school system; the last such history had been published in 1905. I discovered that the system had been decentralized in the nineteenth century. The school reformers of the 1890s demanded centralization as an antidote to low-performing schools and advocated control by professionals as the cure for the incompetence and corruption of local school boards. As I read, I was struck by the ironic contrast between the reformers' demands in the 1890s for centralization and the reformers' demands in the 1960s for decentralization. The earlier group consisted mainly of social elites, the latter of parents and activists who wanted local control of the schools.

So intrigued was I by the contrast between past and present that I determined to write a history of the New York City public schools, which became *The Great School Wars: New York City, 1805–1973*.[5] This was quite a challenge for someone who had graduated from the Houston public schools and—at that time—had no advanced degrees in history or education. As I was completing the book, I earned a doctorate from Columbia University in the history of American education, and the book became my dissertation. While writing and pursuing my graduate studies, I worked under the tutelage of Lawrence Cremin, the greatest historian of American education of his era.

In the mid-1970s, Cremin persuaded me to write a critique of a group of leftist historians who attacked the underpinnings of public schooling. They called themselves revisionists, because they set themselves the goal of demolishing what they saw as a widespread myth about the benevolent purposes and democratic accomplishments of public education. The authors, all of them professors at various universities, treated the public schools scornfully as institutions devised by elites to oppress the poor. This point of view was so contrary to my own understanding of the liberating role of public education—not only in my own life but also in the life of the nation—that I felt compelled to refute it.

The resulting book was called *The Revisionists Revised: A Critique of the Radical Attack on the Schools*.[6] In that book, I defended the democratic, civic purposes of public schooling. I argued that the public schools had not been devised by scheming capitalists to impose "social control" on an unwilling proletariat or to reproduce social inequality; the schools were never an instrument of cultural repression, as the radical critics claimed. Instead, I held, they are a primary mechanism through which a democratic society gives its citizens the opportunity to attain literacy and social mobility. Opportunity leaves much to individuals; it is not a guarantee of certain success. The schools cannot solve all our social problems, nor are they perfect. But in a democratic society, they are necessary and valuable for individuals and for the commonweal.

My next book was a history of national education policy from 1945 to 1980, an era notable for major court decisions and federal legislation. In *The Troubled Crusade: American Education, 1945–1980*, I analyzed the many fascinating controversies associated with McCarthyism, progressive education, the civil rights movement, bilingual education, the women's movement, and other social and political upheavals.[7]

While writing *The Troubled Crusade*, I became increasingly interested in issues related to the quality of the curriculum. I began studying the history of pedagogy, curriculum, and standards, especially the teaching of literature and history and the representation of our culture in schools. In 1987, I coauthored a book with my friend Chester E. (Checker) Finn Jr. called *What Do Our 17-Year-Olds Know?* which reported on the first federal test of history and literature. We lamented what seemed to be a loss of cultural memory, a position that hit a public nerve but was scorned in the academic world, which was then caught up in postmodernism and a revolt against "the canon." Our view was that you can't reject the canon if you have no knowledge of it.[8]

In 1985, California State Superintendent Bill Honig invited me to help write a new history curriculum for the state. Over a two-year period, I worked closely with teachers and scholars to draft a curriculum framework that integrated history with literature, geography, the arts, social sciences, and humanities. With this framework, California would become the first state to require all students to study three years of world history and three years of U.S. history, with a substantial infusion of history and biography in the elementary grades. The framework was adopted by the State Board of Education in 1987 and remains in place to this day with only minor revisions to update it. Over the past two decades, the state of California replaced its reading curriculum, its mathematics curriculum, and its science curriculum, but the history curriculum—touching on some of the most sensitive and controversial topics and events in American and world history—endured.[9]

I had not, to this point in my life, given much thought to issues of choice, markets, or accountability.

Then something unexpected happened: I received a telephone call in the spring of 1991 from President George H. W. Bush's newly appointed education secretary, Lamar Alexander. Alexander, a moderate Republican, had been governor of Tennessee. The secretary invited me to come to Washington to chat with him and his deputy David Kearns, who had recently been the chief executive officer of Xerox. We met for lunch at the elegant Hay-Adams Hotel, near the White House. We talked about curriculum and standards (Secretary Alexander later joked that I talked and he listened), and at the end of lunch he asked me to join the department as assistant secretary in charge of the Office of Educational Research and Improvement and as his counselor.

I went home to Brooklyn to think about it. I was a registered Democrat, always had been, and had never dreamed of working in a government job, let alone a Republican administration. I had no desire to leave Brooklyn or to abandon my life as a scholar. And yet I was intrigued by the thought of working in the federal government. Surely education was a nonpartisan issue, or so I then imagined. I decided that this would be a wonderful opportunity to perform public service, learn about federal politics, and do something totally different. I said yes, was confirmed by the Senate, moved to Washington, and spent the next eighteen months as assistant secretary and counselor to the secretary in the U.S. Department of Education.

During my time at the department, I took the lead on issues having to do with curriculum and standards. The federal government is prohibited by law from imposing any curriculum on states or school districts. Nonetheless, my agency used its very small allotment of discretionary funds (about $10 million) to make grants to consortia of educators to develop "voluntary national standards" in every academic subject. Our assumption was that so long as the standards were developed by independent professional groups and were voluntary, we were not violating the legal prohibition against imposing curriculum on states and school districts. And so we funded the development of voluntary national standards in history, the arts, geography, civics, science, economics, foreign languages, and English. We did this energetically but without specific congressional authorization; the absence of authorization unfortunately lessened the projects' credibility and longevity.

The Department of Education was committed to both standards and choice (choice was even higher on the agenda of Republicans than standards, because Republicans generally opposed national standards, which suggested federal meddling). At meetings of top staff in the department, I sat in on many discussions of school choice in which the question was not whether to support choice, but how to do so. The issue of choice had never been important to me, but I found myself trying to incorporate the arguments for choice into my own worldview. I reasoned that standards would be even more necessary in a society that used public dollars to promote school choice. The more varied the schools, the more important it would be to have common standards to judge whether students were learning. I began to sympathize with the argument for letting federal dollars follow poor students to the school of their choice. If kids were not succeeding in their regular public school, why not let them take their federal funds to another public school or to a private—even religious—school? Since affluent families could choose their schools by moving to a better neighborhood or enrolling their children in private schools, why shouldn't poor families have similar choices?

In the decade following my stint in the federal government, I argued that certain managerial and structural changes—that is, choice, charters, merit pay, and accountability—would help to reform our schools. With such changes, teachers and schools would be judged by their performance; this was a basic principle in the business world. Schools that failed to perform would be closed, just as a corporation would close a branch office that continually produced poor returns. Having been immersed in a world of true believers, I was influenced by their ideas. I became persuaded that the business-minded thinkers were onto something important. Their proposed reforms were meant to align public education with the practices of modern, flexible, high-performance organizations and to enable American education to make the transition from the industrial age to the postindustrial age. In the 1990s, I found myself in step with people who quoted Peter Drucker and other management gurus. I dropped casual references to "total quality management" and the Baldridge Award, both of which I learned about by listening to David Kearns during my stint in the Department of Education.

During this time, I wrote many articles advocating structural innovations. In the past, I would have cast a cold eye on efforts to "reinvent the schools" or to "break the mold," but now I supported bold attempts to remake the schools, such as charter schools, privatization, and specialized schools of all kinds. I maintained that we should celebrate the creation of good schools, no matter what form they took or who developed them.

Both the Bush administration and the Clinton administration advocated market reforms for the public sector, including deregulation and privatization. Bill Clinton and the New Democrats championed a "third way" between the orthodox policies of the left and the right. People in both parties quoted *Reinventing Government* by David Osborne and Ted Gaebler as a guide to cutting down bureaucracy and injecting entrepreneurship into government.[10] Months after his inauguration, President Clinton tasked Vice President Al Gore to devise ways to "reinvent" the federal bureaucracy, and he did. With the help of David Osborne, Gore created the National Partnership for Reinventing Government, whose purpose was to adapt private sector management techniques to the public sector. Many of its recommendations involved privatizing, cutting jobs, and implementing performance agreements in which agencies would receive autonomy from regulations in exchange for meeting targets.[11]

Similar ideas began to percolate in the world of public education. The new thinking—now ensconced in both parties—saw the public school system as obsolete, because it is controlled by the government and burdened by bureaucracy. Government-run schools, said a new generation of reformers, are ineffective because they are a monopoly; as such, they have no incentive to do better, and they serve the interests of adults who work in the system, not children. Democrats saw an opportunity to reinvent government; Republicans, a chance to diminish the power of the teachers' unions, which, in their view, protect jobs and pensions while blocking effective management and innovation.

This convergence explained the bipartisan appeal of charter schools. Why shouldn't schools be managed by anyone who could supply good schools, using government funds? Free of direct government control, the schools would be innovative, hire only the best teachers, get rid of incompetent teachers, set their own pay scales, compete for students (customers), and be judged solely by their results (test scores and graduation rates). Good schools under private management would proliferate, while bad schools would be closed down by market forces (the exit of disgruntled parents) or by a watchful government. Some of the new generation of reformers—mainly Republicans, but not only Republicans—imagined that the schools of the future would function without unions, allowing management to hire and fire personnel at will. With the collapse of Communism and the triumph of market reforms in most parts of the world, it did not seem to be much of a stretch to envision the application of the market model to schooling.

Like many others in that era, I was attracted to the idea that the market would unleash innovation and bring greater efficiencies to education. I was certainly influenced by the conservative ideology of other top-level officials in the first Bush administration, who were strong supporters of school choice and competition. But of equal importance, I believe, I began to think like a policymaker, especially a federal policymaker. That meant, in the words of a book by James C. Scott that I later read and admired, I began "seeing like a state," looking at schools and teachers and students from an altitude of 20,000 feet and seeing them as objects to be moved around by big ideas and great plans.[12]

Anyone who is a policymaker, aspires to be a policymaker, or wants to influence policymakers must engage in "seeing like a state." It is inevitable. Policymaking requires one to make decisions that affect people's lives without their having a chance to cast a vote. If no one thought like a state, there would probably be no highways or public works of any kind. Those who make the most noise would veto almost everything. It is the job of representative government to make decisions without seeking a majority vote from their constituents on every single question. Anyone who recommends a change of federal or state policy engages in "seeing like a state." Improvement also depends on having a mix of views and new ideas to prevent the status quo from becoming ossified. Those who make policy are most successful when they must advance their ideas through a gauntlet of checks and balances, explaining their plans, submitting them to a process of public review, and attempting to persuade others to support them. If the policymaker cannot persuade others, then his plans will not be implemented. That's democracy.

How can I distinguish between thinking like a historian and seeing like a state? A historian tries to understand what happened, why it happened, what was the context, who did what, and what assumptions led them to act as they did. A historian customarily displays a certain diffidence about trying to influence events, knowing that unanticipated developments often lead to unintended consequences. A policymaker, on the other hand, is required to plan for the future and make bets about a course of action that is likely to bring about improvements. Policymakers have a theory of action, even if they can't articulate it, and they implement plans based on their theory of action, their guess about how the world works. Historians are trained to recognize assumptions and theories and to spot their flaws.

Market reforms have a certain appeal to some of those who are accustomed to "seeing like a state." There is something comforting about the belief that the invisible hand of the market, as Adam Smith called it, will bring improvements through some unknown force. In education, this belief in market forces lets us ordinary mortals off the hook, especially those who have not figured out how to improve low-performing schools or to break through the lassitude of unmotivated teens. Instead of dealing with rancorous problems like how to teach reading or how to improve testing, one can redesign the management and structure of the school system and concentrate on incentives and sanctions. One need not know anything about children or education. The lure of the market is the idea that freedom from government regulation is a solution all by itself. This is very appealing, especially when so many seemingly well-planned school reforms have failed to deliver on their promise.

The new corporate reformers betray their weak comprehension of education by drawing false analogies between education and business. They think they can fix education by applying the principles of business, organization, management, law, and marketing and by developing a good data-collection system that provides the information necessary to incentivize the workforce—principals, teachers, and students—with appropriate rewards and sanctions. Like these reformers, I wrote and spoke with conviction in the 1990s and early 2000s about what was needed to reform public education, and many of my ideas coincided with theirs.

I have long been allied with conservative scholars and organizations. My scholarly work at Teachers College and later at New York University was supported by conservative foundations, principally the John M. Olin Foundation, which never sought to influence anything I wrote. My close friend Checker Finn took over the helm of the Thomas B. Fordham Foundation in 1996, and I was a member of its board until 2009. We previously worked together as organizers of the Educational Excellence Network in 1981, which advocated for a solid curriculum and high standards.

In 1999, I became a founding member of the Koret Task Force at the Hoover Institution at Stanford University; the task force supports education reforms based on the principles of standards, accountability, and choice. Most of the members of the task force are forceful advocates of school choice and accountability. John Chubb and Terry Moe wrote a highly successful book promoting choice. Caroline Hoxby, Eric Hanushek, Paul Peterson, Paul Hill, Checker Finn, Bill Evers, and Herbert Walberg are well-known scholars and/or advocates of choice, competition, and accountability. In a debate at Hoover, Don Hirsch and I argued against Hoxby and Peterson that curriculum and instruction were more important than markets and choice.[13] I enjoyed the camaraderie of the group, and I loved the intellectual stimulation I encountered at the Hoover Institution. But over time I realized that I was no longer fully supportive of the task force's aims. When I told my colleagues that I felt I had to leave, they urged me to stay and debate with them. I did for a time, but in April 2009 I resigned.

I grew increasingly disaffected from both the choice movement and the accountability movement. I was beginning to see the downside of both and to understand that they were not solutions to our educational dilemmas. As I watched both movements gain momentum across the nation, I concluded that curriculum and instruction were far more important than choice and accountability. I feared that choice would let thousands of flowers bloom but would not strengthen American education. It might even harm the public schools by removing the best students from schools in the poorest neighborhoods. I was also concerned that accountability, now a shibboleth that everyone applauds, had become mechanistic and even antithetical to good education. Testing, I realized with dismay, had become a central preoccupation in the schools and was not just a measure but an end in itself. I came to believe that accountability, as written into federal law, was not raising standards but dumbing down the schools as states and districts strived to meet unrealistic targets.

The more uneasy I grew with the agenda of choice and accountability, the more I realized that I am too "conservative" to embrace an agenda whose end result is entirely speculative and uncertain. The effort to upend American public education and replace it with something market-based began to feel too radical for me. I concluded that I could not countenance any reforms that might have the effect— intended or unintended—of undermining public education. Paradoxically, it was my basic conservatism about values, traditions, communities, and institutions that made me back away from what once was considered the conservative agenda but has now become the bipartisan agenda in education.

Before long, I found that I was reverting to my once familiar pattern as a friend and supporter of public education. Over time, my doubts about accountability and choice deepened as I saw the negative consequences of their implementation.

As I went back to work in my freshly painted office and reviewed the historical record of my intellectual wanderings, deviations, and transgressions, I decided to write about what I had learned. I needed to explain why I had returned to my roots as a partisan of American public education. I wanted to describe where we have gone astray in our pursuit of worthy goals. We as a society cannot extricate ourselves from fads and nostrums unless we carefully look at how we got entangled in them. We will continue to chase rainbows unless we recognize that they are rainbows and there is no pot of gold at the end of them. We certainly cannot address our problems unless we are willing to examine the evidence about proposed solutions, without fear, favor, or preconceptions.

It is time, I think, for those who want to improve our schools to focus on the essentials of education. We must make sure that our schools have a strong, coherent, explicit curriculum that is grounded in the liberal arts and sciences, with plenty of opportunity for children to engage in activities and projects that make learning lively. We must ensure that students gain the knowledge they need to understand political debates, scientific phenomena, and the world they live in. We must be sure they are prepared for the responsibilities of democratic citizenship in a complex society. We must take care that our teachers are well educated, not just well trained. We must be sure that schools have the authority to maintain both standards of learning and standards of behavior.

In this chapter, I have touched upon the evidence that changed my views about reforms that once seemed promising. Elsewhere in my writings, I have explained why I have concluded that most of the reform strategies that school districts, state officials, the Congress, and federal officials are pursuing, that mega-rich foundations are supporting, and that editorial boards are applauding are mistaken. I have attempted to explain how these mistaken policies are corrupting educational values. I have described the policies that I believe are necessary ingredients in a good system of public education. I will not claim that my ideas will solve all our problems all at once and forever. I will not offer a silver bullet or a magic feather. I do claim, however, that we must preserve American public education, because it is so intimately connected to our concepts of citizenship and democracy and to the promise of American life. In view of the money and power now arrayed on behalf of the ideas and programs that I have criticized, I hope it is not too late.

Notes

1. Alfred L. Malabre Jr., *Lost Prophets: An Insider's History of the Modern Economists* (Boston: Harvard Business School Press, 1994), 220.
2. Diane Ravitch, "Tot Sociology: Or What Happened to History in the Grade Schools," *American Scholar* 56, no. 3 (Summer 1987): 343–354; Ravitch, "Bring Literature and History Back to Elementary Schools," in *The Schools We Deserve: Reflections on the Educational Crises of Our Time* (New York: Basic Books, 1985), 75–79; Ravitch, *Left Back: A Century of Failed School Reforms* (New York: Simon & Schuster, 2000).
3. William Chandler Bagley, *Classroom Management: Its Principles and Technique* (New York: Macmillan, 1907), 3; William Henry Maxwell, "On a Certain Arrogance in Educational Theorists," *Educational Review* 47 (February 1914): 165–182, esp. 165–167, 171.

4. Diane Ravitch, "Programs, Placebos, Panaceas," *Urban Review*, April 1968, 8–11; Ravitch, "Foundations: Playing God in the Ghetto," *Center Forum* 3 (May 15, 1969): 24–27.

5. Diane Ravitch, *The Great School Wars: New York City, 1805–1973* (New York: Basic Books, 1974).

6. Diane Ravitch, *The Revisionists Revised: A Critique of the Radical Attack on the Schools* (New York: Basic Books, 1978).

7. Diane Ravitch, *The Troubled Crusade: American Education, 1945–1980* (New York: Basic Books, 1983).

8. Diane Ravitch and Chester E. Finn Jr., *What Do Our 17-Year-Olds Know? A Report on the First National Assessment of History and Literature* (New York: Harper & Row, 1987), 10–11.

9. *History–Social Science Framework for California Public Schools, Kindergarten Through Grade Twelve* (Sacramento: California State Department of Education, 1988); see also Diane Ravitch, "Where Have All the Classics Gone? You Won't Find Them in Primers," *New York Times Book Review*, May 17, 1987; Ravitch, "Tot Sociology."

10. David Osborne and Ted Gaebler, *Reinventing Government: How the Entrepreneurial Spirit Is Transforming the Public Sector* (Reading, MA: AddisonWesley, 1992).

11. Jason Peckenpaugh, "Reinvention Remembered: A Look Back at Seven Years of Reform," GovernmentExecutive.com, January 19, 2001, www.govexec.com/dailyfed/0101/011901p1.htm.

12. James C. Scott, *Seeing Like a State: How Certain Schemes to Improve the Human Condition Have Failed* (New Haven, CT: Yale University Press, 1998).

13. Sol Stern, "School Choice Isn't Enough," *City Journal*, Winter 2008.

CHAPTER 5

Disability Justifies Exclusion of Minority Students

A Critical History Grounded in Disability Studies

D. Kim Reid and Michelle G. Knight

From a disability studies (DS) perspective, the authors analyze how the historical conflation of disability with other identity factors and the ideology of normalcy contribute to the disproportionality problem in K–12 special education. They argue that this conflation and ideology make labeling and segregated education seem natural and legitimate for students carrying the high-incidence, legally defined labels Learning Disabled (LD), Mentally Retarded (MR), and Emotion ally Disturbed (ED). The authors then apply their insights to the scant literature on college access for students labeled LD. Although it appears that disabled students are succeeding at increasing rates, the overall picture obscures the *continued* effects of the historical legacy embedded in the intersections of race, class, gender, and disability for K-16 students.

O ur purpose in this article is to demonstrate that a critical history grounded in Disability Studies (DS) sheds productive light on the problem of overrepresentation of minority students in high-incidence disability groups in K-12 special education and the underrepresentation of such students in college admissions. We define DS and suggest that the historical construction of difference makes institutionalized racism, classism, and sexism seem natural in their conflation with *disability*, defined as oppression based on ableism (Hehir, 2002). Ableism, intertwined with the ideology of normalcy, is the assumption, rooted in eugenics, that it is better to be as "normal" as possible rather than be disabled (Baker, 2002). To show how history penetrates current practice, we provide an example of how labeling minority students as Learning Disabled (LD) affects college admissions. We chose LD because it is the highest-incidence disability category in public schools and postsecondary education. Finally, we make suggestions for addressing the disproportionality problems in K-16 settings.

Critical History Grounded in Disability Studies

DS is an interdisciplinary field of scholarship that unites critical inquiry with political advocacy by using approaches from the arts and humanities and humanistic and post-humanistic social sciences to improve the lives of disabled people on the basis of their self-expressed needs and desires (Gabel, 2005). DS historical analysis takes the form of a *critical* history that examines the role of positivist science in legitimizing domination (lggers, 1997)—science's emancipatory functions are not at issue—and provides a rationale for using other methods and perspectives for studying disability (Bentley, 1999). First, DS challenges the idea of normalcy as a regime of truth (Davis, 1997) and exposes the destructive consequences of "Othering"—framing disabled persons as outsiders (Goffman, 1963). Therefore, it eschews labeling. Nevertheless, because federal legislation requires labeling for funding purposes, it is impossible to discuss disproportionality without recourse to labels. Second, DS questions who has the right to speak for whom about disability-related issues (e.g., about where disabled people should receive services), and it elevates the lived experience of disabled people over the knowledge of so-called experts (Longmore, 2003). Third, DS counters hegemony and promotes democratic participation through a critique of pathologizing beliefs about disability and examination of the politics of exclusion (Ware, 2004).

The predominant approach to special education, the "medical model," spawned the problem of disproportionality. It is a deficit oriented perspective that is grounded in positivist science and undergirds (special) educational legislation (Bejoian & Reid, 2005) and practice (Gallagher, Heshusius, lano, & Skrtic, 2004). From this ableist perspective, disability is considered a personal condition to correct or cure. In contrast, DS scholars locate disability in the oppression of a given culture and historical period rather than in impairments per se (Stiker, 2002). We use the term *disabled students* to emphasize that disabled persons constitute a marginalized group "disabled" by physical and social barriers that result in pathologizing, infantilism, exclusion, and poverty (Garland Thomson, 1997). Shifting the focus of our gaze from the individual to society and its institutions provides a different lens through which to examine the problem of disproportionality.

DS also seeks to expose the historical roots of educational labels and policies (Ballard, 2004; Barton, 2004). Adherents of the medical model have regarded disproportionate representation as a contemporary technical problem (Artiles, 2003). Overlooked by technical framing is the conflict between the goal of realizing the principles of democratic social justice and the underlying, widespread belief systems related to ableism, racism, and classism (Garland Thomson, 1997).

The Historical Construction of Difference and Disproportionate Representation

In this section, we discuss the ideology of normalcy and how this legacy has made it seem natural to see students of color and those living in poverty as "Other" by associating them with disability (Gallagher, 1999). By ideology, we mean systems of representations—beliefs, images, and myths—that mediate our understandings of every aspect of life in profound but often unconscious ways (Althusser, 1971). Systemic discrimination provides an example of the power of ideologies: Although discrimination against all groups is illegal, it nevertheless persists. Consequently, some DS scholars (e.g., Brantlinger, 2004; Ware, 2004) argue that it is unlikely that discrimination resides in societal structures alone. Because the problem of disproportionality is limited to the high incidence, psychometrically defined categories of disability (Harry & Klingner, 2006) and is not apparent when impairments are medically defined (e.g., cerebral palsy; Ferguson, 2001), we see how the belief systems rooted in the ideology of normalcy detrimentally position students with these attributed impairments.

Its strong association with abnormality and monstrosity made disability the quintessential marker of hierarchical relations used to rationalize inequality, discrimination, and exclusion. As Mitchell and Snyder (2003) explain, what our society considers the normal standard—Whiteness, middle-class or greater affluence, ability, and so forth—has no need of definition. What needs to be marked and narrated is what people think of as outside the norm, that is, the person of color, the disabled body or mind, the person living in poverty. Historically, non-Whites, women, the lower social classes, and homosexuals routinely have been marked through medicalization and pathologized (Smith & Erevelles, 2004). As one example, now seemingly preposterous medical diagnoses such as "Drapetomania" (a disease that caused slaves to run away) were constructed to label Blacks as defective (Baymon, 2001). Today, disabled people continue to be considered defective and are more segregated educationally and socially than any other minority (Longmore, 2003).

Because many teachers and the public judge students as acceptable or unacceptable (i.e., normal or abnormal; Youdell, 2003) according to a set of standards that conform to the historical White European ideal, they (a) uphold Eurocentric and ableist conceptions of knowledge and decorum (Ferguson, 2001); (b) consider the dialects of American Blacks and Latinas/os inferior to Standard American English (Delpit, 2003); and (c) believe that *specialized* instructional techniques are warranted for students who do not do well in school, often students of color, the poor, and those labeled disabled (Bartolome, 2003). These so-called normal expectations justify teachers' holding students to standards that may not be familiar to those of non-European descent or even possible for students with impairments. Because most people in contemporary society perceive students with impairments as qualitatively distinct (i.e., empirically abnormal; Shapiro, 1999), "hunting for disability" in students— referral, diagnosis, labeling, sorting, and remediating—appears objective, fair, and benevolent (Baker, 2002). One result of perceiving "different" others through this technicalrational lens (i.e., as defective) is that it seems natural to many Americans that students of color, the poor, and immigrants lie outside the predominant norm and, therefore, belong in *special* education.

What serves to perpetuate oppression, then, are widespread conceptions and attitudes about race, class, gender, and disability and the attendant ideologies that shape these systems of (dis)advantage. One example of the impact of the ideology of normalcy is the fact that students of color and poverty receiving LD, Mentally Retarded (MR), and Emotionally Disturbed (ED) labels are segregated within schools at substantially higher rates than are their White counterparts (Losen & Orfield, 2002). This segregation continues to be condoned and defended by educators and the public alike, not on the basis of the students' race (which would be illegal) but because they are labeled *disabled* (Ferri & Connor, 2006). In essence, marking students of color as disabled allows their continued segregation under a seemingly natural and justifiable label.

Because it makes segregation seem appropriate and even preferable, the enduring belief that impairment and disability are empirical facts is at the center of the disproportionality problem. These "facts" are, however, social constructions (Linton, 1998) whose definitions change through time (Longmore & Umansky, 2001) and across cultures (Kalyanpur & Harry, 1999). For example, the definition of MR changed in the 1970s when agencies adjusted the legal requirement for eligibility from one to two standard deviations below the mean on a sanctioned intelligence test. Consequently, thousands of people changed status overnight by way of policy on new statistical requirements (Fleischer & Zames, 2001). Similarly, the meaning of disability in a developing nation may not mean the same as in the industrialized world (Artiles & Dyson, 2005). LD, MR, and ED, in particular, are very ambiguous: Because there is no single way to operationalize these "disabilities," a student may be considered to be impaired in one school setting but not in another (Collins, 2003; McDermott, 1993).

Furthermore, because most Americans read disability as a break with normalcy, they fail to conceptualize it as a *minority status* as DS asserts (Linton, 1998) and, therefore, overlook the societal factors embedded in ideologies that promote it. Relying on the technical analyses of positivist science, many educators frame overrepresentation as evidence of "misdiagnosis" related to poverty and test characteristics (e.g., Losen & Orfield, 2002) and continue to ignore the historical, ideological roots (Artiles, 2003) that suggest systemic discrimination as a root cause (Brantlinger, 2004). Consequently, many think the solution to disproportion ate representation is doing special education better. In framing overrepresentation in technical terms, however, the implementa tion of well-intentioned practices often constitutes a form of widely sanctioned, systematic, and institutionalized oppression (Ferri & Connor, 2006) that is built into the policies (Beratan, 2006) and practices (Tomlinson, 2004) of (special) education.

In sum, the ideology of normalcy creates systems of disadvantage for minority students. Special education often excludes minority learners from the general education curriculum that profits Whites and defines standards. To illustrate, studies suggest that K-12 minority students in special education actually receive *fewer* and *more technically oriented* services in *more segregated* settings (Harry & Klingner, 2006). Proponents of the medical model argue that minorities need special education because of their cognitive, linguistic, or class-related "deficits." This logic assumes that special education will improve these students' school and post-school outcomes. Nevertheless, the evidence on the impact of special education on school outcomes (e.g., academic achievement, school completion) is mixed. If a disability label can enhance educational opportunities for students, how do minority students fare in terms of access to postsecondary education? As we know, college access is a critically important factor in the creation of better op portunities for adult occupational and social success. We review this evidence in the next section.

From High School to Postsecondary Education: Applying the DS Critical Historical Lens

One way that historical conflation with disability continues to affect students of color and the poor beyond K-12 schooling is revealed through college admissions data on students labeled LD.

Improving access to college for underserved populations (i.e., first-generation, low-income, and disabled students and underrepresented minorities) has been designated as a top priority of K-16 educational systems. Recent demographic shifts in college freshman populations highlight the growing numbers of disabled students entering college. In 2000, for example, 66, 197 disabled freshmen, or 6% of full-time, first-time freshmen—including students with hearing, speech, orthopedic, and health-related problems, partial sight or blindness and those labeled LD—were enrolled in 4-year public and private institutions (Henderson, 2001).

These statistics represent an increase in postsecondary students reporting a disability. Yet they obscure two important aspects of the link between the placement of ethnic minority students in special education in high school and their transition to college. First, the statistics mask the inequity of ethnic minority students' overrepresentation in special education in high schools and their subsequent underrepresentation in college. Second, the statistics do not reveal how access to postsecondary education is based on the intersection of race, class, and disability and the inadequate services provided to labeled students in high school. Closer examination of these statistics shows how the history of disproportionate representation of minorities in special education pervades the intersections of race and class with access to college for students also labeled disabled.

Significantly, the number of students labeled LD who attend college has increased from 16% to 40% of the college students with disabilities in the past 12 years, and this group continues to grow (Henderson, 2001). Notably, however, this statistic represents a White, upper-middle-class increase in postsecondary attendance and attainment: In comparison to college freshmen without disabilities, students labeled LD were more often from White families whose annual income exceeded $100,000 (Henderson). Simultaneously, the decrease in the percentage of other disability categories suggests that minority and poor students identified by disability categories other than LD are decreasing in postsecondary attendance and completion. Therefore, it is necessary to disaggregate the statistics demonstrating the apparent increase of disabled students in postsecondary education. They mask the way the intersections of race, class, and disability perpetuate inequitable access and attainment in postsecondary education and how the prevailing, ableist ideologies (e.g., those defining disability as personal defect) embedded in a technical-rational approach to the disproportionality problem serve to advantage White middle-class students while disadvantaging the minority and poor. This advantage lies primarily in the unquestioned notions of individual responsibility for learning related to the assumption that ability and disability reside in the student. DS shifts the focus from these assumptions about individual pathology and responsibility to an analysis of how institutions fail to meet their responsibility to assist minority students in special education to enter college.

Setting Up Exclusion: K-12 Schooling

In questioning how overrepresentation of disabled minority and poor students in K-12 public schools translates into invisibility in college access, we note that the number of disabled students who participated in K-12 federal programs increased by 30% from 1990 to 1999, rising from 4.3 million to 5.5 million students. Much of this increase can be attributed to a rise in the absolute number of students being identified as disabled. The LD category continues to be the most prevalent classification in secondary schools: Of all students aged 6 to 21 who participate in federal programs for disabled students, 51% are identified as LD. Overall, the number of students labeled as LD increased from approximately 2.1 million to 2.8 million in the decade from 1989 to 1999.

However, critically examining policies and practices surrounding who is identified as LD unearths evidence of inequities in educational opportunities for Blacks and Latinas/os with respect to both placement and assessment. Black students are disproportionately represented in special education in general and, in elementary and high school, in the LD category (Warner, Dede, Garvan, & Conway, 2002), regardless of their socioeconomic class. Conversely, White middle-class students are identified in the spectrum of disabilities in ways directly connected to the race-class intersection. Middle- and upper-middle-class parents have the income to pay for expensive testing that allows their children to be labeled with socially acceptable labels that imply a medicalized, neurological substrate, such as *dyslexic* (Carrier, 1986). Conversely, less affluent Whites and minority students typically receive the less palatable label LD, the label conferred by schools that represents eligibility for special education. Nevertheless, if students who are identified as LD (including the so-called dyslexics) are increasing in representation in high schools (Artiles, Rueda, Salazar, & Higareda, 2005) and not in postsecondary institutions (Henderson, 2001), then the issue of underrepresentation of Blacks and other ethnic and linguistic minorities as disabled students substantiates institutional exclusion at the postsecondary level. Similarly, there is emerging evidence that linguistic minority students are overrepresented in secondary special education programs and are underrepresented in advanced placement courses (Artiles, Fierros, & Rueda, 2004). Although the literature is scant on college preparation for students labeled LD in high school, if labeled students are not expected to go to college, the intersections of race, class, and disability may play a substantial role in facilitating differential and inequitable access to college preparation, in the sense that fewer or less effective services are provided. There is some evidence that this is the case.

Individuals and Institutions: Including Disability in Access to College

Consequently, high schools concerned with improving college access for disabled students need to examine their college preparatory practices. Most disabled college students have been part of a special education teacher's caseload in elementary and/or secondary school (Feldmann & Messerli, 1995). However, because of the technical-rational assumption that some students fail to learn rather than that some institutions fail to teach, many (special) educational practices place the burden for college admission on the individual student instead of asking whether institutional practices facilitated access to a rigorous college-preparatory education. Embedding notions of individualism and institutional structures within intersections of race, class, and disability promotes the perpetuation of inequitable access and the ideology of a meritocratic educational system (Hurn, 1993).

Most documents emphasizing disability and college preparation are "how to" guides sponsored by government agencies or universities and written for high school guidance counselors and disabled students and their families. These documents place the onus on the student: They are didactic in tone and emphasize the need for disabled students to determine which colleges provide which accommodations and to recognize the level of responsibility they need to succeed in college. The documents focus on technical aspects which include: (a) self-advocacy skills, (b) initiative, and (c) time management associated with disability-related transition issues such as self-reporting of disability, articulating accommodation needs, coordinating auxiliary assistance, and making living arrangements (Feldmann & Messerli, 1995). Some see this emphasis on self-determination as a form of student empowerment and the key to student success in postsecondary education (Field, Sarver, & Shaw, 2003). However, these documents do not affirm students' cultural contexts or use their racial and ethnic cultures in the development of institutional supports. In short, they fail to provide services that address the intersections of race, class, and disability (Knight & Chae, 2004; Knight & Oesterreich, 2002).

The emphasis on individualism and self-determination, which we noted is closely linked to racialized discourses of White Eurocentric notions of merit (Ladson-Billings, 2000), may unfairly affect ethnic minority and poor students' opportunities for college access while *privileging* White and affluent disabled students (McDonough, 1997). For instance, this onus renders invisible the co-management of upper-class families to leverage institutional supports for college access, including going to Borders to pick up the needed resources, writing the college essay, and paying for test preparation (Oakes, Rogers, Lipton, & Morrell, 2002). Thus the ideologies of individualism and self-determination support upper-middle-class students, whose family resources are not regarded as unfair advantages. However, some researchers note that a shift in emphasis for disabled students' college access is oc curring. Colleges and universities are legally required under both IDEA (Individuals with Disabilities Education Act) and ADA (Americans with Disabilities Act) to provide accommodations for students who are identified as disabled (Jones, 2002). Consequently, there is increasing recognition that high schools, instructors, and colleges must take on greater responsibility.

High schools and postsecondary institutions seeking to provide more equitable access to postsecondary education for disabled minority students must look beyond statistics demonstrating an increase in the population of disabled students attending college. Disaggregating the data to reveal the intersections of race, class, gender, and disability exposes the continued, systematic exclusion of ethnic minorities and the poor. Furthermore, schools have much to learn from a DS perspective. First, recognizing that disability lies in social and educational attitudes and practices, including what amounts to limiting instructional opportunities in much of K-12 special education (Harry & Klingner, 2006), nullifies the validity of many of the technical-rational gatekeeping measures that are currently used in college admissions decisions. Second, familiarity with the impact of ableist ideologies with respect to the conflation of racism, classism, sexism, and disability could predispose college administrators to refocus their admissions programs on ways to recruit and provide positive support for those students typically excluded because of K-12 disability labels. Finally, colleges and universities might benefit from listening to the voices of minority students labeled as disabled. Indeed, those students and their families are the experts who know the limitations of their K-12 educational opportunities and their current needs, and that information could enable colleges and universities to provide the kinds and levels of multicultural support needed to ensure success in postsecondary placements.

Conclusions

The overrepresentation of minorities in special education in elementary and high school and their underrepresentation at the postsecondary level demonstrate clearly how the historical legacies of racism, classism, sexism, and ableism continue to influence educational practice. Applying a critical history grounded in DS has provided insights into the ways that disability has served historically as an instrument of institutionalized systems of disadvantage for ethnic minorities and the poor, largely because of definitional loopholes and assumptions associated with the technical-rational understanding of disability. Moreover, because of the conflation of disability with race and class identity markers, DS scholars question the practice of labeling students at all and argue against the need to deliver remedial instructional services in segregated settings. Many, instead, promote inclusive education based on constructivist, differentiated instruction and universal design (Broderick, Mehta-Parekh, & Reid, 2005; Reid & Valle, 2004). The hope is that providing respectful, integrated, age-appropriate classrooms for students of all races, classes, genders, and abilities will facilitate more equitable K-16 educational opportunities and improve other life chances.

References

Althusser, L. (1971). Ideology and the ideological state apparatus. In F. Jameson (Ed.), *Lenin and philosophy and other essays* (pp. 1–29). New York: Monthly Review Press.

Artiles, A. J. (2003). Special education's changing identity. *Harvard Educational Review, 73,* 164–202.

Artiles, A. J., & Dyson, A. (2005). Inclusive education in the globalization age: The promise of comparative cultural historical analysis. In D. Mitchell (Ed.), *Contextualizing inclusive education* (pp. 37–62). London: Routledge.

Artiles, A. J., Fierros, E., & Rueda, R. (2004, April). *English language learner overrepresentation in special education: A 10-state analysis of placement patterns and opportunity to learn.* Paper presented at the annual meeting of the American Educational Research Association, San Diego.

Artiles, A. J., Rueda, R., Salazar, J., & Higareda, I. (2005). Within-group diversity in minority disproportionate representation: English language learners in urban school districts. *Exceptional Children, 71,* 283–300.

Baker, B. (2002). The hunt for disability: The new eugenics and the normalization of school children. *Teachers College Record, 1 04*(4), 663–703.

Ballard, K. (2004). Ideology and the origins of exclusion: A case study. In L. Ware (Ed.), *Ideology and the politics of (in)exclusion* (pp. 89–107). New York: Peter Lang.

Bartolome, L. I. (2003). Beyond the methods fetish: Toward a humanizing pedagogy. In A. Darder, M. Baltodano, & R. D. Torres (Eds.), *The critical pedagogy reader* (pp. 408–429). New York: Routledge/Falmer.

Barton, L. (2004). The politics of special education: A necessary or irrelevant approach? In L. Ware (Ed.), *Ideology and the politics of (in)exclusion* (pp. 63–75). New York: Peter Lang.

Baymon, D. (2001). Disability and the justification of inequality in American history. In P. Longmore & L. Umansky (Eds.), *The new disability history: American perspectives* (pp. 33–57). New York: New York University Press.

Bejoian, L., & Reid, D. K. (2005). A disability studies perspective on the Bush educational agenda: The No Child Left Behind Act of 2001. *Equity & Excellence in Education, 38,* 220–231.

Bentley, M. (1999). *Modern historiography: An introduction.* London: Routledge.

Beratan, G. D. (2006). Institutionalizing inequity: Ableism, racism, and IDEA 2004. *Disability Studies Quarterly, 26*(2). Available at www. dsq-sds.org/2006_spring_toc. html

Brantlinger, E. A. (2004). Ideologies discerned, values determined: Getting past the hierarchies of special education. In L. Ware (Ed.), *Ideology and the politics of (in)exclusion* (pp. 11–31). New York: Peter Lang.

Broderick, A., Mehta-Parekh, H., & Reid, D. K. (2005). Differentiating instruction for disabled students in inclusive classrooms. *Theory Into Practice, 44,* 194–202.

Carrier, G. (1986). *Learning disability: Social class and the construction of inequality in American education.* New York: Greenwood Press.

Collins, K. M. (2003). *Ability profiling and school failure: One child's struggle to be seen as competent.* Mahwah, NJ: Lawrence Erlbaum.

Davis, L. J. (1997). Constructing normalcy. In L. J. Davis, (Ed.), *The disability studies reader* (pp. 9–28). New York: Routledge.

Delpit, L. (2003). Language diversity and learning. In A. Darder, M. Baltodano, & R. D. Torres (Eds.), *The critical pedagogy reader* (pp. 388–403). New York: Routledge/Falmer.

Feldmann, E., & Messerli, C. (1995, March). Successful transitions: The students' perspective. In D. Montgomery (Ed.), *Reaching to the future: Boldly facing challenges in rural communities* (pp. 151–158). Conference Proceedings of the American Council on Rural Special Education, March 15–18, Las Vegas, NV.

Ferguson, A. A. (2001). *Bad boys: Public schools in the making of Black masculinity.* Ann Arbor: University of Michigan Press.

Ferri, B. A., & Connor, D. J. (2006). *Reading resistance: Discourses of exclusion in desegregation and inclusion debates.* New York: Peter Lang.

Field, S., Sarver, M., & Shaw, S. (2003). Self-determination: A key to success in postsecondary education for students with learning disabilities. *Remedial and Special Education, 24,* 339–349.

Fleischer, D. Z., & Zames, F. (2001). *The disability rights movement: From charity to confrontation.* Philadelphia: Temple University Press.

Gabel, S. (2005). Introduction: Disability studies in education. In S. L. Gabel (Ed.), *Disability studies in education: Readings in theory and method* (pp. 1–20). New York: Peter Lang.

Gallagher, D., Heshusius, L., Iano, R. P., & Skrtic, T. M. (2004). *Challenging orthodoxy in special education: Dissenting voices.* Denver, CO: Love Publishing.

Gallagher, S. (1999). An exchange of gazes. In J. L. Kincheloe, S. R. Steinberg, & L. E. Villaverde (Eds.), *Rethinking intelligence* (pp. 69–83). New York: Routledge.

Garland Thomson, R. (1997). *Extraordinary bodies: Figuring physical disability in American culture and literature.* New York: Columbia University Press.

Goffman, E. (1963). *Stigma: Notes on the management of spoiled identity.* New York: Simon & Schuster.

Harry, B., & Klingner, J. (2006). *Why are so many minority students in special education? Understanding race and disability in schools.* New York: Teachers College Press.

Hehir, T. (2002). Eliminating ableism in education. *Harvard Educational Review, 72,* 1–25.

Henderson, C. (2001). *College freshmen with disabilities, 2001: A biennial statistical profile.* Washington, DC: American Council on Education.

Hurn, C. (1993). *The limits and possibilities of schooling: An introduction to the sociology of education* (3rd ed., pp. 42–131). Boston: Allyn & Bacon.

Iggers, G. G. (1997). *History in the twentieth century: From scientific objectivity to the postmodern challenge.* Hanover, NH: Wesleyan University Press.

Jones, M. (2002). *Providing a quality accommodated experience in preparation for and during post-secondary school* (Information Brief No. 1, Vol. 1). Minneapolis, MN: National Center on Secondary Education and Transition.

Kalyanpur, M., & Harry, B. (1999). *Culture in special education.* Baltimore, MD: Brookes.

Knight, M., & Chae, H. (2004, April). *Using critical race theory (CRT) and critical Latino theory (LatCrit) to examine Black and Latino youth's negotiations of New York State high stakes Regents exams.* Paper presented at the annual meeting of the American Educational Research Association, San Diego.

Knight, M., & Oesterreich, H. (2002). (In)(di)visible youth identities: Insight from a feminist framework. In W. G. Tierney & L. Hagedorn (Eds.), *Increasing access to college* (pp. 123–144). New York: State University of New York Press.

Ladson-Billings, G. (2000). Racialized discourses and ethnic epistemologies. In N. K. Denzin & Y. S. Lincoln (Eds.), *Handbook of qualitative research* (2nd ed., pp. 257–278). London: Sage.

Linton, S. (1998). *Claiming disability.* New York: New York University Press.

Longmore, P. (2003). *Why I burned my book and other essays on disability.* Philadelphia: Temple University Press.

Longmore, P., & Umansky, L. (Eds.). (2001). *The new disability history: American perspectives.* New York: New York University Press.

Losen, D. J., & Orfield, G. (Eds.). (2002). *Racial inequality in special education.* Cambridge, MA: Harvard Education Press.

McDermott, R. (1993). The acquisition of a child by a learning disability. In S. Chaiklin & J. Lave (Eds.), *Understanding practice: Perspectives on activity and context* (pp. 269–305). New York: Cambridge University Press.

McDonough, P. (1997). *Choosing colleges: How social class and schools structure opportunity.* Albany: State University of New York Press.

Mitchell, D. T., & Snyder, S. L. (2003). *Narrative prosthesis: Disability and the dependencies of discourse.* Ann Arbor: University of Michigan Press.

Oakes, J., Rogers, J., Lipton, M., & Morrell, E. (2002). The social construction of college access: Confronting the technical, cultural, and political barriers to low-income students of color. In W. G. Tierney & L. S. Hagedorn (Eds.), *Increasing access to college: Extending possibilities for all students* (pp. 105–121). Albany: State University of New York Press.

Reid, D. K., & Valle, J. W. (2004). The discursive practice of learning disability: Implications for instruction and parent-school relations. *Journal of Learning Disabilities, 37,* 466–481.

Shapiro, A. (1999). *Everybody belongs: Changing negative attitudes toward classmates with disabilities.* New York: Routledge/Falmer.

Smith, R. M., & Erevelles, N. (2004). Toward an enabling education: The difference that disability makes. *Educational Researcher, 23*(8), 31–36.

Stiker, H. (2002). *A history of disability.* Ann Arbor: University of Michigan Press.

Tomlinson, S. (2004). Race and special education. In L. Ware (Ed.), *Ideology and the politics of (in)exclusion* (pp. 76–88). New York: Peter Lang.

Ware, L. (2004). The politics of ideology: A pedagogy of critical hope. In L. Ware (Ed.), *Ideology and the politics of (in)exclusion* (pp. 183–204). New York: Peter Lang.

Warner, T., Dede, D., Garvan, C., and Conway, T. (2002). One size still does not fit all in specific learning disability assessment across ethnic groups. *Journal of Learning Disabilities, 35,* 500–508.

Youdell, D. (2003). Identity traps or how Black students fail: The interactions between biographical, sub-cultural, and learner identities. *British Journal of Sociology of Education, 24*(1), 3–20.

CHAPTER 6

Equality of Educational Opportunity

Race, Gender, and Special Needs

Joel Spring

Define

Equality of educational opportunity means that everyone has an equal chance to receive an education. When defined as an equal chance to attend publicly supported schools, equal educational opportunity is primarily a legal issue. In this context, the provision of equal educational opportunity can be defined solely on the grounds of justice: If government provides a service like education, all classes of citizens should have equal access to that service.

The Law, Race, and Equality of Educational Opportunity

Equality under the law is the great legal principle underlying the idea of equality of educational opportunity. Everyone should receive equal treatment by the law. No one should receive special privileges or treatment because of race, gender, religion, ethnicity, or wealth. This means that if a government provides a school system, then everyone should be treated equally by that system; everyone should have equal access to that educational system.

Added in 1868, the Fourteenth Amendment to the Constitution provided for equality under the law. One of the purposes of the Fourteenth Amendment was to extend the basic guarantees of the Bill of Rights into the areas of state and local government. The clause of the amendment that emphasized the principle of equality under the law stated, "No State shall ... deny to any person within its jurisdiction the equal protection of the laws."

At first glance, "equal protection of the laws" would suggest that if state laws created a school system, then everyone should have equal access. However, the initial interpretation by the U.S. Supreme Court in 1895 was that "equal protection" could also mean "separate but equal." Or, in other words, segregated education based on race could be legal under the Fourteenth Amendment if all the schools were equal.

The separate but equal ruling occurred in the 1895 U.S. Supreme Court decision *Plessy v. Ferguson.* The case involved Homer Plessy, who was one-eighth African American and seven-eighths white. He

Plessy v Ferguson

was arrested for refusing to ride in the colored coach of a train, as required by Louisiana state law. The Supreme Court's decision in this case that segregated facilities could exist if they were equal became known as the separate but equal doctrine.

The 1954 desegregation decision *Brown v. Board of Education of Topeka* overturned the separate but equal doctrine by arguing that segregated education was inherently unequal. This meant that even if school facilities, teachers, equipment, and all other physical conditions were equal between two racially segregated schools, the two schools would still be unequal because of the racial segregation.

In 1964 Congress took a significant step toward speeding up school desegregation by passing the important Civil Rights Act. About school desegregation, Title VI of the 1964 Civil Rights Act was most important because it provided a means for the federal government to force school desegregation. In its final form, Title VI required the mandatory withholding of federal funds from institutions that practiced racial discrimination. Title VI states that no person, because of race, color, or national origin, can be excluded from or denied the benefits of any program receiving federal financial assistance. It required all federal agencies to establish guidelines to implement this policy. Refusal by institutions or projects to follow these guidelines was to result in the "termination of or refusal to grant or to continue assistance under such program or activity."

Title VI of the 1964 Civil Rights Act was important for two reasons. First, it established a major precedent for federal control of American public schools, by making it explicit that the control of money would be one method used by the federal government to shape local school policies. Second, it turned the federal Office of Education into a policing agency with the responsibility of determining whether school systems were segregated and, if they were, of doing something about the segregated conditions.

One result of Title VI was to speed up the process of school desegregation in the South, particularly after the passage of federal legislation in 1965 that increased the amount of money available to local schools from the federal government. In the late 1960s southern school districts rapidly began to submit school desegregation plans to the Office of Education.

In the North, prosecution of inequality in educational opportunity as it related to school segregation required a different approach from that used in the South. In the South, school segregation existed by legislative acts that required separation of the races. There were no specific laws requiring separation of the races in the North. But even without specific laws, racial segregation existed. Therefore, it was necessary for individuals bringing complaints against northern school districts to prove that the existing patterns of racial segregation were the result of purposeful action by the school districts. It had to be proved that school officials intended racial segregation to be a result of their educational policies.

The conditions required to prove segregation were explicitly outlined in 1974, in the Sixth Circuit Court of Appeals case *Oliver v. Michigan State Board of Education*. The court stated, "A presumption of segregative purpose arises when plaintiffs establish that the natural, probable and foreseeable result of public officials' action or inaction was an increase or perpetuation of public school segregation." This did not mean that individual motives or prejudices were to be investigated but that the overall pattern of school actions had to be shown to increase racial segregation; that is, in the language of the court, "the question is whether a purposeful pattern of segregation has manifested itself over time, despite the fact that individual official actions, considered alone, may not have been taken for segregative purposes."

Figure 6.1 presents a time line of significant events in the struggle for equality of educational opportunity.

The Meaning of Race

The question of the meaning of race was highlighted by the original separate but equal case, *Plessy v. Ferguson*. According to the lines of ancestry as expressed at the time, Plessy was one-eighth African

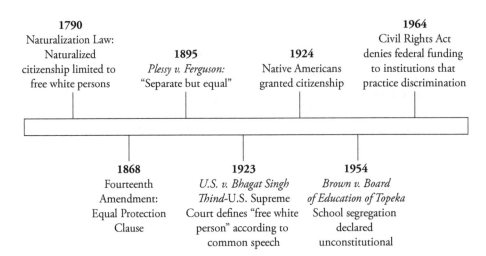

1790		1895		1924		1964
Naturalization Law:		*Plessy v. Ferguson:*		Native Americans		Civil Rights Act
Naturalized		"Separate but equal"		granted citizenship		denies federal funding
citizenship limited to						to institutions that
free white persons						practice discrimination

1868		1923		1954
Fourteenth		*U.S. v. Bhagat Singh*		*Brown v. Board*
Amendment:		*Thind-*U.S. Supreme		*of Education of Topeka*
Equal Protection		Court defines "free white		School segregation
Clause		person" according to		declared
		common speech		unconstitutional

Figure 6.1: Time Line of Events Discussed—Equality of Educational Opportunity

American and seven-eighths white. Was Homer Plessy white or black? What was the meaning of the term *white*? Why wasn't Plessy classified as white since seven-eighths of his ancestry was white and only one-eighth was black? Why did the court consider him black?

Plessy v. Ferguson highlights the principle that race is a social and legal construction. The U.S. legal system was forced to construct a concept of race because the 1790 Naturalization Law limited naturalized citizenship to immigrants who were free white persons. This law excluded Native Americans from citizenship. This limitation remained until 1952. Because of this law, U.S. courts were forced to define the meaning of white persons. Adding to the legal problem was that most southern states had adopted the so-called one drop of blood rule which classified anyone with an African ancestor, no matter how distant, as African American. Under the one drop of blood rule, Homer Plessy was considered black.

The startling fact about the many court cases dealing with the 1790 law was the inability of the courts to rely on scientific evidence in defining white persons. Consider two of the famous twentieth-century court cases. The first, *Takao Ozawa v. United States* (1922), involved a Japanese immigrant who graduated from high school in Berkeley, California, and attended the University of California. He and his family spoke English and attended Christian churches. A key issue in *Takao Ozawa v. United States* (1922) was whether "white persons" referred to skin color. Many Japanese are fair skinned. The Court responded to this issue by rejecting skin color as a criterion. The Court stated, "The test afforded by the mere color of the skin of each individual is impracticable, as that differs greatly among persons of the same race, even among Anglo-Saxons, ranging by imperceptible gradations from the fair blond to the swarthy brunette, *the latter being darker than many of the lighter hued persons of the brown and yellow races* [my emphasis]." Rejecting the idea of skin color, the Court recognized the term *Caucasian* to define white persons—and denied citizenship.

However, the following year the U.S. Supreme Court rejected Caucasian as a standard for defining white persons in *United States v. Bhagat Singh Thind* (1923). In this case, an immigrant from India applied for citizenship as a Caucasian. According to the scientific rhetoric of the time, Thind was a Caucasian. Faced with this issue, the Court suddenly dismissed Caucasian as a definition of white persons. The Court argued, "It may be true that the blond Scandinavian and the brown Hindu have a common ancestor in the dim reaches of antiquity, but the average man knows perfectly well that there are unmistakable and profound differences between them today." Therefore, rather than relying on a scientific definition as it had in *Takao Ozawa v. United States*, the U.S. Supreme Court declared, "What

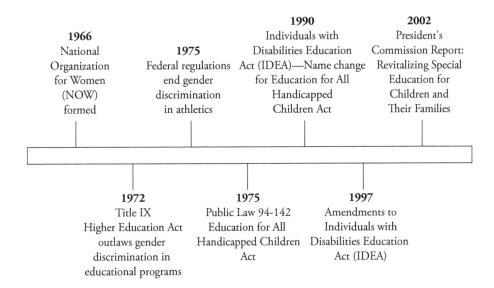

1966
National
Organization
for Women
(NOW)
formed

1975
Federal regulations
end gender
discrimination
in athletics

1990
Individuals with
Disabilities Education
Act (IDEA)—Name change
for Education for All
Handicapped
Children Act

2002
President's
Commission Report:
Revitalizing Special
Education for
Children and
Their Families

1972
Title IX
Higher Education Act
outlaws gender
discrimination in
educational programs

1975
Public Law 94-142
Education for All
Handicapped Children
Act

1997
Amendments to
Individuals with
Disabilities Education
Act (IDEA)

we now hold is that the words "free white persons" are words of common speech, to be interpreted in accordance with the understanding of the common man." The Court never specified who was to represent this common man. Thind was denied citizenship.

U.S. court histories are filled with disputable efforts to define race. My nineteenth-century ancestors on my father's side were denied U.S. citizenship and were recognized as only having tribal citizenship despite the fact that the majority of their ancestors were European. Until Native Americans were granted U.S. citizenship in 1924, many so-called mixed bloods were limited to tribal citizenship. The confusion over legal racial categories was exemplified by an 1853 California court case involving the testimony of immigrant Chinese witnesses regarding the murder of another Chinese immigrant by one George Hall. The California Supreme Court overturned the murder conviction of George Hall by applying a state law that disallowed court testimony from blacks, mulattos, and Native Americans. California's Chief Justice ruled that the law barring the testimony of Native Americans applied to all "Asiatics" since, according to theory, Native Americans were originally Asians who crossed into North America over the Bering Straits. Therefore, the chief justice argued, the ban on court testimony from Native Americans applied to "the whole of the Mongolian race."

The effect of this questionable legal construction of race was to heighten tensions among different groups of Americans. Many of those classified as African American have European and Native American citizenship. However, because of the one drop of blood rule and legal support of segregation, the possibilities for continuing assimilation and peaceful coexistence between so-called whites and blacks were delayed and replaced by a tradition of hostility between the two groups. The law reduced the chances of evolving into a peaceful multiracial society. It will probably take another century to undo the damage created by the legal construction of race and segregation in the nineteenth and early twentieth centuries.

What Race Am I?: Racial and Cultural Self-Identification

In an effort to resolve the problems in defining a person's race, the U.S. Census Bureau is using personal self-identification. The Census Bureau asks people to select their race from a "flash card" listing six groups: White, Black, American Indian, Eskimo and Aleut, Asian or Pacific Islander, and Other races. The Census Bureau also uses the designation "A.O.I.C.," which stands for "alone or in combination" with other races. Thus a census report might indicate "Black A.O.I.C." for a person who indicates that he is only black or has an ancestry of a combination of races or ethnic groups. "Black alone" means those who claim only black ancestry; similar definitions are made for "White A.O.I.C.," "White alone," "Asian A.O.I.C.," and "Asian alone."

Often, Census data refers to "Hispanic (of any race)." Regarding Hispanic self-identification, the U.S. Census Bureau explains its method: "Respondents were asked to select their [Hispanic] origin (and the origin of other household members) from a 'flash card' listing ethnic origins. People of Hispanic origin, in particular, were those who indicated their origin was Mexican, Puerto Rican, Cuban, Central or South American, or some other Hispanic origin. It should be noted that people of Hispanic origin may be of any race."

Regarding its use of racial classification the U.S. Census Bureau attached this footnote to its 2006 report on 2004 income (there is a delay in reporting because of the time required to compile and analyze data):

1. The 2003 CPS [Current Population Survey] asked respondents to choose one or more races. White Alone refers to people who reported White and did not report any other race category. The use of this single-race population does not imply that it is the preferred method of presenting or analyzing data. The Census Bureau uses a variety of approaches. Information on people who reported more than one race, such as "White and American Indian and Alaska Native" or "Asian and Black or African American," is available from Census 2000 through American Factfinder. About 2.6 percent of people reported more than one race in 2000.

2. Black alone refers to people who reported Black and did not report any other race category.

3. Asian alone refers to people who reported Asian and did not report any other race category.

By making racial definitions subjective, self-identification makes race a matter of cultural choice. Consider a person who had a great-grandmother who was Native American while all other ancestors were of European ancestry. This person might prefer to identify with Native American as opposed to European cultures and, consequently, choose Native American from the U.S. Census Bureau's flash card. Or consider a person who has African, European, and Native American ancestry. This combination of ancestry is typical of many U.S. citizens who identify themselves as black. Should this person choose black, white, or Native American when confronted with a U.S. Census Bureau flash card? The choice will probably be based on cultural affiliation through self-identification with white, black, or Native American cultures.

Further, the meaning of "white" continues to be a perplexing issue. In *Shades of White: White Kids and Racial Identities in High School*, Pamela Perry investigates white identity in two high schools in California. One high school is racially mixed while the other is predominantly white. Perry defines white students as those of European ancestry who are not Hispanic. Her central question for white students at both schools is: "What does it mean to be white?" Perry summarizes the responses from both schools: "Most believed that to be white meant that you had no culture. ... Some felt victimized as whites, some felt privileged, many felt both. Some felt 'racist', some felt nonracist, many felt both."

White students said they had no culture, Perry concluded, because they did not recognize that their culture is the standard and dominant culture of the United States. They are unconsciously accepting white culture as the norm. This is exemplified when these white students identify black and Latino students as having a unique culture. In identifying separate black and Latino cultures, white students are unconsciously making a distinction between white and other cultures. Feeling that they lack a culture sometimes causes white students to envy blacks and Latinos. For example, many white students have adopted the clothing and music styles of black student culture.

Black high school students recognize that white students are imitating their clothing and music styles. One black student commented to Perry, "They'll [white students] be listening to rap music and trying to wear clothes that we wear and overdo it. ... You're [in reference to white students] trying to be me, but you're getting only the surface."

As an example of differing views regarding cultural exchanges, some black students feel demeaned rather than proud that white students are imitating their cultural styles. The reaction of black students is in sharp contrast to the envy some white students have of black culture. One black student describes the reason for white adoption of black styles: "They try to overaccommodate. Or they feel bad that we're structurally lower and so they try to be like that so they can relate to your friends that way." This student intimated that she would feel more comfortable with white students if they acted within their own cultural boundaries.

Many white students distinguish whiteness as lacking any ties to the past. For instance, some white students feel that African American, Native American, and Mexican American students have a conscious relationship to a historical past. This historical past is directly related to a distinctive culture. From the perspective of these white students, black students think about their roots in Africa, Native American students feel linked to their pre-Columbian cultures, and Mexican American students identify with the dominant Mexican culture of the Southwest that existed prior to being conquered by the United States. In contrast, white students did not focus on the cultures of their European ancestry.

As I suggested at the beginning of this section, self-identification as a method of defining race is resulting in a focus on cultural differences because of the often and complicated ancestry of American citizens. I find it interesting to ask my college students to identify their race and to discuss the problems associated with self-identification. Sometimes, students who identify themselves as black or white find that they share a common Native American ancestry.

Race and Social Class

Does race or social class determine equal educational opportunity? Take the case of African American Professor Cornel West. While a professor of theology at Princeton University, West, after lecturing on Plato's *Republic*, drove into New York City for a photo session for his new book. Driving an expensive car (as he described it) and planning to have dinner at an expensive restaurant, West felt the burden of the race line when stepping onto the streets of Manhattan. After parking his car, West tried to hail a taxicab to take him to the photo session. In a simmering rage, West watched taxi after taxi stop for white people while ignoring him. After an hour, a cab finally stopped for him. A similar experience occurred to David Dinkins, the former mayor of New York City. The first black mayor of the city watched as taxis responded to whites while ignoring him. Even the former leader of the city could not escape its racist temperament.

There is a correlation between level of education and income. Therefore it is distressing that a 2004 study of high school graduation rates by Jing Miao and Walt Haney concludes: "Despite the graduation rate method used, results indicate that high school graduation rates in the U.S. have been declining in recent years and that graduation rates for black and Hispanic students lag substantially behind those of white students." This would suggest a future increasing income disparity among whites and blacks and Hispanics.

No matter how high a person's status or income, racism is still a problem. However, social class remains important. Opportunities are quite different for an African American growing up in an upper-class household compared with an African American or white child growing up in poverty. Social-class lines are as sharply drawn in the black community as they are in the white community. For this reason, it is important to consider social class as it intersects with race.

As indicated in Table 6.1, wealth is as disproportionately distributed in the African American and Hispanic communities as in the white community. The upper class in the white community commands about the same percentage (49.0 percent) of total white income as the upper class of the African

American and Hispanic communities, 50.0 percent and 47.9 percent, respectively. Indeed, the lower class of each racial grouping shares similar small percentages of the total income of their race—white, 3.9 percent; African American, 3.1 percent; Hispanic, 4.1 percent.

Social Class	White (%)	Black (%)	Hispanic (%)
Upper	49	50	47.9
Upper-middle	23.1	24.0	23.4
Middle	15.0	14.7	15.2
Lower-middle	9.1	8.3	9.5
Lower	3.9	3.1	4.1

Table 6.1. Share of Aggregate Income by Social Class, Race, and Hispanic Origins, 1999

Source: U.S. Census Bureau, "Table B-3. Share of Aggregate Income Received by Each Fifth and Top 5 Percent of Households by Race and Hispanic Origin of Householder: 1967 to 1999," Money Income in the United States—1999 (Washington, DC: U.S. Printing Office, 2000).

Although social class is highlighted by the income distribution within each racial group, race is still a factor in the overall distribution of income in the United States. Table 6.2 indicates these racial differences according to mean household income. According to the table, white and Asian household incomes are significantly above those of blacks and Hispanics with a 2004 "white alone, not Hispanic" mean household income at $65,317 and "Asian alone" mean household income of $76,747 as compared with "black alone" ($40,685) and "Hispanics of any race" ($45,871).

Race or Hispanic Origins	Mean Household Income ($)
All races	60,528
White A.O.I.C.*	62,873
White alone	62,958
White alone, not Hispanic	65,317
Black A.O.I.C.*	40,814
Black alone	40,685
Asian A.O.I.C.*	76,371
Asian alone	76,747
Hispanic (of any race)	45,871

Table 6.2. Income Distribution to $250,000 or More for Households by Race or Hispanic Origins, 2004

*Alone or in combination with other races,
Source: Adapted from U.S. Census Bureau, "Table HINC-06, Current Population Survey," 2005 *Annual Social and Economic Supplement.* http://pubdb3.census.Rov/macro/032005/hhinc/new06 OOO.htm.

Major disparities exist, as indicated in Table 6.3, between racial groups living in poverty with 8.6 percent of whites (not Hispanic) living in poverty as compared to black (24.7 percent), Asian (9.8 percent), and Hispanic of any race (21.9 percent).

School Segregation Today

School segregation for blacks and Latinos increased in recent years as indicated in Table 6.4. "Latino" is used in Table 6.4 in contrast to "Hispanic." Elsewhere in my writing, I have discussed in detail the

Race	Percentage Below Poverty Level
White, not Hispanic	8.6
White	10.8
Black	24.7
Asian	9.8
Hispanic of any race	21.9

Table 6.3. Poverty Status of People by Race, 2004

Source: Adapted from U.S. Census Bureau, "Table 3," *Income, Poverty, and Health Insurance Coverage in the United States: 2004* (Washington, DC: U.S. Printing Office, 2005), p. 10.

problems associated with the distinction between Hispanic and Latino. Here it suffices to say that the decision to use "Latino" was made by the source for the data—Harvard University's The Civil Rights Project. As indicated in Table 6.4, racial segregation increased for black students: from 66 percent of black students attending schools with 50–100 percent minority students in 1991–1992 to 73 percent in 2003–2004. The most segregated were Latino students with 73 percent attending schools with 50–100 percent minority students in 1991–1992 and 77 percent in 2003–2004.

	1991–1992	2003–2004
Percentage of black students in 50–100% minority schools	66	73
Percentage of Latino students in 50–100% minority schools	73	77
Percentage of Native American students in 50–100% minority schools	43	52

Table 6.4. Changes in School Segregation, 1991-2003

Source: Compiled from Tables 3, 4, and 5 in Gary Orfield and Clumgmei Lee, "Racial Transformation and the Changing Nature of Segregation," *The Civil Rights Project* (Cambridge, MA; Harvard University, 2006), pp. 10–11.

In general, schools remain segregated with white students being the most racially isolated: the average white student attends a school where more than 78 percent of the students are white, 9 percent are black, 9 percent are Latino, 3 percent are Asian, and 1 percent is Native American (Table 6.5). As indicated in Table 6.5, the average Latino student attends schools that are 55 percent Latino and the average black student attends schools that are 53 percent black.

In 1999 Gary Orfield, head of Harvard's Civil Rights Project and a long-time advocate of school desegregation, issued a report with the ominous title, "Resegregation in American Schools." The report states, "We are clearly in a period when many policymakers, courts and opinion makers assume that desegregation is no longer necessary. ... Polls show that most white Americans believe that equal educational opportunity is being provided." Responding to the report, Chester Finn, a conservative critic of public schools, faulted Orfield for even worrying about school segregation. "Gary Orfield," Finn said, "must be the only American who still thinks that integration for its own sake is an important societal goal." For Finn, "The price of forced busing and other forms of social engineering is too high to pay when there are more urgent crises facing this country's schools."

In response to increased school segregation in southern states, Gary Orfield, in the summer of 2002, organized a joint conference between Harvard University's Civil Rights Project and the University of North Carolina's Center for Civil Rights. Others reported an increase in school segregation

Race	Average White Student	Average Black Student	Average Latino Student	Average Asian Student	Average Native American Student
Percentage of school that is white	78	30	28	45	44
Percentage of school that is black	9	53	12	12	7
Percentage of school that is Latino	9	13	55	20	11
Percentage of scliool that is Asian	3	3	5	22	3
Percentage of school that is American Indian	1	1	1	1	35

Table 6.5. Racial Composition of Schools Attended by the Average Student of Each Race, 2003–2004

Source: Gary Orfield and Chungmei Lee, "Racial Transformation and the Changing Nature of Segregation." *The Civil Rights Project* (Cambridge, MA: Harvard University, 2006), p. 9.

in cities throughout the South. Experts at the conference gave the following reasons for increased segregation:

1. Recent court decisions outlawing race as a main factor in student assignment.

2. Increased residential segregation.

3. Increased role of private schools in contributing to segregation.

Of course, the larger issue is whether or not racial segregation is still an important issue? Here are some points to consider in answering this question:

- Does school segregation contribute to continuing tensions between racial and ethnic groups?

- Does school segregation result in inequalities in school finances?

- Does school segregation contribute to inequality of educational opportunities?

Second-Generation Segregation

Second-generation segregation refers to forms of racial segregation that are a result of school practices such as tracking, ability grouping, and the misplacement of students in special education classes. Unlike segregation that existed by state laws in the South before the 1954 *Brown* decision, second-generation forms of segregation can occur in schools with balanced racial populations; for instance, all white students may be placed in one academic track and all African American or Hispanic students, in another track.

Nationally, most studies examine the process of great change and no change as integration of schools results in segregation within schools. One collection of studies can be found in Ray Rist's *Desegregated Schools: Appraisals of an American Experiment.* The studies describe the subtle forms of segregation that began to occur as white and African American students were placed in integrated schools for the first time. For instance, in one recently integrated school, African American students were suspended for committing the same offenses for which white students received only a reprimand. A teacher in the school complained that, unlike African American students, when white students were sent to the principal's office, they were immediately sent back to class. In this school, equal opportunity to attend the school did not result in equal treatment within the school.

Unequal treatment of different races within the same school is one problem in integrated schools; the establishment of racial boundaries among students creates another. One study in the Rist book describes how racial boundaries were established in a high school in Memphis, Tennessee, after the students of an all-African American school were integrated with the students of an all-white school. Here, white students maintained control over most student activities. Activities in which African American students began to participate after integration were athletics and cheerleading. When this occurred, the status of these activities was denigrated by white students. On the other hand, whites could maintain control of the student government, ROTC, school clubs, and the staff of the yearbook.

This division of control among student activities reflected the rigid social boundaries that existed in the high school between the two groups. Individuals who crossed these social boundaries had to adapt to the social customs of those on the other side. For instance, African American students changed their style of dress and social conduct to be accepted by white students. African American students who crossed racial lines by making such changes found themselves accused by other African American students of "acting white" and were subsequently rejected by "unchanged" African American students. The same was true of white students who crossed racial boundaries.

The racial boundaries that continue to exist in high schools after integration reflect the racial barriers that continue in the larger society. The social life of a school often reflects the social world outside the school. Integration of a school system can help ensure equality of educational opportunity, but it cannot break down society's racial barriers. Although schools attempt to deal with this problem, its solution requires a general transformation of racial relationships in the larger society.

The Economics of Racism

What is the economic value of being white instead of African American? Elsewhere I have demonstrated the differences in lifetime income according to race. A more subjective approach was used by Andrew Hacker, along with his white students, which determined that being white was worth a million dollars a year. In *Two Nations: Black and White, Separate, Hostile, Unequal*, Hacker describes presenting his students with a fictional account of a white person being visited by representatives of an unnamed institution. The white person is informed that a terrible mistake was made and that he should have been born black. Consequently, the person was now going to be given a black skin and facial features but his memory and ideas would remain the same. Since this was a mistake, the person would be offered financial compensation for being made black. The white students were then asked to name what they felt should be the compensation for becoming black. Their answer was $1 million yearly.

Defining Racism

Racism means prejudice plus power. Racism refers to acts of oppression of one racial group toward another. One form of oppression is economic exploitation. This definition of racism distinguishes between simple feelings of hostility and prejudice toward another racial group and the ability to turn those feelings into some form of oppression. For instance, black people might have prejudicial feelings toward white people, but they have little opportunity to express those prejudicial feelings in some form of economic or political oppression of white people. On the other hand, prejudicial feelings that white people might have toward blacks can turn into racism when they become the basis for discrimination in education, housing, and the job market. Within this framework, racism becomes the act of social, political, and economic oppression of another group.

When discussions of racism occur in my multicultural education classes, white students complain of a sense of hostility from black students and, consequently, accuse black students of racism. Black students respond that their feelings represent prejudice and not racism because they lack the power to discriminate against whites. The troubling aspect of this response is the implication that if these black students had the power, they would be racist. One black student pointed out that there are situations where blacks can commit racist acts against whites. The black student used the example of the killing of white passengers by a black man on a commuter railroad several years ago. The evidence seemed to indicate that the killer was motivated by extreme hatred of whites that the newspapers labeled "black rage." This was a racist act, the black student argued, because the gun represented power.

Racism is often thought of as whites oppressing people of color. Of course, there are many problems with this definition. If one parent is black and another white, are their children considered black or white? Can one white-skinned child of this marriage be considered white while one dark-skinned child is considered black? Jake Lamar recalls how the confusion over skin color sparked the development of his racial consciousness at the age of 3. Jake was sitting at the kitchen table when his uncle Frank commented "about how obnoxious white people were." Jake responded, "But Mommy's white." His uncle replied that his mother was not white but was "just light-skinned." Jake then said that he thought his father, brother, and himself were black while his sister and mother were white. His mother then explained that they had many white ancestors that caused the variation in skin color but they were still "all Negroes." Thinking back on this incident, Jake Lamar reflected, "Black and white then meant something beyond pigmentation … so my first encounter with racial awareness was at once enlightening and confusing, and shot through with ambiguity."

Keeping in mind the complexities of racial classification and the importance of social class, certain generalities can be made about the racial attitudes of whites at the end of the twentieth century. In *Prejudice and Racism*, social psychologist James Jones summarizes the racial attitudes of some whites:

- Whites feel more negatively toward blacks than they do toward Hispanics, Asians, and legal and illegal immigrants.

- Whites perceive blacks as lazy, violent, and less intelligent than Hispanics, Asians, and legal and illegal immigrants.

- Whites believe blacks are receiving more attention from government than they deserve.

- Whites believe blacks are too demanding in their struggle for equal rights.

- High levels of antiblack racism are correlated with white attitudes that police and the death penalty make streets safe, and with opposition to assistance to the poor.

- Antiblack and anti-Hispanic racism are correlated with whites' opposition to open immigration and multilingualism.

Institutional Racism: Relationship Between Racial Segregation and High School Dropouts

There is a clear relationship between racial segregation and dropping out of high school. A 2004 report by the Center for Social Organization of Schools at Johns Hopkins University argues that black and Latino youth, in comparison to white youth, are more likely to attend high schools with high dropout rates. The Johns Hopkins report states that in locations studied, "half or more of high school students do not graduate, let alone leave high school prepared to fully participate in civic life. It is no coincidence that these locales are gripped by high rates of unemployment, crime, ill health, and chronic despair."

The Hopkins report found that half of African American students attend high schools where half or more of high school students do not graduate. Forty percent of Hispanics attend similar high schools. In comparison, only 11 percent of white students attend high schools with these high dropout numbers.

In high schools where minority students are the majority, there is five times less chance of freshmen being eventually promoted to senior status than in a majority white school.

Geographically, the worst-performing high schools are located in northern and western cities and throughout the southern states. Eighty percent of high schools with the worst records in promoting students from freshmen to eventually senior status can be found in 15 states (Arizona, California, Georgia, Florida, Illinois, Louisiana, Michigan, Mississippi, New Mexico, New York, North Carolina, Ohio, Pennsylvania, South Carolina, and Texas). In Illinois, Ohio, Michigan, New York, and Pennsylvania, more than half of African American students attend schools where the majority of students do not graduate on time or at all. Georgia, North and South Carolina, Florida, and Texas collectively lead the nation in "both total number and level of concentration of high schools with weak promoting power."

With the rate of high school dropouts increasing, the Johns Hopkins report casts a pall over hopes to improve the educational and economic conditions of African Americans and Hispanics. The report proclaims that its study is "a call to action. We must no longer tolerate the squandered potential, limited life chances, and social malaise that result from poorly educating our nation's youth."

Disparity in Educational Funding Based on Race

Not only is the picture for high school dropouts racially charged but also the disparities in school spending. "The Funding Gap 2004: Many States Still Shortchange Low-Income and Minority Students" issued by The Education Trust concludes, "[There is] a gap of more than $1,000 per student nationwide, and similar gaps between white and minority students. The majority of states had a funding gap, with large states like New York, Illinois and Pennsylvania leading the nation in their unwillingness to fairly fund education for their most vulnerable children."

Statistics on school spending demonstrate a virulent form of institutional racism. Table 6.6 shows the financial disparities in five states with the largest differences in spending between school districts and for the entire United States. For the entire United States, the gap between per-student funding in school districts with the fewest minority students and those with the most minority students is $1,099. The most shocking figure is for New York, which has a high number of minority students. In New York, $9,739 are spent per student in school districts with the fewest minority students while only $7,573 are spent per student in districts with the most minority students; the difference is $2,166.

	Per-Student Funding in the Districts with the Fewest Minority Students ($)	Per-Student Funding in the Districts with the Most Minority Students ($)	Funding Gap ($)
Delaware	8,950	7,682	-1,268
Illinois	7,398	5,536	-1,862
Kansas	8,115	6,442	-1,674
New York	9,739	7,573	-2,166
Montana	7,593	5,572	-2,022
Entire United States	7,605	6,506	-1,099

Table 6.6. State and Local Minority Funding Gaps, 2002

Source: Kevin Carey, *The Funding Gap 2004: Many States Still Shortchange Low-Income and Minority Students* (Washington, DC: Education Trust, 2004), p. 7.

Race, Social Class, and Equal Educational Opportunities

The Advisory Board for the President's Initiative on Race in *One America in the 21st Century: Forging a New Future* recognized that the problem of equal educational opportunity involves the intersection of social class and race. Wealthy African Americans, whites, Asians, and Hispanics can choose to live in school districts with adequate and exceptional public schools. In the words of the Advisory Board, "Our concern is that educational opportunities and public services are being restricted to those who live disproportionately in areas of concentrated poverty."

This results, as indicated in Table 6.7, in blacks, Hispanics, and Native Americans attending schools that are segregated by socioeconomic class. Forty-eight percent of blacks, 49 percent of Hispanics, and 36 percent of Native Americans in the fourth grade attend schools where more than 76 percent of the students are eligible for free or reduced-price lunches.

Race/Ethnicity	Percentage Attending Schools Where 10% or Less Are Eligible for Free or Reduced-Price Lunch	Percentage Attending Schools Where 11–25% Are Eligible for Free or Reduced-Price Lunch	Percentage Attending Schools Where 26–50% Are Eligible for Free or Reduced-Price Lunch	Percentage Attending Schools Where 51–75% Are Eligible for Free or Reduced-Price Lunch	Percentage Attending Schools Where 76% or More Are Eligible for Free or Reduced-Price Lunch
White	21	23	32	19	5
Black	4	6	18	24	48
Hispanic	4	6	16	24	49
Asian/ Pacific Islander	27	19	21	16	16
Native Americans	4	8	21	31	36

Table 6.7. Race/Ethnicity and Poverty: Percentage of Fourth Graders by Their Race/Ethnicity and the Percentage of Students in the School Eligible for a Free or Reduced-Price Lunch, 2005

Source: National Center for Education Statistics, *The Condition of Education* 2006 (Washington, DC: U.S. Printing Office, 2006), p. 33.

The President's Advisory Board identified the following conditions in areas of concentrated poverty:

• Schools with low expectations and standards.

• Substandard and crumbling school facilities.

• Inadequate public transportation.

• Poorly financed social services.

In addition, the Advisory Board found that students from low-income families were less likely to have access to such educational opportunities and resources as

• Preschool programs

• High-quality teachers

- Challenging curricula

- High standards

- Up-to-date technology

- Modern facilities

In the context of the changing U.S. population and existing educational problems, the Advisory Board recommended the following to achieve equal educational opportunity:

1. Enhance early childhood learning. Data indicate that racial disparities persist in terms of early childhood learning. For example, 1996 data show that 89 percent of white children ages 3 to 5 were read to three or more times per week compared with 74 percent of black children and 62 percent of Hispanic children ... efforts could include providing training and services for parents ... and expanding support for such programs as Head Start, Early Head Start, and Even Start.

2. Strengthen teacher preparation and equity. High-quality teachers are too scarce a resource, especially in high-poverty, high-minority communities ... [action] could include creating incentives to both attract top students to teaching and encourage certified teachers to teach in underserved communities.

3. Promote school construction. It is estimated that building and renovating our public schools to adequately serve all students will cost more than $100 billion.

4. Promote movement from K–12 to higher education. Efforts must be taken to ensure equal opportunity in higher education and to strengthen the pipeline from K–12 through higher education. Such efforts should include support for partnerships between colleges and K–12 schools that increase expectations by exposing students to future educational opportunities ... efforts could include increasing the availability of advanced-placement courses in high-poverty, high-minority school districts and providing financial support, such as loans or grants, for college test preparation courses.

5. Promote the benefits of diversity in K–12 and higher education. Diversity can promote many benefits that accrue to all students and society, including: improve teaching and learning by providing a range of perspectives that enrich the learning environment; strengthen students' critical-thinking skills by challenging their existing perspectives ... improve students' preparation for employment ... and foster the advancement of knowledge by spurring study in new areas of concern.

6. Provide education and skills training to overcome increasing income inequality that negatively affects lower-skilled and less-educated immigrants. The high rates of Hispanic high school dropouts suggest ... there is a clear need for continued English-language training to ensure that limited-English-proficient students can perform and compete in the educational system.

7. Implement the comprehensive American Indian and Alaska Native education policy. To meet the particular needs of American Indian and Alaska Native students, we urge ... improving and expanding educational opportunities.

The Advisory Board's recommendations might have effected the real increase in the number of minority students in college. A 2002 report of the American Council of Education stated that minority student enrollment in colleges and universities jumped by 48 percent in the 1990s. However, the report found that "despite greater numbers of minority students in college, blacks and Latinos lagged behind whites and Asian-Americans in graduating."

In summary, the recommendations for equality of educational opportunity include early childhood education, high-quality teachers in schools serving low-income families, school construction, equal access to higher education, diversity in the classroom, and adequate English instruction for children from non-English-speaking homes.

Teaching about Racism

In many ways it is difficult when schools are becoming more segregated to reduce racist attitudes in the classroom. The Advisory Board for the President's Initiative on Race was primarily concerned about the intersection of poverty and racial differences. It did not deal directly with the role that schools can play in reducing racism through classroom instruction. A variety of approaches to teaching about racism are available. One excellent book is Beverly Tatum's *Why Are All the Black Kids Sitting Together in the Cafeteria?: A Psychologist Explains the Development of Racial Identity*. Educator and African American activist Beverly Tatum worries about the loss of white allies in the struggle against racism and the hostility she feels from white college students when teaching about racism. Reflecting on her teaching experiences, she writes, "White students … often struggle with strong feelings of guilt when they become aware of the pervasiveness of racism. … These feelings are uncomfortable and can lead white students to resist learning about race and racism." Part of the problem, she argues, is that seeing oneself as the oppressor creates a negative self-image, which results in a withdrawal from a discussion of the problem. What needs to be done, she maintains, is to counter the guilt by giving white students a positive self-image of whites fighting against racism. In other words, a self-image of whites being allies with blacks in the struggle against racism.

A popular antiracist curriculum for preschool children is the National Association for the Education of Young Children's "Anti-Bias Curriculum: Tools for Empowering Young Children." This curriculum and related methods of instruction are designed to reduce prejudice among young children regarding race, language, gender, and physical ability differences. The premise of the method is that at an early age children become aware of the connection between power and skin color, language, and physical disabilities. Cited as examples are a 2 1/2-year-old Asian child who refuses to hold the hand of a black classmate because "It's dirty" and a 4-year-old boy who takes over the driving of a pretended bus because "Girls can't be bus drivers."

According to the Anti-Bias Curriculum, research findings show that young children classify differences between people and they are influenced by bias toward others. By the age of 2, children are aware of gender differences and begin to apply color names to skin colors. Between ages 3 and 5, children try to figure out who they are by examining the differences in gender and skin color. By 4 or 5 years old, children engage in socially determined gender roles and they give racial reasons for the selection of friends. Based on these research findings, the advocates of the curriculum believe that prejudice can be reduced if there is conscious intervention to curb the development of biased concepts and activities.

Another antiracist education program is the Teaching Tolerance Project that began after a group of teenage skinheads attacked and beat to death an Ethiopian man on a street in Portland, Oregon, in 1988. After this incident, members of the Southern Poverty Law Center decided it was time to do something about teaching tolerance. Dedicated to pursuing legal issues involving racial incidents and denial of civil rights, the law center sued, for the man's family, the two men who were responsible for teaching violent racism to the Portland skinheads. These two teachers, Tom Metzger, the head of the White Aryan Resistance, and his son, became symbols of racist teachings in the United States. In a broad sense, the Teaching Tolerance Project is designed to provide information about teaching methods and materials that will counter the type of racist teachings represented by Metzger and his son.

Similar to the Anti-Bias Curriculum, the Teaching Tolerance Project primarily defines racism as a function of psychological attitudes, in contrast to an emphasis on racism as a function of economic exploitation. On the inside cover of its magazine *Teaching Tolerance*, tolerance is defined as "the capacity for or the practice of recognizing and respecting the beliefs or practices of others." Within the context of this definition, the project members "primarily celebrate and recognize the beliefs and practices of racial and ethnic groups such as African-Americans, Latinos, and Asian-Americans."

The primary purpose of the Teaching Tolerance Project is to provide resources and materials to schools to promote "interracial and intercultural understanding between whites and nonwhites." There have also been decisions to include material dealing with cultural tolerance, homelessness, and poverty. The Teaching Tolerance Project is only one of many educational attempts to end racism in the United States. The end of racism is essential for the full provision of equality of opportunity and equality of educational opportunity in U.S. society.

The Recent Struggle for Equal Education for Women

The reader should check the Web sites of the following organizations for current issues, policies, and the history of struggle regarding women's education: American Association of University Women (http://www.aauw.org), National Organization for Women Foundation (http://www.nowfoundation.org), and Education Equality of the Feminist Majority Foundation (http://www.feminist.org/education). These organizations are in the forefront in protecting women's rights in education.

Since the nineteenth century, the struggle for racial justice paralleled that of justice for women. Demands for equal educational opportunity pervaded both campaigns for civil rights. In the second half of the twentieth century the drive for equal educational opportunity for women was led by the National Organization for Women (NOW), which was organized in 1966. The founding document of the organization declared, "There is no civil rights movement to speak for women as there has been for Negroes and other victims of discrimination. The National Organization for Women must therefore begin to speak." In NOW's founding document, education is called "the key to effective participation in today's economy … [and public schools should educate a woman] to her full potential of human ability."

During its first years of activism, NOW focused on

- Eliminating discriminatory quotas against women in college and professional school admissions.

- Urging parents, counselors, and teachers to encourage women to pursue higher education and professional education.

- Eliminating discriminatory practices against women in the awarding of fellowships and loans.

- Investigating the problem of female school dropouts.

NOW's activities and that of other women's organizations turned to legal action with the passage of Title IX of the 1972 Higher Education Act. Title IX provided for sexual equality in employment in educational institutions and for sexual equality in educational programs. The legislation applied to all educational institutions, including preschool, elementary and secondary schools, vocational and professional schools, and public and private undergraduate and graduate institutions. A 1983 U.S. Supreme Court decision, *Grove City College v. Bell*, restricted Title IX in its application to specific educational programs within institutions. In the 1987 Civil Rights Restoration Act, Congress overturned the Court's decision and amended Title IX to include *all* activities of an educational institution receiving federal aid.

Armed with Title IX, NOW and other women's organizations placed pressure on local school systems and colleges to ensure equal treatment of women in vocational education, athletic programs, textbooks and the curriculum, testing, and college admissions. Following is a brief chronological list of achievements in providing equality of educational opportunity for women:

- 1972: Legal action against school systems with segregated courses in home economics and industrial arts.

- 1974: With backing from NOW, more than 1,000 women's studies departments created on college campuses.

- 1975: Federal regulations to end sex discrimination in athletics.

- 1976: Lawsuits regarding female participation in athletics and gender-biased hiring in school administration.

- 1976: Educational Equity Act authorizes Office of Education to prepare "non-sexist" curricula and non-discriminatory vocational and career counseling, sports education, and other programs designed to achieve equity for all students regardless of sex."

- 1983: Last all-male school in the Ivy League, Columbia University, becomes coeducational.

- 1986: FairTest organized to counter sex bias in high-stakes tests.

- 1996: Virginia Military Institute and the Citadel become coeducational.

The struggle for equality of educational opportunity is reflected in the following changes in educational programs:

- The number of female graduates from medical school increased from 8.4 percent in 1969 to 34.5 percent in 1990.

- The percentage of doctoral and professional degrees awarded to women increased from 14.4 percent in 1971 to 36.8 percent in 1991.

- Most discrimination in vocational programs ended.

- Female participation in high school athletics increased from 7 percent in 1972 to 37 percent in 1992 and in college athletics from 15.6 percent in 1972 to 34.8 percent in 1993.

Sexism and Education

In *Failing at Fairness: How America's Schools Cheat Girls*, Myra and David Sadker summarize current research on educational discrimination against girls. One surprising result of their research and analysis of other data was that girls are equal to or ahead of boys in most measures of academic achievement and psychological health during the early years of schooling, but by the end of high school and college, girls have fallen behind boys on these measurements. On entrance examinations to college, girls score lower than boys, particularly in science and mathematics. Boys receive more state and national scholarships. Women score lower than men on all entrance examinations to professional schools.

An explanation for the decline in test scores is that girls suffer a greater decline than boys in self-esteem from elementary school to high school. (Of course, an important general question about the following statistics is why both boys and girls decline in feelings of self-esteem.) As a measure of self-esteem, the Sadkers rely on responses to the statement, "I'm happy the way I am." The Sadkers report that in elementary school 60 percent of girls and 67 percent of boys responded positively to the statement. By high school these positive responses declined to 29 percent for girls and 46 percent for boys. In other words, the decline in self-esteem for girls was 31 percentage points as compared with 21 percentage points for boys. Why is there less self-esteem and a greater decline in self-esteem among girls as compared with boys?

To get an answer to the question, the Sadkers asked students how their lives would be different if they suddenly were transformed into members of the opposite sex. Overall, girls responded with feelings that it wouldn't be so bad and that it would open up opportunities to participate in sports and politics. In addition, girls felt they would have more freedom and respect. Regarding self-esteem, girls expressed little regret about the consequences of the sex change. In contrast, boys expressed horror at the idea, and many said they would commit suicide. They saw themselves becoming second-class citizens, being denied access to athletics and outdoor activities, and being racked with physical problems. Concerning self-esteem, and in contrast to girls, boys expressed nothing but regret about the consequences of the sex change.

Contributing to the lack of self-esteem among girls, the Sadkers argue, are modes of classroom interaction, the representation of women in textbooks and other educational materials, and the discriminatory content of standardized tests. In one of their workshops with classroom teachers, the Sadkers illustrate classroom sex bias by asking four of the participants—two men and two women—to act like students in a middle-school social studies classroom. The lesson is about the American Revolution and it begins with an examination of homework. Acting as the teacher, David Sadker perfunctorily tells one woman that two of her answers are wrong and comments to the group on the neatness of the other woman's homework. He tells one man that two of his answers are wrong and, unlike his response to the woman with wrong answers, he urges the man to try harder and suggests ways of improving his answers. David then states to the other man that he failed to do his homework assignment. In contrast to the woman with the neat paper, this man illustrates what the Sadkers call the "bad boy role."

David Sadker then continues the lesson by discussing battles and leaders. All of the Revolutionary leaders are, of course, male. During the lesson he calls on the males 20 times each while only calling on one woman twice and completely ignoring the other woman. The one woman called on misses her question because she is given only half a second to respond. When questioning the men, David Sadker spends time giving hints and probing. At the end of this demonstration lesson, the Sadkers report, one woman commented that she felt like she was back in school. She often had the right answer but was never called on by the teacher.

What this workshop demonstration illustrates, based on the Sadkers' findings on classroom interaction, is that boys receive more and better instruction. Boys are more often called on by the teacher and boys interact more with the teacher than do girls. In a typical classroom situation, if both boys and girls have their hands raised to answer a question, the teacher is most likely to call on a boy. A teacher will spend more time responding to a boy's question than to a girl's question. In other words, girls do not receive equal educational opportunity in the classroom.

In addition, women are not so well represented as men in textbooks. The Sadkers found in 1989 elementary school language arts textbooks that there were from two to three times as many pictures of men as women. In one elementary history text, they found four times as many pictures of men as women. In one 1992 world history textbook, of 631 pages they found only 7 pages related to women. Two of those pages were devoted to a fifth grade female student who had made a peace trip to the Soviet Union.

It is most likely that the treatment received by girls in the classroom and in textbooks contributes to their low self-esteem and to their decline, as compared with boys, in performance on standardized tests from elementary school to high school. It seems logical that if less instructional time is spent with girls than boys, then boys would more rapidly advance academically. In addition, without equal representation in textbooks, girls might value themselves less and have less incentive to achieve. Less instructional time and representation in textbooks contribute to the glass ceiling of the classroom.

The lowering of self-esteem and content bias may contribute to the significant gender gap in scores on standardized college entrance examinations and entrance examinations to professional schools. For instance, on the widely used Scholastic Aptitude Test (SAT) males score 50 points higher on the math section and up to 12 points higher on the verbal section. It is important to understand that discrimination in standardized testing involves the denial of economic rewards, specifically scholarships and career opportunities.

The content bias and economic value of standardized tests were recognized in a 1989 ruling by a federal judge in New York. The judge ruled that the awarding of New York State scholarships using the SAT discriminated against female students. The case was brought to court by the Girls Clubs of America and NOW. The court argued that the scholarships were to be awarded based on academic achievement in high school and that the SAT was not constructed to test achievement but to determine college performance. The court's decision states, "The evidence is clear that females score significantly below males on the SAT while they do equally or slightly better in high schools."

In this court case, academic achievement was defined according to grades received in high school courses. Interestingly, the Sadkers argue that this apparent paradox between girls' high grades and low standardized-test scores is a result of grade inflation. This grade inflation results from female passivity and their willingness to follow classroom rules. Often, teachers formally and informally incorporate evaluations of student behavior in their academic grading practices. For girls, good behavior can result in good grades.

But the issue of grade inflation still doesn't solve the puzzle of lower performance by girls on tests like the SAT. The Sadkers suggest that one possible reason for the differences in scores between males and females is that the content of standardized tests is biased. Boys are more familiar with organized sports, financial issues, science, wars, and dates. Consequently, test items referring to these areas tend to favor boys. As an example, the Sadkers describe a gifted high school girl who lost her concentration on the preliminary SAT when she encountered an analogy question comparing "a football and a gridiron." The analogy baffled her because she had little knowledge of football.

One possible solution to teacher bias in classroom interaction, the Sadkers suggest, is to have an observer code classroom interaction so that the teacher becomes aware of any possible bias. If teachers are unconsciously favoring boys, then this observation provides the opportunity for them to change their behavior. One teacher told the Sadkers that she distributed two chips to all students. When students want to comment or ask a question, they have to give up one chip. Before the class is over, all students must use their two chips. This guarantees equal participation of all students and ensures that classroom interaction is not dominated by only a few students. In addition, the Sadkers recommend that teachers consciously search for books portraying strong female characters in a variety of occupational and social roles. They point to the work of the National Women's History Project, which since the 1970s has published materials emphasizing women's roles in history. In addition, the Sadkers recommend the use of workshops to heighten teachers' awareness of their own possible sexist behavior and to understand how to find nonsexist educational material for the classroom.

Another possible solution is single-sex education. This would eliminate the problem of female students having to compete with male students for teachers' attention. In classrooms of only girls, teachers would not tend to push girls aside and focus their instructional efforts on boys. In an all-girls school or classroom, female students might receive the equal educational opportunity denied to them in a coed classroom.

Writing in favor of girls' schools, Susan Estrich, professor of law and political science at the University of Southern California, notes that 60 percent of the National Merit Scholarship finalists are boys. Echoing the Sadkers' findings, she reports from a 1992 study of the American Association of University

Women, "that even though girls get better grades (except in math), they get less from schools." While she does not dismiss efforts to equalize opportunities for girls in coed schools, she argues that currently single-sex education is working. For instance, in all-girls schools 80 percent of girls take four years of math and science, whereas in coed schools the average is two years of math and science. In Fortune 1000 companies, one-third of the female board members are graduates of women's colleges even though graduates of women's colleges represent only 4 percent of all female college graduates. In addition, graduates of women's colleges earn 43 percent of the math and 50 percent of engineering doctorates earned by all women, and they outnumber all other females in *Who's Who*.

Estrich does see the possibility of offering single-sex classes within a coed institution. She cites the example of the Illinois Math and Science Academy, which experimented with a girls-only calculus-based physics class. Instead of sitting meekly at their desks while boys command all the attention, girls are actively asking and answering questions. In an all-girls algebra class in Ventura, California, the teacher reports spending time building self-confidence along with teaching math. For Estrich, at least at this point in time, all-girls schools are a means for ending sexism in education.

Of course, for an all-girls school or classroom to overcome the problems of sexism completely it would require the maintenance of the same educational expectations as there are for boys and the use of textbooks and other educational materials that provide strong female role models. As I discussed previously in this chapter, one of the problems with segregated female education in the nineteenth century was the belief that women did not have the physical and mental stamina to undergo the same academic demands as men. Consequently, to avoid sexism, there should be no watering down of the curriculum in female schools and classrooms. In addition, sex-segregated education would have to avoid the pitfalls of tracking women into a sex-segregated labor market. One of the problems in the development of the high school in the early twentieth century was that it tended to track women into certain occupations. For an all-girls school or classroom to avoid this form of discrimination, there would have to be an emphasis on opening up all career opportunities for women.

There are many critics of proposals for all-female schools. One University of Michigan researcher, Valerie Lee, found that many all-girls classrooms still contained high levels of sexist behavior on the part of the teacher. In one case, a history teacher assigned a research paper and told students that she would provide "major hand-holding" to help the students. Lee argued that the offer of major hand-holding would not occur in a boys' school. In addition, she found male bashing taking place in some all-female schools.

Moreover, Lee found boys in all-male schools engaging in serious sexist comments about women. In other words, all-female schools do not do anything about the sexist attitudes of men. In fact, all-male schools might reinforce male sexist behavior. For instance, in a 1994 court case involving a suit by Shannon Faulkner to gain entrance to the all-male military college, The Citadel, one of the witnesses, a 1991 graduate of the school, reported that the word *woman* was used on campus in a derogatory manner "every day, every minute, every hour, [it was] a part of the life there."

Therefore, there is the possibility that single-sex education might result in greater academic achievement for girls while doing nothing about sexist attitudes among men. The academic gains made by women might mean little in a world dominated by sexist males. Also, the courts may not approve of singlesex public schools, because of a decision regarding all-boys African American schools in Detroit. The Court argued that the all-boys schools were a violation of the 1954 *Brown* decision that declared as unconstitutional separate but equal schools that were racially segregated.

In 1998, the American Association of University Women (AAUW) released a follow-up report to its earlier charges that public schools were shortchanging girls. The new study found that the number of girls enrolled in algebra, trigonometry, precalculus, and calculus was growing at a faster rate than the number of boys. Probably the most impressive statistic was that the differences between boys and girls was the smallest in the world on international tests in math and science. However, the report found that technology, particularly computer technology, is emerging as the new boys' club. The report found that girls have less exposure to computers inside and outside school and that girls feel less confident about using computers. The gap between boys and girls in computer knowledge and use increases from grades 8 to 11. Only 17 percent of students taking the College Board's Advanced Placement Test in computer science were women.

In reference to the technological gap between males and females, Janice Weinman, the executive director of the Washington-based AAUW said, "This is becoming the new club [computer technology] from which girls are feeling disenfranchised. Consequently, girls are not going to be appropriately prepared for the technology era of the new 21st century."

However, there are areas where girls outperform boys. More girls than boys are enrolled in advanced English, foreign language, and art courses. In addition, girls outscore boys by wide margins on reading and writing tests in middle and elementary grades.

Education Week reporter Debra Viadero provides the following summary of other findings in the AAUW study:

1. In school-to-work programs, which combine challenging academics with vocational training, girls still tend to cluster in traditional female occupations.

2. Although girls are taking more advanced-placement courses and getting better grades than boys, their scores on those exams still tend to be lower.

3. On large-scale exams, such as the National Assessment of Educational Progress, the top scorers in math and science still tend to be boys.

What's Happening to the Boys in the New Gender Divide?

"At Colleges, Women Are Leaving Men in the Dust," declares *New York Times* reporter Tamar Lewin in her 2006 article on "The New Gender Divide." College men study less and socialize more than college women. Lewin writes, "with sex discrimination fading and their job opportunities widening, women are coming on much stronger, often leapfrogging the men to the academic finish. Rick Kohn, a male undergraduate at the University of North Carolina, told reporter Lewin that women work harder in school: "I take the path of least resistance. ... The girls care more about their G.P.A. and the way they look on paper." Some small colleges, according to another *New York Times* reporter Bill Pennington, are so desperate that they are starting football programs to attract men. Lewin found some college administrators complaining that undergraduate men are spending more time playing video games than studying.

The reality is that fewer males than females are graduating from high school and entering college. Research has indicated that 72.7 percent of females graduated from high school in 2003 while only 65.2 percent of males did. In 2005, according to *The Condition of Education 2006*, there were 8,538,000 women in undergraduate programs as compared to 6,376,000 men. The growth of female versus male undergraduate enrollments occurred after the late 1970s when enrollment figures for women and men were about equal. Prior to the 1970s, male undergraduate enrollment was larger than female. Why the change?

A report of the American Council of Education, *Gender Equity in Higher Education: 2006*, noted that age was a factor in the numerical differences between male and female undergraduates. As noted in Table 6.8, the American Council of Education reports that the percentage of undergraduate males declines among the older student population. For those under 25 years old the undergraduate attendance by racial classification is 46 percent (white), 42 percent (black), 43 percent (Hispanic), and 50 percent (Asian) as compared to those over 25 years old—41 percent (white), 32 percent (black), 38 percent (Hispanic), and 40 percent (Asian). The report suggests that the lower percentage of males over 25 years old is the result of the difficulty for some men to leave the workforce and return to school. As noted in Table 6.8, these differences exist across income levels.

Race	Percent of Males under Age 25	Percent of Males over Age 25	Percent of Males under Age 25, Top 25% Family Income	Percent of Males over Age 25, Top 25% Family Income	Percent of Males, under Age 25, Middle 25% Family Income	Percent of Males over Age 25, Middle 25% Family Income	Percent of Males under Age 25, Bottom 25% Family Income	Percent of Males over Age 25, Bottom 25% Family Income
White	46	41	51	41	47	39	44	39
Black	40	32	54	40	44	29	42	32
Hispanic	43	38	51	42	46	36	43	34
Asian	50	40	54	40	52	39	48	45

Table 6.8. Undergraduates by Age, Sex, Race, and Income, 2003–2004

Source: Adapted from American Council of Education tables printed in Tamar Lewin, "A More Nuanced Look at Men, Women and College," *The New York Times*, July 12, 2006, p. B8.

No one has a clear answer as to why male educational attainment is declining. In *Hopeful Girls, Troubled Boys: Race and Gender Disparity in Urban Education*, Nancy Lopez explored the gender issue among second-generation immigrants from the Caribbean in a New York City high school. She concluded that school officials treated black males as being "at-risk" and these youth responded by cutting class and demonstrating "willful laziness" by not studying or striving for good grades. Researcher Lopez claims that the school primarily supports "'feminine traits' such as passivity, silence and obedience." Further, females attending high school assumed more responsibility for maintaining the home than did males in high school. Males spent more time playing basketball or other sports than helping with family chores. The result, according to Lopez, "Women were institutionally engaged with their schools and maintained high aspirations."

Students with Disabilities

By the 1960s, the civil rights movement encompassed students with disabilities. Within the context of equality of educational opportunity, students with special needs could only participate equally in schools with other students if they received some form of special help. Since the nineteenth century many of the needs of these students have been neglected by local and state school authorities because of the expense of special facilities and teachers. In fact, many people with disabilities were forced to live in state institutions for the mentally ill or retarded. For instance, consider "Allan's story," a case history of treatment prior to the 1970s, provided by the U.S. Office of Special Education Programs:

Allan was left as an infant on the steps of an institution for persons with mental retardation in the late 1940s. By age 35, he had become blind and was frequently observed sitting in a corner of the room, slapping his heavily callused face as he rocked back and forth humming to himself.

In the late 1970s, Allan was assessed properly for the first time. To the dismay of his examiners, he was found to be of average intelligence; further review of his records revealed that by observing fellow residents of the institution, he had learned self-injurious behavior that caused his total loss of vision.

> Although the institution then began a special program to teach Allan to be more independent, a major portion of his life was lost because of a lack of appropriate assessments and effective interventions. (*Source:* U.S. Office of Special Education, "History: Twenty-Five Years of Progress in Educating Children With Disabilities through IDEA," www.ed.gov/offices/osers/osep/, 2002.)

The political movement for federal legislation to aid students with disabilities followed a path similar to the rest of the civil rights movement. First, finding themselves unable to change educational institutions by pressuring local and state governments, organized groups interested in improving educational opportunities for students with special needs turned to the courts. This was the path taken in the late 1960s by the Pennsylvania Association for Retarded Children (PARC). PARC was one of many associations organized in the 1950s to aid citizens with disabilities. These organizations were concerned with state laws that excluded children with disabilities from educational institutions because they were considered uneducable and untrainable. State organizations like PARC and the National Association for Retarded Children campaigned to eliminate these laws and to demonstrate the educability of all children. But, as the civil rights movement discovered throughout the century, local and state officials were resistant to change and relief had to be sought through the judicial system.

In *Pennsylvania Association for Retarded Children (PARC) v. Commonwealth of Pennsylvania*, a case that was as important for the rights of children with disabilities as the *Brown* decision was for African Americans, PARC objected to conditions in the Pennhurst State School and Hospital. In framing the case, lawyers for PARC focused on the legal right to an education for children with disabilities. PARC, working with the major federal lobbyist for children with disabilities, the Council for Exceptional Children (CEC), overwhelmed the court with evidence on the educability of children with disabilities. The state withdrew its case, and the court enjoined the state from excluding children with disabilities from a public education and required that every child be allowed access to an education. Publicity about the PARC case prompted other lobbying groups to file 36 cases against different state governments. The CEC prepared model legislation and lobbied for its passage at the state and federal levels.

Public Law 94–142: Education for All Handicapped Children Act

In 1975, Congress passed Public Law 94–142, the Education for All Handicapped Children Act that guaranteed equal educational opportunity for all children with disabilities. In 1990, Congress changed the name of this legislation to Individuals with Disabilities Education Act (IDEA). The major provisions in the Public Law 94–142 were to provide for equal educational opportunity for all children with disabilities. This goal included the opportunity for all children with disabilities to attend regular school classes. As stated in the legislation, "all children with disabilities [should] have available to them … a free appropriate public education which emphasized special education and related services designed to meet their unique needs."

Writing an IEP

One of the issues confronting Congress during legislative debates was that of increased federal control over local school systems. Congress resolved this problem by requiring that an individual education plan (IEP) be written for each student with disabilities. This reduced federal control since each IEP would be written in local school systems. IEPs are now a standard part of education programs for children with disabilities. Public Law 94–142 requires that an IEP be developed for each child jointly by the local educational agency and the child's parents or guardians. This gives the child or the parents the right to negotiate with the local school system about the type of services to be delivered.

Teachers, school administrators, and parents work together to arrive at an IEP statement. It is important that school officials and teachers understand the regulations governing the writing of IEPs. As provided for in the original legislation, an IEP includes:

1. A statement of the present levels of educational performance of such child.

2. A statement of annual goals, including short-term instructional objectives.

3. A statement of the specific educational services to be provided to such child, and the extent to which such child will be able to participate in regular educational programs.

4. The projected date for initiation and anticipated duration of such services.

5. Appropriate objective criteria and evaluation procedures and schedules for determining, on at least an annual basis, whether instructional objectives are being achieved.

Which Children Have Disabilities?

The category of "learning disability" created a continuing controversy in determining which children should be classified as disabled. Some critics of special education, as I discuss in a later section on the report of President George W. Bush's Commission on Excellence in Special Education, think the "learning disabilities" category is too broad and includes children who have not received adequate classroom instruction in reading. This controversy is caused by federal regulations defining disabilities.

As reported in *The Condition of Education 2005*, there were 12.2 percent of school-age children with disabilities in the 2001–2002 school year. As indicated in Table 6.9, the major disabilities are learning (6 percent), speech and language impairments (2.3 percent), and mental retardation (1.3 percent).

Disabilities	Percentage with Disability
Specific learning disabilities	6.0
Speech or language impairments	2.3
Mental retardation	1.3
Emotional disturbance	1.0
Hearing impairments	0.2
Orthopedic impairments	0.2
Other health impairments	0.7
Visual impairments	0.1
Multiple disabilities	0.3
Autism	0.2
Developmental delay	0.1

Table 6.9. Children (Aged 6-21) with Disabilities in Public Schools, 2001-2002

Source: National Center for Education Statistics, *The Condition of Education* 2006 (Washington, DC; U.S. Printing Office, 2006), p. 124.

Inclusion

The 1975 Education for All Handicapped Children Act called for the integration of children with disabilities into regular classes. Similar to any form of segregation, the isolation of children with disabilities often deprives them of contact with other students and denies them access to equipment found in regular classrooms, such as scientific equipment, audiovisual aids, classroom libraries, and computers. Full inclusion, it is believed, will improve the educational achievement and social development of children with disabilities. Also, it is hoped, bias against children and adults with disabilities decreases because of the interactions of students with disabilities with other students. The integration clause of the Education for All Handicapped Children Act specified that:

> to the maximum extent appropriate, handicapped children, including children in public or private institutions or other care facilities, are educated with children who are not handicapped, and that special classes, separate schooling, or other removal of handicapped children from the regular educational environment occurs only when the nature or severity of the handicap is such that education in regular classes with the use of supplementary aids and services cannot be achieved satisfactorily.

The term *inclusion* is the most frequently used word to refer to the integration of children with disabilities into regular classrooms. The phrase *full inclusion* refers to the inclusion of all children with disabilities.

In 1990, advocates of full inclusion received federal support with the passage of the Americans with Disabilities Act. This historic legislation bans all forms of discrimination against the disabled. The Americans with Disabilities Act played an important role in the 1992 court decision *Oberti v. Board of Education of the Borough of Clementon School District*, which involved an 8-year-old, Rafael Oberti, classified as educable mentally retarded. U.S. District Court Judge John F. Gerry argued that the Americans with Disabilities Act requires that people with disabilities be given equal access to services provided by any agency receiving federal money, including public schools. Judge Gerry decided that Rafael Oberti could manage in a regular classroom with special aides and a special curriculum. In his decision, Judge Gerry wrote, "Inclusion is a right, not a privilege for a select few."

The 1997 Congressional amendments to this legislation, now called the Individuals with Disabilities Education Act, emphasized the importance of including children with disabilities in regular classes. In the text of the 1997 amendments, it was claimed that since the passage of the original legislation research, inclusion in regular classes improved the academic performance of children with disabilities. In the words of the Amendments, "Over 20 years of research and experience has demonstrated that the education of children with disabilities can be made more effective by … having high expectations for such children and ensuring their access in the general curriculum to the maximum extent possible."

During Congressional hearings leading to the passage of the 1997 Individuals with Disabilities Education Act Amendments, there were complaints that appropriate educational services were not being provided for more than one-half of the children with disabilities in the United States. Also, more than 1,000,000 of the children with disabilities in the United States were excluded entirely from the public school system and were not educated with their peers. In addition, there were complaints that many disabilities were going undetected.

The inclusion of children with disabilities in regular classrooms created a new challenge for regular teachers. Classroom teachers, according to the legislation, were to be provided with "appropriate special education and related services and aids." The legislation specified that teachers should receive extra training to help children with disabilities. In the words of the legislation, school districts must provide: "high-quality, intensive professional development for all personnel who work with such children in order to ensure that they have the skills and knowledge necessary to enable them to meet developmental goals." Also, teacher education programs were to give all student teachers training in working with students with disabilities.

Inclusion and No Child Left Behind

On 9 December 2003, federal regulations, Title I—Improving the Academic Achievement of the Disadvantaged, from the U.S. Department of Education were posted in the Federal Register requiring children with disabilities be included in the state testing systems under the No Child Left Behind Act of 2001. However, states are allowed to create alternative tests and standards for students with disabilities. The scores of these students are to be utilized in determining whether a school has made adequate yearly progress. Schools not making adequate yearly progress will be targeted for improvement and parents will be allowed to choose other schools.

Inclusion is one reason given for requiring the assessment of students with the most significant cognitive disabilities to be included in state testing programs. The argument is made that teachers will expect more of students and work harder at teaching students with significant cognitive disabilities if they are included in the state testing system. "Students with disabilities," the federal regulation states, "accrue positive benefits when they are included in school accountability systems. Educators realize that these students also count, just like all other students; they understand that they need to make sure that these students learn to high levels, just like other students. When students with disabilities are part of the accountability system, educators' expectations for these students are more likely to increase."

Also, federal regulations indicate a fear that if these students are not included in the state testing programs then school administrators will attempt to raise their school's test scores by classifying more students as having disabilities. In other words, excluding students with disabilities raises the specter of school administrators cheating by overenrolling students in these programs. As the federal regulation states: "For example, we know from research that when students with disabilities are allowed to be excluded from school accountability measures, the rates of referral of students for special education increase dramatically."

The federal regulations included the testimony of an unnamed Massachusetts state official about the benefits of including students with the most significant cognitive disabilities in its assessment. The state official claimed that these students were taught concepts not normally developed in their classes. "Some students with disabilities," the state official explained, "have never been taught academic skills and concepts, for example, reading, mathematics, science, and social studies, even at very basic levels." The official asserted his/her belief in inclusion in state testing programs under No Child Left Behind: "Yet all students are capable of learning at a level that engages and challenges them."

The federal regulation provides an emphatic endorsement of inclusion:

Teachers who have incorporated learning standards into their instruction cite unanticipated gains in students' performance and understanding. Furthermore, some individualized social, communication, motor, and self-help skills can be practiced during activities based on the learning standards. Too often in the past, students with disabilities were excluded from assessments and accountability systems, and the consequence was that they did not receive the academic attention they deserved. Access and exposure to the general curriculum for students with disabilities often did not occur and there was no systemwide measure to indicate whether or what they were learning. These regulations are designed to ensure that schools are held accountable for the educational progress of students with the most significant cognitive disabilities, just as schools are held accountable for the educational results of all other students with disabilities and students without disabilities.

As indicated in Table 6.10 there has been a small but steady increase in the number of students with disabilities included in regular classrooms for more than 80 percent of the school day—from 44.5 percent in 1994–1995 to 49.9 percent in 2003–2004.

An Inclusion Success Story

In the 10 July 2002 issue of *Education Week*, Allison Shelley tells the story of Down syndrome student Chris Vogelberger, whose first experience with inclusion was in a third grade classroom. During the first year, his spoken-language abilities increased by two years. Now attending middle school, Chris has a full-time assistant, Debbie Beiling, whom he calls Bean.

School Year	80% of Day in Regular Classroom	79–40% of Day in Regular Classroom	Less Than 40% of Day in Regular Classroom	Not in Regular School
1994–1995	44.5%	28.7%	22.4%	4.3%
1998–1999	46.1%	29.8%	20.1%	4.1%
2001–2002	48.4%	28.3%	19.2%	4.0%
2003–2004	49.9%	27.7%	18.5%	3.9%

Table 6.10. Percentage Distribution of Students (aged 6-21) with Disabilities in Regular Classrooms
Source: Adapted from Table 27–1 in National Center for Education Statistics, *The Condition of Education* 2005 (Washington, DC: U.S. Printing Office, 2005), p. 172.

His daily lessons are loaded onto his iMac laptop by the school's special education resource teacher. His iMac lessons are modified versions of what the teacher will be presenting in class. During class instruction, the regular teacher can focus on the rest of the class while Chris works on his laptop. At times, the teacher directly helps him begin one of the modified lessons. For instance, in science class as other students are learning about the periodic table and properties of metals and nonmetals, Chris is studying the parts of the atom. In language arts, he studies words on flash cards.

Most importantly, Chris is learning to interact with other students and other students are learning to accept him. He has developed a circle of friends. One of those friends, Dan O'Connell, told reporter Allison Shelley, "I've had a better year with him here. I started out the school year thinking that everyone would be perfect in a sense, the way that they would talk and act. But then I found out that people can really be different. You learn how to deal better with everyone."

Praising the idea of inclusion, Chris's mother said, "He will not be living in a special education world. He'll be living in our world."

The Inclusion Debate

While Chris Vogelberger's story is a model of successful inclusion, there has been sharp criticism of the concept. The lack of training of classroom teachers and the limited availability of aides and special education resources make implementing inclusion difficult. Not surprisingly, the lack of adequate funding underlies all.

One critic of inclusion is the American Federation of Teachers (AFT), one of the major teachers' unions. The organization's resolution on "Inclusion of Students with Disabilities" complains that teachers and support staff are not receiving adequate training for educating children with disabilities in regular classrooms. The teachers' union charges that inclusion is just a method for reducing costs in local school districts because separate special education classrooms could be eliminated. Also, the resolution expresses concern about the extra burden inclusion places on classroom teachers. Consequently, the union declares,

> Resolved that the AFT oppose inclusion—that is, any movement or program that has the goal of placing all students with disabilities in general education classrooms regardless of the nature or severity of their disabilities, their ability to behave or function appropriately in the classroom, or the educational benefits they and their general education peers can derive.

In addition, the AFT in the same resolution denounced what it called "the appalling administrative practices that have accompanied the inclusion movement." The following lists the practices objected to by the AFT:

1. Placing too many students with disabilities in individual general classrooms.

2. Placing students with disabilities in general education classrooms without services, professional development, or paraprofessional assistance.

3. Refusing to assist teachers who are having problems meeting the unique needs of students with disabilities.

4. Changing IEPs en masse so that students with disabilities may be placed in general education classrooms without supports and services and irrespective of the appropriateness of the placement.

In contrast to the American Federation of Teachers, the National Association of State Boards of Education supports full inclusion in its report *Winners All: A Call for Inclusive Schools*. The report calls for a fundamental shift in the provision of services for students with disabilities. As the report envisions the full-inclusion process, rather than teaching in a separate classroom, special education teachers would provide their services in regular classrooms by team-teaching with the regular teacher or providing other support.

The idea of inclusion is resisted by some parents who believe that separate special education classrooms provide important benefits for their children. For instance, 20 parents of children with disabilities attending the Vaughn Occupational High School in Chicago carried signs at the board of education meeting on 7 September 1994, reading "The board's inclusion is exclusion." The parents were protesting the board's decision to send their children to neighborhood schools for inclusion in regular classrooms. Traditionally, Vaughn provided vocational training for students with disabilities. The students would hold low-level jobs at McDonald's, an airline food service company, and a glass-installation business.

The board's action regarding the Vaughn students was the result of a 1992 complaint by the Illinois state board that Vaughn students were not spending time with nondisabled peers. The state board threatened to remove all federal and state funds from the school district if the students were not included in regular classrooms. Martha Luna complained about the decision because it denied her 15-year-old son, Tony, vocational training to meet his needs. Ms. Luna stated, "I know Tony won't go to college so I don't expect that, just for him to learn everyday living and work skills."

Reflecting the American Federation of Teachers' complaint about the extra burden inclusion places on classroom teachers, a survey found that over 70 percent of practicing teachers object to including students with disabilities in their classrooms. The West Virginia Federation of Teachers released a survey of 1,121 teachers showing that 87 percent did not believe that inclusion helped general education students and 78 percent did not believe that inclusion helped students with disabilities. A survey of teachers in Howard County, Maryland, reports that 64 percent of middle school teachers believe "that inclusion detracts from their ability to fully serve the needs of the general student population." Only 21 percent believed inclusion benefitted children with disabilities. The complaints about inclusion are occurring as the proportion of disabled students receiving their education in regular classrooms increases. In 1991, for instance, 32.8 percent of disabled students were receiving their educations in regular classrooms. By 1995, the figure had risen to 44.5 percent.

The preceding figures indicate the complications in implementing inclusion programs. Following is a list of objections by teachers to inclusion programs:

- Disabled students are moved into regular classrooms without any support services.

- Experienced teachers have never received training in teaching students with disabilities or in teaching in an inclusive classroom.

- School districts implementing inclusion policies do not provide adequate training for general education teachers.

- Education schools do not provide prospective teachers with a basic knowledge of learning disabilities or situations they are likely to confront in inclusive classrooms.

- General education teachers are often excluded from the individualized education plan (IEP) team.

- Parents of nondisabled students worry that their children's education will be compromised in inclusive classrooms.

The preceding issues contain their own solutions, which include (1) more education and training for experienced and future teachers, (2) adequate support services for teachers in inclusive classrooms, (3) teacher participation on the individual planning team, and (4) education of parents about inclusive classrooms. Model full-inclusion schools and teacher education programs do exist that address the preceding issues. Teachers and administrators at the Zachary Taylor Elementary School, a suburban Washington, DC, community, operate a model full-inclusion school that they believe is improving the academic and social performance of disabled students and has made other students more caring and tolerant. Syracuse University, in response to the problem of inadequately prepared teachers, instructs general education and special education teachers together. At the end of four years, both groups receive dual certification. In answer to worried parents of students in general education, John McDonnell, chair of the special education department at the University of Utah, states, "There really has been no effect on the educational progress of kids without disabilities by including kids with disabilities at the classroom level."

Commission on Excellence in Special Education

In its 2002 report, "Revitalizing Special Education for Children and Their Families," President George W. Bush's Commission on Excellence in Special Education decries the condition of special education despite over 25 years of federal involvement. The Commission lists the following problems regarding students with disabilities:

- Young people with disabilities drop out of high school at twice the rate of their peers.

- Enrollment rates of students with disabilities in higher education are still 50 percent lower than enrollment among the general population.

- Most public school educators do not feel well prepared to work with children with disabilities. In 1998, only 21 percent of public school teachers said they felt very well prepared to address the needs of students with disabilities, and another 41 percent said they felt moderately well prepared.

In addition, the Commission is particularly concerned with the classification "specific learning disabilities" whose numbers grew by 300 percent since 1976. The Commission report claims that 80 percent are classified as learning disabled because they do not know how to read. As a result, out of the total population of children with disabilities, the Commission maintains, 40 percent "are there because they weren't taught to read. The reading difficulties may not be their only area of difficulty, but it's the area that resulted in special education placement."

The Commission also worried about racial bias in special education placements particularly in the areas of mental retardation. The Commission's report contends that African American children are overrepresented among those children classified as mentally retarded and emotionally disturbed. This overrepresentation illustrates another form of second-generation segregation for children who received insufficient reading instruction.

In addressing these problems, the Commission made the unique recommendation of using federal funds designated for children with disabilities to provide parents whose children are in failing schools with vouchers that would allow them to transfer to another public school or private school. From the perspective of the Commission, vouchers would give parents greater power to control their children's educational futures. As I have discussed elsewhere in my writing, there exists a heated debate about school voucher plans.

The Commission report reiterates the concept of equality of educational opportunity for students with disabilities and the importance of inclusion. The Commission report expresses concern about many instances of local schools' segregating children with disabilities from the general population. The Commission report declares: "We affirm our commitment to the fundamental belief that children with all types of disabilities must be included to the maximum extent appropriate in their school community."

And, of course, the key to any improvement in education and the education of children with disabilities is the training of future teachers. The Commission's recommendations went beyond concerns with just the proper preparation of classroom teachers for inclusion and the education of special education teachers. The Commission called for the recruitment of candidates for teacher education with high levels of verbal ability. In addition, they suggested majoring in the subject they are planning to teach and instruction in the school curriculum they are expected to transmit.

Adequate teacher training, proper classification of students, and providing the equipment and teachers for inclusion require greater investment of local, state, and federal funds. The lack of funding continues as an ongoing problem for the education of children with disabilities. However, Chris Vogelberger's story demonstrates how the struggle for equality of educational opportunity has improved the condition of human beings. Sixty years ago, people with Down syndrome might have spent their entire lives in state institutions, cut off from the rest of society.

Conclusion

Unequal educational opportunities continue to plague American schools. Even though the civil rights movement was able to overturn laws requiring school segregation, second-generation segregation continues to be a problem. Differences between school districts in expenditures per student tend to increase the effects of segregation. Many Hispanic, African American, and Native American students attend schools where per-student expenditures are considerably below those of elite suburban and private schools. These reduced expenditures contribute to unequal educational opportunity that, in turn, affects a student's ability to compete in the labor market.

However, the advances resulting from the struggle for equal educational opportunity highlight the importance of political activity in improving the human condition. In and out of the classroom, teachers assume a vital role in ensuring the future of their students and society. In the areas of race, gender, and children with disabilities, there have been important improvements in education since the nineteenth century. The dynamic of social change requires an active concern about the denial of equality of opportunity and equality of educational opportunity.

Suggested Readings and Works Cited

Advisory Board for the President's Initiative on Race. *One America in the 21ˢᵗ Century: Forging a New Future*. Washington, DC: U.S. Printing Office, 1998. Report predicting future of race relations in the twenty-first century.

American Association of University Women, http://www.aauw.org. This organization plays a major role in protecting women's rights in education. The reader should check the organization's annual reports on current issues.

American Council of Education. *Gender Equity in Higher Education: 2006*. Washington, DC: American Council of Education, 2006. This is a report on gender differences in enrollment in higher education.

American Federation of Teachers. "Resolution on Inclusion of Students with Disabilities." http://www.aft.org/about/resolutions/1994/inclusion.htm. This resolution describes the concerns of one of the two teachers' unions about the improper administration of inclusion programs. It also contains a description of the problems that might be encountered by administrative implementation of inclusion programs.

Anyon, Jean. *Ghetto Schooling: Political Economy of Urban Educational Reform*. New York: Teachers College Press, 1997. This book demonstrates how the combination of politics and economics creates segregated and underfunded urban schools.

Balfanz, Robert, and Nettie Legters. *Locating the Dropout Crisis: Which High Schools Produce the Nation's Dropouts? Where Are They Located? Who Attends Them?* Baltimore: Center for Social Organization of Schools, Johns Hopkins University, 2004. This study shows that a majority of African American and 40 percent of Hispanic students attend high schools where the majority of students do not graduate.

Carey, Kevin. *The Funding Gap 2004: Many States Still Shortchange Low-Income and Minority Students*. Washington, DC: Education Trust, 2004. Carey shows disparities in funding based on racial concentrations in school districts.

Commission on Excellence in Special Education. "Revitalizing Special Education for Children and Their Families, 2002." Washington, DC: Department of Education, 2002. This report of George W. Bush's commission on special education recommends the use of federal funds to support vouchers for students with disabilities.

Education Equality. Feminist Majority Foundation. http://www.feminist.org/education. This site provides links and information on the history of and current problems in achieving gender equality, including criticisms of recent political attempts to reduce the impact of Title IX on schools.

Estrich, Susan. "For Girls' Schools and Women's Colleges, Separate Is Better." *The New York Times Magazine* (22 May 1994): 39. Estrich argues against coeducation.

Hacker, Andrew. *Two Nations: Black and White, Separate, Hostile, Unequal*. New York: Charles Scribners' Sons, 1992. This is a study of racial divisions in the United States.

Heller, Carol, and Joseph Hawkins. "Teaching Tolerance: Notes from the Front Line." *Teachers College Record* (Spring 1994): 1–30. A history and description of the Teaching Tolerance project is presented.

IDEA '97 Regulations. www.ideapractices.org/law/regulations/regs/SubpartA.php. These are the federal regulations issued in 1997 that regulate the education of children with disabilities.

Ignatiev, N., and John Garvey. *Race Traitor*. New York: Routledge, 1996. This important book for antiracist education is based on the idea of the importance of deconstructing and reconstructing "whiteness."

Jones, James. *Prejudice and Racism*, 2nd ed. New York: McGraw-Hill, 1996. Jones conducts an important study of the sources and issues surrounding racism in American society.

Kluger, Richard. *Simple justice*. New York: Random House, 1975. Kluger provides a good history of *Brown v. Board of Education* and the struggle for equality.

Lamar, Jake. *Bourgeois Blues: An American Memoir*. New York: Plume Books, 1992. This autobiography deals with the racism encountered by an upper-class African American.

Lee, V. E., H. M. Marks, and T. Byrd. "Sexism in Single-Sex and Coeducational Secondary School Classrooms." *Sociology of Education*, Vol. 67, no. 2 (1994): 92–120. This is an important study of sexism in single-sex classrooms.

Lemann, Nicholas. *The Promised Land: The Great Black Migration and How It Changed America*. New York: Vintage Books, 1991. This is a definitive history of African American migration from the South to the urban North.

Lewin, Tamar. "A More Nuanced Look at Men, Women and College." *The New York Times* (12 July 2006): p. B8. http://www.nytimes.com. This review of the 2006 report by the American Council of Education shows that the gender gap in undergraduate enrollments is greater among students over 25 years old.

——. "The New Gender Divide: At Colleges, Women Are Leaving Men in the Dust." *The New York Times on the Web* (9 July 2006). http://www.nytimes.com. This important newspaper article highlights the growing disparity between female and male attainment in college.

Lopez, Ian F. Haney. *White by Law: The Legal Construction of Race*. New York: New York University Press: 1996. Legal cases involved in defining the legal meaning of "white" are discussed.

Lopez, Nancy. *Hopeful Girls, Troubled Boys: Race and Gender Disparity in Urban Education*. New York: Routledge, 2003.

Meier, Kenneth Joseph Stewart, Jr., and Robert England. *Race, Class, and Education: The Politics of Second-Generation Discrimination*. Madison: University of Wisconsin Press, 1989. This book studies the politics of second-generation segregation.

Miao, Jing, and Walt Haney. "High School Graduation Rates: Alternative Methods and Implications." *Educational Policy Analysis Archives* Vol. 12, no. 55 (15 October 2004). Tempe: College of Education, Arizona State University. This study concludes that there is a declining high school graduation rate among black and Hispanic students.

National Center for Education Statistics. *The Condition of Education 2006*. Washington, DC: U.S. Printing Office, 2006. This report contains recent information on race and ethnicity in U.S. public schools.

——. "Indicator 27 of Students with Disabilities in Regular Classrooms." *The Condition of Education 2005*. Washington, DC: U.S. Printing Office, 2005. Data on students with disabilities in U.S. public schools are provided.

National Organization for Women Foundation. http://www.nowfoundation.org. The annual reports of NOW's foundation list current educational issues involving gender equity.

"National Organization for Women's 1966 Statement of Purpose" (Adopted at the Organizing Conference in Washington, DC, 29 October 1966). http://www.now.org. This historic document establishes the foundation for the participation of women in the civil rights movement.

Orfield, Gary. *Schools More Separate: Consequences of a Decade of Resegregation*. Cambridge, MA: Harvard University, The Civil Rights Project, 2001. Details of the resegregation of American schools in the last quarter of the twentieth century are presented.

———. *The Reconstruction of Southern Education: The Schools and the 1964 Civil Rights Act*. New York: Wiley-Interscience, 1969. Orfield presents a study of the desegregation of southern schools following the passage of the 1964 Civil Rights Act.

Orfield, Gary, and Chungmei Lee. *Racial Transformation and the Changing Nature of Segregation*. Cambridge, MA: Harvard University, The Civil Rights Project, 2006. This is the latest report from the Harvard Civil Rights Project on the problem of segregation in American schools.

Pennington, Bill. "The New Gender Divide: Small Colleges, Short of Men, Embrace Football." *The New York Times on the Web* (9 July 2006). http://nytimes.com. This article discloses that colleges are trying to increase male enrollments by instituting football programs.

Perry, Pamela. *Shades of White: White Kids and Racial Identities in High School*. Durham, NC: Duke University Press, 2002. Perry performs an important study of how white high school students form their racial identities.

Richard, Alan. "Researchers: School Segregation Rising in South." *Education Week on the Web* (11 September 2002). http://www.edweek.org. This report discusses the rise of school segregation in the South.

Rist, Ray. *Desegregated Schools: Appraisals of an American Experiment*. New York: Academic Press, 1979. This book provides many examples of second-generation segregation.

Sadker, Myra, and David Sadker. *Failing at Fairness: How America's Schools Cheat Girls*. New York: Scribner's, 1995. This is the landmark study on the treatment of women in American schools.

Schemo, Diana Jean. "Report Finds Minority Ranks Rise Sharply on Campuses." *The New York Times on the Web* (23 September 2002). http://www.nytimes.com. Schemo summarizes the American Council on Education report on increased minority students on college campuses.

Schnaiberg, Lynn. "Chicago Flap Shows Limits of 'Inclusion,' Critics Say." *Education Week* (5 October 1994): 1, 12. This article describes parent protest about inclusion in Chicago.

Shelley, Allison. "Brave New World." *Education Week* (10 July 2002). Shelley tells the story of Down syndrome student Chris Vogelberger's inclusion in regular classes.

Tatum, Beverly Daniel. *"Why Are All the Black Kids Sitting Together in the Cafeteria?": And Other Conversations about Race*. New York: Basic Books, 1997. This landmark book on antiracist education discusses methods of creating positive antiracist models for white students.

U.S. Census Bureau. "Current Population Survey (CPS)—Definitions and Explanations." http//www.census.gov/population/www/cps/cpsdef.html. This is a guide to the racial and other terms used in the collection of the national census.

———. "Current Population Survey 2005. Annual Social and Economic Supplement." http://www.census.gov/hhes/www/income/dinctabs.html. Data on relationship between race and income are provided.

U.S. Department of Education. "Title I—Improving the Academic Achievement of the Disadvantaged." *Federal Register*, Vol. 68, no. 236 (9 December 2003). Washington, DC: U.S. Government Printing Office, 2003. Title I outlines the regulations requiring students with disabilities to be tested under the requirements of No Child Left Behind Act of 2001.

U.S. Office of Special Education Programs. "History: Twenty-Five Years of Progress in Educating Children with Disabilities Through IDEA, 2001." www.ed.gov/offices/osers/osep. This document provides a history of federal legislation for children with disabilities beginning with the passage of Public Law 94–142.

Viadero, Debra. "VA. Hamlet at Forefront of 'Full Inclusion' Movement for Disabled." *Education Week* (18 November 1992): l, 14. This article describes the implementation of a full-inclusion plan in a community in Virginia.

———. "NASBE Endorses 'Full Inclusion' of Disabled Students." *Education Week* (4 November 1992): 1, 30. This article discusses the report supporting full inclusion of students with disabilities. The report *Winners All: A Call for Inclusive Schools* was issued by the National Association for State Boards of Education.

———. "'Full Inclusion' of Disabled in Regular Classes Favored." *Education Week* (30 September 1992): 11. This is a report on the court case *Oberti v. Board of Education of the Borough of Clementon School District*, which involves full inclusion.

Walsh, Mark. "Judge Finds Bias in Scholarships." *Education Week* (15 February 1989): 1, 20. This article describes the court ruling that found the awarding of scholarships by using test scores to be biased against female students.

West, Cornel. *Race Matters*. New York: Vintage Books, 1994. This set of essays emphasizes the continuing importance of race in social relationships in U.S. society.

Wilson, William J. *The Declining Significance of Race: Blacks and Changing American Institutions*. Chicago: University of Chicago Press, 1979. This book argues that social class is a more important factor than race in determining equality of opportunity among African Americans.

Wolf, Carmen, et al. *Income, Poverty, and Health Insurance Coverage in the United States: 2003*. Washington, DC: U.S. Census Bureau, August 2004. The authors provide important census material on the relationship between race and income.

Wollenberg, Charles. *All Deliberate Speed: Segregation and Exclusion in California Schools, 1855–1975*. Berkeley: University of California Press, 1976. This is a good history of segregation in California. It includes a discussion of the important Court decision regarding Mexican Americans, *Mendez et al. v. Westminster School District of Orange County*, and of the segregation of Asian Americans.

Reflection Questions

1. Think about the aims and purposes of education for 21st century schools. What role do schools play in our society today? What happens to different groups of students when we define schooling as a site for job preparation and not a place for knowledge production and creation? Consider how demographics, social trends, politics and economics have impacted how we think about public schools. Finally, attempt to create a list of aims and purposes for 21st century schools. Include aims and purposes for the areas of the intellectual, political, economic and social, but also consider additional areas that have emerged in the 21st century, for example, technology. Provide a rationale for your thinking.

2. After reading the essays in this section, attempt to answer the following questions: Who profits from both the successes and failures of public education? Who ultimately determines the content of the curriculum and makes decisions regarding how that varies from school-to-school? How do we go about reconciling private and public interests in public education?

3. Are public schools dominated by pedagogies of hope or hopelessness? Is change possible? How can we engage the voices of all major constituencies (parents, educators, politicians, community members, etc.) in this discussion? What changes would you see in the local schools (aims, purpose and curriculum) if the voices of the local community took precedence over private, political and economic interests?

4. Schools (and teachers) are frequently blamed for social problems? Should schools be responsive to solving larger social and political problems, e.g. racism, poverty, teenage pregnancy, etc.? How does the answer to this question impact the ways in which we view the aims and purposes of public education and the content of the curriculum?

5. A focus on privatization, efficiency and profit are steering many public schools away from social justice concerns. Should corporate interests have a voice in discussions regarding the process, progress and product of public schools? What are the issues in this discussion and how do we go about resisting these efforts?

SECTION II

Social Justice and Critical Theory in the Schoolhouse

Introduction

Eleanor J. Blair

Today, we see educators regularly trying to reconcile accountability efforts with mounting evidence of the failures of large educational bureaucracies to meet the needs of increasingly large numbers of children coming from less advantaged, diverse backgrounds. Critical theory provides a framework for reconsidering the aims and purposes of education generally, but more specifically, it provides a guide for the kinds of questions that we need to be asking regarding how and why we serve some groups more effectively than others. Critical theory embraces the notion that teaching and learning are value-infused activities that require a critical analysis of attempts to provide all children with educational opportunities that facilitate equal access to knowledge and is culturally responsive to the needs and values of diverse groups. Public schools must be held accountable for their failures and be required to initiate a dialogue that revisits the public's commitment to the democratic ideals represented by American public education and seeks to negotiate a new vision of public education, one that seeks to address the needs of all children, not just a few.

Earlier reform efforts have highlighted the need for teachers to be both critical pedagogues and advocacy leaders. The contemporary focus on outcomes has often obscured any discussion of the context and conditions of teachers' work, and certainly ignored any consideration of multiple pedagogies, some more responsive to changing populations of students than others. The facts, however, are clear: teachers' work is stagnant and resistant to change and, among poor children from diverse backgrounds, achievement is low and dropout rates are high. At times it is difficult to keep pessimism at bay when one considers the viability or sustainability of any significant paradigm shift that will impact public schools in a meaningful way. In my work, I keep exposing my students to the transformative ideas of critical pedagogy, but I frequently encounter anger and outright resistance that is couched in the concern that I don't understand the reality of schools; a reality that equates good teachers to good technicians. Giroux (1988) discussed the impact of this threat to the teaching profession in the following:

> One of the major threats facing prospective and existing teachers within the public schools is the increasing development of instrumental ideologies that emphasize a technocratic approach to both teacher

preparation and classroom pedagogy. At the core of the current emphasis on instrumental and pragmatic factors in school life are a number of important pedagogical assumptions. These include: a call for the separation of conception from execution; the standardization of school knowledge in the interest of managing and controlling it; and the devaluation of critical, intellectual work on the part of teachers and students for the primacy of practical consideration. (pp. 122–123)

To this day, I am not sure that I am adequately preparing teachers to deal with the morass they will encounter in the schools; I know the major issues that will present impediments to the process of creating schools and classrooms that are amenable to the changing needs of teachers and students, but I keep trying. Despite frequent bouts of cynicism regarding the future of public education, I am still hopeful that the future of public schools, and the teaching profession, will hinge on the ability of teachers to move forward and claim their rightful places as teacher leaders whose voices must be central to all meaningful and substantive reform of schools and classrooms.

Thus, inherent to meaningful change in public education is a vision that recognizes meaningful change will only occur when the debate over public education expands to include the voices of teachers in the articulation of a "renewed" and "re-envisioned" conception of the future of public schools that mediates ideas of a "just democracy" with a commitment to social justice and an overriding concern for future conceptions of teachers' work. Unfortunately, the public has been led by politicians and corporate America to believe that testing and accountability measures—as they are presently being defined and redefined in increasingly more stringent and restrictive ways—are the only viable solutions to the problems that afflict American schools. As I always tell my students, "how we define the problem determines the solution." If we simply define the ills of American education as low test scores, the solutions that we consider will only focus on raising test scores; however, an exclusive focus on test scores obscures the possibility that real reform must address begin with a redefinition of the problem. Problems associated with race and poverty are messy, and not easily solved; however, there are many individuals working in education today who have myriad perspectives on how to change schools. Many of those individuals are teachers, who, given the opportunity, could begin to translate research into practice. At the very crux of teachers' work is the idea that teachers working in collaboration with other professionals can ultimately influence lasting, sustainable change in schools and classrooms across America.

In this section of the book, readers are presented with five essays that define and explore the role of critical theory and social justice in schools. Carr, Gresson, Kincheloe, Medina, and Sensoy and DiAngelos provide both an introduction to the fundamental concepts associated with critical pedagogy, but also apply these principles to the work we do in schools and classrooms. After reading the work of these authors, it should be clear that teachers' work, by necessity, requires both skill and a commitment to the values associated with social justice. It is only in this way that the work of creating public spaces that are relevant and responsive to the needs of all children will be successful.

References

Giroux, H. (1988). *Teachers as intellectuals: Toward a critical pedagogy of learning.* Westport, CT: Bergin & Garvey.

CHAPTER 7

Transforming Educational Leadership Without Social Justice?

Looking at Critical Pedagogy as More Than a Critique, and a Way Toward "Democracy"[1]

Paul R. Carr

One thing we know for sure, as common wisdom has it, is that you can always count on change. *Change is everywhere*, we are told constantly. *We are about change*, political parties extol. *If you don't change, you'll be left behind*, is what we are taught. While advertisers, business gurus, pundits, and highly remunerated futurists all agree that change is in the air, that progress is the way to go, and that evolution means embracing change, I'm left wondering: what type of change, defined by whom, for whom, contextualized, understood, and embraced in what manner, by whom, and why? If change is a certainty, as we are led to believe, then why is there still poverty? One would think that social inequities—including racism, sexism, income gaps, homelessness, religious intolerance, discrimination of all forms, and so on—would be history; that, with all of the change going on, there would be no room for such anti-change variables. While, undoubtedly, much *has* changed—and there is evidence of this—social inequities, in many regards, are widening, not dissipating. This, I would argue, relates to power and how it is exercised, challenged, and considered. This chapter on transformative leadership, building on the work of Carolyn Shields (2004, 2010), takes the posture that power is directly related to the educational project and, moreover, that it can only take place within a broad framework that acknowledges social inequities (Kincheloe, 2007, 2008a, 2008b; Macrine, 2009). Critical pedagogy provides such a framework, and I will use that framework here to position an argument in favor of a more engaged, politically meaningful, and counter-hegemonic transformative leadership, one that deemphasizes neo-liberalism, the reproduction of social relations, and the solidification of a rigid educational system that too willingly weeds out those with lower cultural capital, incongruent lived experiences, and divergent identities (see the work of Paulo Freire, 1973, 1985, 1998, 2004, 1973/2005).

In discussing the transformative leadership project, I will focus on democracy as a means of reframing a way of understanding change in education within a critical pedagogy–pedagogical perspective (Carr, 2007, 2008a, 2008b, 2008c, 2010; Lund & Carr, 2008). Democracy is key to this debate because if democracy is not an objective of education, then what is its purpose (Westheimer, 2008; Westheimer & Kahne, 2003, 2004)?[2] Principals and vice-principals, along with superintendents and other senior education officials, form a group that I, and others, call administrators, and they are the focus of the first line of implementation in the quest for transformative leadership. Added to this group, we must also consider policymakers, decisionmakers, and other leaders, who have a direct stake in what happens in schools. Interest groups, think-tanks, teachers' federations, parents' groups, and others are also enmeshed in how we define, orchestrate, evaluate, and produce education. Transformative leadership, therefore, involves many sectors, interests, concepts, and realities (Shields & Edwards, 2005). Significantly, it is something that is a product of society; is socially, economically, and politically constructed, and is an appendage of the power structures in which it exists. For this chapter, I will argue that democracy is a useful concept to guide our thinking here because it forces us to acknowledge the broader macro-portrait of society, something that inevitably impinges on the individual actions of administrators and, moreover, is shaped by the concerns and priorities of various groups in society. Thus, the critical pedagogy of democracy in relation to transformative leadership is the focus of this chapter and will guide the analysis and discussion throughout. The chapter presents thoughts, concepts, and research related to democracy, critical pedagogy, and the critical pedagogy of democracy, and concludes with some proposals for more engaged, critical, and meaningful transformative change in education, with particular attention being paid to the leadership role.

Democracy and Transformative Leadership

What can be done to contribute to democracy in and through education, and how does leadership fit into the equation? Clearly, there is no one answer, especially not an easy or simplistic one. A fundamental, and perhaps obvious, argument is that democracy and education must be inextricably linked. One might ask: What kind of education? Part of the formulation of a response comes in the form of how we choose to elucidate what we mean by *democracy*. My interpretation surpasses the electoral politics (representative) model, embracing a *thicker* version of inclusion, participation, dialog, interrogation, and critical engagement, which is underpinned by a vigorously and humbly formulated critical pedagogy (Carr, 2008c). This form of democratic education seeks to embrace the experiences and perspectives of diverse peoples, including those traditionally marginalized from the national narratives that have enshrined a partisan allegiance to patriotism; these narratives were not often included and accepted military conquest as a normative value, and, conversely, often excluded and rejected those groups and actions that ran counter to hegemonic reasoning (Carr, 2010). It is problematic, therefore, to consider democracy in exclusion of a meaningful analysis of inequitable power relations, and this links directly with the notion of transformative leadership as opposed to traditional forms of leadership that privilege maintaining the status quo (Kincheloe & Steinberg, 2006; Macrine, 2009; McLaren & Kincheloe, 2007).

I caution that there is no one thing, menu, or recipe that can be produced to inculcate a democratic state, government, citizen, or education system (Carr, 2008a). Indeed, even addressing an amalgam of concerns is no guarantee of reinforcing democracy. However, the desire for a more meaningful, just, and decent form of democracy is something that requires—borrowing from the contemporary vernacular within mainstream politics—a certain measure of *hope*. One must remain confident and strident in order to improve the current situation, because to simply endorse it uncritically is to further entrench vast swaths of the landscape, figuratively and literally, to a permanently deceptive existence in which the quest for human rights becomes a mere fictional legal maneuver reserved largely for those with their hands firmly on the economic levers of power.

Ultimately, seeking a more democratic society in and through education is tantamount to seeking the truth. Never comfortable, nor easily achieved, such a proposition requires a multitude of measures as well as the belief that people can, ultimately, function together without self-destruction. War is not the answer, nor is violence. Corruption and greed are also areas that can be addressed, provided that the will of the people is respected. Racism, sexism, and poverty are not virtues—they are man- and woman-made, and can be addressed. Cycles of disenfranchisement do not mesh well with the oft-repeated mantra of American "greatness" and the superiority of a highly developed, advanced nation, one often invoked as being blessed by God. Rather than reducing inequities, society is actually (according to all of the standard measures used to demonstrate development and superiority) becoming less united, less equal, less resolutely inclusive, and ultimately, I would argue, less democratic. The space provided for elections has usurped the place of education in many regards (Carr, 2010; Denzin, 2009).

Critical Pedagogy and Democratic (Sur)Realities

Can we have democracy without democratic literacy? Without democratic engagement? Is critical pedagogy an appropriate means for achieving democratic literacy and democratic engagement? Relying, in large part, on the critical pedagogical foundation of Paulo Freire, it is helpful here to highlight the epistemological salience of Freire's work, which Au (2007) argues is steeped in the Marxist tradition. Epistemological interrogation is a necessary function in the quest for transformative change in education. Although the terminology may change from context to context, Freire's "conscientization" has meaning across diverse milieus and environments. Achieving meaningful experiences in and through education, cognizant of differential power relations, is the core of a critical pedagogical, democratic education. Whether or not a critical Marxist perspective is germane in nurturing democratic education should not obfuscate the reality that critical pedagogy can lead to the process of personal and collective transformation.

Brosio (2003), in citing leading radical political philosopher Michael Parenti, highlights that normative neo-liberal, capitalistic structures have, and continue to have, a significant effect on people and societal development:

> What we need is a 180-degree shift away from unilateral global domination and toward equitable and sustainable development among the peoples of the world. This means U.S. leaders would have to stop acting like self-willed unaccountable rulers of the planet. They must stop supporting despots, and stop opposing those democratic movements and governments that challenge the status quo. The struggle is between those who believe that the land, labor, capital, technology, markets, and natural resources of society should be used as expendable resources for transnational profit accumulation, and those who believe that such things should be used for the mutual benefit of the populace. What we need is to move away from liberal complaints about how bad things are and toward a radical analysis that explains why they are so, away from treating every situation as a perfectly new and befuddling happening unrelated to broader politico-economic interests and class power structures. What we need is a global anti-imperialist movement that can challenge the dominant paradigm with an alternative one that circumvents the monopoly ideological control of officialdom and corporate America. (Brosio, 2003)

Bellamy Foster, Holleman, and McChesney (2008) support this perspective, arguing for a more comprehensive, critical, and global analysis of the American empire, suggesting that the degree to which U.S. society is controlled by militarization is poorly understood by the population, which then leads to the military having far-reaching potential to dominate, marginalize, and diminish the vibrancy of vast swaths of society. Willinsky (1998) further addresses the need to critique empire as a necessary step in bringing forth the prospect for change, which relates to Freire's (1973/2005) oppressor-oppressed dichotomy. Anticolonial education should, therefore, not be uniquely a discussion reserved for the archives, as the historical is intertwined with the present, and appreciating how current problems and issues are connected with previous actions is pivotal to avoiding simplistic, essentialized education responses.

Taking account of the dialectical relationship between hegemony and ideology (Fischman & McLaren, 2005) is a fundamental part of the critical pedagogical equation. As highlighted in the first section of their book, critical epistemological interrogation is fundamental to the dissection and unravelling of how power is infused in and through (supposed) democratic processes. The relevance for education, therefore, is clear:

> Critical pedagogy problematizes the relationship between education and politics, between socio-political relations and pedagogical practices, between the reproduction of dependent hierarchies of power and privilege in the domain of everyday social life and that of the classroom and institutions. In doing so, it advances an agenda for educational transformation by encouraging educators to understand the socio-political contexts of educative acts and the importance of radically democratizing both educational and larger social formations. In such processes, educators take on intellectual roles by adapting to, resisting, and challenging curriculum, school policy, educational philosophies, and pedagogical traditions. (Fischman & McLaren, 2005, p. 425)

A critical pedagogy of democracy can cultivate a vigorous and meaningful interrogation of the various strands underpinning power structures, including the functioning of the military, the limited but populism-laden visions of politics, and the infusion of right-wing Christian fundamentalism into decision-making (Giroux, 2005; Steinberg & Kincheloe, 2009). Giroux and Giroux (2006) provide a thoughtful synthesis of critical democratic pedagogy:

> The democratic character of critical pedagogy is defined largely through a set of basic assumptions, which holds that power, values, and institutions must be made available to critical scrutiny, be understood as a product of human labor (as opposed to God-given), and evaluated in terms of how they might open up or close down democratic practices and experiences. Yet, critical pedagogy is about more than simply holding authority accountable through the close reading of texts, the creation of radical classroom practices, or the promotion of critical literacy. It is also about linking learning to social change, education to democracy, and knowledge to acts of intervention in public life. Critical pedagogy encourages students to learn to register dissent as well as to take risks in creating the conditions for forms of individual and social agency that are conducive to a substantive democracy. (p. 28)

Challenging neo-liberalism is a central feature to this project, shining a light on nefarious practices, marginalization, and conservative interpretations of success that serve to blame the victim rather than critique the trappings and inner-working of power (Giroux & Giroux, 2006). Decoding signals, omissions, directives, and the meaning of rhetoric is a key component of the critical pedagogy of democracy (Engels, 2007; Kellner & Share, 2007; Macedo & Steinberg, 2007). State authority is not obliged to be oppressive, and ingratiating students with a critical pedagogy of democracy can lead to thicker experiences and interpretations of democracy.

A radical democratic pedagogy, as outlined by Denzin (2009), speaks to hope: "Hope is ethical. Hope is moral. Hope is peaceful and nonviolent. Hope seeks truth of life's sufferings. Hope gives meaning to the struggles to change the world. Hope is grounded in concrete performative practices, in struggles and interventions that espouse sacred values of love, care, community, trust, and well-being" (p. 385).

Compelling arguments can be made for a more deliberately conscious, engaged, and loving connection to others (Darder & Miron, 2006). Freire spoke of radical love and the inescapable prospect of indignation, which need not be considered weakness, cynicism, or hopelessness (Freire, 2004). The capacity, and necessity, to love is entrenched in the very essence of the human condition. Accepting human and humane interactions and relations, without exploitation and discrimination, is a fundamental consideration for a critical pedagogy of democracy. Darder and Miron (2006) emphasize that our experiences are not disconnected from the broader politico-economic context but, as Brosio (2003) maintains, are interwoven into a socially constructed narrative:

> Capitalism disembodies and alienates our daily existence. As our consciousness becomes more and more abstracted, we become more and more detached from our bodies. For this reason, it is absolutely

imperative that critical educators and scholars acknowledge that the origin of emancipator possibility and human solidarity resides in our body. (p. 16)

As Darder and Miron (2006) argue, everyone is capable of contesting, resisting, and challenging nefarious neo-liberal policies and manifestations:

> If we, as citizens of the Empire, do not use every opportunity to voice our dissent, we shamefully leave the great task of dissent to our brothers and sisters around the world who daily suffer greater conditions of social, political, and economic impoverishment and uncertainty than we will ever know. For how long will our teaching and politics fail to address the relevant and concrete issues that affect people's daily lives? (p. 18)

Not every action or gesture need be representative of a grandiose, sweepingly transformative manifestation. For transformative leadership to be meaningful, individuals can, and must, make their voices heard: They can resist imperialism, hegemony, and patriotic oppression, and, importantly, they can choose love over hate, peace over war, and humanity over inhumanity. This may seem abstract and outside of the boundaries of the proverbial three *R*s, student-based learning, high academic standards, No Child Left Behind—like system reforms, and the like, but, as argued throughout this chapter, there is a direct, visceral relation between power and change, and transformative leadership is hinged, according to this thinking, on a broad platform of macro-level thinking combined with micro-level transformative leadership within school and educational sites.

Fifty Proposals That Could Contribute to Democracy Through Education

Building on the backdrop outlined above—at the risk of being criticized for including some ideas that may not mesh with a democratic education focus, or others that seem to be superfluous to the debate or that may not seem too original or innovative—what follows is a list of 50 proposals that could contribute to a thicker democratic education. Importantly, these proposals should be considered as an ensemble, not as disparate, individual efforts at reform. Within the spirit of this chapter and book, all of these proposals would require a vigorous, engaged, and critical transformative leadership. Based on a critical pedagogical conceptualization of education, change, and democracy, these proposals are offered as an alternative to the neo-liberal, hegemonic reform models currently in place, which have largely overlooked and underplayed social justice.

1. Make education a *societal* responsibility, removing the false narrative of it somehow being only a *local* responsibility. The nation-state should undertake a public education campaign to acknowledge and promote public education as the engine behind societal growth, development, harmony, and ingenuity.

2. Democratic conscientization should be integrated into educational planning, and political, critical, and media-centric forms of literacy should become mandatory aspects of teaching and learning.

3. Eradicate the mainstream representation of education as being neutral and devoid of politics. Emphasize that education can lead to change and that regressive forms of education can lead to docile, compliant citizens, the antithesis of thick democracy.

4. Redefine the notion of accountability in education to more centrally focus on ethics, bona fide diversity, social justice, and thick democracy. Just because No Child Left Behind (NCLB) declares that there is greater accountability does not necessarily mean that this is true.

5. The state should only fund public education, and charters, vouchers, private schools, and other offshoots should be discouraged and not be eligible for public support. Public education is a public good, benefitting all of society, and it should be viewed as a collective, global responsibility.

6. End the ranking of schools and school boards. Such efforts are divisive, punish the marginalized, are not appropriately contextualized, and serve to disintegrate rather than integrate, thus diminishing the possibility of enhancing the public good and the notion of education being a fundamental pillar to solidifying the thicker and more humane elements of a democracy.

7. Do not let high cultural capital areas—those with high property values and other advantages—graduate their high schools without having them work closely with schools in their areas that are facing serious challenges. The notion here is that all schools will see that they are part of a common struggle, existence, and society, and are not simply, as within the neo-liberal mindset, individuals demonstrating how hard they work as opposed to others who are supposedly not committed.

8. All subject areas of the curriculum should explicitly diagnose how power works as well as the meaning of social justice. This should include a critical pedagogical analysis of whiteness; racial, gender, and class inequities; and other forms of marginalization, discrimination, and disenfranchisement. It may be considered impolite to discuss such matters, but to avoid them is only to further entrench and ingratiate harm, damage, and the antithesis of democracy.

9. Education systems and educators should embrace the following saying: *"The more I know, the less I know."* If education is to sincerely be about lifelong learning, then it should involve an endless process of critical interrogation, lived experiences, and dialectical questioning and dialog, which far overshadows the notion of standards, high-stakes testing, and a prescriptive curriculum.

10. Men and women of all origins, races, ethnicities, and backgrounds should be involved in teaching and education. Some elementary schools lack male teachers, and some schools have no racial minorities or no females in leadership positions, which can further lead to false stereotypes about leadership, role models, and learning.

11. Educational policymaking and curriculum development should involve more consultation and collaboration with diverse groups and interests, and the decision-making process should necessarily become more transparent. Educators, parents, students, and the broader community should be able to understand how decisions are made and why, and they should be involved in these processes that will, ultimately, have an effect on all of society.

12. All schools should be twinned within local areas (for example, an urban school could be twinned with a suburban school, and a suburban school twinned with a rural school, or schools from different demographic areas could be twinned in the same area). This twinning would involve bona fide academic and curriculum work in addition to cultural exchange. No student should be allowed to say that they do not know, understand, or experience diversity because "everyone in their school is white," which does not sufficiently encapsulate a thicker version of critical thinking and engagement with pluralism.

13. School boards should use technology to twin classrooms in the United States with those around the world so that educators can exchange language and culture with colleagues in other countries. The government should provide seed funding to schools that require it in order to undertake this program.

14. If there must be standards in education, there should be standards for democratic education, citizenship education, peace education, media literacy, and social justice. Standards should be focused on building a more decent society, not on testing basic skills that are predefined largely because of cultural capital.

15. Teachers should not be remunerated on how well their students do. Teachers' salaries should be increased and other measures of acknowledgment for their contributions should be pursued. The objective should not be to diminish those working in more challenging situations or those whose students have lower levels of cultural capital. The role of the teacher has to be understood in a broader societal context, not simply related to mercantilist outcomes.

16. The curriculum should be significantly revamped. Freire's generative themes and Dewey's constructivism should be incorporated into classrooms at all levels, instilling values of respect, critical interrogation, engagement, and appreciation of how power works.

17. All schools should emphasize deliberative democracy and young people should learn how to listen, articulate, debate, and diagnose difference. Significantly, students should learn how to respectfully seek to construct further knowledge in a peaceful way. Condemning those with critical opinions needs to be stopped as group-think can lead to societal paralysis and a nefarious form of patriotism.

18. Rather than protecting students from controversial subject matter, they should be encouraged to critically understand not only the *what* but also the *how* and *why* behind significant events, issues, and concerns. The mythology that politics is about Democrats and Republicans needs to be rectified, and students need to learn that critical reflection can lead to more appropriate and effective resolutions of systemic problems and conflicts than the use of force, whether it be wars, racial profiling, or the neglect of impoverished groups.

19. Peace and peace education should become centerpieces of the educational project. If peace is not a fundamental part of education, what then is its purpose?

20. A thicker interpretation of the environment and environmental education should be taught throughout the educational program. The effects of war and military conflict on the environment, for example, should be explored.

21. Poorer areas should not be punished because of wealth concentration, and everyone should be able to enjoy the outdoors without cost.

22. Accessible, fair-play, sportsmanlike values should be reasserted in place of a win-at-all-costs mission and the drive for notoriety and the supremacy of money.

23. All students should be introduced to critical service learning. The experiences should be accompanied by courses and debriefings on why societal problems exist. To do a service-learning placement without some sociopolitical contextualization may only reinforce the opposite of what is sought through the actual experience.

24. Contracts for superintendents of education and principals should contain a clause that they will be evaluated on how well they inculcate democratic education, political literacy, and social justice. Their renewal should hinge, in part, on how well they address these matters within their educational institutions.

25. There should be no place in schools for military recruitment, especially not in schools in poorer areas. All students should be afforded the possibility of higher education, not just those with

higher levels of cultural capital, and the message should not be transmitted, either explicitly or implicitly, that poor people have no other option than to join the army.

26. All American students should learn at least one foreign language starting in first grade and then be introduced to a second language in high school. The notion that English will get Americans everywhere they wish to go at all times and will lead to intercultural development, not to mention the visible concern of achieving peace and good relations with the world, must be recast in a more holistic and democratic form of education.

27. The enticement to enter into contracts with for-profit enterprises as a way of funding schools should be eliminated. Communities should be made aware of economic situations that pressure and coerce some localities more than others, and should also be invited to critique the role of marketing, advertising, and the drive to capture market share within schools. Educational policymaking should also address this area. Programs such as Channel One should be prohibited from schools. They are not benevolent services; moreover, they come with strings attached, and are not problematized.

28. The differentiated experiences of schools that have a larger wealth base, as compared to poorer districts, should be addressed. The research on this reality, including the social context, should be concisely and critically presented to parents, students, educators, and the broader community. The approach should not be to illustrate blame, pity, guilt, or incompetence but, rather, to seek to underscore systemic problems, resource allocation, and ineffectual curriculum and policy development.

29. The limited accessibility to field trips to museums, cultural events, and even foreign countries only serves to further increase the educational, cultural, and political gap between Americans. Governments should provide an appropriate level of funding so that all schools can benefit from such indispensable activities.

30. Parents should be required, except in extraordinary circumstances, to provide one half day of service per month to their children's schools. The objective is to make all parents knowledgeable of what happens at school, to create support for progressive activities, and to provide a vehicle to discuss education and democracy. Legislation should be passed to ensure that no parent would be penalized for participating in such a program (and these days would not count as formal vacation days). School principals should be supported in finding the appropriate ways to liaise with parents.

31. Teacher-education programs should focus on qualitative teaching and learning experiences and develop assessment schemes that monitor and support innovation, engagement, collaboration, and critical pedagogical work that emphasizes learning and the *construction* of knowledge over the *acquisition* of knowledge. Similarly, these programs should forge meaningful relationships with local school boards. All education faculty should have some type of formal relationship with their schools.

32. All schools should implement a guest program, whereby a range of professionals, academics, and people with diverse experiences could liaise with students. The access to a diversity of guests should be distributed equally throughout all schools, and no schools should be without some form of a regular, regimented, and engaging program in place. Special attention should be paid to diversity and the public good (i.e., high cultural-capital schools should not be the only ones exposed to leading business and political figures; conversely, critical alternative movements and grassroots figures should not be invited only to working-class schools).

33. Public officials, including politicians, diplomats, and mainstream media, should be invited into schools to dialog with students, all the while being open to critical questions about social justice, bias, patriotism, propaganda, and why systemic issues exist, in addition to the traditional reasons that such figures visit schools (e.g., to extol the virtues of democracy, to sell support for a particular platform, to discuss career choices, how to be a good citizen, etc.).

34. All schools should embark on a range of community projects that could count for credit toward graduation. These projects could involve service-learning, undertaking research, writing narratives and ethnographies, and making presentations on how social problems might be addressed.

35. State departments of education, overseen by a board of professionals and activists, should gather data on inputs and outputs of the education system, and report on how diversity, social justice, media literacy, democracy, and other program areas are relevant. These reports should be available online, free of cost, through the state's Department of Education website.

36. The study of democracy and elections should not be concentrated within a single course (often labelled as a Civics or Government course). Democracy must be demonstrated, acted upon, and lived, not relegated to a course that focuses on encouraging voting.

37. Require school boards and schools to implement participatory budgeting in an inclusive and meaningful fashion, involving diverse interests in determining the allocation of funds for education.

38. Prohibit fundraising within schools, and have educators focus exclusively on critical teaching, learning, and engagement. If schools are not concerned with raising funds they will then be able to freely target the best interests of the students and also to not be beholden to any outside interests.

39. Schools should focus on the prevention of bullying and violence, and work with communities, families, and students at various levels to establish a conducive environment for learning, and, at the same time, seek to avoid the nefarious zero-tolerance, criminalization route.

40. Schools should undertake community violence and criminality projects, examining the form, substance, and degree of violence and criminality in their localities. The data-collection and analysis should include white-collar crime, corruption, racial profiling, and un- and underdocumented crimes, including abuse against women, gang activities, and police misconduct. The results, which would form part of a process of critical interrogation, could be publicly presented on an ongoing basis in order to lead to a more rigorous understanding of how and why criminal activities and violence take place, and, moreover, what is done about it.

41. Similar to point 40, schools should undertake community health projects to determine the types of diseases, infections, and illnesses that exist in local communities, with a view to undertaking critical comparative analyses. Are poorer people more at risk, do they live shorter lives, do they have access to adequate health care, do they contribute equally to the formulation of health policy, and so on? The ongoing results of the research should be exposed, and acted upon.

42. Students should be invited, per Lawrence Kohlberg's moral-development model, to determine some of the rules, guidelines, and conditions of their school experience. Students should not be uniquely the recipients of the formal education experience but should also be full participants in shaping their knowledge and reality.

43. No child should be placed in special education without a full determination of the socio-economic context, thus diminishing the possibility of marginalized and racialized communities being disproportionately streamed into these programs. Despite formal procedures outlined in present processes, there is still widespread concern about the types of children directed to special education.

44. Make humility a virtue for teaching and learning, and downgrade the emphasis placed on economic gain accrued by business leaders, actors, and professional athletes.

45. All schools should have a garden that produces fruits and vegetables. While working one to two hours a week on the garden, students will also learn, and will have opportunities to make concrete curricular connections to the environment, agriculture, nutrition, the economics of food, and globalization. The fruits and vegetables produced could also be consumed by the students.

46. All schools should have music, arts, and physical education programs. Funding and wealth should not be an impediment to children having access to a broad liberal arts education.

47. A war tax of 20% should be applied to all spending on the military and militarization, and the resultant funding should be applied to education. In present times, with approximately $1 trillion being spent annually on the military in the United States, the government would be obligated to allocate an additional $200 billion to the education section. Education should not be used to subsidize war, nor should poorer people be forced into fighting other people's battles.

48. The federal government should organize an annual education summit, in which diverse civil society, educational, and *alter-mondialiste/counter-globalization* organizations could contribute to a debate on the formal measures, data, policies, resources, and goals of public education. This education summit could be considered as an accountability forum for governments and education authorities. The summit would generate a detailed annual report and plan, which would be reviewed the following year.

49. Humility should be emphasized over nationalism and patriotism.

50. Radical love should be the starting point for the conceptualization of education.

Whether or not the above proposals appear to be realistic is not the fundamental question. The reality that there are diverse proposals, movements, interests, and people seeking a different kind of democracy should be kept in mind. Transformative leadership, being ideologically positioned to engage and act upon inequitable power relations, is afforded unique and meaningful access to formal educational structures in which myriad dialogs, debates, and decisions are hashed out. The above set of proposals could be considered and massaged by transformative leaders, who might be able to shift some portions of the bedrock underpinning the neo-liberal monopoly within mainstream education circles that prevents many progressive and social-justice–based reforms from making it to the table.

A Democratic Education Planning Model

This democratic education planning model (Figure 2.1) can assist in mapping what individuals, schools, and communities are thinking and experiencing in relation to democracy and democratic engagement. Schools could document the context, content, experiences, and outcomes of what takes place within the realm of education. There are many ways of promoting constructive collaboration, and I would encourage critical, dialectical, and harmonious efforts aimed at understanding and constructing more meaningful experiences, rather than imposing haphazard, incongruent, and inauthentic ones. For this model, schools could work with diverse interests—or stakeholders, in public-policy jargon—who are not, to use the neo-liberal terminology, clients. Involving teachers, parents, students, members of the community, and others, and being cognizant of differential power relations, may facilitate some important synergetic planning as well as the formulation of proposals. This approach is inspired by the participatory budget planning process (Gandin & Apple, 2005), established in Porto Alegre, Brazil, in which the community comes together to consider how portions of the budget will be spent. Using a critical pedagogical analysis, participants in the democratic education planning model should be highly sensitized to systemic and institutional barriers to change and should also consider the *lived* experiences of individuals and groups, being vigilant to grasp the nuanced existence of marginalized interests.

	Context	Content	Experiences	Outcomes
Individual				
School				
Community				

Figure 7.1: Democratic Education Planning Model

This model does not seek the typical (supposed) accountability report that is skewed toward illustrating the virtue of the funder or the institutional interest. Rather, the focus should be on bona fide, tangible critical engagement, questioning why policies and programs have been developed, in whose interest, and to what end. For example, how do individuals, the school, and the community contribute to the democratic foundation, growth, and tension of what takes place locally within an educational site?

One way to use this model would be to chart out the context for democratic education: to define it, to highlight the historic and contemporary achievement, issues, and challenges, and to address fundamental concerns, such as those related to patriotism, socio-economic development, and political participation, in an inclusive and thick way. The notion is not to draft volumes here but, rather, to attempt to link to our actions the epistemological and philosophical foundation of what we know, and how we know and believe it (Kincheloe, 2008b). Often, education policies seem to drop from the sky, disconnected from the lived realities of students, and are inconsistent with scientific research—although NCLB specifically prescribes that reforms be based on scientific research, can educational leaders enumerate the literature that has informed their philosophies? (Gordon, Smyth, & Diehl, 2008).

Concluding Thoughts

In focusing on democracy, it is clear that a thicker, more critical version of democracy—outside of representative, electoral politics—necessarily involves an inter-disciplinary approach (touching on sociology, history, philosophy, political science, economics, education, cultural studies, and the social sciences in general), and close consideration should be given to a number of directly related subjects and issues (peace studies, media literacy, environmental education, intercultural relations, etc.). There is no set answer, list, or menu to the question of how to *do* democracy, or how to create a *thicker* democracy. Rather, as suggested in the earlier list of what might be done, an amalgam of thinking, interrogation, critical analysis, experience, and humility may lead to a more meaningful and sustainable democracy, one that seeks to inspire and cultivate critical engagement of all people and interests. A more radical determination toward a more radical democracy requires thinking well outside of constricted, hegemonic boundaries, and must address how power works (Hill & Boxley, 2007).

How does transformative leadership fit into this discussion? One might argue that the discussion would remain theoretical, conceptual, and academic without considering the real-world problems and challenges that encapsulate the educational arena, experience, and institution. How do we actually promote change—not just the discourse of change, which is surely important—but the actual process of change? For it to be transformative, it would be important to consider diverse epistemologies, values, strategies, and variables, and, especially, to understand how power works (Shields, 2010). Power is not neutral, nor is democracy, and change of a transformative type can only happen when there is serious, critical engagement. Thus, for the purposes of this chapter, the administrative class must be attuned to the power dynamic. Administrators are not employed simply to carry out orders: They are not soldiers on the battlefield. They provide, one would hope, insight, knowledge, intelligence, and compassion as to how to consider change.

If administrators, individually and as a group, are dissuaded from considering alternative perspectives, as was once the case when women were not taken seriously within the leadership realm, then meaningful transformative change in and through education would be almost impossible. Transformative leaders must be courageous to point out institutional deficiencies that harm groups and populations, and they must be open to that which they do not know. How they are taught, trained, cultivated, and promoted are important pieces of the equation. I have argued that critical pedagogy may be one area in which administrators could benefit a great deal, even if they, at first, react negatively. In a nutshell, administrators are a necessary piece of the puzzle of promoting change in formal education. The issue of whether change is transformative or not depends on how we evaluate power, from what angle, and who is doing the evaluating.

Regarding the 50 proposals enunciated earlier, it is clear that administrators would have an important role to play in endorsing, debating, accepting, shaping, implementing, and evaluating the implications, ramifications, and measures related to them. Such change requires vision and transformative leadership, not merely leaders who oversee incremental change. Are the proposals too radical or not radical enough; too precipitous, too poorly conceived, too costly, too jarring, and so on? I can only answer that they form part of what I call the critical pedagogy of democracy, and they could lead to transformative change. Are they the only proposals to transform education? Most certainly not, but, given the history, political economy, traditions, and context of education, I believe that they are certainly worth considering.

Neither Paulo Freire, nor Joe Kincheloe, nor other well-known critical pedagogues, I believe, would want students, educators, and others to simply replicate what they've done or to simply believe that what they've experienced and developed in theory and in praxis is the ultimate answer. The quest for critical humility and radical love encourages all of us to seek new, innovative, and reflective thoughts and actions in the quest for a more decent society. What Freire, Kincheloe, and others offer us, however, is an enormous wealth and insightful archive of *constructed* knowledge, something that is, I would argue, of tremendous value to those wishing to have a more conscious connection to what society was, is, and is evolving into. The critical pedagogy of democracy is not about counting votes, but relates more fundamentally to an unending critical interrogation of the human experience, focused on humane encounters, social justice, peace, a more equitable and respectful distribution of resources, a more dignified and just recognition of indigenous cultures, and an acknowledgement that hegemonic forces exist that marginalize peoples at home and abroad.

Does your vote count? (Or we might ask, *Are our schools democratic?*) It might (or they might be), but there are a multitude of other factors that are most likely more germane—not to mention that voting, in and of itself, does not make a democracy. As argued throughout my book, any definition of democracy that omits a central place for a meaningful, engaged, and critical education is problematic. *People* construct a democracy, not political parties and institutions (albeit they are relevant), and, therefore, *people* must construct their political, economic, social, cultural, and philosophic destinies. The people are the ones who define their circumstances, values, affiliations, interpersonal relations, and essence to live. Yet, as per the central hypothesis of this book, the people must also be vigilant and suspicious of how power affects their daily lives, their abilities, their relations, and their connection to the world. Education is the key intersecting vehicle that can reinforce or, conversely, interrupt patriotic bondage, racialized marginalization, essentialized visions of poverty and impoverishment, and an uncritical assessment of how power works. Freire and Kincheloe offer much inspiration for this journey, and their willingness to question and accept questions provides for a vibrant, dynamic, and engaged democracy within the spirit of critical pedagogy. Alongside the mantra of the *alter-mondialiste* movement that *another world is possible*, I would like to conclude by suggesting that *another democracy is possible*.

Postscript: Good People in Difficult Jobs

For five years, from 2005 to 2010, I had the pleasure to teach in an educational leadership doctoral program at Youngstown State University. I taught three of the mandatory courses—Qualitative Methods, Theories of Inquiry, and Diversity and Leadership—providing me with significant exposure to the students, in addition to sitting on dissertation committees. The students, who were largely white, with a majority being male, and were, for the most part, principals and superintendents, came from rural, suburban, and urban school boards within a roughly two-hour radius. My learning experience in working with the students was not only important but also transformative. I learned that my views, concerns, opinions, beliefs, values, ideology, proclivities, idiosyncrasies, and way of being may not be common, shared, accepted, and embraced by others.

I learned that sustained and meaningful critical analysis, discussion, and engagement can help transform thinking. I refer to myself because I learned a great deal from the students, from their questions, critiques, presentations, papers, justifications, and positioning as students, people, and colleagues. Much of the material I presented was not necessarily what might come quickly to mind when thinking of educational leadership; for instance, we focused on epistemology and what we do not know, which is not easy for educational leaders, when thinking about theory. We started with what we did and did not know about Cuba, and why, and what the signification was for us in deconstructing political reality and intercultural relations; and when we started to study diversity, I had them focus on white power and privilege rather than the much-vaunted benefits of a heterogeneous society. In both cases, the initial reaction was: *Why this?* and *What does this have to do with what we're all about?*

I recall a professor of political science from my undergraduate studies warning that we should not focus too narrowly on the target, lest we miss the framework. Thus for me, during this period, the objective was to engage and accept, with humility, that we were limited in our knowledge, and, moreover, that knowledge is socially constructed. We also sought to ingratiate ourselves in the comfort that we could change, perhaps not as radically and quickly as we would like, but for the better, in seeking to refocus our comprehension of our limitations. Ultimately, the process of dialectical engagement in this way aimed to liberate us from the strictures and structures that are ensconced in hegemonic relations, which limit how we consider and address social justice.

Did the students benefit? I can only speak for myself, but the experience was one that instilled in me the notion that transformative leadership requires a process, humility, and a rejection of rubrics, matrices, tools, instruments, and measures that provide one answer only (or, rather, one hegemonic viewpoint only). Administrators are surely a fundamental part of the change equation, and engaging them in ways that encourage transverse thinking can help facilitate change. As important as this is, the next and even more transformative step involves confronting power, not sustaining it, and transformative leadership will reach its full potential when this becomes a central feature of the educational debate, not a peripheral one.

Notes

1. Parts of this chapter borrow from a book I recently completed: Carr, P. (2010). *Does Your Vote Count? Democracy and Critical Pedagogy*. New York: Peter Lang.
2. As elaborated in Carr (2010), formal, normative, hegemonic interpretations of democracy based on electoral processes to the behest of critical, meaningful engagement through education can be understood through a thin to thick spectrum of democracy, with the former (electoral processes) being more at the thin end, and the latter (critical engagement) being more at the thick end.

References

Au, W. (2007). Epistemology of the oppressed: The dialectics of Paulo Freire's *Theory of knowledge. Journal for Critical Education Policy Studies, 5*(2). Retrieved from http://www.jceps.com/index.php?pageID= article&articleID=100

Bellamy Foster, J., Holleman, H., & McChesney, R. (2008). The U.S. imperial triangle and military spending. *Monthly Review, 60*(5), 1–19.

Brosio, R. (2003). High-stakes tests: Reasons to strive for better Marx. *Journal for Critical Education Policy Studies, 1*(2). Retrieved from http://www.jceps.com/index.php?pageID= home&issueID=17

Carr, P. R. (2007). Experiencing democracy through neo-liberalism: The role of social justice in education. *Journal of Critical Education Policy Studies, 5*(2). Retrieved from http://www.jceps.com/index.php?pageID=article&articleID=104

Carr, P. R. (2008a). "But what can I do?": Fifteen things education students can do to transform themselves in/through/with education. *International Journal of Critical Pedagogy, 1*(2), 81–97. Retrieved from http://freire.mcgill.ca/ojs/index.php/home/article/view/56/31

Carr, P. R. (2008b). Educating for democracy: With or without social justice? *Teacher Education Quarterly*, fall, 117–136.

Carr, P. R. (2008c). Educators and education for democracy: Moving beyond "thin" democracy. *Inter-American Journal of Education and Democracy, 1*(2), 147–165. Retrieved from http://www.riedijed.org/english/articulo.php?idRevista=4&idArticulo=16

Carr, P. R. (2010). *Does your vote count? Democracy and critical pedagogy*. New York: Peter Lang.

Darder, A., & Miron, L. F. (2006). Critical pedagogy in a time of uncertainty: A call to action. *Cultural Studies—Critical Methodologies, 6*(1), 5–20.

Denzin, N. K. (2009). Critical pedagogy and democratic life or a radical democratic pedagogy. *Cultural Studies—Critical Methodologies, 9*(3), 379–397.

Engels, J. (2007). Floating bombs encircling our shores: Post–9/11 rhetorics of piracy and terrorism. *Cultural Studies—Critical Methodologies, 7*(3), 326–349.

Fischman, G. E., & McLaren, P. (2005). Rethinking critical pedagogy and the Gramscian and Freirean legacies: From organic to committed intellectuals or critical pedagogy, commitment, and praxis. *Cultural Studies—Critical Methodologies, 5*(4), 425–447.

Freire, P. (1973). *Education for critical consciousness*. New York: The Continuum Publishing Company.

Freire, P. (1985). *The Politics of education*. South Hadley, MA: Bergin & Garvey Publishers.

Freire, P. (1998). *Pedagogy of freedom: Ethics, democracy, and civic courage*. Lanham, MD: Rowman & Littlefield.

Freire, P. (2004). *Pedagogy of indignation*. Boulder, CO: Paradigm Publishers.

Freire, P. (1973/2005). *Pedagogy of the oppressed*. New York: Continuum.

Gandin, L. A., & Apple, M. (2005). Thin versus thick democracy in education: Porto Alegre and the creation of alternatives to neo-liberalism. *International Studies in Sociology of Education, 12*(2), 99–116.

Giroux, H. (2005). The passion of the right: Religious fundamentalism and the crisis of democracy. *Cultural Studies—Critical Methodologies, 5*(3), 309–317.

Giroux, H., & Giroux, S. S. (2006). Challenging neo-liberalism's new world order: The promise of critical pedagogy. *Cultural Studies—Critical Methodologies, 6*(1), 21–32.

Gordon, S. P., Smyth, J., & Diehl, J. (2008). The Iraq War, "sound science," and "evidence-based" educational reform: How the Bush administration uses deception, manipulation, and subterfuge to advance its chosen ideology. *Journal for Critical Education Policy Studies, 6*(2), 173–204. Retrieved from http://www.jceps.com/PDFs/6-2-10.pdf

Hill, D., & Boxley, S. (2007). Critical teacher education for economic, environmental and social justice: An ecosocialist manifesto. *Journal for Critical Education Policy Studies, 5*(2). Retrieved from http://www. jceps.com/index.php?pageID=article&articleID=96

Kellner, D., & Share, J. (2007). Critical media literacy, democracy, and the reconstruction of education. In Macedo, D., and Steinberg, S. (Eds.), *Media literacy: A reader* (pp. 3–23). New York: Peter Lang.

Kincheloe, J. L. (2007). Critical pedagogy in the twenty-first century. In McLaren, P., & Kincheloe, J. (Eds.), *Critical pedagogy: Where are we now?* (pp. 9–42). New York: Peter Lang.

Kincheloe, J. L. (2008a). *Critical pedagogy: Primer*. New York: Peter Lang.

Kincheloe, J. L. (2008b). *Knowledge and critical pedagogy: An introduction*. London: Springer.

Kincheloe, J. L., & Steinberg, S. R. (2006). An ideology of miseducation: Countering the pedagogy of empire. *Cultural Studies—Critical Methodologies, 6*(1), 33–51.

Lund, D. E., & Carr, P. R. (Eds.). (2008). *"Doing" democracy: Striving for political literacy and social justice*. New York: Peter Lang.

Macedo, D., & Steinberg, S. (2007). *Media literacy: A reader*. New York: Peter Lang.

Macrine, S. (Ed.). (2009). *Critical pedagogy in uncertain times: Hopes and possibilities*. New York: Palgrave Macmillan.

McLaren, P., & Kincheloe, J. L. (Eds.). (2007). *Critical pedagogy: Where are we now?* New York: Peter Lang.

Shields, C. M. (2004). Dialogic leadership for social justice: Overcoming pathologies of silence. *Educational Administration Quarterly, 40*(1), 109–113.

Shields, C. M. (2010). Transformative leadership: Working for equity in diverse contexts. *Educational Administration Quarterly, 46*(4), 558–589.

Shields, C. M., & Edwards, M. M. (2005). *Dialogue is not just talk: A new ground for educational leadership*. New York: Peter Lang.

Steinberg, S., & Kincheloe, J. (Eds.). (2009). *Christotainment: Selling Jesus through popular culture*. Boulder, CO: Westview Press.

Westheimer, J. (2008). *No child left thinking: Democracy at-risk in American schools* (Democratic Dialog series, no. 17). Ottawa, Canada: Democratic Dialog, University of Ottawa.

Westheimer, J., & Kahne, J. (2003). Reconnecting education to democracy: Democratic dialogs. *Phi Delta Kappan, 85*(1), 9–14.

Westheimer, J., & Kahne, J. (2004). What kind of citizen? The politics of educating for democracy. *American Educational Research Journal, 41*(2), 237–269.

Willinsky, J. (1998). *Learning to divide the world: Education at empire's end*. Minneapolis: University of Minnesota Press.

CHAPTER 8

Race and Pedagogy

Aaron David Gresson III

We blame P–12 teachers and university professors for the "failure" of the schools. We blame them on a lot of levels. We blame their professional teacher education; we blame what they teach; we blame how they teach. The simplistic and punitive reform efforts that have resulted in the creation of standards and the development of high stakes testing reflect the fact that, for over twenty years, teachers in public schools and institutions of higher education have been blamed for all that is wrong with education. —*Perry Marker (2003, 1)*

When Frederick Douglass's master insisted that he not be taught to read and write, he was addressing the role of pedagogy in learning. Defined broadly as the theory and practice of teaching, pedagogy has been alternatively defined by Henry Giroux (1994, 281) as "a vehicle for transmitting knowledge." According to Giroux, pedagogy not only transmits knowledge: it shapes, enhances, and limits what we are aware of and how we use and broaden our minds.

Given this view of pedagogy, Douglass was exposed to several pedagogies: the master's; the master's wife's; and his own evolving lived experience of slavery and White people. From these diverse pedagogies, he learned to challenge slavery and yet remain positive toward the White abolitionists who helped him gain his own freedom and advocate for slavery's termination. Further, Douglass's life was clear evidence that the education gap created by slavery could be overcome. For hundreds of years, moreover, African Americans have achieved academically and assumed a significant role in the growth of the nation (Benson-Hale, 1986).

A major achievement gap continues to exist between African Americans and White Americans. As a result, "race and pedagogy" has become an increasingly significant subtheme in the race and education discourse. This subtheme of "race and pedagogy" is made more complex and pressing for prospective teachers because of another issue: blaming teachers for a wide range of national problems.

In the epigraph, Perry Marker identifies the main race-related issue raised with respect to teachers: the role of curriculum and instruction in continuing the gap in achievement. Given that people have very different notions of what "race" and "pedagogy" do or ought to mean, there are tensions that continue to plague efforts to reduce the education gap. Some put the failure of certain minorities to do better in school down to human factors, including cultural, familial, and individual flaws (Thernstrom & Thernstrom, 2003). On the other hand, some see racism as the continuing underpinning for both social and educational inequality (Bell, 1992). In this chapter, we will review some of the tensions and interventional trends associated with the topic of "race and pedagogy." We begin with a closer look at what it means to be an effective teacher for those students identified as academically underachieving.

Some Aspects of Effective Teaching for Educational Equity

Pedagogy is concerned ultimately with teaching. What makes for quality teaching? Different people will identify different things: teacher preparation or excellence, teacher care, supportive administrators, sufficient material resources, parental and community involvement, and so on. Here, I want to focus on several elements that bear more specifically on the matter of equitable education—that is, an education that allows all students to achieve to their abilities and potential.

Scholars have identified many critical elements of quality teaching that move toward or promote equity. These are:

- Teachers' content knowledge and pedagogy (Saphier, 1997; Wiggins & McTighe, 1998)

- Teachers' cultural responsiveness (Gay, 2000; Howard, 2003; Ladson-Billings, 1994; Milner, 2003)

- School organization and structures that promote and support ongoing collaborative learning among the stakeholders—students, parents, teachers, and community

- Teacher-pupil relationships

[handwritten margin note: "essential for quality teaching"]

These four foci or elements have been identified as essential for quality teaching. They have been viewed as especially significant for students identified as struggling or at risk of failure in public schools. Minorities, especially African American and Latino students, have been among the most often cited groups requiring quality teachers (Darling-Hammond, 1998, 2006). For this reason, reform efforts have paid particular attention to these four elements. But what precisely do these elements refer to?

School Knowledge and Pedagogy

The first of these elements pertains to the observation that beyond school knowledge as curriculum content and material, there is a "school knowledge" (Anyon, 1981) that gets expressed differently in schools according to class and other differentiating characteristics. That is, quite often, very different content is presented to different students according to their class. For instance, consider Jean Anyon's study of five schools, distinguished by class (working, middle, elite). She found that even when the textbooks were similar in some courses, the way the material was presented was very different, with important consequences for how students saw themselves both as learners and as future citizens and workers.

Research has shown that student achievement and performance is very much influenced by teacher assumptions and beliefs (Brophy, 1983; Brophy & Good, 1986; Rist, 1970). This is important to understand because a variety of reforms have been based on understanding and influencing teacher beliefs. We will return to this issue below. Summarizing research on the importance of quality teachers, the following passage from the Teachers 21 Web site illustrates a basic attitude and pedagogical orientation characterizing effective teaching:

> Teaching rigorous content knowledge means teaching not only facts, but also deconstructing and explicitly teaching the habits, skills, and practices … associated with a discipline or academic practice. For example,

a science teacher might break apart and teach discrete aspects of writing a laboratory report, including understanding terms and concepts (e.g.: hypothesis, conclusion), the purpose and function of each section of the lab report, communicating results in different forms (text, graph, pictures), etc. If the laboratory report required students to work in groups, the teacher might also explicitly discuss and teach expectations, roles, and routines regarding working in groups, and have in place a system for students to discuss with the teacher not only benefits, but also problems or obstacles that arise through working in groups.

Rigorous teaching, as described above, can and does take place across classes and racial groups (Haberman, 1995; Ladson-Billings, 1994). In addition to the strategic deconstructive skills described as important for effective teaching, effective practitioners have been identified by others. For instance, Martin Haberman has identified excellent teachers of minority children identified as "star teachers." These teachers are both warm and fair; they also model or personify discipline. They do not blame the students' underachievement on possible personal weaknesses, family background, or the community at large. Rather, they provide safe, secure environments for their students and identify ways of avoiding the institutional pitfalls that can hurt their pupils.

The reform implication of this element—teacher mastery of knowledge and pedagogy—is simple: the teacher must not only know what and how to teach subject matter content (math, science, social studies), she or he must also recognize that students learn from teachers things not in the books. This has been called "the hidden curriculum" (Jackson, 1968) because these ideas, values, and beliefs are not always stated. Nonetheless, students learn attitudes and strategies about life and learning through the things said and done in schools by teachers, administrators, parents, and other students (Meighan, 1981).

Efforts have been made to make sure that all teachers are well prepared, especially those chosen to teach minorities. Citing the research evidence for this policy goal, Linda Darling-Hammond (1998, 1) notes:

> Studies of underprepared teachers consistently find that they are less effective with students and that they have difficulty with curriculum development, classroom management, student motivation, and teaching strategies. With little knowledge about how children grow, learn, and develop, or about what to do to support their learning, these teachers are less likely to understand students' learning styles and differences, to anticipate students' knowledge and potential difficulties, or to plan and redirect instruction to meet students' needs. Nor are they likely to see it as their job to do so, often blaming the students if their teaching is not successful.

Darling-Hammond's ending thought echoes Martin Haberman's view cited earlier. Recall how Haberman's star teachers do not blame the students for their own lack of preparation. But the problem goes further: teacher expertise and the quality of the curricula taught are interrelated. This relationship pertains to the relevance of the materials being taught. This is the second element of effective teaching identified above.

Culturally Relevant Curriculum and Pedagogy

We begin with another passage from Darling-Hammond (1998, 1):

> Teacher expertise and curriculum quality are interrelated, because a challenging curriculum requires an expert teacher. Research has found that both students and teachers are tracked: that is, the most expert teachers teach the most demanding courses to the most advantaged students, while lower-track students assigned to less able teachers receive lower-quality teaching and less demanding material. Assignment to tracks is also related to race: even when grades and test scores are comparable, black students are more likely to be assigned to lower-track, nonacademic classes.

I often begin my courses in education and human services by helping my students to see their "shared fate" (Kirk, 1964) with their future students and clients. As future teachers and human service workers, my students have already been tracked. Like those teachers discussed by Darling-Hammond, my student teachers will be working most often with the less advantaged students and "multiproblem families." They will, like their clientele, frequently find less than favorable work conditions, institutional resources, and social approval (Pinderhughes, 1995). In addition, they will often be misunderstood by the very people they seek to help. This mutual mistrust and shared distress with the system will frequently pit them against each other (Gresson, 2004).

I include this kind of thinking in my students' coursework as a part of my pedagogy; more precisely, I try to share these kinds of thoughts and reflections as part of the "hidden curriculum" that I believe to be relevant to them. If they can see me working to give them things beyond the book, outside the typically spoken classroom ideas, perhaps they can learn additional ways of relating to their students and clients when they get out into the world.

Culturally relevant curriculum and pedagogy means that the teacher recognizes that the learner begins with a worldview—including ways of taking in new information—that reflects the home and community environments. What is taught in the classroom, if it is relevant to this dimension of the student, becomes powerful precisely because it invites or draws the student into developing or adopting more powerful ways of seeing, relating, and working.

Ladson-Billings (1990) views culturally relevant or sensitive pedagogy as teaching that uses the student's culture to help them achieve success. As I indicated above, all successful teachers must respond at some level to the students' cultural context to help them succeed. As it applies to minorities such as African Americans and Latinos, this means that such pedagogy focuses on teaching the academic subject matter with rigor but in a manner that does not dislodge or alienate the student from her or his culture or personal sense of self or identity.

The critical concern with curriculum that is culturally relevant is captured by Sharon Nelson-Barber and Elise Trumbull Estrin (1995, 174) in their discussion of making mathematics and science culturally relevant to Native American students:

> Many American Indian students have extensive knowledge of mathematics and science-knowledge that is rooted in naturalist traditions common to Native communities and arrived at through observation and direct experience. Because many Indian communities follow traditional subsistence lifestyles, parents routinely expose their offspring to survival routines, often immersing the children in decision-making situations in which they must interpret new experiences in light of previous ones. … Unfortunately, a majority of teachers recognize neither Indian students' knowledge nor their considerable learning strategies.

These authors go on to make a parallel observation regarding the interconnection of culturally relevant content and pedagogy:

> American Indian ways of teaching, such as modeling and providing for long periods of observation and practice by children, are quite harmonious with constructivist notions of learning. "Mainstream" teachers can look to their American Indian colleagues for such examples of culturally-responsive practice as well as insights into how to interpret student performance on classroom tasks.

The competent or effective teacher must learn to learn from her or his students, and from their families and communities. The inevitable differences in lived experience among humans mandate that we all engage in a certain degree of intercultural communication if we are to work effectively together. The emphasis on collaborative school communities is one consequence of this perspective. Collaboration thus constitutes a third element in the promotion of effective teaching.

Collaborative School Communities as Pedagogy

Collaboration is a conscious strategy for teaching in diverse, racially mixed communities. This strategy derives, in part, from evidence that teacher interactions and relationships with minorities and their families have often failed to promote quality education (Epstein, 1995). In addition, research on effective collaborative community-school partnerships has strengthened the belief that shared governance is important.

There are at least two important dimensions or forms of collaboration: that among teachers and that between teachers, their schools, and the community at large. The first form of collaboration has particular significance for the ways that instruction in literacy, mathematics, and other subjects might be taught within a given team of teachers. Here, for instance, teachers' pedagogy becomes more inclusive and pertinent to student interests and needs by a willingness to share decision making. This sharing feature is inclusive of differences; it also assumes or mandates mutual caring and support (Irwin & Farr, 2004; Newmann & Wehlage, 1995). The relevance of such collaboration to issues of race and difference in the classroom and school has been stated in this way by Teachers 21:

> Within a collaborative culture, educators can work together to ensure that issues of race, class, and achievement are not undiscussable …, but become a central focus of all conversations about student performance. These conversations would have the potential to inform not only individual teacher practice and shared school beliefs, but might also have the power to shape organizational structures. For example, a learning community might examine student achievement patterns (as measured by standardized tests, attendance, disciplinary actions, etc.) to critically evaluate and reform the ways aspects of the school itself might contribute to these patterns.

Working with one's colleagues is very important to the achievement of educational equity. But there is another dimension of collaboration that must also be addressed. This is teacher-student interaction and relationships.

Teacher-Student Relationships

The vast literature on minority student dropouts has been particularly concerned with unproductive teacher-student interactions (Faith, 2007; Miller, 1998). In this context, the overriding observation has been that teachers, especially new and inexperienced ones, frequently fail to develop relationships with minority students that foster resilience and a sense of belonging. Resilience and a sense of belonging are two of the most critical factors helping high school completion.

The *failed relationship* is itself pedagogical: it teaches the child that he or she is not valued by the context. Moreover, the child experiences that he or she is not expected to achieve. This has been the critical, repeated finding of research dealing with teaching practices and attitudes. As the educational publishing company ScholarCentric argued on their Web site:

> Not surprisingly, researchers have found strong links between school connections and student resiliency. When researchers compared high-risk Mexican-American students with significantly high grades and those with significantly low grades, they found that the resilient students reported significantly higher levels of family and peer support, positive ties to school, high levels of teacher feedback, and placed higher value on school. The most significant predictor of success was the student's sense of belonging to the school.

Other studies report similar findings. According to Loyce Caruthers (2006, 1):

> The nature of teacher-student relationships strongly affects student performance, including the decision to drop out of school. A study of high school dropouts among Native American students concluded that dropouts perceived teachers as not caring about them and not providing them sufficient assistance in their work.

These four elements of effective teaching are not discrete in any final sense; they work together to bring about the desired outcome of an effective teacher-pupil exchange that can be described as academic success. But knowing what is needed is one thing, achieving it another. For this reason, in part, there have been many educational reform efforts made in the past twenty-five years (Hampel, 1996; Ravitch,

1983). These have met with varying degrees of success (Stringfield, 2000). Several of these have, nonetheless, commanded considerable attention, both positive and negative.

Some Reform Initiatives in "Race and Pedagogy"

There have been many initiatives aimed at changing the ways schools are structured, teachers are prepared, and curriculum constructed and presented. There have also been broader reform initiatives or positions developed and championed. These initiatives are not always distinguishable from each other or mutually exclusive. Nonetheless, for our purposes, we may divide and consider them in two categories: (1) race-focused initiatives and (2) critical pedagogies. Both categories have social justice and educational equity as important goals. However, they differ in their emphases on achieving these ends.

Some Race-Focused Initiatives

Multiculturalism as Pedagogy. Multicultural education became a major theme and initiative within education in the 1970s (Banks, 2000; Gresson, 2004). Because education prior to the 1960s emphasized a one-sided, Eurocentric understanding of values, beliefs, and the way things ought to be, some challenged it. The argument was that the nation is pluralistic, made up of diverse groups with multiple perspectives on reality and what is important; accordingly, schools should reflect these various perspectives, particularly with respect to ancestry and cultural traditions. The belief was and is that so much of school success is due to how a person fits into the school culture.

From this view, for example, it was argued that curricular materials in reading that talked only about Dick, Jane, baby Sally, and Spot did more than merely teach one how to read: it also taught one that the world that these fictional children inhabited was the only, the best, and the preferred world. Certainly, I as a child saw the world through their eyes and never even associated myself with having the things and experiences common to them. To be sure, I did learn to read and write despite the common minority experience in segregated schools of the pre-1960s: less learning resources, including the discarded textbooks and materials of White students (Kozol, 1991, 2005).

Multiculturalism, according to some scholars, largely concerns itself with being sure that everyone gets some recognition in the curriculum. From this view, attitudes of "prejudice" due to ignorance must be replaced with tolerance. Tolerance can lead to an intervention or prescription "inclusive knowledge" or curricular enrichment. The goal is cultural pluralism—different cultures living harmoniously side by side in democratic unity.

This view of multiculturalism is simplistic, but it does represent the picture many have of this vast initiative. The reasoning behind the rejection of multiculturalism is complex. It actually has several elements and critics. These include:

- Conservative critics who believe that America's greatness is due to everyone more or less accepting a single, necessarily Euro-American cultural orientation (Bork, 1996; Kirk, 1993; Schlesinger, 1998)

- Radical critics who see multiculturalism as failing to sufficiently characterize and challenge the structural inequities that fuel the political, cultural, and social dominance of the Euro-American and capitalist forces (Kincheloe & Steinberg, 1997)

- Progressive critics who see the assumptions underpinning multiculturalism as flawed (Carter, 2000; Marable, 1992)

- Afrocentric critics who see Eurocentric cultural dominance as deadly to the ultimate forging of a worldview that African peoples (and others) can use to further their collective interests (Asante, 1980/1987)

These various perspectives on multiculturalism seem not to greatly alter the commitment to promote the democratic ideal of cross-educating people about the positives of diversity and pluralism in the United States (Banks, 2000, 2004). They do, nonetheless, point to the perceived need for ways of getting beyond the specifics of race, if not racism, in the effort to further an all-inclusive educational agenda. Recent illustrations of this shift include renewed interest in teaching and modeling social justice and democracy (Ayers, Hunt, & Quinn, 1998). This model has much to commend it, especially the focus on traditional American values regarding liberty, equality, and fair play. But the ultimate viability of such initiatives depends on a critical mass of individuals and groups prepared to undergo the explorations of self, oppression, and the discovery of mutually enhancing experiences (Gresson, 2004).

Afrocentric Education and Culturally Appropriate Pedagogy. Thomas Jefferson said that observers should not return to Africa to judge whether or not enslaved Africans were intellectually equal to Europeans or Asians. His view regarding the Africans has been championed by many since the eighteenth century. It has also been challenged by many, including several African Americans. The movement associated with those who have looked to Africa for evidence of cultural equality or superiority has been called Afrocentrism. This movement emphasizes the contributions of African cultures and a distinctive group or racial identity to the world. It necessarily challenges the attitude expressed by Jefferson and the educational practices traditionally associated with views of European superiority (Eurocentrism). Some of the ideas associated with an Afrocentric worldview—a view that claims African peoples share distinctive, perhaps essential qualities—have generated both opposition (Ginwright, 2004) and support (Allen, 2004).

Afrocentrism begins with Africa, not the United States, to forge a set of images or narratives regarding how African peoples constructed their values and worldview. This strategic return to Africa has been aimed, in part, at offsetting the near total refusal to acknowledge that Blacks had civilizations or compelling cultural traditions prior to the arrival of the White man. Molefi Asante (1980/1987) has viewed the return to places such as Egypt to reclaim a civilized past to construct an "Afrocentric idea" as a necessary corrective to the intentional erasure of historical facts and cultural ways by those oppressing Africans and their descendents.

Nigerian-born Afro-Canadian scholar George Dei (1994, 17) offers a related understanding of the theory:

> Afrocentricity as an intellectual paradigm must focus on addressing the structural impediments to the education of the African student by engaging her or him to identify with her or his history, heritage, and culture. To be successful the Afrocentric pedagogue must move away from a manipulation of the "victim status and exploiting white guilt" to work toward finding solutions to pressing problems of educating students of African descent. (Moses, 1991, 88)

From this perspective, African American academic achievement is aided by positive self-esteem; however, this self-affirmation has been truncated by the repeated, mass advertising campaign that presents everything important as the achievement of White men. Without necessarily denying the importance of positive self-esteem for academic achievement, some scholars have called a return to Africa a myth (Mary Lefkowitz, 1996). This dimension of the debate regarding Afrocentrism continues. Still, some have been willing to place African traditions and values in the forefront of curriculum and pedagogy. Dei has described the matter in this way in his essay on Afrocentric education (1994, 17):

> For the Afrocentric educator, Afrocentricity is a commitment to a pedagogy that is political education. It is a form of education intended to equip students and teachers with the requisite cultural capital to work toward the eradication of the structural conditions that marginalize the existence of certain segments of the school population.

A major aspect of the Afrocentric initiative has been to identify traditions, beliefs, values, and styles of survival that were lost to African Americans with enslavement. The hope has been, in part, to gain a legitimate enhancement of self-esteem. The argument has been that much of the education gap for African Americans is that they have been "miseducated" (Woodson, 1935); they lack knowledge of their past and many of the habits needed to compete in the contemporary world. In such a context, moreover, they are seen to permit maltreatment or misrepresentation by White educationalists—teachers, administrators, policymakers, and researchers.

The rise of Afrocentric pedagogy has been due to this particular perspective on traditional minority educational practice and policy. A wide range of discussion has accompanied the pursuit of a specific set of curricular and pedagogical practices aimed at improving the intellectual (cognitive) and emotional (affective) life of African Americans. For instance, the focus on addressing the language needs of those students who come to school with speaking habits different from the middle-class teacher has led to the so-called Ebonics debate. Ebonics is a term used to describe the dialect associated with many African Americans who have learned a variant of English that has been influenced by traditional African languages. These children, according to mainstream views, merely don't know how to speak proper English. They, like their Latino and Asian peers for whom English is not the first language, are seen as needing to learn English—pure and simple.

But from the Afrocentric view, like that held by many bilingual educators and scholars, knowledge of the non-English, first language is helpful in teaching both English and the other subject matters. Language has been a major theme in discussions of academic achievement. Native Americans were among the first to be "reeducated" about the relative place of English in their lives (Spring, 2004). African Americans, more recently, featured in debates around the role of Ebonics in learning; and there has been a persistent tension around bilingual education and its relation to learning among subgroups such as Latinos (Soto, 2001), Native Americans (Garcia, 2002), and Asian Americans (Mouw & Xie, 1999).

Moreover, the Afrocentric focus shares another feature with bilingualism and biculturalism: all reflect the fact that minorities are increasingly less a "deficit" than an "asset" for the United States. More precisely, the student population is increasingly made up of students from bilingual and bicultural backgrounds. As Eugene Garcia (2002, 74) wrote in his integrative essay on Native American language recovery:

> Initial signs from efforts by the Navajo and Pueblo cultures in reclaiming indigenous languages are hopeful. Others, including a more optimistic Hinton (1994), conclude that limited progress is being made in retarding the overall phenomenon of language loss among US indigenous people. Clearly, as we address issues of bilingualism and schooling in the US, this issue will continue to require attention. In the US, with the roots of bilingual education in the domain of social justice, attention to the human, particularly education costs, can be related to Native language extinction. At the core of this extinction, Fishman (1991) reminds us, is the issue of "rooted identity." Cesar Chavez also reminded us that in the struggle for education equities in the US, "equities are not about equalities but about dignity." In essence, bilingual educators in the US have come to realize that self-worth is a critical element of educating language-minority students. Crawford (1995) appropriately points out that language and cultural loss is a characteristic of dispersed and disempowered communities; those that may need their language and culture most. It is not a phenomenon of privileged communities.

The emphasis on *self-worth* as a central feature of academic achievement is what has inspired supporters of Afrocentric and other bicultural educational initiatives. The importance of this emphasis seems self-evident to those who recall that race-based oppression has always sought to strip away self-esteem and self-care. Thus, while there are those who point to the apparent "reverse racism" of Afrocentric perspectives on education, this continues to be a preferred strategy among those concerned with helping African American youth to succeed within seemingly hostile environments (Morris, 2003, 2004).

Culturally appropriate teaching pedagogies for African American males, within such a context, might include hip-hop culture—that is, music, songs, poetry, and videos (Hall, 2007). The goal of this form of urban pedagogy is to engage the students by forming a bridge between their lived world and that of the teacher and school. In making her argument for the use of hip-hop as a pedagogy of engagement, Hall (2007, 40) said:

> Several scholars and socially and politically conscious artists are advocating liberatory education and pedagogy to educate a new generation of hip hoppers. Liberatory education has its roots in the teachings of Carter G. Woodson, Anna Julia Cooper and W. E. B. Du Bois. Aldridge wrote that Woodson, the father of African American history month, believed that education for African Americans should be realistic, rigorous, and firmly rooted in the culture and historical experiences of African people. This sentiment is shared by socially and politically conscious rappers such as Ishues and KRS-One who believe that "education and schooling as practiced in the United States denies students access to the truth and provides them with illusions rather than an understanding of reality." (Alridge, 2005, 240)

Other emergent instructional approaches share the emphasis on engagement. The idea of culturally appropriate pedagogy has been introduced to address this issue. From this perspective, the overall academic program—mathematics, science, and social studies—should attempt to make cultural sense vis-à-vis the background of students from different racial and ethnic groups. Assuming that cultural context strongly impacts learning, this orientation advocates for such practices as the hip-hop curriculum. Among the various ideas associated with culturally appropriate pedagogy is that of constructivism. This theory of learning suggests that humans learn or construct knowledge by relating new information to their prior knowledge and experience. As pedagogy, culturally relevant teaching uses the learner's experience to introduce new knowledge.

Many assume that the constructivist approach is merely good commonsense teaching. But the idea of culturally relevant pedagogy, which employs constructivist thinking, has been challenged for its potential inappropriateness. In particular, Guoping Zhao (2007) has noted the potential for over-emphasizing differences that are not pertinent to a given instructional task. Zhao cautions against pigeonholing students merely because of an assumed cultural relevance in their learning style. Nonetheless, some scholars have found it useful to explore alternative pedagogical strategies for teaching some minorities. For instance, Sean Coleman (2002) has reported preliminary findings of research employing culturally appropriate teaching pedagogies on specific mathematic exercises with fourth- and sixth-grade at-risk students. Placing students in both individualistic and communal learning situations, he found "that learning and performing fraction problem solving tasks under a communal condition allows for significant improvement on individual performance of such tasks than in the individual cultural condition."

Prospective teachers can perhaps best view these and related reform initiatives as strategies that can complement their own self-reflective, constructive efforts. The possible temptation to adopt approaches unfamiliar to one, even in the name of cultural sensitivity, can be problematic; so it is best to only adopt new techniques thoughtfully.

Antiracist Education. Audrey Thompson (1995, 1) has noted:

> To many critics, anti-racist pedagogy has all the earmarks of propaganda. Certainly the popular media portray anti-racist and other progressive pedagogies as extremist, humorless, strident, and biased. The catch phrase "politically correct" has become shorthand for an ideologically mandated equality that violates common sense, a superficial rhetoric thrust upon a sensible populace by out-of-touch academics with a personal ax to grind. To its advocates, on the other hand, anti-oppressive pedagogy represents an important chance to help marginalized students flourish and to engage privileged students in knowledge-seeking that sets aside assumptions allowing them to condescend to, or dismiss, alternative perspectives.

Some might say that all education aimed at achieving social justice will be antiracist. Thus, both multicultural and Afrocentric education and pedagogy are antiracist. But some view the seeming flaws of multiculturalism and Afrocentrism as requiring an alternative reform initiative: antiracist education. This perspective grew chronologically from the failed attempts to bring about social justice by infusing diverse content about groups and their histories, achievements, and contributions to the American mosaic. Racism was and remains the focus of this perspective.

There are problems associated with this approach (Arora, 2005; Thompson, 1995). Perhaps the most notable pertains to the idea of forcing people to be nonracist. Some believe that a democratic value includes the right to be racist and that any effort for schools to try to influence students deemed as racist is undemocratic (Butin, 2001; Kumashiro, 2004).

Nonetheless, efforts continue to introduce policies and practices believed to be nonoppressive to all people (Gresson, 2004). In particular, focus is placed on the structures or institutional arrangements that promote discrimination and oppression. Expressions of racism by individuals are thus deemphasized; the rationale being that individual behaviors are largely influenced by social arrangements of rules, roles, and relationships. For instance, policies such as zero-tolerance to fighting in schools that seem to disproportionly affect African American or Latino males might be critiqued and eliminated or revised to be more fair (Heckman & Kruger, 2003; House, 1999; Insley, 2001; Wagstaff, 2004).

The primary concern in much antiracist or antioppressive activity at the individual level is largely related to helping willing individuals to explore "power" and "ideology" as factors that tie individuals to systematic arrangements that promote inequality. The goals here are aimed at alerting people to a variety of practices seen as racist in effect. These include

- Use of intelligence test to measure human potential along static "racial" lines

- Acceptance of unequal opportunities along racial lines,

- The creation and dissemination of ideas that normalize—or present as naturally occurring—racially patterned disparities.

These basic goals result in a variety of school-related efforts aimed at changing through challenging the accepted or given social ideas underpinning racism. Of course, as mentioned above, many people believe that their ideas about "race" are the truth and may not want to be a part of an initiative they see as wrong. Many school-based goals of antiracist education are held by most people. Thus, some critics question whether it does enough or is merely hype (Troyna, 1985). Nonetheless, scholars such as Harvard University Professor Mica Pollock (2006) have identified a number of commonplace antiracist practices in education that may seem contradictory but actually complement each:

> These four … [antiracist practices]—rejecting false notions of human difference, engaging lived experiences shaped along racial lines, enjoying versions of such difference, and constantly critiquing and challenging systems of racial inequality built upon these notions of difference—are actually not self-contradictory. Rather, they demonstrate that everyday anti-racism requires doing each situationally on a daily basis. Antiracism requires not treating people as race group members when such treatment harms, and treating people as race group members when such treatment assists. Deciding which move to take when requires thinking hard about everyday life in educational settings as complex, conflict-ridden and deeply consequential.

Audrey Thompson (1995, 1) offers an instructional orientation to the implicit contraction in her illustration of inviting people with different perspectives or lived experience to move toward antiracist perspectives:

What would this mean for a specific classroom undertaking—say, an inquiry into the debate between Booker T. Washington and W. E. B. Du Bois? It might mean framing the debate as a specific genre within the performance tradition so that particular moves would be identifiable as "playing the game" or "advancing the narrative." What counts as meaningful and persuasive would then be understood in light of the *kind* of public performance that the debate constitutes, including its audiences over time. One way to accomplish that framing would be to enter the debate from an altogether different perspective— that offered by Barbara Fields and James Anderson, for example, or by Toni Morrison or Carter G. Woodson. Taking up the debate in a performance vein also would mean treating each of the sides of the argument as opening up possibilities, rather than as describing "realistic" or "rational" positions. Thus, one would not simply read the positions literally and argue, for example, "Washington was being realistic; there was a very real danger of lynching at the time," or, alternatively, "I agree with Du Bois. The Constitution provides us with our rights; no one is required to earn them." Instead, the classroom project would involve understanding, appreciating, and critiquing each of the positions as a complex move in the attempt to shape race relations against a particular historical backdrop. Developing such an understanding might take any number of directions, but it could not be referred simply to abstract principles or to individuals' experience. Instead, it would involve *creating* an experience in which the elements of the debate were a point of departure rather than themselves setting the limits of the educational experience.

This is a very large passage. It says a great deal. It requires some reading and rereading, but it is a very thoughtful effort to address the enduring, underlying issue of racism as a preferred way of dealing with difference and exercising power in word and deed over others. The prospective teacher, as seen by the above statements from Thompson and Pollock, must be flexible, knowledgeable, and committed in order to address the moment to moment actions that give shape to human identity and positive interactions among students.

Partly because antiracist curricula and pedagogy involve so much work by individuals, many doubt whether this kind of initiative is sufficient. Rather, these other critics of race-based policies and practices that reproduce social inequalities call for perspectives that can assist more systemic or large-scale change. A brief review of a few of these will round out our discussion of race-focused reform.

Race and the Critical Perspectives on Education

Elsewhere, I have defined *criticality* as an attitude or perspective that forefronts looking at reality—issues, beliefs, values, and behavior—in terms of ideas such as power, ideology, race, gender, and class. These concepts encourage us to see beyond the surface meaning or understanding of a thing. For instance, the term "gender" prompts us to ask whether how we define "male" and "female" influences development and behavior in ways that we assume are "natural" but really are socially prescribed and created. Gender bias in the classroom is one consequence of applying critical ideas to education and schooling.

Several scholarly efforts have emerged to offer other critical insights into education and schooling. Among the theories that have gained attention are

- Postmodernism

- Feminism

- Postcolonialism

- Queer theory

- Critical pedagogy

These different areas offer both concepts and explanations for understanding issues, including schooling and education. These new concepts do not necessarily claim to have the whole truth or total knowledge regarding an issue; rather, they generally try to challenge perspectives that attempt to talk about issues in non-negotiable terms. That is, they attempt to create a space for alternative voices and perspectives. They are based on the fact that some people have more power than others; and one aspect of this power is the creation and control of knowledge through control of schools, media, and other institutions of finance and governance.

Language, identity, and power can be seen as stable, unchanging and well-defined; they can also be seen as changing, unclear in aspects of their meaning and possible meaning. Change comes, in part, from resistance. When Frederick Douglass resisted enslavement, he was participating in the change in the ideas of the time about the necessary and unchanging nature of "race," "intelligence," and future race relations.

Critical Pedagogy and Constructivism. More radical perspectives have evolved to shape the role of the larger society in creating inequality. Critical Pedagogy is perhaps the most notable of these orientations and initiatives. The term has many meanings because it is not static; its meaning has evolved as different scholars and educators describe and develop their own efforts to make an impact on the way schooling occurs in different times and places. With roots in the 1930s social activism in Europe among the so-called Frankfurt School (Kincheloe, 2004) and exemplified in the work of Brazilian educator Paulo Freire, critical pedagogy attempts to achieve educational equity through a variety of strategies.

These strategies aim, in particular, at raising the learner's critical consciousness. Elsewhere, I have indicated my own critical perspective and commitment through the introduction of the thinking of Kurt Lewin and C. Wright Mills. Both men pursued social justice through ideas or theories aimed at helping us to think more fully about the consequences of human action. Similarly, in other writings, I have introduced critical theory as a corrective to some of the oppressive limitations of social theory that would not address issues such as power, ideology, and oppression.

Critical theory and pedagogy are two aspects of a single thrust: to use ideas or analytical tools to influence how learning and teaching are arranged to achieve the enlargement of the individual's perspectives on the world and things occurring around her/him. From this view, of course, critical theory and pedagogy are related to issues facing minorities, women, and other collectivities forced to the margins of society by rules, roles, and relationships that are exclusionary. A major aspect of critical pedagogy, then, is the examination of how communication and language are used to continue domination of some by others.

Critical pedagogy is also a collaborative and democratic form of human action. It seeks to link personal liberation to collective transformation of the institutions and social arrangements that undermine greater freedom and social justice. It is with respect to social justice, moreover, that critical pedagogy has been most profoundly related to teacher education and the preparation of future teachers who will challenge those practices that lump individuals into categories and essentialize them and their possibilities.

Many scholars and educators have been identified with this initiative (Darder, Torres, & Baltadano, 2002). These include Henry A. Giroux (2006), Peter McLaren (1998), bell hooks (1994), Debbie Britzman (2003), and Joe L. Kincheloe (2004). Kincheloe, for instance, has given sustained attention to the relation of teacher education and critical pedagogy in his primer. He notes, "The dominant culture's conversation about education simply ignores questions of power and justice in the development of educational policy and classroom practice" (2004, 99). Because of this neglect, moreover, Kincheloe emphasizes, as we have in other writings, the importance of contextualizing knowledge. That is, it is important to recognize that there are different types of knowledge claiming a voice or hearing and that the teacher must learn to work with the uncertainties that accompany this fact.

Some critical theorists have focused on "critical race theory" and education. For instance, Ladson-Billings and Tate (1995) used ideas from critical race theory to clarify aspects of the continuing presence of unequal or unfair treatment for minorities in schooling despite the apparent improvements.

They base their discussion on three ideas taken from legal studies, where the idea of critical race theory first arrived (Taylor, 1998). Ladson-Billings and Tate argue that the relevance of critical race theory to education is based on three central propositions:

1. Race continues to be a significant factor in determining inequity in the United States.

2. U.S. society is based on property rights.

3. The intersection of race and property creates an analytic tool through which we can understand social (and, consequently, school) inequity.

From their discussion of these propositions, Ladson-Billings and Tate affirm a general tenet of critical race theory: as long as Whites continue to control the most powerful institutions, they will continue to manipulate circumstances to their advantage. Thus, a positive shift in the plight of minorities such as African Americans is linked to White self-interests (Bell, 1992). To illustrate this basic assumption of critical race theory and education, they cite a study reported by Kofi Lomotey and John Statley on the education of African Americans in Buffalo Public Schools in the 1980s:

> Lomotey and Statley's examination of Buffalo's "model" desegregation program revealed that African-American and Latino students continued to be poorly served by the school system. The academic achievement of African-American and Latino students failed to improve while their suspension, expulsion, and dropout rates continued to rise. On the other hand, the desegregation plan provided special magnet programs and extended day care of which whites were able to take advantage. What, then, made Buffalo a model school desegregation program? In short, the benefits that whites derived from school desegregation and their seeming support of the district's desegregation program. ... Thus, a model desegregation program becomes defined as one that ensures that whites are happy (and do not leave the system altogether) regardless of whether African-American and other students of color achieve or remain.

This interpretation of desegregation efforts is only one lens on the issue. Others see important progress with respect to the success of school integration. Still, the dominant trend, called resegregation, does seem to support this tenet of critical race theory, at least for some of the scholars and activists concerned with race in education. Ladson-Billings and Tate (1995, 65) illustrate why this perspective clashes with the more mainstream interest in multiculturalism:

> We argue that the current multicultural paradigm functions in a manner similar to civil rights law. Instead of creating radically new paradigms that ensure justice, multicultural reforms are routinely "sucked back into the system" and just as traditional civil rights law is based on a foundation of human rights, the current multicultural paradigm is mired in liberal ideology that offers no radical change in the current order. ... Thus, critical race theory in education, like its antecedent in legal scholarship, is a radical critique of both the status quo and the purported reforms.

There have been many efforts to address the failures of the nation to act on the promises and expectations of the Civil Rights Movement, including the Supreme Court decision of 1954. Critical race theory, in general, derived out of the perception that too many things did not change despite the things that have changed. But there are those who caution against too much pessimism regarding the stranglehold of racism. In addition, and perhaps most important, critical race theory assumes that Blacks and Whites are rigidly and essentially different collectivities about which we can theorize easily and accurately. They counter that a balanced perspective recognizes both the need for a critical voice for the oppressed and the consequential presence of Whites pursuing social justice as part of the human family (Taylor, 1998).

Critical race theory reflects a frustration, a fear that things are changing less than many want to claim. It is a way of viewing reality that keeps the pressure on those committed to racial and social equality. Prospective teachers are invited by both critical pedagogy and critical race theory to confront those ways of relating—whether in the classroom or elsewhere—that come down on the side of those who control most of the resources and institutions in society. Teachers may also be encouraged in this invitation by the growing range of globally significant perspectives on attaining social justice and educational equity. One of the most exciting areas for this new thinking and advocacy around race and pedagogy is Whiteness studies and postcolonial pedagogy.

Whiteness Studies and Postcolonial Pedagogies

Whites have always recognized that unequal privileges are built into our society. But what is new, perhaps, is the evolving discourse about "Whiteness" (McIntosh, 1988). Whiteness is an idea foreign to many Whites. But it is, in part, this very unfamiliarity that constitutes an aspect of what is meant by "Whiteness" (Nakayama & Krizek, 1995). Many have attempted to offer a definition for this term that gets at the heart of the issue of privilege based on racial categorization (Hill, 2004; Lipsitz, 1995; McKinney, 2005).

Joe L. Kincheloe (1999, 162) wrote:

> In the emerging sub-discipline of whiteness studies scholars seem better equipped to explain white privilege than to define whiteness itself. Such a dilemma is understandable: the concept is slippery and elusive. Even though no one at this point really knows what whiteness is, most observers agree that it is intimately involved with issues of power and power differences between white and non-white people. Whiteness cannot be separated from hegemony and is profoundly influenced by demographic changes, political realignments, and economic cycles. Situationally specific, whiteness is always shifting, always reinscribing itself around changing meanings of race in the larger society. As with race in general whiteness holds material/economic implications—indeed, white supremacy has its financial rewards. The Federal Housing Administration, for example, has traditionally favored housing loans for white suburbs instead of "ethnic" inner cities.

Several important ideas are contained in this passage, notably the relation between power and whiteness. The elusiveness of the term is also part of its power. As Kincheloe continues:

> Indeed, critical multiculturalists understand that questions of whiteness permeate almost every major issue facing Westerners at the end of the twentieth century: affirmative action, intelligence testing, the deterioration of public space, and the growing disparity of wealth. In this context the study of whiteness becomes a central feature of any critical pedagogy or multicultural education for the twenty-first century. The effort to define and reinvent the amorphous concept becomes the "prime directive" of what is referred to here as a critical pedagogy of whiteness.

The idea of Whiteness has angered or offended many who view "race talk" as inappropriate or out of step with "colorblind" policy (Gresson, 2004). They see such talk as aimed at playing the "race card" or as intended to induce "White guilt" (Steele, 2006; Thernstorm, 2006). Some note that efforts to expose the disingenuous or the "bad faith" among those who speak of any systematic or enduring White racial oppression involve true courage.

However, some see postcolonial analysis of Eurocentric pedagogy in other terms. For instance, in their comparative case study of indigenous youth in Australia and the United States, Hickling-Hudson and Ahlquist (2003, 67–68) write:

> White blindness to the difference race makes in people's lives has a powerful effect on schools and other institutions in white dominant societies. It keeps white people from learning about the role that their privilege plays in personal and institutional racism. If white teachers want to challenge the authority of the white, western world-view, and build an anti-racist, socially just and global curriculum, they need

to acknowledge their power and privilege. This is the foundation for learning to give up that power and instead working to build anti-racist alliances across ethnic, racial, and cultural differences. A key component of such alliances is the principle of self-determination for indigenous peoples and peoples of color in public schooling. The goal is not to elicit feelings of guilt for white racism but to encourage insight into the racialized nature of oppression, as a foundation for working towards the redistribution of power and resources along more equitable lines.

What is going on within a postcolonial context? The term connotes a time after colonial rule. The specific task is to understand precisely how "Whiteness" works. How do those who have gained power by a variety of methods including enslavement of others organize things to keep their control? This is the question. Since schooling has a pivotal role in this process, the postcolonial perspective considers the curriculum in places across the world that have suffered from colonialism and racism:

> It explores the ways in which the Eurocentric curriculum, which includes the practices and assumptions of "whiteness," is often so accepted as the norm that it is invisible and beyond question for many teachers. It is rarely admitted at any level of the education system that today's curriculum still draws from the white imperialist projects of "fostering a science and geography of race, renaming a good part of the world in homage to its adventurers' homesick sense of place, and imposing languages and literatures on the colonized in an effort to teach them why they were subservient to a born-to-rule civilization" … Poststructural theories offer opportunities to think about how teachers are positioned within discourses of identity. Our research (and others') suggests the need for teachers to interrogate their assumptions about class and culture and how these are played out in their pedagogical relationships with students. (Hickling-Hudson & Ahlquist, 2003, 67–68)

Race, Pedagogy, and Higher Education

Much of the focus thus far has been on issues associated with K–12 settings. But a large part of the race and pedagogy discourse pertains to postsecondary settings (Cabrera et al., 1999, 2002). Historically, minorities, especially African Americans in the South, were not able to pursue higher education. After desegregation in the 1950s, many minorities began attending previously all-White institutions in the South and elsewhere. Aided by affirmative action policies, the minority population increased significantly.

However, a variety of problems emerged. Ranging from issues of minority student academic readiness to campus climate, these problems have seemed to both ebb and flow over the past several decades. The wide education gap between minorities and majority group students continues. In an incisive article, Anthony Carnevale, vice president at the Educational Testing Service, wrote in the spring of 2000:

> But the current diversity on U.S. campuses falls short of the diversity we need in our workplaces. Minorities still are underrepresented in higher education. The share of minorities among college students should at least equal their share of the 18- to 24-year-old college-age population. By that measure, there are currently 200,000 African Americans and 430,000 Hispanics missing on today's college campuses. As time passes, the opportunity gap in minority education is likely to widen because our educational policies will not provide sufficient support. Decades, even generations, of equal opportunity in elementary and secondary education will be required to produce equal educational outcomes in postsecondary education. In the meantime, only affirmative action can ensure that those occupying the most elite positions in our society mirror the racial and cultural composition of the United States.

The three important areas of focus in higher education have been teacher education, retention of minorities through pedagogical improvements, and knowledge production by universities. The first of these focuses has been improving teachers' abilities to matriculate minority students, especially those from the most disadvantaged circumstances. The second focus has been on college classroom practices that can either help or hinder minorities performing their best and reaching graduation. The third area of focus is the knowledge production arm of the university itself. With the arrival of area studies—African American, Women's, Gender, Latino, and Asian—the university has been forced to address its own role in the production and reproduction of knowledge that can be a force of either oppression or liberation. A brief comment on each of these initiatives will help clarify the overall concern with race and pedagogy in higher education.

Teacher Education, "Race," and Pedagogy

Ask most prospective teachers if their expectations for students differ, and few will likely say "yes." It is not that they are intentionally denying an awareness of differences. Rather, they truly believe that they treat all students the same. But they don't. This was shown in a now famous study of gender bias in the classroom (Sadker & Sadker, 1994). In this study, female teachers showed preferential treatment toward White male students and were able to believe this only when they were shown on video favoring boys in subtle but important ways. Their behavior reflected often unconscious but very real differences in expectations for the females and males in their classes.

Teacher expectations also differ for racial and ethnic groups. Among findings reported by researchers are:

- White students are expected to achieve higher than African American students (Baron, Tom, & Cooper, 1985).

- Parsons (cited in Weinberg, 1977) reported that teachers praise and encourage White students more, respond to them more, and pay more attention to them than to Mexican American students.

On the other hand, teachers have been found to be incredibly positive influences for disadvantaged students if they are able to care for or support these students (Nettles et al., 2003; Noddings, 1992/2000). This is important to bear in mind because the teaching force is largely made up of White females; hope for overcoming the education gap is dependent partly upon their being successfully connected with certain minority students and their families. The emergent trends in race and pedagogy are premised, in large measure, on evidence of such success in the past and a conviction that it can be improved.

There are two basic objectives of race-related curricula and pedagogy for student teachers. These are:

- providing a set of critical tools or concepts for understanding the contexts of teaching (Kincheloe, Slattery, & Steinberg, 2000)

- encouraging the development of the attitudes and emotions needed for classroom success (Gresson, 2004)

It must be stated from the outset that there are critics of any initiative that seems to point a finger at the dominant group. The above objectives thus are problematic. An excellent illustration of this alternative perspective is offered by McElroy (2005, 1) in a Fox News article where she relates the concept of cultural competence to the notions of "diversity" and "multiculturalism":

> "Cultural competency" advances the same basic goals as those buzz words. Certain groups (such as minorities) and certain ideas (such as gender feminist interpretations of oppression) are to be promoted by institutionalizing policies that encourage them. Of course, this means that other groups and other ideas are de facto penalized or discouraged.

Perspectives such as the above are important for teacher educators to be sensitive when trying to teach about social justice, democracy, and the educational enterprise. The reasons are many, but perhaps the most important is that prospective teachers have a lived experience and a perspective on issues of social justice and oppression that may lead them to resist learning that they may need to disidentify with aspects of their traditions (Gresson, 2004; Kincheloe, 2004). Consequently, much of the race-related literature on teacher education preparation seeks to understand what perspectives a predominately White female teaching force have (Carr & Klassen, 1997; Zembylas, 2003), as well as the impact these perspectives have on their understandings and behaviors regarding issues of educational equity, social justice, and democratic inclusion.

Student Teachers and "Race Pedagogy." The issue of pedagogy is such a complex one, it will be helpful to first contextualize what is being discussed when people talk about "Eurocentric" or "Multiculutral" pedagogy. To do this, let us return once again, briefly, to the case of Frederick Douglass and his master. They had very different needs and intentions. Education did not mean the same thing to them. The master did not fear that Douglass learning to read would in and of itself be the problem; rather he was concerned that the emotional and cognitive growth that comes with such learning would enable Douglass and other slaves to challenge the "facts" and "figures" that the master used to control things.

This is important. It says something about the very idea of education. In this regard, Paulo Freire (1970, 67–68) wrote: "Education as the practice of freedom … denies that [people] are abstract, isolated, independent and unattached to the world; it also denies that the world exists as a reality apart from people. Authentic reflection considers neither abstract [people] nor the world without people, but people in their relations with the world."

For Freire, becoming educated is becoming a part of the action, a part of the construction of what is and can be. It is liberating. Referring back to slavery, the slave master fears the liberating potential of education. This is what anyone who controls information or knowledge as a means of controlling another person fears. Whether one believes it or not, many feel that "Eurocentric" educational thought and practice have this oppressive potential.

When Frederick Douglass fully understood this fact in relation to his own denial of an education, he had a profound awakening. His education became liberating; he understood not just new information but also ways of relating to the challenging and changing world he inherited. Let me repeat here part of his quotation: "I now understood what had been to me a most perplexing difficulty—to wit, the White man's power to enslave the Black man. It was a grand achievement, and I prized it highly. From that moment, I understood the pathway from slavery to freedom. It was just what I wanted, and I got it at a time when I the least expected it." Here Douglass illustrates resistance pedagogy. Moreover, he offers a clue to what is called culturally powerful or relevant pedagogy: that form of teaching and learning that enables one to make one's own decisions. This type of pedagogy has traditionally required that the minority person both accept and resist much of the information present in the dominant society—for instance, to simultaneously learn that "White is pretty" and "Black is ugly," on the one hand, and yet forge for oneself and family, on the other, an image of "Black is Beautiful!" (Gresson, 1982).

This idea, or even talking about it, has often been viewed as offensive by many, especially those who have escaped the lived experience of group oppression due to race, ethnicity, or the like (Gresson, 1995, 2004). It is perhaps less important that the prospective teacher agrees with this implied accusation of the dominant society than it is that she or he is aware that there are those who do feel this way. This awareness is not limited to the majority group teacher, however; as a minority teacher of predominantly White students, I have also had to acknowledge that descriptions of my own experiences with segregated education and racial oppression can be experienced and interpreted as attacks on how they both see themselves and understand the world (Gresson, 2004).

My own curricula and pedagogy, although approved or sanctioned by some teacher educators as sound, are not acceptable to every scholar. Moreover, my students may resist learning something—however sound or scholarly—that seems to undercut their biographies, histories, and daily life. The same is true for millions of minorities who may experience not only school as oppressive, but aspects of the larger White society as well. With this tension or irony in mind, we can perhaps see why some educators concerned with social oppression have focused on pedagogy. In particular, the teacher-student relationship has been a major concern, since student academic achievement has been often seen as positively affected or influenced by how the teacher feels about her or him.

An excellent summary of the teacher education and "race" is provided by Allard and Santoro (2004, 14) in their study of teacher beliefs and teaching practices in Australia:

> If we accept that identities are constantly in the act of becoming, then how student teachers see themselves, locate themselves within discourses of "difference" e.g.—of social justice, of economic imperatives, of teacher professionalism—depends in part on the experiences, contexts and discourses they are offered. As teacher educators, part of our role is to offer experiences to our students that enable them to understand and examine their own positionings within and through current discourses. While some researchers (e.g., Britzman, 1991; Causey et al., 2000) argue that a way of helping pre-service teacher-education students is to begin from their personal constructs, we recognise that this is an extraordinarily difficult task to undertake, not just for our students, but for anyone. However, while this may serve as a starting point for developing understanding and insights into taken-for-granted beliefs about culture and class, it does not necessarily address the fundamental question: how does one work with difference in classrooms in ways that acknowledge cultural and class values and beliefs without essentialising identities or stereotyping groups?

Minority Retention and Pedagogy

Pedagogy has been especially interesting with respect to minority higher education. The two trajectories that have evolved are the HBCU and Predominately White Institution models. Each has taken a certain minority constituency and each faces challenges today that reflect the clash between historical and contemporary needs.

Pedagogy and HBCUs. The years immediately following the abolition of slavery saw an almost frenzied effort to achieve an education among the former slaves (Anderson, 1988; Williams, 2005). G. Stanley Hall described how postwar Blacks were anxious for learning, so much so that presumably Booker T. Washington declared that one of his missions was to lower the sights of his people. Whatever the extent of truth to Hall's observation, it was true that the years immediately following the Civil War were marked by a comprehensive, unrelenting effort to gain an education. The belief then, and to some degree even now, was that "racial uplift" lay at the heart of achieving full equality in America.

The major role of the historically Black colleges and universities was to teach the ex-slaves to read and write. The curriculum was largely precollegiate until after the Civil War. For example, the earliest such institution, Cheyney University in Pennsylvania was organized in 1837 as an Institute for Colored Youth. It taught an elementary and secondary curriculum. Today, more than one hundred HBCUs are in operation (Gasman & Jennings, 2006; Reddick, 2006). Unlike the development of higher education in White private and state postsecondary institutions, the Black schools followed a different path.

The years after the Civil War saw the growth of American colleges and universities; higher education, in general, spread through the passage of the Morrill Act of 1862. This act provided the basis for land-grant institutions financed largely by public taxes. In particular, according to James Anderson (undated):

> African American higher education took a different path. From the Reconstruction era through World War II (1939–1945) the majority of Black students were enrolled in private colleges. Northern religious

mission societies were primarily responsible for establishing and maintaining the leading Black colleges and universities. African American religious philanthropy also established a significant number.

Given the virtual nonexistence of public education for Blacks in the South, these institutions had to provide preparatory courses at the elementary and high school levels for their students. Often they did not offer college-level courses for years until their students were prepared for them. Nonetheless, the missionary aims of these early schools reflected the ideals of classical liberal education that dominated American higher education in general in that period, with its emphasis on ancient languages, natural sciences, and humanities. Blacks were trained for literacy, but also for teaching and the professions.

The curriculum found in the historically Black postsecondary institutions reflected the complex needs of the newly enfranchised African American group. And as William Watkins (1993) has shown, the curriculum has evolved in different directions to capture needs grounded in the diverse experiences of African Americans. This diverse set of needs continues unto the present. However, the pursuit of fuller participation in the American democracy underlay the shape of much of this curricular focus. In *The Education of Blacks in the South, 1860–1935*, the 1990 recipient of a best book award from the American Educational Research Association, James D. Anderson (1988, 29) explains:

> Black leaders did not view their adoption of the classical liberal curriculum or its philosophical foundations as mere imitation of white schooling. Indeed, they knew many whites who had no education at all. Rather, they saw this curriculum as providing access to the best intellectual traditions of their era and the best means to understanding their own historical development and sociological uniqueness.

Throughout African American history, education has been seen as crucial to the argument for full inclusion. It has been the experience of failing to attain inclusion even when academically prepared that has influenced some to question the efficacy of education. This, however, remains a minority perspective among the various minorities. Recent research indicates that education continues to be seen by African Americans, in particular, as very important.

Still, the historical value placed on education by Booker T. Washington and White benefactors of Black Education (Watkins, 2001) was seen as serving both curricular and pedagogical functions. On the pedagogical end, vocational or hands-on instructional practices were seen as facilitating discipline and other qualities some Whites felt the Africans lacked (Anderson, 1988). Another factor affected the way that schools were designed and instruction carried out in these institutions. Because so many of the students accepted for postsecondary education lacked college preparation, they often needed remedial work. Much like the community college, HBCUs have accepted students needing remedial work as part of the mandate for uplift.

At the same time, partly under the influence of leaders in education such as W. E. B. Du Bois, these schools saw their mission to include the cultivation of the brightest and the best students to assume leadership roles within African American communities.

Pedagogy and Predominately White Institutions. Minorities outside of the South traditionally attended the private schools up North. Though numerically small, these students typically excelled and returned to African American communities to assume leadership roles. As might be expected, even though their career opportunities were significantly fewer than their White counterparts, they did well. But, interestingly, they did not do as well as students attending historically Black institutions. However, things have changed. According to Fryer and Greenstone (2007), economists at Harvard and MIT, respectively:

> Until the 1960s, Historically Black Colleges and Universities (HBCUs) were practically the only institutions of higher learning open to Blacks in the US. Using nationally representative data files from 1970s

and 1990s college attendees, we find that in the 1970s HBCU matriculation was associated with higher wages and an increased probability of graduation, relative to attending a Traditionally White Institution (TWI). By the 1990s, however, there is a wage penalty, resulting in a 20% decline in the relative wages of HBCU graduates between the two decades. ... The data provide modest support for the possibility that HBCUs' relative decline in wages is partially due to improvements in TWI effectiveness at educating blacks.

These results do not necessarily tell the full story regarding the curricular and pedagogical functions traditionally assumed by the HBCUs. That is, the greatest dropout rates for minorities are at the predominately White institutions. Moreover, there is considerable evidence that the various minorities do not necessarily achieve wage parity with Whites as a result of attending predominately White institutions (Darity & Myers, 1998).

There have been a wide range of issues associated with minority higher education in predominately White institutions. These include:

- Preferential treatment—fairness and affirmative action policies

- Effective mentoring of diverse students

- Racial intolerance on campus

- Retention of minority students

- Diversity and cultural autonomy of campus Minority faculty at predominately White institutions

These are just some of the areas of concern that have been prevalent in minority higher education. They all touch on issues of school climate and organizational structure. The more precise issue of pedagogy and race has also been an enduring one. Perhaps the one area in which it has been most notable is with respect to minority underachievement in mathematics and science. It is here that important differences between HBCUs and HWCUs might be seen (Inniss & Perry, 2003). Ebony McGee (2005, 1) has framed the challenge in this way:

> The disturbingly low rates of math achievement by students of color (African Americans, Latinos, Native Americans), women, and low-income students have gained increasing attention in the education community. ... Although African Americans, Latino/as, and Native Americans made up 28 percent of the college-age population in 1995, they received only 9 percent of the bachelor's degrees and 2 percent of the doctorates in engineering. On the other hand in that same year, 50 percent of high school Asian graduate students took advanced mathematics, while 31 percent of African-American and 24 percent of Hispanic graduates took remedial mathematics courses compared to 15 percent of white and Asian students. (National Science Foundation, 2000)

This higher education racial gap has been the rationale for advocating for new pedagogies. For instance, Annie Howell and Frank Tuitt (2003) have advocated for the need to adjust modes of instruction or pedagogy. The traditional modes of pedagogy, including lectures, have potentially harmful consequences. Chief among these is the potential creation of a variant of hostility that turns students away from engagement.

Traditional forms of classroom teaching include such things as lectures and independent laboratory work. This form of pedagogy is considered teacher-centered; information is decontextualized (that is, isolated from a specific relevant situation). In addition, the textbooks that are used are routinely treated as the truth rather than partial truth or knowledge. Emphasis is on memorization and giving it back to the instructor (regurgitation). Recitation, multiple-choice test items, and selecting the one "right" or correct answer are emphasized.

This type of pedagogy is familiar to most of us. And it works reasonably well, or so it seems. Where and when it does not, we accept this as evidence that the learner has some flaw, individual or group. We have already discussed the consequence of this type of teaching elsewhere, noting that this form of teaching is one way of tracking youth into prescribed positions within society (Clark, 1960).

Of course, elite institutions do not necessarily follow this precise model of teaching. There is evidence that elite schools, both K–12 and postsecondary, do vary their pedagogies (Anyon, 1981; Bartlett, 2005). In particular, elite institutions tend to provide a wide range of instructional or learning opportunities for their students. Interestingly, within the predominately White institutions, emphasis on minority-related pedagogy found a special expression and focus within the newly emerging area studies programs.

Area Studies: Curricula and Pedagogy. We have noted elsewhere that institutionalized education such as found in universities and colleges was promoted by those who believed that a unified, cumulative knowledge base would promote civilization. As a consequence, certain people became the official producers of knowledge and shared beliefs that were considered "the truth." Of course, humans have probably always competed to determine whose vision or version of truth was the accepted one. The term "canon" has been used to refer to knowledge we have come to accept as true and worthy of passing on from generation to generation.

In the 1960s, with the arrival of the various liberation movements—Black, women's, gay and lesbian, and so forth—there were parallel efforts to influence the knowledge accepted as the truth. Within the academy, one form this new effort took was the creation of departments and programs that focused on histories of the minorities and the disenfranchised. In addition, new information or research studies were initiated to correct or update what was traditionally thought and taught about minorities.

Two aspects of area studies might be mentioned just briefly. The first pertains to the very idea of an area studies as a field of inquiry. According to James B. Stewart (2006):

> As disciplines evolve sub-disciplines develop enabling researchers to pursue specialized inquiries. However, sub-disciplines subscribe to a set of shared values and interests that provide a coherent macro-level disciplinary identity. Distinctive schools of thought typically develop within disciplines as a result of differing interpretations of some aspects of the discipline's mandate, for example, disagreements regarding the relative merits of quantitative and qualitative research. Different schools of thought can also exist within individual sub-disciplines. In several disciplines there are disagreements within sub-disciplines regarding the relative importance of race and class in perpetuating disparities.

> Africana Studies can be appropriately characterized as an "academic discipline" with distinctive intellectual assumptions and values. Afro-American Studies, Critical Race Studies, Diaspora Studies, African Studies, Afro-Latino/a Studies, and Africana Women's Studies can be treated as sub-disciplines within the discipline of Africana Studies and rational judgments can be made about whether a school of thought within each sub-discipline is best identified with Africana Studies, per se, or some other intellectual tradition. (See Stewart, 1992, 2004)

From the pedagogical side, Tunde Adeleke (2002, 1) has noted:

> History has shown that oppressed and subordinated groups often invoke "liberation pedagogy." This pedagogy has come in the form of revisionist critique of prevailing body of thought—as was the case in the United States, with the struggles for Black Studies—and for the intellectual recognition and legitimacy of the historical and cultural heritage of blacks. … In both the United States and Africa, the emergent intellectual tradition served to correct the misconceptions and fallacies of a dominant tradition, and moved toward creating a holistic body of knowledge that more accurately depicts and represents marginalized and indigenous people's historical experiences.

Together, Stewart and Adeleke address the emerging race-based questions stimulated by an ever-evolving vision of the possible and how it affects what is traditionally viewed as essential and unchanging. More specifically, the notion of "race" and its relation to education and pedagogy is in constant flux. Where we go in the realms of both research and pedagogy depends in large measure on what choices are made on the global stage.

Suggested Readings

Three themes are taken up in this chapter on race and pedagogy. These include the broad areas of culturally sensitive teaching, school reforms, and higher education and minorities. Much of the literature presented in this chapter is the best starting place for further reading on these themes. But a few additional sources might be mentioned here. First, you might start with T. C. Howard's (2003, Summer), "Culturally Relevant Pedagogy: Ingredients for Critical Teacher Reflection." *Theory into Practice*, 42(3), 195–202. In this piece, Tyrone Caldwell focuses on the role of reflection in preparing teachers for culturally relevant teaching.

Another useful resource deals with teacher expectations and responsibility. Diamond, J. B., Randolph, A., & Spillane, J. P. (2004, March), "Teachers' Expectations and Sense of Responsibility for Student Learning: The Importance of Race, Class, and Organizational Habitus." *Anthropology & Education Quarterly*, 35(1), 75–98. This article focuses on the educational needs of African American students; particular emphasis is placed on showing how school leaders can help teachers to assume greater responsibility for student learning. Because of the emphasis on school administrator leadership, the article contributes to the clarification of the relation between student learning and effective building level leadership. One useful review of the influence of "school culture"—values, beliefs, and relationships—on success is at the Southwest Educational Development Laboratory Web site: Victoria Boyd, "School Context: Bridge or Barrier to Change," http://www.sedl.org/change/school/culture.html.

Racial identity as a construct or theory has been long acknowledged when thinking of African Americans or "Blacks." It is a less well thought about idea with respect to "Whites." But since the 1970s, a growing number of scholars and researchers have turned their attention to the complex dimensions that constitute "racial identity" for everyone who has been racialized. How people understand themselves as a racial being is related to what some scholars refer to as "resolutions." This term refers to the successive steps people go through as they solve or resolve previous ways of seeing themselves and others. An excellent illustration of this orientation is Mark M. Leach, John T. Behrens, & N. Kenneth La Fleur's (2002, April), "White Racial Identity and White Racial Consciousness: Similarities, Differences, and Recommendations." *Journal of Multicultural Counseling and Development*, 30, 66–80.

Postcolonial studies are a new field that addresses many of the issues and themes discussed throughout this chapter. What kinds of research ought to be conducted and the methods to be followed are two such themes. In addition, shifting identity—as student, teacher, and researcher—is another related theme. A recent special issue of the very important journal *Race Ethnicity and Education* brings these themes together in several essays. A good starting point here is S. L. Daza's (2008, March), "Decolonizing Researcher Authenticity." *Race Ethnicity and Education*, 11(1) (2008, March), 71–85. Daza's article is concerned with the researcher's relationship to her or his focus of inquiry and asks how this relationship is affected and negotiated in terms of three axes of difference: ethnolinguistic affiliation, sexual orientation, and race/skin color.

Another related article in this issue of the journal is C. Dillard's (2008, March), "Remembering Culture: Bearing Witness to the Spirit of Identity in Research." *Race Ethnicity and Education*,

11(1), 87–93. Dillard's essay is very interesting because it tries to show how a postcolonial agenda invites, even forces, us to shift from using race as a way of identifying ourselves in the search for a more inclusive and socially healing identity, perhaps in spiritual terms.

Much confusion exists around the nature of minority parents' and students' thinking and behaviors with respect to higher education. Do they think about it at all? How do they participate in thinking about funding college, school selection, and successful completion of college?

A very useful way of entering this area of minority higher education is through a study aimed at revealing families in action: Knight, M. G., Norton, N. E. L., Bentley, C. C., & Dixon, I. R. (2004, March), "The Power of Black and Latina/o Counterstories: Urban Families and College-Going Processes." *Anthropology & Education Quarterly*, 35(1), 99–120. These scholars examined the college-related experiences of 27 African American and Latina/o families in order to understand the diversity of practices utilized by working-class and poor families to support their children's college-going processes. Using ethnographical methods they were able to expand the typically reported understanding of what positive efforts these families made to see that their children might get into college.

References

Adeleke, T. (2002). Globalization and the Challenges of Race-Based Pedagogy. Retrieved January 9, 2008, from http://globalization.icaap.org/content/v2.2/adeleke.html.

Allard, A., & Santoro, N. (2004). Making Sense of Difference? Teaching Identities in Postmodern Contexts. Retrieved February 17, 2008, from http://www.aare.edu.au/04pap/all04561.pdf.

Allen, T. D. (2004, December). Review of Black in School: Afrocentric Reform, Urban Reform, and the Promise of Hip-Hop Culture. *E-Journal of Teaching and Learning in Diversity Settings*, 2(1), 177–181. Retrieved February 15, 2008, from http://www.subr.edu/coeducation/ejournal/Allen%20Book%20Review.htm.

Alridge, D. (2005, Summer). From Civil Rights to Hip-Hop: Toward a Nexus of Ideas. *Journal of African American History*, 90(2), 226–252.

Anderson, J. (1988). *The Education of Blacks in the South: 1860–1935*. Chapel Hill: University of North Carolina Press.

Anderson, J. D. (undated). Colleges and Universities, Historically Black, in the United States. Retrieved February 15, 2008, from www.pbs.org/itvs/fromswastikatojimcrow/blackcolleges_2.html.

Anyon, J. (1981). Social Class and School Knowledge. *Curriculum Inquiry*, 11(1), 3–42.

Arora, R. K. (2005). *Race and Ethnicity in Education*. Burlington, VT: Ashgate.

Asante, M. (1980/1987). *The Afrocentric Idea*. Philadelphia: Temple University Press.

Ayers, W., Hunt, J. A., & Quinn, T. (Eds.). (1998). *Teaching for Social Justice: A Democracy and Education Reader*. New York: New Press.

Banks, J. A. (2000). *An Introduction to Multicultural Education*, 3rd edition. Boston: Allyn & Bacon.

Banks, J. A. (Ed.). (2004). *Diversity and Citizenship Education: Global Perspectives*. San Francisco, CA: Jossey-Bass.

Baron, R. M., Tom, D. Y. H., & Cooper, H. M. (1985). Social Class, Race and Teacher Expectations. In J. B. Dusek (Ed.), *Teacher Expectancies*, 251–269. Hillsdale, NJ: Lawrence Erlbaum Associates.

Bartlett, L. (2005, August). Dialogue, Knowledge, and Teacher-Student Relations: Freirean Pedagogy in Theory and Practice. *Comparative Education Review*, 49(3), 344–364.

Bell, D. (1992). *Faces at the Bottom of the Well: The Permanence of Racism*. New York: Basic Books.

Benson-Hale, J. (1986). *Black Children, Their Roots, Culture, and Learning Styles*. Baltimore, MD: Johns Hopkins University Press.

Bork, R. H. (1996). *Slouching towards Gomorrah: Modern Liberalism and American Decline*. New York: Regan Books/HarperCollins.

Britzman, D. (2003). *Practice Makes Practice: A Critical Study of Learning to Teach*, revised edition. Albany, NY: SUNY Press.

Brophy, J. (1983). Research on the Self-fulfilling Prophecy and Teacher Expectations. *Journal of Education Psychology*, 75(5), 631–661.

Brophy, J. E., & Good, T. L. (1986). Teacher Behavior and Student Achievement. In M. C. Wittrock (Ed.), *Handbook of Research on Teaching*, 3rd edition, 328–375. New York: Macmillan.

Butin, D. W. (2001). If This Is Resistance I Would Hate to See Domination: Retrieving Foucault's Notion of Resistance within Educational Research. *Educational Studies*, 32(2), 157–176.

Cabrera, A. F., Crissman, J. L., Bernal, E. M., Nora, A. P. T., & Pascarella, E. T. (2002). Collaborative Learning: Its Impact on College Students' Development and Diversity. *Journal of College Student Development*, 43(2), 20–34.

Cabrera, A. F., Nora, A., Terenzini, P. T., Pascarella, E., & Hagedorn, L. S. (1999). Campus Racial Climate and the Adjustment of Students to College: A Comparison between White Students and African-American Students. *The Journal of Higher Education*, 70(2), 134–160.

Carnevale, A. (2000, Spring). The Opportunity Gap: Campus Diversity and the New Economy. *National Crosstalk*. Retrieved February 17, 2008, from http://www.highereducation.org/crosstalk/ct0500/voices0500-carnevale.shtml.

Carr, P. R., & Klassen, T. R. (1997). Different Perceptions of Race in Education: Racial Minority and White Teachers. *Canadian Journal of Education*, 22(1), 67–81.

Carter, R. T. (2000). Reimaging Race in Education: A New Paradigm from Psychology. *Teachers College Record*, 102(5), 864–897.

Caruthers, L. (2006, Fall). Using Storytelling to Break the Silence That Binds Us to Sameness in Our Schools. *Journal of Negro Education*, 75(4), 661–676.

Clark, B. (1960). The Cooling Out Function in Higher Education. *American Journal of Sociology*, 65, 569–576.

Coleman, J. S. (2002, Spring). From Kindergarten to College (K–16): Preparing Students to Meet the Academic, Social, Technological, and Professional Challenges in the 21st Century. *SIG Newsletter*, 3(1). Retrieved March 5, 2008, from http://www.geocities.com/talentdevelopment/newsletter/newsletter.html

Crawford, J. (1995). Endangered Native American Languages: What Is to Be Done and Why? *Bilingual Research Journal*, 19(1), 17–38.

Darder, A., Torres, R. D., & Baltodano, M. (Eds.). (2002). *The Critical Pedagogy Reader*. New York: RoutledgeFalmer.

Darity, W. A., & Myers, S. L. (1998). *Persistent Disparity: Race and Economic Inequality in the United States since 1945*. Northampton, MA: Edward Elgar.

Darling-Hammond, L. (1998, Spring). Unequal Opportunity: Race and Education. *The Brookings Review*, 16(2), 28–32. Retrieved September 29, 2007, from http://www.brookings.edu/press/review/spring98/darling.htm.

Darling-Hammond, L. (2006). *Powerful Teacher Education: Lessons from Exemplary Programs*. San Francisco, CA: Jossey-Bass.

Dei, G. J. S. (1994, March). Afrocentricity: A Cornerstone of Pedagogy. *Anthropology & Education Quarterly*, 25(1), 3–28.

Epstein, J. (1995). School, Family, Community Partnerships. *Phi Delta Kappa*, 76(9), 701–712.

Faith, E. (2007). Finding Healing and Balance in Learning and Teaching at the First Nations University of Canada. *First Peoples Child & Family Review*, 4(3), 8–12. Retrieved February 10, 2008, from http://www.fncfcs.com/pubs/vol3num4/Faith_pp8.pdf.

Fishman, J. (1991). What Is Reversing Language Shift (RLS) and How Can It Succeed? *Journal of Multilingual and Multicultural Development*, 11(1–2), 5–36.

Freire, P. (1970). *Pedagogy of the Oppressed*. Trans. Myra Bergman Ramos. New York: Continuum Press.

Fryer, R. G., & Greenstone, M. (2007, April). The Causes and Consequences of Attending Historically Black Colleges and Universities. NBER Working Paper No. 13036. Retrieved February 15, 2008, from http://www.nber.org/papers/w13036.pdf.

García, E. (2002). Bilingualism and Schooling in the United States. *International Journal of the Sociology of Language*, 155/156(1), 1–92.

Gasman, M., & Jennings, M. (2006). New Research, New Questions: Social Foundations Scholarship on Historically Black Colleges and Universities. *Educational Foundations*, 20(1–2), 3–8.

Gay, G. (2000). *Culturally Responsive Teaching: Theory, Research & Practice*. New York: Teachers College Press.

Ginwright, S. A. (2004). *Black in School: Afrocentric Reform, Urban Reform, and the Promise of Hip-Hop Culture*. New York: Teachers College Press.

Giroux, H. A. (1994, Fall). Doing Cultural Studies: Youth and the Challenge of Pedagogy. *Harvard Educational Review*, 64(3) 278–308.

Giroux, H. A. (2006). *The Giroux Reader (Cultural Politics and the Promise of Democracy)*, Nick Couldry (series ed.). Boulder, CO: Paradigm.

Gresson, A. D. (1982). *The Dialectics of Betrayal: Sacrifice, Violation and the Oppressed*. Norwood, NJ: Ablex.

Gresson, A. D. (1995). *The Recovery of Race in America*. Minneapolis: University of Minnesota Press.

Gresson, A. D. (2004). *America's Atonement: Racial Pain, Recovery Rhetoric and the Pedagogy of Healing*. New York: Peter Lang.

Haberman, M. (1995). *Star Teachers of Children in Poverty*. West Lafayette, IN: Kappa Delta Pi.

Hall, T. D. (2007). *A Pedagogy of Freedom: Using Hip Hop in the Classroom to Engage African-American Students*. Unpublished doctoral dissertation, University of Missouri-Columbia. Retrieved March 1, 2008, from http://edt.missouri.edu/Fall2007/Dissertation/HallT-120507-D8654/short.pdf.

Hampel, R. (1996, Winter). Forum: History and Education Reform. *History of Education Quarterly*, 36, 473–502.

Heckman, J. J., & Kruger, A. B. (2003). *Inequity in America: What Role for Human Capital Policies?* Cambridge, MA: MIT Press.

Hickling-Hudson, A., & Ahlquist, R. (2003). Contesting the Curriculum in the Schooling of Indigenous Children in Australia and the United States: From Eurocentrism to Culturally Powerful Pedagogies. *Comparative Education Review*, 47, 64–91.

Hill, M. (2004). *After Whiteness: Unmaking an American Majority*. New York: NYU Press.

Hinton, L. (1994). *Flutes of Fire: Essays on California Indian Languages*. Berkeley, CA: Heyday.

hooks, b. (1994). *Teaching to Transgress: Education as the Practice of Freedom*. New York: Routledge.

House, E. (1999, April). Race and Policy. *Education Policy Analysis Archives*, 7(16). Retrieved on January 11, 2008, from http://epaa.asu.edu/epaa/v7n16.html.

Howard, T. C. (2003, Summer). Culturally Relevant Pedagogy: Ingredients for Critical Teacher Reflection. *Theory into Practice*, 42(3), 195–202.

Howell, A., & Tuitt, F. (Eds.). (2003). *Race and Higher Education: Rethinking Pedagogy in Diverse College Classrooms*. Cambridge, MA: Harvard University Press.

Inniss, L., & Perry, R. (2003, November). A Retrospective Profile of Electrical Engineering Graduates from the FAMU-FSU College of Engineering. *Frontiers in Education Annual*, 1(5–8), T2A-5–10.

Insley, A. C. (2001). Suspending and Expelling Children from Educational Opportunities: Time to Reevaluate Zero Tolerance Policies. *American University Review*, 50, 1039–1074.

Irwin, J. W., & Farr, W. (2004, October). Collaborative School Communities That Support Teaching and Learning. *Reading and Writing Quarterly*, 20(4), 343–363.

Jackson, P. W. (1968). *Life in Classrooms*. New York: Holt, Rinehart and Winston.

Kincheloe, J. L. (1999). The Struggle to Define and Reinvent Whiteness: A Pedagogical Analysis. *College Literature*, 26(3), 162–195.

Kincheloe, J. L. (2004). *Critical Pedagogy: A Primer*. New York: Peter Lang.

Kincheloe, J. L., Slattery, P., & Steinberg, S. R. (2000). *Contextualizing Teaching: Introduction to Education and Educational Foundations*. Boston: Allyn & Bacon.

Kincheloe, J. L., & Steinberg, S. R. (1997). *Changing Multiculturalism*. Buckingham, UK: Open University Press.

Kirk, H. D. (1964). *Shared Fate: A Theory of Adoption and Mental Health*. New York: Free Press.

Kirk, R. (1993). *America's British Culture*. New Brunswick, NJ: Transaction.

Kozol, J. (1991). *Savage Inequalities: Children in America's Schools*. New York: Crown.

Kozol, J. (2005). *The Shame of the Nation: The Restoration of Apartheid Schooling in America*. New York: Crown.

Kumashiro, K. (2004). *Against Common Sense: Teaching and Learning toward Social Justice*. New York: RoutledgeFalmer.

Ladson-Billings, G. (1990). Culturally Relevant Teaching: Effective Instruction for Black Students. *The College Board Review*, 155, 20–25.

Ladson-Billings, G. (1994). *The Dreamkeepers: Successful Teachers of African American Children*. San Francisco, CA: Jossey-Bass.

Ladson-Billings, G., & Tate, W. F. (1995). Toward a Critical Race Theory of Education. *Teachers College Record*, 97, 47–68.

Lefkowitz, M. (1996). *Not Out of Africa: How Afrocentrism Became an Excuse to Teach Myth as History*. New York: Basic Books.

Lewin, K. (1948). *Resolving Social Conflicts*. New York: Harper & Row.

Lipsitz, G. (1995, September). The Possessive Investment in Whiteness. *American Quarterly*, 47(3), 369–386.

Lomotey, K., & Statley, J. (1990). The Education of African Americans in Buffalo Public Schools. Paper presented at the annual meeting of the American Educational Research Association, Boston.

Marable, M. (1992). *Black America*. Westfield, NJ: Open Media.

Marker, P. M. (2003). Another Brick in the Wall: High Stakes Testing in Teacher Education—The California Teacher Performance Assessment. *Workplace*. Retrieved February 3, 2008, from http://www.louisville.edu/journal/workplace/issue5p2/marker.html

McElroy, W. (2005, October 19). Cultural Competence: Coming to a School Near You? Retrieved November 15, 2007, from Fox News Online: http://www.foxnews.com/story/0,2933,172816,00.html.

McGee, E. (2005). Chronicles of Success: Black College Students Achieving in Mathematics and Engineering. Retrieved February 17, 2008, from http://www.blacksuccessfoundation.org/Achieving%20in%20Math%20and%20Engineering.htm.

McIntosh, P. (1988). White Privilege and Male Privilege. Wellesley College, Centre for Research on Women. Working Paper No. 189.

McKinney, K. (2005). *Being White: Stories of Race and Racism*. New York: Routledge.

McLaren, P. (1998). *Life in Schools: An Introduction to Critical Pedagogy in the Foundations of Education*, 3rd edition. New York: Longman.

Meighan, R. (1981). *A Sociology of Educating*. London: Holt, Rinehart & Winston.

Miller, R. E. (1998, September). The Arts of Complicity: Pragmatism and the Culture of Schooling. *College English*, 61(1), 10–28.

Mills, C. W. (1959). *The Sociological Imagination*. London & New York: Oxford University Press.

Milner, R. (2003). Teacher Reflection and Race in Cultural Contexts: History, Meanings, and Methods in Teaching. *Theory into Practice*, 42(3), 173–180.

Morris, J. E. (2003). What Does Africa Have to Do with Being African-American: A Micro-ethnographic Analysis of a Middle School Inquiry Unit on Africa. *Anthropology & Education Quarterly*, 34(3), 255–276.

Morris, J. E. (2004). Can Anything Good Come from Nazareth? Race, Class, and African-American Schooling and Community in the Urban South and Midwest. *American Educational Research Journal*, 41(1), 69–112.

Moses, W. J. (1991). Eurocentrism, Afrocentrism, and William Ferris's *The African Abroad*, 1911. *Journal of Education*, 173(1), 76–90.

Mouw, T., & Xie, Y. (1999, April). Bilingualism and the Academic Achievement of First- and Second-Generation Asian Americans: Accommodation with or without Assimilation? *American Sociological Review*, 64(2), 232–252.

Nakayama, T., & Krizek, R. (1995). Whiteness: A Strategic Rhetoric. *Quarterly Journal of Speech*, 81, 291–309.

National Science Foundation. (2000). *Science and Engineering Indicators*. Washington DC: NSF.

Nelson-Barber, S., & Estrin, E. T. (1995, Summer). Bringing Native American Perspectives to Mathematics and Science Teaching. *Theory into Practice*, 34(3), 174–185.

Nettles, M. T., Millett, C. M., & Ready, D. D. (2003). Attacking the African American-White Achievement Gap on College Admissions Tests. *Brookings Papers on Education Policy*, 215–238.

Newmann, F., & Wehlage, G. (1995). *Successful School Restructuring*. Madison, WI: Center on Organization and Restructuring of Schools.

Noddings, N. (1992/2000). The Challenge of Care in Schools: An Alternative Approach to Education. In R. Reed & T. Johnson (Eds.), *Philosophical Documents in Education*, 2nd edition, 247–257. New York: Longman (Reprinted from *The Challenge to Care in Schools: An Alternative Approach to Education*, by Noddings, 1992, New York: Teachers College Press).

Pinderhughes, E. (1995). Empowering Diverse Populations: Family Practice in the 21st Century. *Families in Society: The Journal of Contemporary Human Services*, 76, 131–139.

Pollock, M. (2006). Everyday Antiracism in Education. Retrieved November 23, 2007, from http://www.understandingrace.org/resources/pdf/rethinking/pollock.pdf

Ravitch, D. (1983). *The Troubled Crusade: American Education, 1945–1980*. New York: Basic Books.

Reddick, R. J. (2006). The Gift That Keeps Giving: Historically Black College and University-Educated Scholars and Their Mentoring at Predominantly White Institutions. *Educational Foundations*, 20(1–2), 61–84.

Rist, R. (1970). Student Social Class and Teacher Expectations. *Harvard Educational Review*, 40, 411–451.

Sadker, M., & Sadker, D. (1994). *Failing at Fairness: How America's Schools Cheat Girls*. New York: Charles Scribners Sons, Macmillan Publishing Co.

Saphier, J. (1997). *The Skillful Teacher: Building Your Teaching Skills*. Acton, MA: Research for Better Teaching.

Schlesinger, A. M. (1998). *The Disuniting of America: Reflections on a Multicultural Society*, revised edition. New York: W. W. Norton & Company.

ScholarCentric. (undated). Success Highways. Retrieved November 21, 2007, from http://www.scholarcentric.com

Soto, L. D. (2001). *Making a Difference in the Lives of Bilingual/Bicultural Children*. New York: Peter Lang.

Spring, J. (2004). *How Educational Ideologies Are Shaping Global Society*. Mahwah, NJ: Lawrence Erlbaum Associates.

Steele, S. (2006). *White Guilt: How Blacks and Whites Together Destroyed the Promise of the Civil Rights Era*. New York: HarperCollins.

Stewart, J. B. (1992). Reaching for Higher Ground: Toward an Understanding of Black/Africana Studies. *The Afrocentric Scholar*, 1(1), 1–63.

Stewart, J. B. (2004). *Flight in Search of Vision*. Trenton, NJ: Africa World Press.

Stewart, J. B. (2006, April). Sub-disciplinary Specializations and Disciplinary Maturation: Relationships among Afro-American Studies, Critical Race Studies, Diaspora Studies, African Studies, Afro-Latino/a Studies, and Africana Women's Studies at the Conversations for Sustaining Black Studies in the 21st Century. Ford Foundation Conference, New York City.

Stringfield, S. (2000, June). A Synthesis and Critique of Four Recent Reviews of Whole-School Reform in the United States. *School Effectiveness and School Improvement*, 11(2), 259–269.

Taylor, E. (1998, Spring). A Primer on Critical Race Theory. *The Journal of Blacks in Higher Education*, 19, 122–124.

Teachers21. (undated). Critical Actions for Promoting Educational Equity. Retrieved February 10, 2008, from http://www.teachers21.org/documents/EquityPaper.doc.

Thernstrom, A. (2006, May 10). Steele Sense: From White Racism to White Guilt, America Still Struggles with Race. *National Review Online*. Retrieved February 16, 2008, from http://www.thernstrom.com/pdf/National%20Review%20Online_May10_2006.pdf.

Thernstrom, S., & Thernstrom, A. (2003). *No Excuses: Closing the Racial Gap in Learning*. New York: Simon & Schuster.

Thompson, A. (1995). Anti-racist Pedagogy—Art or Propaganda? Retrieved February 12, 2008, from http://www.ed.uiuc.edu/eps/PES-Yearbook/95_docs/thompson.html.

Troyna, B. (1985). The Great Divide: Policies and Practices in Multicultural Education. *British Journal of Sociology of Education*, 6(2), 209–224.

Wagstaff, L. H. (2004). *Zero-Tolerance Discipline: The Effect of Teacher Discretionary Removal on Urban Minority Students*. Unpublished dissertation, University of Texas, Austin.

Watkins, W. H. (1993, Fall). Black Curriculum Orientations: A Preliminary Inquiry. *Harvard Education Review*, 63(3), 321–338.

Watkins, W. H. (2001). *The White Architects of Black Education: Ideology and Power in America, 1865–1954*. New York: Teachers College Press.

Weinberg, M. (1977). *A Chance to Learn: The History of Race and Education in the United States*. Cambridge, UK: Cambridge University Press.

Wiggins, G., & McTighe, J. (1998). *Understanding by Design*. Arlington, VA: Association for Supervision and Curriculum Development.

Williams, H. A. (2005). *Self-taught African American Education in Slavery and Freedom*. Chapel Hill: University of North Carolina Press.

Woodson, C. G. (1935/2000). *The Mis-education of the Negro*. Chicago: African-American Images.

Zembylas, M. (2003, March). Interrogating "Teacher Identity": Emotion, Resistance, and Self-formation. *Educational Theory*, 53, 107–127.

Zhao, G. (2007, February). The Making of the Modern Subject: A Cross-cultural Analysis. *Educational Theory*, 57(1), 75–88.

CHAPTER 9

Critical Pedagogy in Action

Joe L. Kincheloe

Educators walk minefields of educational contradictions in the contemporary pedagogical landscape. On some levels teachers and students discover that schools pursue democratic goals and education for a democratic society; on other levels they find that schools are authoritarian and pursue anti-democratic goals of social control for particular groups and individuals. Sometimes participants learn that schools are grounded on cooperative values; in high-stakes test-driven curricula they find that a competitive ethic is dominant. At other junctures students and teachers are told that the knowledge of schools is based on a diversity of cultural and global sources; when the curriculum is delineated, however, they often find that school knowledge comes primarily from dominant cultural, class, and gender groups (Apple, 1999; Schubert, 1998).

Advocates of critical pedagogy are aware that every minute of every hour that teachers teach, they are faced with complex decisions concerning justice, democracy, and competing ethical claims. Although they have to make individual determinations of what to do in these particular circumstances, they must concurrently deal with what John Goodlad (1994) calls the surrounding institutional morality. A central tenet of pedagogy maintains that the classroom, curricular, and school structures teachers enter are not neutral sites waiting to be shaped by educational professionals. Although such professionals do possess agency, this prerogative is not completely free and independent of decisions made previously by people operating with different values and shaped by the ideologies and cultural assumptions of their historical contexts. These contexts are shaped in the same ways language and knowledge are constructed, as historical power makes particular practices seem natural—as if they could have been constructed in no other way (Bartolomé, 1998; Berry, 2000; Cochran-Smith, 2000; Ferreira and Alexandre, 2000).

Thus, proponents of critical pedagogy understand that every dimension of schooling and every form of educational practice are politically contested spaces. Shaped by history and challenged by a wide range of interest groups, educational practice is a fuzzy concept as it takes place in numerous settings, is shaped by a plethora of often invisible forces, and can operate even in the name of democracy and justice to be totalitarian and oppressive. Many teacher education students have trouble with this political dimension and the basic notion that schooling can be hurtful to particular students. They embrace the institution of education as "good" because in their own experience it has been good to them. Thus, the recognition of these political complications of schooling is a first step for critical pedagogy-influenced educators in developing a social activist teacher persona. As teachers gain these insights, they understand that cultural, race, class, and gender forces have shaped all elements of the pedagogical act. They also discover that a central aspect of democratic education involves addressing these dynamics as they systematically manifest themselves (Crebbin, 2001; Gergen and Gergen, 2000; Knobel, 1999; Noone and Cartwright, 1996).

Critical pedagogy is a complex notion that asks much of the practitioners who embrace it. Teaching a critical pedagogy involves more than learning a few pedagogical techniques and the knowledge required by the curriculum, the standards, or the textbook. Critical teachers must understand not only a wide body of subject matter but also the political structure of the school. They must also possess a wide range of education in the culture: TV, radio, popular music, movies, the Internet, youth subcultures, and so on; alternative bodies of knowledge produced by marginalized or low-status groups; the ways power operates to construct identities and oppress particular groups; the modus operandi (MO) of the ways social regulation operates; the complex processes of racism, gender bias, class bias, cultural bias, heterosexism, religious intolerance, and so on; the cultural experiences of students; diverse teaching styles; the forces that shape the curriculum; the often conflicting purposes of education; and much more. This introduction to critical pedagogy issues a challenge to teachers, to educational leaders, and to students to dive into this complex domain of critical pedagogy. Many of us believe that the rewards for both yourself and your students will far outweigh the liabilities.

Nothing is impossible when we work in solidarity with love, respect, and justice as our guiding lights. Indeed, the great Brazilian critical educator Paulo Freire always maintained that education had as much to do with the teachable heart as it did with the mind. Love is the basis of an education that seeks justice, equality, and genius. If critical pedagogy is not injected with a healthy dose of what Freire called "radical love," then it will operate only as a shadow of what it could be. Such a love is compassionate, erotic, creative, sensual, and informed. Critical pedagogy uses it to increase our capacity to love, to bring the power of love to our everyday lives and social institutions, and to rethink reason in a humane and interconnected manner. Knowledge in this context takes on a form quite different from its more accepted and mainstream versions. A critical knowledge seeks to connect with the corporeal and the emotional in a way that understands at multiple levels and seeks to assuage human suffering.

radical love

The version of critical pedagogy offered here is infused with the impassioned spirit of Freire. I experience this spirit in my life when watching and listening to

- an A.M.E. church choir from New Orleans singing gospel songs

- Native American women making tremolo at a Sioux college graduation

- a rock band in a groove that shakes an audience to its core

- a Spanish calypso singer squeezing out every last note as the audience fills the air with heartfelt "olés"

- a dedicated and well-informed teacher bringing a group of students to life with her knowledge, passion for learning, and her ability to engage them in the process of teaching themselves and others.

I'm sure you sense this impassioned spirit in your own spaces. Critical pedagogy wants to connect education to that feeling, to embolden teachers and students to act in ways that make a difference, and to push humans to new levels of social and cognitive achievement previously deemed impossible. Critical pedagogy is an ambitious entity that seeks nothing less than a form of educational adventurism that takes us where nobody's gone before.

This impassioned spirit moves critical teachers to study power inscriptions and their often pernicious effects. The actions such teachers take to address them constitute one dimension of putting a critical pedagogy into action. Critical teacher educators must model this complex behavior for their education students in every dimension of professional education. This approach becomes extremely important when we understand the fear of the impassioned spirit and the hostility of many teacher education programs toward ideas that consider the effects of power on shaping and misshaping the pedagogical act. There are still too many teacher education programs that assume schooling is unequivocally a good thing serving the best interests of individual students, marginalized groups of students, and the culture in general. Such programs assume that the curriculum, institutional organizations, hiring practices, and field placements of the educational world are just and equitable and do not need examination on these levels. Critical teacher educators possess the difficult task of inducing students to challenge the very practices and ways of seeing they have been taught in their professional programs. Do "best practices," critical students ask, "help create a democratic consciousness and modes of making meaning that detect indoctrination and social regulation?"

Such critical pedagogical ways of seeing help teacher educators and teachers reconstruct their work so that it facilitates the empowerment of all students. In this context, critical educators understand that such an effort takes place in an increasingly power-inscribed world in which dominant modes of exclusion are continuously "naturalized" by power wielders' control of information. "What does this have to do with teacher education?" Critics may ask. "We live in a democracy," they assert. Why do we have to spend all this time with such political issues? Isn't our focus teaching and learning? However, democracy is fragile, critical educators maintain, and embedded in education are the very issues that make or break it. Are teachers merely managers of the predetermined knowledge of dominant cultural power? Is teacher education merely the process of developing the most efficient ways for educators to perform this task? Do teachers operate as functionaries who simply do what they are told? Contrary to the views of many, these questions of democracy and justice cannot be separated from the most fundamental features of teaching and learning (Cochran-Smith, 2000; Grimmett, 1999; Horton and Freire, 1990; McLaren, 2000; Powell, 2001; Rodriguez and Villaverde, 2000; Vavrus and Archibald, 1998).

This chapter analyzes and expands upon these themes of critical pedagogy. Throughout, I focus on questions of democracy, justice, and quality in the pedagogical context. There is no doubt that these issues are complex and passionate feelings surround them. In this context, I attempt to provide a fair picture of critical pedagogy but not a neutral one. As a political animal, I hold particular perspectives about the purpose of schooling and the nature of a just society. These viewpoints shape what follows. The best I can do is to reflect on where such perspectives come from and decide whether or not I want to maintain my dedication to them. Be aware of these biases and make sure you read what I have to say critically and suspiciously. Furthermore, be certain to read all texts in this same way, especially the ones that claim an objective and neutral truth. As I tell my students, whenever individuals tell me they are providing me with the objective truth I guard my wallet. As critical pedagogy maintains, little in the world and certainly little in the world of education is neutral. Indeed, the impassioned spirit is never neutral.

The Central Characteristics of Critical Pedagogy

All descriptions of critical pedagogy—like knowledge in general—are shaped by those who devise them and the values they hold. The description offered here is no different. Many will agree with it and sing its praises, while others will be disappointed—and even offended—by what was included and what was left out. As with any other description I would offer about any social or cultural phenomenon, my delineation of the central characteristics of critical pedagogy is merely my "take" and reflects my biases and perspectives.

Critical Pedagogy Is Grounded on a Social and Educational Vision of Justice and Equality

Educational reformers can discuss collaborative school cultures and reflective practices all they want, but such concepts mean very little outside a rigorous, informed vision of the purpose of education. Many educational leaders and school boards are crippled by the absence of informed discussion about educational purpose. Without this grounding their conversations about what to do in schooling go around in circles with little direction and less imagination. Clichés abound as wheels are perpetually reinvented and old wine seeks new packaging. In the contemporary era there are endless attempts at school reform with little improvement to show for the efforts. Without an educational vision, most educational reforms create little more benefit than applying Aspercreme to ease the pain of a massive head wound. The educational vision, the purpose of schooling promoted here, demands a fundamental rethinking, a deep reconceptualization of

- what human beings are capable of achieving

- the role of the social, cultural, and political in shaping human identity

- the relationship between community and schooling

- the ways that power operates to create purposes for schooling that are not necessarily in the best interests of the children that attend them

- how teachers and students might relate to knowledge

- the ways schooling affects the lives of students from marginalized groups

- the organization of schooling and the relationship between teachers and learners.

A critical pedagogical vision grounded as it is in social, cultural, cognitive, economic, and political contexts understands schooling as part of a larger set of human services and community development. Any viable vision of critical education has to be based on larger social and cognitive visions. In this context, educators deal not only with questions of schooling, curriculum, and educational policy but also with social justice and human possibility. Understanding these dynamics, critical educators devise new modes of making connections between school and its context as well as catalyzing community resources to help facilitate quality education with an impassioned spirit. With this larger vision in mind and knowledge of these different contexts, educators are empowered to identify the insidious forces that subvert the success of particular students. This ability is not generally found in typical educational practice. Without it, educators and school leaders experience great difficulty in determining what is important knowledge in their particular school or school district. Without it, such individuals cannot determine why some policies and pedagogies work to accomplish some goals and not others (Bamburg, 1994; MDRC, 2002; Wang and Kovach, 1996).

This stunting of potential takes place in the pedagogy of low expectations where concern with disciplining the incompetent poor to create a more ordered and efficient society takes the place of a democratic critical social vision. Historical accounts of schools designed for these regulatory purposes alert us to the dangers of such educational structures (see Kincheloe, Slattery, and Steinberg, Chapter 5 for a discussion of this theme). Throughout history, such schools have served to categorize, punish, restrict, and restrain those students who failed to fit the proper demographic. Our critical vision of education enables us to see education in a systemic context. In this context, we gain an appreciation of the importance of the relationship between education and other social dynamics (FAUSSR, 1998). These interactions are complex, as all social, political, economic, cultural, and educational decisions are interrelated. With such an understanding, we can begin to reshape these relationships and the educational decisions we make in relation to them in new and previously unexplored ways.

In concrete terms, the implementation of this vision means that teachers can begin to develop distinct practices to help particular students flourish in schools located in specific communities. In this context, critical teachers draw on their larger vision to help them determine what types of human beings they want to graduate from their schools. Do we want socially regulated workers with the proper attitudes for their respective rung on the workplace ladder? Or do we want empowered, learned, highly skilled democratic citizens who have the confidence and the savvy to improve their own lives and to make their communities more vibrant places in which to live, work, and play? If we are unable to articulate this transformative, just, and egalitarian critical pedagogical vision, then the job of schooling will continue to involve taming, controlling, and/or rescuing the least empowered of our students. Such students do not need to be tamed, controlled, and/or rescued; they need to be respected, viewed as experts in their interest areas, and inspired with the impassioned spirit to use education to do good things in the world.

Critical Pedagogy Is Constructed on the Belief That Education Is Inherently Political

Whether one is teaching in Bangladesh or Bensonhurst, Senegal or Shreveport, East Timor or West New York, education is a political activity. Who is hired for the third-grade position at Scarsdale Elementary, the decision to adopt the Success for All curriculum in District Nine in Brooklyn, the textbook chosen for the eighth-grade science class at Cedar Bluff Middle School, the language used to teach math at Coconut Grove Elementary School in Miami—these decisions all hold profound political implications. They refer to power and how it is distributed and engaged in the world of education and life in schools. For example, the decisions made in the previous examples will often privilege students from dominant cultural backgrounds—upper middle class, white, heterosexual, first language English, and Christian—while at the same time undermining the interests of those who fall outside these domains.

By utilizing IQ tests and developmental theories derived from research on students from dominant cultural backgrounds, schools not only reflect social stratification but also extend it. This is an example of school as an institution designed for social benefit actually exerting hurtful influences. Teachers involved in the harmful processes most often do not intentionally hurt students; they are merely following the dictates of their superiors and the rules of the system. Countless good teachers work every day to subvert the negative effects of the system but need help from like-minded colleagues and organizations. Critical pedagogy works to provide such assistance to teachers who want to mitigate the effects of power on their students. Here schools as political institutions merge with critical pedagogy's concern with creating a social and educational vision to help teachers direct their own professional practice. Any time teachers develop a pedagogy, they are concurrently constructing a political vision. The two acts are inseparable.

Many times, unfortunately, those who develop pedagogies are unconscious of the political inscriptions embedded within them. A district supervisor who writes a curriculum in social studies, for example, that demands the simple transference of a body of established facts about the great men and great events of American history is also teaching a political lesson that upholds the status quo (Degener, 2002; Keesing-Styles, 2003; 21st Century Schools, 2003). There is no room for students or teachers in such a curriculum to explore alternate sources, to compare diverse historical interpretations, to do research of their own and produce knowledge that may conflict with prevailing interpretations. Such acts of democratic citizenship may be viewed as subversive and anti-American by the supervisor and the district education office. Indeed, such personnel may be under pressure from the state department of education to construct a history curriculum that is inflexible, based on the status quo, unquestioning in its approach, "fact-based," and teacher-centered. Dominant power operates in numerous and often hidden ways.

Peter McLaren (2000) writes that this power dimension of critical pedagogy is central and that practitioners must be aware of efforts to dilute this power literacy. Today, critical pedagogy has been associated with everything from simply the rearrangement of classroom furniture to "feel-good" teaching directed at improving students' self-esteem. Simply caring about students, while necessary, does not constitute a critical pedagogy. The power dimension must be brought to bear in a way that discerns and acts on correcting the ways particular students get hurt in the everyday life of schools. When critical pedagogy embraces multiculturalism, it focuses on the subtle workings of racism, sexism, class bias, cultural oppression, and homophobia. It is not sufficient for a critical multiculturalism (Kincheloe and Steinberg, 1997; Kincheloe, Steinberg, Rodriguez, and Chennault, 1998) to build a program around supposedly depoliticized taco days, falafels, and Martin Luther King's birthday.

The ability to act on these political concerns is one of the most difficult tasks of critical pedagogy. Over the decades many conservative educators have participated in a Great Denial of the political dimension of education. In this denial, curricula and syllabi that fail to challenge the status quo are viewed as neutral documents presenting essential data. Students who want to become teachers have oftentimes encountered courses in political denial. Throughout elementary and secondary schools they were presented the facts unproblematically as if they were true. In college their liberal arts and sciences courses many times simply delivered the facts in biology, physics, sociology, psychology, or literature. The idea that these courses presented only one narrow perspective on the field in question, that they left out competing forms of knowledge produced by scholars from different schools of thought or from different cultures, was never mentioned. The political assumptions behind the curricula they encountered were erased. To ask such students to start over, to relearn the arts and sciences in light of these political concerns, is admittedly an ambitious task. Even so, this is exactly what critical pedagogy does, and those of us in the field believe such an effort is worth the time invested. A first-year teacher cannot accomplish such a huge task in the first year of his or her practice, but over a decade one can. Critical pedagogy challenges you to take the leap.

An important aspect of the Great Denial is that politics should be kept out of education and that is what mainstream curricula do. Critical pedagogy argues that such pronouncements are not grounded on an understanding of power. The political dimensions of education should be pointed out in all teaching and learning—critical pedagogy included. We must expose the hidden politics of what is labeled neutral. Such calls are often equated with a pedagogy of indoctrination. The critical educator Henry Giroux (1988) responds to such charges, contending that such criticism is flawed. Giroux argues that it confuses the development of a political vision with the pedagogy that is used in conjunction with it. Advocates of critical pedagogy make their own commitments clear as they construct forms of teaching consistent with the democratic notion that students learn to make their own choices of beliefs based on the diverse perspectives they confront in school and society. Education simply can't be neutral. When education pretends to be politically neutral like many churches in Nazi Germany, it supports the dominant, existing power structure. Recognition of these educational politics suggests that teachers take a position and make it understandable to their students. *They do not, however, have the right to impose these positions on their students.* This is a central tenet of critical pedagogy.

In this context it is not the advocates of critical pedagogy who are most often guilty of impositional teaching but many of the mainstream critics themselves. When mainstream opponents of critical pedagogy promote the notion that all language and political behavior that oppose the dominant ideology are forms of indoctrination, they forget how experience is shaped by unequal forms of power. To refuse to name the forces that produce human suffering and exploitation is to take a position that supports oppression and powers that perpetuate it. The argument that any position opposing the actions of dominant power wielders represents an imposition of one's views on somebody else is problematic. It is tantamount to saying that one who admits her oppositional political sentiments and makes them known to students is guilty of indoctrination, while one who hides her consent to dominant power and the status quo it has produced from her students is operating in an objective and neutral manner. Critical pedagogy wants to know who's indoctrinating whom. These political dynamics won't go away and teachers must deal with them.

Critical Pedagogy Is Dedicated to the Alleviation of Human Suffering

Knowing and learning are not simply intellectual and scholarly activities but also practical and sensuous activities infused by the impassioned spirit. Critical pedagogy is dedicated to addressing and embodying these affective, emotional, and lived dimensions of everyday life in a way that connects students to people in groups and as individuals. In this context, the advocates of critical pedagogy are especially concerned with those groups and individuals who are suffering, whose lives are affected by the sting of discrimination and poverty. Acting on this concern critical educators seek out the causes of such suffering in their understandings of power with its ideological, hegemonic, disciplinary, and regulatory dimensions.

Indeed, the very origins of critical pedagogy—the tradition that lays the groundwork for critical pedagogy and is concerned with power and its oppression of human beings and regulation of the social order—are grounded on this concern with human suffering. Herbert Marcuse, one of the founders of the Frankfurt School of Critical Theory, and Paulo Freire were profoundly moved by the suffering they respectively witnessed in post–World War I Germany and Brazil. Although I am committed to a critical pedagogy that continues to develop and operates to sophisticate its understandings of the world and the educational act, this evolving critical pedagogy in education should never, never lose sight of its central concern with human suffering. One does not have to go too far to find suffering. In the United States, suffering is often well hidden, but a trip to inner cities, rural Appalachia, or Native American reservations will reveal its existence. Outside of the United States, we can go to almost any region of the world and see tragic expressions of human misery. Advocates of critical pedagogy believe such suffering is a humanly constructed phenomenon and does not have to exist. Steps can be taken to eradicate such suffering if the people of the planet and their leaders had the collective will to do so. In recent years, however, market-driven, globalized economic systems pushed on the world by the United States and other industrialized nations via the World Trade Organization (WTO) and the International Monetary Fund (IMF) have exacerbated poverty and its attendant suffering.

Understanding at the theoretical level, both how diverse influences insidiously shape what we perceive and don't perceive about the world and how we can better cultivate the intellect, is a central dimension of critical pedagogy and must always be connected to the reality of human suffering and the effort to eradicate it. Sometimes scholarship and teaching operating exclusively on the theoretical level remove us from and anesthetize us to human pain and suffering. This insensitivity is unacceptable to the critical educator. In critical pedagogy the theoretical domain always interacts with the lived domain, producing a synergy that elevates both scholarship and transformative action. Indeed, the very definition of a critical consciousness involves the development of new forms of understanding that connect us more directly to understanding, empathizing with, and acting to alleviate suffering. Sophisticated understandings and engagement in the struggle against inequality characterize a critical consciousness. Such a struggle engages the lived suffering that comes out of oppression while it studies its consequences in the realm of knowledge production (Barone, 2000; Giroux, 1997; Hicks, 1999; Madison, 1988; McLaren, 2000; 21st Century Schools, 2003).

Pedagogy That Prevents Students From Being Hurt

Critical pedagogy mandates that schools don't hurt students—good schools don't blame students for their failures or strip students of the forms of knowledge they bring to the classroom. In a recent book

I coedited with Alberto Bursztyn and Shirley Steinberg (2004), I began the introductory essay with the proclamation that "I don't trust schools." What I was trying to get across involved the understanding that those of us concerned with critical pedagogy have to be very wary of the goals schools embrace and the ways they engage particular individuals and groups. To exemplify my concern, I often ask students in my classes and audience members in my speeches if any of them have ever studied at any point during their schooling the story of the European colonization of Africa and the effects of the slave trade. The slave trade killed at the very least tens of millions of Africans; some scholars say two hundred million—estimates vary.

I often find that no one in a classroom or audience has encountered this human tragedy in any systematic detail in his or her schooling. In this context, I typically point out that I simply could not trust an institution that routinely ignored such information. The very idea that these millions of unnecessary deaths would not rate as one of the most important events of the last millennium is hard to understand. An institution that would not engage students in wrestling with the moral responsibilities accompanying acquaintance with such knowledge is both intellectually and ethically impaired. Something is wrong here. In no way do advocates of critical pedagogy blame teachers for this failure. They, too, have been victimized by the same social systems that have produced this situation. Indeed, their job is hard enough and so little respected that they don't need flack from this domain. The arts and sciences programs in colleges and universities that were responsible for this aspect of teacher education failed them.

Understanding that education is always political as it supports the needs of the dominant culture while subverting the interests of marginalized cultures, critical pedagogy does not allow such omissions in the curricula it develops. In this context advocates of critical pedagogy work to make sure schools don't continue to be hurtful places. The same institutions that don't teach about the mass killings in Europe's African slave trade—and scores of other atrocities that could be listed here—also blame students for their academic problems. In many schools and especially those shaped by the George W. Bush administration's "No Child Left Behind" legislation in the early twenty-first century, teachers are discouraged from taking into account the social, cultural, and economic backgrounds of their students and the needs and interests that emerge from them.

The exclusion of the social, cultural, and economic ways of knowing from the development of curriculum often holds tragic consequences for students. Many educational leaders influenced by psychometrics (the discipline that measures intelligence) and mainstream versions of educational psychology construct schools around the belief that intelligence and academic ability are individual dynamics free from social, cultural, and economic influences. Since the time of Plato, theories of intelligence have been employed to justify socioeconomic disparity and scholarly inferiority. The "dregs" at the bottom have always been said to be deficient and/or pathological. Critical educators feel that it is an outrage to separate environmental factors from efforts to measure ability or intelligence.

It doesn't take a brain surgeon to uncover the process that occurs when a culturally different and/or poor student encounters the middle-class, white-culture-grounded practice of school and the intelligence-testing establishment. The middle-class mind-set often views poverty as a badge of failure. Many educational leaders and psychologists seem to be unconcerned with the psychic toll that declarations of failure inflict on marginalized children and adolescents. Advocates of critical pedagogy understand how hard it is to go day after day to a school where you are viewed as a failure in all aspects of your life. Should we be surprised when such students express hostility and anger about having to be in such schools or when they reject the value of academic work in their lives? In many ways such responses are logical reactions; they are strategies of self-protection in a hostile and hurtful environment. When tracking policies are added to this mix, the hurtful nature of schools is enhanced. Operating on the simple-minded assumptions of psychometrics and achievement and standards tests, students are deemed capable or incapable of academic work. Those who score poorly are relegated to the "slow" classes that serve to further undermine their academic performance (Beck, 1991; Grubb et al., 1991; Kincheloe and Steinberg, 1997; Kincheloe, Steinberg, and Gresson, 1996; Oakes, 1985).

Critical pedagogy will not stand for these mechanisms of social and educational stratification that hurt socially, linguistically, and economically marginalized students so badly. The cultural backgrounds of African American, Native American, poor Appalachian, and Latino students are often deemed by middle-class, white schools to be inferior to those of the dominant culture. Because of such perspectives, students from such backgrounds come to realize that success in school may come only with a rejection of their ethnic and/or class backgrounds and the cultural forms of knowledge that accompany them. Lilia Bartolomé (1996) refers to this process as the robbing of students' "culture, language, history, and values" (p. 233). Critical teachers work to foil this robbery by helping students recall what they already know. Such teachers take student knowledge seriously and examine it as part of their curriculum. Students who possess particular insight about a topic can become the teacher for a day and share their knowledge with other students in the class. Knowing that they possess valuable knowledge, such students begin to realize that they are capable of learning much more. With this realization, teachers work with students to delineate what else they can learn and how it can be useful in their lives.

The Importance of Generative Themes

Critical pedagogy is enacted through the use of generative themes to read the word and the world and the process of problem posing. Critical pedagogy applies Paulo Freire's notion of generative themes used to help students read the word and the world. This reading of the word and the world helped students connect what they decoded on the printed page to an understanding of the world around them. Thus, a synergistic relationship emerged between word and world. After exploring the community around the school and engaging in conversations with community members, Freire constructed generative themes designed to tap into issues that were important to various students in his class. As data on these issues were brought into the class, Freire became a problem poser. In this capacity, Freire used the knowledge he and his students had produced around the generative themes to construct questions. The questions he constructed were designed to teach the lesson that no subject matter or knowledge in general was beyond examination. We need to ask questions of all knowledge, Freire argued, because all data are shaped by the context and by the individuals that produced them. Knowledge, contrary to the pronouncements of many educational leaders, does not transcend culture or history.

In the context of reading the word and the world and problem posing existing knowledge, critical educators reconceptualize the notion of literacy. Myles Horton spoke of the way he read books with students in order "to give testimony to the students about what it means to read a text" (Horton and Freire, 1990). Reading is not an easy endeavor, Horton continued, for to be a good reader is to view reading as a form of research. Thus, reading becomes a mode of finding something, and finding something, he concluded, brings a joy that is directly connected to the acts of creation and re-creation. One finds in this reading that the word and world process typically goes beyond the given, the common sense of everyday life. Several years ago, I wrote a book entitled *Getting Beyond the Facts* (2001b). The point of the title was to signify this going beyond, to represent a form of reading that not only understood the words on the page but the unstated dominant ideologies hidden between the sentences as well.

This going beyond is central to Freirean problem posing. Such a position contends that the school curriculum should in part be shaped by problems that face teachers and students in their effort to live just and ethical lives. Such a curriculum promotes students as researchers (Steinberg and Kincheloe, 1998) who engage in critical analysis of the forces that shape the world. Such critical analysis engenders a healthy and creative skepticism on the part of students. It moves them to problem-pose, to be suspicious of neutrality claims in textbooks; it induces them to look askance at, for example, oil companies' claims in their TV commercials that they are and have always been environmentally friendly organizations. Students and teachers who are problem posers reject the traditional student request to the teacher: "just give us the facts, the truth and we'll give it back to you." On the contrary, critical students and teachers ask in the spirit of Freire and Horton: "please support us in our explorations of the world."

By promoting problem posing and student research, teachers do not simply relinquish their authority in the classroom. Over the last couple of decades several teachers and students have misunderstood the subtlety of the nature of teacher authority in a critical pedagogy. Freire in the last years of his life was very concerned with this issue and its misinterpretation by those operating in his name. Teachers, he told me, cannot deny their position of authority in such a classroom. It is the teacher, not the students, who evaluates student work, who is responsible for the health, safety, and learning of students. To deny the role of authority the teacher occupies is insincere at best, dishonest at worst. Critical teachers, therefore, must admit that they are in a position of authority and then demonstrate that authority in their actions in support of students. One of the actions involves the ability to conduct research/produce knowledge. The authority of the critical teacher is dialectical; as teachers relinquish the authority of truth providers, they assume the mature authority of facilitators of student inquiry and problem posing. In relation to such teacher authority, students gain their freedom—they gain the ability to become self-directed human beings capable of producing their own knowledge.

Teachers as Researchers

In the new right-wing educational order that exists in the twenty-first century, knowledge is something that is produced far away from the school by experts in an exalted domain. This must change if a critical reform of schooling is to ever take place. Teachers must have more say, more respect, in the culture of education. Teachers must join the culture of researchers if a new level of educational rigor and quality is ever to be achieved. In such a democratized culture, critical teachers are scholars who understand the power implications of various educational reforms. In this context, they appreciate the benefits of research, especially as they relate to understanding the forces shaping education that fall outside their immediate experience and perception. As these insights are constructed, teachers begin to understand what they know from experience. With this in mind they gain heightened awareness of how they can contribute to the research on education. Indeed, they realize that they have access to understandings that go far beyond what the expert researchers have produced.

In the critical school culture, teachers are viewed as learners—not as functionaries who follow top-down orders without question. Teachers are seen as researchers and knowledge workers who reflect on their professional needs and current understandings. They are aware of the complexity of the educational process and how schooling cannot be understood outside of the social, historical, philosophical, cultural, economic, political, and psychological contexts that shape it. Scholar teachers understand that curriculum development responsive to student needs is not possible when it fails to account for these contexts. With this in mind, they explore and attempt to interpret the learning processes that take place in their classrooms. "What are its psychological, sociological, and ideological effects?" they ask. Thus, critical scholar teachers research their own professional practice (Kraft, 2001; Norris, 1998).

With empowered scholar teachers prowling the schools, things begin to change. The oppressive culture created in twenty-first-century schools by top-down content standards, for example, is challenged. In-service staff development no longer takes the form of "this is what the expert researchers found—now go implement it." Such staff development in the critical culture of schooling gives way to teachers who analyze and contemplate the power of each other's ideas. Thus, the new critical culture of school takes on the form of a "think tank that teaches students," a learning community. School administrators are amazed by what can happen when they support learning activities for both students and teachers. Principals and curriculum developers watch as teachers develop projects that encourage collaboration and shared research. There is an alternative, advocates of critical pedagogy argue, to top-down standards with their deskilling of teachers and the "dumbing-down" of students (Jardine, 1998; Kincheloe, 2003; Norris, 1998; Novick, 1996).

Promoting teachers as researchers is a fundamental way of cleaning up the damage of deskilled models of teaching that infantilize teachers by giving them scripts to read to their students.

Teacher says:	Class, take out your pencils.
	[teacher waits until all students have their pencils in hand.]
Teacher then says:	Class, turn to page 15 of your textbook.
	[teacher waits until all students have turned to correct page.]
Teacher says:	Read pages 15–17. When you are finished, close your books and put your hands on the top of your desk. You have ten minutes.

Deskilling of teachers and dumbing-down of the curriculum take place when teachers are seen as receivers, rather than producers, of knowledge. A vibrant professional culture depends on a group of practitioners who have the freedom to continuously reinvent themselves via their research and knowledge production. Teachers engaged in critical practice find it difficult to allow top-down content standards and their poisonous effects to go unchallenged. Such teachers cannot abide the deskilling and reduction in professional status that accompany these top-down reforms. Advocates of critical pedagogy understand that teacher empowerment does not occur just because we wish it to. Instead, it takes place when teachers develop the knowledge-work skills, the power literacy, and the pedagogical abilities befitting the calling of teaching. Teacher research is a central dimension of a critical pedagogy.

Teachers as Researchers of Their Students

A central aspect of critical teacher research involves studying students, so they can be better understood and taught. Freire argued that all teachers need to engage in a constant dialogue with students that questions existing knowledge and problematizes the traditional power relations that have served to marginalize specific groups and individuals. In these research dialogues with students, critical teachers listen carefully to what students have to say about their communities and the problems that confront them. Teachers help students frame these problems in a larger social, cultural, and political context in order to solve them.

In this context, Freire argued that teachers uncover materials and generative themes based on their emerging knowledge of students and their sociocultural backgrounds. Teachers come to understand the ways students perceive themselves and their interrelationships with other people and their social reality. This information is essential to the critical pedagogical act as it helps teachers understand how they make sense of schooling and their lived worlds. With these understandings in mind, critical teachers come to know what and how students make meaning. This enables teachers to construct pedagogies that engage the impassioned spirit of students in ways that move them to learn what they don't know and to identify what they want to know (Degener, 2002; Freire and Faundez, 1989; Kincheloe and Steinberg, 1998).

It is not an exaggeration to say that before critical pedagogy can work, teachers must understand what is happening in the minds of their students. Freire, Giroux, McLaren, Shirley Steinberg, bell hooks, Patti Lather, Deborah Britzman, and Donaldo Macedo are all advocates of various forms of critical teaching who recognize the importance of understanding the social construction of student consciousness, focusing on motives, values, and emotions. Operating within this critical context, the teacher researcher studies students as living texts to be deciphered. The teacher researcher approaches them with an active imagination and a willingness to view students as socially constructed beings.

When critical teachers have approached research on students from this perspective, they have uncovered some interesting information. In a British action research project, for example, teachers used student diaries, interviews, dialogues, and shadowing (following students as they pursue their daily routines at school) to uncover a student preoccupation with what was labeled a second-order curriculum. This curriculum involved matters of student dress, conforming to school rules, strategies of coping with boredom and failure, and methods of assuming their respective roles in the school pecking order. Teacher researchers found that much of this second-order curriculum worked to contradict the stated aims of the school to respect the individuality of students, to encourage sophisticated thinking, and to engender positive self-images. Students often perceived that the daily lessons of teachers (the intentional curriculum) were based on a set of assumptions quite different from those guiding out-of-class teacher interactions with students. Teachers consistently misread the anger and hostility resulting from such inconsistency. Only in an action research context that values the perceptions of students could such student emotions be understood and addressed (Armstrong, 1981; Kincheloe, 2001b; Oldroyd, 1985; Steinberg, 2000; Wood, 1988).

Social Change and Cultivating the Intellect

Critical pedagogy is interested in maintaining a delicate balance between social change and cultivating the intellect—developing a rigorous education in a hostile environment that accomplishes both goals. Freire always maintained that pedagogy has as much to do with the effort to change the world as with developing rigorous forms of analysis. In other words, a critical pedagogy is not only interested in social change but also in cultivating the intellect of teachers, students, and members of the larger society. There is nothing simplistic about this delicate and synergistic relationship. We cannot simply attempt to cultivate the intellect without changing the unjust social context in which such minds operate. Critical educators cannot just work to change the social order without helping to educate a knowledgeable and skillful group of students. Creating a just, progressive, creative, and democratic society demands both dimensions of this pedagogical process.

Freire and Horton were adamant about connecting these dimensions. Social change pursued in isolation can insidiously promote anti-intellectualism if critical educators are not careful. As Horton (Horton and Freire, 1990) put it, a teacher cannot be a coordinator or facilitator "if you don't know anything. What the hell are you around for, if you don't know anything? Just get out of the way and let somebody have the space that knows something" (p. 154). As Freire told me shortly before his death: "No teacher is worth her salt who is not able to confront students with a rigorous body of knowledge. This is not to endorse a banking education but to support the idea that teachers often provide students with knowledge that students then react to, reject, reinterpret, analyze, and put into action." Teachers, Freire and Horton agreed, must model rigorous thinking and compelling ways of being a scholar for their students.

Often in my own writing about critical pedagogy I use the concept of complexity to help signify the importance of bringing together the goals of social change and the cultivation of the intellect. In doing so, I use the phrases "complex critical pedagogy" and "a critical complex education" (Kincheloe and Weil, 2001). Accomplishing these two goals is always complex and must be understood in great detail by critical teachers. In order to construct and enact a pedagogy that is socially transformative as well as rigorous in its cultivation of the intellect, teachers must be acutely aware of the complicated world of education with its diverse cultural settings and wide range of student backgrounds. Such goals cannot be accomplished without a compelling understanding of the goals themselves and the complicated context in which education takes place. Advocates of top-down standards, for example, assume that if we lay out the minimum content requirements that all students must meet and then teach everyone in the same way, schools will be improved. They don't seem to recognize the diverse needs and dispositions toward the schooling process that different students bring to the classroom. Would we teach the same skills and content in the same way to a group of students in a classroom where most students read below grade level as opposed to one where all students read above grade level? How do we develop and enact a pedagogy that takes into account this and a thousand other levels of diversity? Any pedagogy that doesn't address such issues is mere window dressing, a public relations campaign for particular political operatives.

Obviously, there are thousands of different ways to learn and critical teachers must gain an awareness of such cognitive differences in their efforts to teach in more sophisticated ways. Often these cognitive differences are connected to cultural issues such as race, ethnicity, socioeconomic class, gender, religious beliefs, and other factors. A critical complex pedagogy must understand the effects of these contextual factors, in particular the ways they affect school performance. Without such an understanding, cultural and cognitive *difference* are confused with academic *deficiency*. Learning to make this distinction and then developing a curriculum to address the difficulties students experience is a necessary teaching ability in a critical complex pedagogy.

In the twenty-first century, classrooms in this society are structured by multiple layers of complexity. Typically ignoring this reality, top-down, standards-oriented reforms often view the educational world as one homogenous group—everyone comes from an upper-middle-class, white, English-speaking background. Even relatively simple distinctions such as the difference between the goals of elementary and secondary education are often overlooked by the present standards conversation. Elementary educators teach all subjects and are expected to be content generalists. Of course, secondary teachers teach particular areas in the present school configuration and are expected to be content specialists. Elementary teachers are now being presented with stacks of content standards in a variety of fields with little, if any, help in integrating them or making sense of how these bodies of content might fit into an elementary education.

Secondary teachers are now being provided with large collections of top-down content standards in their disciplines. If such teachers possess the skills such standards dictate, then they are induced to discard their disciplinary knowledge and experience and embrace without question a body of externally imposed data. Such a pedagogy fails to produce transformative action or intellectual challenge. Teachers always deserve to be a part of the conversation about standards and educational reform, not deskilled functionaries who mechanically do what they are told by external inquisitors. In a complex critical pedagogy, teachers must not only engage in a dialogue with standards devisors but also need to buy into the logic of such a critical complex rigor if improvements are to be made. Advocates of a critical pedagogy must be prepared to convince teachers that such goals are worthy. Such advocates must be prepared to help teachers move from their present understandings to a more complex view of the teaching act that includes social transformation and the cultivation of the intellect. No educational reform can work if teachers are excluded from the negotiations about its development and implementation.

Marginalization and Critical Pedagogy

Critical pedagogy is interested in the margins of society, the experiences and needs of individuals faced with oppression and marginalization. It is not merely interested in the experiences and needs of students who come from the mythical center of the social order. Thus, critical teachers seek out individuals, voices, texts, and perspectives that had been previously excluded. Mainstream scholarship and the education it supports often drop the margins from consideration in order to concentrate on the so-called typical. Critical pedagogy, thus, amplifies the voices of those who have had to struggle to be heard. Unfortunately, in contemporary U.S. society and its schooling, there are many excluded voices coming from multiple margins. Several times in the last few years, critical pedagogy itself has been accused of ignoring particular voices. The critical pedagogy that I am describing here must not marginalize the voices of any subjugated individual or group.

A complex critical pedagogy is always searching for new voices that may have been excluded by the dominant culture or by critical pedagogy itself. Poor, non-English as first language, gay, lesbian, and bisexual, physically challenged, nonathletic, nonwhite, overweight, shy, and short students often find themselves oppressed in various ways in school. Students who don't come from such groups and are deemed talented and popular in the school culture often find it very difficult to understand this oppression. From the privileged perspective of the dominant culture, it may be difficult to empathize with the travails of those who have been deemed to be "different." When one is a part of different privileged groups, he or she is less likely to notice the ways that the marginalized are judged by particular norms.

Advocates of critical pedagogy understand that all students can be silenced to some extent by top-down, memory-based classroom arrangements that dictate the issues to be studied, the nature of the lessons, and the arguments employed to support various positions. But marginalized students from the previously enumerated groups are vulnerable to personal humiliation by teachers, administrators, and other students. Such humiliation often follows from the assumption that a lack of familiarity with the habits, problems, values, rituals, and ways of seeing common to the school culture constitutes no mere difference but deficiency on the part of the marginalized. Critical teachers understand the anger, depression, and anxiety such practices incite in such students.

Antonia Darder described one middle-aged African American college student who experienced these emotions in school. In a journal the student kept for one of her classes she explained how she had repressed her anger over her school experiences for years because she always worked to evade trouble with white people. Although she kept quiet for the first several weeks of the term, a class discussion in which white students expressed their resentment about being held accountable for the past racism of others pushed her over the edge. As she listened to white students explain that racism is a relic of history not found in the present, the student exclaimed: "Things may look better to you because you're white and middle class, but maybe you should come to my neighborhood in Watts. Things there are still a mess" (Darder, 1991).

After decades of silence, the student—by way of her own words—gained a new empowerment and developed a new public voice in racially mixed groups. Thinking back on the conversation, the student later wrote that she felt good about expressing her frustrations and rage. Reflecting on her school and work lives, she had come to understand that she had always put on two faces: one for African Americans and another for white people. Like countless other African Americans in offices and classrooms, she did what she had to do to survive in white-dominated institutions. Critical teachers appreciate the cultural dynamics at work in situations such as this one and operate to create safe classrooms that enable rather than repress marginalized students. In no way is this to imply that supporting such students is easy. When race, class, gender, sexual orientation, religion of teachers and students differ, numerous and complicated conflicts can develop. Critical teachers constantly have to deal with the ramifications of these differences.

In this context, advocates of critical pedagogy maintain that teachers must study the ways that a world that is unjust by design shapes the classroom and the relations between teachers and students. By doing this, teachers can begin to discern concrete manifestations of the abstract concept of a world unjust by design. Here critical teachers make use of this knowledge not to "save" marginalized students but to provide a safe space for them and to learn with them about personal empowerment, the cultivation of the intellect, and the larger pursuit of social justice. In a racial context, oftentimes the notion of saving students involves a paternalistic effort to help them become more culturally white. This is not what critical pedagogy is attempting to accomplish. Instead, critical pedagogy is profoundly concerned with understanding subjugated forms of knowledge coming from these various oppressed groups and examining them in relation to other forms of academic knowledge.

Critical teachers explore non-Western, subjugated, and indigenous voices in order to better appreciate the nature and causes of human suffering and the process of domination. Such forms of knowledge are very important to the critical project because of the unique perspective they bring to scholars saturated with the Eurocentric, patriarchal, and elitist ways of seeing. As important as they are, however, indigenous forms of knowledge are not exempt from critique. Advocates of critical pedagogy always respect such forms of knowledge but refuse to turn them into icons that are too precious to analyze and interpret (McLaren, 2000; Semali and Kincheloe, 1999). Understanding such dynamics and putting them into practice in the everyday life of school is a central task of critical teaching. In this context, such understanding helps shape the nature of teacher-student interactions, the curriculum, the culture of the school, and educational purpose in general (Grange, 2003; Keesing-Styles, 2003; Kilduff and Mehra, 1997).

Such studies move critical educators to a larger awareness—so important in light of U.S. efforts at empire-building in the twenty-first century—of the sense of Western superiority embedded in knowledge production and curriculum development. The non-Western, subjugated, and indigenous forms of knowledge previously mentioned are viewed in this context as unsophisticated, backward, and unscientific. What the West has historically labeled reason has been associated with high levels of maturity of human civilization. Those who exercise reason enter a new stage of human maturity. Those who don't are viewed as depraved and underdeveloped. Thus, Western reason is a developmental notion. Different groups of people—races and nations, for example—can be located on a developmental continuum based on reason.

Such developmentalism is found at the individual level in schools as students are placed on a developmental continuum based on their capacity to employ reason. The point advocates of critical pedagogy are making in this context is that reason comes in many forms—the one used by many Western observers and educators is a particular form of reason that is particular to Western societies after the Scientific Revolution. To use one's own worldviews to judge other peoples can be a dangerous enterprise. It can be used to justify the marginalization of groups who are different. There's no such thing as oppression, supporters of the status quo often argue, it's just that "those people" are inferior; they're not as intelligent and civilized as we are. Throughout history, Europeans have made such arguments from the Crusades against the heathen Muslims, the African slave trade and slavery, to the Third Reich's efforts to exterminate Jews, Gypsies, homosexuals, and physically challenged people.

The Importance of Positivism

Critical pedagogy focuses on the importance of positivism in shaping what goes on in education and knowledge production. The critique of positivism is central to critical theory and critical pedagogy. Positivism is an epistemological position. Epistemology is the study of knowledge, its production, the nature of truth, and the criteria we use to determine whether a statement is valid. Epistemology has shaped the education, the way we think, the way we see the world, and our view of ourselves. Epistemological questions might include: How do you know? Is that true? Is that a fact or an opinion? Is that an objective test? The epistemological position of Western Cartesian modernism is positivism. Few philosophical orientations have been so influential on the way we live our lives and shape education as has modernist positivism.

There is no difference, positivists argue, between the ways knowledge is produced in the physical sciences and in the human sciences—one should study sociology in the same way one studies physics. Social and educational knowledge about humans would be subjected to the same decontextualizing forces as the study of rocks. Positivist social and behavioral scientists continue to pull people out of their cultural settings and study them in laboratory-like conditions. They don't understand that we can't be understood outside of the context that helped shape us. Society, positivists maintain, like nature, is nothing more than a body of neutral facts governed by immutable laws. Therefore, positivists conclude that social actions should proceed with law-like predictability. In this positivistic context, education is also governed by unchanging laws. Thus, the role of the teacher is to uncover these laws and then act in accordance with them. For example, educational laws would include universal statements regarding how students learn and how they should be taught.

The positivist educator, in other words, sees only one correct way to teach, and scientific study can reveal these methods if we search for them diligently. This is the logic, the epistemology on which top-down standards and other standardized forms of education are based. Everyone is assumed to be the same regardless of race, class, or gender. I know if I go into a poor area where I'm from in the Appalachian Mountains of East Tennessee with this positivistic framework I'm going to run into trouble. When I bring out the same curriculum and the same teaching strategies used in the wealthy suburbs of Scarsdale, New York, I'm going to find that because of the backgrounds of many of my poor Appalachian students, there will be problems. They're not going to be ready to study the same curriculum in the same ways as the New York students. This is not because of their inferiority—they are not inferior—but simply because they don't have the same experiences as the upper-middle-class students from Scarsdale. Good critical pedagogy dictates that I start where they are and teach them in ways that are culturally relevant to them.

In my book on social studies education (*Getting Beyond the Facts: Teaching Social Studies/Social Sciences in the Twenty-First Century*, 2001b), I list and discuss the characteristics of positivism. Critical teachers would do well to understand positivism and the ways it insidiously shapes schooling and what we know. Here is the list without extended discussion:

- All knowledge is scientific knowledge

- All scientific knowledge is empirically verifiable

- One must use the same methods to study the physical world as one uses to study the social and educational worlds

- If knowledge exists, it exists in some definite, measurable quantity

- Nature is uniform and whatever is studied remains consistent in its existence and behavior

- The factors that cause things to happen are limited and knowable, and, in empirical studies, these factors can be controlled

- Certainty is possible, and when we produce enough research, we will understand reality well enough to forgo further research

- Facts and values can be kept separate, and objectivity is always possible

- There is one true reality, and the purpose of education is to convey that reality to students

- Teachers become "information deliverers," not knowledge-producing professionals or empowered cultural workers

There's an impudent dimension to critical pedagogy that says "who said teaching has to be done in this standardized way?" There's no one right way to teach. Such impudence is based on a cynicism toward the notion that positivistic ways of operating get us to the "right place" in research and education. We should use the research methods that are best suited to answering our questions about a phenomenon and the teaching methods that are designed for the special needs of the students we are teaching. Teaching and producing knowledge always encounter multiple inputs and forces. The best teacher in the world may not, for example, be able to reach a student on Thursday morning who watched her father beat up her mother on Wednesday night. The critical researcher-teacher does not allow these unexpected complexities to be dismissed by the excluding, reducing impulses of positivism. Refusing such reductionism is a subversive act in a school system shaped by positivist reforms such as "No Child Left Behind."

Advocates of a critical pedagogy understand that all human experience is marked by uncertainties and that order is not always easily established. "Order in the court" has little authority when the positivist judge is resting in his quarters. Indeed, the rationalistic and reductionistic quest for order refuses in its arrogance to listen to a cacophony of lived experience and the coexistence of diverse meanings and interpretations. The concept of understanding in the complex world viewed by critical teachers is unpredictable. Much to the consternation of many, there exists no final meaning that operates outside of historical and social context. As critical pedagogues create rather than discover meaning in the everyday world, they explore alternate meanings offered by others in diverse circumstances. If this weren't enough, they work to account for historical and social contingencies that always operate to undermine the universal positivist pronouncement of the meaning of a particular phenomenon. Jean Piaget may have studied how middle-class Swiss boys develop cognitively, but do African villagers from rural Malawi develop the same way? Critical psychologists don't think so, and such scholars discern big problems when positivists claim that the Malawi children should. When they don't, they are deemed cognitively deficient, not just culturally different. When educators fail to discern the unique ways that historical and social context make for special circumstances, they often provide reductionistic forms of knowledge and teaching that impoverish our understanding of everything connected to them (Burbules and Beck, 1999; Cary, 1998, 2003; Marijuan, 1994).

The Force of Science to Regulate

Critical pedagogy is aware that science can be used as a force to regulate and control. Science—especially the social, behavioral, and educational—developed in a time of much upheaval in the European world. As nineteenth-century inventions, the social, behavioral, and educational sciences—sociology, psychology, economics, political science, and anthropology, in particular—were directed toward managing and regulating the emerging populations of the urban-industrial world. The landed, moneyed, and industrial classes were frightened by the prospect of a working-class revolution and hoped that such disciplines would help in the regulatory process. Indeed, the development of public schooling in the United States cannot be understood outside this desire to control the population. The social sciences, contrary to conventional wisdom, shaped the societies that they sought to study. Unlike the claims they put forward, they were not disinterested scientific observers seeking only objective knowledge.

With these dynamics in mind, advocates of critical pedagogy recognize the contributions of physical and social science but are always suspicious of this regulatory dimension. Thus, they always study science in cultural and historical contexts, asking questions of the uses to which it has been put and whose interests it serves. Critical observers understand that science—like any system of discourse and practice—involves more than can be seen on the surface. Science carries with it a social, cultural, political, and economic history replete with pain, suffering, and privilege. It is never wise, advocates of critical pedagogy warn, to take one way of seeing the world and assume that it provides a picture of what the world is really like—critical pedagogy included. Indeed, a key element of the type of critical pedagogy I'm promoting here involves the importance of gaining multiple perspectives (in this context, see my work on bricolage, Kincheloe, 2001a; Kincheloe and Berry, 2004; Kincheloe and McLaren, 2004).

With this understanding of science as a regulative discourse, critical teachers are "on alert" to the ways Western elitist vantage points are normalized in education ("The Human Sciences," 1999; Kilduff and Mehra, 1997; Pickering, 2000). We see them at work in the world of art and art education when dominant power produces accepted modes of representing the world while excluding others (Cary, 1998, 2003). Concurrently, we see such dominant modes of perceiving in history, government, literature, and scientific curricula. Students

- study Western history and views of "others,"
- are exposed to little criticism of the structure of the nation's government,
- read the white male canon with a few gratuitous additions,
- are shielded from a view of science as a human construction by a particular cultural group at a specific historical time.

The promulgation of such ways of seeing is a form of education as regulation, reducing student and citizen resistance to the interests of dominant groups. Regulated individuals are more likely to accept their places in the workplaces of global capitalism. Teachers are not exempt from the dominant power's attempts to regulate. Critical pedagogy works to expose and confront the dominant power's appropriations of what were supposed to be democratic processes. The electronic world of the twenty-first century is vulnerable to power in ways never before imagined. Not only through schooling but also by way of television and other modes of communication, dominant power attempts to produce more compliant forms of consciousness and identity (Cannella and Kincheloe, 2002; Steinberg and Kincheloe, 1997). With nearly twenty-four-hour-a-day access to individuals in their most private spaces, the dominant power struggles to produce ways of seeing that allow it more freedom to operate. Thus, the regulatory power of science now uses media as well as schooling to accomplish its work.

The Importance of Understanding Context

Critical pedagogy is cognizant of the importance of understanding the context in which educational activity takes place. The more teachers and students understand the various social contexts in which education takes place, the more we appreciate the complexity of the process. The more of these contexts with which teachers are familiar, the more rigorous and critical education becomes. The problems of teacher education and teaching are multidimensional and are always embedded in a context. The more research sociocognitives produce, for example, the more it becomes apparent that a large percentage of student difficulties in school results not as much from cognitive inadequacy as from socially contextual factors (Kincheloe, Steinberg, and Gresson, 1996; Kincheloe, Steinberg, and Villaverde, 1999; Lave and Wenger, 1991; Snook, 1999; Wertsch, 1991). Critical teachers need a rich understanding of the social backgrounds of students, the scholarly context in which disciplinary and counter-disciplinary forms of knowledge are produced and transformed into subject matter, and the political context that helps shape school purpose.

In positivistic schools, learners' lives are decontextualized. When they examine the contexts and relationships connecting learner, culture, teaching, knowledge production, and curriculum, teachers move into a more complex paradigm. In this "zone of complexity," learning is viewed more as a dynamic and unpredictable process. As a complex, changing, unstable system, it resists generalized pronouncements and universal steps detailing "how to do it." Complex systems interact with multiple contexts and possess the capacity for self-organization and creative innovation. Each teaching and learning context has its unique dimensions that must be dealt with individually. Our understanding of educational purpose is also shaped by the complexity of these contextual appreciations. Teachers who are aware of this complexity embrace an evolving notion of purpose ever informed and modified by encounters with new contexts (Capra, 1996; Kincheloe and Weil, 2001; Schubert, 1998).

Teachers act on these contextual insights to not only help understand the various educational forms of knowledge but to grasp the needs of their students. In the critical orientation, such concerns can never be separated from the sociopolitical context: macro in the sense of the prevailing Zeitgeist and micro as it refers to the context immediately surrounding any school. In this context, critical teachers listen for marginalized voices and learn about their struggles with their environments. As such teachers delineate the effects of the contemporary political context shaped by corporations and economic interests, they build deep relationships with local communities, community organizations, and concerned individuals in these settings. With this in place, students gain new opportunities to learn, not only in classrooms but also in unique community learning environments. Here they can often address particular sociopolitical dynamics and learn about them in very personal and compelling ways (Cochran-Smith, 2000; Grimmett, 1999; Hoban and Erickson, 1998; Thomson, 2001; Vavrus and Archibald, 1998).

Critical educators place great emphasis on the notion of context and the act of contextualization in every aspect of their work. When problems arise, they stand ready to connect the difficulty to a wider frame of reference with a wide array of possible causes. When pedagogical problems fail to meet the criteria of an archetype, critical teachers research unused sources and employ the information acquired to develop a larger understanding of the interaction of the various systems involved with the problem. When teachers fail to perform such an act of contextualization, students get hurt. When teachers do not contextualize, they tend to isolate various parts of a pedagogical circumstance and call each a problem (Bohm and Edwards, 1991). They tinker with components of the problem but never approach its holistic nature. Educational data, for example, derive meaning only in the context created by other data. Context may be more important than content. These insights change the way educators approach their work.

Decades ago, John Dewey wrote about these contextual dynamics. In the second decade of the twentieth century, Dewey observed that many thinkers saw knowledge as self-contained, as complete in itself. Knowledge, he contended, could never be viewed outside the context of its relationship to other information. We only have to call to mind, Dewey wrote, what passes in our schools as acquisition of knowledge to understand how it is decontextualized and lacks any meaningful connection to the experience of students. Anticipating the notion of a critical pedagogy, Dewey concluded that an individual is a sophisticated thinker to the degree in which he or she sees an event not as something isolated "but in its connection with the common experience of mankind" (Dewey, 1916, pp. 342–343). To overcome the reductionism that has plagued teaching and allowed for its technicalization and hyperrationalization, critical educators must take Dewey's insights into account.

The Importance of Resisting the Dominant Power

Critical pedagogy is dedicated to resisting the harmful effects of dominant power. Advocates of critical pedagogy work to expose and to contest oppressive forms of power as expressed in socioeconomic class elitism, Eurocentric ways of viewing the world, patriarchal oppression, and imperialism around the world. In this context, white people must learn to listen to nonwhites' and indigenous people's criticism of them and of the cultural norms they have established and imposed on people of a lower socioeconomic class and non-European peoples at home and abroad. The struggle to resist the harmful effects of dominant power and the empowerment of marginalized and exploited peoples must include everything from engaging such individuals in a rigorous, empowering education to a more equitable distribution of wealth. Indeed, as Western societies have moved to the political right, traditional concerns about the welfare of the working class have faded. Too often in the contemporary global economy we find unemployed and underemployed individuals with insecure, temporary, part-time, and low-paying jobs. The exploitation of working people has intensified in the contemporary era, as free market economics and globalization have fragmented and disoriented the working class.

Too often, mainstream education teaches students and teachers to accept the oppressive workings of power—in the name of a neutral curriculum, in the attempt to take politics out of education. Critical pedagogy moves students, workers, and citizens to question the hidden political assumptions and the colonial, racial, gender, and class biases of schooling and media education. Critical pedagogy induces students to question these power plays that lead to human suffering. Many members of Western societies in the first decade of the twenty-first century see overtly political pronouncements as somehow inappropriate and out of place in institutions such as schools. Teachers, they say, should remain neutral. Students, however, need to understand the covert political implications of almost everything that presents itself as objective information, disinterested science, and balanced curricula. Of course, advocates of critical pedagogy know where they're coming from: they are making a case for fairness, for delineation of both sides of a question. Students have been taught to believe that objectivity is an attainable virtue that should be practiced by everyone involved with education. They have never been exposed to the argument that education is never neutral and that when we attempt to remain neutral we fail to expose the political inscriptions of so-called neutrality. In the name of neutrality, therefore, students are taught to support the status quo. It is a highly complex and difficult task, but critical teachers believe we should resist this tyranny of alleged neutrality.

Such resistance is accomplished not only by speaking in gender terms about race, class, sexual, and colonial oppression. The curriculum of critical pedagogy "names names" as it focuses its attention on corporate power wielders (e.g., Enron), agents of colonialism (e.g., Donald Rumsfeld and his actions in relation to Iraq), and the promoters of specific types of race, class, gender, sexual, cultural, and religious prejudice (e.g., Rev. Franklin Graham and Rev. Jerry Falwell in relation to Muslims and Islam; Charles Murray and Richard Herrnstein in relation to African Americans, Latinos, and the poor of all races; and Michael Savage in relation to gays and lesbians). While names are named and conscious oppressors are delineated, critical pedagogues also appreciate the fact that many aspects of race, class, gender, sexual, cultural, and religious prejudice are not intentional and often take place in the name of good intentions.

Without an understanding of these specific dynamics, teachers are too often unable—even with love in their hearts and the best intentions—to protect students from the radioactive fallout of hidden structures of racism, class bias, patriarchy, homophobia, colonialism, and religious prejudice. Students of critical pedagogy must understand that college teacher education both in liberal arts and sciences and schools of education has often ignored these issues, focusing instead on inculcating a body of "neutral" facts into teachers' heads, rearranging the physical layout of the classroom, the format of the curriculum, lesson planning, and behavioral objectives. Too often such matters served only, in Donaldo Macedo's (1994) words, "to stupidify" those who took them seriously, as they pushed questions of how both school purpose and teacher/student identities are shaped vis-à-vis larger sociopolitical and cultural formations off the table.

In the context of these questions of power, oppression, and struggle, advocates of critical pedagogy understand, even as they document the insidious operations of racism, class elitism, patriarchy, heterosexism, colonialism, and religious intolerance, that such structures have holes with numerous tunnels for escape. Even when educational purposes are consciously oppressive, Clint Allison (1995) reminds us, purposes and outcomes are not the same thing. Even though they have operated as tools of dominant power, schools are places that often teach literacy—an essential skill in the process of empowerment. Many students use those portions of education that they find applicable to their lives, concurrently identifying and rejecting hegemonic attempts to win their consent to "dumbing-down" perspectives.

Of course, these are the students who are deemed to have bad attitudes, who may be labeled surly and unteachable, but they also may be the students who are sufficiently empowered to lead pro-democracy and anticolonial movements in Western societies. Thus, proponents of critical pedagogy recognize the possibility for resistance, even successful resistance, to the forces of the dominant power. Because patriarchal, white supremacist, class elitist, colonial, and homophobic oppression is not deterministic, because it is mediated by countless factors, the dominant power's intentions may mutate in the kaleidoscope of everyday school life. In this context, critical teachers and students can seize opportunities to expose the oppressive workings of power and offer democratic, pluralistic, more power-sharing alternatives in their place.

Understanding Complexity

Critical pedagogy is attuned to the importance of complexity in constructing a rigorous and transformative education. Because of the importance of complexity, I often refer to my version of critical pedagogy as a critical complex pedagogy (Kincheloe, 2001b; Kincheloe, Bursztyn, and Steinberg, 2004). Many observers have come to the conclusion over the last several decades that the simplicity of Cartesian rationalism and mainstream forms of knowledge production does not meet the needs of educators and scholars. The web of reality is composed of too many variables to be taken into account and controlled. The scientist Ilya Prigogine labels this multitude of variables "extraneous perturbations," meaning that one extraneous variable, for example, in an educational experiment can produce an expanding, exponential effect. So-called inconsequential entities can have a profound effect in a complex nonlinear universe. The shape of the physical and social world depends on the smallest part. The part, in a sense, is the whole, for via the action of any particular part, the whole in the form of transformative change may be seen. To exclude such considerations is to miss the nature of the interactions that constitute reality. The development of a counter-Cartesian reconceptualization of critical pedagogy does not mean that we simplistically reject all empirical science. It does mean, however, that we conceive of such scientific ways of seeing as one perspective on the complex web we refer to as reality.

This theme of complexity is central to any critical pedagogy that works to avoid reductionism. Critical pedagogues who take complexity seriously challenge reductionistic, bipolar, true-or-false epistemologies. As critical teachers come to recognize the complexity of the lived world with its maze of uncontrollable variables, irrationality, non-linearity, and unpredictable interaction of wholes and parts, they begin to also see the interpretative dimension of reality. We are bamboozled by a science that offers a monological, one-truth process of making sense of the world. Complex critical scholars and cultural workers maintain that we must possess and be able to deploy multiple methods of producing knowledge of the world. Such methods provide us diverse perspectives on similar events and alert us to various relationships between events. In this complex context we understand that even when we use diverse methods to produce multiple perspectives on the world, different observers will produce different interpretations of what they perceive. Given a variety of values, different ideologies, and different positions in the web of reality, different individuals will interpret what is happening differently. Charles Bingham (2003) argues that we must understand this complexity in order to appreciate the complications of gaining knowledge. Humans, Bingham maintains, are not isolated agents in their efforts to acquire knowledge—they must receive help from others to engage in learning.

Bingham's notion of the relationship between knower and known changes the way we approach knowledge, learning, teaching, and social action. Indeed, critical activity in this complex process is not something employed by solitary students operating on their own. Critical agents use language developed by others, live in specific contexts with particular ways of being and ways of thinking about thinking, have access to some forms of knowledge and not others, and live and operate in circumstances shaped by particular dominant ideological perspectives. In its effort to deal with previously neglected complexity, the mode of critical pedagogy offered here appreciates the need to understand these contextual factors and account for them. Complex critical analysts are not isolated individuals but people who understand the nature of their sociocultural context and their overt and their occluded relationships with others. Without such understandings of their own contextual embedding, individuals are not capable of understanding from where the prejudices and predispositions they bring to the act of meaning making originate. Any critical activity that attempts to deal with the complexity of the lived world must address these contextual dynamics.

As we look back from the perspective of the first decade of the twenty-first century to the innovative scholarly work on epistemology and research of the last several decades, one gains understanding: producing knowledge about the world is more complex than we originally thought. What we designate as facts is not as straightforward a process as it was presented to us. Critical pedagogues with an understanding of complexity know that what most people consider the natural social world is a conceptual landmine wired with assumptions and inherited meanings. Critical researchers have learned that what is unproblematically deemed "a fact" has been shaped by a community of inquirers. Such uncritical researchers accept, often unconsciously, a particular set of theoretical assumptions. Engaging in knowledge work without a deep understanding of the tacit rules of the game is not a manifestation of rigor. Indeed, such a lack of knowledge of complexity profoundly undermines the effort to understand the world around us (Fischer, 1998; Horn, 2003). Great scholars in diverse historical and cultural settings have admonished individuals not to take fixed viewpoints and concepts as reality (Varela, 1999).

Roymeico Carter (2003) extends this concept into the world of the visual. The complexity of researching the visual domain is often squashed by the formal methods of Cartesian aesthetics. Carter reminds us that the intricate layers of visual meaning must be studied from numerous perspectives as well as diverse cultural and epistemological traditions (Rose and Kincheloe, 2003). But such diversity of perception lets the cat out of the bag; it relinquishes control of how we are to see the world. According to Ilya Prigogine, complexity demands that researchers give up the attempt to dominate and control the world. The social and physical worlds are so complex that they can only be understood like human beings themselves: not machine-like, unpredictable, dependent upon context, and influenced by minute fluctuations (Capra, 1996). Thus, critical complex scholars focus their attention on addressing the complexity of the lived world, in the process understanding that the knowledge they produce should not be viewed as a transhistorical (not influenced by its historical context) body of truth. In this framework, knowledge produced is provisional and "in process." Critical scholars and educators know that tensions will develop in social knowledge as the understandings and insights of individuals change and evolve (Blackler, 1995).

A researcher, for example, who returns to an ethnographic study only a few years after completing it may find profound differences in what is reported by subjects. The categories and coding that worked five years ago may no longer be relevant. The most important social, psychological, and educational problems that confront us are untidy and complicated. As we wade through the swamp of everyday life, ways of seeing that fail to provide multiple perspectives at macro, meso, and micro levels do not provide the insights needed in a critical pedagogy. It is one thing to find out that schools do not provide many poor students a path to social mobility. It is quite another to take this macro finding and combine it with the meso dynamics of the ways particular schools and school leaders conceptualize the relationship between schooling and class mobility. It is also important that these findings be viewed in a context informed by everyday classroom and out-of-classroom interactions between teachers and students and students and their peers. Obviously, different research strategies will be used to explore the differing questions emerging at the different levels. Once data from these diverse layers are combined, we begin to discern an emerging picture of the multiple dynamics of the relationship between socioeconomic class and education. Only a multidimensional, complex picture such as this can help us formulate informed and just strategies to address such issues.

Avoiding Empire Building

Critical pedagogy is aware of and opposed to contemporary efforts to build a new American Empire around the world. In the present era, emerging forms of U.S. colonialism and imperialism move critical pedagogues to examine the ways American power operates under the cover of establishing democracies all over the world. Advocates of critical pedagogy argue that such neocolonial power must be exposed, so it can be opposed in the United States and around the world. The American Empire's subversion of democratically elected governments from Iran (Kincheloe, 2004), Chile, Nicaragua, to Venezuela— when its real purpose is to acquire geopolitical advantages for future military assaults, economic leverage in international markets, and access to natural resources—is justified in the name of freedom. Critical teachers need to view their work in the context of living and working in a nation state with the most powerful military industrial complex in history. It is a complex that has shamefully used the monstrous terrorist attacks of September 11 to advance an imperialist agenda fueled by corporate accumulation by means of force. Indeed, the war on terror is a cloaking device to hide broader, imperialistic political and economic goals.

David G. Smith (2003) argues that such imperial dynamics are supported by particular epistemological forms. The United States is an epistemological empire based on a notion of truth that undermines the forms of knowledge produced by those outside the good graces and benevolent authority of the empire. Thus, in the twenty-first century, critical teachers must develop sophisticated ways to address imperialist conquests (whether accomplished through direct military intervention or indirectly through the creation of client states) and the epistemological violence that helps discipline the world. Smith refers to this violence as a form of "information warfare" that spreads deliberate falsehoods about countries such as Iraq and Iran. U.S. corporate and governmental agents become more sophisticated in the use of such epistoweaponry with every day that passes.

In many ways, September 11 was a profound shock to millions of Americans who obtain their news and worldviews from the mainstream, corporately owned media and their understanding of American international relations from what is taught in most secondary schools and in many colleges and universities. Such individuals are heard frequently on call-in talk radio and TV shows expressing the belief that America is loved internationally because it is richer, more moral, and more magnanimous than other nations. In this mind-set, those who resist the United States hate our freedom for reasons never quite specified. These Americans, the primary victims of a right-wing corporate-government-produced miseducation (Kincheloe and Steinberg, 2004), have not been informed by their news sources of the societies that have been undermined by covert U.S. military operations and U.S. economic policies (Parenti, 2002). Many do not believe, for example, the description of the human effects of American sanctions on Iraq between the first and second Gulf Wars. Indeed, the hurtful activities of the American Empire are invisible to many of the empire's subjects in the United States itself.

The hostile relations that now exist between the West (the United States in particular) and the Islamic world demand that critical pedagogues be very careful in laying out the argument we are making about this new era of U.S. imperialism in the world. The activities of the American Empire have not been the only forces at work creating an Islamist extremism that violently defies the sacred teaching of the religion. But American imperial misdeeds have played an important role in the process. A new critical orientation toward knowledge production, scholarship, and teaching based on this and the other dimensions of critical pedagogy can help the United States redress some of its past and present policies toward the diverse Islamic world and other nations victimized by U.S. aggression. While these policies have been invisible to many Americans, they are visible to the rest of the world. And, unfortunately, many Americans reading this book will pay for such national policies over the next few years.

In my chapter on U.S. imperialism in Iran in *The Miseducation of the West: Constructing Islam* (2004), I explore the inability of American leaders to understand the impact of empire-building in the Persian Gulf on the psyches of those personally affected by it. Indeed, the American public was ignorant of covert U.S. operations that overthrew the democratically elected government of Iran, so a totalitarian regime more sympathetic to the crass needs of the American Empire could be installed. The citizens of Iran and other peoples around the Muslim world, however, were acutely aware of this imperial action and the contempt for Muslims it implied. When this was combined with a plethora of other U.S. political, military, and economic initiatives in the region, their view of America was less than positive. In the second Gulf War, American leaders simply disregarded the views of nations around the world—the Muslim world, in particular—when opposition to the American invasion of Iraq was expressed. History was erased as Saddam Hussein was viewed in a psychological context as a madman. Times when the United States supported the madman were deleted from memory. The empire, thus, could do whatever it wanted, regardless of its impact on the Iraqi people or the perceptions of others (irrational others) around the world. Critical teachers struggle to change these imperial policies.

References

Allison, C. (1995). *Present and past: Essays for teachers in the history of education.* New York: Peter Lang.
Apple, M. (1999). *Power, meaning, and identity: Essays in critical educational studies.* New York: Peter Lang.
Armstrong, M. (1981). The case of Louise and the painting of landscapes. In J. Nixon (Ed.), *A teachers' guide to action research.* London: Grant McIntyre.

Bamburg, J. (1994). Raising expectations to improve student learning. Available from http: //www.ncrel.org/sdrs/areas/issues/educatrs/leadrshp/ie0bam.htm

Barone, T. (2000). *Aesthetics, politics and educational inquiry: Essays and examples*. New York: Peter Lang.

Bartolomé, L. (1996). Beyond the methods fetish: Towards a humanizing pedagogy. In P. Leistyna, A. Woodrum, and S. Sherblom (Eds.), *Breaking free: The transformative power of critical pedagogy* (pp. 229–252). Cambridge, MA: Harvard Educational Review Press.

Bartolomé, L. (1998). *The misteaching of academic discourses: The politics of language in the classroom*. Boulder, CO: Westview Press.

Beck, R. (1991). *General education: Vocational and academic collaboration*. Berkeley, CA: NCRVE.

Berry, K. (2000). *The dramatic arts and cultural studies: Acting against the grain*. New York: Falmer.

Bingham, C. (2003). Knowledge acquisition. In D. Weil and J. Kincheloe (Eds.), *Critical thinking and learning: An encyclopedia*. Westport, CT: Greenwood Press.

Blackler, F. (1995). Knowledge, knowledge work, and organizations: An overview and interpretation. *Organization Studies, 16*(6), 1021–1046.

Bohm, D., and Edwards, M. (1991). *Changing consciousness*. San Francisco: Harper.

Britzman, D. (1986). Cultural myths in the making of a teacher: Biography and social structure in teacher education. *Harvard Educational Review, 56*(4), 442–455.

Britzman, D. (1991). *Practice makes practice: A critical study of learning to teach*. Albany: State University of New York Press.

Burbules, N., and Beck, R. (1999). Critical thinking and critical pedagogy: Relations, differences, and limits. In T. Popkewitz and L. Fendler (Eds.), *Critical theories in education*. New York: Routledge.

Cannella, G., and Kincheloe, J. (2002). *Kidworld: Childhood studies, global perspectives, and education*. New York: Peter Lang.

Capra, F. (1996). *The web of life: A new scientific understanding of living systems*. New York: Anchor.

Carter, R. (2003). Art education and critical thinking. In D. Weil and J. Kincheloe (Eds.), *Critical thinking and learning: An encyclopedia*. Westport, CT: Greenwood Press.

Cary, R. (1998). *Critical art pedagogy: Foundations for postmodern art education*. New York: Garland.

Cary, R. (2003). Art and aesthetics. In D. Weil and J. Kincheloe (Eds.), *Critical thinking and learning: An encyclopedia*. Westport, CT: Greenwood Press.

Cochran-Smith, M. (2000). *The outcomes question in teacher education*. Paper presented at AERA, New Orleans.

Crebbin, W. (2001). The critically reflective practitioner. Available from http://www.ballarat.edu.au/~wcrebbinTB780/critreflect.hyml

Darder, A. (1991). *Culture and power in the classroom*. Westport, CT: Bergin and Garvey.

Degener, S. (2002). Making sense of critical pedagogy in adult literacy. *The Annual Review of Adult Learning and Literacy*. Available from http://www.gse.harvard.edu/~ncsall/ann_rev/vol2_2.html

Dewey, J. (1916). *Democracy and education*. New York: The Free Press.

Ferreira, M., and Alexandre, F. (2000). Education for citizenship: The challenge of teacher education in postmodernity. Available from http://www.ioeoe.ac.uk/ccs/conference2000/papers/epsd/ferreiraan-dalexandre.html

First Annual Urban Schools Symposium Report (FAUSSR). (1998). Relationship, community, and positive reframing: Addressing the needs. Available from http://www.inclusiveschools.org/procsho.htm

Fischer, F. (1998). Beyond empiricism: Policy inquiry in postpositivist perspective. *Policy Studies Journal, 26*(1), 129–146.

Freire, P. (1970). *Pedagogy of the oppressed*. New York: Herder and Herder.

Freire, P. (1972). *Research methods*. Paper Presented to a Seminar, Studies in Adult Education, Dar-es-Salaam, Tanzania.

Freire, P. (1978). *Education for critical consciousness*. New York: Seabury Press.

Freire, P. (1985). *The politics of education: Culture, power, and liberation*. South Hadley, MA: Bergin and Garvey.

Freire, P. (1998). *Pedagogy of the heart*. New York: Continuum.

Freire, P., and Faundez, A. (1989). *Learning to question: A pedagogy of liberation*. New York: Continuum.

Freire, P., and Macedo, D. (1987). *Literacy: Reading the word and the world*. South Hadley, MA: Bergin and Garvey.

Gergen, M., and Gergen, K. (2000). Qualitative inquiry: Tensions and transformations. In N. Denzin and Y. Lincoln (Eds.), *Handbook of qualitative research* (2nd ed.). Thousand Oaks, CA: Sage.

Giroux, H. (1981). *Ideology, culture, and the process of schooling*. Philadelphia: Temple University Press.

Giroux, H. (1983). *Theory and resistance in education*. South Hadley, MA: Bergin and Garvey.

Giroux, H. (1988). *Schooling and the struggle for public life*. Minneapolis: University of Minnesota Press.

Giroux, H. (1992). *Border crossings: Cultural workers and the politics of education*. New York: Routledge.

Giroux, H. (1997). *Pedagogy and the politics of hope: Theory, culture, and schooling*. Boulder, CO: Westview Press.

Goodlad, J. (1994). *Educational renewal: Better teachers, better schools*. San Francisco: Jossey-Bass.

Grange, L. (2003). Educational research as democratic praxis. Available from http://www.kas.org.za/publications/seminarreports/democratictransformationofeducation/le%20grange.pdf

Grimmett, P. (1999). Teacher educators as mettlesome mermaids. *International Electronic Journal for Leadership in Learning, 3*(12). Available from htttp://www.ucalgary.ca/~iejll

Grubb, N., Davis, G., Lum, J., Plihal, J., and Marjaine, C. (1991). *The cunning hand, the cultured mind: Models for integrating vocational and academic education*. Berkeley, CA: NCRVE.

Hicks, E. (1999). *Ninety-five languages and seven forms of intelligence*. New York: Peter Lang.

Hoban, G., and Erickson, G. (1998). *Frameworks for sustaining professional learning.* Paper Presented at the Australasian Science Education Research Association, Darwin, Australia.

hooks, b. (1994). *Teaching to transgress: Education as the practice of freedom.* New York: Routledge.

Horn, R. (2003). Scholar-practitioner leaders: The empowerment of teachers and students. In D. Weil and J. Kincheloe (Eds.), *Critical thinking and learning: An encyclopedia.* Westport, CT: Greenwood Press.

Horton, M., and Freire, P. (1990). *We make the road by walking: Conversations on education and social change* (B. Bell, J. Gaventa, and J. Peters (Eds.)). Philadelphia: Temple University Press.

The Human Sciences. (1999). What is it to be human? Available from http://www.barnaed.ua.edu/~stomlins/607/607w3ahs1.html

Jardine, D. (1998). *To dwell with a boundless heart: Essays in curriculum theory, hermeneutics, and the ecological imagination.* New York: Peter Lang.

Keesing-Styles, L. (2003). The relationship between critical pedagogy and assessment in teacher education. *Radical Pedagogy.* Available from http://radicalpedagogy.icaap.org/content/issue5_1/03_keesingstules.html

Kilduff, M., and Mehra, A. (1997). Postmodernism and organizational research. *Academy of Management Review, 22*(2), 453–481.

Kincheloe, J. (2001a). Describing the bricolage: Conceptualizing a new rigor in qualitative research. *Qualitative Inquiry, 7*(6), 679–692.

Kincheloe, J. (2001b). *Getting beyond the facts: Teaching social studies/social sciences in the twenty-first century.* New York: Peter Lang.

Kincheloe, J. (2003). Into the great wide open: Introducing critical thinking. In D. Weil and J. Kincheloe (Eds.), *Critical thinking and learning: An encyclopedia.* Westport, CT: Greenwood Press.

Kincheloe, J. (2004). Iran and American miseducation: Cover-ups, distortions, and omissions. In J. Kincheloe and S. Steinberg (Eds.), *The miseducation of the West: Constructing Islam.* Westport, CT: Greenwood Press.

Kincheloe, J., and Berry, K. (2004). *Rigor and complexity in qualitative research: Constructing the bricolage.* London: Open University Press.

Kincheloe, J., Bursztyn, A., and Steinberg, S. (2004). *Teaching teachers: Building a quality school of urban education.* New York: Peter Lang.

Kincheloe, J., and McLaren, P. (2004). Rethinking critical theory and qualitative research. In N. Denzin and Y. Lincoln (Eds.), *Handbook of qualitative research* (3rd ed.). Thousand Oaks, CA: Sage.

Kincheloe, J., Slattery, P., and Steinberg, S. (2000). *Contextualizing teaching: Introduction to education and educational foundations.* New York: Longman.

Kincheloe, J., and Steinberg, S. (1997). *Changing multiculturalism.* London: Open University Press.

Kincheloe, J., and Steinberg, S. (1998). *Unauthorized methods: Strategies for critical teaching.* New York: Routledge.

Kincheloe, J., and Steinberg, S. (2004). *The miseducation of the West: Constructing Islam.* New York: Greenwood Press.

Kincheloe, J., Steinberg, S., and Gresson, A. (Eds.). (1996). *Measured lies: The "bell curve" examined.* New York: St. Martin's Press.

Kincheloe, J., Steinberg, S., Rodriguez, N., and Chennault, R. (1998). *White reign: Deploying Whiteness in America.* New York: St. Martin's Press.

Kincheloe, J., Steinberg, S., and Villaverde, L. (Eds.). (1999). *Rethinking intelligence: Confronting psychological assumptions about teaching and learning.* New York: Routledge.

Kincheloe, J., and Weil, D. (Eds.). (2001). *Standards and schooling in the United States: An encyclopedia.* Santa Barbara, CA: ABC-CLIO.

Knobel, M. (1999). *Everyday literacies: Students, discourse, and social practice.* New York: Peter Lang.

Kraft, N. (2001). Certification of teachers—A critical analysis of standards in teacher education programs. In J. Kincheloe and D. Weil (Eds.), *Standards and schooling in the United States: An encyclopedia* (3 vols.). Santa Barbara, CA: ABC-CLIO.

Lather, P. (1991). *Getting smart: Feminist research and pedagogy within the postmodern.* New York: Routledge.

Lave, J., and Wenger, E. (1991). *Situated learning: Legitimate peripheral participation.* New York: Cambridge University Press.

Macedo, D. (1994). *Literacies of power: What Americans are not allowed to know.* Boulder, CO: Westview Press.

Madison, G. (1988). *The hermeneutics of postmodernity: Figures and themes.* Bloomington: Indiana University Press.

Marijuan, P. (1994). *Information revisited.* Paper Presented to the First Conference on the Foundations of Information Science, Madrid, Spain.

McLaren, P. (1989). *Life in schools: An introduction to critical pedagogy in the foundations of education.* New York: Longman.

McLaren, P. (1995). *Critical pedagogy and predatory culture: Oppositional politics in a postmodern era.* New York: Routledge.

McLaren, P. (1997). *Revolutionary multiculturalism: Pedagogies of dissent for the new millennium.* Boulder, CO: Westview Press.

McLaren, P. (1998). Revolutionary pedagogy in post-revolutionary times: Rethinking the political economy of critical education. *Educational Theory, 48*(4), 431–462.

McLaren, P. (2000). *Che Guevara, Paulo Freire, and the pedagogy of revolution.* Lanham, MD: Rowman & Littlefield.

MDRC for the Council of the Great City Schools. (2002). Foundations for success: Case studies of how urban school systems improve student achievement. Available from http://www.cgcs.rg/reports/foundations.html

Noone, L., and Cartwright, P. (1996). Doing a critical literacy pedagogy: Trans/forming teachers in a teacher education course. Available from http://www.atea.schoools.net.au/ATEA/96conf/noone.html

Norris, N. (1998). Curriculum evaluation revisited. *Cambridge Journal of Education, 28*(2), 207–219.

Novick, R. (1996). Actual schools, possible practices: New directions in professional development. *Education Policy Analysis Archives, 4*(14), 1–15.

Oakes, J. (1985). *Keeping track: How schools structure inequality.* New Haven, CT: Yale University Press.

Oldroyd, D. (1985). Indigenous action research for individual and system development. *Educational Management and Administration, 13*(2), 113–118.

Parenti, M. (2002). *The terrorism trap: September 11 and beyond.* San Francisco: City Lights.

Pickering, J. (2000). Methods are a message. In M. Velmans (Ed.), *Investigating phenomenal consciousness: Methodologies and maps.* Amsterdam: John Benjamins.

Powell, R. (2001). *Straight talk: Growing as multicultural educators.* New York: Peter Lang.

Rodriguez, N., and Villaverde, L. (2000). *Dismantling White privilege.* New York: Peter Lang.

Rose, K., and Kincheloe, J. (2003). *Art, culture, and education: Artful teaching in a fractured landscape.* New York: Peter Lang.

Schubert, W. (1998). Toward constructivist teacher education for elementary schools in the twenty-first century: A framework for decision-making. Available from my.netian.com/~yhhknue/coned19.htm

Semali, L., and Kincheloe, J. (1999). *What is indigenous knowledge? Voices from the academy.* New York: Falmer.

Smith, D. (2003). On enfraudening the public sphere, the futility of empire and the future of knowledge after 'America.' *Policy Futures in Education, 1*(3), 488–503.

Snook, I. (1999). Teacher education: Preparation for a learned profession. Available from http://www.aare.edu.au/99pap/sno99148.htm

Steinberg, S. (2000). The new civics: Teaching for critical empowerment. In D. Hursh and E. Ross (Eds.), *Democratic social education: Social studies for social change.* New York: Falmer.

Steinberg, S. (Ed.). (2001). *Multi/intercultural conversations: A reader.* New York: Peter Lang.

Steinberg, S., and Kincheloe, J. (1997). *Kinderculture: Corporate constructions of childhood.* Boulder, CO: Westview Press.

Steinberg, S., and Kincheloe, J. (1998). *Students as researchers: Creating classrooms that matter.* London: Falmer.

Thomson, C. (2001). Massification, distance learning and quality in INSET teacher education: A challenging relationship. Available from http://www.ru.ac.za/academic/adc/papers/Thomson.htm

21ˢᵗ Century Schools. (2003). Philosophical foundations of critical theory and critical pedagogy. Available from http://www.21stcenturyschools.com/philosophical_foundation.htm

Varela, F. (1999). *Ethical know-how: Action, wisdom, and cognition.* Stanford, CA: Stanford University Press.

Vavrus, M., and Archibald, O. (1998). *Teacher education practices supporting social justice: Approaching an individual self-study inquiry into institutional self-study process.* Paper Presented to the Second International Conference on Self-Study of Teacher Education Practice, Herstmonceux Castle, UK.

Wang, M., and Kovach, J. (1996). Bridging the achievement gap in urban schools: Reducing educational segregation and advancing resilience-promoting strategies. In B. Williams (Ed.), *Closing the achievement gap: A vision for changing beliefs and practices.* Alexandria, VA: ASCD.

Wertsch, J. (1991). *Voices of the mind: A sociocultural approach to mediated action.* Cambridge, MA: Harvard University Press.

Wood, P. (1988). Action research: A field perspective. *Journal of Education for Teaching, 14*(2), 135–150.

CHAPTER 10

Art Education Programs

Empowering Social Change

Yolanda Medina

The aim of this article is to bring attention to an important connection between art education programs and the development of social justice practices in K–16 classrooms. This article is organized into three sections. The first is an analysis of the hierarchical and unilateral approach to education that urban students experience throughout their schooling, and how this educational model fails to develop traits that can empower students to promote social justice for those who are marginalized or oppressed. The second section advocates for the promotion of art education programs infused with particular aesthetic experiences that can help students develop the missing traits. The closing section discusses the changes that will be required to institute these programs in the United States in general and New York City (NYC) in particular, and the challenges this will entail. The author is a lifelong resident of NYC, which is both her hometown and one of the largest urban cities in the world.

The Banking Approach

My teaching experiences in urban K–16 settings indicate that students' educational experiences are being formed by a pedagogical system that is hierarchical and non-interactive. Freire (2000) refers to this model as the "banking concept of education" (p. 71) in which students are reduced to storing bits of information provided by the instructor, who considers her/himself a superior authority, and "turns them [students] into receptacles to be filled" (p. 72). In this educational model, students' experiences and ways of interpreting the world are not valued. The learning process has no personal relevance, and students are discouraged from creating meaning in the classroom or their lives. Over the course of time, this educational approach can weaken students' faith in their own power to transform the world, leaving them at the mercy of authority figures who tell them how to live. This process separates students from what somatic theorists call their *somatic sensibility*.

Tomas Hanna defines *soma* as "the body as perceived from within by first-person perception" (Green, 2001, p. 2). The *soma* represents a subjective understanding of our emotions and motivations as we perceive them inside our selves, as opposed to the objective viewpoint of a detached observer. Somatic Theory focuses on embodied experiences such as sensation, movement, and intention, which carry memories connected with feelings of love, joy, passion, compassion, and sorrow. I suggest that our understanding of the world is not restricted to our minds, but also deeply embedded in our bodies in the form of experiential memories. If we take a minute to consider, we realize that memory is triggered not only by language or thought, but sometimes by odors, sensations, or colors. A disembodied experience is emotionless; it can be recalled by our memory, but this recollection does not arouse the feelings that accompanied the experience when it entered our lives. Somatic sensibility allows us to recall the emotions connected with our experiences, and this gives us a stronger visceral understanding of how they affect our lives and shape the way we see ourselves and others.

Students come into our classrooms already accustomed to the banking model of education, in which their individual ways of interpreting the world are disregarded and the learning process is detached from personal experience. They have learned to see the world as fixed, with units of knowledge set and defined by authority figures pontificating in front of the class. Over time, students lose both the ability to question the status quo and the confidence to change it. The world they are to inherit is seen as unchangeable and static. Greene (1995) describes this situation well:

> My argument is simply that treating the world as predefined and given, as simply there, is quite separate and different from applying an initiating, constructing mind or consciousness to the world. When habit swathes everything, one day follows another identical day and predictability swallows any hint of an opening possibility. (p. 23)

Because this type of learning process is predetermined and leaves little room for critical and independent thinking, it reduces students' capacity to imagine, which Greene (1995) defines as the "ability to look at things as if they could be otherwise" (p. 19). This is the same skill displayed by an interior designer who walks into an empty room and creates a mental image of how s/he wants it to look, then works towards the realization of that image. We must be capable of imagining things as we want them to be before we can see ourselves as agents of change. If students cannot develop their imagination, they cannot envision their own power to create and re-create the world.

The next section will briefly explain how certain types of aesthetic experience can enable students to engage in social change by encouraging them to identify with others who share similar experiences. I will advocate for infusion of the arts into K–16 classrooms as a way of producing focused aesthetic experiences that can facilitate this process. The goal is to bring the body (soma) and its somatic sensibilities into the classroom along with our students' minds.

The Aesthetic Process

Greene (2001) defines the field of aesthetics as "concerned about perception, sensation, imagination, and how they relate to knowing, understanding, and feeling about the world" (p. 5). An aesthetic experience can be described as the relationship created between an observer and a specific artwork, and the way that work of art affects the observer in light of his/her background and personal history. Aesthetic experiences differ in their effects depending upon what each observer brings to the encounter. Susan Stinson (1985) discusses three different levels of aesthetic experience and explains why they must be used carefully in educational contexts, because not all of them will encourage constructive engagement with the world. This article will briefly discuss the first two, but the third level of experience is the one I am interested in promoting as an educational resource. This is the type of experience that will help students to embrace their own power to create positive social change.

Stinson's first dimension is limited to appreciation of the particular beauty of the artwork. According to her analysis, the observer is not deeply moved at this level of perception because the artwork bears no connection with his/her previous experiences. For this reason, the first level of aesthetic experience cannot release the imagination or empower the observer. This is analogous to the banking method of education, in which students are limited to storing new information without applying critical thought or interpretation.

Stinson's second level of aesthetic experience concerns the way in which the artwork moves the observer. The effect the work will have in this dimension depends upon the life experiences the observer brings to the encounter, and thus upon the degree to which the observer can relate to the piece in question. Some will see this level of experience as a transcendental moment that can give the observer the strength and security to create positive change in her/his life. Stinson (1985) describes this kind of experience as a "source of knowledge of God and a major source of meaning in life" (p. 77).

Aesthetic experiences at Stinson's second level can release the imagination and allow the observer to see a path towards a better life, but this does not necessarily encourage movement beyond the personal into the social realm. The experience fails to engender compassion, which according to Fox (1999) "is political as well as personal" (p. 109). I share Fox's belief that "compassion leads to work" (p. 8), and that without it, social empowerment will have no relevant effect. For this reason, I agree with Stinson's concern that "transcendent experiences may too often simply refresh us—like a mini vacation—making us better able to tolerate some things which we ought not tolerate" (p. 78). Though I would not wish to devalue the positive effects felt at this level of aesthetic experience, the particular type of educational encounter I am promoting is intended to engender both personal empowerment and a desire for social change. Stinson describes a third level of aesthetic experience that strengthens the relationship between the observer and the world around her/him. The work of art becomes a vehicle for appreciating other people's suffering and connecting it with our own. Stinson elaborates by quoting Maxine Greene:

> … certain works of art are considered great primarily because of their capacity to bring us into conscious engagement with the world, into self reflectiveness and critical awareness, and to sense moral agency, and it is these works of art which ought to be central in curriculum. (Greene cited in Stinson, 1985, p. 79)

In order to create an environment in which students can reach this third level of aesthetic experience, we must offer quality education programs that expose them to artworks that will help them to recognize common sources of oppression. These encounters must involve the body (soma) as a mediator of experience and employ its somatic sensibilities to explore the work of art. This is the only way in which observers can fully appreciate the human emotions that are represented in the work. This process helps students to achieve what Greene (2001) refers to as "uncoupling" (p. 69), or using our imagination and our own personal history to help us *feel* what the artist means, rather than simply seeing or hearing it. Encounters of this kind have an extraordinary capacity to release the imagination and engender compassion, because they engage our personal experience at the bodily level. This process reconnects us to our somatic sensibility, which is the source of our power to create and recreate the world in which we live.

I have briefly explained how creating a particular type of educational aesthetic experience is of the utmost importance in empowering students to promote social justice for those who are marginalized or oppressed. On the one hand, this process helps students understand how oppression affects them personally, which will allow them to initiate a healing process. On the other hand, students can use this critical lens to see how, consciously or unconsciously, they have oppressed others, and this will help them to appreciate the commonalities in all human suffering. The compassion they develop through this kind of encounter will eventually empower them to create social change. The final section of this article will discuss the challenges involved in establishing this kind of art program in our urban classrooms, and the changes that will be required.

Challenges and Changes

Infusing the arts into K–16 classrooms will involve substantive change in our educational system, and will therefore present serious challenges for administrators and teachers alike. This final section will examine some of these challenges, and in particular, how to achieve the level of financial support required for educational programs that use the techniques I have described. Finally, speaking as a New Yorker and a Teacher Educator involved with Aesthetic Education, I will end the discussion by demonstrating the limited value that has been placed on art education by the New York City Department of Education in the past few decades, and by describing the changes needed to ensure the implementation of art programs at the local and national levels.

Interest in new progressive pedagogies will always be initiated by concerned educators who submit requests to administrators for the adoption of new or revised curricula. A difficult step in the introduction of arts-driven curricula is convincing education administrators of the importance of this approach. Before they will agree to the necessary changes, administrators must come to value the arts as an indispensable part of the education of all children. Then they will be more willing to allot funds for the use of artistic venues that are available in the community, and to allow teachers to use aesthetic curricular approaches that develop skills not measured by the No Child Left Behind (NCLB)–mandated tests or the National Council for Accreditation of Teacher Education (NCATE) standards. Educators must advance strong arguments in favor of the idea that artistic programs can be implemented successfully in all curricular areas and will develop qualities in students that strengthen academic performance.

At the Local Level

The likelihood of the arts playing an important role in a child's education is ironically slim in New York City, the artistic capital of the world. Since the fiscal crisis of the 1970s, art education has essentially been eliminated in New York City's public schools. The situation has barely improved in recent years, despite the efforts of Mayor Giuliani, who in 1997 created Project ARTS (Art Restoration Throughout the Schools) with the assistance of the Department of Education. This program was designed to restore arts education to all New York City public school curricula over a three-year period, with one third of all schools joining the program each year. Seventy-five million dollars were allocated for this project, but "as of the 2004–2005 academic year, out of 1,356 public schools over 152 schools have no art education program, and more than 160 elementary schools that have more than 500 students have one or no art teacher" (Moskowitz, 2005, p. 2).

Although funding for this program has been in place since 1997, the New York City Department of Education has repeatedly found ways to put these monies out of reach, with the explanation that "nearly half of its middle schools are already deemed in need of improvement" (NY1, 2004, p. 4). Luckily for the children of NYC, the city's artistic and cultural institutions recognize the importance of art education and the effects of restrictions posed by low per-pupil budgets and wide funding gaps between urban and suburban schools. Whenever possible, organizations such as the Lincoln Center Institute and Project ARTS have shouldered a large portion of the financial responsibility for promoting the arts in NYC public schools. However, in a city served by over 1,350 public schools with an average of 1,000 students per school, the monies allocated for arts education are spread very thin. Some urban districts that educate large numbers of poor minority children and cannot count on the support of local artistic and cultural institutions have even fewer opportunities to expose their students to the arts.

Quality art programs are indispensable in the schooling of urban children. Through the arts, children can learn to imagine possibilities, to "look at things as if they could be otherwise" (Greene, 1995, p. 19). The aesthetic learning process can enable students to broaden their perspectives, to overcome the taken-for-granted, and to envision a better world. If we prevent underprivileged children from developing these capacities, we close the door to a brighter future for them and for our country. Greene (1995) argued that "Too rarely do we have poor children in mind when we think of the way imagination enlarges experience. And what can be more important for us than helping those called at risk overcome their powerlessness?" (p. 36). Unfortunately, the essential capacities for imagination, compassion, and social responsibility are not measured in the state mandated standardized tests, nor are they considered in the standards required by NCATE.

At the National Level

Before quality art education programs can reestablish roots in our urban schools, we must take a long hard look at our required learning standards and traditional assessment tools. Existing standards should be amended to allow educators more flexibility, and better criteria should be devised for measuring student learning. This will allow teachers to abandon "banking" models of education, and to experiment with alternative methods such as I have described—using the arts to help children understand the world, their roles within it, and their capacity to change it.

Each state should commit to providing an adequate and equitable funding system for its public schools. As things stand today, public schools in urban neighborhoods receive much smaller annual per-pupil allowances than those in the suburbs and other privileged areas. The year-by-year perpetuation of this disparity demonstrates our politicians' inadequate concern for the education of our urban youth, and it seems increasingly unlikely that they will voluntarily pursue the establishment of art programs that could teach students to question the inequalities and injustices of the existing system.

This is the biggest challenge that promoters of aesthetic educational methods will face when approaching education administrators for approval of art-related curricula. The challenge to the system is twofold: the new methods will require additional expenditure, and they will empower students to question the status quo. Individuals educated through the exploration of aesthetic experience are more likely to challenge existing power structures and imagine how they can be changed to benefit the socially disadvantaged. If students feel empowered in this way, they will develop a sense of entitlement that will allow them to take a stand when necessary in the name of social justice.

Final Thoughts

The absence of arts programs in urban public schools constitutes a violation of human rights, harming the neediest of our children. I can attest that art education programs are well worth fighting for, because after infusing arts into my teacher education curricula, I have witnessed powerful changes in students' consciousness as they exit my classrooms and transition into their teaching careers. They have blossomed into newly empowered individuals with a strong desire to change the lives of the children they will teach. I believe in the ability of a committed community to create change because I have seen this process in action. By infusing art education programs into K–16 classrooms, we can teach students to appreciate and exercise their power to change the world. The educational communities they go on to build will contribute to the empowerment of all people.

References

Carey, K. (2004). *The funding gap 2004*. Washington, DC: The Education Trust.

Fox, M. (1999). *A spirituality named compassion: Uniting mystical awareness with social justice*. Rochester, VT: Inner Traditions.

Freire, P. (2000). *Pedagogy of the oppressed* (30th anniversary ed.). New York: Continuum.

Green, J. (2001, April). Somatic knowledge: The body as content and methodology in dance and arts education. Paper presented in the NDEO Conference.

Greene, M. (1995). *Releasing the imagination. Essays on education, the arts, and social change*. San Francisco: Jossey-Bass.

Greene, M. (2001). *Variations on a blue guitar: The Lincoln Center Institute lectures on aesthetic education*. New York: Teachers College Press.

Marcuse, H. (1969). *An essay on liberation*. Boston: Beacon Press.

Moskowitz, E. (2005, May 9). From the mouths of babes: New York City public school kids speak out. New York City Council. City Hall.

Moskowitz, E. (2005, October 31). Oversight: Arts education. Briefing paper of the Human Services division. New York City Council. City Hall.

NY1. (2004, October 28). First student transferred from failing city schools. [Online]. Retrieved October 28, 2004, from http://www.ny1.com/ny1/content/index.jsp?&aid=44661 &search_result=1&stid=4.

Stinson, S. (1985). Curriculum and the morality of aesthetics. *Journal of Curriculum Theorizing*, (6), 66–83.

CHAPTER 11

The Invisibility of Oppression

Ozlem Sensoy and Robin DiAngelos

"I'm a slave 4U"

In 2004 Britney Spears, one of the world's highest paid entertainers, married then unknown dancer Kevin Federline. Britney's marriage was shocking for many reasons: She was fairly young (22 at the time of this marriage), she had just married someone else 9 months earlier (that marriage was annulled 55 hours after the ceremony), and she had only known Kevin for a few months. At the time Kevin and Britney met and became engaged, Kevin's girlfriend Shar Jackson was pregnant with their second child. Kevin and Britney's wedding was ridiculed in the press for many of its "unclassy" elements: the bridesmaids' pink track suits with the words "The Maids" on the back, complementing the groomsmen's white track suits with the words "The Pimps," the menu of chicken wings and ribs, and a cash bar. So what, you might wonder, do the sordid tabloid details of a pop star's life have to do with critical social justice literacy?

Our socialization shapes our below-the-surface ideas about groups of people. These ideas are the result of myriad institutional forces. Among the most powerful forces are media and popular culture. In this chapter we trace a specific form of oppression—sexism—in media and popular culture in order to examine how our seemingly objective ideas, views, and opinions are the product of interlocking and ongoing social messages. These messages make it difficult to see oppression and are central to how oppression is normalized.

Today, women have the right to vote and a multitude of other rights afforded to them by law, and many women in the United States and Canada would argue that women's oppression is a thing of the past. However, sexism is a cogent example of how oppression adapts over time and how the cultural "water" is difficult to see while we are swimming in it.

What Is an Institution?

The term *institution* refers to a large-scale and established set of laws, customs, practices, and organizations that govern the political or social life of a people. Institutions make and enforce a society's rules and norms. Examples of institutions include marriage and family, religion, schooling, military, prison, government, law, mass media, and corporations.

From a critical theory perspective, institutions serve as primary socializing forces in society. Institutions are the systems that guide our practices in daily life. For example, consider again how schools regulate students. Schools establish the hours of attendance, decide what will be studied and how, define good and bad behavior and then reward students for good behavior and punish them for bad, determine which holidays will be celebrated and how, establish dress codes, define play, establish the norms and language with which to speak to authority, and so on. Thus there is more going on within schools than intentional instruction of subject matter.

Institutions produce, circulate, and maintain the dominant culture's norms, values, definitions, language, policies, and ideologies—and do so in ways that are above as well as below the surface of the cultural "water." Institutions are directly connected to (and reflective of) larger dynamics (interests, power relations, fears) of a given society.

To think critically about institutions requires us to move beyond our personal experiences with them and consider the big picture. We must consider the interlocking outcomes institutions produce collectively and the impact of these outcomes in society.

An Example: Sexism Today

A key challenge in understanding current manifestations of oppression is that they are often much easier to see in the past than in the present. For example, it is easy for most people to accept that denying women the right to vote, enslaving Blacks, or forcing Indigenous people into residential schools are all examples of oppression. Because our attention is directed to isolated events and specific changes from the past, rather than the overall picture, oppression becomes harder for us to see. We are led to believe that once women got the right to vote (or slave, were freed, or residential schools closed), the issue of oppression was over. What is important to understand about oppression is that it can adapt and change over time, while still maintaining inequitable outcomes overall.

Let's trace a specific example of oppression today: sexism. The following statistics demonstrate the importance of addressing overall outcomes in order to understand current manifestations of sexism.

In the global context:

- There are an estimated 12.3 million adults and children in forced labor, bonded labor, and forced prostitution around the world. Women and girls comprise at least 80% of the world's trafficking victims (U.S. Department of State, 2007).

- Women are working as commercial sex workers; working in sweatshop factories sewing garments, peeling shrimp, weaving carpets, picking cotton, mining minerals, harvesting rice; and working in households as domestic care workers. They are bonded by debt that is almost impossible to pay off and must do this menial, degrading, and debilitating labor for long hours with no rights or protections in order to survive (U.S. Department of State, 2010).

- Violence against women is the most pervasive yet least recognized human rights violation in the world, affecting one in three women (United Nations Population Fund, n.d.; Watts & Zimmerman, 2002). If we take a conservative global population estimate that 3 billion of the world's people are women (Nation Master, 2005), then that means that approximately 1 billion women are affected by gender-based violence.

- Assault and violence based on trafficking (the illegal trade in human beings that constitutes a modern form of slavery) of women and girls for forced labor and sex are widespread (Watts & Zimmerman, 2002; World Health Organization, 2009).

- Among the most common forms of violence against women is sexual violence. Rape is a frequent product of war, commonly called "war rape" (MacKinnon, 1994), and is universally declared a crime against humanity (Copelon, 2000).

- In the 1994 Rwandan genocide, it is estimated that up to 500,000 women were raped during a 100-day period (Surf Survivors Fund, n.d.).

- In 1992 Croatian and Bosnian women were subjected to rape and gang rape by soldiers in rape/death camps (Allen, 1996).

While war rape is considered a crime against humanity, and trafficking affects women in developing nations at higher rates than women in the United States or Canada, violent crimes against women and other forms of exploitation are not restricted to developing nations. Sexism occurs in U.S. and Canadian women's lives in many ways, including:

- One in four women in the United States will experience domestic violence in her lifetime, and one in six women has been a victim of rape—in a single year, that is approximately 300,000 women (Tjaden & Thoennes, 2006).

- Less than 10% of sexual assaults in Canada are reported to the police (Statistics Canada, 2006b).

- Fifty-one percent of Canadian women report having experienced at least one incident of physical or sexual violence; four out of five female

- Undergraduates at Canadian universities have been victims of violence in a dating relationship; and 83% of women with disabilities will be sexually assaulted during their lifetime (SACHA, n.d.).

- In the United States, an estimated 1.3 million women are victims of physical assault by an intimate partner *each year* (NCADV, 2007).

- Women are underemployed and make up the overwhelming population of unpaid workers in the home. When women do work outside the home, they are overrepresented in minimum-wage positions (Sussman & Tabi, 2004).

- Women in Canada and the United States earn, on average, 65–80% of their male counterparts (Statistics Canada, 2010; U.S. Bureau of Labor Statistics, 2010).

- Since life expectancy for women on average is longer than for men, we know that women account for a greater percentage of the population of elderly people and therefore more likely to be the victims of elder abuse (Hightower, 2002; Straka & Montminy, 2006).

What these statistics reveal is not only that rape, sexual assault and violence against women (perpetrated primarily by men) occur at extraordinary rates in Canada and the United States, but that many of us are unaware of the severity and pervasiveness of this violence. In addition to direct experiences of gender violence, there are indirect ways that many of us support violence against women and girls. For example, Canada and the United States are primary consumers of clothing, accessories, and household goods produced by sweatshop labor.

What Makes Sexism Difficult to See?

Given the extent of violence against women globally as well as locally, how are so many of us able to deny its existence? Why does mainstream culture position women's oppressions as a problem of marginalized societies (developing nations or people living in poverty) rather than as a pervasive system that affects *all* women throughout the world, mediated by their additional social positions (of race, class, sexuality, and other identities)? In order to understand how the pervasiveness of violence against women, and violence against women of color, poor women, and women with disabilities in particular, becomes so normalized as to be virtually invisible, one must practice seeing the interconnections between socialization, institutions, and culture.

There are several reasons why sexism is difficult to see. First, the way that dominant culture focuses on individuals obscures group-level patterns. If we view oppression as isolated events (such as suffrage or reproductive rights), or as an extreme example of violence against a single woman, the broader patterns become obscured. It is harder to see everyday and ongoing sexism when placed alongside of the sensationalized examples (e.g., a woman whose nose is chopped off to "restore honor" or a woman locked away in a basement for years and forced to bear children by her father/abuser). When we define oppression solely as individual acts that individual bad people do, we conceal the everyday ways that social institutions organize and hold sexism in place. Further, there is a silence that surrounds most individual cases, which helps keep gender violence hidden.

Second, corporate-produced popular culture has become a more pervasive institution in our lives through multiple points of entry such as advertising, sponsored curriculum in schools, and mass media (e.g., the Internet). For example, corporate-produced toys amplify rigid gender roles, socializing girls into femininity (nurturing, caring, beauty play) and boys into masculinity (aggressive, violent, physical play). Walk through any major toy store and peruse the aisles and you will see that rather than definitions of masculinity and femininity expanding, these definitions have become more narrow. Male musculature in toys and media repre sentations has become more exaggerated, the emotional range has become more limited—usually to some variation of rage—and violent play for boys has become more realistic through video games (Morrison & Halton, 2009; Pope, Olivardia, Gruber, & Borowiecki, 1999). At the same time, girls' toys and imagery have become more passive as girls' play is focused primarily on self-grooming or performing domestic duties.

As corporate culture represents masculinity as dominance, disconnection from feelings, invulnerability, and immunity from emotional attachment, it simul taneously represents femininity as passive, pleasing, and above all else attractive to boys. In this way, sexism is naturalized very early on in children's popular culture. At the same time, corporate-produced advertising promotes the idea of individualism and free choice. According to corporate culture, it is through their products (and the lifestyles advertisers associate with them) that we can demonstrate our uniqueness and freedom of choice. Sexism is thus sold to us and continually reinforced, while at the same time it is denied.

Third, the sexism in our everyday lives is obscured through the ideology of the "West" as civilized and liberated, in contrast to places that are uncivilized and backwards, such as the "East." For example, "The Muslim Woman" is an archetypal oppressed woman, standing in stark contrast to our own perceived liberation in the United States and Canada (places that are presumed to be free of Muslim women). Indeed, many of our female students frequently deny that sexism is a socializing force in their own lives and support this denial by giving the example of the Muslim woman as the woman who is *truly* oppressed (Sensoy & DiAngelo, 2006). When our students look to the Muslim woman in this way, they see the opposite of themselves. Think about the following list and consider which side is associated with "Western" women and which side is stereotypically associated with Muslim women:

- Modern/Primitive

- Active/Passive

- Individual/Group

- Industrious/Idle

- Pretty/Ugly

- Open/Covered

- Free/Restricted

Notice that although one can be both a Muslim woman *and* a Western woman, the binary view positions these identities as opposites and therefore prevents us from seeing the complex and intersecting nature of identity. Because we have not been taught to see the complexity of social identity, without further study we can only understand forms of social oppression such as sexism through the most simplistic explanations. These simplistic explanations cannot account for the ways that other social positions such as race and class also determine women's experiences under sexism. Thus these binaries also reinforce racism, classism, and other forms of oppressions.

At the same time that corporate interests are amplifying rather than reducing rigid gender roles, we are socialized to believe that in the United States and Canada, we are liberated and free; the way we "do gender" just seems normal, even healthy, and certainly better than the way *they* do it (for example, we can wear whatever body-revealing clothes we choose from chain stores in the local mall where our brand choices are believed to demonstrate our individuality, while *they* "have to" wear clothes that cover their bodies and all look the same). While our attention is continually drawn to examples of sexism that occur "over there"—in non-White, non-Western contexts—examples of sexism "over here" are usually situated in the past. Together, these dynamics hide the patterns and outcomes of sexism that surround us all. Let's examine a few contemporary locations in which patterns of sexism are normalized.

Discourses of Sexism in Advertising

Many people cite sports as now open to women, and a strong emphasis on sports often begins in schools. But what is emphasized between boys and girls varies.

There is often a lack of support for "girls'" sports in school, and even when there is funding for girls, the broader culture reinforces the idea that girls' sports are not as valuable since girls in sports don't "go" anywhere in terms of professional leagues. The results of games between women's teams are not announced daily on local and national television as they are for men's teams (men's teams of course are not identified as "men's" teams at all, but just as "teams").

Girls and women in sports are not taken seriously in the mainstream culture, except in contexts such as the diet/fitness industry or as male-oriented "entertainment" such as the Lingerie Football League (LFL) wherein attractive female athletes wearing lingerie compete in "real" football matches. While society's interest in women athletes increases during the Olympics, the final matches that end the Games (and most other competitions, such as the U.S. Open or Wimbledon) are between men.

Once girls who are highly interested in sports reach puberty, a new pressure to establish their heterosexuality (by demonstrating their interest in boys and by re maining "feminine") emerges. One of the clearest recent examples of establishing the heterosexuality and gender normativity of female athletes through advertising was illustrated with Canadian ice hockey player Hayley Wickenheiser, a four-time Olympic medalist and seven-time World championship medalist. As an athlete, Wickenheiser has logged an impressive resume of accomplishments. However, the stereotype of women hockey players not being feminine follows Wickenheiser, as it does all female players. Despite their strength and skill at their sport, their lack of traditional femininity is problematic.

Since the 2010 Olympic Games Wickenheiser has been featured in ads for Betty Crocker. In these ads the audience sees Hayley in a domestic setting; she sits with her husband and son around the kitchen table eating Hamburger Helper. Hayley tells us that just like us, she's a busy mom and the last thing she wants is to come home and spend a lot of time in the kitchen making dinner for her family.

What's powerful about these ads is how quickly they reinforce important ideas about the social construction of gender in relation to the institution of marriage and family. Hayley is separated from her athleticism as the viewer is explicitly asked to identify with her as "a mom just like you" presented in a typical nuclear family. Her heterosexuality is confirmed, along with her commitment to her traditional family responsibilities (for example, that she will do the cooking for her husband and son is taken for granted). Regardless that she is an athlete at the pinnacle of athletic accomplishment, as a woman, she is still expected to come home and put dinner on the table for her family.

The rates at which women's hockey is funded are relevant to her participation in a campaign for a product that any health-conscious athlete is unlikely to consume. The ten highest paid professional male hockey player salaries are 8–10 million U.S. dollars per season (not including bonuses that players are usually awarded when they enter the playoffs). The newly created professional women's hockey league in Canada (holding its first draft in 2010) draws some of the greatest Olympic-level athletes from the United States and Canada. Yet the players in the league, including Hayley Wickenheiser, one of the world's best hockey players, receive *no* league salary, and while their travel costs and ice time are covered, they pay for their own equipment (Canadian Press, 2010). Were Hayley male, she would receive the top contract that the most skilled male players receive. Thus many women athletes must depend on endorsements and contracts with European leagues and other sources to fund their sport.

While kids may spend 6 hours a day for 180 days per year in school receiving instruction, they interact with media every day. A 2010 study by the Kaiser Family Institute reports that youth between the ages of 8–18 spend approximately 7.5 hours per day, 7 days a week with media such as video games, TV, music, and books (Rideout, Foehr, & Roberts, 2010). And according to the Campaign for a Commercial-Free Childhood, "Children ages 2–11 see at least 25,000 advertisements a year on TV alone, a figure that does not include product placements within shows. They are also targeted with advertising on the Internet, cell phones, mp3 players, video games, school buses, and even in school" (n.d., p. 2; see also Federal Trade Commission, 2007). Yet when discussing the power of advertising with our students, we often hear, "I don't pay any attention to the ads. They don't affect me at all."

Advertising is a multibillion-dollar industry based on copious research. There are no accidents in ads—every aspect of an ad is designed to affect us, even if we only glance at it for a moment. This is important because one of the ways that media and popular culture work to perpetuate sexism and androcentrism is by normalizing particular kinds of people and relationships. Over and over, as we see these kinds of women and girls (and not others) playing out certain scripts of behavior (and not others), those women and relations become normal (and ideal) to us.

Virtually everything in advertising is gendered, furthering the strict division between men and women and their roles in society and shaping our seemingly neutral and personal consumer "choices." Food is a cogent example of gender divisions reinforced through marketing. According to advertisers, women drink iced tea and eat yogurt, salads, chocolate, and cake, while men drink beer and eat pizza, hamburgers, bacon, and other red meat. Even smell is gendered. While there is no biological difference in hair between women and men, we cannot use the same shampoo. What makes a shampoo masculine or feminine? Smell. The smell of fruit or flowers is for women, while smells associated with the "rugged outdoors," such as pine and musk, are for men.

Alcohol and cigarettes are another example of gendering in advertising. Marlboro, Winston, and Camel cigarettes are top-selling brands. Their iconic ad campaigns are heavily geared toward men, often depicting very tough and masculine men riding horses or driving pickup trucks. Yet women as well as men smoke these brands. On the other hand, Virginia Slims are heavily marketed to women. Because of this, men will not typically smoke them. Remember that a cigarette is a cigarette. It is its *association* with women that prevents men from consuming the product.

This association and its impact on our behavior indicate the direction of power. The minoritized group can emulate the dominant group because in doing so they are emulating the higher status group and thus gain status, but the dominant group does not emulate the minoritized group because they are emulating the lower status group and thus lose status. This is why women wear pants as well as dresses, but men do not wear dresses as well as pants (there has been a small resurgence of kilts for men in an alternative subculture, but these kilts are acceptable because they are masculinized by their association with ancestry and battle). Men who order cosmopolitans or other "fruity" drinks risk ridicule (because fruit is gendered female). This is an illustration of how powerful gender roles, unequal power, and marketing are in shaping our everyday "choices."

Discourses of Sexism in Movies

Because we all share the same socialization through the wider culture, familiar stock characters and plots are an effective way to quickly communicate an emotion, story element, or plot tension. For example, if a director wants to convey ideas about a "studious female," he can quickly signal this idea by visually coding the character as someone who wears glasses, has brown hair, and dresses conservatively.

Conversely, in a slasher film, we know from the start which females will be murdered (all but one) and which won't (only one will survive). The women who will be murdered are sexually promiscuous and often unintelligent and thus "deserve" to die. This is quickly signaled through cues in dress, behavior, and music. The audience, because it has seen these signifiers repeatedly, immediately under stands the character types. This process normalizes these outcomes for women and what they deserve. What women deserve is always tied to their relationship to men, whether she will be killed by a man if she is bad, or "get the man" if she is good. Further, because the women who die in slasher films are highly sexualized, the violence toward them is also sexualized. The repetitiveness of these story lines makes these roles and outcomes for women normal and unremarkable, while reinforcing these concepts "under the surface" of our conscious awareness.

Another typical character and plot sequence is in the subgenre of romance movies (often called "chick flicks"). The script usually follows the fairy-tale story line: The main character is a young woman who is in a metaphorical "coma" of some kind, usually by circumstances of her life such as taking care of an ailing charge *(The English Patient, The Wedding Planner, Dying Young)* or being ultra career oriented *(27 Dresses, The Proposal, How to Lose a Guy in 10 Days)* or because she is too involved in her work/ school to realize how wonderful she is "inside and out" and doesn't "fix herself up" or "accept herself for who she is" *(Miss Congeniality, My Big Fat Greek Wedding, The Holiday, Bridget Jones's Diary)*.

In this coma she is often encouraged by her friends (or sister or gay best friend) to get out more, try something new, take a chance, and/or fix her hair and makeup. Despite her career success, family commitments, and fulfilling friendships, this state of being without Prince Charming is presented as problematic. She is not as beautiful, desirable, or fulfilled as she *could* be were she to also have that perfect man in her life. When she meets Prince Charming through a serendipitous encounter, she often does not realize that he is "the one," He must break her coma in order to complete her life. After Prince

Charming breaks her coma, she becomes more beautiful, which is signaled to the audience through "improvements" in hair, makeup, clothes, and softer lighting.

Mainstream movies like *Pretty Woman* and *Maid in Manhattan* (as well as many reality makeover shows) *normalize* the idea that it is important for women to transcend their race and class status and realign with traditional

> Just as we might find ourselves laughing at a racist joke, we might find ourselves enjoying a film that reproduces sexism. Indeed, it's likely that due to how normalized these narratives are, we won't *see* them as *sexist* at all. Yet the more a narrative appeals to us (especially if we are women), the more important it is for us to be able to think critically about it so that we can resist its effects. Recall the concept of internalized oppression and that minoritized groups often collude with dominant ideology. Thus, no socially constructed text can or should be off. limits to a critical analysis, regardless of how popular or "enjoyable" it is.

notions of femininity. Prince Charming facilitates her transformation, as through him, she acquires access to a better life, self-esteem, and often a better wardrobe. These movies reinforce the ideology that women are fundamentally incomplete without a man. This man brings not only personal fulfillment and definition, but also increased social status through heterosexual marriage and a middle- or upper-class consumer lifestyle.

Discourses of Sexism in Music Videos

If we add music videos to this popular culture landscape, we can see that media are so extraordinarily consistent in rigid gender divisions that it is virtually impossible to escape sexist messages. Our concerns here are not with sex per se or with a return to prudish mores, but with the relentless gender-based narratives of domination and subordination in popular culture. We are also concerned with the increasing sexualization of girls at earlier ages and the near total reduction of female value to their bodies. The messages conveyed to girls are that their value depends solely on how attractive they are to men and how well they can please them. Although music videos as we know them are relatively phenomena (MTV debuted in 1981 and MuchMusic in 1984), they are among the most powerful media for normalizing sexism. What dominant culture may view to be *transgressive* in music videos—for example, the Katy Perry video, "I kissed a girl and I liked it," or Britney Spears's "If you seek Amy" [F-U-C-K me], or Lady Gaga and Christina Aguilera crawling on all fours with leashes around their necks—are actually very traditional representations of women performing classic porn tropes as defined by men. In fact, virtually all of these videos are written and directed by men.

Scholars such as Diane Levin and Jean Kilbourne (2008), Gail Dines (2010), Sut Jhally (2007, 2009), Chyng Sun and Miguel Picker (2008), and Robert Jensen (2007) have offered compelling evidence that the line has been blurred between popular and porn culture, and this blurring is most evident in music videos. Through music videos the narratives of pornography have merged into the everyday worlds of young people. It is not uncommon for female porn stars to appear in music videos (and in mainstream movies; Academy Award winning director Steven Soderbergh cast porn star Sasha Gray in one of his films), and porn directors such as Gregory Dark direct music videos for artists such as Britney Spears. Pole dancing and lap dancing classes are offered at many health clubs and bridal showers, and it is now common for young women to remove all of their pubic hair (giving them a prepubescent look), which was first normalized in pornography.

Pornography increasingly amplifies the most violent aspects of the rigid gender divisions between men and women. The physical brutalization and emotional degradation of women in porn, particularly in "gonzo" (amateur or "reality") porn that is ubiquitous on the Internet, has become more normalized as men become desensitized and need ever more intense images to feel stimulated (Dines, 2010; Jensen, 2007).

To some, it may seem an exaggeration to connect pornography to music videos and popular culture. However, consider that in 2006 the worldwide porn industry was worth 96 billion dollars (Dines, 2010). Each year over 13,000 porn films are released (compare that to the approximately 600 Hollywood film releases in a given year, according to the Motion Picture Association of America's website), and there are 420 million Internet porn pages, 4.2 million porn websites, and 68 million search engine requests for porn *daily* (Dines, 2010). The porn site LiveJasmin has more visitors worldwide than BBC Online, CNN, and the *New York Times*; and it ranks just after the most visited sites such as Google, Facebook, and Craigslist (Alexa, 2010). Many of us regularly receive unsolicited pornographic spam in our workplace and other e-mail accounts. In addition, consider that the largest consumers of online pornography are children between the ages of 12 and 17. In fact, many porn websites target children by using the names of popular characters from kid culture, such as Pokemon, on their websites. These techniques trick children into early exposure (Gomez, 2007).

Porn is ubiquitous in popular culture and an increasing presence in young people's lives. In addition to the misogyny (hatred of women) in gonzo porn, the racist discourses are extreme and unparalleled in their degradation of people of color. Yet pornography is simultaneously everywhere and nowhere, as few people talk openly about their porn consumption. For these reasons—among others—it is critical that we set aside whatever discomfort about or attachment to porn we may personally feel and think deeply about the power of porn to shape our sexuality and normalize misogyny, racism, and classism.

The representation of men as dominant, aggressive, and in control of women's bodies depends upon the representation of women as submissive, pleasing, and available for every aspect of *men's* desire. If the narratives of pornography were to acknowledge women as human beings with thoughts, feelings, and desires of their own rather than as "suffering sluts" and "stupid whores" (Dines, 2010, pp. xx–xxi), the viewer could not tolerate the pain, physical damage, and humiliation inflicted upon women that are a basic feature of gonzo porn (Dines, 2010; Jensen, 2007; Sun & Picker, 2008). Yet over time, even as we are looking directly at men brutalizing women, the ideology of sexism rationalizes it as a natural outcome of biological roles, personal choice, and mutual desire.

In many music videos, the characters and plots are predictable and include the obligatory cheerleaders, schoolgirls, strippers, and prostitutes. Peep shows, sex clubs, and sex parties are primary settings, and money is often being thrown on women's seminude bodies (the epitome of this trope is Nelly's "Tip Drill" video, showing him sliding a credit card between a woman's buttocks). Women of color fare especially poorly in music videos, as Black women are most likely to be portrayed as whores and reduced to their "booties" and Asian and Latina women are virtually absent.

An ad for MTV featured a woman in a G-string having the MTV logo branded onto her bare buttocks with a hot iron as smoke emanates from her flesh. No male (unless he was Black and it was a reenactment of pre–Civil War slavery) would be shown being painfully branded like cattle. Ironically, these representations of female sexuality are packaged as empowerment, control, and liberation for women. Consider what it means then that women's empowerment, control, and liberation are depicted as inseparable from their sexual submission to men.

Told over and over, these clichés construct an ideal female who is always available for sex with any, every, and multiple partners; who wants to be watched, touched by strangers, and objectified; who enjoys humiliation and abuse; and who has no real power, other than the illusory and temporary "power" of sexual attractiveness. It is impossible to ignore the parallels between music videos and mainstream pornography. Through repetition, rigid gender roles, as presented in movies, videos, pornography, and ads, come to seem normal and natural and make it difficult to conceptualize any other reality. As elements of porn cross over into the mainstream, our sexuality is ever more rigidly defined and we become less free, not more.

We may see these videos as a matter of choice—the women choose to perform in them and we can choose to watch them or not. But if the most popular pop stars, such as Britney Spears, Christina Aguilera, Lady Gaga, Rihanna, and Katy Perry, can choose the story lines of their music videos, why do they all choose the same stories? And at what cost could they make different choices in an industry dominated by men? As for our choice to watch them or not, we would first have to be able to avoid them, which is difficult given how ubiquitous they are. Perhaps we do intentionally watch and enjoy them but insist that we don't take them seriously. Perhaps we should, for what does it mean to *not* take seriously a woman being branded with a hot iron for "entertainment"? What does it mean to not take seriously (or be unaware of) how corporate culture has co-opted hip-hop, stripped it of its critique of racism and classism, and sold it back to us filled with misogyny and the worst possible stereotypes about Black people and urban life? How might oppressive forces depend on our not taking these dynamics seriously?

But on a deeper level, we *are* influenced by these images. No one is outside of socialization, and marketers spend billions on research to find ever more effective techniques for infiltrating our subconscious. Money spent on advertising to children alone was estimated at over $15 billion annually in the early

2000s (Linn, 2004), and corporations now spend $17 billion annually marketing to children, a significant increase from what was $100 million in the 1980s (Crane & Kazmi, 2010). The next time you are sitting in a classroom or conference room, look around. How different are the choices that you have made in dress, hairstyle, accessories, and lifestyle from those around you? Where do you shop and what brands do you chose? How different are these locations and brands from those chosen by your peers? The insistence that the women of music videos or porn can just chose to not participate, or that we can just chose not to watch them, or if we do watch them that we can just choose to be unaffected by them, is naive.

Returning to the Britney Spears example that began this chapter, let's reinterpret the gossip and titillation surrounding her wedding through the lens of sexism. The story of Britney's wedding has many layers that illustrate how popular culture facilitates the normalization of gender roles that obscure women's inequality. Consider "The Pimps" on the groomsmen's jackets. The pimp caricature is a dominant man who is surrounded by beautiful women of all races. "His" women are ready and willing to hook up with him or any number of his friends any time. There is nothing that his women won't consent to, and they happily obey his commands and compete with other women for his attention. The pimp character, once relegated to illicit magazines and films, has crossed into the mainstream and is seen more and more frequently in popular culture: the WWE's "Ho-Train," Hugh Hefner's "reality" show *The Girls Next Door,* and in a multitude of music videos, television shows, and bar, club, and party culture. Rather than reflecting her unique tastes and creativity, Britney's choice is completely in line with broader cultural discourses circulating in society.

The pimp caricature is the ultimate symbolic representation of men's domination over women and parallels dynamics in the broader society. In contrast to the glamorous representation in music videos of sexy pimps and happy whores, the reality can be harsh. The average age of entry into prostitution for girls in the United States is 12–13 (Shared Hope International, 2009). As a trainer might do with a wild animal, the pimp "breaks" his women in order to control them (indeed, the women are referred to as his "stable"), exploits and profits from their labor, and keeps them impoverished and dependent on him. These women are at daily risk of violence, which he uses to control them, as well as at risk for violence at the hands of their johns. The murder rate for female prostitutes in 2004 was estimated at 229 per 100,000, compared to, for example, the rate for male cabdrivers an occupation at higher-than-average risk for homicide), which is estimated as 29 per 100,000 (Potterat et al., 2004). Once they reach a certain age (or "condition"), they are no longer of use and so are discarded. Sex trafficking enslaves millions of women and children. These women and children don't enslave themselves—they are enslaved by people (primarily men) working as pimps. When the pimp caricature is glorified in mainstream culture to the degree that a young woman wants to put the label on her groomsmen, sexism has been utterly normalized and its violent and exploitative foundation neutralized, rendered invisible, and reduced to a funny joke. The life and work of Rachel Lloyd illustrates the impact of prostitution on the lives of women and girls, as well as the possibility to challenge it.

Intersectionality. Of course sexism doesn't stand in isolation from other forms of oppression. Women are not *just* women with one shared experience under sexism. In the example of Britney's wedding and the public response to it, we can also see dynamics of class and race. The classic image of a pimp is one of a crude and uneducated Black man who "owns" a poor woman (either White or of color) who is typically a drug addict with little other option but to work the street (women who service upper-class men don't have to work the streets and are generally referred to as "high-class call girls" or "escorts"). In addition to the pimp stereotype, other details of Britney's wedding are also stereotypically associated with southern Blacks or other "low-class" group stereotypes: chicken wings, ribs, and a cash bar. The public reaction to this wedding is in part an illustration of the contempt we have for people associated with these race and class stereotypes. The public ridicule makes it clear—class is about more than money.

Readers may find themselves thinking that we are making too much of this; Britney is no longer married, it was just a joke and we should lighten up. But this misses the symbolic power of the elements of her wedding. These elements illustrate how sexism adapts over time in ways that render the oppressive relations between men and women normal and unremarkable in the culture. Meanwhile, in every institution women are unequal and gender-based violence is a global epidemic. At what point and by whom should that be taken seriously? Whose interests does it serve for that violence and injustice to be trivialized and relegated to the realm of humor? We would argue that these interests are certainly not women's.

In this chapter we briefly traced a specific form of oppression—sexism—through popular culture and examined some of the ideologies, discourses, and market interests that work to make sexism normal, invisible, and even *desirable* to us. What might we find if we were to trace other forms of oppression through popular culture? That is, what ideologies about *race* are circulating in popular culture in ways that make racism appear normal and unremarkable to us? What ideologies are circulating that work to rationalize racism by positioning people of color as *deserving* of their oppression, such as in the relentless association of Blacks and Latinos with crime? What ideologies circulate about *social class,* for example, on shows such as *Jerry Springer,* where poor and working-class guests act in crude ways and on "reality" shows such as *Cops,* wherein we continually see poor Whites, Blacks, and Latinos, often shirtless, being taken away in handcuffs? How are classism and racism reinforced and reproduced in these media representations? What messages do we get from the virtual absence of Asian heritage people in media, except as Kung Fu fighters or geeks? Developing critical social justice literacy enables us to *see,* and thus gives us the opportunity to *resist,* these discourses.

Discussion Questions

1. According to the authors, oppression is difficult to see. Discuss some of the reasons why this is so.

2. Pick a social group and describe how that group is represented in advertising, music videos, movies, magazines, and wider popular culture. As an extension activity, you might collect some data on how that group is represented in various institutions besides media (remember, a group's absence is also significant).

3. The authors argue that there are three reasons why sexism.is difficult to see: the focus on individuals rather than patterns, the influence of corporate culture, and the ideology of *civilized* versus *uncivilized* people in the world. Explain in your own words what each of these are and how they work.

Extension Activities

1. The authors argue that one of the most common patterns in dominant culture that makes oppression difficult to see is the focus on individual people or issues, rather than broader patterns. Identify a well-known individual from a minoritized group who has been held up as "making it" (e.g., Michael Oher featured in the film *The Blind Side*) and generate a list of the ways in which oppression (organized at the group level) is obscured by mainstream representations of that individual. What does focusing on a single person prevent us from seeing?

2. Spend an evening recording information contained in commercials depicting the "average family." What is the composition of the average family? What do they do? What kinds of activities does each member of the family engage in? Record all the places you have seen this "average family" in mainstream culture. How do they communicate to us what is normal in terms of race, class, gender, ability, and sexuality? How does their presence function as a kind of "looking-glass self"?

3. Watch the documentary film *Very Young Girls* (2007) by David Schisgall and Nina Alvarez, an expose on the sex trafficking of adolescent girls (http://I www.gems-girls.org). Imagine that you are a journalist investigating this issue. Research at least two other anti-sex-trafficking activists/ organizations in addition to Rachel Lloyd and GEMS. Based on what you learn, convey the issue to the broader public or your peers, in ways such as (but not limited to) the following: a poster, stencil art, article, graph, or short public service announcement video (3–5 minutes long).

References

Alexa: The web information company. (2010). The top 500 sites on the web. Available at http://www.alexa.com/topsites/global

Allen, B. (1996). *Rape warfare:* The *hidden genocide in Bosnia-Herzegovina and Croatia.* Minneapolis: University of Minnesota Press.

Allen, B. Campaign for a Commercial-Free Childhood. (n.d.). Marketing to children overview. Available at http://www.commercialfreechildhood.org/factsheets/overview.pdfCanadian Press. (2010, August 9).

Canadian Women's hockey league to have lst draft. *CBC News.* Available at http://www.cbc.ca/sports/hockey/story/2010/08/09/sp-cwhl-draft.html

Copelon, R. (2000). Gender crimes as war crimes: Integrating crimes against women into international criminal law. *McGill Law Journal, 46*(1), 217–240.

Crane, A., & Kazmi, B. A. (2010). Business and children: Mapping impacts, managing responsibilities. *Journal of Business Ethics, 91*(4), 567–586.

Dines, G. (2010). *Pornland: How porn has hijacked our sexuality.* Boston: Beacon.

Federal Trade Commission, Bureau of Economics. (2007, June 1). Children's exposure to TV advertising in 1977 and 2004 (Staff Report). Available at http://www.ftc.gov/os/2007/06/cabecolor.pdf

Gomez, R. A. (2007, Fall). Protecting minors from online pornography without violating the first amendment: Mandating an affirmative choice. *SMU Science & Technology Law Review.* Available at https://litigation-essentials.lexisnexis.com

Hightower, J. (2002). Violence and abuse in the lives of older women: Is it elder abuse and violence against women? Does it make any difference? *INSTRAW Electronic Discussion Forum.* Available at http://www.un-instraw.org/

Jensen, R. (2007). *Getting off. Pornography and the end of masculinity.* Boston: South End Press.

Jhally, S. (Producer & Director). (2007). *Dreamworlds 3: Desire, sex, & power in music video* [Motion Picture]. Northhampton, MA: Media Education Foundation.

Jhally, S. (2009). Advertising, gender, and sex: What's wrong with a little objectification? In R. Hammer & D. Kellner (Eds.), *Media/cultural studies* (pp. 313–323). New York: Peter Lang.

Levin, D. E., & Kilbourne, J. (2008). *So sexy so soon:* The *new sexualized childhood and what parents can do to protect their kids.* New York: Ballantine Books.

Linn, S. (2004). *Consuming kids: The hostile takeover of childhood.* New York: New Press.

MacKinnon, C. A. (1994, Spring). Rape, genocide, and women's human rights. *Harvard Womens Law Journal, 17,* 5–16.

Morrison, T. G., & Halton, M. (2009, Winter). Buff, tough, and rough: Representations of muscularity in action motion pictures. *The Journal of Men's Studies, 17*(1), 57–74.

National Coalition Against Domestic Violence (NCADV). (2007, July). Domestic violence facts. Available at http://www.ncadv.org/files/DomesticViolenceFactSheet (National).pdf

Pope, H. G., Jr., Olivardia, R., Gruber, A., & Borowiecki, J. (1999). Evolving ideals of male body image as seen through action toys. *International Journal of Eating Disorders, 26*(1), 65–72.

Potterat, J. J., Brewer, D. D., Muth, S. Q., Rothenberg, R. B., Woodhouse, D. E., Muth, J. B., et al. (2004). Mortality in a long-term open cohort of prostitute women. *American Journal of Epidemiology, 159*(8), 778–785.

Rideout, V., Foehr, U., & Roberts, D. (2010). *Generation M2: Media in the lives of 8–18-year-olds.* Menlo Park, CA: Henry J. Kaiser Family Foundation. Available at http://www.kff.org/entmedia/mh012010pkg.cfm

Schisgall, D., & Alvarez, N. (Directors). (2007). *Very young girls* [Documentary]. New York: Swinging T Productions.

Sensoy, O., & DiAngelo, R. (2006). "I wouldn't want to be a woman in the Middle East": White female student teachers and the narrative of the oppressed Muslim woman. *Radical Pedagogy, 8*(1). Available at http://radicalpedagogy.icaap.org/content/issue8_1/sensoy.html

Sexual Assault Centre of Hamilton Ontario (SACHA). (n.d.). Sexual assault statistics. Available at http://www.sacha.ca/home.php?sec=l 7&sub=43

Shared Hope International. (2009). *The national report on domestic minor sex trafficking: America's prostituted children.* Vancouver, WA: Shared Hope International. Available at http://www.sharedhope.org/Portals/O/Documents/SHl_National_Report_on_DMST_2009%28without_ cover%29.pdf

Statistics Canada. (2006). *Measuring violence against women: Statistical trends.* Ottawa, ON: Author.

Statistics Canada. (2010, June). Average earning by sex and work pattern. Available at http://www40.statcan.gc.ca/IO1IcstO1/laborO1a-eng.htm

Straka, S. M., & Montminy, L. (2006). Responding to the needs of older women experiencing domestic violence. *Violence Against Women, 12*(3), 251–267.

Sun, C., & Picker, M. (Director and Producer). (2008). *The price of pleasure: Pornoraphy, sexuality, and relationships* [Motion picture]. Northampton, MA: Media Education Foundation.

Surf Survivors Fund. (n.d.). Statistics on Rwanda. Available at http://www.survivorsfund.org.uk/resources/history/statistics.php

Sussman, D., & Tabi, M. (2004). Minimum wage workers. *Perspectives on Labour and Income, 5*(3), 5–14.

Tjaden, P., & Thoennes, N. (2006). *Extent, nature, and consequences of rape victimization: Findings from the National Violence Against Women survey.* Washington, DC: U.S. Department of Justice.

United Nations Population Fund. (n.d.). Ending widespread violence against women. *UNFPA Gender Equality.* Available at http://www.unfpa.org/gender/violence.htm

U.S. Bureau of Labor Statistics. (2010, June). Highlights of women's earnings in 2009. *U.S. Bureau of Labor Statistics.* Available at http://www.bls.gov/cps/cpswom2009.pdf

U.S. Department of State. (2007, June). *Trafficking in persons report.* Washington, DC: Author. Available at http://www.state.gov/ documents/organization/82902. pdf

U.S. Department of State. (2010, June). *Trafficking in persons report* (10th ed.). Washington, DC: Author. Available at http://www.state.gov/documents/organization/142979.pdf

Watts, C., & Zimmerman, C. (2002). Violence against women: Global scope and magnitude. *The Lancet, 359*(9313), 1232–1237.

World Health Organization. (2009). Violence against women: Factsheet no. 239. Available at https://www.who.int/mediacentre/factsheets/fs239/en/index.html

Reflection Questions

1. Both parents and students complain about the lack of relevance of public education. Research identifies many successful and innovative models of schooling, for example, KIPP Schools, Harlem Children's Zone, charters, etc. Why do you think that there is tremendous resistance to attempts to establish alternative schools for the general school population? How are these alternative programs more successful in addressing the needs of diverse students?

2. As you think about critical theory and social justice, consider what a school based on these principles would look like. What would be the aims and purposes around which this school is organized? What would be the content of the curriculum? And finally, what would be the role of assessment?

3. Are there problems associated with students being involved in shaping and directing a school program? Describe and discuss. How do student roles and responsibilities shift when students take more active roles in the schools? In what ways can the curriculum accommodate the changing roles and responsibilities of students?

4. Technology has had an impact on the ways in which teaching and learning occur in schools today. Will technology provide more access to knowledge for all students or will the increased use of technological resources create a greater chasm between the "haves" and the "have-nots"? Why or why not? How will the roles and responsibilities of students and teachers change in response to these changes?

5. Identify the educational practices that limit the educational opportunities of some students. Do these practices reinforce preconceived notions about groups of students who have not traditionally succeeded in schools? Describe and discuss your answers to these questions.

SECTION III
Teaching, Learning and Leading Against the Grain

Introduction

Yolanda Medina

One of my favorite teaching moments is when I speak to teacher education students about oppression, privilege, and discrimination. As I look around the classroom, I see them nodding their heads in agreement and taking notes on new vocabulary terms discussed from the readings. Often, in their reflective papers, students state that my class lectures have given them the language needed to express what they have always felt. They convey to me a sense of personal identification with the injustices discussed in our classroom and the sense of helplessness that came with not having the language to communicate their feelings or actively express resistance to oppressive, discriminatory practices. A student once wrote, "There is a certain level of authority that only language can give you." Acquiring a critical language to discuss these issues helps these students embrace a sense of empowerment needed to assertively discuss and react to situations of oppression, and to stand up for what they believe to be just, to do the right thing, and to go against the grain. We believe that one of the most important traits that teachers need to have is the capacity to stand up for what is right for their students, schools, and communities and go against the grain when it is needed.

The group of essays chosen for this section examine how education can be used as a form of resistance to or rejection of an educational structure that often perpetuates social, cultural and economic inequalities. This educational structure that is embodied by public schooling was created in the mid- to late-1800s for the primary purpose of preparing individuals for two main goals: first, preparation for a differentiated workforce that has almost become obsolete, rendering the current system archaic and useless. And second, to acculturate or "Americanize" the children of immigrants through the imposition of White, Anglo-Saxon, Protestant (WASP) values and compliance to previously defined social norms. Through the years, this system has played an important role in shaping, and reaffirming, the values and norms of American society. Unquestioning obedience to authority, the value of rote knowledge, and the unwavering acceptance of an educational system based on meritocracy were just a few of values and norms that the schools nurtured and rewarded. Over the course of time, this approach to education ultimately weakened an individual's faith in her/his power to shape the world and left them at the mercy of those in positions of authority to tell them how to lead their lives.

The authors in this section of the book write with passion from a very personal place—their own subversive experiences as educators, leaders, activists and parents. The essays present the perspective that the true purpose of education is to create individuals capable of living in peace, of accepting the human range of diverse ways of living—be they religious, social, cultural or sexual—and of embracing all living beings as equals. Freire (2000) believed that "people's vocation is humanization and this vocation is constantly negated" (p. 43). We agree, as do the authors in this section, that education can be a path toward humanization. Through education and knowledge acquisition, we either support individual growth and expansion or we can hinder it. We support the development of humanization when, as educators, we encourage individuals to critically analyze the societal structures that maintain the religious, social, economic and sexual inequalities that negate this human growth and begin conversations about healing and change. Simultaneously, we hinder this growth when we perpetuate a system that continues to reflect the desires of the past and ignore the needs of the future. True education is about questioning the world, our capacity to change it for the better, and participating in the struggle to make that happen. This section is about teaching, learning, and leading against the grain for humanization.

To go against the grain takes a lot of guts, a strong desire for social change, and a tremendous amount of trust in our capacities, as a community of educators, to persevere and triumph. To go against the grain takes an extraordinary amount of hope and an imaginative capacity that will allow us to "look at things as if they could be otherwise" (Greene, p. 19) so that we do not perpetuate old habits and fail to create new ones in the name of equality and justice. Going against the grain requires a sense of empowerment that begins with the acquisition of the language needed to communicate these issues, constant critical self reflection, and a willingness to struggle for positive change. That is the essence of what these authors promote in the following chapters.

There are multiple ways to look at the experiences and beliefs of the authors in this section of the book. Collay, Cowhey, Gorlewski, Love, Medina, and Pucci and Cramer use both research and life experiences to explore how a commitment to social justice and critical theory situates and grounds their understanding of teachers' work. They also discuss the contradictions and challenges that require us to constantly re-evaluate and revise our understanding of the aims and purposes of public education. The stories told in these essays speak to the struggles that teachers encounter in their efforts to create schools with transformative pedagogies and integrated curriculums that reflect pedagogical values where there is a conscious honoring of the diverse backgrounds of all students.

All of the authors in this section teach, learn and lead against the current educational system that dehumanizes individuals. Hopefully, these essays encourage other educators to consider alternative forms of education that shape and nurture individual capacity for critical reflecting, questioning, and changing the world through knowledge, respect and an understanding of our differences.

References

Freire, P. (2000). *Pedagogy of the oppressed* (30th anniversary edition). New York: Bloomsbury.
Greene, M. (1995). *Releasing the imagination. Essays on education, the arts, and social change*. San Francisco: Jossey-Bass.

CHAPTER 12

Teaching Is Leading

Michelle Collay

Why do we feel that we need to apply the word *leader* to only certain teachers? One reason is that most of us think of a leader as someone who takes on additional roles outside the classroom. The perception that "regular" teachers are not leaders is reinforced by historical patterns of school management, such as physical isolation, exclusion of teachers from decision-making roles, and the chronic de-skilling of teachers through a constant barrage of misguided mandates (Cochran-Smith & Lyttle, 2006).

Yet effective teaching *is* leadership. Leadership in schools means holding fast to a vision of democratic learning communities and taking actions, small and large, to disrupt inequity and to create real opportunities for students, families, colleagues, and community members. And in spite of inadequate funding, social factors that limit teacher professionalism, and outdated school structures, effective teaching and learning happen in all kinds of schools every day, as teachers lead by leveraging relationships within and beyond their classrooms.

Leading from the Classroom

Teachers lead by using their professional knowledge and judgment to support the learning of all students, by guiding the professional development of colleagues, and by participating in communities of practice (Barth, 2001; Danielson, 2006; Donaldson, 2007). Teaching is a vocation requiring everyday acts of leadership—courage, a clear vision of what matters, strong relationships with others, and resistance to the bureaucracy that can grind teachers down.

The following four dimensions of powerful classroom-based leadership are exemplified by 50 experienced teachers working in some of the most challenging urban districts in the United States (Collay, 2011). As program director and instructor in a teacher leadership master's degree program, I documented these experienced teachers' reflections about leadership over five years. I visited their classrooms, observed their courage and efficacy in action, and witnessed what transformative teacher leaders do.

Teachers Lead by Teaching Well

Teaching well means embracing the tensions of being in relationship with students, colleagues, parents, and the community (Gergen, 2009). Teaching is a messy business, requiring us to be theoretically grounded and purposeful while we respond to the ups and downs of the school day: providing one student with more structure and another student with less; staying in at lunchtime with a recalcitrant student in one case and sending her out for extra recess in another.

Those who teach are quite conscious of the countless decisions that influence relationships and build connections that lead to learning. Such intricate and subtle decision making requires professional expertise.

Teaching has been compared to jazz improvisation (Cuban, 2011), and like jazz musicians, teachers draw on deep knowledge of the art, technique, and emotional work of making meaning together. Here are some examples of how teachers lead by establishing and nurturing relationships:

Sheila finds out that a student failing her English class will be kicked off the soccer team because of his low grades. She meets with the soccer coach and student to brainstorm some ways to raise his English grade.

When Richard e-mails the parents of one of his high-performing students because she has stopped turning in homework, he discovers that her mother has been deployed with the National Guard. He asks the student to come by his room one morning each week so that they can send her mother updates. He also uses the sessions to check her homework and provide tutoring.

Cristina has noticed a pattern of bullying by a group of 8th grade girls. She refers them to the guidance counselor, as required by school policy, but in her own classroom she also assigns each of them to tutor an English language learner. She meets with the girls weekly to learn about their tutees' progress.

Teachers Lead by Collaborating

Teacher collaboration with students, families, and colleagues is essential to create conditions for learning. Unlike directing a meeting or managing a staff, this collaboration is often invisible. School cultures and physical structures—from policies that forbid teachers to leave their class rooms unsupervised to long hallways that separate staff members from one another—often limit collaboration among adults. The very act of talking with a colleague during the day can be an accomplishment.

Teachers overcome such boundaries in creative ways, including developing study groups or professional learning communities. They lobby the school administration for designated prep time, use that time for relevant work, use emerging technologies to communicate, meet outside school, and find and share resources. But this kind of collaboration takes persistence (Collay, Dunlap, Enloe, & Gagnon, 1998).

Schooling traditions also limit collaboration between parents and teachers. Teacher–parent collaboration is evident in many elementary classrooms, typically decreases by middle school, and virtually disappears in high school. Partnering with parents can be fraught with tension on both sides, but some teachers seem to have a knack for building trust with even the most anxious parent or caretaker. It takes additional courage and leadership to share the path of coteaching and coparenting which divisions of race, language, and class complicate the relationship (Keyes, 2000; Miretsky, 2004).

Communication with parents is essential in teachers' efforts to make sense of students' lives within and beyond the classroom, a capacity that is often underrated and overlooked, even by teachers themselves. As a parent of two school-age children, my main concern at the parent conference is, does this teacher *see* my child?

What I'm really asking is, Does this important adult in my child's life know her as a whole person, with all her warts and gifts, or is she just a name in the grade book? The quality of their relationship has a profound influence on the quality of her learning.

The following examples show how teachers lead by building connections within and beyond the classroom:

Dan calls three parents each night and shares something positive about their child.

Maria organizes a term-long literacy project requiring her 5th graders to write reviews of Newbery Award books for primary students, interview primary teachers about their literacy curriculum, suggest age and topic-appropriate chapter books, and volunteer as readers in the primary teachers' classrooms. The 5th graders send their reviews to the books' authors.

Philomina arranges for students from her 7th grade life science classes to participate in a local non-profit group's "Save the Creek" cleanup event. In preparation, they study urban watershed ecology in class, interview a local ecologist from the Environmental Protection Agency, and e-mail members of the nonprofit group about examples of successful trout reintroduction in the same watershed. Students joining the cleanup receive a membership in the nonprofit group, and skeptical neighbors now see students from the local middle school as an asset to the community.

Tai uses resources available through the California History–Social Science Project (http://chssp. ucdavis.edu) to take high school students through a study of their family's journey to or across North America. Each student interviews an immigrant from his or her ethnic or language community, often a family member. The videotaped interview and key events of that family's and ethnic group's journey are portrayed on a web-based timeline, with audio explanations provided in two languages. The materials are made available at the community library and are used by teachers of English as a second language for their adult literacy classes.

Teachers Lead through Inquiry

Studies conducted by education researchers often use "scientific" research methods that exclude the important factor of relationships between students and teachers. But classrooms are not laboratories, and students are not rats (fortunately). Classrooms are communities of practice, some more evolved than others. Measuring student "outcomes" on standardized tests provides *some* information about what students know, but it captures only a small part of a larger picture of complex, socially constructed knowledge.

When teachers lead through inquiry, they must begin with asking the right questions. Teachers must learn to trust their instincts, develop their own questions, deliberately document what they observe, and determine what action is needed. The hard-won knowledge they glean from such inquiry can empower them to hold their ground in the face of the next mandate or initiative. Thus, classroom-based inquiry is a requirement for good teaching and learning, not a luxury.

Formal teacher-led inquiry may include asking specific questions about how students learn: for example, conducting a child-study of one student's emotional development or comparing the progress of early readers who experience a new reading program with the progress of past cohorts of early readers. In addition, teachers conduct multiple forms of informal inquiry every day—from observing that a student is acting withdrawn and unhappy as he arrives at school to glancing at students' math tests and noting that almost the whole class missed problem 23. In the first case, the teacher may draw on her knowledge of the child, the family, and the school to sensitively explore why the student is upset and to respond constructively. In the second case, the teacher uses her awareness of curriculum flaws, knowledge of effective instruction, and interpretation of test results to conclude that students did not understand the material and she must teach it in a different way.

Here are some examples of teachers leading through inquiry:

Jessie, Andrea, Jake, and Melissa are differentiating a math curriculum for middle school prealgebra. Their department adopted a lesson-study framework for professional development. These teachers meet weekly to review their lesson plans, critique one another's instruction, and collect and organize unit assessment data. They observe and discuss one teacher's lesson each month. They record their observations of students' engagement with the math materials, collect assessment data from their own students, and use the test scores to identify target areas for instruction.

A school implements Response to Intervention (RTI) to differentiate instruction for its students. Although grade-level teams agree that the concept has merit, even experienced teachers are challenged to find time and space for assessing students and adapting their instruction. In addition to following the required protocol for identifying students and documenting their progress, grade-level teams use their shared prep time to discuss the challenges they have encountered and to strategize about the logistics of making RTI work. They invite the school's data coach to facilitate the development of student case studies, which they use to analyze individual students' strengths as learners, to compare writing samples from early efforts to final drafts, and to assess the fluency of English language learners. This enables them to form a comprehensive portrayal of student ability and to design instruction accordingly.

Teachers Lead by Developing Partnerships

Some partnerships are teacher initiated, as productive teachers embrace expertise beyond the classroom and school. Teachers must also navigate partnerships that are not of their own making, such as those resulting from a mandate, a reform effort, or an external grant.

Good teaching in the context of either a welcome or an uninvited partnership requires a strategic response to the resources provided. Although experienced teachers may hold a healthy and understandable skepticism when told that this next initiative is "the answer," such skepticism should not keep them from taking advantage of useful parts of a grant, such as a coaching framework or materials that can improve learning in their classrooms. Good teaching unfolds when teachers broker resources for their students, strengthen existing collaborations within their schools, and build relationships with individuals who can provide relevant support.

For example, a nonprofit preschool agency in the county established a formal partnership with one elementary school's preschool staff. The agency provided training and resources for preschool teachers—including curriculum materials and manipulatives for math and language literacy—and trained staff to supervise recreation time. The preschool funding formula initially excluded kindergarten and 1st grade teachers Jamilla and Eduardo, who had worked with the preschool team to establish program coherence. Together, the preschool and primary staff asked the program director to include the primary grades in the initiative. This potentially divisive partnership now supports a reliable sequence of learning experiences for children ages 3–8, strengthening early literacy development.

Looking at Teaching through the Lens of Leadership

It takes courage to trust our intuition, observations, and interpretations and to take action in the face of outside pressures and little support. But teachers lead every day by teaching well, collaborating with others, con ducting well-designed inquiry, and forming partnerships. We should not underestimate the powerful leadership role played by teachers who build relationships from their classrooms outward, thus transforming themselves, their students, their students' families, their colleagues, and their communities.

References

Barth, R. (2001). Teacher leader. *Phi Delta Kappan, 82*(6), 443–449.

Cochran-Smith, M., & Lytle, S. (2006). Troubling images of teaching in No Child Left Behind. *Harvard Educational Review, 76*, 668–697.

Collay, M. (2011, June 16). *Everyday teacher leadership: Taking action where you are.* San Francisco: Jossey-Bass.

Collay, M., Dunlap, D., Enloe, W., & Gagnon, G. (1998). *Learning circles: Creating conditions for teacher professional development.* Thousand Oaks, CA: Corwin.

Cuban, L. (2011). Jazz, basketball, and teacher decision-making [blog post] Retrieved from *Larry Cuban on School Reform and Classroom Practice* at http://larrycuban.wordpress.com/2011/06/16/ jazz-basketball-and-teacher-decision-making

Danielson, C. (2006). *Teacher leadership that strengthens professional practice.* Alexandria, VA: ASCD.

Donaldson, G. (2007). What do teachers bring to leadership? *Educational Leadership, 65*(1), 26–29.

Gergen, K. (2009). *Relational being: Beyond self and community.* Oxford, UK: Oxford University Press.

Keyes, C. (2000). Parent-teacher partnerships: A theoretical approach for teachers. *Issues in early childhood education: Curriculum, teaching education, and dissemination of information* (Proceedings of the Lilian Katz Symposium, Champaign, Illinois). Retrieved from http://ecap/crc/illinois.edu/pubs/katzsym/keyes.pdf

Miretsky, D. (2004). The communication requirements of democratic schools: Parent-teacher perspectives on their relationships. *Teachers College Record, 106*, 814–851.

CHAPTER 13

Going Against the Grain

Mary Cowhey

People are unreasonable, illogical, and self-centered; forgive them anyway.
If you are kind, people may accuse you of selfish, ulterior motives; be kind anyway.
If you are successful you will win some false friends, and some true enemies; be successful anyway.
What you spend years building, someone could destroy overnight; build anyway.
If you find serenity and happiness, others may be jealous; be happy anyway.
The good you do today, people will often forget tomorrow; do good anyway.
Give the world the best you have, and it may never be enough; give the world your best anyway.
In the final analysis, it is between you and God. It was never between you and them anyway. —Mother Teresa

*D*uring my first year of teaching, there was a school shooting tragedy in Kentucky, in which some students who felt like they didn't fit in brought weapons from home and shot a bunch of students and a couple of teachers. It was tragic, to be sure. A group of teachers clamored at our staff meeting that we had to "tighten up security" at our school. When asked for suggestions, their first idea was that parents not be allowed to walk children to their classrooms, because that allowed an unregulated flow of "strangers" in our building. I pointed out that if they were parents who came to the classroom, the teachers would know their names and faces and they would no longer be strangers; they would be family members. No, they argued, someone with a violent agenda could slip in. I said that by getting to know the families, I will know if there are issues of alcoholism, mental illness, domestic violence, child abuse, custody disputes, or other issues about which I need to be especially vigilant.

I pointed out that in the recent tragedy, the shooters were not violent strangers or even disturbed family members who "slipped in" but troubled students who were required to be there. No matter, they thought we should have a system in place so that parents and guardians couldn't go past the front lobby. I said that the school would be more secure if we had parents in the hallways, because they love their children. If they saw anyone acting suspiciously or causing trouble, they'd be all over them in a minute.

In the end, it was decided to set up a system where all nonstaff had to sign in and get a visitor badge before going down the hallways, and that a person without a visitor badge could be stopped. A counter was *put across the front lobby to control the traffic flow. This created a need for volunteers to handle the visitor badge distribution and collection, and caused bottlenecks, which caused children to be tardy.*

A week or two after this new system had been implemented, I was walking from my apartment to the Dumpster in my neighborhood when I saw Magda, a parent who continued to walk her sons to my classroom every morning. She smiled broadly and said hello. I noticed that on her coat she was still wearing the school visitor badge. I realized she wore it all the time. I was glad to see her creative resistance to the new rule. Later the fire department said the counter in the lobby was a hazard and could block quick evacuation in case of a fire, so it had to go.

* * *

We live in a competitive society. For many people, competition is more natural than cooperation. Some people feel defensive when others do things differently. They may feel compelled to criticize or humiliate the one who is different. They may want the one who is different to go away or to be removed. If you teach critically, and if teaching critically is different from the dominant culture in your school, you may feel like you are going against the grain, swimming against the tide. I often felt this way. I feel it less often now.

When I started teaching, I had a one-year contract. I knew that my district laid off the new teachers every spring for the first three years. Many were not hired back after that first layoff. I wanted a chance to teach. I wanted this school and this principal. I was willing to take a year. I taught like I had a year to live. I don't mean that in a "Damn the torpedoes!" way, but rather that I was gung ho to try out all the ideas I had read about in my own classroom.

I set up my classroom using tables instead of desks, so that we could work in cooperative groups. I made home visits. I did not have cute classroom decorations. I hung up Romare Bearden's colorful collages and large beautiful photos of children, torn from old UNICEF calendars. I set up a woodworking center. Skeptical colleagues stood in my doorway and shook their heads, saying things like, "You'll get sued for that." (No child ever injured herself, and even my most aggressive students never whacked anyone with a hammer; I use it now only during my simple machines unit, because the hammering is so noisy.)

I felt self-conscious on the first day of school when all the other first-grade classrooms had monarch butterfly caterpillars and thought, "Are we supposed to do that?" I had shown a veteran teacher my lesson plans for the first week and asked her advice. She laughed at me and said, "You're planning to *teach* on the first day of school?" Of course, I felt rather stupid and asked what she was planning to do. She just laughed some more.

I did a lot of things differently from the other first-grade teachers and most other teachers at my school. Some of those things were ideas and practices from research. Many others were the children's ideas. Some were just based on my own hunches and opinions. I initially shunned some practices, like the teaching of handwriting, on the basis that it was conformist and uncreative. No one required me to teach handwriting, so I didn't.

A couple of years later, I had a first grader whose handwriting (I realized in retrospect) actually had gotten worse in the course of the school year. Because I did not teach it and had not established clear expectations in relation to it, I just thought she was rushing because she was so excited to get her story out. That summer, a brain tumor was diagnosed in her, and she later lost a good deal of her vision. I felt terribly guilty for not having pursued that casual observation about her handwriting.

In the meantime, my district decided to implement a new handwriting program. I was quick to sign up for the training and appreciated the thoughtful (if not exciting) approach to teaching this useful and necessary skill. Of course, handwriting gets a little more exciting when used for authentic purposes, such as making signs and banners that need to be standard, bold, and legible. I pay much closer attention and intervene more quickly now when one of my students doesn't meet the clear expectation. If my intensive interventions with family support don't work well enough (usually they do), I can consult with our occupational therapist to determine whether it is a difference I need to be concerned about, or just a difference.

That handwriting thing was a mistake none of my colleagues noticed or criticized. I criticized myself for it a lot, and took constructive action to improve my practice. There were plenty of things, however, especially my first year, that my colleagues *did* notice and criticize. I cried many times that year because I wasn't sure what to do. I just wanted to teach and teach well.

Crimes of Nonconformity

One day that first spring, some of my colleagues asked to meet with the principal regarding their complaints about me, which were all in the realm of nonconformity. In fact, they'd made a list of my crimes of nonconformity. It included the following:

- Doesn't eat lunch in the faculty room
- Allows parents into the classroom
- Has family events in the evenings
- Students do not walk in a straight line in the hallway
- Students are loud when they walk in the hallway

Of course, I was guilty on all counts. In an effort to fit in, I *had* gone to the faculty room to eat at the start of the year, but the conversations were extremely unpleasant. There was one loud teacher in particular who liked to "hold court" in the faculty room. I was uncomfortable with his frequent racist and classist comments about families who came from the subsidized apartments "across the street" and "welfare mothers" and stereotypical imitations of African American and Puerto Rican students. Students and often whole families were given unflattering labels.

I felt very uncomfortable and wasn't sure what I should do or say. I was new in the school and didn't want to alienate new colleagues. I didn't want to appear uptight or self-righteous. I didn't laugh, heartily or nervously, just watched. A few times I asked friendly teachers what they thought about that commentary and they would shake their heads or roll their eyes, saying, "Just ignore him," or "He always acts like that."

That first winter, I took a course that another first-grade teacher, Lisa, recommended about antiracism for educators. I read Beverly Daniel Tatum's *"Why Are All the Black Kids Sitting Together in the Cafeteria?"* I knew it wasn't enough to just not laugh. I had to say something to interrupt the cycle of racism. The next time he made a comment about the neighborhood across the street, I calmly said, "You know, I live across the street. Do you think that about me and my family?" Another day he made a joke about welfare mothers. I said, "You might not realize this, but I was a welfare mother for a couple of years, and I don't think that's funny." When he did another one of his stereotypical impressions of an African American student I said, "I find that offensive."

Things would get real quiet. Conversation would stop when I entered the faculty room, and I'd receive a couple of icy stares. The racist diatribes subsided, at least in my presence, but I didn't feel welcome. That was when I started to eat lunch in my classroom with Lisa. We could talk about readings from the antiracism course, or questions about teaching without static. The complaint almost struck me funny, like they minded my absence.

My principal was aware of the faculty room scene, and she began to make changes over time. She had the very large square table removed and replaced it with four or five smaller round tables so there could be different and even semiprivate conversations there instead of a single dominated and loudly moderated one. Lisa and I went back to eating in the faculty room and had our conversations there. A staff social committee cleaned and painted the faculty room, and installed a carpet, couch, and comfy chairs in one area, in addition to the tables. Over time, the loud teacher was transferred to another school and then stopped working for the district.

I remember Sonia Nieto once said she advised new teachers not to go to the faculty room, because conversation there was often so jaded and discouraging. She said her thinking on that issue changed over time, and now she urges new teachers to go eat in the faculty room. I don't go every day, but I go on a fairly regular basis and enjoy the company of other staff members in what has become a less-biased, more collegial place.

I never quite understood why some teachers so resented parents of first graders dropping their children off at the classrooms. I don't know what they suspected Puerto Rican parents of whispering to their children in Spanish—"Go poke the teacher with scissors," perhaps? I listened and quickly learned that all of those whispered Spanish conversations ended with "Give me a kiss," "Bless you," or "Behave yourself" (literally, "carry yourself well"). Who could ask for more than blessed, kissed, hugged, well-behaved children? I was not in a hurry to make those parents go away.

It was also true that I had organized family events in the evening, like bilingual Family Math Nights. I started organizing them because parents unfamiliar with the new district-mandated "Investigations" math curriculum were angered by what they perceived to be a dumbing down of the curriculum. Some of those parents weren't playing the assigned math games with their children at home, not recognizing the value of that homework. Many of these parents expected a traditional rote approach and did not understand the constructivist philosophy behind the new curriculum.

I had gotten training from the local educational collaborative in running Family Math and Science Nights and had organized a series at the school the year before, when I was a student teacher, as part of my research on most effective family involvement practices to support student learning. I invited the other first-grade teachers to participate in organizing the Family Math Nights for our grade level and offered them the option of just sending home the leaflets inviting their students and families.

Lisa was enthusiastic about organizing it with me. Several parents, as well as Kim, the bilingual teacher who worked with my class, and Kathy, the ESL teacher who worked with Lisa's class, volunteered to help with outreach, translation, and running the activities. Two other first-grade teachers were discouraging, saying that no one would come, that it was a waste of time, and besides, it would set a negative precedent. One explained that if teachers did things like this on an unpaid basis, they would be considered "past practice" in future negotiations, and teachers who didn't want to would be required to do them. Because I was new in the teachers' union, I hadn't been aware of that. Teachers still aren't paid enough, and without teachers' unions, we'd be paid even less. It was a valid point. I located some grant money to pay all of the teachers involved, but no more teachers chose to help or to invite their students.

The Family Math Nights were a tremendous success. Hispanic parents who had been skeptical of the new math curriculum were impressed and better understood how to support their children. They also felt more empowered to ask questions and discuss math with teachers. The parents who attended were enthusiastic and spoke to their friends and neighbors. Eventually the nonparticipating teachers got notes from parents in their classes asking if they could have a Family Math Night too. Those teachers who had not distributed the leaflets to invite their families complained to our principal that Family Math Nights should be stopped.

Our principal, who was new in her position, had been supportive of the bilingual Family Math Nights and had helped me locate the grant money. We had already completed the planned series of three events in the fall, so it was not a problem to "stop" that year. My principal chose not to tangle with the complaining teachers on this point. The following year, two parents who had been involved the first year went to the Parent-Teacher Organization and volunteered to organize the Family Math Nights for all of the second grades. The parents of all second graders were automatically invited through the school newsletter. Because it was entirely organized by parents, there was little anyone could complain about.

The year after that, the Family Center, an organization within the school to promote family involvement, had a chunk of grant money and was interested in running Family Math Nights. The director came to ask my advice about it. I explained that research showed that the most effective way to involve parents least likely to participate with children who were most likely to benefit (lower income, less educated, nonnative English speakers, folks with math anxiety) was to hold a series of smaller events, instead of one schoolwide event. I said that I could train volunteers the Family Center recruited, which would give the school a base of Family Math leaders for years to come. She said, "Considering school politics, I think it would be best if you weren't involved." Later, I learned that the Family Center planned to hire a trainer who lived across the state.

I was very upset. I had organized a successful series of events at the school while a student teacher and again as a first-year teacher, and had worked as a trainer. The Family Math programs were very popular with parents and, if properly implemented, could have a major effect on reducing the achievement gap in math. I had been prevented from providing Family Math for my class and grade level because it upset some teachers. Now I heard that some stranger who had no rapport with our families and no clue about our school culture would be a better choice than me for training the parent volunteers to run it.

I felt sick over the whole thing. I knew my ego was getting wrapped up in it. In addition to teaching, I was in graduate school and had a new baby. I didn't need more work or more battles. I cared deeply about Family Math, the principle and the actual program, but I realized I had to let it go and just focus on teaching. I wished them luck and said no more. The trainer from across the state backed out because it was too far for her to travel. They never implemented the program.

I can't fight every battle and still have the energy, sanity, and focus to keep teaching positively, keep loving my family, keep having a life. Even with allies among colleagues, families, and administrators, I can't win every battle. Sometimes, however sadly, I have to let go.

Learning to Walk with Silent Dignity

It was also terribly true that my class did not walk in straight lines (there was clearly some clumping going on) and that we were not completely silent. In fact, if we ever were silent, it was more by accident than design. I had observed that my class was not the only nonstraight, nonsilent class in the school, but this was not the time to mention that. It was not my students' fault; I had never taught them, never expected or demanded this behavior from them. I had not fostered this straight and silent behavior because I thought it was authoritarian and conformist.

I had to think about it again. Our classroom was near the end of a hallway, so not much traffic passed our door, which was sometimes closed if we were engaged in a noisy activity of our own. This meant that we passed lots of other classrooms whenever we went anywhere in the school. I could understand that a classroom closer to the center of the school might feel annoyed or distracted if they had to put up with noisy hallway traffic interrupting their lessons. I discussed this criticism with my class. They agreed it was true and hadn't considered that it might be annoying and distracting to students and adults who were trying to concentrate on their work. Getting consensus about the silence wasn't too hard.

We had to think more strenuously about reasons to walk in a straight line. We finally came up with these:

- If your hands are not at your sides, you could feel tempted to run your hand along the walls and this could mess up, knock down, or tear the artwork of other students displayed in the hall. That would be disrespectful.

- If you are walking next to your friends, you might forget that you shouldn't talk and just start talking with them when you should be quiet.

- If you walk in bunches, it might be hard for another class to pass in the opposite direction.

- If you want to walk and talk in clumps or bunches with your friends, you could do that outside at recess time.

All of this criticism had gotten me thinking about my friend Ruth, and a conversation I had heard her have with her son, Frankie, a couple of years earlier when we were both single mothers in college. She had picked him up from the private school he attended, and we were riding in the car. A biracial first grader, he was complaining that his teachers were punishing him for things that White kids did too, but they went unpunished.

I was surprised at what seemed to be the harshness of Ruth's tone as she spoke to him. She said, "Look, Frankie. I'm not saying it's right, and I know it isn't fair. You're young to have to hear this, but you are just going to have to learn to be better and work harder than the others, because people are going to be looking at you. There will always be somebody who thinks you don't belong at their school because you're not White or because we don't have as much money as they do. Don't let anyone provoke you. They're wanting to make a bad example of you because they think you don't belong here, so you're just going to have to get used to having to act better than everybody else." Those words were hard to hear, but she loved her son fiercely. As a woman of color, she spoke from the wisdom of her own experience, and I knew she was right. It wasn't right or fair, but it was true.

I looked at my own students, their eyes shining with excitement and adventure. We were a loud and energetic bunch. I didn't want to handcuff and blanket them to stifle their lively nature. I asked if they remembered the part of the video about Martin Luther King Jr. we had watched earlier that year, about the march to Selma. They recalled it vividly. I said, "Martin Luther King taught those activists to walk with silent dignity. People threw rocks and bottles and garbage at them, called them names, and sprayed fire hoses on them, and still they walked with silent dignity, like no insult could hurt them. Do you think we could walk with silent dignity?" We tried it, a very slow, tall, dignified, silent walk, like we were marching to Selma, all the way to the cafeteria and back. We had found a way.

After that, instead of dreading the hallway walks and nasty rebukes, we anticipated them. We thought of other historical examples, such as Gandhi's salt march to the sea and Harriet Tubman conducting a group on the Underground Railroad (*extra* quietly). The leader got to announce, "We're going to walk to the gymnasium now. We're going to walk with silent dignity, like we're marching to Selma," and we'd step off. Finally, my class looked straight and silent, but more important, they looked sharp and proud. There wasn't another complaint about our hallway behavior all year.

Let no man drag you down so low as to make you hate him.

—George Washington Carver

When I first started teaching at my school, bullying was a problem—among the teachers. It had been that way for a long time, so it had become part of the faculty culture at the school. It was especially strong the first year. Intimidation was not subtle. A teacher came up to me in the faculty room and said, "You know why my nickname is The Terminator?" I didn't know. "Because the teachers I don't like, I get fired." Her friends laughed and a couple of other teachers smiled uncomfortably. I wondered how and if a teacher could have the power to get another teacher fired, but I didn't ask. I just said, "Thanks, I'll remember that."

One day a teacher came in my room and announced that my first graders would be taking a standardized test the next day. I was surprised, asked the purpose of the testing, and began to give my objections to standardized testing. She raised her hand to silence me, and then waved it dismissively, saying, "I've heard all that before. The other teachers who had those arguments, they're gone now."

I walked into a teacher meeting my first week and set my notebook on a table, about to take my seat. A teacher sitting nearby said, "You don't want to sit there. I'm pretty nasty." I smiled, said, "Thanks for the tip," and sat elsewhere.

I found that wonderful George Washington Carver quote that year and made it into a sign that I hung in my classroom. I taught the quote to my students and reminded myself of it daily. It was a hard year.

There's something to be said for staying, for quietly doing what you do, however strange it may seem to skeptical colleagues. Like Ruth said, you just have to act better and work harder. I was nervous when one of my students was assigned to The Terminator's class for the next grade. I was worried she would somehow find fault with his education. I got even more worried when I heard her in the office saying that she had scheduled a meeting with his parents and the principal the first week of school. It turned out that he was reading and doing math on such an advanced level that he didn't "fit" in her groups, so she wanted to send him to the next grade.

I do more assessment than our principal and district require. Many of my students are below grade level when they arrive in the fall. We are required to use the Developmental Reading Assessment in the early fall and again in late spring. I also use it in December and March and aggressively look for interventions (whole class or individual) or additional help to bring every student to or above grade level by the end of the year. My main motivation is to teach my students well, but I would not be truthful if I failed to say that I am also conscious of the critics out there who would be quick to pounce if my students were not making strong progress.

My principal has always made a point of honoring diversity, including a diversity of teaching styles. She believes that different children thrive in different environments and that it is important to offer a variety. Our classrooms range from the traditional to the progressive. In the nine years I've been in the district, expectations and frameworks have been clarified and some things have been implemented on a districtwide or schoolwide basis.

On any given morning at our school, you can walk in one classroom and see teacher, children, and parent volunteer gathered on the rug for a morning meeting and in another class see students standing to recite the Pledge of Allegiance. In the next room, they may be starting the day with silent reading at their tables. In the next one, they may be doing punctuation worksheets at their individual desks. Within a shared set of constraints, we all have a certain amount of freedom to develop our own teaching styles, to collaborate with colleagues, to engage in research, to work on our own projects.

I appreciate that freedom and don't try to impose my style of teaching on others. Increasingly, teachers check in to borrow books and other materials for lessons or units they have heard about and would like to try. The faculty bullying that characterized my school eight years ago has receded significantly. In its place is more collaboration and respect … not perfect, but much better.

I take all criticism seriously, whatever the source. Even if the motivation is less than well intentioned, I try to find what is valid in what is being said. Even if there is no direct complaint to my principal, I will often ask to discuss the criticism with her to get another perspective on it and get her advice. Even if the critic did not demand action, I try to take the criticism constructively and make some plan of action that would improve my teaching.

To Pledge or not to Pledge

One September about five years ago, a third-grade teacher came up to me and said, "I have to tell you a funny story." She said that John, who was in my class for first and second grade, failed to recite the Pledge of Allegiance when she directed the class to do so. She asked him why he didn't recite it. He said,

"We never did that in Ms. Cowhey's class." She asked why not. He shrugged and said, "Because she's a protester, I guess."

The story got me thinking. It was true: I had not taught my students that traditional morning routine of saying the Pledge of Allegiance. Why not? On a gut level, I would have felt fraudulent. It seemed like one more conformist thing that I wasn't going to do if I wasn't told to. I thought back to my first-grade experience in Catholic school in the 1960s. Every morning I stood up and faithfully recited,

I pledge a legion to the flag of the Union States of America
And to the public, four witches stand,
One nation, invisible under God,
With liberty and justice for all.

I didn't know what *pledge, allegiance, united, republic, nation, indivisible, liberty* or *justice* meant. I'd heard of the American *Legion* Hall, where old men went. I knew there was a *public* school, where my Jewish neighbors went. I knew my dad was in the *union*, and that it had something to do with work. I knew what *invisible* meant, and I knew that you couldn't see God, so that line sort of made sense. The nuns were very enthusiastic about this, so I figured it was a kind of prayer. We always followed it up with this:

Hail Mary, full of grapes,
The Lord is swishy
Blessed ot thou among swimming
And blessed is the fruit of thy room JESUS [head bow]
Holy Mother, Mother of God,
Pray for us sinners
Now at the hour of our death. Amen.

That one was equally mysterious. I understood the "full of grapes" part because my mother had explained to me that the wine used for Communion was made of grapes. The nuns in their long habits were swishy when they walked, so I supposed the Lord could be swishy too. I wasn't sure about that swimming part, but I let that go, because I knew there were fishermen in the story. The fruit in her room went with the grapes okay. I knew Mary (for whom I was named) was the Mother of God, and we were obviously the sinners in this prayer. I never understood "now at the hour of our death" because we never died when we said it. I tried hard to make sense of all this, but in the end, I recited it without question because everyone else did. And I didn't want to get whacked with a ruler.

The more I thought about it, the more I realized I did not make the children recite the Pledge of Allegiance because I think it is developmentally inappropriate. As a native English-speaking first grader with a strong vocabulary, I hadn't understood many of the words in it. What about my students with more limited vocabularies, and those learning English, and those who are not citizens? I think it sets a negative precedent to teach children to repeat and promise to do things they don't understand or believe. It makes a promise worthless. It trains people to be nonthinkers.

No parents or students had ever complained about my lack of pledge recitation. I checked the latest revision of the state curriculum frameworks and saw that I was now supposed to teach "national symbols, holidays, heroes and songs." All right, then, I would *teach* the Pledge of Allegiance.

I wrote out the Pledge of Allegiance on a chart. One of my students recognized it and shouted enthusiastically, "I know how to do that! I learned that in kindergarten." I asked if he would like to demonstrate for the class. He and several of his kindergarten classmates rose and recited it, in a rendition that sounded like mine in first grade. I thanked them and asked if they or other students could help me define some of the very tricky words in it. The first graders who had learned to recite it in kindergarten showed little advantage over those who had not when it came to defining words such as *pledge, allegiance, united, states,* and so on.

After we developed definitions for the new vocabulary, I distributed sheets with the pledge, typed double-spaced. Because we now understood that a pledge was a promise and had discussed that you should never promise to do something you don't understand or believe, I asked them to go through and make whatever changes necessary so that they could understand every word of the pledge. Here are Michael's changes:

> *I promise you can count on me to the flag of the together governed*
> *   places of America,*
> *And to the Republic, for which it stands,*
> *One country, can't break up, under God,*
> *With freedom and fairness for all.*

Next, I distributed lined paper and asked them to rewrite the pledge in their own words. Here is Michael's rewrite:

> *I promise you can count on me to respect the flag of the United States of*
> *   America and the government it stands f or,*
> *One country that God is watching. Indivisible,*
> *With freedom and fairness.*

Since then, I've taught the Pledge of Allegiance every year. I explain that we don't say it every day because I think that's a mighty big promise for first or second graders to make. I also explain that I don't think noncitizens should be pressured to recite it, because I would feel uncomfortable pledging allegiance to a country of which I was not a citizen. I tell them that as they grow up, they'll decide whether they want to just stand respectfully during the pledge or actually recite it, but they'll do so knowing what it means.

Over the years as I've taught this lesson, we had many discussions about the last line, "With liberty and justice *for all*." "What about Iraq?" my students wanted to know. "Does that mean *all* in the world or just *all* in the United States?" Other students pointed out discrimination against Blacks and gays and said, "It's not even fair to *all* in the United States."

All this to say that even if I shut my classroom door when I teach critically, eventually, word will leak out. My students will go forth to other classrooms, ask questions, and think differently. So will their parents. Sooner or later, people will know.

For example, we always do a lot of learning about family diversity and honoring all families. Last year our school hired a new secretary. One hectic afternoon, heavy snow developed, causing after-school-program cancellations. The new secretary came over the public address system and concluded her cancellation announcement by saying, "So if you need to call your mom and dad to let them know, you can come to the office to use the phone." Several students looked up from their math problems, eyebrows raised. Astrid raised her hand and said, "The announcer lady just made a mistake. She said, 'call your mom and dad,' but a lot of kids at this school don't have a mom and dad. They have one mom or two moms or an aunt or a grandmother or other guardian. Saying that could make them feel left out. They should say 'parents and guardians' instead."

I said, "She's new, and maybe she doesn't know that yet or hasn't thought about it. Would you please write her a kind note about that?" So Astrid did. I was pleased that Astrid had listened critically to something as mundane as a cancellation announcement and that she recognized exclusive language. She did not respond in anger or act like a wounded victim. She took prompt action, using oral and written language, to correct a mistake, to make our school a better place.

Thinking Critically about Teaching Differently

When I first started teaching, I felt pretty alone, like an odd duck. Some of my early teaching decisions were based on little more than a sense of social justice and my well-worn tendency to reject conformity. I cried a lot that first year and doubted myself often. My husband, Bill, a former engineer who had just become a first-year teacher himself, listened; we consoled and encouraged each other. I was able to talk with my teaching friend, Lisa, to process what was happening at school, with my students, their families, the faculty and administration. I could talk with my principal about major concerns. Although she couldn't solve all the problems with the wave of a wand, I felt she was an ally who shared my concerns and was working to address them (maybe not as fast as I wished) from the administrative end.

It took me months to develop a sense of who my allies were on the faculty and to gain the confidence to risk interrupting the status quo. The reality is that the forces that maintain the status quo have allies, often loud and numerous. When you go against the grain, you enter a world of complex dynamics that can't all be studied out beforehand. Some folks show their true colors right away.

When my husband went for a second interview for his first teaching job, he asked the principal, "What kind of diversity do you have here?" There was a long pause, and then the principal answered, "We've got a few of them, but they don't give us much trouble." When the principal called to offer my husband the job the next day, Bill turned him down. There's no sense in starting to work for an educational leader with whom you have major disagreements from the start.

I've learned to observe carefully what happens when I make changes, noticing who my allies and opponents are. I may find allies in administration and opponents among colleagues, or vice versa, but more likely, I'll find some of both. The reasons they oppose and the methods they use are complex. I tread more carefully now; I am less likely to charge around like a bull in a china shop. My principal has demonstrated that one can often make deeper, more lasting institutional changes through a series of sometimes subtle, thoughtful, deliberate moves over years than by hasty, bold actions and decrees that generate backlash and resentment.

It is not easy to go against the grain, to challenge the status quo in an institution as established as a school. I sometimes rock the boat by doing something different, doing something new, or not doing something that was always done before. When I choose to do something different, I think first about what my reasons are, and am prepared to talk with students, parents, colleagues, and administrators about those reasons. As a bottom line, I consider whether my idea is developmentally appropriate and safe (physically and emotionally). Can I articulate the educational benefit? Is the topic or skill the children will gain through it relevant to the curriculum frameworks? How will this help the children? I think about what is expected and required and why. I rethink it each time I do it.

Sometimes, I go with my gut and the rationale evolves over time, as I observe the results. My ability to articulate that rationale also develops over time. I need to be able to talk through ideas with someone I really trust (partner, friendly colleague, principal, mentor) so I can reflect on these questions. If I can't talk through it, I probably am not ready to do it.

I try to be brave in the face of intimidation, but I always listen carefully to criticism. I'm no Mother Teresa, but I try not to provoke critics unnecessarily by dressing inappropriately, chatting on a cell phone, or doing personal e-mail in the presence of students, or otherwise acting unprofessional. This is not to be judgmental, but to be aware that plenty of other people may be. People may criticize, but let them criticize the educational changes I make, not that I showed my navel.

CHAPTER 14

Teaching from the Test

Using High-Stakes Assessments to Enhance Student Learning

Julie A. Gorlewski

Introduction

Prepositions matter. One of my favorite academic cartoons depicts a pig standing on a corner, holding a sign that reads, "Will work as food." The caption offers an ironic epilogue: the pig's grammar mistake led to a position, but not one that he wanted. I generally share this image with my English education students early in the semester, intending to remind them of the importance of accuracy in language—even with seemingly innocuous words like prepositions. A more subtle but equally relevant example of preposition power is reflected in the title of this chapter. Educators—with good reason—bemoan the causes and effects of teaching *to* standardized tests. In this chapter, I explore the considerable possibilities that arise from a shift in the preposition; instead of teaching *to* the test, we can encourage educators to plan instruction with standards and assessments in mind. That is, we can show future educators how to avoid the deleterious consequences of standardization and retain their professional roles by teaching *from* the test.

The purpose of this chapter is to explore how the typically negative effects of standardization on curriculum and instruction can be used to develop critical pedagogies intended to advance student empowerment and promote social justice. Specifically, this chapter describes how I used high-stakes tests to expand (rather than narrow) the curriculum and enhance (rather than inhibit) student learning in a teacher education program.

Context

Despite a wealth of scholarship demonstrating the reductive effects of high-stakes examinations on curriculum and instruction (Hillocks, 2003; Ketter & Pool, 2001; Neill & Gayler, 2001; Nelson, 2001; Nichols & Berliner, 2007; Popham, 2001), in the United States today the trend in education is toward increasing accountability with more and more standardized assessments. These assessments then drive curriculum and instruction (Gorlewski, 2011; Garrison, 2010; Apple, 1996). Although standards, as broad frameworks for setting learning targets, are not necessarily problematic, when they

are operationalized as high-stakes assessments, test-based pedagogies emerge and freque
curriculum, leaving little room for construction of knowledge or critical pedagogies.
enon is evident at all educational levels. Energies that might be devoted to social justice and critical
pedagogies are drowned in the ocean of norm-referenced data that serve political ends without doing
much to improve the teaching/learning process. Legislation that legitimizes testing as the central measure of learning undermines the ability of educational institutions to inspire excellence and ameliorate
inequities. In addition, critics maintain that high-stakes assessments serve to perpetuate current class
structures by maintaining skill gaps and controlling ideology, particularly beliefs in individualism, meritocracy, and what counts as knowledge (Dorn, 2003; Hillocks, 2002).

The experience described in this chapter began with the results of a critical ethnography I conducted
in 2006 which investigated the experiences of students and teachers in a working-class high school. The
study consisted of participant and non-participant observation, in-depth semi-structured interviews with
11th grade students and teachers across the four major disciplines (English language arts, social studies,
science, and mathematics), and analysis of a wide range of documents created by teachers, administrators, students, and state education department officials. Data analysis, grounded in constant-comparison
methodology, indicated that high-stakes standardized assessments resulted in narrowed curriculum,
teacher deprofessionalization, and student alienation from schooling. In this K–12 setting, it was clear
that teaching to the test, particularly in the area of writing (which connects closely to thinking), had negative effects on student performance, teacher professionalization, and writing instruction.

In an attempt to reduce the effects of standardization, I implemented instructional activities
designed to integrate aspects of standardization while simultaneously reinforcing tenets of critical pedagogy, i.e., the awareness that "every dimension of schooling and every form of educational practice are
politically contested spaces" (Kincheloe, 2007, p. 2). To be effective, the activities could not be strictly
strategic (focused on measuring bits of knowledge easily assessed on multiple choice tests). Addressing
student performance from a critical pedagogical perspective required, instead, that students understand that the assessments themselves are socially constructed and that using assessments as means of
self-reflection could offer possibilities of bridging the gap between standards and culturally responsive
instruction. This view of standardized assessments, grounded in the concept of "resistance literacy"
(Gorlewski, 2011), provides a context in which high-stakes tests can be a lever for critical pedagogy, a
context that certainly seemed transferable to a higher education classroom.

From K–12 to Teacher Education

Although I had taught graduate-level teacher education courses on a part-time basis over the previous
five years, in 2009 I began teaching full time in a teacher certification program in western New York
State. This program had two unique characteristics. First, it was an accelerated, cohort-based program;
students began classes in the fall, and in most cases were student teaching by the following fall. Second,
although the college was a U.S. institution, the cohort was primarily composed of Canadian students,
many of whom drove for hours to attend classes.

This college program was particularly attractive to Canadian students who had been closed out of
teacher education programs (which were quite selective) in their native country because Ontario (the
province from which most of our Canadian students came) accepted New York State teacher certification as equivalent to its own certification. Therefore, if the Canadian students in our program earned
New York State certification, they would also be certified to teach in Ontario (which, for most of them,
was the ultimate goal). In addition to course work, to earn state certification in New York, students are
required to pass a set of assessments. Generally, the Canadian students who enrolled were solid students
who had little difficulty meeting the requirements of our New York State certification program. There
was, however, one significant hurdle.

Julie A. Gorlewski

The Content Specialty Test

For these students, New York State certification requisites included three examinations: the Liberal Arts and Sciences Test (LAST), the Assessment of Teaching Skills—Written (ATSW), and the Content Specialty Test (CST). Pearson Education, Inc. (2008) which publishes the assessments as part of its New York State Teacher Certification Examinations, describes these tests as follows:

> The New York State Teacher Certification Examinations are criterion referenced and objective based. A criterion-referenced test is designed to measure a candidate's knowledge and skills in relation to an established standard rather than in relation to the performance of other candidates. The explicit purpose of these tests is to help identify for certification those candidates who have demonstrated the appropriate level of knowledge and skills that are important for performing the responsibilities of a teacher in New York State public schools. (CITE, p. 2)

The CST, as its name implies, is specific to the core area discipline that adolescent education students intend to teach. Its development and format are explained in the test booklet:

> Each test is designed to measure areas of knowledge called subareas. Within each subarea, statements of important knowledge and skills, called objectives, define the content of the test. The test objectives were developed for the New York State Teacher Certification Examinations in conjunction with committees of New York State educators.

> Test questions matched to the objectives were developed using, in part, textbooks; New York State learning standards and curriculum guides; teacher education curricula; and certification standards. The test questions were developed in consultation with committees of New York State teachers, teacher educators, and other content and assessment specialists.

> An individual's performance on a test is evaluated against an established standard. The passing score for each test is established by the New York State Commissioner of Education based on the professional judgments and recommendations of New York State teachers. Examinees who do not pass a test may retake it at any of the subsequently scheduled test administrations. (Pearson, 2008, p. 2)

In New York State, the CST is required for certification in the following subject areas:

- Agriculture
- American Sign Language
- Biology
- Blind and Visually Impaired
- Business and Marketing
- Cantonese
- Chemistry
- Dance
- Deaf and Hard of Hearing
- Earth Science
- Educational Technology Specialist
- English Language Arts
- English to Speakers of Other Languages
- Family and Consumer Sciences
- French
- German
- Gifted Education
- Greek
- Health Education
- Hebrew
- Italian
- Japanese
- Latin
- Library Media Specialist
- Literacy
- Mandarin
- Mathematics
- Multi-Subject
- Music
- Physical Education
- Physics
- Russian
- Social Studies
- Spanish
- Students with Disabilities
- Technology Education
- Theatre
- Visual Arts

The graduate students had no difficulty with the LAST and the ATSW; their undergraduate experiences had prepared them well with respect to general studies and literacy skills necessary to achieve a passing score on these examinations. In fact, many students opted to take these exams just after acceptance and had already passed them before taking the methods class I taught. The CST, however, posed a challenge. Despite the fact that these students had earned bachelor's degrees in English, the scope of the exam and its focus on American literature created anxiety that was not entirely without merit. That is, students had reason to be concerned about this exam, since they could not assume that the material it covered would have been included in their English degree programs at Canadian colleges and universities.

Even though students had the option of retaking the exam if they earned an inadequate score, the fee ($79 per administration) and the efforts associated with the test increased anxiety associated with the possibility of failing to achieve certification.

In short, the intent of the test is to serve as an assurance that New York State certified teachers possess and can demonstrate particular sets of knowledges, dispositions, and skills—characteristics that are set forth through the "established standards" claimed by the assessors in their descriptive document. This is certainly a laudable goal; no educator would support the certification of candidates unworthy of the designation. However, in a school of education, we faced a specific, significant challenge as we sought to help our candidates meet the standards meant to be measured by this assessment. Primarily, the challenge involved preparing students for the assessment without resorting to test-prep pedagogy. In fact, I believe that we, in schools of education, have an obligation to model—consistently—critical pedagogies. Therefore, in this class, the challenge for me was to foster critical pedagogies even as we explicitly prepared students for the CST.

Course Goals

Since I had no intention of subordinating our program or course goals to the assessment (however positive its intent), I decided to begin instructional planning with the course goals, which had been developed through a collaborative process aligned with Teacher Education Accreditation Council (TEAC) standards. The goals for this course, which was entitled Methods of Adolescence Education: English, were:

Teacher candidates will understand

1. Student diversity and how to be effective with a variety of students.

2. National and State standards and how to build units and lessons that meet these standards.

3. Formative and summative assessment techniques that can be used to guide practice.

4. A wide variety of proven techniques from which to select to teach English effectively.

Naturally, these goals were supported and extended by a detailed set of course objectives—none of which were explicitly aligned with the certification examinations.

The course goals and objectives had been developed in accordance with a set of four claims that the department faculty had composed as part of the accreditation process. These claims were aligned with the guiding principles and the mission of the department, the college, and the accrediting agency.

Claim 1: (Our) College graduates know the subject matter in their certification area(s).

Claim 2: (Our) College graduates meet the needs of diverse learners through effective pedagogy and Best Teaching Practices.

Claim 3:   (Our) College graduates demonstrate scholarship supported by the use of technology.

Claim 4:   (Our) College graduates are caring educators.

In addition, the school of education faculty had created a set of common core assessments linked to specific courses. Within the context of the comprehensive program, these assessments were meant to target the specified claims and goals of the department. Common core assessments included a Philosophy of Education, an Annotated Bibliography, a Lesson Plan, and a Unit Plan. Materials associated with the common core assessments incorporated descriptors and rubrics; however, the content allowed for academic freedom with respect to both substance and pedagogical approach. As might be expected, the common core assessments associated with the methods class consisted of lesson plans and a unit plan.

From Standards to Critical Pedagogy

As I began to *think* about planning the course—a component of the process that seems always to precede actual planning by many, many hours—I kept returning to the two aspects of the course and the program over which I had the least control: the certification examinations (in particular, the CST, which related directly to our content area) and the common core assessments. How could I model critical pedagogical practices while ensuring that students adhered to the guidelines necessary for them to succeed at these essential tasks? The answer (or, more accurately, an answer) came to me as I reflected on my experiences in secondary education when I sought to prepare students for mandatory examinations relative to earning a high school diploma without contributing to the alienating, commodifying, and exploitative experiences of learning that standardized assessments tend to foster. Critical approaches that had been effective in this setting included transparent explication of the tasks as the social construction that they are, intentional efforts to explore and validate the knowledges and skills that students bring to the tasks (whether or not these knowledges or skills seem to be valued on the assessments), deliberate exploration of the emotional and social pressures connected to the assessments, and finally—once the cultural considerations have been unpacked and investigated—focused development of the skills necessary to succeed on the assessments. These strategies had worked well with high school students and had allowed me to connect critical pedagogies to standardized requirements without subjugating our identities (mine or my students) to state or institutional mandates. Could these ideas transfer to a graduate-level classroom? And, if so, how?

One of my recurrent professional and personal survival strategies is to seek synergy. If I am in a situation that seems confounding and overwhelming, it feels natural to find connections in order to help organize my thoughts and maximize the effects of my efforts. In this case, a possibility emerged that combined the CST with the common core assessments and was in harmony with the principles of critical pedagogy.

Embracing Assessments

In accordance with curriculum planning principles of backward design, I began the semester by presenting the expectations for the course and asking students to identify connections between department claims, course goals, and their aspirations as teacher candidates. Rather than casting the common core assessments (the unit plan and lesson plan) as obstacles or impediments that hindered our ability to engage in effective learning experiences (as such assignments are often portrayed and performed in courses that require them), I introduced the assessments as opportunities for us to demonstrate the learning that would occur over the course of the semester. Furthermore, I organized our instructional activities to support the creation of unit and lesson plans; for example, when we delved into the topic of essential questions, students used the opportunity to craft essential questions related to their unit plans and lesson plans. Each week, students made progress in their understanding of the methods and strategies relative to English language arts in secondary schools, and their progress would be apparent, in part, through the development of their unit plans (of course, other assignments were built into the course, as well, both formative and summative). In addition, we discussed the terminology of the lesson plan and unit plan descriptors and rubrics with respect to the importance of common language, as well as the power relations involved in determining whose language is used. Students applied the rubrics to one another's plans during peer review sessions and, in doing so, cultivated a sense of appreciation for the challenges inherent in the development of such tools. Deep understanding of the core assessments, themselves, assisted students in two ways. First, they demonstrated planning ability and knowledge that went beyond the surface of the assessment expectations. Second, their confidence in their capacities as teachers and learners was strengthened. This increased confidence was expressed in their individual conferences with me, in their final presentations, and in their course evaluations. By rethinking the assignment in terms of its framework, analyzing it as a socially constructed instrument, and focusing on its indefinite spaces—areas that allowed for choice and exploration—I was able to shift the experience from externally focused and restricted, to authentic and purposeful.

It is important to note one significant advantage that contributed to my ability to apply critical pedagogical principles to the unit plan and lesson plan assessments: I was the evaluator of these assignments. Although the documents, along with the completed rubrics, were submitted to the school of education assessment coordinator, I was the final arbiter in terms of the grades that students received on the projects. Therefore, if we, as a class, chose to accept a more inclusive definition of "reflection," for example, I—as the instructor/evaluator—would incorporate that definition in my appraisal of the student work. Unfortunately, such flexibility is utterly absent from a standardized assessment like the CST.

To apply a critical pedagogical approach to the CST required that I bring together my students, the course goals (as addressed through the common core assessments), and the examination, itself. Fortunately, after many stressful hours of deliberation as I planned the course, inspiration struck. And the idea was much simpler than I had ever imagined: I decided to have students incorporate content from the CST into their unit/lesson plans so that their development of these plans would address potential aspects of students' content area deficiency. But how could I make this happen?

On the first day of class, we discussed the requirements of the course and the requirements for New York State certification. Reviewing the expectations for a semester's worth of work, as well as the complex, lengthy regulatory and bureaucratic specifications for certification, is an overwhelming experience for students; however, I believe that knowledge—even knowledge that is intimidating—is always more empowering than ignorance. Furthermore, I was determined to help students develop the confidence and capacity to meet the challenges they faced. Therefore, after introducing the unit plan, I distributed the 59-page Preparation Guide for the English language arts CST.

It is a daunting document. It lists the examination's six subareas:

Subarea I.   Listening and Speaking

Subarea II.   Writing

Subarea III.   Reading

Subarea IV.   Fundamentals of Literature

Subarea V.   Language and Literature

Subarea VI.   Fundamentals of Literature: Constructed-Response Assignment

These subareas incorporate 24 objectives which are explicated by a series of focus statements. The objectives embody an exceptional range and scope of knowledge, skills, and information. Some are extremely general, such as Objective 0012: Understand writing for literary response and expression; Objective

0007: Understand reading for information and understanding; Objective 0019: Understand literature written for adolescents; and Objective 0017: Understand the characteristic features of various types of nonfiction.

Others are more specific but also comprehensive, such as Objective 0011: Understand the use of reading comprehension strategies; Objective 0015: Understand the historical, social, and cultural aspects of literature, including the ways in which literary works and movements both reflect and shape culture and history; Objective 0022: Understand significant themes, characteristics, trends, writers, and works in American literature from the colonial period to the present, including the literary contributions of women, members of ethnic minorities, and figures identified with particular regions; Objective 0018: Understand the characteristic features of various forms of poetry; and Objective 0024: Understand the literatures of Asia, Africa, continental Europe, Latin America, and the Caribbean, including major themes, characteristics, trends, writers, and works.

Students were understandably frustrated and anxious by the preparation guide, which seemed to warn them that everything that they had ever learned about English—as speakers, listeners, writers, and readers—was fodder for a prospective test question. No one could be expected to demonstrate proficiency in relation to all these objectives and focus statements. How might such a broad content area be focused in order to provide students with strategies to address their deficiencies without destroying their sense of expertise with respect to the assessment? Here's what I did.

After providing a few minutes for students to peruse the guide to sample questions and study tips, I instructed them to read each of the objectives (and its related focus statements) and rank the objectives 1–24 according to the students' sense of their own level of expertise and proficiency. Then I asked them to identify, in their rankings, the lowest 5 objectives and share these objectives aloud with me and their classmates. We discussed overlapping concerns, possible interpretations of overly general objectives, and ways to make the comprehensive objectives manageable. Next, I divided them into groups and asked them to each select one objective, eliminating duplication among group members and taking into consideration our previous class discussion. At the end of this process, each student had identified an objective that addressed a content area deficiency *and*—among our 25 candidates—*all* the CST objectives were accounted for.

Then, and only then, I informed them that each student's self-assigned objective was going to be the focus for his or her unit plan. I must admit that their initial reactions were hardly joyful. Many students admitted that they had envisioned creating unit plans that were devoted to areas of English language arts that reflected their passions, not their deficits. However, once I clarified the purpose of this method of selecting unit plan topics, they appreciated its intent, as well as its promise. If all went well, I informed them, the whole class would benefit from this range of unit plan topics. The advantages of purposeful application of their weakest objective were obvious; they would be immersed in an area in which they were now the least confident. Moreover, as students presented pieces of their units to their classmates over the course of the semester, our learning community would extend its expertise with respect to all the CST objectives.

Remarkably, that is exactly what happened. The unit plans and lesson plans enabled students to develop strengths in matters that many had previously avoided. In addition, the range of topics was broad and offered possibilities for applying methods and strategies that a more restricted set of selections would not have provided. When the course ended, several student comments—in person and on course evaluations—indicated that they were gratified, and even a bit surprised, to learn that they enjoyed a topic they had once disliked. Although they were still anxious about the exam, they were more confident about their ability to pass the CST.

And all of them passed on their first attempt.

Reflection

As enjoyable as it is to report the positive results, it is not the main point of this account. While passing is required to earn certification, passing was not the primary intent of the activities described in this chapter.

To me, what really matters is that teacher candidates experience and develop a critical approach to standardized assessments—wherever they appear.

The work that we did was intended to help students meet—then move beyond—the requirements of these high-stakes standardized assessments. As a result of these approaches, students developed increased confidence and expertise—characteristics that promote performance on assessments without resorting to test-based pedagogies. While the negative effects of standardization are well known, it is sometimes difficult for educators to imagine ways in which resistance can be enacted without dire consequences for teachers and students. Reconsidering our own perceptions of standards as something we can use *with* and *for* our students (rather than *on* or *against* them) enables educators to avoid having our profession devoured by high-stakes assessments.

I hope we can escape the sad fate of the unemployed cartoon pig who offered to work *as* food.

References

Apple, M. W. (1996). *Cultural Politics and Education.* New York: Teachers College Press.

Dorn, S. (2003). High-Stakes Testing and the History of Graduation. *Education Policy Analysis Archives, 11*(1), p. 1–29.

Garrison, M. (2009). *A Measure of Failure.* New York: SUNY Press.

Gorlewski, J. (2001). *Power, Resistance, and Literacy: Writing for Social Justice.* Charlotte, NC: Information Age Publishing, Inc.

Hillocks, G. J. (2003). Fighting Back: Assessing the Assessments. *English Journal, 92*(4), 63–70.

Ketter, J., & Pool, J. (2001). Exploring the Impact of Direct Writing Assessment in Two High School Classrooms. *Research in the Teaching of English, 5,* 344–393.

Kincheloe, J. L. (2007). *Critical Pedagogy.* New York: Peter Lang Publishing.

Neill, M., & Gayler, K. (2001). Do High-Stakes Graduation Tests Improve Learning Outcomes? Using State-level NAEP Data to Evaluate the Effects of Mandatory Graduation Tests. In G. Orfield & M. L. Kornhaber (Eds.), *Raising Standards or Raising Barriers* (pp. 107–126). New York: Century Foundation Press.

Nelson, G. L. (2001). Writing beyond Testing: "The Word as an Instrument of Creation." *English Journal, 91*(1), 57–61.

Nichols, S. L., & Berliner, D. C. (2007). *Collateral Damage: How High-Stakes Testing Undermines Education.* Cambridge, MA: Harvard Education Press.

Panofsky, C. P. (2003). The Relations of Learning and Student Social Class: Toward Re-"Socializing" Sociocultural Learning Theory. In A. Kozulin et al. (Eds.), *Vygotsky's Educational Theory in Cultural Context* (pp. 411–431). New York: Cambridge University Press.

Pearson, Inc. (2008). *New York State Teacher Certification Examinations Preparation Guide: English Language Arts CST.* Albany, NY: New York State Education Department.

Popham, W. J. (2001). *The Truth about Testing: An Educators Call to Action.* Alexandria, VA: Association for Supervision and Curriculum Development.

CHAPTER 15

"Too Young for the Marches but I Remember These Drums"

Recommended Pedagogies for Hip–Hop–Based Education and Youth Studies

Bettina L. Love

The first function of education is to provide identity. —Akbar (1998)

I Don't Know Much, but I Know What Moves Me!

My mother and father never really shared much with me about how they met, where they grew up, who my great-grandparents were, or how two people with Southern roots landed in upstate New York. Similarly, my teachers never discussed my culture or heritage, and never linked my experiences at school to my community or home life. Of course, in school, we discussed the usual Black History events and icons—the Underground Railroad, Dr. Martin Luther King, Jr., Rosa Parks, and the Civil Rights Movement. As a youth, I respected those events and viewed those freedom fighters as heroes, but I could not emotionally connect to such larger-than-life figures. I had trouble comprehending how my life and struggles as an urban youth linked to that of Parks or King—perhaps because they were only discussed during Black History Month, or maybe because I was never told the full story of their brilliance, sacrifice, and humanity. Moreover, the process of schooling and the marginalization of Black History left me less connected to my history as an urban youth, someone of African descent, and an African American. I had little understanding of who I was in relation to my community and heritage. While I was not completely lost—as my skin, speech, and body movements connected me to my local community—I ultimately had no sense of who I was outside of my zip code.

When I was around twelve or fourteen years old, something happened to my view of the world that changed my relationship to my culture completely. I had listened to Hip Hop music throughout my childhood through my older brother, who is fourteen years my senior, but as I reached adolescence, Hip Hop became more than just music to me. I began to view Hip Hop as my culture, my teacher, and, most importantly, my way of grasping concepts that adults claimed eluded my young mind.

For example, in the late 1980s and early 1990s, my working-class neighborhood fell to drugs and crime, one corner at a time. Rappers like Chuck D, Nas, Queen Latifah, Jay Z, and KRS-One boldly explained to me the nature of this transformation, and all its consequences. KRS-One taught me about my African and African American history, Jungle Brothers and De La Soul introduced me to jazz and Afrocentrism, and Lauryn Hill became my big sister with powerful advice to conquer the social ills of my community.

For me, Hip Hop connected my everyday life and the lives of my friends to the greater contributions and struggles of African people and African Americans living in the United States. Furthermore, Hip Hop's sound—influenced by the African drums, slave songs coded in metaphors and euphemisms, jazz, soul, rhythm and blues, funk, and Civil Rights freedom songs—sonically transported me to the Motherland, the March on Washington, the L.A. janitors' strikes, the 1968 Chicano student walkouts, and the 1992 L.A. riots (Love, 2012). Thus, in the words of Common (2007), I was, "too young for the marches but I remember these drums" (track 12). Hip Hop gave me a sense of identity and an emotional wholeness filled with love, anger, hope, and youthfulness.

Thus, I know firsthand the transformative power of Hip Hop. It is an unflinching culture of urban youth rooted in the principles of democracy. Hip Hop represents youths' "critical modes of self-expression," reflective of their yearning to be heard, recognized, and included in the democratic process (Prier, 2012, p. xxxv). From an educational perspective, when Hip Hop merges with the pedagogies of "cultural connectedness" (Paris, 2012), the "funds of knowledge" (Moll & Gonzalez, 1994) and everyday realities of students, a form of education arises that "recognizes and celebrates how youth move, speak, think, create, and relate to the world" (Love, 2012, p. 109).

This chapter will explore the significance of merging the field of youth and Hip Hop studies with the transformative and empowering teaching methods of culturally sustaining pedagogy (CSP) and reality pedagogy (RP). The integration and amalgamation of pedagogies like CSP and RP within the field of youth and Hip Hop studies build on the long-standing use of critical pedagogy in the field to position the culture, social context, learning styles, and experiences of students at the center of the learning experience. More specifically, I will argue that Hip Hop music and culture can be a catalyst for ensuring that Black and Brown youth know their rich African, African American, and Latina/o heritage, which is the foundation of Hip Hop and the fight against oppression. In that same vein, I contend that before youth can attempt the critical endeavor of examining issues of race, class, power, and place, they must first understand their cultural heritage and its significance, as well as their everyday realities as urban youth.

Theory

In 2009, Christopher Emdin introduced the teaching framework of RP to the field of science education. Emdin (2011) defined RP as a teaching method that "focuses on the cultural understandings of students within a particular social space, like a science classroom" (p. 286). RP consists of what Emdin (2011) called the "5 Cs": cogenerative dialogues, coteaching, cosmopolitanism, context, and content. Cogenerative dialogues, the first C, are structured dialogues that build on students' Hip Hop identities and familiarity with the Hip Hop communal tradition of cyphers. Cyphers are one of the most long-standing cultural rituals of Hip Hop (Love, 2013). The second C, coteaching, encourages students to be the "expert at pedagogy … while the teacher is positioned as a novice who is learning how to teach" (Emdin, 2011, p. 288). Coteaching allows teachers to study how students learn from one another in order to better understand students' learning styles, and provides an opportunity for students to learn in ways that reflect their realities.

The third C, cosmopolitanism, is based on the philosophical construct that human beings are responsible for each other, and that individual differences should be valued. Context, the fourth C, connects students' home lives and culture to their classrooms through community and culture artifacts.

Context allows students to bring to the classroom artifacts that represent who they are and where they come from. Emdin (2011) wrote, "[w]hen students can physically see and examine artifacts both in the classrooms and in their home communities, the divides between the school world and their real lives are broken down" (p. 291). Finally, content, the fifth C, evolves out of the willingness of the teacher to acknowledge his or her limitations with academic content, and to explore and learn with students.

As a teaching framework, RP sets the stage and tone for constructing classrooms where both teach ers and students are co-creating and learning from the realities of students' lives and cultural knowledge. Although Emdin's work is situated for urban science classrooms, his five Cs can transform education through all disciplines. However, I recommend combining RP with CSP, as explained in further detail below, due to the dire need in the field of youth studies to embrace the realities of students, while main taining and enhancing students' knowledge of their culture, history, and traditions. Only then can educators begin the process of examining oppression, especially in the field of Hip Hop and youth studies.

Turning now to CSP, Django Paris introduced this teaching method in 2012 with his article "Culturally Sustaining Pedagogy: A Needed Change in Stance, Terminology, and Practice." Paris (2012) wrote that CSP "seeks to perpetuate and foster—to sustain—linguistic, literate, and cultural pluralism as part of the democratic project of schooling" (p. 93). CSP embraces students' heritage while recognizing that culture is fluid and ever-changing. Furthermore, CSP is rooted in the ideological premise of cultural pluralism and schooling as a fundamental component of democracy. Establishing a teaching framework that embraces cultural pluralism is vital, because U.S. schools, more than ever before, are multiethnic and multilingual spaces. Schools are vibrant with culture, yet indolent with curriculum and teaching practices that reflect the diversity of students.

Both RP and CSP are outgrowths of "culturally relevant pedagogy" (CRP), inspired by the seminal work of Gloria Ladson-Billings, who coined the term in 1995. CRP "produce[s] students who can achieve academically, produce[s] students who can demonstrate cultural competence, and develop[s] students who can both understand and critique the existing social order" (Ladson-Billings, 1995, p. 474). However, Paris (2012) contended that CRP does not explicitly support the "linguistic and cultural dexterity and plurality necessary for success and access in our demographically changing U.S. and global schools and communities" (p. 95). Today's schools are filled with Black and Brown faces, especially in urban areas. Overall, more than 45% of school-age students are minorities, according to the Pew Research Hispanic Center (2013). In 2011, the Hispanic student population among grades pre-K through 12 reached 23.9%. Furthermore, in 2011, there were more than 2 million Hispanics aged 18–24 years old enrolled in college, a record high. Put another way, Hispanics make up 16.5% of college enrollment. By the year 2043, Hispanics will be the majority, and Whites will be the minority in the population (Pew Research Hispanic Center, 2013). Moreover, Hip Hop is the common culture of Black and Brown students. Cohen, Celestine-Michener, Holmes, Merseth, and Ralph (2007) found that 97% of Black youth and 88% of Hispanic youth listened to rap music. Their research also uncovered that youth of various ethnicities were using Hip Hop to express their cultural identity. Watkins (2005) explained that:

> Whatever social or political impact hip hop has had on young people has come primarily in the world of popular culture. Hip hop's evolution launched a revolution in youth culture. All the things that traditionally matter to young people—style, music, fashion, and a sense of generational purpose—have come under the spell of hip hop. (p. 148)

Based on the above statistics and research, there is a clear need for a pedagogy that meaningfully responds to the cultural and linguistic diversity of our youth. For too long, educators have responded to diversity through deficit approaches that ignore cultural pluralism, cultural equity, and the day-to-day realties of urban youth from multiethnic and multilingual backgrounds. Both RP and CSP teaching theories have focused on using the customs, traditions, and the language of students who identify with Hip Hop music and culture to explicitly link students' culture to schooling. Hip Hop can at once build solidarity among youth and represent modes of cultural expression that give them a sense of purpose and knowledge about who they are. My own story that I shared at the beginning of this chapter reflects how Hip Hop can inform youth and youth culture. In light of that power, educators need to help youth question that influential "spell" of Hip Hop. However, there is not necessarily one pedagogy that captures the heritage of all youth (at times both fluid and fixed), corporate America's media attack on youths' humanity by way of Hip Hop, and the oppressive social structures that complicate the lives of urban youth. Therefore, I suggest a hybrid of RP and CSP as a starting point to begin transforming the field of youth studies, since both pedagogies build upon the work of critical pedagogy, which is the foundation of critical youth studies. In short, these two pedagogies serve as a fitting starting place to engage in real educational reform which cannot take place unless it is rooted, I believe, in the principles of critical pedagogy.

This Has Been Done Before

Critical pedagogy and Hip Hop share two very important common principles:

1. Raising the critical consciousness of people who have been or who are being oppressed (Ginwright, 2004; Morrell, 2002; Williams, 2009), and

2. Firmly acknowledging that schools are places that maintain the status quo.

For example, KRS-One (1989) rapped that "[i]t seems to me in a school that's ebony, African his tory should be pumped up steadily, but it's not and this has got to stop" (track 8). Freire (1970/2003) suggested that education could be transformative and empowering if poor and oppressed people had the pedagogical space to understand how their lived experiences have been shaped by social institutions (Akom, 2009). Yet, Freire (1970/2003) noted that many schools rely on the "banking method of education" (p. 71) that turns students into passive receptacles of knowledge and fails to make a connection between school and their lives.

Akom, Cammarota, and Ginwright (2008) contended that traditional and nontraditional educational spaces that are "youth driven cultural products" can be places "that embody a critique of oppression, a desire for social change, and ultimately lay the foundations for community empowerment and social change" (p. 4). The authors called for Youth Participatory Action Research (YPAR) in the field of critical youth studies. The authors defined YPAR as a "research methodology in which young people study their own social contexts to understand how to improve conditions and bring about greater equity" (p. 4). They argued that YPAR must be linked to critical race theory and critical media literacy in order to "develop pedagogical spaces for resistance, resiliency, hope, and healing" (p. 4). I am inspired by the work of Akom, Ginwright, and Cammarota—individually and jointly—because they conduct their research within the field of youth studies with the actual youth. Thus, their merging of theories is rooted in their understanding of the needs of youth on the ground. I witnessed this approach firsthand in the spring of 2013, when I attended a presentation by the organization Speak Out in Oakland, California. Akom partnered with human-rights activist, Ninotchka Rosca, through Speak Out to work with a group of students and examine their community, media, and oppressive social structures through tradi tional research methods (quantitative and qualitative data collection, and analysis). However, they also disrupted traditional research methods by using Spoken Word and Hip Hop to report their findings.

That experience solidified for me the power of integrating theories to shape youth studies grounded in critical pedagogy. Therefore, combining CSP and RP is in no way an alternative to YPAR; it is an other powerful pedagogical tool to transform our society through the experiences and culture of youth. Thus, I am proposing a hybrid pedagogical method that can reach similar goals of YPAR through a different format. Teachers, community organizers, youth, Hip Hop studies scholars, and all individuals concerned with the body, mind, and spirit of youth must engage them with empowering pedagogies. If not, we are simply maintaining the status quo by not equipping students with the tools to effectively fight injustice.

Moving from Theory to Practice: RP and CSP

I believe that traditional and nontraditional educational spaces that are anchored by the experiences of youth will fundamentally transform education for the better. However, in implementing new classroom practices that address how educators begin to value and maintain the languages and cultures of urban youth, traditional youth learning spaces must meet the needs of innovative pedagogies like Paris's CSP. In short, CSP cannot be an effective pedagogical resource if learning structures do not provide the space for innovation. It is for that reason that a merger of Paris's CSP and Emdin's RP is necessary to afford teachers the time, space, and classroom procedures to effectively create a classroom where cultural pluralism and cultural equality are possible.

The five C's of RP provide the learning structure for CSP to function in a classroom on a daily basis. For example, taking from Emdin's (2011) classroom cyphers concept,

> a small group of students are given the opportunity to reflect on their classroom experiences, critique the instruction, discuss the inhibitors to the classroom learning, and most importantly, provide teachers with insight into what can work well in the classroom from the students' perspective. (p. 287)

Cyphers provide a space for students to not only critique instruction, but also society, in ways that reflect their language and cultural understanding of social structures, which is fundamental to CSP. I have written in the past on the way in which cyphers can be culturally relevant spaces for urban youth to express themselves and their culture (Love, 2013). Through the work of Paris, I contend that cyphers can be culturally sustaining spaces as well. Likewise, Emdin's work is the foundation for my premise of using cyphers to encourage youths' social-emotional learning and community-building skills (Love, 2013). Educator and youth advocates attempting CSP need, first and foremost, to create spaces that provide opportunities for youth from various ethnicities and "linguistic realities" to discuss inequities and how to value people's differences in hopes of creating "cultural pluralism" (Paris, 2012). CSP can only function if the learning spaces allow it to do so. Emdin's RP provides this space.

Emdin's (2011) notion of students possessing a "cosmopolitan ethos" that cultivates youth who are invested in sustaining "each other's livelihoods and happiness" (p. 290) is also fundamental to CSP. Cosmopolitism and cultural pluralism go hand in hand, but traditional and nontraditional learning structures must engage differently with youth to create youth-driven spaces. Furthermore, Emdin's fourth and fifth Cs, context and content, help define Paris's CSP in ways that allow students to develop and sustain school curriculum and pedagogy that is co-created by students and teachers. When students are allowed to change the physical space where they learn to reflect their lives, this act affirms youths' culture, and allows youth to take ownership of the space. The final C of Emdin's RP, content, amplifies Paris's CSP, because it involves teachers acknowledging what they do not know in relation to science. By extending context to culture, language, and the everyday realities of youth, it could be transformative if educators acknowledged to students that they actually knew very little about the languages that were spoken by youth every day, or their cultural backgrounds, but at the same time demonstrate a willingness to learn about that language and culture. Thus, content allows CSP to form organically from the community of youth. Lastly, Emdin (2011) stressed that for RP to be successfully implemented, educators must develop the "appropriate mind-set" (p. 292) for creating learning spaces that value diversity and social justice, matched with instructional practices that allow for this mind-set to flourish. That mind-set is transformative when teachers, community members, youth advocates, and researchers enter into students' culture and teach from a place of cultural pluralism that unites all youth. This concept demonstrates the pedagogical power of CSP and RP. Additionally, the amalgamation of CSP and RP—inspired by youths' Hip Hop identity—can create a pedagogical third space where classroom activities are informed by the lives of students and official school curriculum (Gutiérrez & Stone, 2000; Kirkland, 2008, 2009; Love, 2013).

Teaching in the Third Space

A conglomeration of Hip Hop, CSP, and RP frameworks offers a complex space for critical reflection by allowing educators and students to examine students' lives and communities within the ever-changing cultural practice of Hip Hop. However, Hip Hop education, coupled with the principles of RP and CSP, which are rooted in democratic education, moves beyond the official and unofficial dimensions of pedagogical space into a "third space" (Dyson, 2001; Kirkland, 2008, 2009) where youth counternarratives are reflective of youths' social, economic, political, and cultural realities and conditions.

In the third space model, educational text, discussion, and activities emerge from students' lives. The third space creates a reciprocal relationship between school and out-of-school practices, values, and beliefs of students because instruction and classroom procedures are so closely tied to the everyday realities of youth (Dyson, 2001; Gutiérrez & Stone, 2000; Love, 2013). The elements of CSP and RP assist educators in creating classrooms that are pedagogical third spaces, while embracing students' heritage. For example, when students coteach, learn in classrooms that resemble their communities, and have artifacts present in the classroom that are of importance to their cultural identity, traditional class room ways are then overshadowed by new configurations of instruction informed by youth. Further, when educational spaces are informed by youth who identify with Hip Hop music and culture, critical dialogue concerning racism, sexism, love, language, cultural differences and pride, sexual orientation, capitalism, classism, drugs, crime, hard work, and violence are at the center of the curriculum. Hip Hop is rich with examples of society's ills and what uplifts us all. Tupac Shakur is a great example of how a Hip Hop artist can inspire, educate, and express what it means to be young and full of life. Moving the topics discussed in Hip Hop, mentioned above, to the center of the curriculum is key to fostering CSP and RP.

Apple and Beane (2000) emphasized that democratic education must not be consumed within "glossy political rhetoric" (p. 105), but within the everyday realities of youth. Put another way, democratic education must acknowledge that young people learn from their everyday sociocultural activities (Cole, 1996; Moll, 2000) in and outside of school walls. A combination of CSP and RP—rooted in Hip Hop—provides educators committed to democratic education and cultural pluralism with a pedagogical space to understand the importance and educational value of situating instruction within the realities of their students' lives. Furthermore, curriculum focused on students' lives is "supported by cognitive research demonstrating that learning is a process of making meaning out of new or unfamiliar events in light of familiar ideas or experiences" (Darling-Hammond, 1997, p. 74). This ideological and pedagogical shift recognizes that urban youth consume Hip Hop as a site of epistemological development linked to youths' everyday language and literacy practices (Mahiri, 2004; Richardson, 2006, 2007). Alim (2006) argued that "Hip Hop is a cultural practice embedded in the lived experiences of Hip Hop-conscious beings existing in a home, street, hood, city, state, country, continent, hemisphere near you" (p. 12). Educators have used Hip Hop to help students make sense of the classics (Morrell & Duncan-Andrade, 2002), the academic writing process (Cooks, 2004), and teach literacy interpretation (Hill, 2006).

As empowering as Hip Hop education is for students and educators alike, Hip Hop is created and disseminated in the contested and ever-shifting space of Black popular culture. Although Hall (1993) contended that Black popular culture represents the culture of Black folks, it is still created in the space of homogenization and formulaic narratives of Black life fueled by cultural, social, economic, and technological conditions of today. David Kirkland (2008) added that Hip Hop, which is grounded in Black popular culture, operates within postmodern Blackness. He wrote:

> Postmodern blackness reiterates the idea that cultural, social, economic, and technological conditions of our age are constantly shifting. These shifts have given rise to a decentralized, multimedia dominated society in which norms are continuously revised, ways of living are continually improvised, and new technologies for communication and meaning making are regularly being devised. … Human conditions, or human experiences, are rich and diverse, elaborated on in tension through texts and conversations that take into account the contexts in which they are composed. (Kirkland, 2008, p. 72)

For youth to successfully grapple with the sly and shifting landscape in which Hip Hop is created and disseminated, they must engage in pedagogical practices that are fluid, dexterous, and rich in critical discussion that teaches youth how societal norms are reinvented to maintain the status quo, perpetuate stereotypes, and label Black and Brown youth as society's problem. RP and CSP combined is a ripe teaching framework for promoting and sustaining a classroom that is fluid enough to teach youth how to enjoy Hip Hop as consumers and critique the music and its culture as intellectuals.

Never Too Young

> Must be a bond, a connection between us here and us what are across the sea. A connection, the last of the old, first of the new. —Nana Peazant in *Daughters of the Dust* (Dash, 1991)

I have never been to Africa, but I am African. I cannot rap, dance, or DJ, but I am Hip Hop. As a teenager, I grew angry when I began to learn about my culture, my history, and my language outside of school, because in school I was forced to deny those aspects of my humanity every day. I found solace in Hip Hop, along with knowledge of self. I define knowledge of self as "[t]he study of Hip Hop culture, music, and elements, alongside the examination of issues within one's surroundings to create positive change in one's community" (Love, 2013, p. 19). More broadly, Akbar (1998) argued that knowledge of self is part of an effective education that allows students to understand who they are and the dilemmas they may face in life. In short, knowledge of self is empowerment. To empower youth through schooling, students must know where they come from, feel connected to their heritage, and be able to then link that heritage to that of others, thus forming cultural connectedness. Joining the structured principles of RP to the teaching framework of CSP creates a structure for CSP to flourish. In my experience, most teachers who are concerned with integrating RP or CSP into their classrooms feel overwhelmed by the task. While they possess the fortification to transform how we teach, research, and work with young folk, they lack the knowledge base as to how to accomplish that goal on a grand scale and on a day-to-day basis. However, when incorporated, the 5 Cs of RP provide a daily structure for CSP. Merging these two theories together will create the structure needed for adults to learn and see "the brilliance the students bring with them in their blood" (Delpit, 1992, p. 248). As an educator and scholar in Hip Hop and youth studies, I am encouraged by the work of Paris and Emdin, as both of these scholars push the boundaries of the youth studies field and education to create new ways of thinking and teaching urban youth. Through such work, Hip Hop Education is alive and well.

References

Akbar, N. (1998). *Know thyself.* Tallahassee, FL: Mind Productions & Associates.
Akom, A. A. (2009). Critical hip hop pedagogy as a form of liberatory praxis. *Equity and Excellence in Education*, *42*(1), 52–66.

Akom, A. A., Cammarota, J., & Ginwright, S. (2008). Youthtopias: Towards a new paradigm of critical youth studies. *Youth Media Reporter, 2*(4), 1–30.

Alim, H. S. (2006). *Roc the mic right: The language of hip hop culture.* New York, NY: Routledge.

Apple, M. W., & Beane, J. A. (2000). Democratic schools: Lessons from the chalk face. Buckingham, UK: Open University Press.

Cohen, C. J., Celestine-Michener, J., Holmes, C., Merseth, J. L., & Ralph, L. (2007). *The attitudes and behavior of young Black Americans: Research summary.* Retrieved from http://www.resourcelibrary.gcyf.org/node/290

Cole, M. (1996). *Cultural psychology: A once and future discipline.* Cambridge, MA: Belknap Press of Harvard University Press.

Common. (2007). Finding forever. On *Finding Forever* [CD]. New York, NY: G.O.O.D. Music.

Cooks, J. A. (2004). Writing for something: Essays, raps, and writing preferences. *English Journal, 94*(1), 72–76.

Darling-Hammond, L. (1997). *The right to learn: A blueprint for creating schools that work.* San Francisco, CA: Jossey-Bass.

Dash, J. (Writer & Director). (1991). *Daughters of the dust* [Motion picture]. USA: Kino International.

Delpit, L. D. (1988). The silenced dialogue: Power and pedagogy in educating other people's children. *Harvard Educational Review, 58*(3), 280–299.

Delpit, L. D. (1992). Education in a multicultural society: Our future's greatest challenge. *Journal of Negro Education, 61*(3), 237–249.

Dyson, A. H. (2001). Donkey Kong in Little Bear country: A first grader's composing development in the media spotlight. *Elementary School Journal, 101*(4), 417–433.

Emdin, C. (2009). Reality pedagogy: Hip hop culture and the urban science classroom. In W. M. Roth (Ed.), *Science education from people for people: Taking a stand(point)* (pp. 72–90). New York, NY: Routledge.

Emdin, C. (2011). Moving beyond the boat without a paddle: Reality pedagogy, Black youth, and urban science education. *Journal of Negro Education, 80*(3), 284–295.

Freire, P. (2003). Pedagogy of the oppressed (Rev. ed.). New York, NY: Continuum.

Ginwright, S. (2004). *Black in school: Afrocentric reform, urban youth, and the promise of hip hop culture.* New York, NY: Teachers College Press.

Gutiérrez, K. D., & Stone, L. D. (2000). Synchronic and diachronic dimensions of social practice: An emerging methodology for cultural-historical perspectives on literacy learning. In C. D. Lee & P. Smagorinsky (Eds.), *Vygotskian perspectives on literacy research: Constructing meaning through collaborative inquiry* (pp. 150–164). Cambridge, UK: Cambridge University Press.

Hall, S. (1993). What is this 'Black' in Black popular culture? *Social Justice, 20*(1–2), 104–114.

Hill, M. L. (2006). Using Jay-Z to reflect on post-9/11 race relations. *English Journal, 96*(2), 23–27.

Kirkland, D. E. (2008). "The rose that grew from concrete": Postmodern Blackness and new English education. *English Journal, 97*(5), 69–75.

Kirkland, D. E. (2009). Standpoints: Researching and teaching English in the digital dimension. *Research in the Teaching of English, 44*(1), 8–22.

KRS-One. (1989). You must learn. On *Ghetto music: The blueprint of hip hop* [CD]. New York, NY: Jive Records.

Ladson-Billings, G. (1995). Toward a theory of culturally relevant pedagogy. *American Educational Research Journal, 32*(3), 465–491.

Love, B. L. (2012). *Hip hop's li'l sistas speak: Negotiating hip hop identities and politics in the new South.* New York, NY: Peter Lang.

Love, B. L. (2013). Urban storytelling: How storyboarding, moviemaking & hip hop-based education can promote students' critical voice. *English Journal, 103*(5), p. 53–58

Mahiri, J. (2004). *What they don't learn in school: Literacy in the lives of urban youth.* New York, NY: Peter Lang.

Moll, L. (2000). Inspired by Vygotsky: Ethnographic experiments in education. In C. Lee & P. Smagorinsky (Eds.), *Vygotskian perspectives on literacy research: Constructing meaning through collaborative inquiry* (pp. 256–268). New York, NY: Cambridge University Press.

Moll, L. C., & Gonzalez, N. (1994). Lessons from research with language-minority children. *Journal of Reading Behavior, 26*(4), 439–456.

Morrell, E. (2002). Toward a critical pedagogy of popular culture: Literacy development among urban youth. *Journal of Adolescent and Adult Literacy, 46*(1), 72–77.

Morrell, E., & Duncan-Andrade, J. M. R. (2002). Promoting academic literacy with urban youth through engaging hip hop culture. *English Journal, 91*(6), 88–92.

Paris, D. (2012). Culturally sustaining pedagogy: A needed change in stance, terminology, and practice. *Educational Researcher, 41*(3), 93–97.

Pew Research Hispanic Center. (2013). *A nation of immigrants.* Retrieved from http://www.pewhispanic.org/files/2013/01/statistical_portrait_final_jan_29.pdf

Prier, D. C. (2012). *Culturally relevant teaching: Hip hop pedagogy in urban schools.* New York, NY: Peter Lang.

Richardson, E. (2006). *Hip hop literacies.* Hoboken, NJ: Taylor & Francis.

Richardson, E. (2007). "She workin' it like foreal": Critical literacy and discourse practices of African American females in the age of hip hop. *Discourse and Society, 18*, 789–809.

Watkins, S. C. (2005). *Hip hop matters: Politics, pop culture, and the struggle for the soul of a movement.* Boston, MA: Beacon Press.

Williams, A. D. (2009). The critical cultural cypher: Remaking Paulo Freire's cultural circles using hip hop culture. *International Journal of Critical Pedagogy, 2*(1), 1–29.

CHAPTER 16

The Issue of Identity

Yolanda Medina

In order to discover and describe the core of my educational philosophy, I have been reflecting on my personal history, examining it as if I were watching an old home movie of my life, searching through the memories and experiences that I believe shaped my identity. This journey has been painful, therapeutic, and life affirming. It was painful because revisiting my past revived memories of learning and maturing through sorrows; therapeutic because it helped me develop a sense of closure, empathy, and forgiveness; and life affirming because by analyzing my past, I came to understand my reasons for being and my life choices, and I began to envision my future.

This personal search has been complicated, because identity is like a false mirror. As soon as you think you understand and accept it as a definition of your self, it begins to shift and mutate, and before you know it, you turn into someone else. An individual's identity is created from a number of elements that can include but are not limited to race, culture, language, gender, social class, religion, and abilities. These elements engender connections that Amin Maalouf (2000) refers to as "allegiances" (p. 2), and these allegiances can change over time, as we move in and out of the various groups that define our lives as social beings. It is never easy to trace the influences that have helped to shape us as individuals, but the search becomes even more challenging when our lives have crossed multiple cultural and geographical borders.

As I tried to understand the construction of my identity, I realized that it is rife with paradoxes and tugs-of-war that have prevented me from compartmentalizing long enough to define who I am. I am a Dominican and a New Yorker; a rebel and a hyper-achiever; a Latina with a Southern past; a bad student but a caring teacher; a dancer and a teacher educator; a Salsera and a feminist. These characteristics are often contradictory, yet none of them could have developed without the influence of the others. I am a mixture of all of them, though at times I choose to express more of one than of the others.

Thinking about the development of my identity reminds me of the movie *How to Make an American Quilt,* which tells the story of a group of women creating a marriage quilt for the granddaughter of one of their members. The movie combines flashbacks of each woman's story, connecting their narratives to the individual quilt section each one is creating. As the movie unfolds, we learn how each woman's life has been affected by another member of the group. At the end, when all the stories are sewn together, they compose a quilt of personal connections.

My identity can be seen as a quilt with a narrative sequence, each patch representing a flashback onto a story from my life or an allegiance to one group or another. All these patches of experience are held together by a common theme, like a gold thread running through the quilt in its entirety. This thread represents what I have come to understand as my perpetual feeling of displacement and need to prove my worth.

I cannot remember a time in my life when I felt a sense of completely belonging. I have always felt that for one reason or another I do not fit into the mold created by my surroundings. Throughout my life, I have compensated for these feelings of maladjustment in one of two ways: either by rebelling against authority and refusing to comply with expectations, or by hyper-achieving and striving to become the best at everything, in order to prove wrong all those who seem to lack faith in my moral and intellectual capacities.

In the following pages I will relate the stories connected with some of the patches in my identity quilt, some briefly and others in more detail. Some of these stories will overlap, and some will be contradictory, but they are all pieces of the complex self that I have become. The story of my development as a person, my discovery and definition of who I am, and my delineation of the paths I have chosen to follow is inseparable from my philosophy of education; I could not have become the teacher I am had I not made the journey I will now describe.

My Life in Two Countries

Born in Queens, New York, I am the only child of two teenagers who divorced before I could form memories of them as a couple. After the divorce, my mother and I moved to the Dominican Republic, her country of origin. The explanation she gave for this decision was that in the Dominican Republic she could provide better educational opportunities for both of us, a better upbringing for me than the one I was receiving in New York City, and a lifestyle she had never enjoyed and would be unable to afford to give me if we stayed. It was during those early years that I first began to feel different from my classmates, relatives, and friends.

The Dominican Republic is a country of extreme social and racial stratification with a strict social structure that resembles a caste system. A very small upper-class group controls the wealth of the country, and the members of this elite have Spanish surnames and light skins, which entitles them to better jobs, greater respect, and more opportunities for advancement. In contrast, the members of the underclass majority have darker skin and a closer genetic link to our shared African heritage. Membership in the latter group condemns an individual to second-class citizenship, inferior education, if any, and few opportunities for financial growth. Most members of this subordinate group serve the members of the elite.

I did not belong to either of these social groups. I was not part of the upper class, because although I attended their schools, my last name did not connote personal wealth. I was not part of the subordinate group, because although I lived with and befriended children in poorer neighborhoods, I attended an upper-class school. Furthermore, I was not interested in the games the children in my neighborhood played, the music they listened to, or the places they frequented. I preferred the activities that the children at my school took pleasure in and the places they frequented, but I could not afford them financially.

Later in life I began to understand that belonging to a higher social class meant not only having money or a particular kind of surname, but also embracing a system of values, interests, and behaviors that I unconsciously absorbed throughout my school years. I had assimilated the ideals of a privileged class even though I was constantly reminded that I did not fulfill all the requirements for membership. At the same time and for the same reason, I was considered a *comparona* (a stuck-up person) by the children of the other, much larger social group. No matter where I was or who I was with, I was always aware of my otherness.

Years after my mother and I moved to the Dominican Republic, I still found excuses to return to New York City. For months on end I stayed with relatives we had left behind, until my life story was split in two, with half in each country. However, while I frequently traveled to both of these places throughout my teenage years, I always felt homesick for one when I lived in the other, and guilty for leaving loved ones behind. I became what Villaverde (2008) calls a "border dweller," a term she borrows from Anzaldúa and defines as "a person who straddles or lives across two or more borders (literal, theoretical, social, cultural, geographic, etc.)" (p. 11). Consequently, I grew up with one foot in New York City and the other in the Dominican Republic, emotionally torn between two countries, two languages, and two cultures.

In addition to my constant homesickness and guilt, there was another reason for my lingering sense of alienation. I was always seen as a *Dominicanita* in New York City and thus perceived as a naïve little girl who needed to be protected, while in the Dominican Republic I was called a *gringita*, or "little American girl." The latter was more painful to me because Dominicans hold a stereotyped view of American children as a decadent influence on their culture, since the children of American transplants are notorious for using drugs, indulging in sex, and answering back to elders. This stereotype was used to warn those around me, including my mother, that my trips to the United Stated would make me too *americanizada*. Because their cultural stereotype held that American children were loud and *malcriados*, or disrespectful, Dominicans thought that I needed to be controlled. I spent most of my teenage years trying to prove to my relatives, teachers, and peers in both countries that I was as trustworthy, normal, and intelligent as my cousins and classmates.

A dancer with scars

During all those years of displacement, no matter what country I was in, there was always one thing that remained constant in my life—I was always enrolled in some kind of dance class. There, no one cared what I had done before I arrived, or how I arrived—by plane, car, or foot. No one asked if I was Dominican or *gringa*. No one cared about my last name, just my first. All that mattered was that I wanted to dance, and because of that, I was welcome.

I now understand why to this day dancing remains such a significant part of my life. The dance floor was my first encounter with social justice. It was the only place that offered me an equal opportunity to succeed—a place where achieving success was not connected to my social class or nationality, and where my heritage did not matter. All that truly mattered in this community was my love for dancing. For this reason, ballet, jazz, modern, and Latin dances were at thecenter of my life as I pivoted precariously across lines of social class, culture, and language.

Consequently, I grew up dancing, and never doubting that I was going to dance for the rest of my life. After graduating high school, I joined a dance group in the Dominican Republic, which greatly reduced the frequency of my trips to New York City. Dancing thus became my whole life. Then, at the peak of my dancing career, I stumbled into a sliding-glass door that shattered, slit three tendons in my left leg, and caused cuts requiring over 1,800 stitches. I was left with little hope of ever dancing again.

Scarred for life, not only physically but also emotionally, I realized that I had reached a turning point and would have to decide where to go and what to do next. My friends and family did not know what advice to give me because they wondered, what could a dancer do but dance? Perhaps they believed that since I had spent so much time on point shoes, my brain had atrophied.

My old feelings of displacement and need to prove my worth returned in full force: I had lost the only place where they could not haunt me, the dance floor. This time, in order to prove everybody wrong, I promised myself that I would completely forget about dancing. I enrolled in college and became an elementary school teacher. This was a pathway I had never envisioned for myself, and I naturally experienced a sense of mourning for the losses I had suffered. However, my reentry into the world of the classroom set my life on a new path that would eventually bring healing, joy, and a deep sense of fulfillment. Although I did not understand this at the time, I was beginning a journey of discovery that would give me new ways of understanding my place in the world and the contributions I could offer.

"Sunk in the everydayness of life"

A few years after my life-changing accident, I had become a different person. I was living a so-called "normal life"—I had earned a bachelor's degree, I had stable employment teaching at an elementary school, and I had even married. Yet in spite of it all, I was still unhappy.

Looking back on that time, I see that I was what Maxine Greene (1995) refers to as "sunk in the everydayness of life" (p. 14). I felt trapped in what I considered a mediocre life, with no escape in sight. I had lost the capacity to question my life, evaluate its flaws, and consider how to rebuild it. I had forgotten that I had the right and the power to change my world. Before the accident, though feelings of displacement had always haunted me, I still knew with all the strength of my body exactly what I wanted from life, and that conviction had kept me going even when my only goal was to prove my worth. After I stopped dancing, I lost that strength and stopped all my questionings. As a result, I had begun to comply with the expectations of my surroundings regarding social behavior.

After I had been married for several years, teaching primary grades at a private school and living a "normal life," the owner of the school where I worked suggested that I continue my own education. He recommended that I enroll in a master's degree program in Elementary Education at Western Carolina University, where he knew people who could facilitate my entry into the program. I remember that during this conversation I began to imagine a different life for myself, and to believe that I had the power to make that change. I did not hesitate to take advantage of this opportunity, and in a matter of three months, I had moved to North Carolina to continue my formal education.

Today I understand that this choice was, in part, a cowardly escape from a loveless marriage that I knew was bound to fail, and from a life that I had unconsciously rejected. However, at the time I could only see (and admit) as much as my pain would allow. I also knew that my new choices would bring as much pain to my loved ones as the happiness they had felt for me before, unaware as they were that I was secretly miserable. Launching myself into the unknown, I left my home, my marriage, my friends, and my mother to move to the United States to pursue a master's degree in Elementary Education, and subsequently a Ph.D. in Educational Leadership and Cultural Foundations at the University of North Carolina at Greensboro.

My feelings about leaving home were again very complex. I wanted to avoid being "sunk in the everydayness of life," and I felt excited about starting a new life full of possibilities. Yet at the same time, I felt guilty for abandoning my home, my memories, and those whom I loved. My new and unfamiliar surroundings filled me with apprehension, and I was unsure of my ability to speak and write in English at the graduate level. Most of all I was insecure about fitting into the strange Southern culture, something I so desperately needed to do in order to succeed.

Who am I?

Life in the South was very different from life in the Dominican Republic, and based on what I remembered, from life in New York City. On the one hand, I was the only Latina in both of my graduate programs. On the other hand, the racial issues that take precedence in the South are in regard to Black and White. For this reason, I felt very uncomfortable participating in class discussions about race and ethnicity. Although Latinos and African Americans share a history of slavery and oppression, race is a social construct and therefore a lived experience. I was not African American and I was not White. I felt like a plantain in a basket of fruits.

Furthermore, this feeling of social discomfort inhibited my ability to communicate in English. Sometimes after gathering the courage to participate and stating my opinion about an issue raised in class, I would immediately realize that my comment had not come out the way I had intended. Nevertheless, my statement would initiate a discussion among my classmates, and by the time I could mentally organize what I had really meant to say, the moment was gone, and the class had moved on to something else, leaving me with a sour taste of stupidity and inadequacy. Maalouf describes the total alienation I experienced during this period:

> The secret dream of most immigrants is to try to pass unnoticed. Their first temptation is to imitate their host, and sometimes they succeed in doing so. But more often they fail. They haven't got the right accent, the right shade of skin, the right first name, the right family name or the proper papers, so they are soon found out. (Maalouf, 2000, p. 39)

My biggest fear was indeed of being "found out." I was terrified that my professors would eventually realize that I did not belong in the program because of my limited intellectual capacity, insufficient English proficiency, and horrible writing skills, or just because I was a woman who had somehow squeezed into the program through the back door.

To preserve my sanity, confront my feelings of inadequacy, and find a way to feel comfortable when speaking about issues of race, I began a search to define my own racial identity. Not being White or Black, what was I? Was I Hispanic? Latina? American? Latin American? Who was I, and what did I stand for?

After months of reflection and reading the work of various Latin American intellectuals on the construction of race, I decided to call myself Latina. I did not choose the term Hispanic, because it is linked to my people's colonizers and oppressors, the Spaniards. I did not choose American, because although I was born in the United States, I was raised primarily by Dominicans in the Dominican Republic, and I felt a strong connection to that country and its culture.

I must point out that I use the word *Latina* with caution, because I understand that the term *Latina/o* can also function as a reductionist social construct that places all people from Spanish-speaking countries into one category, thus perpetuating the belief that we all belong to a single culture and therefore must all act the same way. In addition, this term is problematic because it is used only in the United States. People from the Spanish-speaking countries of Latin America do not think of themselves as Latinos; they define their identity according to the specific country of their origin.

Nevertheless, I believe that in the past few decades, the rush of immigration into the cities of the United States by so many Spanish speakers of different nationalities, including Cubans, Puerto Ricans, Dominicans, Colombians, and Mexicans, has engendered interracial relations with both Whites and Blacks that have allowed for the development of a common political discourse. This discourse has produced a cultural category that I will refer to as Latin American. It has also defined my choice of racial identity: I am Latina.

Awakening in my body

I must admit that the years in graduate school were intellectually challenging. I spent that time searching for a place of belonging, reading books that stretched the boundaries of my understanding, and participating in extraordinary class discussions. However, I also spent those years in denial. The intellectual demands of graduate school could not keep me from thinking about the void I felt in my body and soul because I was not dancing. I wanted to show everyone that I had a brain and that I knew how to use it, and to prove this point, I had even been willing to leave my loved ones behind. By the time I graduated with my master's degree, I realized that I had everybody fooled: they all thought the dancer in me was completely gone. I had convinced them that I was nothing but an oversized brain walking around with no body attached to it—and that is exactly how I felt. I enjoyed my new intellectual identity, but it was hard to keep from thinking about dancing, even though those thoughts were so painful for me.

In order to make sense of new information, people process it first by relating it to previous experiences. In my case, because I had decided to concentrate on my intellectual development and reject the memories of my life as a dancer, I had to create a new way of understanding that was completely disassociated from my earlier experiences. I was practicing what Paulo Freire (2000) has called the "banking concept of education" (p. 72), in which the learning process is disconnected from the student's life. I was bottling in the new knowledge to separate it from my lost life as a dancer, and when I found a way to do that successfully, I was in good shape ... *or so I thought.*

It was during my doctoral work at the University of North Carolina at Greensboro that I first learned about the notion of the body-mind split. This idea haunted me for a long time, because although it resonated with my experience, I still could not draw a direct connection with what I was going through at the time. Then one day I met a man named Oren, who became my friend and later my dance partner. He invited me to go Salsa dancing, and I will never forget that night. As I danced, I awakened in my body for the first time in years.

Suddenly I understood the real meaning of the body-mind split. This concept holds that in our society the mind is more important than the body, thoughts are more important than feelings, and reason takes precedence over emotions, in an ideology that separates thinking from being and devalues experience as a creator of meaning. The alternative view is what Sherry Shapiro (1999) refers to as *body knowledge*: "both mind and body mingle together in a continuous informational stream creating the interpretations we call knowledge. As such, we experience our interpretations as reality" (p. 33).

I was a living example of this concept of body-mind separation. My mind was divorced from my body, not because I had given up dancing, but because I had thrown away the most valuable tool I had for creating meaning and understanding the world. I cannot understand how I could have gone for so long without that vital connection to my body, which had previously channeled all my expressions of love, joy, passion, and compassion. When I look back at that time in my life, those disembodied memories appear in black and white—blurry, odorless, and tasteless. When I began to dance again, the emptiness I had felt for so long, and had tried so hard to ignore, simply disappeared. Since then, I have continued dancing as an essential part of my integrated identity.

Latina Salsera

At that point, my allegiances shifted once again, and I became a *Latina Salsera*, an allegiance that I still carry with pride. Consequently, during my last few semesters in graduate school and after a hiatus of many years, I again began traveling to New York City, the capital of Salsa, for training and exposure.

Little did I expect that in New York I would discover a new community among the *Salseros Dominican-Yorks*, or Dominicans living in New York. Finally, I found a place where I belonged, full of people who saw the world and created meaning in the same way I did: *through our bodies and our culture.* Kathleen Casey (1995) calls this kind of discovery "a Collective Subjective, [where] in the process of articulating a common political discourse, individual isolation is overcome, and identity is created in community" (p. 223). Needless to say, as soon as I finished my Ph.D., I moved back to New York City.

However, to my dismay, it did not take long before I began to feel displaced in my new surroundings once again. Now the feminist in me was screaming accusations that I was perpetuating machismo and traditional sexism by conforming to the demands of a dance style that is sold as a "lead-and-follow" dance, in which men are the leaders and women follow.

One way in which Salsa instructors typically sell their lessons to the public is by claiming that in this age of women's liberation, Salsa dancing is one of the few arenas where men are still in charge.

I often heard a particular instructor say during a lesson, "Women, you may be the bosses everywhere else now, but here, men are still in charge." The men would often cheer and applaud this kind of statement. These comments were disturbing to me as a feminist, because although I love Salsa, I felt that by allowing a man to lead me I was giving in to traditional sexism.

This internal dissonance motivated me to attend classes at different studios to compare how other Salsa instructors taught the "follow-and-lead" techniques. I hoped to find a way of easing the tension between the feminist angel (in cap and gown) who stood firmly on my right shoulder, hitting me over the head with my Ph.D. diploma and insisting that I was perpetuating female oppression, and the *Salsera* angel (in a red, glittery outfit) on my left shoulder, shaking her hair and moving her hips to the sound of the congas.

Finally, I found a Salsa school called Santo Rico Dance, Inc., where I would learn how to resolve this conflict. The owner, Tomas Guerrero, was also a teacher with a more acceptable philosophy: "to lead and follow is to know the right moment to react to the actions of your partner." With his help, I came to understand that leading and following are both learned behaviors and equally important skills. Following is not a natural capacity that women are born with, any more than cooking is. Both men and women have to learn and master all the skills necessary to create a well-balanced partnership. Dancing is about two partners giving each other just the right amount of body tension so that when one initiates a move, the other translates it into a shift of weight that will complete the paired movement. If either partner does not give the right amount of tension back to the other, they both fail to create the dance move. In other words, to lead and to follow means knowing the precise moment in which to "act" and "react." Thus, despite the macho sales pitch I had heard so often in other dance schools, I concluded that Salsa dancing is based on mutuality, partnership, communication, and the sharing of equal strengths at precise moments. *Imagine my relief!*

Why did I become a teacher?

Based on the early memories I have described so far, it may be difficult to understand my choice of teaching as a profession. I have analyzed my negative feelings of displacement and intellectual inadequacy, and my positive experiences of reawakening to the truth of my body and finding a *collective subjective* among the Salseros Dominican-Yorks. However, none of this explains why I became a passionately committed teacher and later a teacher educator. Perhaps after my life-changing accident, I was subconsciously motivated to choose teaching as a career, as a way of helping others. Yet I needed to search deeper into my life to discover my true motivations.

Another journey through my memories took me back to my middle- and high-school years in the Dominican Republic. This was a difficult and problematic passage, because I have very little recollection of that time. At first, all I could remember was the sheer boredom of sitting for hours on end in rooms where teachers "blah blah blahed" their way to the end of the period. I remembered taking notes and memorizing a lot of information, not because it had any relevance or appeal for me, but because I knew that later I would have to spill it out on a test. I also remembered skipping many classes. Then I began to recall punishments and complaints made against me, and I felt a renewed hostility toward some of my old teachers. I could not think of a single reason why I should have wanted to become a teacher. I had detested school!

Then I thought that perhaps those hateful memories of school were precisely what drove me to become an educator and made me so passionate about education and social justice. I did not have a wonderful schooling experience, and my teachers did not serve as positive role models. In fact, my few recollections of school are oppressive, painful, and silencing. Worst of all are the memories of those moments in which I acquired the reputation of a *malcriada*—a disrespectful girl—because I could not keep my mouth shut and spoke up whenever I felt injustices had been committed toward my peers or me. This reputation in turn made me rebel even more. "Unquestioned authority" was not in my vocabulary. Nevertheless, with time, the punishments and complaints had served to silence me and fueled my feelings of inadequacy and my compulsion to prove my normalcy.

The truth is that I became a teacher despite these horrible experiences, but also because of them. Intuitively, I knew that there were other ways of approaching students, and I needed to discover them. I wanted to see children as more than "deficit pieces, [for when they are] unable to be affirmed for the strength they possess, children come to know themselves only in the places where they need extra help, whether those places mean academics, social skill or their bodies" (Pennell, 2010, p. 41). Perhaps I wanted to do my best, first as an elementary school teacher and later as a teacher educator, so that the children whose lives I touched—directly and indirectly—would have a different schooling experience than I had endured.

As I searched for alternative pedagogies that empower students to become embodied learners and teaching methods that do not perpetuate pain, disconnection, and oppression, I attended numerous graduate courses and education conferences with professors and speakers known to promote alternative classroom environments. Most of these encounters were wonderful. The professors and speakers helped me shape and understand my world, affirmed my radical views as legitimate, and—most importantly—helped me to determine the type of classroom I wanted to create, by modeling mostly positive and some negative pedagogical examples.

A story with three lessons

In one particular graduate course, I was very disappointed with a White male professor who claimed to follow a liberating feminist pedagogy when in fact his course mirrored a conservative, patriarchic, and silencing educational model. This class was composed mostly of women, with one White male student. Throughout the course, the professor and the male student managed to monopolize the discussion to the point of silencing the rest of the class. Worst of all, this environment of patriarchal camaraderie blinded the professor to the fact that on the few occasions when female students managed to participate, we were always interrupted by the male student with corrections of our words, based on what he believed we meant to say.

After a few months of bearing with this situation, I found myself repeatedly interrupted one day in the middle of an oral presentation, and I could not restrain myself from walking out of the class, never intending to return. My advisor subsequently arranged a meeting for me with this professor so that we could discuss this situation. I was horrified by the prospect of confronting him and speaking up for myself, after years of being socialized to believe that doing so was a sign of disrespect. I felt as if I was back in grade school; once more I was little Jolie Medina, *la malcriada*.

To prevent my emotions from getting the better of me in this meeting, I wrote down what I wanted to say and went to meet my nemesis. Then, in a flood of tears, I expressed my extreme discomfort with his class and explained how oppressive it was for me and for the other female students. He listened to everything that I had to say, handing me tissues to dry my tears. Then he proceeded to inform me that although he was saddened at this situation, he felt that his class was not a therapy session, and that it was not his job to pamper students. He also said that it was our responsibility as graduate students to fight for the right to speak when we wanted to participate. After that day, I never returned to his class, nor did I speak to him again. There would be no point in it, as we viewed education through very different frameworks that would always prevent us from seeing eye-to-eye.

I include this anecdote because, as a spiritual person, I believe that everything happens for a reason, and that no matter how painful an experience may be, I should learn from it and turn it into a life lesson. In this spirit, I would like to describe the three lessons that I learned from my encounter with this professor.

First, I learned that while educators may have the best intentions of promoting a liberating classroom environment, they still can inadvertently perpetuate ideologies of oppression. Although this professor called himself a liberationist pedagogue and a feminist thinker, he failed to see that his method of conducting class was based on masculine ideals of independence, detachment, and competition, as opposed to connection, care, and compassion, which are the primary characteristics of a liberating feminist pedagogy. Second, although I do not propose that classrooms should become group therapy sessions, I do believe that education should be healing, rewarding, and constantly respectful of human dignity. Finally, this experience made me realize how important it is to ensure that every student's voice is acknowledged in the classroom. This can only happen if we, as the facilitators of discussion, become actively involved in providing each student with the opportunity to speak, even if this means limiting the participation of the most vocal individuals in the group.

Santo Rico Kids Cultural Center

> *The Santo Rico Kids Program is my life and soul …*
> *It is my legacy.*
> *Once upon a time I wished I could teach children, I wished I could teach dance,*
> *I wished I could honor my culture by creating a space for others to rejoice with me,*
> *I wished I could gather families together,*
> *I wished to live surrounded by friends,*
> *I wished I could bring together a sense of what it means to be a New Yorker, a*
> *Latina, and an American, and not feel confused about it.*
> *The Santo Rico Kids Cultural Center made my wishes come true.*
> *For that I live in blessings.*

Yolanda Medina, Founder

I had been living in New York City and dancing Salsa at Santo Rico Dance, Inc., for several years when Tomas Guerrero, the school's owner and dance instructor who had helped me to incorporate the true spirit of Salsa into my feminist worldview, suggested that I start a children's dance program at the school. Honored and enthused about the possibilities this project offered, I launched into the creation of the Santo Rico Kids Cultural Center.

This fulfilling work connected with so many of my allegiances: the educator, the dancer, the Salsera, and the Dominican-York. Thinking back at the time, I realized that I had taught children and I had danced, but I had never taught children how to dance. This project also offered me the opportunity to create an environment for children and their parents that promoted the democratic values of inclusion, acceptance, equality, and diversity—values that I had searched for as a student and tried to promote as an educator. In other words, creating this program provided me with an opportunity to offer others the safe haven that the dance floor had given me as a child—a place to feel welcome regardless of heritage.

Thus the Santo Rico Kids Cultural Center was born, first offering classes in Salsa, and later including other genres such as Hip-Hop, Afro-Cuban, and Jazz. The program's mission statement articulated all of my educational ideals:

> The Santo Rico Kids Cultural Center is dedicated to providing outstanding multicultural awareness and acceptance to children ages 4–18 through the study and performance of the arts in a democratic, non-competitive, and non-discriminatory environment. Santo Rico Kids Cultural Center intends to offer all types of arts representing the population it serves as a way to support parents of the community in the teaching of cultural pride.

Through the study and performance of diverse cultural arts, children will learn to:

- accept difference

- recognize the importance of multiple perspectives in a democratic society

- work in collaboration

- understand the importance of community

- interact with other children and adults in a non-competitive environment

- take pride in their own culture

By the third year of its operation, the Santo Rico Kids Cultural Center was blooming into one of the most respected children's Salsa schools in the city. Located in Spanish Harlem, the program enrolled over 100 students of diverse social classes, cultures, and languages. It sponsored two professional children's dance teams: The Santo Rico Kids, consisting of boys and girls, and the Santoriquitas (Little Santo Rico girls), an all-girls team. These groups frequently traveled to perform in world-renowned events such as the Orlando Children's Salsa Conference, the New York Salsa Congress, and the Puerto Rican Day Parade. The children attended summer dance camps on full scholarships and were interviewed by Telemundo, a Spanish-speaking television channel.

The school offered various levels of dance instruction in multi-age settings. Every June, we gave a recital in a public theater, and all the children's family members and friends, and even their schoolteachers, gathered together, filling the hall to capacity to see the children show what they had learned that year. There were new choreographies, costumes, makeup, and glitter—lots of glitter and laughter.

Best of all, the Santo Rico Kids Cultural Center was a family. The children, instructors, and parents organized every trip, party, and meeting, and these events were always fully attended. Parental involvement always exceeded my expectations, and dance classes were filled with chatter and joy—instructors teaching, children dancing, and parents laughing and enjoying each other's company.

One memory that I hold especially dear was the birthday party we held for Julie, the youngest of the founding students. Her mother had to travel abroad to attend a relative's funeral, and before leaving, she asked if it would be possible for us to celebrate Julie's seventh birthday at the studio. The day of the party, the studio was full of students, parents, and instructors, all gathered to support and celebrate Julie's birthday. When her mother returned, she presented us with a framed composition Julie had written describing her birthday party and her joy at sharing this happy day with our extended "family." To this day, that memento remains in my office as a reminder that simple expressions of care can seed children's memories and influence them deeply in positive ways.

Of course, not everything at the studio was smiles and hugs; there were occasional conflicts, as can be expected in any truly democratic environment. Some of these were resolved immediately, some took a little longer, and others simply faded in the course of time as the point became irrelevant. In any case, whenever families walked into the dance studio they always felt welcomed, and everyone eagerly looked forward to dance classes, parents and children alike.

Ten years have passed since the inception of the Santo Rico Kids Cultural Center, and the program continues to offer a safe haven for children in Spanish Harlem and vicinity. The founding students have outgrown the program, and most have moved on to college, some with full scholarships, while others are still completing high school. Some of these children continue to dance Salsa, and Julie is dancing for Tomas Guerrero in the Santo Rico Dance Company at the age of 15. Other children have found different forms of expression such as cheerleading, break dancing, Hip-Hop, sports, and playing various musical instruments.

Most importantly, all of them have successfully continued their education and have developed leadership skills that will help them to be successful members of their communities. I feel a humble gratitude for the gifts the program has given me, and I am proud to think that I may have contributed something to the students' successes.

The importance of imagination

During the period when I was founding and running the Santo Rico Kids Cultural Center, I also held a two-year position as an Instructor in Elementary and Early Childhood Education at Queens College, where I taught Social Foundations of Education at both graduate and undergraduate levels. Today I am an Assistant Professor in the Teacher Education Department at the Borough of Manhattan Community College of The City University of New York. I teach Social Foundations of Education and coordinate the Childhood and Bilingual Childhood Education programs. The majority of my students are Black or Latina women of limited means.

These community college students, like me, are mostly non-traditional students. They return to school after experiencing life for a number of years, and/or they belong to marginalized groups based on their race, gender, and/or social class. They often report having to juggle their lives in various worlds. In the context of the college environment, their struggle is to become members of an academic community while trying to retain their identities as members of their own local communities; like me, they are "*border dwellers.*" For this reason, my students come into the classroom with a rich background of experiences that can easily be connected to the issues of oppression and privilege discussed in Teacher Education courses that are geared toward addressing social justice concerns.

I believe that my students share my views about how issues of discrimination and privilege affect children and their schools. Yet I still hear a tone of despair in their voices, and very little if any hope for a better future. They are doubtful of their authority and power to change the current systems of domination. As future educators, they want to become healers of children's suffering, but it seems as if a huge wall stands before their eyes, and they cannot see any better alternative. They cannot imagine a life that differs from their experience.

Hearing my students express the same desire and mental blockage semester after semester made me realize that in developing my educational model, which was based on the inclusionary principles of critical pedagogy, I had neglected an important factor that I now consider indispensable for the empowerment of students to create social change. I had failed to take into account the influences of my students' previous learning experiences, which, like my own, had been limited to "the banking concept of education" as Freire (2000) described it. In this approach, students' individual ways of interpreting the world are not valued. The learning process is disconnected from their lives, so they can never truly embody the knowledge they receive, or understand that they can use it to transform the world. Furthermore, because this approach to learning is one-dimensional and hierarchical, it leaves little room for critical and independent thinking. Even worse, it reduces one's capacity to imagine. Thus, students come to see the world as fixed and given.

This was the flaw in my teaching model: my students' underdeveloped powers of imagination limited their ability to actualize the knowledge they gained through participation in my courses. They were coming to my classroom, sharing their experiences, and linking them to issues of oppression and the need for change, but they still could not imagine a better future and therefore did not believe in their own power to create and recreate their world.

After coming to this realization, I began to think about my own life story and compare it to those of my students. Correlating our lives and experiences, I found that I shared five or six characteristics with many of them: they were mostly women, non-traditional students, and people of color who grew up poor, spoke English as a second language, and were either immigrants or children of immigrants. However, there was one basic yet crucial difference between us: my students lacked the capacity to "see things as if they could be otherwise." Recalling that my own sense of identity and personal power was rooted in my experiences as a dancer and a participant in artistic encounters, I came to believe that this was the missing piece in my educational model. I believe that my involvement with the arts has allowed me to imagine possibilities that my students cannot (yet) envision, and that exposure to artistic expressions of suffering, longing, redemption, peace, and renewal can help them connect with their own power to change the world they have inherited, and will lead.

This journey has helped me define the kind of pedagogy that I am committed to creating, which has two key characteristics. First, it must promote models of learning that embrace human beings with dignity and respect; this must be a pedagogy in which students' interests and experiences become the most important tools in the classroom, and knowledge is shaped using their own ways of understanding the world. Second, these educational models must feature encounters with the arts that will help students develop their capacity to imagine an end to unnecessary suffering, and to create much-needed social change.

My mission as a teacher educator is to model this new pedagogy to future teachers, so they in turn can model it to their future students. To rephrase a quotation from Tupac Shakur in the film *Resurrection* (Lazin, 2003), I may not be the one who changes the world, but I want to spark the minds of those who will.

References

Casey, K. (1995). The new narrative research in education. *Narrative Research, 21.* 211–253.

Freire, P. (2000). *Pedagogy of the oppressed,* (30th anniversary edition). New York: Continuum.

Greene, M. (1995). *Releasing the imagination: Essays on education, the arts, and social change.* San Francisco: Jossey-Bass.

Lazin, L. (Producer). (2003). *Tupac-Resurrection.* [Motion Picture]. Amaru/MTV and Paramount Entertainment.

Maalouf, A. (2000). *In the name of identity: Violence and the need for belonging.* New York: Penguin.

Pennell, A. (2010). Toward compassionate community: What school should be about. In Y. Medina & H. S. Shapiro (eds.), *Schooling in a diverse American society* (pp. 41–48). New York: Pearson Learning Solutions.

Shapiro, S. (1999). *Pedagogy and the politics of the body: A critical praxis.* New York: Garland.

Villaverde, L. E. (2008). *Feminist theories and education.* New York: Peter Lang.

CHAPTER 17

The Story of Cesar Chavez High School

One Small School's Struggle for Biliteracy

Sandra Liliana Pucci and Gregory J. Cramer

A growing body of literature suggests important benefits of smaller high schools in comparison to their traditional "comprehensive" counterparts (Darling-Hammond, Acess, & Wichterle Ort, 2003; Shear et al., 2008). Such benefits reside in both the affective and academic domains. Proponents of small schools have reported more personalized environments in which teachers know all students, more positive feelings about self and school exhibited by students, more parental choice and involvement, and other relevant climate issues (Conchas & Rodriguez, 2008).

The transformation of two low-performing comprehensive high schools into smaller schools by the Coalition Campus School Project in New York City produced startling improvements in several areas: attendance, reading and writing assessments, graduation rates, and college-going rates (Darling-Hammond et al., 2003; Iatarola, Schwartz, Stiefel, & Chellman, 2008). Other research shows more access to higher level academic offerings and more equitable achievement gains (Lee & Ready, 2007). Data from the high school dropout literature focusing on school structure indicate that the social and academic organization of a school can have a significant impact (Lee & Burkham, 2003). Smaller school size can serve to "constrain" the curriculum, limiting offerings to more challenging, academic material rather than lower level courses, which in turn leads to higher and more equitably distributed learning (Lee, Croninger, & Smith, 1997).

At the present moment there is little research examining how Latino students fare in these smaller schools. The school that is the center of the case study described in this chapter was founded on the principles of best practices for language minority students, such as primary language instruction and support, preteaching vocabulary, and context-embedded instruction (Cloud, Genesee, & Hamayan, 2009; Garcia, 2005; Goldenberg & Coleman, 2010). This research has shown that utilizing and developing the native language enhances academic achievement and English proficiency. Bilingual education in this school district is defined as a K-12 developmental program.

Studying Cesar Chavez High School

The focal school for this chapter is Cesar Chavez High school (CCHS, a pseudonym), a bilingual, university-preparatory high school in the urban Midwest. CCHS was founded by nine bilingual high school teachers, their students, a university professor, and a group of parents. Their coming together was a product of several years of joint effort in a large, comprehensive high school, and the desire for a more effective and equitable education for bilingual students. The previous institution had a population of 1,500 and a 50% graduation rate. The group of nine teachers felt that their efforts to foster student achievement were "diluted" by other personnel in the building who clearly did not share their vision. They had previously worked with the university professor as part of a federal grant aimed at effecting important changes, but when the principal of the school retired, things began to unravel. The group decided to found a new school. The climate to participate in such an undertaking was favorable, given that the district had just received funding fom the Bill and Melinda Gates Foundation to support the start-up of a group of small high schools.

CCHS is categorized as an "instrumentality charter" of the district; in other words, all teachers are union members and employees of that school district. The chartering document, which states the mission of the school, cites transformative pedagogy, integrated curriculum, constructivism, college preparation, and the development of bilingualism/biliteracy as the shared vision. There is also an explicit commitment to antiracist, antilinguicist, antisexist, and anticlassist pedagogy. CCHS opened its doors in September of 2004 and is currently in its seventh year of operation.

CCHS enrolls 250 students, 95% of whom are Latino, with the majority being of Mexican or Caribbean origin. The students are largely placed in grade-level groups according to English and Spanish proficiency levels; these are malleable groups of "English-dominant," "Spanish-dominant," and "transitional." A *constrained curriculum,* which posits one set of academic objectives for all students regard less of individual needs (Lee et al., 1997), is the norm at the school, with students at each grade level receiving the same courses, all aca demic in nature. Enrollment goes through the same process used by the district and there are no entrance requirements. The school has no administrator and runs as a *teachers' cooperative—a* structure in which administrative duties are distributed among teaching staff.

This chapter presents a descriptive study of CCHS. Data collection began during the second year of the school's operation and focuses on exploring and describing the efforts of "founding members" in their struggle against "playing host to the system" (Bowles & Gintis, 1976) through the establishment of a progressive, university-preparatory school serving an overwhelmingly Latino English-language-learning population.

The researchers—a university professor (Pucci), who is also one of the founding members of the school, and two teachers (Cramer and one other teacher) enrolled in graduate studies at the university—used mixed methods to study CCHS. Data collection included classroom observations, observations of teacher meetings, and focus-group interviews of a purposive sample of students across grade levels. Selected classrooms were observed twice weekly by one of the researchers. Ethnographic field notes and audio recordings were collected during observations and interviews (Emerson, Fretz, & Shaw, 1995), and student artifacts were also collected. This chapter reports on data collected during the school's first five years of operation, with the student focus groups taking place in Year 3. The researchers have served in multiple roles: nonparticipant observers in the classroom, participant observers at meetings, full participants at meetings, as well as classroom teachers who acted as complete participants in their own teaching contexts (Gold, 1958; Junker, 1960). Observational field notes, audiotapes, student artifacts, online parent surveys, publicly available institutional data, and focus group and interview data (of students and teachers) were also collected during this time.

The data were analyzed, categorized, compared, and contrasted using a methodology that seeks to "elicit meaning from the data" (Lecompte & Preissle, 1993, p. 235), rather than codify and compute it. Instead, categories and domains are constructed (Spradley, 1980). A domain analysis was used to sort the data into multiple categories, allowing a portrait to emerge that is reflective of the big picture of the systems and issues affecting operation.

Successes and Challenges: Emerging Themes

The purpose of this study was to examine and describe factors that support or hinder the success of CCHS and its students. Several major themes emerged from the analysis of data collected over the first five years: community, political engagement, academics and curriculum, intellectual freedom, school district bureaucracy, and teacher consciousness.

Community

The majority of students and teachers in the school feel a strong sense of community and belonging. Students report that "everyone knows each other, and nobody got problems with each other." Several students and teachers used the term "family-like" to describe the atmosphere at the school. One student said "people actually pay attention to you here." The students feel that the teachers are "different, cool with us," and that they can discuss anything with the teachers. However, others felt that certain teachers "try to control us, and they can't." It is interesting to note that despite the fact that many students used the term "family-like" to describe the atmosphere, there are still important teacher-student tensions and misunderstandings. Yet we find an overwhelming *social* buy-in on the part of students.

Despite different cliques, the general sentiment is one of great respect among students; this fact is borne out by the extremely low incidence of any type of violence or fighting between students, in con trast with most large high schools in the district. Most students live in the neighborhood. There are also many siblings and cousins at CCHS and some of the teachers and staff have enrolled their own children. The majority of teachers also feel that the quality of student-teacher relationships on the school level is remarkably close. Although they had experienced close relationships with students while working in previous settings, they commented that the size of the school also influenced their interactions. Some teachers reported significant mentoring relationships with students whom they had never had in class. Clearly, the establishment of community is one of the successes of the school.

Political Engagement

Students and teachers from CCHS are very active in the larger political context of immigration rights. Participation in locally and nationally organized protest marches is a regular event. Several of the teachers and the university professor continue to push for college opportunities for "undocumented" students, who constitute a considerable portion of the school's population. The state in which the school is located recently passed a provision enabling undocumented students to be assessed resident tuition. Previously, according to statute they were assessed as international students, regardless of their graduation from a high school clearly located within the boundaries of the state. However, some state campuses continue to require the students to "apply" for such a tuition waiver—it is not automatic. Thus the students must expose themselves as undocumented in order to apply for the in-state tuition remission, something that is obviously problematic.

Furthermore, present and past students continue to be active in protesting what they view as interference in their school by the dis trict, due to low test scores and NCLB regulations. They have regularly attended school board and other district-level meetings. In October 2011 there was a walkout, during which many former students and community members joined the students and staff.

Academics and Curriculum

Both teachers and students report high expectations for the quality of work students are required to complete. In the first three years CCHS was able to maintain its commitment to 6 years of mathematics in 4 years of high school, offering a full array of courses taught by qualified licensed teachers. Courses such as the Spanish for Native Speakers (SNS) offerings have proven useful to a significant num ber of students. In 2010, 13 students scored well enough on the Advanced Placement (AP) Spanish language examination to obtain the retroactive college credits. Similarly, the social studies/language arts connection with Latino history and Latino literature courses, which all freshmen receive, has remained consistent despite staff turnover. By the fifth year of operation the World History curriculum had been transformed from a typical chronological representation of "facts" into a thematic, critical examination of the sociopolitical forces that have shaped the world. Unfortunately, this has not been true in all content areas. Science, for example, has been plagued by the general shortage of bilingual science teachers as well as significant teacher turnover.

The Advanced Placement Debate. During Year 3 some important questions were raised regarding AP courses. Some teachers felt that their content and manner of delivery were incompatible with the CCHS mission of a truly culturally relevant and engaging curriculum. This is of particular importance, since despite the students' social buy in, there are still those who remain academically unengaged. This theme also arose during student focus groups, with several students describing their courses as being "boring," or "something my grandmother would like." Students know they are "advanced" but want content they can relate to, "stuff we are going through," rather than "things that happened even before Christ was born."

The AP debate came to a head during the third year of operation. A group of teachers acting independently began to program the junior class (for their second semester) into two groups, students who wanted to combine AP U.S. history with an advanced English course entitled American Authors, and others who preferred "regular" English Eleven and "regular" U.S. history. Subsequent intervention and discussion led to more students in the "advanced" classes, but the result was, in effect, a tracked junior class, which students interpreted as separating the *"más cerebritos"* (brainiest) from the others, and as they were being separated from their friends, their lament was both academic and social. This set off an ideological alarm for some staff, who maintained that tracking was clearly against the school's philosophy. A new teacher, who was eventually assigned the regular U.S. history course, raised issues of both equity and pedagogy, as in his opinion, the "mix of higher and lower" achievers would have been healthier, resulting in more learning and prosocial behavior. One group of teachers was especially dismayed at the tracking, as the 11th graders were products of the school, meaning that most had attended since the beginning of their high school careers, so there was no one else to blame for their "lack of preparation."

"Explain." Students were eager to discuss their classroom experiences and were clear about what they expected from teachers. In other words, they did not want to have books "thrown at them," but they wanted teachers to *"explain"* and to keep explaining until the students understood, to show them how, not just tell them. In their eyes, a good teacher was a person who didn't give up, who "stayed with the students" during the lesson, made sure they understood, and tried different ways of getting things across. In some instances, students complained about material being covered too quickly. One student recounted that she went to school one day asking about the previous day's work, and the attitude of the teacher was "like it is already tomorrow." Other students reported being loaded with homework they were unable to complete due to after-school obligations such as jobs, helping their parents at their workplace, or picking up and taking care of younger siblings and cousins. Compounding those realities was the issue that the students sometimes did not understand the material well enough to do the homework independently and were penalized if they do not complete it. As one student commented, *"No es que no queramos, es que no entendemos"* [It's not that we don't want to do it, it's that we don't understand].

A Print-Rich Environment. The original chartering document for CCHS included a heavy emphasis on biliteracy development. An important part of the school's mission is to develop academic registers in both English and Spanish and enable students to express themselves powerfully and bilingually in multiple genres of written communication.

Space for the new school was carved out from an existing middle school with dwindling enrollment, and there was no library at the site. The teachers decided to use an available classroom to set up a literacy center, stocking it with a large quantity of high-interest books both in Spanish and English. However, this center did not effectively function until Year 3 of the CCHS operation, as the demands of start-up, as well as an underestimation of the library skills needed for such an undertaking, resulted in slow progress. By the end of Year 2 the teachers, as well as the university professor, decided to prioritize getting the center functioning. After further surveying the students, more high-interest materials were purchased and made accessible.

The school also has a daily sustained silent reading (SSR) program which began in Year 5; the literacy center is the source for most of these reading materials. While the SSR program is most likely respon sible for the modest increases in reading scores on standardized tests, not all the students have bought into the activity. Inadequate buy-in and lack of modeling on the part of some teachers are at the heart of the problem. Despite a great deal of support and education on its implementation and value, several teachers have been resistant to submitting to its discipline.

Intellectual Freedom

During the first three years of operation there was a general air of professional fulfillment and satisfaction among the staff with re gard to course offerings. Teachers were able to offer Latino history, Latino literature, Spanish for native speakers, an array of mathematics courses, art history, holistic literature-based ESL, different music courses, film analysis, psychology, and sociology. Obtaining a charter license through the state enabled teachers to teach outside their licensure. The ability to offer a culturally relevant, broad-reaching, "Latino-centric" curriculum has been one of the major successes of the school. Additionally, grants that were awarded for charter school operation, as well as a district-level Gates Foundation grant for "smaller high schools," enabled CCHS to purchase substantial amounts of non-textbook print materials and technology. Although some staff felt that special electives were sometimes based more on teachers' tastes and expertise rather than on student interests, overall morale around these issues was high.

During Years 4 and 5 the tide shifted. The state changed the ability of teachers to teach outside their areas with charter licenses. The "highly qualified teacher" clause of No Child Left Behind (NCLB), which prohibits teaching outside of one's licensed content areas, began to be enforced by the district. Thus the charter license, a tremendous boon for small high schools, was trumped by NCLB. The school was no longer able to draw upon the "unlicensed" talents of the teaching staff. Bilingual teachers could not teach ESL, professional but unlicensed musicians could not teach music, college athletes could not teach physical education (PE), and trained, passionate dancers could not teach dance. Presently, the school is severely limited in what electives it can offer. Furthermore, the district has been threatening to shut down schools that cannot offer PE or art; yet being a small school, CCHS simply does not have the resources to hire full-time art and PE teachers. For a short period, while there was still a middle school in the building, art and PE teachers were shared. However, due to declining enrollment the middle school was shut down, and the school has returned to the same staffing dilemma.

School District Bureaucracy

All of the founding-member teachers had worked for the same large urban school district for a number of years before starting their school. Nevertheless, the bureaucracy of the district continues to present unexpected challenges. There is considerable tension between the school's unique vision of autonomy, originality, and flexibility, and the district's structures requiring accountability and conformity. The school's smaller size, teachers' cooperative structure, and corresponding lack of layers of support staff found in larger, more traditional settings became a heavy burden on the lead teacher as well as other individuals assuming leadership roles. In addition, many "central of fice" meetings at the district took teachers' time away from their students and teaching. Other challenges included managing the budget, meeting testing requirements, and various tasks that were unconnected to student learning.

School Improvement Plan. Additionally, the school has come under scrutiny for not meeting "adequate yearly progress" (AYP) according to NCLB guidelines in its test scores since inception. The majority of the students are English language learners (ELLs) who, by definition, are a "nonproficient" subgroup. Standardized tests are given in the tenth grade, and each year schools need to demonstrate AYP, regardless of whether the students understand the language of the test. The resulting classification as a "school in need of improvement" with in a "district in need of improvement" has resulted in the invasion of what we characterize as an NCLB "middle management." Many consultants and school district personnel visited the school to deliver mandatory professional development, often on such elementary topics as "Bloom's taxonomy," a session in which pocket-reference flip charts were distributed. Instead of focusing on the specific needs of the teachers, students, and school, professional development sessions emphasized general topics geared to instruction in English, and most presenters had no expertise in bilingual education. Rather, the sessions consisted of a series of generic sessions that form part of the district's overall response to NCLB. Furthermore, in 2010 the district, acting under NCLB guidelines, mandated a "School Improvement Plan" (SIP), which has come to dominate all staff meetings. Whereas in the past the CCHS staff devoted common meeting times to developing integrated courses and schoolwide Socratic seminars based on engaging, culturally responsive literature, all staff meetings focused on figuring out how to get "local data" into the SIP. Thus the focus of such gatherings has shifted from working on larger issues or developing rich curricula for the school's unique population to putting data into the SIP. Although NCLB has posed challenges for many urban schools, the impact on CCHS has been particularly acute as it openly threatens the mission of the school and disproportionately penalizes ELLs.

Staffing. Although CCHS can interview and select their teachers, a shortage of high school bilingual personnel continues to plague the district. It is important to note that programs in this district are "developmental" rather than "transitional," so teachers must be fluent in Spanish. Years 1 and 2 were particularly difficult, with "long-term substitutes" assigned to the building by the district and philosophically incompatible with the school. At the end of Year 1, two of the founding members exited from the school on "incompatibility transfers." In the middle of Year 2, a highly skilled science teacher decided to return to Puerto Rico. A new teacher, who had been chosen through the school's interview process, walked out after 3 weeks. Another new teacher spent the academic year afraid of his students and was not invited to return for Year 3. Pleas to the school district for qualified teachers were often answered by *"no hay"* ("there aren't any"). Years 3 and 4 started with the school in a slightly better position regarding staffing, with the hiring of a few new teachers, but the shortage of bilingual high school teachers remained, with no relief on the horizon.

Further, the "highly qualified teacher" clause of NCLB continues to stymie efforts to find truly qualified educators. For example, an excellent licensed teacher from Mexico who worked effectively with students for the Spanish for native speakers classes was unable to pass the PRAXIS I, a "preprofessional skills" examination, and was eventually replaced by a monolingual substitute.

Teacher Consciousness: Constructing "El Hombre Nuevo"

The CCHS founding teachers moved from a large comprehensive high school with multiple layers of personnel performing various tasks (i.e., administrators, counselors, clerical personnel, and so on). Forming a teachers' cooperative and opening a new school has been a continuous struggle to transform their ways of thinking about professional responsibilities, the students, and each other. This was seen in two forms: inequitable work burdens, particularly felt by the lead teachers, and "baggage" in the form of unproductive attitudes and beliefs, which have proved difficult to shed, gone unexamined, or in some cases, reified.

As previously mentioned, of particular concern was the push to track the eleventh graders by some teachers. Reasons given for separating the students included some having "low skills" or others "being capable but not willing" to do the work. Individual staff blamed the lack of skills on one or two particularly poor teachers who eventually left the school, while others saw this issue as representing a retreat from the original CCHS mission. In Year 3 a "junior meeting" was called, which resulted in previously detracked students deciding for the AP offerings and others "choosing the easier class." The staff came to loggerheads: Tracking is against the original mission of the school, but the teachers of these advanced courses did not see all students as being capable of succeeding in this curriculum and would not teach them. In Year 4 the staff decided to disband the offering of the AP U.S. history and American Authors combination in favor of a more engaging theme-based curriculum they agreed was more consistent with best practices for language minority students. However, there are still many important conversations that need to take place, some of which go straight to the heart of the AP system and the high school curriculum itself.

With the small numbers of students and close monitoring of their progress, the school is fostering a great percentage of students on track to graduate on time. In fact, as previously noted, the graduation and college-going rates are far above district averages. But there are bumps along the way. A critical incident at the end of Year 2, when four ninth graders who had not passed all their classes were "flunked," again sounded alarm bells. This was not a staff consensus decision; it was made by a teacher responsible for programming. Interestingly, in this case, the small size of the school worked against these students, who were programmed again as ninth graders, repeating the entire first semester ninth-grade curriculum, including classes they had actually passed. Those who had completed sufficient credits by January were "promoted" to the tenth grade. This situation caused much hurt and resentment on the part of these students, who eventually left the school—one never graduated.

Another ideological tension identified is the relationship between the teacher as individual and the school as a whole. There are a few teachers who do not make sufficient effort to implement collectively agreed-upon schoolwide initiatives, such as SSR, rules about school uniforms, tardiness, use of cell phones, "hall walking," and other issues. Nonimplementation of SSR was observed well into the second year of its inception, with some teachers using the SSR 45-minute time slot for homework, correcting papers, not monitoring student activity, and so on. A few individuals view their noncompliance with various policies as righteous acts of resistance. At times, an oppositional situation developed, in which some teachers are the "bad guys," or the "enforcers," and the "righteous resisters" are the "cool" teachers. There was also misunderstanding of a few teachers who seemingly did not understand what it meant to be part of a teachers' cooperative, or were not willing to work together as a collective.

What Have We Learned at Cesar Chavez High School?

Despite these bumps, graduation rates in the first five years were well above the district average of 50%; CCHS rates hovered between 88% and 96%. Ten students graduated with full tuition scholarships to the state's flagship university as a result of their participation in a summer precollege program as well as meeting admission requirements. Students are regular recipients of scholarship money from private sources. For example, in 2006 seven of the CCHS seniors received scholarships for a total of $178,000 to assist in their university studies. These available figures for college enrollment data are impressive. From the first graduating class of 47 (in 2005), 23 students immediately enrolled at either a 2- or 4-year college, a rate of 49%; the average college-going rate of subsequent classes is 43%.

Results from this study highlight the significant, if not unexpected, challenges in founding and sustaining a small bilingual high school. They point to several meaningful accomplishments, as well as critical work to be done.

In many ways the concept of a constrained curriculum (Lee & Burkam, 2003) has worked both in principle and practice. Being a small school with limited staff, it *is* almost impossible to change a student's schedule if conflict occurs. CCHS is quite different from a large comprehensive high school, where students can often be reprogrammed—sometimes on teacher whim—into a "lower level" class or a nonacademic elective. In the context of the school in this study, this constrained curriculum has the power to mitigate against tracking, embracing one academically oriented curriculum for all. Although some teachers were left unsatisfied by the outcome of the AP U.S. history decision, they were able to resolve the issue collectively, then found themselves embroiled in the curricular fall-out from NCLB.

An examination of student transcripts shows that there is little or no variation of courses in the freshman and sophomore years. Yet even with the liberationist vision of the original chartering documents, adults sometimes find it hard to enact truly transformative stances toward students and each other. Some students report differential treatment in terms of access to information, flexibility regarding independent studies, attendance, grading, discipline, and "second chances." Institutional capital, although seemingly distributed on a communitarian basis, still has "competitive" leaks (Stanton-Salazar, 2001) with certain students or groups of students able to curry more favor than others. Staff agree that more face-to-face time where philosophical and ideological questions can be raised is needed, yet meeting times are inevitably consumed by the nuts-and-bolts work needed to simply keep the school floating. In addition, the demands of NCLB paperwork—most notably the School Improvement Plan—eat up time the staff could devote to critical issues. But CCHS is not the first to be faced with this challenge; it is a situation that has been previously discussed in small teacher-led schools (Meier, 2002). Yet, as Meier insightfully points out, there needs to be time to "safely" navigate critical issues, and this time has been severely lacking.

Our work at CCHS has led us to call for the rethinking of what defines a challenging, academically oriented curriculum. The notion of AP constituting a "gateway" to college success seems to be a relatively unchallenged concept by the majority of educators in the United States. Discussions of equal access to AP take center stage (Solorzano & Ornelas, 2002), rather than a critical analysis of the stifling, traditional AP curriculum itself, the financial interests of the College Board, or the underbelly of this system. The fact that passing AP examinations can lead to retroactive university credits at some—not all—institutions of higher learning certainly could be used as a justification, a so-called return on the investment. At CCHS we have seen some utility in the case of AP Spanish, but a deeper analysis of the system—who wins and who loses—is required. At this school, the leap between a Latino-centric freshman year and the culturally subtractive emphasis and narrow scope and sequence of AP courses in subsequent years created a disjointed curriculum, which sent mixed messages.

Teachers' ideologies and beliefs must also be explored and clarified. In Year 3, with the calming of the "start-up" waters, other issues were able to float to the surface. There are differing beliefs among teachers; some feel that the school is for everyone and that we should work with all students no matter what the challenge, and others maintain that if a student does not comply with the disciplinary and academic demands of the school, "it's time to look for another school." These ideologies are also manifested in individual teachers' perceptions that they care more than others or that they understand the students better, and falling into the trap of commiserating with students in their complaints against other teachers, justified or not. Yet others seem to want to be "friends" with their students.

While the need for caring educators (Valenzuela, 1999) is undeniable, caring must not be substituted for a political commitment to challenge students to acquire the type of skills and knowledge necessary to become critical, active citizens (or noncitizens, as the case may be with so many of our students). Thus the notions of caring and advocacy need to be interrogated. To do so teachers must acknowledge the inevitable contradiction between individual and community. Both Bowles and Gintis (1976) and Freire (1970) are very clear on these concepts. In the case of schooling, this contradiction consists of teachers educating students in the interests of society, however those interests may be defined. Students, for their part, often seek to use their schooling for personal ends. Thus conflicts between students and teachers are inevitable because schools, even and perhaps especially schools that seek to educate students to become critical actors, are inherently constraining. Schools and teachers that deny this contradiction or wish it away forfeit their historic roles as institutions that mediate the passage of students from childhood to adulthood. Teachers must understand that this contradiction characterizes every school. It is independent of particular students and particular teachers, and stands above whatever warmth or personal regard that individual students and teachers have for each other (Bowles & Gintis, 1976).

Ernesto "Che" Guevara, in his essay "Socialism and Man in Cuba," (1989), discusses the difficulty of constructing a new society with individuals who were born and conditioned in the old. While our comparison to the Cuban revolution may seem hyperbolic, what the founding documents of the school show, is just that: An attempt to forge a new school society, a different, more equitable way of relating and being. But the transition is difficult. Guevara comments:

> I think the place to start is to recognize this quality of incompleteness. … The vestiges of the past are brought into the present in the individual consciousness, and a continual labor is necessary to eradicate them. … The new society in formation has to compete fiercely with the past. The past makes itself felt not only in the individual consciousness—in which the residue of an education systematically oriented toward isolating the individual still weighs heavily—but also through the very character of the transition period in which commodity relations still persist. So long as it exists its effects will make themselves felt in the organization of production and, consequently, in consciousness. (p. 5)

As this study shows, changing the size of a school alone cannot transform a system resistant to accommodating innovation, or an inequitable educational culture that has been unconsciously reproduced. Though each individual (teacher) is both "a unique being and a member of society" (p. 5), it is clear that more consciousness needs to be developed in order to obtain the collective rewards of liberationist schooling.

Conclusions

The national high school graduation rates of Latino and other students of color in the United States reveal an ongoing system of inequity. Although there seems to be controversy in the literature as to what constitutes a "dropout" (Fry, 2010), all agree that a substantial number of Latinos either drop out of a U.S. high school—37% according to Fry—or simply do not complete high school, 42% according to figures disseminated by the National Council of La Raza (http://www.nclr.org). Extensive commentary on this is beyond the scope of this paper, but one interesting point is Fry's distinction between ELL and English-proficient Latino dropouts. His figures assert that lack of English language ability is an important characteristic of Latino dropouts, almost 59% of whom do not speak English well (p. 9). One can only speculate as to the negative impact of the lack of quality bilingual programs for most secondary students. The dropout rate for Latinos in the Midwestern district where this school is located hovers at around 40%. There is a definite need to expand the research literature examining institutional factors and the utility of a constrained curriculum, as well as to identify the factors that lead to the positive affective and academic results of smaller, bilingual high schools.

Differential access to university preparatory courses has been repeatedly documented in the literature (Stanton-Salazar, 2001; Valenzuela, 1999). Although some, including Kozol (2005), insist that integration and/or busing students of color to more affluent suburban high schools is the key to high school graduation, few have actually tried to construct, along with families, a school with culturally/linguistically relevant curriculum *for them*. This study examines one such school attempting to do so. If supporting and hindering factors can be identified through an examination of data, this research may provide substantial indications of how to more effectively fight educational inequity.

References

Bowles, S., & Gintis, H. (1976). *Schooling in capitalist America*. New York, NY: Basic Books.

Cloud, N., Genesee, F., & Hamayan, E. (2009). *Literacy instruction for English language learners*. Portsmouth, NH: Heinemann.

Conchas, G., & Rodriguez, L. (2008). *Small schools and urban youth: Using the power of school culture to engage*. Thousand Oaks, CA: Corwin Press.

Darling-Hammond, L., Acess, J., & Wichterle Ort, S. (2003). Reinventing high school: Outcomes of the Coalition Campus School Project. *American Educational Research Journal, 39*(3), 639–673.

Emerson, R., Fretz, R., & Shaw, L. (1995). *Writing ethnographic fieldnotes*. Chicago, IL: University of Chicago Press.

Freire, P. (1970). *Pedagogy of the oppressed*. New York, NY: Seabury Press.

Fry, R. (2010). *Hispanics, high school drop outs and the GED*. Washington, DC: Pew Hispanic Center.

Garcia, E. (2005). *Teaching and learning in two languages: Bilingualism and schooling in the United States*. New York, NY: Teachers College Press.

Gold, R. (1958). Roles in sociological field observation. *Social Forces, 36*, 217–223.

Goldenberg, C., & Coleman, R. (2010). *Promoting academic achievement among English learners. A guide to the research*. Thousand Oaks, CA: Corwin Press.

Guevara, E. (1989). *Socialism and man in Cuba*. New York, NY: Pathfinder Press.

Iatarola, P., Schwartz, A., Stiefel, L., & Chellman, C. (2008). Small schools, large districts: Small school reform and New York City's students. *Teachers College Record, 110*(9), 1837–1878.

Junker, B. (1960). *Field work*. Chicago, IL: University of Chicago Press.

Kozol, J. (2005). *Shame of the nation: The restoration of apartheid schooling in America*. New York, NY: Crown.

Lecompte, M., & Preissle, J. (1993). *Ethnography and qualitative design in educational research*. San Diego, CA: Academic Press.

Lee, V., & Burkam, D. (2003). Dropping out of high school: The role of school organization and structure. *American Educational Research Journal, 40*(2), 353–393.

Lee, V., Croninger, R., & Smith, J. (1997). Course taking, equity, and mathematics learning: Testing the constrained curriculum hypothesis in U.S. secondary schools. *Educational Evaluation and Policy Analysis, 19*(2), 99–12.

Lee, V., & Ready, D. (2007). *Schools within schools: Possibilities and pitfalls of high school reform*. New York, NY: Teachers College Press.

Meier, D. (2002). *The power of their ideas: Lessons for America from a small school in Harlem*. Boston, MA: Beacon Press.

Shear, L., Means, B., Mitchell, K., House, A., Gorges, T., Oshi, A., Smerdon, B., & Shkolnik, J. (2008). Contrasting paths to small-school reform: Results of a 5-year evaluation of the Bill & Melinda Gates Foundation's National High Schools Initiative. *Teachers College Record, 110*(9), 1986–2039.

Solorzano, D., & Ornelas, A. (2002). A critical race analysis of advance placement classes: A case of educational inequality. *Journal of Latinos and Education, 1*(4), 215–229.

Spradley, J. (1980). *Participant observation*. Orlando, FL: Harcourt, Brace, & Jovanovich.

Stanton-Salazar, R. (2001). *Manufacturing hope and despair: The schooling and kin support networks of U.S.-Mexican youth*. New York, NY: Teachers College Press.

Valenzuela, A. (1999). *Subtractive schooling: U.S.-Mexican youth and the politics of caring*. Albany: State University of New York Press.

Reflection Questions

1. After reading this section, think about what 2–3 values you consider most important and that you would like your students to value as well? Explain each and why.

2. What are the things you can do as a teacher to help create spaces of critical reflection in your classroom?

3. As an educational leader, what are the things you can do to make sure that you are addressing the needs of the children, the school, and the community?

4. What are the benefits of teaching to humanize in poor, diverse settings? What are the benefits of teaching to humanize in more affluent, homogeneous settings?

5. Make a list of terms that you find important for you to incorporate in your teacher vocabulary. Discuss your selections with a partner.

SECTION IV
Teachers in 21st Century Schools

Introduction

Yolanda Medina

Every teacher should realize the dignity of his calling; that he is a social servant set apart for the maintenance of proper social order and the securing of the right social growth. In this way the teacher always is the prophet of the true God and the usher of the true kingdom of God. —Dewey (1897)

Every semester on the first day of my Social Foundations of Education class I write this quote on the board and ask my students to think about what it tells them about the teaching profession. This conversation introduces, what I consider to be, one of the most important discussion that I will have with my teacher education students. Many preservice teachers enter teacher education classrooms without having ever questioned what the true role of the teacher is in the lives of students and even a larger number of them never have thought of the power teachers have to change the world. They think that their future job only entails the passing of knowledge already set and written in the textbooks (and somehow make it fun so the kids enjoy it) and, with clear disciplinary expectations, maintain order in the classroom. This first day discussion opens their eyes to a whole new perspective on their future careers and helps them realize that teaching is not as easy as they think. Teaching entails a whole lot more than simply teaching the three Rs. The roles and responsibilities associated with teaching give teachers the power to make education a liberating force or a crippling experience in the lives of children.

The introductory lecture in my class leads the way to a semester full of discussions on the purpose of education, one that expands students' original understanding of what it means to teach. Henry Giroux (2012), in the essay included in this section, states,

While I believe that public education should equip students with skills to enter the workplace, it should also educate them to contest workplace inequalities, imagine democratically organized forms of work, and identify and challenge those injustices that contradict and undercut the most fundamental principles of freedom, equality, and respect for all people who constitute the global public sphere. (p. 9)

Class discussions often start with the sharing of painful experiences in conventional classrooms where students were given material to memorize and regurgitate for a grade, student-teacher relationships were non-existent and students felt invisible. They share their pains and aches for a week or two, but then these discussions turn to memories of caring, dedicated teachers and what they do that makes them remarkable. These teachers, they say, believe in their students. They guide learning instead of forcing and defining it for students and they encourage students to question everything and be active participants in their own learning. These teachers believe in their power to change the future and they take it seriously.

This section contains five essays that we consider to be important when discussing the roles and responsibilities of teachers in schools and classrooms. These essays explore the multiple roles that teachers must play in 21st century schools; roles that have previously been diminished by narrow visions of how teachers are educated and function in their work. Delpit, Giroux, Hinchey, Ladson-Billings, and Madeloni and Gorlewski all share a commitment to the importance of teachers working as empowered leaders in public educational spheres. The authors in this section would agree with me when I say that the true purpose of teachers' work is to create critical thinking individuals prepared to live in a democratic society, who stand up for what is just, and who feel empowered to change their lives and the lives of those around them. With this in mind, the authors in this section speak to teachers and future teachers, reminding us of our true calling as educators and helping us to understand that how we teach and what we teach are important dimensions of teachers' work, and ultimately, the primary influence on what the future will look like for the students we teach.

References

Dewey, J. (1897). My pedagogic creed. *School Journal, 54*, 77–80.
Giroux, H. (2012). *Education and the crisis of public values: Challenging the assault on teachers, students, & public education.* New York: Peter Lang.

CHAPTER 18

Warm Demanders

The Importance of Teachers in the Lives of Children of Poverty

Lisa Delpit

"My teacher treated me as a diamond in the rough, someone who mostly needed smoothing." —Mary Frances Berry, *USA Today*

"There comes that mysterious meeting in life when someone acknowledges who we are and what we can be, igniting the circuits of our highest potential." —Rusty Berkus, *To Heal Again*

I've taught many young teachers, and they all seem so tired when they arrive at my evening classes. I know they work hard, and I know that for many of them "the system," "the parents," "the paperwork," "the high-stakes tests" all make it seem that what they do doesn't make much of a difference. If there is one message I try to convey to them, it is that *nothing* makes more of a difference in a child's school experience than a teacher. As I have written before, when I interviewed a group of African American men who were successful but "should not" have been, based on their socioeconomic status, their communities, their parents' level of education, and so on, all of them insisted that their success was due in large part to the influence or intervention of one or more teachers during their school careers. These were teachers who *pushed* them, who *demanded* that they perform, even when they themselves thought that they could not. The teachers gave them additional help and insisted that they were capable of doing whatever anyone else could do.

Gloria Ladson-Billings says that successful teachers of low-income, culturally diverse children know that their students are "school dependent."[1] What she means is that while children from more privileged backgrounds can manage to perform well in school and on high-stakes tests in spite of poor teachers, children who are not a part of the mainstream are dependent upon schools to teach them whatever they need to know to be successful.

I am reminded of my own experience with my daughter in softball. To say that I am unknowledgeable about sports is an extreme understatement. Yet I wanted to make sure that my daughter was not handicapped by my limitations, so I took her to become a member of a locally sponsored team. Since my own knowledge of the sport did not extend beyond the names of the bat and ball, I was amazed that after two practices my seven-year-old actually knew where left field was! After practice, the coach came to talk to the parents. He told us that we needed to "work with" our kids at home, practicing softball skills and going over the rules. My first thought was panic, my second was, "Look, I get her here; you're the coach. It's your job to teach her. I can't do a thing." Suddenly I understood fully what many parents who are not school-savvy or educated themselves must think about schools and teachers who insist that they "work with" their children at home! If the coach didn't teach Maya, there was little hope for my child's future softball career.

For children of poverty, good teachers and powerful instruction are imperative. While it is certainly true that inequity, family issues, poverty, crime, and so forth all affect poor children's learning opportunities, British educator Peter Mortimore found that the quality of teaching has *six to ten times* as much impact on achievement as all other factors combined.[2] This can explain why I have found, like educator Robert Marzano, that two schools serving the same population can have vastly different success rates.[3] In a recent study of schools in a southern city, I visited two public elementary schools located less than a mile apart, both serving very low-income African American children. One school's state test scores were at the top of the district—higher than the average score of the district's well-to-do schools, and the other school's scores were at the very bottom of the district. What was the cause of such a discrepancy? The schools essentially served the same population. The difference could only be the quality of teaching and instruction. In each of the classrooms in the higher-scoring school I saw teachers engaged with their students, actually teaching. In the lower-performing school, I saw most teachers sitting while students completed seat work.

What gave me even more reason to pause was the realization that the teachers in the lower-performing school apparently believed that it was okay to remain seated and not involved with the students when a visitor came into the room. This was even the case when she or he observed my conversations with the students that made it clear that many of them did not understand what they were supposed to be doing on the worksheet. That observation led me to conclude that somehow the culture of the school signaled to the teacher that "not teaching" was okay. If there is not a strong culture of achievement in a school, many teachers may not be teaching as effectively as they are capable of doing.

Indeed, Mike Schmoker in his remarkable book *Results Now* cites a 2001 study by K. Haycock and S. Huang that shows that "the best teachers in a school have *six times as much impact* as the bottom third of teachers."[4] Much of Schmoker's work centers on the notion that poor children are not learning because schools and teachers are not adequately teaching them. He records instances of researchers and administrators visiting large numbers of classrooms and observing very little effective teaching and, despite district- or state-mandated curricula, very little coordinated, integrated instruction.

In my own recent visits to a number of schools and classrooms during a six-month stay in one mid-sized, predominantly African American district where I observed the two schools mentioned above, I was shocked to find how little teaching was actually occurring in many classrooms in a variety of schools. I saw an inordinate number of classrooms where students were doing seat work for an entire period—mostly busywork that had little connection to deep learning. Few if any questions were asked, and those that were demanded little thought on the part of student or teacher. Children who chose not to do the worksheet were ignored as long as they were quiet.

In one classroom of over-age high schoolers who had recently switched to a new schedule, the teacher told me that the periods were too long and the students got tired so she allowed them to take naps if they chose to take a break from doing their assigned seat work. In this language arts classroom, the teacher was apparently unaware that two students, instead of using the computers to complete their assignment, were instead comparing cell phone plans!

It is no surprise, but still a jolt, to realize the implications of such non-teaching. Schools that had been designated as "failing" had large numbers of teachers like those described. In contrast, schools that performed at high levels had larger numbers of teachers who were actually teaching. They were visible in the classroom. They held students' attention. They were explaining concepts and using metaphors to connect the knowledge students brought to school with the new content being introduced. They used different kinds of media. They asked students to explain concepts to their peers. They posed questions that required thought and analysis and demanded responses. *No one* was allowed to disengage.

One of the most poignant aspects of this reality is that students are quite aware when the instruction they are receiving is subpar. While many are willing to play the game to avoid being challenged, others are distraught at the realization that they are being shortchanged. In a Florida high school that has been designated as "failing" for several years in a row, the students were primarily low-income Haitian immigrants, many of whom were from Haitian Creole-speaking families. Many of those teaching in this school were substitutes or Spanish-speaking new immigrants with limited English skills themselves who were recruited from Central American countries because they knew a specific subject area but who had no teaching experience. A district math supervisor told me that she once visited the school and had to hold back tears when the students in one class looked at her pleadingly and said, "Miss, can you please teach us something?"

During my sojourn visiting schools, I also had the opportunity to talk with high school students who were involved in a citywide after-school spoken-word poetry-writing program. As I always do when I have the opportunity, I asked the primarily African American students to talk to me about what problems they saw in their schools. Most of the students' comments focused on what teachers did or did not do in classrooms.

Students were also very aware of the culture of their schools, the attitudes their teachers have toward teaching, and the effort those teachers put into their craft:

- It's bad when they say you go to a bad school. It's like then they think you are automatically a bad person. Even when it's just one bad seed that acts crazy, people think everyone in the school is like that.

- Sometimes the teachers won't give you help. Some of them say things like, "I got mine; all I have to do is get my paycheck."

- In high school a lot of teachers are about occupying us, not teaching us.

- The bookwork and the tests have nothing to do with us.

- Our teachers don't understand how much impact they have. It's hard when they act about as serious about what they're doing as our little sisters or brothers.

- One teacher said she didn't want to teach today because she was having a bad day. But then she would have about four or five bad days in a row!

I also asked them to describe a good teacher they had encountered in their school lives:

- A good teacher takes time, makes sure you understand.

- One who enjoys being there.

- One who doesn't put on a movie when they're tired.

- A teacher who asks questions to help get the students closer to the answers.

- For each chapter there should be a lecture, activities and games, and reading outside of the text from different sources (from a future teacher, perhaps?).

- One who has a sense of humor, but can be serious when necessary.

- Someone you can find outside of class for help.

- Someone who is patient, understanding, ready to teach if you're ready to learn.

- One who is willing to learn about you and about new things.

- A good teacher inspires you and pushes you to the point of no return.

Many researchers have identified successful teachers of African American students as "warm demanders." James Vasquez used the term to identify teachers whom students of color said did not lower their standards and were willing to help them. Warm demanders expect a great deal of their students, convince them of their own brilliance, and help them to reach their potential in a disciplined and structured environment.[5]

Franita Ware in her research describes several such teachers, including Ms. Willis, a sixteen-year veteran, who taught third through fifth grades. In one example of Ms. Willis's no-nonsense approach, she spoke loudly and clearly to her students about the importance of completing and submitting homework:

> Chris, pass out the workbooks while I'm doing some housekeeping and I want everybody to … listen. Yesterday I checked for two things; number one, homework. I had about half of the class that turned in their homework. I do not give you homework every day, but when I do it's a practice skill that needs to be done. It's something that you need: it's not just something for you to do. … And I expect you to do it. Now from now on, if you cannot do it, then you need to write me a note of explanation. And the only reason I'll tell you that you cannot do your homework is that you are dead—and you won't be here then. Because if you go to Grady [a local hospital with a reputation for long waits], I told you all the time … take your book with you and do it while you're sitting there. … We are not here to play, I'm getting you ready for middle school. … I am thoroughly disappointed with you. … Excuse me for hollering.[6]

Ware comments that what was remarkable when observing this classroom is that the students were "*absolutely quiet and looked at her with respect* while she spoke."[7] They did not indicate any anger or resentment, but rather their facial gestures suggested remorse. Ms. Willis was explicit about why these students in a remedial class needed to do homework; at the same time she acknowledged that students were not always in control of their lives (e.g., perhaps having to spend the evening in the hospital). However, she gave students ideas for ways to resolve issues that might arise and take control of unforeseeable eventualities. There were no excuses.

Ms. Willis would tell her students who could not read that they *would* read and that she would teach them. Poverty is not seen as an excuse for failure with warm demanders. Although they recognize the difficult circumstances of their students, they demand that they can and will rise above them.

Another teacher studied by Ware, Mrs. Carter, expressed similar beliefs. She refused to accept poverty as an excuse for lack of academic achievement. When a student didn't own a computer, she still had to finish a computer-based assignment. Mrs. Carter allowed the student to come early and/or stay after school, and she wrote a pass for her to use the computer during the homeroom period. The point is, there are no excuses.

I know of another warm demander with an excellent reputation for producing high achievement levels with her low-income students. This elementary teacher sympathized with her young charge who would fall asleep every day in reading class. Although she knew that the child's home life was in shambles, she told the child that, no matter what, she had to work to learn in school. In order to keep the child awake and alert, the teacher had her stand during reading instruction. There was no ridicule involved, only support and praise for her efforts. If the child wished to sleep at recess, she could.

Teachers who are warm demanders help students realize that they can achieve beyond anything they may have believed. One of my favorite stories about a warm demander comes from well-known motivational speaker Les Brown. After being abandoned as an infant by his young, single mother, who gave birth to him on a filthy floor in an unused warehouse in Liberty City, Miami, Brown and his twin brother were adopted by a single cafeteria worker. Because of his high energy and inability to focus, he was placed in an educable mentally retarded class in fifth grade. He says that because he was called slow, he lived up to the label. He languished in these classes until a chance encounter in his junior year in high school changed his life.

As he was waiting outside a classroom for a friend, the substitute teacher inside the class called out to him,

"Young man, go to the board and work this problem out for me."

"Well, I can't do that sir."

"Why?"

"I'm not one of your students, first of all."

"Go to the board and work it out anyhow."

"Well, I can't do that, sir."

"Look at me. Why not?"

"Sir, because I'm educable mentally retarded. I'm not supposed to be in here."

Brown says that as the students in the class erupted in laughter, the teacher, Mr. Leroy Washington, said, "Don't ever say that again. Someone's opinion of you does not have to become your reality."[8]

That comment was the turning point of Brown's life. Mr. Washington became his mentor. Brown followed Washington around, watched him, modeled his behavior, and wanted to be a great speaker like him. Brown believes that it was because of Mr. Washington's comment and his continued insistence that Brown would be what he believed he could be, that Brown became the remarkable success that he is today.

Brown spoke about Mr. Washington in an interview: "In his presence he made you feel, without uttering a word, that you had greatness within you. That man triggered something in me that reminds me of what Goethe said, 'Look at a man the way that he is and he only becomes worse, but look at him as if he were what he could be, then he becomes what he should be.'"[9]

Warm demanders are sometimes spoken of by their students as being "mean." For those teachers who master this pedagogy, their "meanness" is often spoken of with pride by their students, and often with a smile, "She so mean, she *makes* me learn."[10]

Tyrone Howard studied a teacher, Ms. Russell, who, although stern and self-identified as authoritarian, would always treat her students with respect. She referred to them as "Ms." or "Mr." and always explained why she chose to take various actions. Her students sometimes expressed discontent with her domineering ways of teaching, but most thought that the ends justified the means: "She's mean and she hollers a lot, but you learn. I know that I have learned a lot this year, especially in reading and math. And if you look at all of the kids who make the honor roll or honor society, they're mostly in her class, so I guess it's worth it."[11]

I have written elsewhere that we cannot assume that a raised voice carries the same meaning in all cultures. My great niece DeMya at five years old turned to me one day and said out of the blue, "When people's mamas yell at them, it just means they love them." Tyrone Howard found similar beliefs when he sought to get young students' responses to their teachers.

Jaylah, a fourth-grade student stated, "If you [a teacher] holler, it just means you care. But you can't holler for no reason at all. If we did something bad and she didn't holler, I would think that something's wrong, and maybe she [doesn't] care [any]more."[12]

My own caveat about interpreting the raised voices with which some teachers, usually African American, talk to children, is that it is important to listen to their words, not just their tone. Good teachers may be telling the children that they are "too smart" to be acting the way they are acting, or submitting the kind of work they are turning in (or not turning in). When a teacher expresses genuine emotion and a belief in a child's ability to do better, that is a message that many children are eager to hear, regardless of the medium.

Howard wrote of one teacher who became upset with one of her fourth-grade students because of the student's failure to complete a task. The teacher angrily told the student she was capable of better work. The student stood humbly without response. To an outsider this might have seemed harsh, but shortly after the teacher expressed her disappointment, she approached the girl, put her arm around her shoulders, and had a private conversation. The next day the teacher showed Howard a note she found on her desk in which the chastised student thanked the teacher for being so terrific and thanked her for her "toughness," because it "really got me back on track."[13]

I need to pause for an aside here, however. I want to make it clear that I am not suggesting that everyone should proceed to be mean to or yell at black children. That model typically works only when, as Mrs. Carter in Ladson-Billings's work suggests, your own cultural background is so similar that you also associate a raised voice with concern and caring. And there are certainly times when "yelling" by a teacher of whatever color is intended to belittle and degrade students. What I am saying is that real concern about students' not living up to their academic potential should be transmitted in the teacher's genuine mode of emotional expression. For many teachers, that mode could more likely be quietly expressed as disappointment. It could be expressed through humor. The point is to make sure the students know that the teacher believes they are capable and expects a lot of them.

It may be surprising to some that the students respond to such high expectations and strong demands. It is important to point out, however, that high expectations and strong demands are insufficient. The other necessary components are care and concern. When students believe that the teacher cares for them and is concerned about them, they will frequently rise to the expectations set. When students believe that teachers believe in their ability, when they see teachers willing to go the extra mile to meet their academic deficiencies, they are much more likely to try.

Recent empirical research has also supported the educational value of the "warm demander" model. In a study in Chicago that sought to determine what differentiated schools that improved from those that did not, Valerie Lee and colleagues found that schools that were the most successful maintained two elements. The first she calls "academic press," meaning that the content that students are to learn is made clear, expectations for academic learning are high, and students are held accountable for their performance and provided the assistance needed to achieve. This is the "demand" aspect of warm demanders. The second is termed "social support," meaning there are strong social relationships among students and adults in and out of school, the "warm" part of the warm demander equation. These relationships are imbued with a sense of trust, confidence, and psychological safety that allows students to take risks, admit errors, ask for help, and experience failure along the way to higher levels of learning. The greatest achievement occurred when both factors were present. When both existed, students made four times the yearly growth in math and three times the yearly growth in reading than when neither was present. If one existed without the other, the gains were much less impressive.[14] In schools with high academic press and low social support, the resulting performance of students was almost as low as if neither academic press nor social support was present. In other words, having high academic standards without providing the necessary social support essentially wiped out all potential gain. On the other hand, social support without academic press resulted in minimally higher performance than the inverse but still did not provide adequate academic growth.

Seminal scholar in multicultural education Geneva Gay has this to say about caring in the service of academic achievement:

> Teachers have to care so much about ethnically diverse students and their achievement that they accept nothing less than high-level success from them and work diligently to accomplish it. … This is a very different conception of caring than the often-cited notion of "gentle nurturing and altruistic concern" which can lead to benign neglect under the guise of letting students of color make their own way and move at their own pace.[15]

A part of this caring goes beyond academics. Warm demanders who are successful with children from poor families play other roles as well. They see themselves as advocates for the young people within a system that may not be so caring. They adopt many of the attributes of parents. They consider the whole child, not just his or her mind. They are concerned with the kind of people they are helping to mold—they focus on promoting character, honesty, responsibility, respect, creativity, and kindness.

I have seen miracles performed by many warm demanders over the years. Mr. Orlando Moss, a music teacher in Atlanta, for example, has been consistently able to mold young people with little or no musical background into a prize-winning orchestra—The William Still Sinfonia Orchestra. He demands hours of concentrated practice, much beyond the endurance (and attention span) of most adults. He tells the children, "I know you are tired, but I know you can play that measure with better tone. We will stay here all night if we need to." And the youngsters willingly put in more effort—even after their parents are grumbling and falling asleep in the bleachers. Of course, Mr. Moss will come in early or stay even later to help a young person who needs special attention.

I first met Mr. Moss when I brought my eight-year-old daughter to his orchestra class. He quickly said hello to me but directed intense attention to Maya. As he shook her hand, he looked deeply into her eyes and said, "Hello, prodigy." And that is how he greeted all of his new students—all black and Hispanic, most from low-income families.

I have seen the same warm demander pedagogy in teachers of all ethnicities. One of my daughter's young white high school teachers, Melissa Maggio, "read" my daughter's attitude of academic indifference correctly when she sat down with Maya for a long talk. Ms. Maggio finally broke through Maya's shell of nonchalance when she said, "You just don't think you're very smart, do you?" Through sudden tears, my child admitted the truth of that revelation. From then on, Ms. Maggio proceeded to prove to this child that she was indeed intelligent by pushing her relentlessly to excel.

It is the quality of relationship that allows a teacher's push for excellence. As I have previously written, many of our children of color don't learn *from* a teacher, as much as *for* a teacher. They don't want to disappoint a teacher who they feel believes in them. They may, especially if they are older, resist the teacher's pushing initially, but they are disappointed if the teacher gives up, stops pushing. One veteran high school teacher observed:

> Teaching anywhere today is hard work. It's especially hard in the cities because there are so many forces out there fighting against you. Teachers take the kids' resistance as not wanting to learn. But as soon as the teachers stop pushing, the students say that teachers didn't care because they would have kept on pushing them. The kids see it as a contest. Every day when I went into the classroom, I knew I had to be up to the challenge. I never understood, but I never gave up because I'm not a quitter.[16]

The caring, the persistence, the pushing—all these create trust. It is the trust that students place in these strong teachers that allows them to believe in themselves. It is the teachers' strength and commitment that give students the security to risk taking the chance to learn. These teachers do not shy away from a student challenge, but deal with issues when they arise. They seldom send a disruptive student to the office. They maintain their own discipline. They engage in conversations with disrupters outside of class to build the relationships that are the basis of cooperation. And these students know that if the teacher is strong enough to control them, then the teacher is strong enough to protect them.

Ware interviewed Mrs. Carter before the start of the school year and asked her about her disciplinary procedures:

> Sometimes I *mean-talk* them in varying degrees of severity. And sometimes when you do yell, it is not always right to yell. Sometimes you have to go back and say—"What was really going on with you when I yelled at you? I'm so sorry"—you know, but what was really happening? … Sometimes

with these kids, you have to [address the behavior] right then and there. ... They are accustomed to a certain response and if you don't give them that response they will read that as weakness. "She's weak; I can do this and she won't even say anything to me." But if you turn around and you get them right there, where it is, and it doesn't matter who's there or what's going on, you don't have that problem.[17]

Although I contend that teachers of all ethnicities are capable of successfully teaching African American children, most of the teachers I have described here are themselves African American. Their success is not because their skin color matches their students' but because they know the lives and *culture* of their students. Knowing students is a prerequisite for teaching them well. There are several ways to become knowledgeable about one's students—living in their community, spending a lot of time there, talking extensively with students and their parents. But one of the most effective and efficient means is learning from excellent teachers who already know the students and their culture. One young European American teacher I met at a conference told me that she and an African American teacher in her school began some tough discussions about race, culture, and teaching after an incident had left them both upset. Eventually, in order to attempt deeper understanding of the positions each adopted after the incident, they decided to spend time observing in each other's classrooms. The teacher who spoke to me at the conference said that those observations and discussions were so enlightening that they changed her teaching forever.

Similarly, African American Jennifer Obidah, then a young professor, and Karen Teel, a seasoned white high school teacher, found themselves arguing about issues of race and teaching when they tried to work together on a research project. Rather than move away from the conflict, they agreed to move deeper into exploring their differences. The result was a co-authored book titled *Because of the Kids*, which can serve as an example of what white teachers can learn from black educators.[18]

And so, to my students who are teachers, and to all teachers, I reiterate: Your work *does* matter more than you can imagine. Your students, particularly if they are low-income children of color, cannot succeed without you. You are their lifeline to a better future. If you put energy and expertise into your teaching, learn from those who know your students best, make strong demands, express care and concern, engage your students, and constantly ensure that your charges are capable of achieving, then you are creating for your students, as Professor Bill Trent once said about his own warm demander teachers, "a future we could not even imagine for ourselves."[19]

Notes

1. Gloria Ladson-Billings, "'Yes, but How Do We Do It?' Practicing Culturally Relevant Pedagogy," in *City Kids, City Schools*, ed. William Ayres, Gloria Ladson-Billings, Gregory Michie, and Peter Noguera (New York: New Press, 2008), 165.
2. Peter Mortimore and Pamela Sammons, "New Evidence of Effective Elementary Schools," *Educational Leadership* 45, no. 1 (September 1987): 4–8.
3. Robert J. Marzano, *What Works in Schools: Translating Research into Action* (Alexandria, VA: Association for Supervision and Curriculum Development, 2003).
4. Mike Schmoker, *Results Now* (Alexandria, VA: Association for Supervision and Curriculum Development, 2006), quoting K. Haycock and S. Huang, "Are Today's High School Graduates Ready?" *Thinking K–16* 5 (Winter 2001): 3–17.
5. Jacqueline Jordan Irvine and James Fraser, "Warm Demanders," *Education Week* 17 (May 13, 1998): 42, 56.
6. Franita Ware, "Warm Demander Pedagogy: Culturally Responsive Teaching That Supports a Culture of Achievement for African American Students," *Urban Education* 41 (July 2006): 436–37.
7. Ibid., 437.
8. Dennis Wholey, *The Miracle of Change* (New York: Simon & Schuster, 1987), 223.
9. Lilly Walters, *Secrets of Superstar Speakers* (New York: McGraw-Hill, 2000).
10. Lisa Delpit, *Other People's Children* (New York: The New Press, 2006), 37.
11 Tyrone C. Howard, "Telling Their Side of the Story: African-American Students' Perceptions of Culturally Relevant Teaching," *The Urban Review*, 33, no. 2, (2001): 139. (See also Tyrone Howard, "Powerful Pedagogy for African American Students: Conceptions of Culturally Relevant Pedagogy." *Urban Education*, 36, no. 2, (2001): 179–202.)
12. Howard, "Telling Their Side of the Story," 138.

13. Ibid., 138–39.

14. Valerie Lee et al., *Social Support, Academic Press, and Student Achievement: A View from the Middle Grades in Chicago* (Chicago: Consortium on Chicago School Research, October 1999). http://ccsr.uchicago.edu/publications/p0e01.pdf.

15. Geneva Gay, *Culturally Responsive Teaching: Theory, Research, and Practice* (New York: Teachers College Press, 2000), 109.

16. Michele Foster, *Black Teachers on Teaching* (New York: The New Press, 1997), 49.

17. Ware, "Warm Demander Pedagogy," 438.

18. Jennifer E. Obidah and Karen Manheim Teel, *Because of the Kids: Facing Racial Differences in Schools* (New York: Teachers College Press, 2001).

19. Lisa Delpit, *Other People's Children*, 158.

CHAPTER 19

In Defense of Public School Teachers in a Time of Crisis

Henry A. Giroux

The noble tradition that once viewed public school teaching as an important public service is in rapid decline in the United States. This democratic legacy, advanced by important scholars such as Jane Addams and John Dewey, valued teachers for providing a crucial educational foundation in the service of the greater social good. Educators were viewed as a valuable resource in teaching students how to take responsibility for their future, develop an unrelenting fidelity to justice, and hone their ability to discriminate between rigorous arguments and heavily charged opinions. Such an education focused on enabling young people to develop the values, skills, and knowledge required for them to enter adult life as critical citizens capable of questioning "common sense," official knowledge, public opinion, and the dominant media. Developing the conditions for students to be critical agents was viewed as central to the very process of teaching and learning and was part of the broader project of enabling students to both shape and expand democratic institutions. Since the 1980s, however, teachers have faced an unprecedented attack by those forces that view schools less as a public good than as a private right. Seldom accorded the well-deserved status of public intellectuals in the current educational climate, teachers remain the most important component in the learning process for students, while also serving as a moral compass to gauge how seriously a society invests in its youth and in the future. Yet teachers are now being deskilled, unceremoniously removed from the process of school governance, largely reduced to technicians, or subordinated to the authority of security guards. They are also being scapegoated by right-wing politicians who view them as the new "welfare queens" and their unions as a threat to the power of corporations and the values of a billionaire-sponsored market-driven educational movement that wants to transform schooling into a for-profit investment rather than a public good. Underlying these transformations are a number of forces eager to privatize schools, substitute vocational training for education, govern schools that serve poor white and minority students through the axis of crime, and reduce teaching and learning to reductive modes of testing and evaluation.

Indications of the poisonous transformation of both the role of the public school and the nature of teacher work abound. The passage of laws promoting high-stakes testing for students and the use of test scores to measure teacher quality have both limited teacher autonomy and undermined the possibility of critical teaching and visionary goals for student learning.[1] Teachers are no longer asked to think critically and be creative in the classroom. On the contrary, they are now forced to simply implement predetermined instructional procedures and standardized content at best and at worst put their imaginative powers on hold while using precious classroom time to teach students how to master the skill of test taking. Subject to what might be labeled as a form of "bare" or stripped-down pedagogy, teachers are removed from the processes of deliberation and reflection and reduced to implementing lockstep, time-on-task pedagogies that do great violence to students. Behind the rhetorical smokescreen justifying this kind of pedagogical practice, there is a separation of conception from execution that was originally hatched by bureaucrats and "experts" from mainly conservative foundations. Questions regarding how teachers motivate students, make knowledge meaningful in order to make it critical and transformative, work with parents and the larger community, or exercise the authority needed to become a constructive pedagogical force in the classroom and community are now sacrificed to the dictates of an instrumental rationality largely defined through the optic of measurable utility.

Little is said in this discourse about allocating more federal dollars for public schooling, replacing the aging infrastructures of schools, or increasing salaries so as to expand the pool of qualified teachers. Teachers are no longer praised for their public service. Despite the trust we impart to them in educating our children, we ignore and devalue the firewall they provide between a culture saturated in violence and idiocy and the radical imaginative possibilities of an educated mind and critical agent capable of transforming the economic, political, and racial injustices that surround us and bear down so heavily on public schools. Teachers are stripped of their worth and dignity by being forced to adopt an educational vision and philosophy that has little respect for the empowering possibilities of either knowledge or critical classroom practices. Put bluntly, knowledge that can't be measured or defined as a work-related skill is viewed as irrelevant, and teachers who refuse to implement a standardized curriculum that evaluates young people through "objective" measures of assessment are judged as incompetent. Any educator who believes that students should learn more than how to obey the rules, take tests, learn a work skill, or adopt without question the cruel and harsh market values that dominate society "will meet," as James Baldwin's "A Talk to Teachers" insists, "the most fantastic, the most brutal, and the most determined resistance."[2] And while the mythic character of education has always been at odds with its reality (as Baldwin notes in talking about the toxic education imposed on poor black children), the assault on public schooling in its current form truly suggests that "we are living through a very dangerous time."[3]

As education is reduced to a mindless infatuation with metrics and modes of testing, the space of public schooling increasingly enforces this deadening experience with disciplinary measures reminiscent of prison culture. Moreover, as the vocabulary and disciplinary structures of punishment replace education, a range of student behaviors are criminalized resulting in the implementation of harsh mandatory rules that push many students deeper into the juvenile or adult criminal justice systems.[4] With the rise of the governing through crime complex, war becomes a powerful mode of governance in schools, and one consequence is that teachers are increasingly removed from dealing with children as an important social investment and democratic symbol of the future. As the school is militarized, student behavior becomes an issue handled by either the police or security forces. Removed from the normative and pedagogical framing of classroom life, teachers no longer have the option to think outside of the box, to experiment, be poetic, or inspire joy in their students. They no longer have the freedom or power to teach, as W. E. B. Du Bois poetically states "to learn to communicate with the stars."[5]

Instead, school has become a form of dead time, designed to kill the imagination of both teachers and students. For years, teachers have offered advice to students, corrected their behavior, offered help in addressing their personal problems, and gone out of their way to understand the circumstances surrounding even the most serious of student infractions. But this role of teachers, as both caretakers and engaged intellectuals, has been severely restricted by the imposition of a stripped-down curriculum that actually disdains creative teacher work while relegating teachers to the status of clerks. Ignorance, fear, and learning how to take bubble tests are what now give schools a sense of mission and community. Needless to say, the consequences for both teachers and students have been deadly. Great ideas, modes of knowledge, disciplinary traditions, and honorable civic ideals are no longer engaged, debated, and offered up as a civilizing force for expanding the students' capacities as critical individuals and social agents. Knowledge is now instrumentalized, and the awe, magic, and insight it might provide are rendered banal as it is redefined through the mindless logic of quantification and measurement that now grips the culture of schooling and drives the larger matrix of efficiency, productivity, and consumerism shaping broader society. As testing becomes an end in itself, it both deadens the possibility of critical thinking and removes teachers from the possibility of exercising critical thought and producing imaginative pedagogical engagements. These modes of bare pedagogy that take their cues from a market-driven business culture treat teachers as fast-food, minimum wage workers and disdain the notion that public schools may be one of the few remaining places where students can learn how to deal with complicated ideas. As public schools become more business friendly, teachers are rendered more powerless and students more ignorant. In fact, in some public schools students are turning up for classes in which teachers are completely absent, replaced by computers offering online modes of education. As many as one million students are now finding themselves in classrooms where the only adult is a computer technician. In the Miami-Dade County Public Schools over 7,000 students are enrolled in classrooms with no teachers. The only answers to questions are provided by lab facilitators, who are simply technicians. Many students in Florida sign up for classes and are quite surprised when they find themselves in what are called virtual classrooms. Chris Kurchner, an English teacher at Coral Reef Senior High School in Miami, calls this approach to teaching "criminal" and insists that "They're standardizing in the worst possible way, which is evident in virtual classes."[6] The only value this approach to pedagogy seems to have is that it means school districts spend less on teachers and buildings.[7] Unfortunately, this approach to teaching is less about learning than about a deep-seated disdain for teachers, students, and critical modes of education. It is also an approach to teaching supported by billionaire reformer Bill Gates, who stands to make millions in profits selling online courses to schools.

One current example of the unprecedented attack being waged against teachers, meaningful knowledge, and critical pedagogy can be found in Senate Bill 6, which is being pushed by Florida legislators. Under this bill, the quality of teaching and the worth of a teacher are solely determined by student scores on standardized tests. Teacher pay would be dependent on such test scores, while the previous experience of a teacher would be deemed irrelevant. Moreover, advanced degrees and professional credentials now become meaningless in determining a teacher's salary. Professional experience and quality credentials are rendered inconsequential next to the hard reality of an empiricism that appears divorced from the daily challenges most teachers face. But there is more at stake in this proposed legislation than a regressive understanding of the role of teachers and the desire to eliminate the very conditions, places, and spaces that make good teaching possible. The real point of Bill 6 is both to weaken the autonomy and authority of teachers and to force the Florida teachers' union to accept merit pay. The bill also mandates that the power of local school boards be restricted and that new teachers be given probationary contracts for up to five years, then humiliated further by being given a contract to be renewed annually. Moreover, salaries are now excluded as a subject of collective bargaining, thereby degrading the purpose of schooling, teaching, and learning. This bill is not only harsh and cruel, but educationally reactionary. It is designed to turn public schools into political tools for corporate-dominated legislators, while simultaneously depriving students of any viable notion of teaching and learning. Bad for schools, teachers, students, and democracy, Bill 6 lacks any viable ethical and political understanding of how schools work, what role they should play in a democracy, and what the myriad forces are that are working to undermine both critical teaching and critical learning. Yet this degradation of teaching and the dumbing down of the curriculum do not capture what is perhaps the most detrimental effect of Bill 6:

namely, that it promotes modes of stratification that favor existing class, racial, and cultural hierarchies. David Price, in criticizing what he calls the tyranny of outcome-based, high-stakes testing, points to the forces at work in promoting such tests and how they are used politically. He writes:

> Today a lucrative industry of test designers (estimated to be worth between $700 million and one billion dollars a year) is followed by a kowtowing curriculum industry rolling across America like a fleet of ambulance chasers—pitching textbooks, worksheets and bric-a-brac designed to help districts more effectively "teach to the test."… Curricula are narrowed as underfunded districts struggle to meet external standards. The culture of American primary and secondary schools is increasingly dominated by the needs of standardized tests. These tests are no longer diagnostic aids helping teachers identify the status of individual students—they have become ends unto themselves, and as such they have taken on punitive roles in which test scores are assisting in the acceleration of stratification in America's primary and secondary education system.[8]

We need a new language for understanding public education as formative for democratic institutions and for the vital role that teachers play in such a project. When I wrote *Teachers as Intellectuals* in 1988, I argued that education should be viewed as a moral and political practice that always presupposes particular renditions of what constitutes legitimate knowledge, values, citizenship, modes of understanding, and views of the future. In other words, teaching is always directive in its attempt to shape students as particular agents and offer them a particular understanding of the present and the future. And while schools have a long history of simply attempting to reproduce the ideological contours of the existing society, they are capable of much more, and therein lies their danger and possibilities. At their worst, teachers have been viewed as merely gatekeepers. At best, they are one of the most valued professions we have in educating future generations in the discourse, values, and relations of democratic empowerment. Rather than being viewed as disinterested technicians, teachers should be viewed as engaged intellectuals. They should be supported in their efforts to construct the classroom conditions that provide the knowledge, skills, and culture of questioning that are necessary for students to participate in critical dialogue with the past, question authority, struggle with ongoing relations of power, and prepare themselves for what it means to be active and engaged citizens in the interrelated local, national, and global public spheres.

The need to define teachers as public intellectuals and schools as democratic public spheres is as applicable today as it was when I wrote *Teachers as Intellectuals*. Central to fostering a pedagogy that is open, discerning, and infused with a spirit of critical inquiry, rather than mandates, is the assumption that teachers should not only be critical intellectuals but also have some control over the conditions of their own pedagogical labor. Academic labor at its best flourishes when it enhances modes of individual and social agency and respects the time and conditions teachers need to prepare lessons, research, cooperate with each other, and engage valuable community resources. Put differently, teachers are the major resource for what it means to establish the conditions for education to be linked to critical learning rather than training, to embrace a vision of democratic possibility rather than a narrow instrumental notion of education, and to honor the specificity and diversity of children's lives rather than treat them as if such differences do not matter. Hence, teachers deserve the respect, autonomy, power, and dignity that such a task demands.

The basic premise here is that if public education is a crucial sphere for creating citizens equipped to exercise their freedoms and learn the competencies necessary to question the basic assumptions that govern democratic political life, then public school teachers must be allowed to shape the conditions that enable them to assume their responsibility as citizen-scholars. Being able to take critical positions, relate their work to larger social issues, offer multiple forms of literacies, and foster debate and dialogue about pressing social problems makes it possible for teachers to provide the conditions for students to conjure up the hope and belief that civic life matters. Students should see teachers modeling in the classroom the principle that they *can* make a difference in shaping society so as to expand its democratic possibilities for all groups. Of course, this is not merely a matter of changing the consciousness of teachers or the larger public or the ways in which teachers are educated. These are important considerations, but what must be embraced in this recognition of the value of public school teachers is that such an investment in young people is an issue of politics, ethics, and power, all of which must be viewed as part of a larger struggle to connect the crisis of schooling and teaching to the crisis of democracy itself.

Teachers all over America are now flanked on both sides by a number of anti-democratic tendencies. One side can be linked to a shadowy form of ruthless market fundamentalism that mistakes students for products and equates learning with the practice of conformity and disciplinary mindlessness. On the other side are those anti-intellectual and residual religious and political fundamentalists who view schooling as a threat to orthodoxy. Appealing to "tradition," they want to silence critical forms of pedagogy as well as eliminate those teachers who value thinking over conformity, teaching over training, and empowerment over deskilling. There is also the resurgent movement of Tea Party politicians in Wisconsin, Michigan, and Florida. The most notorious is the union-busting campaign being waged by Governor Walker who, under the guise of calls for austerity and deficit reductions, is attempting to pass legislation that would take away the collective bargaining rights of teachers. This represents not only an attack on teacher unions but on the very nature of public and higher education. As Chris Hayes pointed out in *The Nation*, "What is driving it is the ultimate aim of permanently scrapping the model of public education that has sustained this country for years. Teacher unions are the stewards of preserving public education, which is the core element of our civil life."[9] Paul Krugman is a bit more forceful, if not accurate, in arguing that Walker is not just trying to be fiscally responsible "by ending workers' ability to bargain"; he is trying, along with his backers, "to make Wisconsin—and eventually America—less of a functioning democracy and more of a third-world-style oligarchy."[10] What all of these anti-democratic tendencies share is a disregard for critical teaching, a disdain for the notion of teachers as critical and public intellectuals, and a deep hatred for those organizations that fight for such issues. To oppose these anti-democratic tendencies, we must take up the challenge of redefining and re-imagining teaching as a vital public service and schools as democratic public spheres. This means reminding teachers and everyone concerned about education of their responsibility to take ethical and risky positions and engage in practices currently at odds with both religious fundamentalism and the market-driven values that now dominate public schooling.

Today's educators face the daunting challenge of creating new discourses, pedagogies, and collective strategies that will offer students the hope and tools necessary to revive education as a political and ethical response to the demise of democratic public life. Such a challenge suggests struggling to keep alive those institutional spaces, forums, and public spheres that support and defend critical education and enable students to come to terms with their own power as individual and social agents. Students should learn to exercise civic courage and engage in community projects and research that are socially responsible. None of this will happen unless the American public refuses to allow schools and teachers to surrender what counts as knowledge, values, and skills to the highest bidder. In part, this requires pedagogical practices that connect language, culture, and identity to their deployment in larger physical and social spaces. Such pedagogical practices are based on the presupposition that it is not enough to teach students how to read the word and knowledge critically. They must also learn how to act on their beliefs, reflect on their role as engaged citizens, and intervene in the world as part of the obligation of what it means to be a socially responsible agent. As critical and public intellectuals, teachers must fight for the right to dream, conceptualize, and connect their visions to classroom practice. They must also learn to confront directly the threat from fundamentalisms of all varieties that seek to turn democracy into a mall, a sectarian church, or an adjunct of the emerging punishing state. What the concept of teachers as public intellectuals means, once again, is that the most important role of teachers involves both educating students to be critical thinkers and preparing them to be activists in the best sense of the term—that is, thoughtful and active citizens willing to fight for the economic, political, and social conditions and institutions that make democracy possible. The reason why the public in education has become so dangerous is that it associates teaching and learning with civic values, civic courage, and a respect for the common good—a position decidedly at odds with the unbridled individualism, privatized discourse, excessive competition, hyper-militarized masculinity, and corporate values that now drive educational policy and practice.

There are those critics who in tough economic times insist that providing students with anything other than work skills threatens their future viability in the job market. While I believe that public education should equip students with skills to enter the workplace, it should also educate them to contest workplace inequalities, imagine democratically organized forms of work, and identify and challenge those injustices that contradict and undercut the most fundamental principles of freedom, equality, and respect for all people who constitute the global public sphere. Public education is about much more than learning how to take a test, job preparation, or even critical consciousness raising; it is about imagining a more democratic society and a better future, one that does not simply replicate the present. In contrast to the cynicism and political withdrawal fostered by mainstream media culture, a critical education demands that its citizens be able to translate the interface of private considerations and public issues, recognize those anti-democratic forces that deny social, economic, and political justice, and give some thought to their experiences as a matter of anticipating and struggling for a more just world. In short, democratic rather than commercial values should be the primary concerns of both public education and the university. Professor Mark Slouka, an insightful cultural critic, takes on some of these issues in asking what may be the most important question at the heart of any proposed notion of educational reform, "What is the purpose of education in an aspiring democracy?" He writes:

> The questions are straightforward enough: What do we teach, and why? One might assume that in an aspiring democracy like ours the answers would be equally straightforward: We teach whatever contributes to the development of autonomous human beings; we teach, that is, in order to expand the census of knowledgeable, reasoning, independent-minded individuals both sufficiently familiar with the world outside themselves to lend their judgments compassion and breadth (and thereby contribute to the political life of the nation), and sufficiently skilled to find productive employment. In that order. Our primary function, in other words, is to teach people, not tasks; to participate in the complex and infinitely worthwhile labor of forming citizens, men and women capable of furthering what's best about us and forestalling what's worst. It is only secondarily—one might say incidentally—about producing workers.[11]

If the right-wing educational reforms now being championed by the Obama administration and many state governments continue unchallenged, America will become a society in which a highly trained, largely white elite continues to command the techno-information revolution while a vast, low-skilled majority of poor and minority workers is relegated to filling the McJobs proliferating in the service sector. The children of the rich and privileged will be educated in exclusive private schools, and the rest of the population, mostly middle-class, poor and non-white, will be offered bare forms of pedagogy suitable only for working in the dead-end, low-skill service sector of society, assuming that these jobs will even be available. Teachers will lose most of their rights, protections, and dignity and will be treated as clerks of the empire. And as more and more young people fail to graduate from high school, they will join the ranks of those disposable populations now filling up our prisons at a record pace.

In contrast to this poisonous vision, I strongly believe that genuine, critical education cannot be confused with job training. At the same time, public schools have to be viewed as institutions just as crucial to the security and safety of the country as national defense. If educators and others are to prevent the distinction between education and training from becoming blurred, it is crucial to challenge the ongoing corporatization of public schools, while upholding the promise of the modern social contract in which all youth—guaranteed the necessary protections and opportunities—are seen as a primary source of economic and moral investment and as symbolizing the hope for a democratic future. In short, those individuals and groups concerned about the promise of education need to reclaim their commitment to future generations by taking seriously the Protestant theologian Dietrich Bonhoeffer's belief that the ultimate test of morality for any democratic society resides in the condition of its children. If public education is to honor this ethical commitment, it will have to not only re-establish its obligation to young people but reclaim its role as a democratic public sphere and uphold its support for teachers.

Defending teachers as engaged intellectuals and public schools as democratic public spheres and a public good is not a call for any one ideology in the political spectrum to determine the future direction of public and university education. But at the same time, such a defense reflects a particular vision of the purpose and meaning of public and higher education and their crucial role in educating students to participate in an inclusive democracy. Teachers have a responsibility to engage critical pedagogy as an ethical referent and a call to action for educators, parents, students, and others to reclaim public education as a democratic public sphere—a place where teaching is not reduced to learning how to either master tests or acquire low-level job skills but flourishes as a safe space where reason, understanding, dialogue, and critical engagement are available to all faculty and students. Conceived as such, education becomes a site of ongoing struggle to preserve and extend the conditions in which judgment and freedom of action are informed by the democratic imperatives of equality, liberty, and justice. Teaching becomes another site of struggle to ratify and legitimate the role of teachers as critical and public intellectuals, despite attempts to undermine their autonomy. Viewing public schools as laboratories of democracy and teachers as critical intellectuals offers a new generation of educators an opportunity to understand education as a concrete reminder of the great struggle for democracy. This struggle entails an attempt to liberate humanity from the blind obedience to authority. Individual and social agency gain meaning primarily through the freedoms guaranteed by the public sphere, where the autonomy of individuals becomes meaningful under those conditions that ensure the workings of an autonomous society.

The current vicious assault on public school teachers is a reminder that the educational conditions that make democratic identities, values, and politics possible and effective have to be fought for more urgently at a time when democratic public spheres, public goods, and public spaces are under attack by market fanatics and other ideological fundamentalists. These enemies of democracy believe that corporations can solve all human problems or that dissent is comparable to aiding terrorists—positions that share the common denominator of disabling a substantive notion of ethics, politics, and democracy. The rhetoric of accountability, privatization, and standardization that now dominates both major political parties in the United States does more than deskill teachers, weaken teacher unions, dumb down the curriculum, punish students, and create a culture of ignorance. It also offers up a model for education that undermines it as a public good while disinvesting in a formative culture necessary to creating critical citizens. In this state of fragile democracy, the opportunity for students to learn how to govern and be critical citizens is at serious risk of being hijacked.

As James Baldwin reminds us, we live in dangerous times. Yet as educators, parents, activists, and workers, we can address the current assault on democracy by building local and global social movements that fight for the rights of teachers and students to teach and learn under conditions that foster the autonomy, resources, and respect necessary for successful classroom teaching. Democratic struggles cannot overemphasize the special responsibility of teachers as intellectuals to shatter the conventional wisdom and myths of those ideologies that would relegate educators to mere technicians or adjuncts of the corporation. As the late Pierre Bourdieu argued, the "power of the dominant order is not just economic, but intellectual—lying in the realm of beliefs," and it is precisely within the domain of ideas that a sense of utopian possibility can be restored to the public realm.[12] Teaching in this instance is not simply about critical thinking but also about social engagement—a crucial element of both learning and politics itself. More precisely, democracy necessitates quality teachers and critical pedagogical practices that provide a new ethic of freedom and a reassertion of collective responsibility as a central preoccupation of a vibrant democratic culture and society. Such a task, in part, suggests that any movement for social change needs to put education and the rights of students and teachers at the forefront of the struggle. Teachers are more crucial in the struggle for democracy than security guards and the criminal justice system. Students deserve more than to be trained to be ignorant and willing accomplices of the corporation and the state. Teachers represent a valued resource and are one of the few groups left that can educate students in ways that enable them to resist the collective insanity that now threatens this country. We need to take teachers seriously by giving them the autonomy, dignity, labor conditions, salaries, freedom, time, and support they deserve. The restoration, expansion, and protection of public school teaching as a public service may be the most important challenge Americans will face in the twenty-first century.

Notes

1. For a brilliant critique of high-stakes testing, see Sharon L. Nicholas and David Berliner, *Collateral Damage: How High-Stakes Testing Corrupts America's Schools* (Cambridge: Harvard Educational Press, 2007). David Berliner has also written a class defense of public education, see David Berliner and Bruce Biddle, *The Manufactured Crisis: Myths, Fraud, and the Attack on America's Public Schools* (New York: Basic Books, 1996).
2. James Baldwin, "A Talk to Teachers," *Saturday Review* (December 21, 1963). Online at: http://richgibson.com/talktoteachers.htm
3. Ibid.
4. I take this up in Henry A. Giroux, *Youth in a Suspect Society: Democracy or Disposability?* (Boulder: Paradigm, 2009).
5. Cited in Gayatri Chakravorty Spivak, "Changing Reflexes: Interview with Gayatri Chakravorty Spivak," *Works and Days*, 55/56: Vol. 28, 2010, p. 8.
6. Laura Herrera, "In Florida, Virtual Classrooms with No Teachers," *The New York Times* (January 17, 2011), p. A15.
7. Trip Gabriel, "More Pupils Are Learning Online, Fueling Debate on Quality," *The New York Times* (April 6, 2011), p. A1.
8. David H. Price, "Outcome-Based Tyranny: Teaching Compliance While Testing Like a State," *Anthropological Quarterly*, 76: 4 (Fall 2003), p. 718.
9. Chris Hayes, cited in Sara Jerving, "The Future of Public Education, as Much as Unions, Is at Stake in Wisconsin," *The Nation* (February 21, 2011). Online: http://www.thenation.com/blog/158754/future-public-education-much-unions-stake-wisconsin
10. Paul Krugman, "Wisconsin Power Play," *The New York Times* (February 20, 2001), p. A17.
11. Mark Slouka, "Dehumanized: When Math and Science Rule the School," *Harper's Magazine* (September 2009), pp. 33–34.
12. Pierre Bourdieu and Günter Grass, "The 'Progressive' Restoration: A Franco-German Dialogue," *New Left Review*, 14 (March–April 2003), p. 66.

CHAPTER 20

Starting Points

Assumptions and Alternatives

Patricia H. Hinchey

I think that it is a profoundly democratic thing to begin to learn to ask questions. —Antonio Faundez

My dad's been dead a long time, but one piece of his advice still kicks in every time I get behind the wheel of a car: *Pat, never trust a blinker.* I never do. As a result (and unlike my husband), I have never found myself in the path of a car coming straight at me after failing to make the turn promised by its cheerily flashing—and lying—blinker. I'm still acting on Dad's instructions, though I don't generally get into the car chanting *Don't trust a blinker ... Don't trust a blinker. ...* Long ago I translated his principle into what is now my automatic behavior.

All of us move through every day exhibiting countless similar behaviors, habits we acquired from someone, somewhere, that now seem simply the best or right way to do something. Driving easily offers many more examples: Maybe we never exceed the speed limit, or routinely exceed it by five miles per hour. Maybe we never let the gas gauge fall below a half or quarter tank, or maybe we routinely wait until it falls to the E line.

What's interesting and important to notice about these habits—and what also has important implications for educators, as I'll explain shortly—is that they resulted from someone or other, at some time or other, making some assumptions, or holding some beliefs, or reaching some conclusions, about the nature of the driving experience. My dad assumed, for example, that other drivers are not trustworthy, and so he always drove defensively. Many people assume that all laws should be obeyed, to the letter, at all times, whether they deal with driving or stealing, and so they automatically obey the speed limit just as they automatically return lost wallets and tell the whole truth on their income tax returns. Other drivers assume that the police ticket only drivers exceeding the speed limit by more than five miles an hour, and so they speed by just that much. Still others assume that all automakers set the fuel gauge to register E long before a tank is actually perilously close to empty.

The point here is simple but essential: Our lives overflow with countless daily acts that are essentially habits, actions we take without thinking about them. We no longer question whether the assumptions underpinning them are sound—if, in fact, we ever did think about those assumptions when authorities like parents were schooling us in certain behaviors (like not trusting a blinker—certainly I never asked my dad for his evidence that other drivers were untrustworthy). And yet, unexamined assumptions are critical; they shape our behavior, and our behavior has consequences for ourselves and others.

For example, a driver who assumes that the speed limit is really five miles over the posted limit may be headed for an expensive encounter with a police officer; a driver who believes the E on a gas gauge is meaningless may be in for a long walk. While we generally choose actions we believe are safe or productive, what we actually experience depends on whether the assumptions behind our actions are sound. My dad, an authority figure I never doubted, was usually right—but that's just my good luck. Other authority figures, including adults who insist that it's safe to speed moderately or that a car will never stop running until the gauge registers below empty, are often wrong.

It's essential, then, to take a conscious look at our assumptions because they largely determine the effectiveness of our strategies and the quality of our results: sound assumptions usually lead us to effective actions and satisfying results, whereas unsound ones more often prompt unwise actions and unhappy consequences. Driving habits are a simplistic example, but the principle is a sound one that applies to far more important examples. Most especially, assumptions about schools, students, teaching, and learning all influence teachers' actions—and teachers' actions have enormous consequences not only for the students whose future they shape, but also for the American society those students will eventually join as workers and democratic citizens. Most of us can afford a speeding ticket, but this text will argue that we can no longer afford schools peopled by educators who act without being conscious of their assumptions, their choices, and the likely consequences.

Why Theory and Philosophy Matter: From the Abstract to the Practical

Having themselves been students for at least eight to twelve years, and possibly sixteen years or more, most people have countless ideas about what constitutes the right or best things for teachers, students, and parents to do: Teachers should talk, and students should listen. Teachers should assign homework, and students should do it. Teachers should give tests and assign grades, and parents should accept the grades as good indicators of what a child is or is not learning. Teachers should tell parents what their children need to do, and parents should impose the teacher's strategies on their children.

Precisely because these routines have been part of American public education for so long, teachers might be hard pressed to explain the assumptions underpinning them, even though they've probably completed several courses on teaching and learning. It is not difficult, however, to discredit many assumptions once they are exposed. For example, once I was working with a group of student teachers who complained vehemently that their students would not do homework. In response, I asked why they were assigning homework—and they were, to a person, baffled by the question. *What do you mean?* they asked. *We have to give homework.* When I asked why again, the best they could come up with was *Because that's what teachers do* (Hinchey 1992).

As my own research has indicated, however, many widespread but unconscious assumptions about the need to assign homework can be identified: *assigning homework ensures that students get essential practice*, for example, or *assigning homework is an effective way to keep students, who have too much time on their hands, out of trouble after school.* Once exposed, many such assumptions are easily refuted with readily available, abundant evidence to the contrary. For example: simply assigning homework does not mean students will benefit from doing it (Strauss 2002). Common homework assignments often force students to practice a skill they have long since mastered, as when senior high students are routinely required (as are third graders) to underline subjects and verbs or to circle adjectives in sentences; tasks like these are also time-wasters because they are not useful in life outside the classroom. Moreover, many students are already heavily scheduled with sports, church, work, parenting and other activities, so that their problem is too little discretionary time rather than too much. And, these examples merely scratch the surface of why there is often a great deal more sense in students' refusal to do nightly homework than in teachers' insistence on assigning it.

Despite the power of such faulty assumptions to shape classroom habits, and despite the frustration those ill-founded routines often produce, there are several reasons that practitioners rarely articulate and examine the unconscious ideas driving their practice. First, American schools have changed little in over a century (Cuban 1993), making for very long and very ingrained traditions. Second, teacher education courses focus most often not on the *whys* but on the *hows* of schooling: not on why to assign homework or to use multiple choice tests, but on how much homework to assign and on how to word a distractor on an exam. And, the *hows* are usually presented as prescriptions from educational researchers who have tried to attain the institutional status of natural scientists by conducting research in pursuit of definitive findings about what is called "best practice." As a result, much of their work reaches teachers in the form of authoritative directives to be followed, not ideas to be examined. The teacher is not to probe Bloom's Taxonomy for weaknesses, but to be sure that questions on an exam go beyond recall to other levels of cognitive skill; the teacher is not to question limitations of the Skinnerian principle of positive reinforcement, but to provide stickers to students who have spelled every word correctly.

And finally, even if teacher educators were inclined to ask students to examine the theory and assumptions underpinning practice (as they often are not), experience tells me that it is exceedingly difficult to get students to take theory and philosophy seriously (Hinchey 1992). As they approach the terrifying prospect of being alone in a classroom with thirty unpredictable young people, education students themselves generally demand recipes for what to do and scorn abstractions offered for thoughtful reflection.

The result is, naturally, a lot of people going through motions they do not fully understand and have never consciously chosen, a situation unlikely to produce results matching even the best and most earnest of good intentions. It is this situation that provides the impetus for this book, which asks readers to take time now, wherever they may be in their careers, to think through a variety of educational ideas that have startlingly different implications for classroom action. Our assumptions, beliefs, theories, and philosophies about schools and learning have a direct impact on how we conduct ourselves in classrooms, consciously or not; every action we take reflects some particular line of thinking and eliminates another at the same time. If we assume we have to assign homework, for example, then we won't have classrooms without it, whether it's effective or not.

Developing a Personal Stance

This being the case, I suggest that all educators need to start thinking much more consciously about classroom routines they've accepted as desirable or necessary without scrutinizing them, simply because they constitute "what teachers do." Given that assumptions produce behaviors and behaviors have consequences, educators need to make informed choices for themselves. Instead of passively accepting classroom advice and practices as revered hand-me-downs from teachers who have come before, or routinely assuming that distant experts like Bloom and Skinner always know better than a parent what a particular child may need, teachers need to think for themselves in terms of what to believe about, what to offer, and how to treat the children who actually populate their classrooms.

This text offers readers an opportunity to identify their own assumptions, to explore alternatives, and to make conscious choices about their own practice—although it does so in a context that unabashedly endorses the choices of the critical educator. Despite the philosophical orientation of this work, however, the choice of where to stand ultimately will be the reader's own. Perhaps even more important than which stance a reader chooses is the act of consciously choosing a stance, rather than mindlessly defaulting to one out of habit.

A first step toward careful reflection and choice is recognizing that consciously or not, anyone who has ideas about what schools "should" be or do is already aligned with one paradigm of education or another. Accordingly, the balance of this chapter will sketch two competing paradigms, providing a context for readers to begin reflecting on their own past and future alliances. Identifying an existing alliance is only a preliminary step, however. To begin evaluating their initial inclination, readers will need to understand the assumptions that undergird it—and that means, in turn, that they need to understand how particular kinds of life experiences shape the thinking of teachers and students alike. Chapter Two, therefore, focuses on teacher experience and thinking, while Chapter Three focuses on the life experiences of students who often come from very different backgrounds, and so experience the world very differently, than their teachers. Taken together, these three introductory chapters are intended not only to help readers become aware of the nature and sources of their thinking, but also to help them expand their thinking about teachers and students different from themselves.

In addition to better understanding and expanding their own thinking, readers working to choose consciously between paradigms need an in-depth understanding of how their objectives and consequences differ. Therefore, Chapters Four and Five offer a detailed look at the rhetoric and results of dominant educational rhetoric and policy, while Chapter Six offers a more detailed look at elements of the critical alternative sketched below. These last chapters will make clear that the choices teachers make between paradigms not only dictate very different behaviors on their part, but also promise dramatically different consequences for students as well as for the future of American democracy. For those who begin identifying themselves as critical educators, an appendix listing resources and allies provides an immediate bridge to next steps in developing a personal critical practice (or *praxis*—action based on conscious reflection).

Following below, then, are preliminary overviews of deeply rooted historical assumptions embedded in contemporary American educational practice as well as of critical theorists' starkly contrasting vision. Both sketches are necessarily oversimplified, intended to provide only a skeletal framework for the chapters that follow.

Historical Possibilities: Traditional Goals

The influence of historical thinking on contemporary education is strong, as recent legislation illustrates. As the twenty-first century opened, politicians of every persuasion took every opportunity to echo widespread voter dissatisfaction with public schools (Robelen 2000), and over time, standards and standardized testing emerged as popular responses to perceived problems with student achievement. That President George Bush succeeded in promoting legislation forcing each state to implement statewide testing (Robelen 2001) suggests that many people see little problem with the task of identifying what students should learn and then assessing their learning through standardized tests. Generally, the thinking behind such testing seems to be *We pretty much know what students need to know, and we know how to find out if they've learned it; we just need accountability to keep teachers and students on task in classrooms.* As is common in much public discourse, the assumptions behind this assertion are unarticulated (and unsupported).

However, any assertion about what students should learn in schools depends ultimately on the answers to other questions: *What, exactly, are schools for?* That is, what are they supposed to accomplish? For example, a school whose primary purpose is to prepare students for jobs immediately after graduation, as technical schools do, would define "what students need to know" very differently from a school whose primary purpose is to prepare them for application to Ivy League universities, for example, as

Stuyvesant High School in New York City does. As this example demonstrates, there is (or should be) a direct link between a school's goals, or what it intends for students to be able to do or be, and its curriculum, or what information and practice students need to realize the school's goals.

The fact that politicians have imposed statewide testing despite the obvious diversity of individual public schools (where a single district may house separate vocational and academic high schools, or may have a concentration of English-speaking students in one elementary school and Spanish-speaking students in another) indicates an enormous assumption on their part: *however different individual schools and students may be, we can expect thousands of American schools to share some inherent crucial goal or goals that can be met if all students and teachers are forced to focus on a single core of information and skills.* What kind of goals could be so critical and so widespread as to justify statewide testing? What curriculum is likely to ensure that those goals are realized? The answers lie in historical conceptions of the purposes of public schools and traditional notions of curriculum.

Many people have heard the United States described, as it so often is, as a melting pot, but few are likely to have thought much about what that phrase signifies: gathering together a diverse group of individuals, applying a process intended to blend the individuals into one mass, and eventually producing a homogeneous standard product. Historically, and for clear political purposes, public schools have been responsible for the process of transforming individual students from a wide variety of backgrounds into some ideal *American*.

While the United States has always prided itself on welcoming immigrants, it has also historically preferred that immigrants be white, Anglo-Saxon and Protestant (WASP)—or, in the case of non-Protestants, Native Americans and other people of color, to immediately learn to look, sound, and behave as if they were WASPs. The country has never welcomed any cultural elements (language, for example) from those outside that mold, because the Founding Fathers placed all social, political and economic power into white, male, Anglo-Saxon Protestant hands. Not surprisingly, those hands have historically kept a firm grip on their power. In fact, the white, male elite specifically looked to the first government-sponsored schools, common schools, to ensure that the social structure and values they endorsed remained dominant. As increasing tensions developed between the Anglo-Saxon community and between immigrant Irish, enslaved and free African Americans, and Native Americans, there was growing worry about the possibility of intermarriage and contamination of Anglo-Saxon blood and culture by "less civilized" others. The common school was intended to defend the theoretically superior Anglo culture from the influence of these others by educating the young as the Anglos thought desirable (Joel Spring 1997, 79). In this tradition, schools were expected to demonstrate to students the *American*—or right—way to think and act, erasing the traditions of their native cultures.

While the historical goal of producing a homogenous American citizen is certainly linked to bigotry, many offer a more defensible rationale for political purposes in schools, including efforts to promote an American identity among diverse student populations. For example, violence is common among disparate groups competing for survival in a new environment, and there are always such groups in American society; once they were Irish and Polish, and now they are perhaps Hmong or Palestinian, but immigrants are always with us. Many still believe that schools can reduce violence among ethnicities by encouraging immigrants to shed their old identities in favor of becoming *American*.

Moreover, no government can exist indefinitely without a loyal citizenry, and governments everywhere—in Japan and Germany and Saudi Arabia as well as the United States—have used schools to inculcate the young with political doctrine. All leaders, monarchists and socialists and democrats alike, want to stay in power and maintain political stability, and that is possible only if the young in every country grow up believing that their particular political system is the best possible political system. To that end, schools are expected to produce citizens who trust and support their government and its policies.

It is easy to see that such political purposes as cultivating a national identity and encouraging enthusiastic patriotism have produced many of the strongest traditions in American public schools. For example, teachers lead students daily in pledging allegiance to the flag, and every February profiles of national heroes George Washington and Abraham Lincoln mushroom in school windows nationwide. History books highlight military might and glory to stimulate pride, and simultaneously ignore the country's less glorious moments, like the genocide of Native Americans, to maintain trust in government authority. The curriculum becomes a list of sanitized and carefully selected facts that all Americans are supposed to know: *Who was the first president of the United States? When was the Declaration of Independence signed? What is the significance of December 7, 1941?* Political purposes, then, are always embedded in public schools and account to some degree for lawmakers' confidence that a one-size-fits-all curriculum and accountability system is feasible.

Closely related to the political goal of creating loyal citizens, and also essential to maintaining the country's status quo, is the economic goal of creating loyal capitalists. In the United States, democracy has become synonymous with capitalism, which schools are to promote as the American way. Essentially, schools are expected not only to extol the merits of capitalism, but also to produce hard workers and energetic consumers.

In practice, these goals shape the curriculum via exclusion: no criticism of capitalism is allowed in schools. Perhaps the strongest example of historic intolerance is an attack on a social studies textbook written by Harold Rugg, who was a professor at Columbia University when the controversy started in 1939.

Believing that schools should educate students to be intelligent and critical consumers, Rugg designed several lessons on those topics. His cautions to consumers inflamed the Advertising Federation of America, which issued a pamphlet titled "Facts You Should Know about Anti-Advertising Propaganda in School Textbooks." To support the charge that the textbook was anti-American (anti-capitalist) propaganda, the pamphlet cited an exchange between two men from Rugg's book in which one man dismissed advertising claims that a motor oil was superior, noting that when he personally tested the oil on copper, it proved corrosive (Spring 1996, 251). The combined efforts of the Federation, the Hearst newspapers, and B. C. Forbes himself reduced sales for Rugg's text from 289,000 in 1938 to 21,000 in 1944—and prompted the spectacle of the Binghamton, NY school board calling for the books to be burned (Spring 1996). The late 1990s demonstrated that the same spirit of censorship is functioning today, when school officials in Ridgewood, NJ, on three days' notice, canceled the performance of an original fourth-grade play critical of Nike and Disney's exploitation of Third World labor (Rana 1998).[1] As demonstrated here, critics of questionable business practices have been traditionally, and strenuously, excluded from American public schools.

Other elements of the economic agenda for schools are less explicit but nonetheless pervasive. If capitalism is to thrive, it must not only have workers, but it must have workers ready, willing, and able to do whatever work businesses need done. And, it needs a large pool of appropriately trained labor in order to keep wages down. When common schools were founded, the country was moving from an agrarian to an industrialized economy, and factories needed hordes of docile workers prepared to accept long hours of tedious labor. Rote and restrictive routines in the form of lining up, marching, and maintaining silence were considered beneficial training for the routines of factory life. Much of modern schooling comes from this tradition.

The authoritative teacher (like the factory supervisor) set tasks and determined how long the obedient students (like employees) worked at them. If students found every day filled with repetitive and boring labor, if their own interests and opinions were rigidly excluded from the classroom, and if they complained—well, what of it? Such was life, in schools and factories both, and students might as well get used to it. In fact, such *is* life in schools, which Bowles and Gintis have described—in their original 1976 text as well as subsequent editions through intervening decades—as "prepar[ing] people for adult work rules by socializing people to function well and without complaint in the hierarchical structure of the modern corporation" (1).

So pervasive and tenacious is the rhetoric exhorting students to prepare themselves for tedious and uninteresting work that many readers, no doubt, will hear their own parents and teachers echoed in common and apparently timeless injunctions: *Of course it's not fun, it's not supposed to be fun—learning is hard work. … I go to the office/plant/store and work and get paid in money; you go to school and work and get paid in grades. … The teacher isn't there to entertain you, s/he's there to teach you, so just do as you're told.* By the time students reached the factory (or the corporation), they were (or are) well-trained to quietly endure its tedious labor and authoritarianism.

The idea that schools should shape workers is also evident in the ubiquitous tracking system, where curricular options like the college preparatory track or the vocational track are designed to prepare students for the next step toward their work life, whatever it might be. Indeed, the schools' responsibility to prepare workers to fill labor needs of all kinds is so zealously embraced that it sometimes manifests itself even in the lowest grades of elementary school. I actually know a kindergarten teacher who, forced by administrative injunction in the late 1990s to design vocational education for five-year-olds, settled on having the children try on different hats. Of the school's many possible and historical purposes, preparing students for jobs is among the most entrenched. It would be no surprise, then, for both the twenty-first century lawmakers who mandated statewide testing and the state officials who designed those tests to simply take for granted that any state curriculum *will* include basic job training, however that might be defined.

Finally, schools have traditionally been expected to prepare students appropriately for social life in the democracy, adopting mainstream values that, again, keep daily life—and the status quo—humming: respect for authority, for example, and belief that hard work and education provide a sure route to success. The country needs citizens who can live together peacefully, who respect laws, who cause others no problems, and schools have a very long tradition of working to produce such citizens. According to Spring (1996), sociologist Edward Ross first conceived of education as serving a police function by inculcating values that had formerly been imposed by church and family; if schools could do a good enough job at what might be called character education, citizens would learn to police themselves (12). Schools, then, appeared to be potentially useful mechanisms for producing the kinds of people that certain elements of society deemed desirable.

Certain personal characteristics have always been hallmarks of Protestantism and what is thought of as "the American character": hard work, competitiveness, self-reliance, pursuit of wealth, respect for authority. While these may not appear on the official curriculum, much of school routine still certainly intends to instill these values—which, not coincidentally, also work to reinforce capitalism. If all it takes to succeed is hard work, for example, then anyone who is poor must be lazy—an idea that helps protect the economic status quo from criticism, despite some harsh social realities. In 1999, for example, nearly one-third of all children in the United States under age 18 were living in poverty (very conservatively defined), with nearly twelve percent of them experiencing moderate or severe hunger (Trends 2001).

The idea that schools can and should work to instill values that will keep American society healthy and happy explains why so many topics outside the traditional academic curriculum have been adopted by schools over the years: driver education, values clarification, sex education … any social imperative that arises. However, precisely because many social topics, especially as they relate to sex—AIDS, homosexuality, birth control—are highly controversial, state and local authorities face enormous challenges when specifying topics for official curricula. Often, such decisions are made in a heated, circus-like atmosphere that leaves communities deeply divided. This was the case in New York City when Chancellor Joseph Fernandez introduced the draft of his Rainbow Curriculum, a multicultural effort intended to alleviate ethnic strife, and lost not only the ensuing curricular battle but also his job. Fernandez was attacked and driven from office because a very few paragraphs in the plan's several hundred pages suggested that schools acknowledge homosexual families (Kelly 1993). Contemporary calls for a more liberal social agenda in schools have consistently been rabidly opposed by many who endorse the traditional, conservative mind-set reflected in such curricular classics as *The Scarlet Letter*.

These, then, are the essential historical purposes of schools: the political, which ask schools to indoctrinate patriotic citizens; the economic, which ask schools to train compliant, productive workers and acquisitive consumers; and the social, which ask schools to nurture hardworking, self-reliant, law-abiding community members. In every instance, the intention is to preserve the American status quo. These ideas—these assumptions—about what schools should accomplish are so ingrained that they function today as taken-for-granted and self-evident facts, sufficiently ingrained to allow lawmakers to confidently impose state curricula and testing.

How these traditional political, economic and social goals are embedded in contemporary educational rhetoric and reform schemes will be detailed in Chapters Four and Five. However, this abbreviated sketch provides enough background for the reader to appreciate the stark contrasts of the alternative, critical vision of goals for schools which follows.

An Alternative Agenda: Critical Goals

Like traditionalists, and for fairly obvious reasons, critical theorists are interested in maintaining a democratic political system. What is very different, however, is how this overarching purpose translates into specific educational goals. Whereas schools have historically focused only on producing a kind of autopilot patriotism *(My country, right or wrong—but it's always right)*, critical theory suggests that schools instead try to educate active and thoughtful citizens, interested in having a voice in government and prepared to do so intelligently. Rather than defining patriotism as unquestioning loyalty, the critical theorist assumes a position articulated by John Dewey decades ago that suggests democracy is best protected not by rabid flag-wavers but by an active and skeptical public:

> Only through constant watchfulness and criticism of public officials by citizens can a state be maintained in integrity and usefulness. (1927, 69)

From this perspective, nurturing a patriotic citizen means encouraging a young person to actively question, rather than blindly obey, authority. In this vision for schools, educators act on the belief that the survival of democracy depends not on "bloated calls to force students to say the pledge of allegiance," but instead on schools' ability to nurture active and engaged citizens who will "be informed, make decisions, and ... exercise control over the material and ideological forces" that shape their lives:

> [D]emocracy is not simply a lifeless tradition or disciplinary subject that is merely passed on from one generation to the next. ... [but something that] encourages all citizens to actively construct and share power over those institutions that govern their lives. (Giroux 1993, 12–13)

From this perspective, democracy is not a thing to revere, but a way of living.

In keeping with this definition of democracy as something to be lived rather than studied, a critical curriculum replaces the mindless parroting of patriotic rhetoric (which has taught countless children to pledge allegiance "to the republic of Richard Sands") with efforts to promote genuine civic understanding. Prominent educator Theodore Sizer both details such understanding and sees its potential for shaping a better United States when he argues that students must develop:

> a grasp of the basis for consensual democratic government, a respect for its processes, and acceptance of the restraints and obligations incumbent on a citizen. ... if all American citizens had mastered at the least the complex principles [in the Bill of Rights], this would be a more just society. (1985, 86)

That the society could, and should, be more just is an integral tenet of critical theory, for reasons that will become evident in the following paragraphs.

To help students grow into knowledgeable and engaged citizens, the focus in a critical classroom is not on memorization but on questioning, on examining existing conditions and proposals with a skeptical eye—on the "watchfulness and criticism" that Dewey advocated. Always, the critical educator encourages such questions as *Who made this decision, who devised this plan, based on what criteria? Who will gain what from it? Who will lose what?* From a critical perspective, such questioning is essential because the status quo always privileges one segment of society over another, and the goal of the critical theorist is to promote a more genuinely equitable society—a society that more closely resembles the promise of democratic rhetoric, equal opportunity to all. The critical educator strives to ensure that every group of young people, the disenfranchised as well as the privileged—poor as well as rich; black and red and yellow as well as white; gay as well as straight; female as well as male—enjoys equal opportunity to pursue a better future through education. To that end, critical questioning purposefully challenges the status quo by examining it through the lens of the less privileged.

In schools, such questioning leads to challenges to long-revered curricular assumptions and routines:

> Whose history and literature is taught and whose ignored? Which groups are included and which left out of the reading list or text? From whose point of view is the past and present examined? Which themes are emphasized and which not? Is the curriculum balanced and multicultural, giving equal attention to men, women, minorities, and nonelite groups, or is it traditionally male-oriented and Eurocentric? Do students read about Columbus from the point of view of the Arawak people he conquered or only from the point of view of the Europeans he led into conquest? Do science classes investigate the biochemistry of the students' lives, like the nutritional value of the school lunch or the potential toxins in the local air, water, and land, or do they only talk abstractly about photosynthesis? (Shor 1992, 14)

The curricular implications here are clear and in sharp contrast to tradition.

The traditional educator, wanting students to support the status quo, will continue to quote T.S. Eliot and to insist that students can spell photosynthesis, as teachers have done for decades. In contrast, the critical educator, wanting students to broaden their experience and thinking, will introduce the voices of Sojourner Truth or Lame Deer, since a commitment to non-mainstream groups makes multiculturalism essential. Additionally, in a critical classroom, research becomes not something done by distant authorities in white lab coats, but by students themselves. As Freire suggests, for example, students might research local living conditions:

> Why not, for example, take advantage of the students' experience of life in those parts of the city neglected by the authorities to discuss the problems of pollution in the rivers and the question of poverty and the risks to health from the rubbish heaps in such areas? Why are there no rubbish heaps in the heart of the rich areas of the city? (1998, 36)

Incorporating such changes is a difficult process, however, because it threatens many, teachers and students alike, who are privileged by the status quo.

Questions like those above, for example, are considered "'in bad taste,'" as Freire himself notes (1998, 36); they call attention to conditions that citizens living in clean and safe neighborhoods would rather not think about. And, including multicultural voices in the curriculum suggests that other cultures may well have valuable ideas to offer. Honoring other cultures, however, challenges the presumed superiority of Anglo-Saxon culture and implies that it's time for the mainstream to stop dismissing members of other cultures as uncivilized or savage. Some discomfort for those who currently enjoy a variety of privileges is inevitable, and so resistance is to be expected. Such resistance will be exacerbated as psychological discomfort is compounded by the prospect of economic change.

To suggest that business decisions should be based less on profitability and more on potential health and environmental concerns, for example, challenges the dominant assumption that profitability always matters most. The assumptions that critical educators challenge, like "We have the world's greatest culture" or "We *must* maximize profit" have been used by the powerful to their own advantage, often at significant material cost to the less powerful. For example, the unquestioned primacy of the bottom line allowed politicians in the 1980s to suggest that ketchup might count as a vegetable in school lunches, and even now, it allows American industries to continue puffing toxic gases into the air of industrial areas far removed from the sheltered enclaves of the wealthy and their children. The cigarette industry has profited from its blatant disregard of human health for decades, and the meat packing industry has similarly found it acceptable to maximize profit through unsafe practices that routinely not only injure but maim and kill employees (Killing Zone 2002). The critical educators' agenda directly challenges the conditions produced by exclusive focus on profitability and in doing so, it threatens to decrease not only the sense of cultural superiority that the privileged enjoy, but also the excessive profits that allow for their material well-being.

The rhetorical results of such challenges to existing privilege are not surprising. (The same is true of practical results, but they will be detailed in later chapters.) Despite their commitment to sustaining democracy, critical theorists are often charged with "politicizing" education and promoting unpatriotic practices. Critical theorists themselves, of course, consider such charges nonsense, and they generally answer with the words of Paulo Freire: "education *is* politics!" (Shor & Freire 1987, 46, emphasis added). That is, there is no way to keep politics out of schools. There is also no way to disentangle political goals from economic ones. When schools support the status quo, as they have for almost two centuries, they are in fact supporting the political and economic goals of supporting current distribution of wealth, prestige and power; when they challenge the status quo, they are in fact pursuing a more equitable distribution of wealth, prestige and power—"a different distribution of material force and well-being than that which satisfies those now in control" (Dewey 1927, 119). Far from being unpatriotic, critical educators intend to make the democracy healthier by uncovering societal inequities and biases, promoting social responsibility, and effecting a more just and equitable society. Critical educators insist on including in classrooms the very criticism of the status quo that traditionalists work so hard to exclude.

Inevitably, such criticisms threaten both assumptions and practices essential to maintaining existing privilege. Not only do they call into question the current emphasis on maximum profitability at any cost, as indicated above, but they also challenge the deeply ingrained assumption that schools should be devoted to job training—especially to training hordes of docile workers to the specifications of business and industry.

As Joel Spring notes, "It is not necessarily true that what is good for American business is good for American schools and students" (1996, 24). Among the several reasons Spring offers to support this assertion, the most important is that when schools offer a curriculum specifically designed to meet the needs of employers, the effect is to help business ensure that they'll keep wages as low as possible—good for business, perhaps, but not for the students who will be tomorrow's workers. Wages often depend on the supply of labor; obviously, the more workers trained in a particular skill available to employers, the lower wages employers need to pay. From the standpoint of business, the ideal situation for hiring is a large pool of applicants that will allow business to pay the lowest wages and select the best worker. For example, in the 1950s business put pressure on the schools to educate more scientists and engineers and by the late 1960s there was a surplus of scientists and engineers, causing low wages and unemployment.

Rather than assuming that businesses have the right to dictate to schools the kinds of workers that are needed, critical educators ask questions about what kinds of jobs businesses are trying to fill and whether the worker or the employer is most likely to benefit substantively from such job preparation at public expense. The reality is that most public schools, especially in poor and working class neighborhoods, serve business interests rather than the interests of their students, increasing profits for employers while doing little to help workers significantly better their lives. (Contemporary examples of this assertion are detailed in Chapters Four and Five.)

Helping businesses keep wages low not only disadvantages students economically, but it often harms them psychologically, even spiritually, as well. It's all very well and good to say that hard work and a high school diploma lead to success, but when a particular region and a high school diploma offer graduates only jobs paying minimum wage—a wage that does not even allow a single parent to pay for child care during work hours—young people stop believing traditional rhetoric, and they stop trusting teachers and other authority figures who promote it. This disillusionment partly explains why so many disadvantaged students leave schools without graduating, virtually ensuring they will never legally improve their lives and simultaneously increasing their alienation from mainstream society.

> Teenagers are a throwaway generation, and they resent it. It is not for nothing that no age group has a higher crime rate. … In spite of the rhetoric to the contrary, they are largely tracked by social class and gender. Too few adults believe that poor kids or minority kids can make it. Don't educate their minds, the conventional wisdom goes, because they aren't interested, and anyway, we do them a big service by preparing them for (semiskilled) jobs. (Sizer 1985, 220)

As Barbara Ehrenreich (2001) so richly demonstrates in *Nickel and Dimed*—an account of her efforts to exist while working at a variety of minimum wage jobs—graduating from high school, qualifying for and obtaining the kinds of jobs abundantly available to the poor may not ensure them even minimal housing. Treating students so shabbily, offering them such a bleak and limited future, educators should not be surprised when disadvantaged young people start considering school and schooling irrelevant. For such students, the dreams of democracy become the dreams of the privileged Other, a fantasy— a lie—that the poor cannot afford to sustain.

Such disillusionment, the critical theorist would argue, poses the most significant threat to democracy. When the economically and educationally disenfranchised stop believing that our much vaunted democracy offers them real hope, then the entire society is at risk. If the dream of democracy is a fraud, why continue to support the existing government? If educational and economic opportunity is a myth, why not turn to welfare and welfare fraud, to drug use, to drug sales, to rioting, to looting—to countless activities that undermine the fabric of society? If, in fact, the American dream is a lie, if the existing system does not offer equal opportunity to those who are not already in power, we should not be surprised when the disadvantaged use any means at their disposal to protest mainstream complicity in their disenfranchisement. After all: what do they have to lose?

Again, from a critical perspective the only hope for the future of the democracy is to encourage marginalized groups to develop the power and political will necessary to effect change in the existing systems that serve to keep them in their current places. This goal makes imperative an entirely new social agenda promoting a much wider range of values and viewpoints.

For example, rather than functioning as norms, docility and passivity become the enemies in a critical classroom, characteristics to be replaced with students' critical questioning and quest for self-determination. Rather than believing economic success comes only from hard work, and failure only from laziness, students must learn to ask what *besides* laziness might explain so many families living in poverty and the widening chasm between our wealthiest and poorest citizens. Rather than learning to *go along to get along* in a world not of their making, students must learn to decide for themselves what kind of future might best serve them, their families, and a country that promises equal opportunity to every constituent group.

The critical focus on questioning and self-determination inevitably produces a new social agenda for schools, because critical questioning applies to values as well as to everything else. Inevitably, such questioning challenges traditional values as solitary and unimpeachable criteria for decision-making. For example, as noted above, a willingness to work hard is considered an essential part of American character. However, in contemporary society the definition of a good person/worker as someone willing to work really, *really* hard has allowed many businesses to impose a "normal" work week of

60–80 hours on workers—to the enormous benefit not of the workers themselves, but of stockholders and other elite. "Mandatory overtime" has become routine in many industries, where workers have not had the option of a 40-hour work week in years. Two workers who each work 60 hours per week provide the company with an additional 40 hours of labor, allowing the company to hire one less person and to save the associated cost for benefits, always a major expense. Workers are forced into an unreasonable work schedule because it helps management save a great deal of money; any cost to the workers is considered unimportant next to the financial benefit to the company.

Currently, the idea that working hard means relinquishing an excessive amount of one's time is so widespread that even organizations beyond business have begun to capitalize on it. College football coaches have been skirting NCAA regulations intended to protect players' health and welfare by scheduling "voluntary" practices beyond the hours allowed. Officially, players don't have to attend, but they know that if they don't attend, they are likely to be punished by not playing. Like factory workers, players have accepted the need to give more of themselves than is reasonable. Only the related deaths of two Florida players within five months have brought such "voluntary" practices under public scrutiny (Berkow 2001).

While the current cultural definition of "hard work" has become a very profitable tool for authorities, abuses like those above prompt the critical theorist to question various facets of the contemporary veneration of "hard work": What is the cost of current practices to workers in terms of their health, personal interests, relationships, and family lives? By what right does any authority presume the right to such a vast proportion of anyone else's life? Do work contracts make clear how much of a worker's life will be required? Or, do unwritten and unspoken rules allow authorities to consume the lives of others and undermine their well-being even as they trumpet their commitment to the welfare of those under their control?

Such questions propose not that we discard such traditional values as hard work, but that we consciously examine how they are being defined and implemented. The critical theorist urges that we consider balancing them against other values that are equally legitimate: the need to work hard with the need to maintain a healthy and happy personal life; the need to compete with the need to cooperate; the need for business to make a profit with the need for business to behave ethically; the need to obey laws in a civilized society with the need to challenge and change unfair and unjust laws; the need to cultivate a common American identity with the need to ensure that that identity comfortably fits all of our many citizens. These kinds of balance, often fostered by examining the values paramount in other cultures (like the Native American emphasis on conservation) will open new possibilities much better calibrated to serve the needs of all American constituencies, not just a powerful few.

In this insistence that education serve the interests of the many rather than the few, the critical theorist offers a vision and an agenda far more democratic and patriotic than its privileged critics will ever admit.

The Why and How of Praxis

Unlike the contemporary politician, the critical theorist does not believe that a productive one-size-fits-all curriculum and assessment system is possible. Of course all students need to learn to read and write and calculate, but those processes are far less defined than many assume. What are students to read? (*The Scarlet Letter* and *Tale of Two Cities*? Chief Joseph's last speech? *The Joy Luck Club*? editorials in the local newspaper?) What are they to write? (answers to factual questions about the Globe Theatre? answers to textbook questions in the words of the text? original poetry? their own letters to the editor?). What are they to calculate (how soon two speeding trains will pass in the night? household budgets for a single parent earning minimum wage? the number of children who go to bed hungry based on national poverty percentages?)

Critical educators believe that all such curricular decisions must be based on classroom context. Many choices, of course, are between the content of a traditional curriculum and the content of a critical curriculum. But even within a critical classroom, there are no standard answers. For example, while it is equally important for both privileged and non-privileged students to understand current inequities, their different life experiences require different pedagogical approaches. Students in Oregon might gain a better understanding of their own lives by reading from the speeches of Chief Joseph, while students in California might reach the same goal more efficiently by reading works by Amy Tan or Richard Rodriguez. Classroom discussions informed by such works would also vary. While privileged students might ask themselves how their mainstream status protected them from challenges minority writers faced, marginalized groups might focus instead on the price of trying to remake themselves in the mainstream WASP image.

For this reason, and to the chagrin of many traditionally educated teachers, critical theorists and educators have no standard curriculum and pedagogy to offer. Instead of saying, as traditionalists so often do, "Here's the way to do *xyz* in the classroom," critical educators speak instead of *praxis:* action based upon reflection, the kind of reflection this text supports. No one can tell a critical educator what issue will be most compelling and which strategies most productive in his or her individual classroom. Instead, each teacher must develop individual praxis by first analyzing his or her own context and then designing appropriate, context-specific curricula and strategies.

Recently, good books that describe individual critical classrooms and pedagogies have become available (Shor & Pari 1999, for example). However, it is important for readers to understand that such books do not provide formulas for critical pedagogy. Instead, they tell the stories of how individual teachers arrived at praxis for their own classrooms. The value of these narratives is not in offering class plans for duplication, but in illustrating the path to praxis. This path is always individual, and it always begins with a classroom practitioner identifying a compelling issue in his or her own classroom. For J. Alleyne Johnson, for example, passing by the scene of a shooting led to a new awareness of how death pervades her students' lives and how difficult their lives are. Haunted by the incident, Johnson eventually acted by offering her students a voice in curriculum and they chose to develop a class newspaper. The final product contained several carefully crafted student pieces relevant to the relentless presence of death in their lives. Johnson ends the narrative not by suggesting that all other teachers rush out and begin assigning class newspapers, but instead by stressing the importance of praxis. Rather than trying to impose a single standard and curriculum on students, as the traditionalist educator insists, Johnson stresses the need to adapt classrooms to the specific students who people them, as critical educators urge:

> Whether we as teachers choose to address it or not, students' lives come with them to school, death and other aspects of students' realities come into our classrooms. Instead of wishing for other students, let us gear our work towards the students we have. (Shor & Pari 1999, 49)

Recipes simply are not possible in a critical classroom. Each teacher must undertake a conscious analysis of every element of an individual teaching situation and design action based on that analysis; that is to say, again, every teacher must develop a personal praxis.

The process, however, is fraught with both difficulty and danger, and so educators who choose a critical path must do so with eyes wide open, with the thorough understanding of practical consequences that this text seeks to nurture. Many teachers, for example, are privileged themselves, and they need first to develop an awareness of their own privilege, a difficult and threatening undertaking detailed in Chapter Two.

It's easy to say we all want the poor to have more—much harder to accept the reality of others having less as a result. It's easy to say we want to end discrimination—much harder to accept that the Koran and the Dhammapada merit places alongside the Bible. It's easy to say that students must learn to use their own voices—much harder to give up our own authority over curriculum to students.

And, the educator who implements critical pedagogy is likely to incur the resistance of privileged Others—colleagues, administrators, politicians and religious groups among them—at considerable professional risk. It's easy to say that the disapproval of others will be no big deal—much harder to maintain a new pedagogy when former friendly colleagues become lunchroom adversaries, or when administrators and parents turn hostile in a meeting challenging classroom activities.

However, readers who see the advantages of critical alternatives but nevertheless fear that their reform efforts might be futile or too costly need to remember this: accepting traditional practice without resistance also has a very high cost. Since education *is* politics, no choice is neutral, and all choices have consequences—and so there simply is no neutral ground for an educator to stand on. Teachers who just go along, who never think about the assumptions underpinning their practice, in effect drift with local current, and by their drifting they travel a route charted by others. Teachers committed to a higher standard of professionalism must instead thoughtfully choose a direction, must mindfully and consciously enter one of two metaphorical rivers Shor sketches:

> Two great rivers of reform are flowing in opposite directions across the immense landscapes of American education. One river flows from the top down and the other from the bottom up. The top-down river has been the voice of authority proposing conservative agendas that support inequality and traditional teaching; the bottom-up flow contains multicultural voices speaking for social justice and alternative methods. These two rivers represent different politics, different models for teaching and learning, and finally different visions of the people and society we should build through education. Will conservative agendas succeed in imposing more control, more rote learning, and more unequal funding on public education? Or will emerging groups and networks democratically remake school systems especially divided by race and class, from impoverished inner cities to affluent suburbs to depressed rural areas? (Shor & Pari 1999, vii)

While this may not be a choice that education students and today's educators bargained for when they decided to enter the profession, it is an inescapable choice nonetheless.

Note

1. Students were subsequently invited to perform the play at Broadway's Roundabout Theater and did so to a near-capacity crowd.

For Further Reading

Fine, M., & Weis, L. (2003). *Silenced voices and extraordinary conversations … Re-imagining schools*. New York: Teachers College Press.

Hinchey, P. (1998). *Finding freedom in the classroom: A practical introduction to critical theory*. New York: Peter Lang Publishing.

Kohn, A. (1999). Forward … into the past. *Rethinking Schools Online, 14*(1). Available at http://www.rethinkingschools.org.

Parker, W. (Ed.). (2002). *Education for democracy: Contexts, curricula, assessments*. Greenwich, CT: Information Age Publishing.

Spring, J. (2000). *The American School 1642–2000* (5th ed.). New York: McGraw-Hill.

References

Berkow, I. (2001, July 28). A deadly toll is haunting football [Electronic version]. *New York Times*, p. D1.

Bowles, S., & Gintis, H. (1976). *Schooling in capitalist America: Educational reform and the contradictions of economic life*. New York: Basic Books.

Cuban, L. (1993). *How teachers taught: Constancy and change in American classrooms, 1890–1990* (2nd ed.). New York: Teachers College Press.

Dewey, J. (1927). *The public and its problems* (1998 ed.). Athens, OH: Swallow Press.

Ehrenreich, B. (2001). *Nickel and dimed: On (not) getting by in boom-time America.* New York: Metropolitan Books.

Freire, P. (1998). *Pedagogy of freedom: Ethics, democracy and civic courage.* Lanham, MD: Rowman & Littlefield.

Giroux, H. A. (1993). *Living dangerously: Multiculturalism and the politics of difference.* New York: Peter Lang.

Hinchey, P. (1992). *Using the practical problems novice teachers articulate as routes to the theoretical thinking they dread* (Unpublished doctoral dissertation, Columbia University Teachers College, New York, 1992).

Kelly, D. (1993, July 6). Fernandez proud of his legacy to NYC schools [Electronic version]. *USA Today*, p. 06D.

The Killing Zone. (2002, February 23). [Electronic version]. *The Guardian*, Manchester (UK), p. 26.

Rana, J. (1998, October). Justice, Do It. *Kids Can Make a Difference Newsletter.* Retrieved August 4, 2003, from http://www.kidscanmakeadifference.org/Newsletter/n1098c.htm

Robelen, E. (2000, October 11). Political ads turn spotlight on education issues [Electronic version]. *Education Week*, 1, 32–33.

Robelen, E. (2001, December 31). House overwhelmingly passes sweeping reform bill. Retrieved July 11, 2003, from http://www.edweek.com/ew/ewstory.cfm?slug=15esea_web2.h21&keywords=Robelen%20and%20reform%20bill

Shor, I. (1992). *Empowering education: Critical teaching for social change.* Chicago: University of Chicago Press.

Shor, I., & Freire, P. (1987). *A pedagogy for liberation: Dialogues on transforming education.* South Hadley, MA: Bergin & Garvey.

Shor, I., & Pari, C. (1999). *Education is politics: Critical teaching across differences, K–12.* Portsmouth, NH: Boynton/Cook.

Sizer, T. R. (1985). *Horace's compromise: The dilemma of the American high school.* Boston: Houghton Mifflin.

Spring, J. (1996). *American education* (7th ed.). New York: McGraw-Hill.

Spring, J. (1997). *The American school 1642–1996* (4th ed.). New York: McGraw-Hill.

Strauss, V. (2002, March 19). An assignment to rethink the idea of homework; More parents are questioning whether there aren't better ways to help in their kids' education [Electronic version]. *The Los Angeles Times*, p. E2.

Trends in the well-being of America's children & youth 2001. (2001). Washington, DC: Department of Health and Human Services.

CHAPTER 21

But That's Just Good Teaching! The Case for Culturally Relevant Pedagogy

Gloria Ladson-Billings

FOR THE PAST 6 YEARS I have been engaged in research with excellent teachers of African American students (see, for example, Ladson-Billings, 1990, 1992b, 1992c, 1994). Given the dismal academic performance of many African American students (The College Board, 1985), I am not surprised that various administrators, teachers, and teacher educators have asked me to share and discuss my findings so that they might incorporate them in their work. One usual response to what I share is the comment around which I have based this article, "But, that's just good teaching!" Instead of some "magic bullet" or intricate formula and steps for instruction, some members of my audience are shocked to hear what seems to them like some rather routine teaching strategies that are a part of good teaching. My response is to affirm that, indeed, I am describing good teaching, and to question why so little of it seems to be occurring in the classrooms populated by African American students.

The pedagogical excellence I have studied is good teaching, but it is much more than that. This article is an attempt to describe a pedagogy I have come to identify as "culturally relevant" (Ladson-Billings, 1992a) and to argue for its centrality in the academic success of African American and other children who have not been well served by our nation's public schools. First, I provide some background information about other attempts to look at linkages between school and culture. Next, I discuss the theoretical grounding of culturally relevant teaching in the context of a 3-year study of successful teachers of African American students. I conclude this discussion with further examples of this pedagogy in action.

Linking Schooling and Culture

Native American educator Cornel Pewewardy (1993) asserts that one of the reasons Indian children experience difficulty in schools is that educators traditionally have attempted to insert culture into the education, instead of inserting education into the culture. This notion is, in all probability, true for many students who are not a part of the White, middle-class mainstream. For almost 15 years, anthropologists have looked at ways to develop a closer fit between students' home culture and the school. This work has had a variety of labels including "culturally appropriate" (Au & Jordan, 1981), "culturally congruent" (Mohatt & Erickson, 1981), "culturally responsive" (Cazden & Leggett, 1981; Erickson & Mohatt, 1982), and "culturally compatible" (Jordan, 1985; Vogt, Jordan, & Tharp, 1987). It has attempted to locate the problem of discontinuity between what students experience at home and what they experience at school in the speech and language interactions of teachers and students. These sociolinguists have suggested that if students' home language is incorporated into the classroom, students are more likely to experience academic success.

Villegas (1988), however, has argued that these micro-ethnographic studies fail to deal adequately with the macro social context in which student failure takes place. A concern I have voiced about studies situated in speech and language interactions is that, in general, few have considered the needs of African American students.[1]

Irvine (1990) dealt with the lack of what she termed "cultural synchronization" between teachers and African American students. Her analysis included the micro-level classroom interactions, the "midlevel" institutional context (i.e., school practices and policies such as tracking and disciplinary practices), and the macro-level societal context. More recently Perry's (1993) analysis has included the historical context of the African American's educational struggle. All of this work—micro through macro level—has contributed to my conception of culturally relevant pedagogy.

What Is Culturally Relevant Pedagogy?

In the current attempts to improve pedagogy, several scholars have advanced well-conceived conceptions of pedagogy. Notable among these scholars are Shulman (1987), whose work conceptualizes pedagogy as consisting of subject matter knowledge, pedagogical knowledge, and pedagogical content knowledge, and Berliner (1988), who doubts the ability of expert pedagogues to relate their expertise to novice practitioners. More recently, Bartolome (1994) has decried the search for the "right" teaching strategies and argued for a "humanizing pedagogy that respects and uses the reality, history, and perspectives of students as an integral part of educational practice" (p. 173).

I have defined culturally relevant teaching as a pedagogy of opposition (1992c) not unlike critical pedagogy but specifically committed to collective, not merely individual, empowerment. Culturally relevant pedagogy rests on three criteria or propositions: (a) Students must experience academic success; (b) students must develop and/or maintain cultural competence; and (c) students must develop a critical consciousness through which they challenge the status quo of the current social order.

3 criteria

Academic success

Despite the current social inequities and hostile classroom environments, students must develop their academic skills. The way those skills are developed may vary, but all students need literacy, numeracy, technological, social, and political skills in order to be active participants in a democracy. During the 1960s when African Americans were fighting for civil rights, one of the primary battlefronts was the classroom (Morris, 1984). Despite the federal government's failed attempts at adult literacy in the South, civil rights workers such as Septima Clark and Esau Jenkins (Brown, 1990) were able to teach successfully those same adults by ensuring that the students learned that which was most meaningful to them. This approach is similar to that advocated by noted critical pedagogue Paulo Freire (1970).

While much has been written about the need to improve the self-esteem of African American students (see, for example, Banks & Grambs, 1972; Branch & Newcombe, 1986; Crooks, 1970), at base students must demonstrate academic competence. This was a clear message given by the eight teachers who participated in my study.[2] All of the teachers demanded, reinforced, and produced academic excellence in their students. Thus, culturally relevant teaching requires that teachers attend to students' academic needs, not merely make them "feel good." The trick of culturally relevant teaching is to get students to "choose" academic excellence.

In one of the classrooms I studied, the teacher, Ann Lewis,[3] focused a great deal of positive attention on the African American boys (who were the numerical majority in her class). Lewis, a White woman, recognized that the African American boys possessed social power. Rather than allow that power to influence their peers in negative ways, Lewis challenged the boys to demonstrate academic power by drawing on issues and ideas they found meaningful. As the boys began to take on academic leadership, other students saw this as a positive trait and developed similar behaviors. Instead of entering into an antagonistic relationship with the boys, Lewis found ways to value their skills and abilities and channel them in academically important ways.

Cultural competence

Culturally relevant teaching requires that students maintain some cultural integrity as well as academic excellence. In their widely cited article, Fordham and Ogbu (1986) point to a phenomenon called "acting White," where African American students fear being ostracized by their peers for demonstrating interest in and succeeding in academic and other school related tasks. Other scholars (Hollins, 1994; King, 1994) have provided alternate explanations of this behavior.[4] They suggest that for too many African American students, the school remains an alien and hostile place. This hostility is manifest in the "styling" and "posturing" (Majors & Billson, 1992) that the school rejects. Thus, the African American student wearing a hat in class or baggy pants may be sanctioned for clothing choices rather than specific behaviors. School is perceived as a place where African American students cannot "be themselves."

Culturally relevant teachers utilize students' culture as a vehicle for learning. Patricia Hilliard's love of poetry was shared with her students through their own love of rap music. Hilliard is an African American woman who had taught in a variety of schools, both public and private for about 12 years. She came into teaching after having stayed at home for many years to care for her family. The mother of a teenaged son, Hilliard was familiar with the music that permeates African American youth culture. Instead of railing against the supposed evils of rap music, Hilliard allowed her second grade students to bring in samples of lyrics from what both she and the students determined to be non-offensive rap songs.[5] Students were encouraged to perform the songs and the teacher reproduced them on an overhead so that they could discuss literal and figurative meanings as well as technical aspects of poetry such as rhyme scheme, alliteration, and onomatopoeia.

Thus, while the students were comfortable using their music, the teacher used it as a bridge to school learning. Their understanding of poetry far exceeded what either the state department of education or the local school district required. Hilliard's work is an example of how academic achievement and cultural competence can be merged.

Another way teachers can support cultural competence was demonstrated by Gertrude Winston, a White woman who has taught school for 40 years.[6] Winston worked hard to involve parents in her classroom. She created an "artist or craftsperson-in-residence" program so that the students could both learn from each other's parents and affirm cultural knowledge. Winston developed a rapport with parents and invited them to come into the classroom for 1 or 2 hours at a time for a period of 2–4 days. The parents, in consultation with Winston, demonstrated skills upon which Winston later built.

For example, a parent who was known in the community for her delicious sweet potato pies did a 2-day residency in Winston's fifth grade classroom. On the first day, she taught a group of students[7] how to make the pie crust. Winston provided supplies for the pie baking and the students tried their hands at making the crusts. They placed them in the refrigerator overnight and made the filling the following day. The finished pies were served to the entire class.

The students who participated in the "seminar" were required to conduct additional research on various aspects of what they learned. Students from the pie baking seminar did reports on George Washington Carver and his sweet potato research, conducted taste tests, devised a marketing plan for selling pies, and researched the culinary arts to find out what kind of preparation they needed to become cooks and chefs. Everyone in Winston's class was required to write a detailed thank-you note to the artist/crafts person.

Other residencies were done by a carpenter, a former professional basketball player, a licensed practical nurse, and a church musician. All of Winston's guests were parents or relatives of her students. She did not "import" role models with whom the students did not have firsthand experience. She was deliberate, in reinforcing that the parents were a knowledgeable and capable resource. Her students came to understand the constructed nature of things such as "art," "excellence," and "knowledge." They also learned that what they had and where they came from was of value.

A third example of maintaining cultural competence was demonstrated by Ann Lewis, a White woman whom I have described as "culturally Black" (Ladson-Billings, 1992b, 1992c). In her sixth-grade classroom, Lewis encouraged the students to use their home language while they acquired the secondary discourse (Gee, 1989) of "standard" English. Thus, her students were permitted to express themselves in language (in speaking and writing) with which they were knowledgeable and comfortable. They were then required to "translate" to the standard form. By the end of the year, the students were not only facile at this "code-switching" (Smitherman, 1981) but could better use both languages.

Critical consciousness

Culturally relevant teaching does not imply that it is enough for students to choose academic excellence and remain culturally grounded if those skills and abilities represent only an individual achievement. Beyond those individual characteristics of academic achievement and cultural competence, students must develop a broader sociopolitical consciousness that allows them to critique the cultural norms, values, mores, and institutions that produce and maintain social inequities. If school is about preparing students for active citizenship, what better citizenship tool than the ability to critically analyze the society?

Freire brought forth the notion of "conscientization," which is "a process that invites learners to engage the world and others critically" (McLaren, 1989, 195). However, Freire's work in Brazil was not radically different from work that was being done in the southern United States (Chilcoat & Ligon, 1994) to educate and empower African Americans who were disenfranchised.

In the classrooms of culturally relevant teachers, students are expected to "engage the world and others critically." Rather than merely bemoan the fact that their textbooks were out of date, several of the teachers in the study, in conjunction with their students, critiqued the knowledge represented in the textbooks, and the system of inequitable funding that allowed middle-class students to have newer texts. They wrote letters to the editor of the local newspaper to inform the community of the situation. The teachers also brought in articles and papers that represented counter knowledge to help the students develop multiple perspectives on a variety of social and historical phenomena.

Another example of this kind of teaching was reported in a Dallas newspaper (Robinson, 1993). A group of African American middle school students were involved in what they termed "community problem solving" (see Tate, 1995). The kind of social action curriculum in which the students participated is similar to that advocated by scholars who argue that students need to be "centered" (Asante, 1991; Tate, 1994) or the *subjects* rather than the objects of study.

Culturally Relevant Teaching in Action

As previously mentioned, this article and its theoretical undergirding come from a 3-year study of successful teachers of African American students.

The teachers who participated in the study were initially selected by African American parents who believed them to be exceptional. Some of the parents' reasons for selecting the teachers were the enthusiasm their children showed in school and learning while in their classrooms, the consistent level of respect they received from the teachers, and their perception that the teachers understood the need for the students to operate in the dual worlds of their home community and the White community.

In addition to the parents' recommendations, I solicited principals' recommendations. Principals' reasons for recommending teachers were the low number of discipline referrals, the high attendance rates, and standardized test scores.[8] Teachers whose names appeared as both parents' and principals' recommendations were asked to participate in the study. Of the nine teachers' names who appeared on both lists, eight were willing to participate. Their participation required an in-depth ethnographic interview (Spradley, 1979), unannounced classroom visitations, videotaping of their teaching, and participation in a research collective with the other teachers in the study. This study was funded for 2 years. In a third year I did a follow-up study of two of the teachers to investigate their literacy teaching (Ladson-Billings, 1992b, 1992c).

Initially, as I observed the teachers I could not see patterns or similarities in their teaching. Some seemed very structured and regimented, using daily routines and activities. Others seemed more open or unstructured. Learning seemed to emerge from student initiation and suggestions. Still others seemed eclectic—very structured for certain activities and unstructured for others. It seemed to be a researcher's nightmare—no common threads to pull their practice together in order to relate it to others. The thought of their pedagogy as merely idiosyncratic, a product of their personalities and individual perspectives, left me both frustrated and dismayed. However, when I was able to go back over their interviews and later when we met together as a group to discuss their practice, I could see that in order to understand their practice it was necessary to go beyond the surface features of teaching "strategies" (Bartolome, 1994). The philosophical and ideological underpinnings of their practice, i.e., how they thought about themselves as teachers and how they thought about others (their students, the students' parents, and other community members), how they structured social relations within and outside of the classroom, and how they conceived of knowledge, revealed their similarities and points of congruence.[9]

All of the teachers identified strongly with teaching. They were not ashamed or embarrassed about their professions. Each had chosen to teach and, more importantly, had chosen to teach in this low-income, largely African American school district. The teachers saw themselves as a part of the community and teaching as a way to give back to the community. They encouraged their students to do the same. They believed their work was artistry, not a technical task that could be accomplished in a recipe-like fashion. Fundamental to their beliefs about teaching was that all of the students could and must succeed. Consequently, they saw their responsibility as working to guarantee the success of each student. The students who seemed furthest behind received plenty of individual attention and encouragement.

The teachers kept the relations between themselves and their students fluid and equitable. They encouraged the students to act as teachers, and they, themselves, often functioned as learners in the classroom. These fluid relationships extended beyond the classroom and into the community. Thus, it was common for the teachers to be seen attending community functions (e.g., churches, students' sports events) and using community services (e.g., beauty parlors, stores). The teachers attempted to create a bond with all of the students, rather than an idiosyncratic, individualistic connection that might foster an unhealthy competitiveness. This bond was nurtured by the teachers' insistence on creating a community of learners as a priority. They encouraged the students to learn collaboratively, teach each other, and be responsible for each other's learning.

As teachers in the same district, the teachers in this study were responsible for meeting the same state and local curriculum guidelines.[10] However, the way they met and challenged those guidelines helped to define them as culturally relevant teachers. For these teachers, knowledge is continuously re-created, recycled, and shared by the teachers and the students. Thus, they were not dependent on state curriculum frameworks or textbooks to decide what and how to teach.

For example, if the state curriculum framework called for teaching about the "age of exploration," they used this as an opportunity to examine conventional interpretations and introduce alternate ones. The content of the curriculum was always open to critical analysis.

The teachers exhibited a passion about what they were teaching—showing enthusiasm and vitality about what was being taught and learned. When students came to them with skill deficiencies, the teachers worked to help the students build bridges or scaffolding so that they could be proficient in the more challenging work they experienced in these classrooms.

For example, in Margaret Rossi's sixth-grade class, all of the students were expected to learn algebra. For those who did not know basic number facts, Rossi provided calculators. She believed that by using particular skills in context (e.g., multiplication and division in the context of solving equations), the students would become more proficient at those skills while acquiring new learning.

Implications for Further Study

I believe this work has implications for both the research and practice communities. For researchers, I suggest that this kind of study must be replicated again and again. We need to know much more about the practice of successful teachers for African American and other students who have been poorly served by our schools. We need to have an opportunity to explore alternate research paradigms that include the voices of parents and communities in non-exploitative ways.[11]

For practitioners, this research reinforces the fact that the place to find out about classroom practices is the naturalistic setting of the classroom and from the lived experiences of teachers. Teachers need not shy away from conducting their own research about their practice (Zeichner & Tabachnick, 1991). Their unique perspectives and personal investment in good practice must not be overlooked. For both groups-researchers and practitioners alike-this work is designed to challenge us to reconsider what we mean by "good" teaching, to look for it in some unlikely places, and to challenge those who suggest it cannot be made available to all children.

Notes

1. Some notable exceptions to this failure to consider achievement strategies for African American students are *Ways With Words* (Heath, 1983); "Fostering Early Literacy Through Parent Coaching" (Edwards, 1991); and "Achieving Equal Educational Outcomes for Black Children" (Hale-Benson, 1990).
2. I have written extensively about this study, its methodology, findings, and results elsewhere. For a full discussion of the study, see Ladson-Billings (1994).
3. All study participants' names are pseudonyms.
4. At the 1994 annual meeting of the American Educational Research Association, King and Hollins presented a symposium entitled, "The Burden of Acting White Revisited."
5. The teacher acknowledged the racism, misogyny, and explicit sexuality that is a part of the lyrics of some rap songs. Thus, the students were directed to use only those songs they felt they could "sing to their parents."
6. Winston retired after the first year of the study but continued to participate in the research collaborative throughout the study.
7. Because the residency is more than a demonstration and requires students to work intensely with the artist or craftsperson, students must sign up for a particular artist. The typical group size was 5–6 students.
8. Standardized test scores throughout this district were very low. However, the teachers in the study distinguished themselves because students in their classrooms consistently produced higher test scores than their grade level colleagues.
9. As I describe the teachers I do not mean to suggest that they had no individual personalities or practices. However, what I was looking for in this study were ways to describe the commonalties of their practice. Thus, while this discussion of culturally relevant teaching may appear to infer an essentialized notion of teaching practice, none is intended. Speaking in this categorical manner is a heuristic for research purposes.
10. The eight teachers were spread across four schools in the district and were subjected to the specific administrative styles of four different principals.

11. Two sessions at the 1994 annual meeting of the American Educational Research Association in New Orleans entitled, "Private Lives in Public Conversations: Ethics of Research Across Communities of Color," dealt with concerns for the ethical standards of research in non-White communities.

References

Asante, M.K. (1991). The Afrocentric idea in education. *Journal of Negro Education, 60,* 170–180.

Au, K., & Jordan, C. (1981). Teaching reading to Hawaiian children: Finding a culturally appropriate solution. In H. Trueba, G. Guthrie, & K. Au (Eds.), *Culture and the bilingual classroom: Studies in classroom ethnography* (pp. 69–86). Rowley, MA: Newbury House.

Banks, J., & Grambs, J. (Eds.). (1972). *Black self-concept: Implications for educational and social sciences,* New York: McGraw-Hill.

Bartolome, L. (1994) Beyond the methods fetish: Toward a humanizing pedagogy. *Harvard Educational Review, 64,* 173–194.

Berliner, D. (1988, October). Implications of studies of expertise in pedagogy for teacher education and evaluation. In *New directions for teacher assessment* (Invitational conference proceedings). New York: Educational Testing Service.

Branch, C., & Newcombe, N. (1986). Racial attitudes among young Black children as a function of parental attitudes: A longitudinal and cross-sectional study. *Child Development, 57,* 712–721.

Brown, C.S (Ed.). (1990). *Ready from within: A first person narrative.* Trenton, NJ: Africa World Press.

Cazden, C., & Leggett, E. (1981). Culturally responsive education: Recommendations for achieving Lau remedies. In H. Trueba, G. Guthrie, & K. Au (Eds.), *Culture and the bilingual classroom: Studies in classroom ethnography* (pp. 69–86). Rowley, MA: Newbury House.

Chilcoat, G.W., & Ligon, J.A. (1994). Developing democratic citizens: The Mississippi Freedom Schools as a model for social studies instruction. *Theory and Research in Social Education, 22,* 128–175.

College Board, The. (1985). *Equality and excellence: The educational status of Black Americans.* New York: Author.

Crooks, R. (1970). The effects of an interracial preschool program upon racial preference, knowledge of racial differences, and racial identification. *Journal of Social Issues, 26,* 137–148.

Edwards, P.A. (1991). Fostering early literacy through parent coaching. In E. Hiebert (Ed.), *Literacy for a diverse society: Perspectives, programs, and policies* (pp. 199–213). New York; Teachers College Press.

Erickson, F., & Mohan, C. (1982). Cultural organization and participation structures in two classrooms of Indian students. In G. Spindler (Ed.), *Doing the ethnography of schooling* (pp. 131–174). New York: Holt, Rinehart & Winston.

Fordham, S., & Ogbu, J. (1986). Black students' success: Coping with the burden of "acting White." *Urban Review, 18,* 1–31.

Freire, P. (1970). *Pedagogy of the oppressed.* New York: Herder & Herder.

Gee, J.P. (1989). Literacy, discourse, and linguistics: Introduction. *Journal of Education, 171,* 5–17.

Hale-Benson, J. (1990). Achieving equal educational outcomes for Black children. In A. Baron & E.E. Garcia (Eds.), *Children at risk: Poverty, minority status, and other issues in educational equity* (pp. 201–215). Washington, DC: National Association of School Psychologists.

Heath, S.B. (1983). *Ways with words.* Cambridge, UK: Cambridge University Press.

Hollins, E.R. (1994, April). *The burden of acting White revisited: Planning school success rather than explaining school failure.* Paper presented at the annual Meeting of the American Education Research Association, New Orleans.

Irvine, J.J. (1990). *Black students and school failure.* Westport, CT: Greenwood Press.

Jordan, C. (1985). Translating culture: From ethnographic information to educational program. *Anthropology and Education Quarterly, 16,* 105–123.

King, J. (1994). *The burden of acting White re-examined: Towards a critical genealogy of acting Black.* Paper presented at the annual meeting of the American Educational Research Association, New Orleans.

Ladson-Billings, G. (1990). Like lightning in a bottle: Attempting to capture the pedagogical excellence of successful teachers of Black students. *International Journal of Qualitative Studies in Education, 3,* 335–344.

Ladson-Billings, G. (1992a). Culturally relevant teaching: The key to making multicultural education work. In C.A. Grant (Ed.), *Research and multicultural education* (pp. 106–121). London: Falmer Press.

Ladson-Billings, G. (1992b). Liberatory consequences of literacy: A case of culturally relevant instruction for African-American students. *Journal of Negro Education, 61,* 378–391.

Ladson-Billings, G. (1992c). Reading between the lines and beyond the pages: A culturally relevant approach to literacy teaching. *Theory Into Practice, 31,* 312–320.

Ladson-Billings, G. (1994). *The dreamkeepers: Successful teaching for African-American students.* San Francisco: Jossey-Bass.

McLaren, P. (1989). *Life in schools.* White Plains, NY: Longman.

Majors, R., & Billson, J. (1992). *Cool pose: The dilemmas of Black manhood in America.* New York: Lexington Books.

Mohatt, G., & Erickson, F. (1981). Cultural differences in teaching styles in an Odawa school: A sociolinguistic approach. In H. Trueba, G. Guthrie, & K. Au (Eds.), *Culture and the bilingual classroom: Studies in classroom ethnography* (pp. 105–119), Rowley, MA: Newbury House.

Morris, A. (1984). *The origins of the civil rights movement: Black communities organizing for change.* New York: The Free Press.

Perry, T. (1993). *Toward a theory of African-American student achievement.* Report No. 16. Boston, MA: Center on Families, Communities, Schools and Children's Learning, Wheelock College.

Pewewardy, C. (1993). Culturally responsible pedagogy in action: An American Indian magnet school. In E. Hollins, I. King, & W. Hayman (Eds.), *Teaching diverse populations: Formulating a knowledge base* (pp. 77–92). Albany: State University of New York Press.

Robinson, R. (1993, Feb. 25). P.C. Anderson students try hand at problem-solving. *The Dallas Examiner,* pp. 1, 8.

Shulman, L. (1987). Knowledge and teaching: Foundations of the new reform. *Harvard Educational Review, 57,* 1–22.

Smitherman, G. (1981). *Black English and the education of Black children and youth.* Detroit: Center for Black Studies, Wayne State University.

Spradley, J. (1979). *The ethnographic interview.* New York: Holt, Rinehart & Winston.

Tate, W.E. (1994). Race, retrenchment, and reform of school mathematics. *Phi Delta Kappan, 75,* 477–484.

Villegas, A. (1988). School failure and cultural mismatch: Another view. *The Urban Review, 20,* 253–265.

Vogt, L., Jordan, C., & Tharp, R. (1987). Explaining school failure, producing school success: Two cases. *Anthropology and Education Quarterly, 18,* 276–286.

Zeichner, K.M., & Tabachnick, B.R. (1991). Reflections on reflective teaching. In B.R. Tabachnick & K.M. Zeichner (Eds.), *Inquiry-oriented practices in teacher education* (pp. 1–21). London: Falmer Press.

CHAPTER 22

Wrong Answer to the Wrong Question

Why We Need Critical Teacher Education, Not Standardization

Barbara Madeloni and Julie A. Gorlewski

Teacher education matters. Many future teachers enter preparation programs with deep-seated and unquestioned ideas about teaching and learning. At a moment when the children in our classrooms reflect the growing diversity of our population but our teaching force remains essentially white and middle class, we need our schools of education to ask pre-service teachers to wrestle with identity and race, to explore the historical/cultural contexts of school, and to frame teaching as the political work that it is. After all, teaching always asks us to imagine the kind of society we want to live in.

Teacher education (like K–12) is under attack by those seeking to exploit the public good and privatize education. Teacher educators find ourselves on the defensive, compelled to answer questions about efficacy and accountability that do not reflect our understandings of our work, questions that do not address the most pressing concerns of critical multicultural educators: making schools sites for social justice and advocating for education as liberation.

Into this moment comes edTPA, promoted as an answer to the perceived shortcomings of teacher education. EdTPA is a 40-plus-page document featuring Pearson's logo. The final product is submitted to a "calibrated scorer," whose evaluation reduces student work to a number. As such, it is the wrong answer to the question of how teacher education should be improved.

EdTPA supporters wrongly link the weaknesses of teacher education to a lack of national performance standards, when the real struggle for teacher education is to equip prospective teachers to serve their students and the larger society as public intellectuals and to enable them to teach powerfully about things that matter.

This is a difficult story to tell. Promoters of edTPA say that they are trying to protect and professionalize teaching and teacher education. Their response to attacks on our profession is to develop a system to measure and prove our worth through a standardized certification assessment. We understand the impulses to protect. However, we do not understand how, in the effort to support the profession, so many of its voices are left out. EdTPA has been imposed on teacher education—an imposition that pushes aside work that matters deeply to education scholars. It narrows the possibilities of teaching and learning, distracts us from critical multicultural education, is an invitation for corporate encroachment, and restricts academic freedom.

Narrowing Teaching and Learning

What does teaching look like? We recall moments from our own teaching: plays are performed, songs are sung, students silently write and pass their writing around in a circle, someone asks why there are no black students in the honors class, someone else asks why we are going to war against Iraq, someone gets angry and walks out, someone makes a joke and we can't stop laughing. What in these interactions represents quality teaching? For teachers, that question remains compelling and uncertain. Grounded in their knowledge of content, pedagogy, and relationships with learners, teachers maintain a questioning stance. Much of the work of educating new teachers involves providing the theoretical, practical, and personal support to embrace the ongoing uncertainty of teaching.

EdTPA devalues the uncertainties of teaching; instead it requires a performance of teaching as definitive—a performance that becomes central to the student teaching experience. When the precursor to the edTPA was piloted at her university, Barbara experienced profound changes in the student teaching seminar. Class time became consumed with questions about evidence for rubrics and scoring. The implicit message of edTPA, that teaching can be measured, was contrary to the developmental conversations Barbara and her students were having. Students were frustrated and confused by the contrast. At the end of the semester, one student wrote, "It seems you should either focus on the TPA or ignore it, but I don't see how we can do the TPA and have those other conversations."

Distracting from Social Justice Education

There is a growing disconnect between the primarily white, middle-class students who are becoming teachers and the mostly black and brown children who are entering K-12 schools. Teacher educators must demonstrate powerful and imaginative teaching practices and must help prospective teachers become creators of effective curriculum. But teaching strategies are not enough to resolve the work of the heart required for developing consciousness of racism, classism, and injustice. Strategies alone cannot foster the courage to combat oppression. We must spend time with students questioning the social context of schools, understanding our identities, negotiating painful psychological terrain, and exploring how school can reproduce inequities.

The student teachers with whom we work struggle to acknowledge racism and injustice. As a student recently wrote to Barbara, "[The course] opened my eyes and made me examine myself in ways that forever changed my perceptions of my social identity and challenged my understanding of what education is and means." Teacher educators are constantly balancing a commitment to critical consciousness and students' calls for practical solutions. Indeed, part of our work is to explore the ideologies and values hidden in the "practical" aspects of teaching by examining underlying assumptions about learning, motivation, and the purpose of schooling.

EdTPA invades this experience. Students tend to focus on meeting the requirements at the expense of realizing when they are making value-based ideological choices. As long as they follow the rubrics, which operate in the land of "value-free" language, they can score well. The edTPA's detailed instructions and rubrics communicate that teaching requires following rules and *can be* reduced to a number. Because edTPA is high-stakes, students lock in on it. Class time is taken over by anxious questions about evidence and scoring. What will be left out? Time to reflect on the emotional experience of teaching? Questions about how our identities impact how we see students and they see us? Considering connections between classroom "management" and the school-to-prison pipeline?

One of the undergraduate students in Julie's Introduction to Curriculum and Assessment course, which is taken a year prior to student teaching, came to her with a problem. Visibly distressed, he told Julie that the teacher to whom he had been assigned for fieldwork had invited him to student teach with her. Because he had tremendous respect and admiration for this teacher, he was thrilled. But he was reluctant to accept her offer—he was apprehensive about completing the edTPA in this setting. He had forged relationships with the young people in this urban school populated with many challenging students, but anticipating the judgment of an "objective" distant scorer—one who might not understand why the classroom was not filled with compliant, well-behaved learners—made him hesitate to accept the invitation. The edTPA has already intruded on the relationship between this candidate and his future students.

Student teachers describe edTPA as a constraint on meaningful reflection. Celia Oyler, professor of education at Teachers College, wrote to us recently that a meeting with students who had piloted the edTPA "was the most wrenching, heartbreaking hour of my professional career as a teacher educator." The Teachers College student teachers, who understood they were part of a pilot and that the assessment was not high-stakes for them, still felt that they had "to fabricate and backtrack and lie to make their teaching fit into a coherent narrative." Although edTPA includes questions connecting learning to the community beyond the classroom, the rubrics get in the way of meaningful reflection. As one student teacher wrote to Barbara: "I tried to add some reflection to these questions, but they're just such bad questions that … it still felt like a performance of sorts. It was like a chance to show how flawless my teaching is, rather than to stop and question it."

Valuing the impersonal above the relational is contrary to social justice education, and to teaching as humanizing practice. As one student from another university wrote to Barbara, "I find it annoying and offensive that the powers that be think it is even possible to standardize a field so subjective as teaching! I thought I had a co-operating teacher and supervisor for a reason! They observe and interact with me daily and weekly. Does their opinion count for nothing now?"

Standardization erases relationships, which are the fabric of teaching, and substitutes mechanization. Teaching becomes technical, nuts-and-bolts work vulnerable to review and control by corporations like Pearson.

Corporatizing Teacher Education

EdTPA is a welcome mat for Pearson Inc. to enter teacher education, reap huge profits, exploit the privacy of students and teacher candidates, and outsource teacher educators' labor. The edTPA marketing campaign denies the significance of Pearson's involvement, claiming that Pearson is only necessary for national distribution and scoring. In denying the import of Pearson's role in edTPA, its promoters ignore the international social and political context: The public sphere is under assault. Pearson has infiltrated every level of education, treating this public good as a market to be exploited. It profits from testing and curriculum at all levels, monopolizing the content and process of teaching and learning worldwide.

Although trust is essential in student teacher development, trust in Pearson is misguided. Recently, Pearson scoring mistakes mislabeled more than 2,700 students in New York as ineligible for gifted and talented programs. Given the high stakes of edTPA, the ramifications of scoring errors are serious; they could affect certification. Teaching is not reducible to a number and accuracy in measurement is a dangerous pretense. But belief in numerical data is central to corporate education "reforms." Pearson's involvement reveals how edTPA, designed to answer questions posed by corporate education reformers instead of the questions of teacher educators, leads us dangerously astray.

In most teacher education programs the decision about credentialing is currently made within a working group that includes the student, cooperating teacher, supervisor, and college faculty. Under edTPA, this decision will be made by an anonymous person hired by Pearson on a piecework basis ($75 per test). This scorer will work with neither a long-term contract nor job protections. Thus, the edTPA dilutes the influence and expertise of educators and reinforces the ranks of casual, temporary, outsourced labor.

Pearson's involvement also raises privacy concerns that must not be taken lightly. Promoters of edTPA tell us that it was created by a team from Stanford, which maintains ownership of it. But the bottom line is that Pearson profits from, and keeps possession of, student work—including the videos of K–12 classrooms. During its pilot in Massachusetts, parents and administrators of four school districts refused to send videos of children to Pearson. After edTPA was adopted in New York, regulations were changed to require that schools allow credential candidates to record their practice and send the recordings to a third party. It is not clear how parents will be informed and given the opportunity to decide whether they want their child's likeness sent to Pearson.

Restricting Academic Freedom

One of the most ominous parts of the edTPA story is the way voices of dissent have been silenced by intimidation and job loss. Since she received a letter of nonrenewal after supporting student teachers who refused to participate in last year's field test of the TPA at the University of Massachusetts (see "Stanford/Pearson Test for New Teachers Draws Fire," winter 2012–13), Barbara regularly receives e-mails such as this one from Monica Urbanik at the University of Wisconsin-LaCrosse:

> I am finding myself in hot water regarding my resistance to our School of Education's adoption of the edTPA. I refused to sign a Pearson/Stanford nondisclosure agreement last week and was asked to leave an edTPA training session. … I am considering this latest obstruction as a sign, pushing me into early retirement.

She later wrote: "I decided to leave my position and retire from the state system. I will not return to this insanity in the fall."

Faculty approach Barbara through e-mail and at conferences saying that they wish they could voice their concerns about edTPA but are fearful of the consequences. In April 2012, when comments in an online forum on the Teacher Performance Assessment Consortium shifted from implementation of the test to questioning it as an instrument, the posts were immediately removed. We have led workshops in which teacher educators who had used the earliest iteration of the edTPA, the Performance Assessment for California Teachers, said they found themselves estranged from students as class conversations focused more and more on how to write to the rubrics. These educators choked back tears describing the shame they carry for their silence in the face of mandates that are stealing the soul of their work and preventing them from modeling the kind of critical pedagogy that they hope will inspire teacher candidates.

While critics are being silenced, promoters engage in the hard sell. EdTPA experts from the Stanford Center for Assessment, Learning, and Equity, the American Association of Colleges of Teacher Education, and Pearson Inc. toured the country last fall to meet with teacher educators. They arrived with PowerPoints of purchase plans and implementation schedules that moved from "introductory" to "exploratory," "scaling up," and "implementation." Each level was offered as a package with separate "benefits," "key features," "terms of agreement," and "membership recommendations." They came, not to ask what we know about new teacher readiness, but to promote a product.

In promoting edTPA, developers suggest that edTPA was created by teacher educators. Like all good marketing, this claim includes a kernel of truth; however, it implies that teacher educators clamored for, and now universally endorse, edTPA. This claim disregards how edTPA restricts academic voice and freedom, includes mandatory nondisclosure agreements, and perpetuates a culture of coercion.

Conclusion

These are treacherous times for public education. Schools and colleges are under unprecedented attack by those who seek to undermine public education. While we try to defend ourselves, we must also work to create education that is challenging, creative, joyful, deeply engaging, and liberatory.

How we resist is as critical as that we resist, for within our resistance we create new spaces for imagination. We do not need more technocratic efficiency, simulated objectivity, or corporate incursions. The troubles of teacher education are human troubles, requiring human answers: conversations, time, space for conflict, space for appreciation and love, space for humor and uncertainty. Teacher educators, like all teachers, must be free to disagree and develop questions that are not standardized. Teacher education can create possibilities for radical imagination in which we rehumanize the classroom and develop the theory and heart to practice education as freedom. Let's make our voices heard. Let's reclaim the conversation.

Reflection Questions

1. How important are the personal characteristics of teachers—e.g., age, gender, experience, race, etc.? What are the qualities and skills needed for teachers in 21st century schools? What kind of plan would you propose for recruiting the kinds of teachers we need for today's schools? And, finally, how would schools have to change to accommodate a new generation of teachers?

2. If public schools are not successfully educating all children, who should be held accountable? Teachers? Parents? Administrators? Is it possible for alternative pedagogical models for teaching and learning to coexist in public schools? How relevant are concerns for culturally responsive educational spaces?

3. In most schools, there is a gap between reality and the "promise of public education." Do our attempts to provide equal access to education reflect unattainable goals for public education? Why or why not? What are the broader implications of a growing gap that accelerates the divisions between those who are academically successful and those who are not?

4. As you consider your personal plan for becoming a teacher, what additional skills, knowledge, or attitudes will you need in order to achieve your desired image of a good teacher? How will you acquire and nurture the skills, knowledge, and attitudes that you require? If teachers are viewed as intellectuals, what changes in the professional status of teachers are needed?

5. What are the problems with "one-size-fits-all" approaches to any aspect of education, for example, teacher education, teaching, learning and assessment? What is the impact of these approaches on attempts to make critical thinking and reflection a part of education? Is there a place for corporate concerns of efficiency and profit in public education?

SECTION V

"Shift Happens": Contemporary Issues of Equity and Diversity

Introduction

Yolanda Medina

This section of the book contains some of the most crucial topics that are relevant to the preparation of teachers. The focus is on helping students reflect on the broad range of issues related to human diversity that you will encounter in contemporary classrooms. Essays were chosen that promote critical conversations on topics that range from race, ethnicity, gender, ability, sexual orientation, bilingualism, and social class among others issues. Accepting and accommodating the richness represented by student diversity is acknowledged as an essential ingredient of teaching and learning experiences that are culturally relevant and responsive.

Although, we chose chapters that address each of these issues individually, our intent is not to make them seem as if they will appear in isolation or at different times in your daily interactions with students. Quite the contrary is true; we agree that all of these complex issues are woven together and, in many cases, they overlap each other. Each essay in this section addresses a specific issue, and hopefully, facilitates an in-depth discussion of that issue. However, the reality is that these topics all intertwine to create the rich tapestry that we call public schools. As such, our classrooms are microcosms of the society we live in. The more we address these issues in our teacher preparation classrooms, the better prepared our teachers will be to create a safe and welcoming environment for ALL children to learn and grow. At the same time, the better prepared teachers are to embrace diversity in their classroom, the better prepared children will be to live and lead in the 21st century. The essays by Anselmo and Rubal-Lopez; Butvilofsky; Finn; Kauffman, McGee, and Brigham; Kronen; and Risner challenge us to consider our understanding of the issues faced by children who are perceived as different, and often as problems, in educational institutions that thrive on ignoring differences and attempting to find a "one-size-fits-all" model for teaching and learning. It is the desire of the editors of this book that students will take the ideas from the previous four sections and apply them to a discussion of how differentness and concerns for equity fit into a broader vision of the aims and purposes of education and how that ultimately impacts every other educational decision that we make in schools and classrooms.

As you begin to think about issues of equity and diversity and the "shifts" that have occurred in demographics, politics, economics, and views of school policies and progress, it is important to revisit some of the questions asked in Section I of this book:

1. What are the aims and purposes of public education, and how have those changed due to historical, social and political events?

2. What is the relationship between those aims and purposes and the content of the curriculum?

3. How is one's philosophy of education and expectations for teacher and student roles related to the previous two questions?

4. How do the answers to these questions impact the role of assessment in our schools?

5. Which ideological and philosophical beliefs shape and guide the questions we ask about the roles of equity, privilege, oppression and social justice?

Consider for a minute how the answers to these questions might vary depending upon the ideological commitment that a teacher brings to her/his work. I would argue that many teachers question the need for a commitment to social justice and/or a consideration of how diversity impacts what happens in a classroom; they want to just teach the subject and grade to which they have been assigned. However, I would argue that each teacher needs to acknowledge the importance of understanding who benefits from their teaching and who is disadvantaged by educational practices. Finding congruence between beliefs and actions is an essential part of the process of becoming a teacher. By necessity, issues of diversity and equity intersect and become an inherent part of the discussion.

CHAPTER 23

Community

Angela Anselmo and Alma Rubal-Lopez

Recognizing the makeup of a community is vital in understanding the experiences that children confront both in and out of the classroom. Its structure as well as its composition will ultimately affect their development (Agueros, 1991; Darling-Hammond, 1997; hooks, 1994; Kozol, 1992, 1995; Ladson-Billings, 1994; Macedo, 1996).

Where you live, who teaches you, who your fellow classmates are, and whether you are a member of that community or an outsider will, undoubtedly, mold the climate of the classroom. In essence, your status in a school community will play a significant role in the quality of that experience and in some instances will determine your success or failure in school. Our combined experiences—which include attending public schools, Catholic schools, private independent schools, private colleges, and public institutions of higher learning, as well as being educated in New York City and in Puerto Rico—attest to the fact that who you are and your status within that community can and does affect how you are perceived by those who have your future in their hands. This will ultimately contribute to how you see yourself.

School is a microcosm of society, and a child's status within that society, more specifically within that local community, will have an impact on his or her education. In inner cities it is no secret that the highest performing schools are usually located in affluent white areas. Often, well-intentioned parents such as ours move children from one neighborhood to another in hopes of improving that child's education, without realizing that the child's self-image is being compromised in the name of "a better neighborhood" or a "better school." Prior to school, parents are the principal agents in the formation of the child's self-concept. Once that child starts school, the teacher and his or her classmates become increasingly important in determining how that child will feel about himself/herself, which will ultimately be reflected in the child's attitude regarding the education domain. If the child perceives himself/herself as not capable of succeeding, his or her desire to even attempt to succeed in such an environment will be hampered. Our hats are off to all those children who find themselves in similar situations who cannot articulate what is happening to them but continue to try and succeed in such an environment. They are the ones who silently carry the scars inflicted at a young age by a system that can often be unkind and unwelcoming.

Furthermore, the creation and implementation of educational policy is also very often carried out without such considerations. The academic benefits of having children bussed from one district to another for whatever reason is at times overshadowed by the disruption in the child's life. This is not to say that children cannot benefit from programs outside their local school. However, in order for the child to benefit from the experience, teachers must be cognizant of these social dynamics.

Our status has changed throughout the course of our education, depending on who was teaching us, the location of the school, and the population being taught. Our experience at St. Rita's School, for example, while living in the projects was one of participation and engagement. Community and school were closely connected. Our lives revolved around school and around the major events such as baptism, communion, confirmation, graduation, Sunday mass, and weddings. Furthermore, my mother's function as the principal's secretary, a job that she did in exchange for free tuition, further added to our engagement with school and strengthened the relationship between parental participation, community, and school.

The demographics of the school contributed to this engagement. Although the population of the community was predominantly people of color, the school's demographics reflected pretty much equal representation of whites, blacks, and Puerto Ricans. The equalization of races resulted in no one dominant or preferred group. Although one could not escape the higher status of being Irish in an environment dominated by Irish nuns and priests, there was never a feeling that we did not belong or that this institution was not ours.

We all recognized St. Rita's as ours, and the nuns and priests recognized the importance of each one of us in the survival of this rundown school with broken bathrooms, poor lighting, squeaky floors, substandard heating, and overcrowded classrooms. Nonetheless, the physical condition of St. Rita's did not stand in the way of educating children who came from poor homes with parents who usually had very little formal education and who were more often than not immigrants or southern blacks who were new to a large urban city. This recognition of our similarities played out in the classroom, where we were all expected to learn and thus judged by the same standards.

Once we left the projects and lived in a neighborhood that necessitated our taking public transportation to school, our status changed. Not only were we outsiders, but our ethnicity in a predominantly Irish and Italian neighborhood gave credence to the notion of our not belonging. In a city where Puerto Ricans were concentrated in few ethnic enclaves throughout its boroughs, our presence in a predominantly white neighborhood was often met with fear and unflattering stereotypes. We were looked upon as uneducated hicks, also known as "spics," with pointed shoes, who were gang members and welfare recipients and who spoke very little English. We were also considered to be violent, explosive, and dangerous.

This was a time in which the largest migration of Puerto Ricans to the United States had recently occurred. The fact that our settlement patterns were concentrated in a few selected areas of the South Bronx, Manhattan, and Brooklyn contributed to furthering the misconceptions of who we were, because any knowledge about us came from the media, which usually depicted Puerto Ricans being arrested or in other negative situations. This was a time when television came into our homes and transformed our lives in unimaginable ways; it became progressively more important in informing us about the world (Steinberg & Kincheloe, 1997). The absence of Puerto Ricans in the media helped to perpetuate notions of our marginality in American society, while movies such as *West Side Story* did little to dispel unflattering stereotypes.

Ironically, the isolation and insulation of our communities in the projects and in other similar ghettos, which provided us with security and a feeling of belonging, conversely contributed to our being stereotyped and to separating us from the mainstream. We became marginalized people in what we thought was a "melting pot." These negative images of who we were played out in the classroom. For several years, I sat in the back of the room with the other three Puerto Ricans. I can't remember once ever having a conversation with any of my teachers.

Although the physical conditions of the school were far superior to those found in St. Rita's, the emotional bond was not there, resulting in my perception of school as something that I had to attend, not something that I felt a part of.

In Puerto Rico, our substandard Spanish skills became linguistic markers of our not being from the island. Nevertheless, we were accepted by our peers and eventually became integral members of our classes. Nonetheless, we were still seen as *las Americanas* or *las gringas,* and thus distinguished from the majority of the population. In high school, where we lived did not play a major role in our school experience. The school community was a microcosm of the larger community, with the predominantly white Honor School viewed as the elite group. Students who were a part of the most diverse population of the school, the nonhonors academic programs, were a tier below the honor students. The next and lowest tier of students were those in commercial and general academic tracks. This segment was made up predominantly of blacks and Latinos, and because of the track they were on, they would end up with the lower-paying jobs. As members of the Honor School, we were part of the elite of that community, and the few of us who were Latino or black were seen as "the exceptions." The effects of this labeling and its implications about the other members of our group had a great influence on how we perceived ourselves and on our social dynamics.

References

Agueros, J. (1991). Halfway to Dick and Jane. In C. J. Verburg (ed.), *Ourselves among others: Cross-cultural readings for writers* (pp. 95–112). New York: St. Martin's.

Darling-Hammond, L. (1997). Education for democracy. In W. C. Ayers & J. L. Miller (eds.), *A light in dark times: Maxine Greene and the unfinished conversation* (pp. 78–92). New York: Teachers College Press.

hooks, b. (1994). *Teaching to transgress: Education as the practice of freedom.* New York: Routledge.

Kozol, J. (1992). *Savage inequalities: Children in America's schools.* New York: Harper Perennial.

Kozol, J. (1995). *Amazing grace: Lives of children and the conscience of a nation.* New York: Harper Collins.

Ladson-Billings, G. (1994). *The dreamkeepers: Successful teachers of African American children.* San Francisco: Jossey-Bass.

Macedo, D. (1996). Power and education: Who decides the forms schools have taken, and who should decide? In J. Kincheloe & S. Steinberg (eds.), *Thirteen questions: Reframing education's conversation* (pp. 43–59, part 2). New York: Peter Lang.

Steinberg, S., & Kincheloe, J. (1997). *Kinderculture.* Boulder, CO: Westview.

CHAPTER 24

"What I Know About Spanish Is That I Don't Talk It Much"

Bilingual Fifth-Grade Students' Perceptions of Bilingualism

Sandra A. Butvilofsky

No toda mi familia sabe dos idiomas. Yo soy una de las afortunadas que sabe dos idiomas. Saber dos idiomas me ha ayudado a conseguir muchas cosas. … Una vez yo y mi mamá fuimos a la tienda y necesitabamos una medicina pa mi hermana. Pero la señora que estaba allí no sabía español y mi mamá tampoco sabía ingles. … Si yo no hablara dos idiomas nosotros no hubieramos conseguido lo que queriamos.

[Not everyone in my family knows two languages. I am fortunate to know two languages. Knowing two languages has helped me do many things. … Once, my mom and I went to the store to get some medicine for my sister. But the woman that worked there did not know Spanish and my mom didn't know English. … If I didn't speak two languages we wouldn't have gotten what we needed.] —Flor

This excerpt from a fifth-grade bilingual student's writing reflects one of the many functions bilingualism serves, as identified by Spanish-and-English-speaking Latino students participating in a biliteracy research project. In this instance, the possession of two languages by Flor (a pseudonym, as are all names of participants and schools in the study) serves as a positive attribute of her identity as she considers herself fortunate to know two languages, and Flor's ability to alternate between both languages allowed her family to get what they needed to help her sister. Flor's cognizance of the value of bilingualism is evident. Unfortunately, not all of the emerging bilingual students represented in this particular study acknowledged their bilingualism or the many benefits of knowing two languages (I sometimes replace the term *English language learners* (ELLs) with the term *emerging bilingual students* because it acknowledges the dynamic process of acquiring two languages rather than focusing solely on the acquisition of the English language). This lack of acknowledgment can be attributed to emerging bilingual students' internalization of the external political and ideological pressures for assimilation toward monolingualism, which oftentimes thwarts the development of bilingualism and biliteracy.

Emerging bilinguals make up the fastest growing population of students attending public schools in large urban districts in the United States today (Genesee, Lindholm-Leary, Saunders, & Christian, 2005); however, only 20% of them are in some type of program that promotes and develops their bilingualism (Zehler et al., 2003). Despite the fact that the academic benefits of bilingual education programs have been established and documented within the United States (August & Hakuta, 1997; Ramírez, Pasta, Yuen, & Ramey, 1991; Thomas & Collier, 1997), bilingualism is a highly contested political issue in the realm of public education for certain groups of students, and biliteracy is rarely referenced. Decisions as to who is entitled to bilingualism are paradoxical. This paradox manifests itself in the various stances taken toward language diversity, which are exemplified in education policies. Some policies, like the No Child Left Behind Act, encourage the teaching of foreign languages to students to increase "national security and global competitiveness," while other policies forbid the use of any language other than English, especially for minority language students or ELLs. Since 1988, voters in California, Arizona, and Massachusetts have approved ballot initiatives restricting bilingual education in those states. Initiatives and accountability measures that force emerging bilingual students into English-only instruction limit emerging bilingual students' full linguistic and literate potential.

In this chapter I use emerging bilingual students' voices to support my argument that more must be done to ensure that bilingualism and biliteracy are supported and maintained in bilingual education programs. Often the primary function of developing bilingualism in Spanish-and-English-speaking children living in the United States is only understood to serve as a temporary medium of instruction. That is, once students have developed a certain level of proficiency in English that enables them to receive instruction primarily in English, there is little regard for maintaining their bilingualism. However, as illustrated above in Flor's writing, for many bilingual students, the function of bilingualism exists far beyond the classroom walls. Bilingualism and biliteracy are not only advantageous for the students but also for their communities, as bilingualism and biliteracy provide cognitive benefits not available to monolingual and monoliterate children (Moll & Dworin, 1996).

The purpose of this chapter, therefore, is to present the seldom acknowledged perceptions of emerging bilingual students' experiences as they develop their bilingualism and biliteracy in a biliteracy program. This inquiry provides a different perspective of the functions of bilingualism, as the perspectives come directly from students and therefore puts "children in the center stage in the world as they see it" (Dyson, 1997, p. 9). Through their writing, fifth-grade Latino students describe both the benefits and struggles of learning and maintaining two languages. They bring to light the often-neglected emotional and psychological aspects they experience, as they have to navigate two cultural worlds while learning two languages. The findings from this study illuminate the many functions of bilingualism as identified by bilingual fifth-grade students, and at the same time, students reveal their awareness of the asymmetric relationship between Spanish and English in the United States.

By attending to and understanding students' perspectives, it is my intention, through the voice of emerging bilingual students participating in a biliteracy program, to share and promote the value of developing bilingualism and biliteracy. Through these writing samples, educators, researchers, and policy makers have a unique opportunity to learn firsthand how students who participate in bilingual education programs feel about their experience as they learned two languages and literacies. This chapter reinforces the importance of recognizing the intersection of literacy research that is situated in multiple-language contexts and the critical roles language and literacy development play in the lived experiences of emerging bilingual students. The questions addressed in this chapter are these: What do students say they are doing with their Spanish and English through their writing samples? And how do students perceive the relationship between Spanish and English, as illustrated in their writing?

A Sociolinguistic Perspective

A sociolinguistic theory of bilingualism provides the framework for understanding how students perceive and use their bilingualism. Sociolinguistics stresses the social nature of language and its use in varying contexts, assuming that "language is not only cognitive but also cultural, social, and situated"

(Moschkovich, 2006, p. 122). As such, a bilingual individual's choice in language use is not only influenced by the individual's own attitude or preference toward a certain language, but also by the relative status of the languages within various contexts (Baker, 2001; Coulmas, 2005). Accordingly, sociolinguists attribute language choice to three conditions: with whom the individual is speaking, where the individual is located, and when the interaction is occurring (Fishman, 1965). In other words, the framework for this chapter resides in the notion that an individual's possession of two languages (Mackey, 1962/2000; Wei, 2000) is "the product of a specific linguistic community that uses one of its languages for certain functions and the other for other functions or situations" (Moschkovich, 2006, p. 123).

In addition, sociolinguists are interested in seeing how the language repertoire of bilinguals may change over time (Grosjean, 1998). Changes in the competency of skills between languages may occur as the environment changes or as an awareness of the value and status given to the two languages is understood (Escamilla, 1994; Grosjean, 1989, 2008). This is especially true when the majority group does not have a great level of tolerance for the minority group and its language. This intolerance toward language diversity has been manifested in English-only movements that have dismantled bilingual education in various areas in the United States. The asymmetric relationship between languages may put linguistic minorities under pressure to adopt the majority language and often leads to language shift or loss within three generations (Coulmas, 2005; Fillmore, 1991).

In bilingual education, empirical studies using a sociolinguistic framework have described the status and function of two languages in contact with one another according to the context (Escamilla, 1994; McCollum, 1999; Reyes, 2004). Through sociolinguistic theory, researchers have demonstrated how the status of a language in a multilinguistic context has the capacity to influence a bilingual's choice in language use. Sociolinguistic studies have demonstrated how the status of a language can affect the goals of programs attempting to develop bilingualism and biliteracy (Fitts, 2006). The study that this chapter covers uses a sociolinguistic framework in order to understand students' perceptions of their bilingualism and biliteracy. This framework acknowledges that emerging bilingual students' use of linguistic, literacy, and cultural resources are influenced by situated sociocultural, sociohistorical, and sociopolitical factors.

Context for the Study: Introduction to Literacy Squared®

The students represented herein were part of a larger biliteracy program and research project called Literacy Squared®, in which Spanish and English literacy instruction was provided and maintained from first through fifth grade. The biliteracy program and research project was created to serve Spanish-and-English-speaking bilingual students in transitional bilingual programs (Escamilla & Hopewell, 2010). Literacy Squared® was purposefully designed utilizing theories of bilingualism in which a bilingual individual's languages are not seen as separate entities within the individual, but rather as part of a whole, having the capacity to influence and interact with one another (Grosjean, 1989; Valdés & Figueroa, 1994). Literacy Squared® subscribes to a holistic theory of bilingualism that acknowledges and capitalizes upon the full linguistic repertoire of the bilingual individual.

Literacy Squared® is an innovative approach to literacy teaching for Spanish-speaking students attending urban schools with high percentages of Latinos and the majority of students receiving free or reduced-price lunch. First conceived in 2004, the program and research purpose was twofold: (1) to examine the potential in providing paired literacy instruction in both Spanish and English starting in first grade and continuing through fifth grade, and (2) to develop new paradigms and theories regarding the biliteracy development of Spanish/English bilingual students (Escamilla & Hopewell, 2010). Unlike other bilingual programs, Literacy Squared® ensures that English literacy instruction is not withheld until a minimal threshold is achieved in Spanish literacy and/or oral English proficiency.

Rather, students receive literacy-based English as a second language (ESL) beginning in first grade, alongside Spanish literacy instruction.

Paired literacy instruction has been recommended as a promising practice for ELLs in several recent research syntheses (August & Shanahan, 2006; Slavin & Cheung, 2003). Specific time allocations for Spanish literacy and literacy-based ESL are designated by grade level. Literacy-based ESL considers what children already know about reading and writing in Spanish and how to apply those skills and strategies in English while also focusing on instruction in ESL. Some of the key components of literacy-based ESL include the use of appropriately leveled and culturally relevant texts; explicit and direct instruction of English literacy skills and strategies that utilize explicit cross-language connections; and a focus on oracy, which is intended to help children develop the language necessary for success in reading and writing. In addition, Literacy Squared® continues the practice of providing literacy instruction in Spanish and English through fifth grade, whereas traditional bilingual programs stop the use of native language instruction, thus limiting literacy instruction to only English around third grade.

One of the main constructs of Literacy Squared® involved the creation of a trajectory toward biliteracy. Literacy Squared® recognizes that when emerging bilingual children are instructed simultaneously in Spanish literacy and literacy-based ESL, they will develop literacy in both languages, though the development of each language will not be equivalent. Rather, it was hypothesized that emerging bilingual children's literacy development in Spanish would be slightly more advanced than their English literacy, but a large discrepancy would not exist between the two. This staggered leveling of biliteracy development is referred to as the "zone of scaffolded biliteracy" (Escamilla & Hopewell, 2010). In other words, student achievement in one language has a direct and measurable correspondence in the second language.

Longitudinal findings for cohorts of students participating in the Literacy Squared® research project demonstrated positive gains in Spanish and English reading and writing (Escamilla & Hopewell, 2010; Sparrow, Butvilofsky, & Escamilla, 2012). Findings indicate that the longer students receive paired literacy instruction, the more likely they are to be reading and writing comparably in both languages. While the difference between Spanish and English reading scores appears to be greater in first grade, as students progress through the intervention, the difference between Spanish and English reading achievement decreases. In other words, emerging bilingual children are on a positive trajectory toward developing biliteracy.

Writing Samples for Study on Student Perspectives

Data examined for this particular study included Spanish and English writing samples from 79 fifth-grade students in six schools participating in the Literacy Squared® project, which were collected during the 2007–08 school year, the first year in which fifth-grade data were collected. Spanish and English writing samples were collected annually as part of the research project, and in fifth grade, students were asked to reflect on their bilingualism in response to a prompt. All 79 students included in this particular study are Latino, were classified as ELLs, and qualified for free or reduced priced lunch, which generally serves as a proxy for socioeconomic status.

Spanish and English writing data are collected yearly from all participants in the Literacy Squared® intervention. Students are asked to write to similar prompts in Spanish and English for 30 minutes. Similarity in prompts was used to elicit cross-language transfer, yet sameness was avoided so as to not encourage translation. The fifth-grade writing prompts were as follows:

Spanish: *Piensa en tu vida personal y escolar, ¿Cómo te ha ayudado saber dos idiomas?* [Think about your personal and school lives. How has knowing two languages helped you in school and in your personal life?]

English: Think about your experiences learning Spanish and English. What is hard? What is easy?

Using a sociolinguistic perspective, each student's Spanish and English writing samples were read through, analyzed, and coded. Because language is social and "cannot be defined without reference to its speakers and the context of its use" (Wei, 2000, p. 12), all writing samples were analyzed to identify *which* language was used, with *whom*, and *where* or in which context (Fishman, 1965; Grosjean, 2008). Students cited using Spanish and/or English with family members (parents, grandparents, siblings, cousins, and other extended family), teachers, friends/classmates and others (which included people outside of the school or home context). The number of times a student mentioned using Spanish or English with one of the aforementioned persons was tallied. Codes were also created to account for the context (home, school, and other); and the frequency with which a student wrote about using either language in a specific context was also calculated. An additional analysis was conducted to account for the students' awareness of the asymmetrical relationship between Spanish and English.

Functions of Bilingualism

Using a sociolinguistic perspective, three main functions describing the students' perceived uses of and purposes for bilingualism emerged from their Spanish and English writing samples: communication, brokering, and cultural advantage. Collectively, these themes yield an understanding of what students actually do with their bilingualism and what they perceive as advantageous in knowing two languages.

Communication

> *A mi me ha ayudado mucho aprender 2 idiomas, porque ahora puedo comunicarme con otras personas. Por ejemplo si yo conozco a alguien que no he visto en mi vida y esa persona hable ingles yo le podría preguntar lo que quisiera. Pero si yo no pudiera hablar el ingles yo no le pudiera hablar.*

> [Learning two languages has helped me, because now I can communicate with others. For example if I meet someone I have never seen in my life and that person speaks English I would be able to ask whatever I want. But if I didn't know English I wouldn't be able to speak with him.] (Jasmín)

Being understood by others, understanding others, and communicating with others in Spanish and English was the overarching function of bilingualism. This finding is consistent with the social function of language, which is to communicate (Wei, 2000). As reflected in Jasmín's excerpt above, speaking two languages created opportunities to interact with others in the wider community. The communicative function of language was not only related to individuals, but also to various media sources such as television, movies, and different printed material.

While students wrote about the benefits of being bilingual, they also wrote about the difficulties of learning English. They expressed feelings of frustration, shame, and sadness, especially within the classroom.

> When I came to school the teacher use to talk to me an [in] english. Put a [I] diden understand her she would get mad at me … they wold tell me to do someting and I still thent [didn't] getet [get it] then I got in trobul. (Jaime)

Despite the teacher's repetition of the directions, Jaime could not understand, and as a result of his inability to understand English, he was not only punished by the teacher, but he was also foreclosed from meaningfully participating in learning.

> Learning was so hard because ebery botty [k]new English etsept [except] me … wen we read in grups the teacher maked me read but I was anberest [embarrassed] because I dirent [k]now anyting or how to read soo I cried. (Jaime)

While students may not always externalize their struggles, having an awareness of them can help teachers affirm and acknowledge students' experiences as they become bilingual. Furthermore, if these students, most of whom had the opportunity to use their native language, experienced such emotional stress, imagine what happens to the majority of emerging bilingual children who are in English-only contexts and are not afforded the opportunity to use their native language in school.

Brokering

I have to use my english sometimes to translate what english people are saying, because my family talks mostly Spanish. (Amelia)

Many students wrote about *brokering,* or using Spanish and English to translate for family or friends in the wider community, school, or home. As defined by Tse (1996), *brokering* is "interpretations and translation performed in everyday situations by bilinguals who have no special training" (p. 486). In addition to translating, the following excerpt from José's writing demonstrates the important role his possession of two languages plays for his family.

Mi papá no abla en ingles y no les entiende a las personas. Por eso yo le ayudo a mi papá ablando dos idiomas. El siempre me yeva a donde necesita ayuda ablando ingles. Cuando no entiend[e] me dice a mi que able para el.

[My dad does not speak English and he does not understand other people. That's why I help him because I speak two languages. He always takes me when he needs me to speak English. When he doesn't understand he tells me to speak for him.] (José)

In the above excerpt, José is demonstrating the important role he plays for his father: José is his father's voice in a sense. This specific example demonstrates the complexity of some children's role in their family and their need to alternate between two languages for their survival and decision making.

Cultural Advantage

Sabiendo dos idiomas a mejorado mi vida. Cuando sea grande voy a tener mas oportunidades de trabajo.

[Knowing two languages has improved my life. When I grow up I will have more job opportunities.] (Victor)

Many students discussed the added macrosociolinguistic benefits of being in possession of two languages (Wei, 2000). These added benefits include better grades, potential economic benefits of having greater job opportunities, earning a higher income, attending college, developing relationships with and understanding people from different backgrounds and languages, and helping the wider community. Manuel writes:

Y yo se que sabiendo el inglés y el español me va a ayudar en el futuro para cuando vaya a trabajar. Estoy feliz de saber dos idiomas. También me puede ayudar en poderle enseñar a mi familia en inglés y el español a mis amigos que quieren aprender español. Al saber 2 idiomas puede que me ayude en tener una vida mejor y un mejor trabajo.

[I know that English and Spanish is going to help me when I work in the future. I am happy to know two languages. It can also help me teach my family Spanish and English and my friends that want to learn Spanish. Knowing two languages can help me have a better life and a better job.] (Manuel)

Not only is knowing two languages helpful for this student's future financial life, but he will also be able to teach his family English and his friends Spanish. Manuel's recognition of his bilingualism facilitates his agency in widening his choices for his own life, as well as affecting others around him by teaching them another language.

Another cultural advantage worth discussing, which is particularly pertinent to Literacy Squared, was the students' awareness of how knowing two languages provided them with academic advantages.

The academic advantages did not only include access to better grades and the potential to go to college, but also an awareness that knowing two languages provided students the opportunity to participate in two literacy and cultural systems.

> *Todo me gusta de aprender dos lenguajes pero lo que me encanta mas es leer. Saber dos lenguajes me ayuda en mi lectura. Me deja tener la habilidad de poder leer cualquier libro de mi gusto aunque sea ingles ó español lo podria entender.*

> [I like everything about learning two languages but what most enchants me is reading. Knowing two languages helps me in my reading. It allows me the ability to read whichever book I like, whether it is in English or Spanish, I could understand it.] (Jasmín)

Hegemony of English

The students expressed much more about bilingualism than just its functions. Their writing reflected some of the unspoken realities of the asymmetrical relationship between Spanish and English in the United States. I say unspoken realities because the students did not explicitly write about the "unequal" relationship between the languages: instead, their writing reflected some of the subtle shifts individuals make in language choice when a majority and minority language are in contact with one another. The notion of losing proficiency in Spanish, choosing English over Spanish, and explicitly identifying with being bilingual explain some of the complex perceptions students in this study held about the relationship between Spanish and English.

When analyzing and recording with whom and in which contexts students used a particular language, it became evident that students used Spanish and English in separate contexts and with different individuals. Students used English in school with teachers, friends, and other students more than Spanish. Spanish was mostly used in the home with various family members. While students did write about using Spanish at school, the use of English was accounted for with more frequency. This finding is consistent with other research in bilingual education contexts in the United States, where English holds a higher status than Spanish (Escamilla, 1994; Fillmore, 1991; Gerena, 2010; McCollum, 1999). According to Wei (2000), "typically, multilingual societies tend to assign different roles to different languages; one language may be used in informal contexts with family and friends, while another for the more formal situations of work, education and government" (p. 13). The language used in more formal contexts is thus the language of higher status (Coulmas, 2005; Grosjean, 1985).

Language Shift and Loss

Despite efforts to promote and develop biliteracy and bilingualism within Literacy Squared® schools, hegemonic influences compel students' use of English over Spanish. Mention of language loss and/or language shift appeared in more than half of the writing samples. A writing sample was coded language loss or language shift when a student wrote about using English more than Spanish, their loss in Spanish proficiency, or their parents' concern over them not using Spanish. In the following excerpt taken from Maria's English writing sample, she mentions both her own choice of using English more often than Spanish and her mother's concern with language shift:

> What I know about Spanish is that I don't talk it much. I talk English most of the time. That's why at the dinner table my mom always says, *"hablen español,"* [speak Spanish] So I do. (Maria)

Maria's mother tells her to "speak Spanish" at the dinner table, thus showing her attempts to prevent Maria's language loss. In addition to students choosing to speak English more often than Spanish, the amount of time spent using English in school increases as well, which leads to an eventual increase in English proficiency and a decrease in Spanish proficiency as demonstrated in this statement:

> The sad part of using English in classes was that I was forgetting my Spanish. Spanish was getting harder and harder for me. (Carlos)

For some of the students, the shift toward English use over Spanish use was unintentional, as school, district, and state policies require students to take high-stakes assessments in English even though students are participating in bilingual programs. For Eddy, his preference for English can be attributed to his desire to pass his state's high-stakes test in English, the Texas Assessment of Knowledge and Skills (TAKS).

> This year in fifth grade my only goals are to past the English TAKS. … I like more english than Spanish so I hope I can past the tests in English.

Although the students were aware of their choice in languages, they were also negotiating the maintenance of their Spanish within their homes with their parents or other family members. Take, for example, Daniel. Not only is he in a position to choose between languages, but he can now teach his mom English, while she helps him maintain his Spanish:

> *Mi mamá quiere aprender ingles. Yo le enseño y como se me olvida el español ella me enseña a mi.*

> [My mom wants to learn English. So I teach her and since I am forgetting Spanish, she teaches me.] (Daniel)

For some students, speaking Spanish in the home is not just a choice, but also a necessity as Yessenia explains:

> *Para mi hablar en español es muy importante porque mis padres ablan en español.*

> [Speaking Spanish is very important to me because my parents speak Spanish.] (Yessenia)

This necessity to preserve Spanish in order to communicate with family members is vital to maintaining and developing relationships. When families lose their ability to communicate with one another, "rifts develop and families lose the intimacy that comes from shared beliefs and understanding" (Fillmore, 1991, p. 343).

Even though many students expressed their preference for using English, a few students expressed their preference for speaking Spanish and were adamant about maintaining both their language and their culture:

> I'm happy that I know 2 languages and I haven't forgotten about my Spanish culture and also thanks to my family and my mom I will always talk Spanish but I will never forget english either. (Liliana)

This sense of pride in possessing two languages was conveyed in several other samples and is addressed in students' identification of self as bilingual.

Identification of Self as Bilingual

Although both the English and the Spanish writing prompts made explicit reference to the use of two languages (Spanish and English), not all of the students directly identified themselves as bilingual or in possession of two languages. When students acknowledged their bilingualism explicitly, they sometimes attached a statement of pride or honor to it. For example:

Yo estoy ogulloso de saber dos idiomas haci puedo enceñarle a mi hermanito y mis primitos.

[I am proud to know two languages so I can teach my little brother and my cousins.] (José)

Another interesting acknowledgment of bilingualism, made by Jessica, was the pride she experienced in knowing two languages although the school did not formally recognize her as being proficient academically in English as demonstrated by assessments.

Aunque abeses agarro malos grados porque ago los examenes en ingles yo stoy orgullosa de mi misma porque lla [ya] se otro idioma.

[Although I sometimes get bad grades because I take tests in English, I am proud of myself because I know another language.] (Jessica)

This excerpt from Jessica clearly shows that the possession of two languages has much more to do with one's identity or ability to communicate than just performing academic tasks in school.

Conclusion

The purpose of this study was to present and describe bilingual fifth grade students' personal perceptions of bilingualism as related in their Spanish and English writing samples. Most studies concerning bilingual education programs focus on the cognitive and linguistic aspects of bilingual programs; however, this study highlights some of the emotional and psychological elements of students' experiences in their lives inside and outside school. Many students in this study understood and articulated the benefits of bilingualism. For them, Spanish did not only serve as a bridge to English, but bilingualism served a greater function and purpose. Some students illustrated that their possession of two languages serves as a navigational device in order to develop meaningful relationships, negotiate communication between persons and other media, and achieve both personal and financial security in multiple worlds. These functions of bilingualism emphasize the need for various communities, especially schools, to encourage and nurture the simultaneous development of both Spanish and English. In addition, schools should engage students in discussions about the advantages and needs for bilingualism.

Knowing and understanding students' perspectives and experiences are important as they can inform curriculum development, policies for emerging bilingual students, and reading and writing instruction. I believe that the findings related to students' perceptions of bilingualism can inform educational practices for emerging bilingual children.

If emerging bilingual children are to develop their bilingual and biliterate potential in bilingual programs, we must recognize the possession of two languages and the ability to navigate two cultural worlds and literacy systems as resources. I suggest the following guidelines for nurturing and legitimizing bilingualism and biliteracy:

1. Maintain formal reading and writing instruction in Spanish and English, starting as early as kindergarten and continuing through fifth grade and beyond.

2. Native language use must be legitimized within the classroom and the school, both in bilingual and in English only programs. This can be accomplished by creating environments in which students are afforded the opportunity to use their native language for various purposes such as to express understanding, to read, and to write.

3. The benefits and challenges of being bilingual and biliterate should be discussed openly and directly. These discussions must address the emotional and psychological difficulty of having

to learn another language. Just as important, it is necessary to discuss the macrosociolinguistic benefits of bilingualism.

4. Students should be given multiple opportunities to read books about bilingualism and books about others' experiences navigating two cultural worlds and linguistic systems.

5. School personnel should go out of their way to speak the minority language outside of the classroom to model the utility and worth of the language.

6. Parents need to be encouraged to continue nurturing the home language.

In conclusion, good bilingual and biliteracy programs should explicitly address all of the issues listed above by providing emerging bilingual students opportunities to read and write in two languages and actively discuss bilingualism. In addition, it is important for bilingual educators and researchers to include the voices and perspectives of bilingual students. Listening to bilingual students and understanding what they think about their languages has the potential to improve program development and, ultimately, promote emerging bilinguals' linguistic resources. It is difficult to really understand what we are teaching without asking students what it is they are learning. The questions we need to ask should go beyond asking about the content being taught, but how what it is we teach is affecting our emerging bilingual students and how what we teach may be useful to them outside of the school walls; as was expressed by many of the students in this inquiry, the functions of bilingualism and the potential in biliteracy development reach beyond the classroom and school context.

Acknowledgment. I wish to thank Kathy Escamilla and Olivia Ruiz Figueroa for developing and actualizing the Literacy Squared biliteracy program and research project. Thanks to this project I was able to conduct this inquiry and write this chapter.

References

August, D., & Hakuta, K. (1997). *Improving schooling for language minority students: A research agenda.* Washington, DC: National Academy Press.

August, D., & Shanahan, T. (2006). *Developing literacy in second-language learners: Report of the National Literacy Panel on Language-Minority Children and Youth.* Mahwah, NJ: Erlbaum.

Baker, C. (2001). *Foundations of bilingual education and bilingualism.* Clevedon, UK: Multilingual Matters.

Coulmas, F. (2005). *Sociolinguistics: The study of speakers' choices.* New York, NY: Cambridge University Press.

Dyson, A. H. (1997). *Writing superheroes: Contemporary childhood, popular culture, and classroom literacy.* New York, NY: Teachers College Press.

Escamilla, K. (1994). The sociolinguistic environment of a bilingual school: A case study introduction. *Bilingual Research Journal, 18,* 21–47.

Escamilla, K., & Hopewell, S. (2010). Transitions to biliteracy: Creating positive academic trajectories for emerging bilinguals in the United States. In J. Petrovic (Ed.), *International perspectives on bilingual education: Policy, practice, and controversy* (pp. 69–93). Charlotte, NC: Information Age.

Fillmore, L. W. (1991). When learning a second language means losing the first. *Early Childhood Research Quarterly, 6,* 323–346.

Fishman, J. A. (1965). Who speaks what language to whom and when. *La Linguistique, 2,* 67–88.

Fitts, S. (2006). Reconstructing the status quo: Linguistic interaction in a dual-language school. *Bilingual Research Journal, 29,* 337–365.

Genesee, F., Lindholm-Leary, K., Saunders, W., & Christian, D. (2005). English language learners in U.S. schools: An overview of research findings. *Journal of Education for Students Placed At Risk, 10*(4), 363–385.

Gerena, L. (2010). Student attitudes toward biliteracy in dual immersion programs. *The Reading Matrix, 10,* 55–78.

Grosjean, F. (1985). The bilingual as a competent but specific speaker-hearer. *Journal of Multilingual and Multicultural Development, 6,* 467–477.

Grosjean, F. (1989). Neurolinguists, beware! The bilingual is not two monolinguals in one person. *Brain and Language, 36,* 3–15.

Grosjean, F. (1998). Studying bilinguals: Methodological and conceptual issues. *Bilingualism: Language and Cognition, 1,* 131–149.

Grosjean, F. (2008). *Studying bilinguals*. New York, NY: Oxford University Press.

Mackey, W. F. (2000). The description of bilingualism. In L. Wei (Ed.), *The bilingual reader*. London, UK: Routledge. (Reprinted from *Canadian Journal of Linguistics*, *7*, 51–85, in 1962)

McCollum, P. (1999). Learning to value English: Cultural capital in a two-way bilingual program. *Bilingual Research Journal*, *23*, 113–134.

Moll, L. C., & Dworin, J. E. (1996). Biliteracy development in classrooms: Social dynamics and cultural possibilities. In D. Hicks (Ed.), *Child discourse and social learning* (pp. 221–246). Cambridge, UK: Cambridge University Press.

Moschkovich, J. (2006). Using two languages when learning mathematics. *Educational Studies in Mathematics*, *64*, 121–144.

Ramírez, D., Pasta, D., Yuen, S., & Ramey, D. (1991). *Final report. Longitudinal study of structured English immersion strategy, early-exit and late-exit transitional bilingual education programs for language-minority children*. San Mateo: CA: Aguirre International.

Reyes, I. (2004). Functions of code switching in schoolchildren's conversations. *Bilingual Research Journal*, *28*(3), 77–98.

Slavin, R., & Cheung, A. (2003). *Effective reading programs for English language learners: A best-evidence synthesis*. Washington, DC: Center for Research on the Education of Students Placed at Risk (CRESPAR).

Sparrow, W., Butvilofsky, S., & Escamilla, K. (2012). The evolution of biliterate writing through simultaneous bilingual literacy instruction. In E. Bauer & M. Gort (Eds.), *Early biliteracy development: Exploring young learners' use of their linguistic resource* (pp. 157–181). New York, NY: Routledge.

Thomas, W., & Collier, V. (1997). *School effectiveness for language minority students*. Washington, DC: National Clearinghouse for Bilingual Education.

Tse, L. (1996). Language brokering in linguistic minority communities: The case of Chinese- and Vietnamese-American Students. *Bilingual Research Journal*, *20*, 485–498.

Valdés, G., & Figueroa, R. A. (1994). *Bilingualism and testing: A special case of bias*. Norwood, NJ: Ablex.

Wei, L. (2000). Dimensions of bilingualism. In L. Wei (Ed.), *The bilingualism reader* (pp. 3–25). New York, NY: Routledge.

Zehler, A., Fleischman, H., Hopstock, P., Stephenson, T., Pendzick, M., & Sapru, S. (2003). *Descriptive study of services to LEP students and LEP students with disabilities: Vol. 1. Research Report*. Retrieved from http://onlineresources.wnylc.net/pb/orcdocs/LARC_Resources/LEPTopics/ED/DescriptiveStudyofServicestoLEPStudentsandLEPStudentswithDisabilities.pdf

CHAPTER 25

A Distinctly Un-American Idea

An Education Appropriate to Their Station

Patrick J. Finn

Jean Anyon studied fifth-grade classes in five public elementary schools in rich neighborhoods and not-so-rich neighborhoods in northern New Jersey.[1] In one school, designated *executive elite*, family breadwinners were top corporate executives in multinational corporations or Wall Street financial firms. Their incomes were in the top 1 percent in the United States. In a second school, designated *affluent professional*, family breadwinners were doctors, TV and advertising executives, and other highly paid professionals. Incomes were in the top 10 percent for the nation. In a third school, designated *middle class*, breadwinners were a mixture of highly skilled, well-paid blue- and white-collar workers and those with traditional middle-class occupations such as teachers, social workers, accountants, and middle managers. Incomes were better than average for the United States but below the top 10 percent. In a fourth and fifth school designated *working class*, about one-third of the breadwinners were skilled blue-collar workers, about half were unskilled or semiskilled blue-collar workers, and about 15 percent of the heads of households were unemployed.

First Anyon noted similarities among the schools. They were nearly all white. They were all located in northern New Jersey and subject to the same state requirements. They all used the same arithmetic books. They had the same language arts course of study. Two of the schools used the same basal reading series. There were startling differences, however.

In the two working-class schools, most of the teachers were born in the same city as the school but lived in better sections. Most of them were young and had graduated from the local teachers college; many of them were single.

In the working-class schools, knowledge was presented as fragmented facts isolated from wider bodies of meaning and from the lives and experiences of the students. *Work* was following steps in a procedure. There was little decision making or choice. Teachers rarely explained why work was being assigned or how it was connected to other assignments. Work was often evaluated in terms of whether the steps were followed rather than whether it was right or wrong. For example, one teacher led the students through a series of steps to draw a one-inch grid on their paper without telling them what they were making or what it was for. When a girl realized what they were making and said she had a faster way to do it, the teacher answered, "No, you don't. You don't even know what I'm making yet. Do it this way or it's wrong."

While the same arithmetic book was used in all five schools, the teacher in one working-class school commented that she skipped pages dealing with mathematical reasoning and inference because they were too hard. The teacher in the second working-class school said, "These pages are for creativity—they're extras." She often skipped them as well.

In one working-class school they used a social studies textbook that was described by its publisher as intended for "low-ability students." The teachers guide referred repeatedly to "educationally deficient students"—for whom the book was intended. The book was intended to provide a year's work, but there were only sixteen lessons consisting of a few paragraphs followed by vocabulary drill and exercises to check recall. However, these were not special education classrooms. In the two working-class school classrooms combined, the children's average IQ was above 100 and eight children had IQs above 125.

In the working-class schools, social studies instruction typically consisted of copying teachers' notes, writing answers to textbook questions, and craft projects, such as cutting out and making a stand-up figure of a cowboy roping a steer to represent the Southwest when studying U.S. geography. Compared to the more affluent schools in this study there was less discussion of controversial topics such as labor disputes, civil rights, and women's rights and less attention to the history of these issues.

In language arts, the teacher gave each student a duplicated sheet entitled "All About Me" and directed them to write their answers on the lines following questions such as "Where were you born?" and "What is your favorite animal?" This activity was referred to as "writing an autobiography." Children were presented with rules for where to put commas, but there was never any discussion of how commas made writing easier to understand or of the notion that punctuation called for decisions based on the intended meaning.

In science, children were routinely told to copy the directions for doing an experiment from the book. The teacher then did the experiment in front of the class as the students watched and wrote a list entitled "What We Found" on the board. The students copied it into their notebooks. A test on "What We Found" would follow.

Teachers made every effort to control students' movement. They often kept children after the dismissal bell to finish their work or to punish them for misbehavior. There were no clocks in classrooms. Materials were handed out by the teacher and closely guarded. Students were ordered to remain in their seats unless given specific permission to move. When permitted to leave the room they needed a pass with the time and date.

Teachers made derogatory remarks regarding the students. A principal was reported to have said to a new teacher, "Just do your best. If they learn to add and subtract, that's a bonus. If not, don't worry about it." A second-grade teacher said the children were "getting dumber every year." Only twice did Anyon hear a teacher say "please" to a student in an unsarcastic tone. She heard "Shut up" frequently.

One fifth-grade teacher said the students needed the basics—simple skills. When asked "why?" she responded, "They're lazy. I hate to categorize them, but they're lazy." Another fifth-grade teacher who was asked why she had students endlessly copy notes from the blackboard in social studies replied, "Because the children in this school don't know anything about the U.S., so you can't teach them much." Another teacher said, "You can't teach these kids anything. Their parents don't care about them and they're not interested." Another teacher answered when asked what was important knowledge for her students, "Well, we keep them busy." You have to keep reminding yourself that these children did not have low IQ scores. They were working-class children with average intelligence, some with better than average intelligence.

When Anyon asked these fifth-grade students, "What do you think of when I say the word *knowledge*?" not a single child used the word *think*. Only one mentioned the word *mind*. When asked if they can make knowledge, only one said yes.

In each category of school, Anyon observed what she called a "dominant theme." In the working-class schools the dominant theme was *resistance*. Students vandalized school property and resisted the teachers' efforts to teach. Boys fell out of chairs; students brought bugs into the classroom and released them; children lost books or forgot them; students interrupted the teacher. They showed no enthusiasm for projects into which the teacher put extra effort. They refused to answer questions and were apparently pleased when the teacher became upset. There was less resistance to easy work, and so assignments were rarely demanding.

According to Anyon these children were developing a relationship to the economy, authority, and work that is appropriate preparation for wage labor—labor that is mechanical and routine. Their capacity for creativity and planning was ignored or denied. Their response was very much like that of adults in their community to work that is mechanical and routine and that denies their capacity for creativity and planning. They engaged in relentless "slowdowns," subtle sabotage, and other modes of indirect resistance similar to that carried out by disgruntled workers in factories, sales floors, and offices.

* * *

In the middle-class school, about one-third of the teachers grew up in the neighborhood of the school. Most graduated from the local state teachers college, and many of them lived in the neighborhood of the school. Some were married to other teachers, accountants, police officers, nurses, and managers of local businesses.

Teachers in the middle-class school seemed to believe that their job was to teach the knowledge found in textbooks or dictated by curriculum experts. They valued this more than knowledge taught by experience. For example, when a child said that the plural of *mouse* is not *mouses* because "it wouldn't sound right," the teacher said that was the wrong reason. The right reason was that *mouse* is an irregular noun, *as it says in the book.*

A social studies textbook intended for use in sixth grade was used in the fifth-grade classroom in the middle-class school. According to the publisher, the purpose of the book was to introduce fundamental concepts. There were "understandings" from anthropology, economics, history, geography, or political science listed in the teacher's guide for each chapter.

Social studies classes involved reading the text, listening to the teacher's explanations, answering the teacher's questions, and occasionally doing reports. There was rarely sustained inquiry into a topic. The teacher rarely used a feature of the text entitled "Using the Main Idea" (applying main ideas to current events and personal situations), because she said she had enough to do to get them to understand the generalizations.

Knowledge in the middle-class school was "more conceptual" than in the working-class school. It was less a matter of isolated facts and more a matter of gaining information and understanding from socially approved sources. Knowledge here was like that in the working-class school, however, in that it was not connected with the lives and experiences of the students.

In the middle-class school, *work* was getting the right answer. Answers were words, sentences, numbers, facts, and dates. You could not make them up. They were found in books or by listening to the teacher. You wrote them neatly on paper in the right order. If you got enough right answers, you got a good grade.

You got the right answer by following directions, but the directions allowed for some choice, some figuring, some decision making, and the teacher explained the purpose of assignments and why the directions would lead to the right answer. For example, students were permitted to do steps "in their heads" rather than write them down. They were allowed to do division problems the long or short way. When reviewing homework they had to say *how* they did the problem as well as give their answer. Social studies consisted of reading passages and answering comprehension questions: who, what, when, where, and sometimes why. However, questions that might have led to controversial topics were avoided because parents might complain.

Work rarely called for creativity. There was little serious attention to how students might develop or express their own ideas. In a social studies project, the students were directed to find information on assigned topics and put it "in your own words." Many of the children's products had imaginative covers and illustrations, which were largely ignored by the teacher who graded on information, neatness, and the student's success in paraphrasing the sources used. Lessons that explicitly called for creativity and self-expression were "enrichment" and "for fun." They did not count toward grades.

The teachers in the middle-class school varied from strict to somewhat easygoing, but for all of them, decisions were made on the basis of rules and regulations that were known to the students. Teachers always honored class dismissal bells. There was little excitement in the school work, and assignments did not seem to take into account the students' interests or feelings, but the children seemed to believe that there were rewards: good grades lead to college and a good job. Remember, these were fifth graders.

When children in the middle-class school were asked what knowledge is, seventeen of twenty used words like *learn, remember, facts, study, smartness, intelligent, know, school, study,* and *brains.* When asked if they could make knowledge, nine said no and eleven said yes. When asked how, they said they'd look it up or listen and do what they're told or they'd go to the library.

The dominant theme in the middle-class school was *possibility.* There was widespread anxiety about tests and grades but there was a pervasive belief that hard work would pay off. These students viewed knowledge as a valuable possession that can be traded for good grades, a good college education, and a good job. There was more excited patriotism around holidays here than in any other school. There were frequent auditorium assemblies with a patriotic flavor. The feeling was that America is full of promise and these children were going to cash in on it.

Anyon observed that in the middle-class school the children were developing a relationship to the economy, authority, and work that is appropriate for white-collar working-class and middle-class jobs: paper work, technical work, sales, and social services in the private and public sectors. Such work does not call for creativity.

Such workers are not rewarded for critical analysis. They are rewarded for knowing the answers, for knowing where to find answers, for knowing which form, regulation, technique, or procedure is correct. While this kind of work does not reward creativity or self-expression, it usually pays enough to enable workers to find opportunities for creativity and self-expression outside the workplace.

* * *

In the affluent professional school the teachers came from elsewhere in the state. They all came from middle- or upper-class backgrounds. Most were women married to high-status professionals or executives.

Creativity and personal development were important goals for students at the affluent professional school. Teachers wanted students to think for themselves and to make sense of their own experience. Discovery and experience were important. In arithmetic, for example, students measured perimeters in the classroom and created questions for other students to answer. They collected data in surveys and did experiments with cubes and scales. They made a film on the metric system. In science, students experimented *in their own way* to discover the properties of aluminum, copper, and glass (which heats fastest, for example), and it didn't matter whether they got the right answer. What mattered was that they discussed their ideas. When students asked, "How should I do this?" teachers answered, "You decide," or, "What makes sense to you?"

There were, however, wrong answers. In arithmetic, six plus two was still eight and only eight. In science, the answer had to be consistent with observations. Students were required to have their observations and answers "verified" by other students before handing in assignments.

The social studies textbook emphasized "higher concepts" such as "the roles of savings, capital, trade, education, skilled labor, skilled managers, and cultural factors (religious beliefs, attitudes toward change) in the process of economic development," and the understanding that "the controlling ideas of Western culture come largely from two preceding cultures: The Judaic and Greco-Roman."

Students read and outlined the text and used it as a guide for "inquiry activities" such as baking clay cuneiform replicas, writing stories and plays and creating murals showing the division of labor in ancient societies. Several students had seen the Tutankhamen exhibit in New York—one had seen it in Paris.

They devoted a lot of time to current events because, according to the teacher, "they're so opinionated anyway, and they love it." Children often wrote editorials and brought in clippings on such topics as labor strife, inflation, and nuclear power. The teacher, however, said she had to be very careful of expressing her own opinion. "One year I had the superintendent's son, the mayor's son, and the daughter of the president of the board of education in my room—all at one time. I *really* had to watch what I said."

Knowledge in the affluent professional school was viewed as being open to discovery. It was used to make sense and thus it had personal value. School knowledge was presented as having relevance to life's problems. Unlike the situation in the working-class and middle-class schools, social strife was acknowledged and discussed.

In the affluent professional school, work was creative activity carried out independently. It involved individual thought and expression, expansion and illustration of ideas, and choice of appropriate methods and materials. Products were often stories, essays, or representations of ideas in murals, craft projects, and graphs. Students' projects were to show originality and individuality, but they had to fit with reality—that is, a creative mural could be marked down if it misrepresented the facts or concepts it was supposed to represent.

One assignment was for students to find the average number of chocolate chips in three chocolate chip cookies. The teacher announced gravely, "I'll give you three cookies, and you'll have to eat your way through, I'm afraid." When work was under way, she circulated giving help, praise, and reminders about getting too noisy. The children worked sitting or standing at their desks or at a bench in the back of the room or sitting on the floor.

In their study of ancient civilizations, they made a film on Egypt. One student wrote the script, the class acted it out, and one of the parents edited it. They read and wrote stories depicting ancient times. They did projects chosen from a list, all of which involved graphic representations such as murals. They wrote and exchanged letters with the other fifth grade in "hieroglyphics." The list goes on.

They discussed current events daily and were encouraged to expand on what they said and to be specific. The teacher's questions were designed to help them make connections between events in the news and what they were learning in school.

In language arts, they did not use textbooks because the principal thought textbooks hampered creativity. Each child interviewed a first grader and wrote a rebus story[2] just for that child. They wrote editorials about matters before the school board and radio plays that were sometimes acted over the school intercom. Lessons on punctuation stressed the relationship between meaning and punctuation.

Products of work were highly prized. The affluent professional school was the only school where Anyon was not allowed to take children's work away from the school. If possible, she could duplicate it and take the copy, but if it could not be copied, she could not have it.

Control involved constant negotiation. Teachers rarely gave direct orders unless the children were too noisy. Instead, teachers commented on the probable consequences of student behavior and asked students to decide accordingly. One of the few rules regulating children's movement was that not more than three children could be out of the room at one time. They could go to the school library at any time to get a book. They merely signed their name on the chalkboard and left the room when they needed to. There were no passes.

They sometimes negotiated what work was to be done. For example, children sometimes asked for more time before moving on to the next subject, and the teacher sometimes acquiesced. There is a remarkable footnote to this discussion. The teacher commented that she was "more structured" that year than usual because of the large number of children in the class who were considered discipline problems.

In the affluent professional school, work was not repetitious and mechanical, as it was in the working-class school; it was not knowing the correct answers, as it was in the middle-class school; it was being able to manipulate what Anyon termed *symbolic capital.*

The children in the affluent professional school had the least trouble answering the question "What is knowledge?" Many of them used the word *think* and several alluded to personal activity having to do with ideas. ("Figuring stuff out." "You think up ideas and then find things wrong with those ideas.") When asked, "Can you make knowledge?" sixteen said yes; only four said no.

In the affluent professional school the dominant theme was *individualism* with a minor theme of *humanitarianism.* Emphasis in the classroom was on thinking for oneself, creativity, and discovery in science and arithmetic. But there was also a pervasive climate of mutual help and concern for one another and for humanity. The principal ended morning announcements with "Do something nice for someone today." Social class and class conflict were discussed in social studies, with a liberal spin. Eight of twenty students interviewed expressed antagonism toward "the rich," who they said were greedy, spoiled, and snobby. This is interesting in light of the fact that these students' family incomes were in the top 10 percent for the nation.

Children in this school were developing a relationship to the economy, authority, and work that is appropriate for artists, intellectuals, legal and scientific experts, and other professionals whose work is creative, intrinsically satisfying for most people, and rewarded with social power and high salaries. Although in the workplace they do not have complete control over which ideas they develop and express, affluent professionals are relatively autonomous. Their relationship to people who decide which ideas will be developed (the executive elite whom I'll get to in the next paragraph) involves substantial negotiation.

* * *

In the executive elite school, as in the affluent professional school, the teachers were women married to high-status professionals and business executives, but in the executive elite school the teachers regarded their students as having higher social status than themselves.

Knowledge in the executive elite school was academic, intellectual, and rigorous. More was taught and more difficult concepts were taught. Reasoning and problem solving were important. The rationality and logic of mathematics were held up as the model for correct and ethical thinking.

Social studies knowledge was more sophisticated, complex, and analytic than in the other schools. Questions such as good and bad effects of imperialism and the reasons for conflict between social classes were discussed. However, there was little questioning of the status quo. The present distribution of wealth and power was presented as natural and timeless—going back to the ancient Greeks.

Children were required to plan lessons and teach them to the class. Among other things, they were evaluated on how well they kept control of the class. The teacher said to one child who lost control of his classmates, "When you're up there, you have authority, and you have to use it. I'll back you up."

While strict attention was demanded during lessons, there was little attempt to regulate the children's movement at other times. They were allowed into the classrooms when they arrived at school; they did not have to wait for the bell, as in every other school in Anyon's study.

Students were permitted to take materials from closets and even from the teacher's desk when they needed them. They were in charge of the school office at lunch time. They did not need permission or a pass to leave the room. Because of the amount of work demanded, however, they rarely left the room.

The children were sometimes flippant, boisterous, and occasionally rude. However, they were usually brought into line by reminding them of their responsibility to achieve. "It's up to you." Teachers were polite to students. There was no sarcasm, no nasty remarks, and few direct orders.

When asked, "Can you make knowledge?" half the children in the executive elite school said yes; half said no. Compared with the affluent professional school children, these children took a more passive view toward the creation of knowledge. For many of them knowledge comes from tradition. It's "out there" and you are expected to learn it.

The dominant theme in the executive elite school was *excellence*—preparation for being the best, for top-quality performance. There was no narcissistic coddling here, but insistence upon self-discipline instead. The pace was brisker than in any other school and children were often told that they alone were responsible for keeping up.

In the executive elite school the children were developing a relationship to the economy, authority, and work that is different from all the other schools. They learned grammatical, mathematical, and other vocabularies by which systems are described. They were taught to use these vocabularies to analyze and control situations. The point of school work was to achieve, to excel, to prepare for life at the top.

* * *

The working-class children were learning to follow directions and do mechanical, low-paying work, but at the same time they were learning to resist authority in ways sanctioned by their community. The middle-class children were learning to follow orders and do the mental work that keeps society producing and running smoothly. They were learning that if they cooperated they would have the rewards that well-paid, middle-class work makes possible outside the workplace. The affluent professional children were learning to create products and art, "symbolic capital," and at the same time they were learning to find rewards in work itself and to negotiate from a powerful position with those (the executive elite) who make the final decisions on how real capital is allocated. The executive elite children? They were learning to be masters of the universe.

Anyon's study supports the findings of earlier observers[3] that in American schools children of managers and owners are rewarded for initiative and assertiveness, while children of the working class are rewarded for docility and obedience and punished for initiative and assertiveness. Remember the teacher who said, "Do it this way or it's wrong."

This couldn't be more obvious when you compare Anyon's "gentry" schools—her executive elite and affluent professional schools—with her working-class schools. The surprising thing is where Anyon's middle-class school fits into this picture. Like the children in working-class schools, children in the middle class school were schooled to take orders. They were taught that knowledge in textbooks was more valuable than their own experience. They were taught through traditional, directive methods to look up knowledge, not to create it. They were not taught to manipulate or direct systems, nor was there any effort to connect school knowledge with their daily lives.

On the other hand, Anyon's middle-class school was like her gentry schools in that students saw the knowledge that teachers had to offer as valuable—albeit for the future, for entrance into good colleges, and for procuring highly paid work. And since they valued the teachers' knowledge, they cooperated with the teachers to get it. The theme here was not *resistance*, as it was in the working-class school; it was *possibility*.

Twenty years after Anyon's study Robert Reich,[4] Clinton's first secretary of labor, analyzed America's workforce in the '90s. While Anyon classified Americans in terms of their incomes and the kind of work they do, Reich's analysis added a new criterion on which to classify workers: with whom do they compete for jobs—only other Americans, or with workers in other countries?

Reich identified the top 20 percent as "symbolic analysts." These are the problem solvers and creators of ideas and symbols. They are engineers, bankers, lawyers, writers, designers, and the fastest-growing category—consultants. Theirs is an international job market. The work done by an engineer in Chicago today might go to an engineer in Tokyo or Bonn tomorrow. The same is true of bankers, lawyers, writers, designers, and consultants. Americans educated in our best schools (those Anyon described as executive elite and affluent professional) perform very well in this international competition, and they command enormous salaries.

Reich classifies what I shall refer to as the working class (the bottom 55 percent of American workers) in two ways. He refers to "in-person service workers" and "routine production service workers." In-person service workers are in retail sales, hospital and health care, food services and security. Since these services are delivered to the consumer "in-person," these jobs cannot be easily exported. In-person service work is often characterized as nurturing work or women's work. It has always been and continues to be poorly paid. In-person service jobs make up a little more than half of the working-class jobs in America today.

Slightly less than half of the working class in America today are in "routine production service work." These are the foot soldiers of American industry—assembly line workers in the older "heavy" industries and in the newer electronics industries. These jobs are eminently exportable. While work in newer industries is cleaner and easier, shops are not unionized and the pay is remarkably lower. The number of well-paid jobs in older industries is declining while the number of poorly paid jobs in newer industries is increasing.

What's left is the approximately 20 percent whom I shall refer to as the middle class. Reich refers to them as government workers. These are the teachers, local and federal government employees, and, surprisingly, physicians paid through Medicaid and Medicare.

In the past twenty years numbers have grown at the top and bottom. The number in the middle has declined. Those at the top have gotten a whole lot richer. Those in the middle are in about the same place economically, and those at the bottom have gotten a whole lot poorer. Reich observed that among the fastest-growing occupations in America is that of security guard. Small wonder.

The question is, do the children of the elite and the middle class and the working class still attend schools like those Anyon described? The answer is, you bet! If there were later studies that did not support her findings or that showed a trend in a different direction, I would never have cited her in the first place. But the recent literature supports her conclusions.

In the early '90s, the faculty at California State University at Dominguez Hills (near Los Angeles) described schools attended by children who are disenfranchised because of social class, poverty, or cultural background in much the same way Anyon described the working-class schools in her study a decade earlier.[5] A colleague of mine regularly sends her students out to schools and asks them to compare what they observe to what Anyon observed. They invariably report that matters remain the same. In *Savage Inequalities*[6] Jonathan Kozol reports on schools in upscale communities like Winnetka, Illinois; Cherry Hill, New Jersey; and Rye, New York, and schools in impoverished communities like East St. Louis, Illinois; Camden, New Jersey; and parts of Washington, D.C., Chicago, and New York City. Nothing's changed, unless, perhaps, it's gotten worse.

In February 1998 I asked one of my classes to write papers comparing Anyon's findings to their own personal experiences. The following are excerpts from two of their papers.

I am from Amherst, New Hampshire. Amherst is one of the most affluent places to live in New Hampshire. About five years ago a high school was built entirely for Amherst families. Amherst originally was sharing a high school with a neighboring middle class town that was not as wealthy. Many parents and families in Amherst wanted a better education for their children, so as a result, a brand new high school was built. The high school was a major development in the town of Amherst, and people from other towns were moving to Amherst, just so their children could go to the high school. I would consider Amherst High School to fit into the affluent professional category. The methods of teaching almost duplicated the strategies taught at the affluent professional school in Anyon's study.

I did not attend the high school, because I went to a private school, but many of my close friends did and my younger sister does now. I was told the students were given extreme privileges and were taught knowledge in creative ways, rather than straight from a textbook. For example, students had their own smoking section, they called their teachers by their first name, there were no honor level classes, and a lot of material taught (from science to English) was done through projects involving the kids to the greatest extent. The students were also able to get away with a lot, because they questioned everything that was assigned to them. Parents were relentless in their persistence to have their kids receive the best education possible.

However, the town Amherst broke away from was left with mostly middle class students, because all the Amherst kids left. As a result, the high school resorted to more traditional styles of educating, which meant teaching straight from a textbook and not giving any choices or freedom to the students. Meanwhile, the Amherst students were receiving progressive styles of teaching and were being educated on how to become superior professionals.[7]

[At first] Anyon's conclusions seemed wildly radical and oversimplified to me. I was not willing to admit that limits so tangible and so obvious existed in classrooms in the United States. After all, America is supposedly the "land of opportunity" where you can achieve whatever career goals to which you aspire. This class culture distinction sounded as severe as the caste system in India. However, the more I remembered various teaching situations I have been in, the more clear class culture perpetuation became.

As a student teacher, I had the opportunity to teach in what Anyon would classify as an affluent professional school and a working-class school. Although both schools professed progressive principles, the differences in the two schools were very apparent at the time. However, I never considered how the methods used to teach differed until reading Anyon's study. I find the correlations between my real life experiences and the study frightening. Reading about this type of class tracking in schools is one thing. Realizing that you have experienced it is truly another.

My experience in the affluent professional school was idyllic. The classes I worked with had many activities promoting independence and creativity such as Reading and Writing Workshops. Students had control of how to use their time, and all teacher directed lessons were mini-lessons taking no more than ten minutes of class time. These lessons were often based on questions that students had encountered during their individual reading or writing activities. Students could sit anywhere they pleased in the room, as long as they were working on their projects. All books read and all writing genres exhibited by the students were self chosen. These conditions mirror Anyon's description of the affluent professional school.

Progressive principles were highly prized, and at each staff meeting, the principal began with the statement, "We are here to consider how we can best serve the whole child in each of our students." Staff went out of their way to interact with students individually in and out of class. All the teachers and administration lived in the school district or in adjacent upper class suburbs and most had attended private colleges for their teacher training. It was inspiring. This was how all of my education professors had told me our classes should run. The students flourished. Parents praised the program on Parent's night. They valued their children's creative efforts.

My next assignment contrasted sharply with the first. Before I began in the classroom my sponsor teacher told me that students at the school were not interested in learning, and were often out of control.

She showed me lessons complete with overheads she had designed instructing students on the proper steps to take if they felt they needed to leave the classroom. Everything was outlined in detail. The desks were always in rows. According to my sponsor teacher, the students "couldn't handle" working in groups.

The most effective way to have students take notes, my grade team told me one day, was to give them Xeroxed copies of the teacher's outline notes with some key words missing. This could have been the school Anyon observed in her study. The control and the bitterness directed at students were shocking.

The teachers in the working-class school lived within the community. In the time I was there, I met four teachers from two grade teams of six each who had graduated from this same school. Almost everyone had attended a state school for their teaching certification. While the affluent professional school's teachers were excited and motivated, the most common refrain I heard among the working-class school's teachers was that they planned early retirement.

The dichotomy still amazes me.[8]

And so I ask, "Those who are smartest and work hardest go furthest?" Who's kidding whom? When students begin school in such different systems, the odds are set for them. President Kennedy once said that he hoped that a person's chance to become president was not determined on the day he was baptized (referring to the fact that some said a Catholic could never become president). I'd like to hope that a child's expectations are not determined on the day she or he enters kindergarten, but it would be foolish to entertain such a hope unless there are some drastic changes made.

Notes

1. Jean Anyon, "Social Class and the Hidden Curriculum of Work," *Journal of Education* (1980): pp. 67–92, and "Social Class and School Knowledge," *Curriculum Inquiry* (1981): pp. 3–42.
2. A rebus story is one where pictures and letters are brought together to form words. For example, a cartoon picture of a hand, a plus sign, and the letters *some* make up the word *handsome*.
3. S. Bowles and H. Gintis, *Schooling in Capitalist America: Educational Reform and Contradictions of Economic Life* (New York: Basic Books, 1976); M. W. Apple, *Ideology and Curriculum* (Boston: Routledge and Kegan Paul, 1979); P. Bourdieu and J. Passeron, *Reproduction in Education, Society, and Culture* (Beverly Hills: Sage, 1977).
4. Robert B. Reich, *The Work of Nations: Preparing Ourselves for 21ˢᵗ Century Capitalism* (New York: Vintage Books, 1991). See also Thomas W. Fraser, *Reading, Writing, and Justice: School Reform as if Democracy Matters* (Albany: State University of New York Press, 1997).
5. The grant proposal is described in J. Cynthia McDermott, "An Institute for Independence through Action, Process, and Theory." In John M. Novak, ed. *Democratic Teacher Education: Programs, Processes, Problems, and Prospects* (Albany: State University of New York Press, 1994).
6. Jonathan Kozol, *Savage Inequalities: Children in America's Schools* (New York: Harper Perennial, 1992).
7. Megan Elizabeth Connolly, *Paper 1, LAI 563 Language, Society, and Language Arts Instruction* (Photocopied, Department of Learning and Instruction, State University of New York at Buffalo, 1998).
8. Susan Marie Sampson, *Paper 1, LAI 563 Language, Society, and Language Arts Instruction* (Photocopied, Department of Learning and Instruction, State University of New York at Buffalo, 1998).

References

Anyon, Jean. "Social Class and the Hidden Curriculum of Work." *Journal of Education* 162, 2 (1980).

Anyon, Jean. "Social Class and School Knowledge." *Curriculum Inquiry* 11, 1 (1981).

Apple, M. W. *Ideology and Curriculum.* Boston: Routledge and Kegan Paul, 1979.

Bourdieu, P., and J. Passeron, *Reproduction in Education, Society, and Culture.* Beverly Hills: Sage, 1977.

Bowles, S., and H. Gintis. *Schooling in Capitalist America: Educational Reform and Contradictions of Economic Life.* New York: Basic Books, 1976.

Connolly, Megan Elizabeth. *Paper 1, LAI 563 Language, Society, and Language Arts Instruction.* Photocopied. Department of Learning and Instruction, State University of New York at Buffalo, 1998.

Fraser, Thomas W. *Reading, Writing, and Justice: School Reform as if Democracy Matters.* Albany: State University of New York Press, 1997.

Kozol, Jonathan. *Savage Inequalities: Children in America's Schools*. New York: Harper Perennial, 1992.

McDermott, J. Cynthia. "An Institute for Independence through Action, Process, and Theory." In *Democratic Teacher Education: Programs, Processes, Problems, and Prospects*. Ed. John M. Novak. Albany: State University of New York Press, 1994.

Reich, Robert B. *The Work of Nations: Preparing Ourselves for 21ʰ Century Capitalism*. New York: Vintage Books, 1991.

Sampson, Susan Marie. *Paper 1, LAI 563 Language, Society, and Language Arts Instruction*. Photocopied. Department of Learning and Instruction, State University of New York at Buffalo, 1998.

CHAPTER 26

Enabling or Disabling? Observations on Changes in Special Education

James M. Kauffman, Kathleen McGee, and Michele Brigham

Schools need demanding and distinctive special education that is clearly focused on instruction and habilitation.[1]

Abandoning such a conception of special education is a prescription for disaster. But special education has increasingly been losing its way in the single-minded pursuit of full inclusion.

Once, special education's purpose was to bring the performance of students with disabilities closer to that of their nondisabled peers in regular classrooms, to move as many students as possible into the main stream with appropriate support.[2] For students not in regular education, the goal was to move them toward a more typical setting in a cascade of placement options.[3] But any good thing can be overdone and ruined by the pursuit of extremes, we see special education suffering from the extremes of inclusion and accommodation.

Aiming for as much normalization as possible gave special education a clear purpose. Some disabilities were seen as easier to remediate than others. Most speech and language disorders, for example, were considered eminently remediable. Other disabilities, such as mental retardation and many physical disabilities, were assumed to be permanent or long-term and so less remediable, but movement *toward* the mainstream and increasing independence from special educators were clear goals.

The emphasis in special education has shifted away from normalization, independence, and competence. The result has been students' dependence on whatever special programs, modifications, and accommodations are possible, particularly in general education settings. The goal seems to have become the *appearance* of normalization without the *expectation* of competence.

Many parents and students seem to want more services as they learn what is available. Some have lost sight of the goal of limiting accommodations in order to challenge students to achieve more independence. At the same time, many special education advocates want all services to be available in mainstream settings, with little or no acknowledgment that the services are atypical. Although teachers, administrators, and guidance counselors are often willing and able to make accommodations, doing so is not always in students' best long-term interests. It gives students with disabilities what anthropologist

Robert Edgerton called a cloak—a pretense, a cover, which actually fools no one—rather than actual competence.[4]

In this article, we discuss how changes in attitudes toward disability and special education, placement, and accommodations can perpetuate disability. We also explore the problems of ignoring or perpetuating disability rather than helping students lead fuller, more independent lives. Two examples illustrate how we believe good intentions can go awry, how attempts to accommodate students with disabilities can undermine achievement.

But he needs resource ...

Thomas, a high school sophomore identified as emotionally disturbed, was assigned to a resource class created to help students who had problems with organization or needed extra help with academic skills. One of the requirements in the class was for students to keep a daily planner in which they entered all assignments; they shared their planner with the resource teacher at the beginning of class and discussed what academic subjects would be worked on during that period.

Thomas consistently refused to keep a planner or do any work in resource (he slept instead). So a meeting was set up with the assistant principal, the guidance counselor, Thomas, and the resource teacher. As the meeting was about to begin, the principal announced that he would not stay because Thomas felt intimidated by so many adults. After listening to Thomas' complaints, the guidance counselor decided that Thomas would not have to keep a planner or show it to the resource teacher and that the resource teacher should not talk to him unless Thomas addressed her first. In short, Thomas would not be required to do any work in the class! When the resource teacher suggested that, under those circumstances, Thomas should perhaps be placed in a study hall, because telling the parents that he was in a resource class would be a misrepresentation, the counselor replied, "But he *needs* the resource class."

He's too bright ...

Bob, a high school freshman with Asperger's syndrome, was scheduled for three honors classes and two Advanced Placement classes. Bob's IEP (individualized education program) included a two-page list of accommodations. In spite of his having achieved As and Bs, with just a single C in math, his mother did not feel that his teachers were accommodating him appropriately. Almost every evening, she e-mailed his teachers and his case manager to request more help for Bob, and she angrily phoned his guidance counselor if she didn't receive a reply by the end of the first hour of the next school day. A meeting was scheduled with the IEP team, including five of Bob's seven teachers, the county special education supervisor, the guidance counselor, the case manager, the principal, and the county autism specialist. When the accommodations were reviewed, Bob's mother agreed that all of them were being made. However, she explained that Bob had been removed from all outside social activities because he spent all night, every night, working on homework. The accommodation she demanded was that Bob have *no* homework assignments. The autism specialist agreed that this was a reasonable accommodation for a child with Asperger's syndrome.

The teachers of the honors classes explained that the homework in their classes, which involved elaboration and extension of concepts, was even more essential than the homework assigned in AP classes. In AP classes, by contrast, homework consisted primarily of practice of concepts learned in class. The honors teachers explained that they had carefully broken their long assignments into segments, each having a separate due date before the final project, and they gave illustrations of their expectations. The director of special education explained the legal definition of accommodations (the mother said she'd never before heard that accommodations could not change the nature of the curriculum). The director also suggested that, instead of Bob's sacrificing his social life, perhaps it would be more appropriate for him to take standard classes. What Bob's mother was asking, he concluded, was not legal. She grew angry, but she did agree to give the team a "little more time" to serve Bob appropriately. She said she would "be back with her claws and broomstick" if anyone ever suggested that he be moved from honors classes without being given the no homework accommodation. "He's too bright to take anything less than honors classes, and if you people would provide this simple accommodation, he would do just fine," she argued. In the end, she got her way.

Attitudes Toward Disability and Special Education

Not that many decades ago, a disability was considered a misfortune, not something to be ashamed of but a generally undesirable, unwelcome condition to be overcome to the greatest extent possible. Ability was considered more desirable than disability, and anything—whether a device or a service—that helped people with disabilities to do what those without disabilities could do was considered generally valuable, desirable, and worth the effort, cost, and possible stigma associated with using it.

The disability rights movement arose in response to the widespread negative attitudes toward disabilities, and it had a number of desirable outcomes. It helped overcome some of the discrimination against people with disabilities. And overcoming such bias and unfairness in everyday life is a great accomplishment. But the movement has also had some unintended negative consequences. One of these is the outright denial of disability in some cases, illustrated by the contention that disability exists only in attitudes or as a function of the social power to coerce.[5]

The argument that disability is merely a "social construction" is particularly vicious in its effects on social justice. Even if we assume that disabilities are socially constructed, what should that mean? Should we assume that socially constructed phenomena are not "real," are not important, or should be discredited?

If so, then consider that dignity, civil rights, childhood, social justice, and nearly every other phenomenon that we hold dear are social constructions. Many social constructions are not merely near and dear to us, they are real and useful in benevolent societies. The important question is whether the idea of disability is useful in helping people attain dignity or whether it is more useful to assume that disabilities are not real (i.e., that, like social justice, civil rights, and other social constructions, they are fabrications that can be ignored when convenient). The denial of disability is sometimes expressed as an aversion to labels, so that we are cautioned not to communicate openly and clearly about disabilities but to rely on euphemisms. But this approach is counterproductive. When we are able only to whisper or mime the undesirable difference called disability, then we inadvertently increase its stigma and thwart prevention efforts.[6]

The specious argument that "normal" does not exist—because abilities of every kind are varied and because the point at which normal becomes abnormal is arbitrary—leads to the conclusion that no one actually has a disability or, alternatively, that everyone has a disability. Then, some argue, either no one or everyone is due an accommodation so that no one or everyone is identified as disabled. This unwillingness to draw a line defining something (such as disability, poverty, or childhood) is based either on ignorance regarding the nature of continuous distributions or on a rejection of the unavoidably arbitrary decisions necessary to provide special services to those who need them and, in so doing, to foster social justice.[7]

Another unintended negative consequence of the disability rights movement is that, for some people, disability has become either something that does not matter or something to love, to take pride in, to flaunt, to adopt as a positive aspect of one's identity, or to cherish as something desirable or as a badge of honor. When disability makes no difference to us one way or the other, then we are not going to work to attenuate it, much less prevent it. At best, we will try to accommodate it. When we view disability as a desirable difference, then we are very likely to try to make it more pronounced, not to ameliorate it.

Several decades ago, special education was seen as a good thing—a helpful way of responding to disability, not something everyone needed or should have, but a useful and necessary response to the atypical needs of students with disabilities. This is why the Education for All Handicapped Children Act (now the Individuals with Disabilities Education Act) was written. But in the minds of many people, special education has been transformed from something helpful to something awful.[8]

The full-inclusion movement did have some desirable outcomes. It helped overcome some of the unnecessary removal of students with disabilities from general education. However, the movement also has had some unintended negative consequences. One of these is that special education has come to be viewed in very negative terms, to be seen as a second-class and discriminatory system that does more harm than good. Rather than being seen as helpful, as a way of creating opportunity, special education is often portrayed as a means of shunting students into dead-end programs and killing opportunity.[9] Another unintended negative consequence of full inclusion is that general education is now seen by many as the *only* place where fair and equitable treatment is possible and where the opportunity to learn is extended to all equally.[10] The argument has become that special education is good only as long as it is invisible (or nearly so), an indistinguishable part of a general education system that accommodates all students, regardless of their abilities or disabilities. Usually, this is described as a "unified" (as opposed to "separate") system of education.[11] Special education is thus something to be avoided altogether or attenuated to the greatest extent possible, regardless of a student's inability to perform in a general setting. When special education is seen as discriminatory, unfair, an opportunity-killing system, or, as one writer put it, "the gold-plated garbage can of American schooling,"[12] then it is understandable that people will loathe it. But this way of looking at special education is like seeing the recognition and treatment of cancer as the cause of the problem.

The reversal in attitudes toward disability and special education—disability from undesirable to inconsequential, special education from desirable to awful—has clouded the picture of what special education is and what it should do for students with disabilities. Little wonder that special education stands accused of failure, that calls for its demise have become vociferous, and that contemporary practices are often more disabling than enabling. An unfortunate outcome of the changing attitudes toward disability and special education is that the benefit of special education is now sometimes seen as freedom from expectations of performance. It is as if we believed that, if a student has to endure the stigma of special education, then the compensation should include an exemption from work.

Placement Issues

Placing all students, regardless of their abilities, in regular classes has exacerbated the tendency to see disability as something existing only in people's minds. It fosters the impression that students are fitting in when they are not able to perform at anywhere near the normal level. It perpetuates disabilities; it does not compensate for them.

Administrators and guidance counselors sometimes place students in programs for which they do not qualify, even as graduation requirements are increasing and tests are mandated. Often, these students' *testing* is modified although their *curriculum* is not. The students may then feel that they have beaten the system. They are taught that the system is unfair and that the only way to win is by gaming it. Hard work and individual responsibility for one's education are often overlooked—or at least undervalued.

Students who consistently fail in a particular curriculum must be given the opportunity to deal with the natural consequences of that fact as a means of learning individual responsibility. For example, social promotion in elementary and middle school teaches students that they really don't have to be able to do the work to pass. Students who have been conditioned to rely on social promotion do not believe that the cycle will end until it does so—usually very abruptly in high school. Suddenly, no one passes them on, and no one gives them undeserved credit. Many of these students do not graduate in four years. Some never recover, while others find themselves forced to deal with a very distasteful situation.

No one wants to see a student fail, but to alter any standard without good reason is to set that same student up for failure later in life. Passing along a student with disabilities in regular classes, pretending that he or she is performing at the same level as most of the class or that it doesn't really matter (arguing that the student has a legal "right" to be in the class) is another prescription for disappointment and failure in later life. Indeed, this failure often comes in college or on the job.

Some people with disabilities do need assistance. Others do not. Consider Deborah Groeber, who struggled through degenerative deafness and blindness. The Office of Affirmative Action at the University of Pennsylvania offered to intercede at the Wharton School, but Groeber knew that she had more influence if she spoke for herself. Today, she is a lawyer with three Ivy League degrees.[13] But not every student with disabilities can do or should be expected to do what Groeber did. Our concern is that too many students with disabilities are given encouragement based on pretense when they could do much more with appropriate special education.

Types of Accommodations

Two popular modifications in IEPs are allowing for the use of calculators and granting extended time on tests and assignments. Calculators can be a great asset, but they should be used when calculating complex problems or when doing word problems. Indiscriminate use of a calculator renders many math tests invalid, as they become a contest to see if buttons can be pushed successfully and in the correct order, rather than an evaluation of ability to do arithmetic or use mathematical knowledge.

Extended time on assignments and tests can also be a useful modification, but it can easily be misused or abused. Extended time on tests should mean *continuous* time so that a test is not studied for first and taken later. Sometimes a test must be broken into smaller segments that can be completed independently. However, this could put students with disabilities at a disadvantage, as one part of a test might help with remembering another part. Extensions on assignments need to be evaluated each time they are given, not simply handed out automatically because they are written into an IEP. If a student is clearly working hard, then extensions may be appropriate. If a student has not even been attempting assignments, then more time might be an avoidance tactic. Sometimes extended time means that assignments pile up and the student gets further and further behind. The result can then be overwhelming stress and the inability to comprehend discussions because many concepts must be acquired in sequence (e.g., in math, science, history, and foreign languages).

Reading tests and quizzes aloud to students can be beneficial for many, but great caution is required. Some students and teachers want to do more than simply read a test. Reading a test aloud means simply reading the printed words on the page without inflections that can reveal correct answers and without explaining vocabulary. Changing a test to open-notes or open-book, without the knowledge and consent of the classroom teacher, breaches good-faith test proctoring. It also teaches students dependence rather than independence and accomplishment. Similarly, scribing for a student can be beneficial for those who truly need it, but the teacher must be careful not to add details and to write only what the student dictates, including any run-on sentences or fragments. After scribing, if the assignment is not a test, the teacher should edit and correct the paper with the student, as she might do with any written work. But this must take place *after* the scribing.

How Misguided Accommodations Can Be Disabling

"Saving" a child from his or her own negative behavior reinforces that behavior and makes it a self-fulfilling prophecy. Well-intentioned guidance counselors often feel more responsibility for their students' success or failure than the students themselves feel. Sometimes students are not held accountable for their effort or work. They seem not to understand that true independence comes from *what* you know, not *whom* you know. Students who are consistently enabled and not challenged are never given the opportunity to become independent. Ann Bancroft, the polar explorer and dyslexic, claims that, although school was a torment, it was disability that forged her iron will.[14] Stephen Cannell's fear for other dyslexics is that they will quit trying rather than struggle and learn to compensate for their disability.[15]

Most parents want to help their children. However, some parents confuse making life *easier* with making life *better* for their children. Too often, parents feel that protecting their child from the rigors of academic demands is in his or her best interest. They may protect their child by insisting on curricular modifications and accommodations in assignments, time, and testing. But children learn by doing, and not allowing them to do something because they might fail is denying them the opportunity to succeed. These students eventually believe that they are not capable of doing what typical students can do, even if they are. Sometimes it is difficult for teachers to discern what a student actually can do and what a parent has done until an in-class assignment is given or a test is taken. At that point, it is often too late for the teacher to do much remediation. The teacher may erroneously conclude that the student is simply a poor test-taker.

In reality, the student may have been "protected" from learning, which will eventually catch up with him or her. Unfortunately, students may not face reality until they take a college entrance exam, go away to college, or apply for a job. Students who "get through" high school in programs of this type often go on to flunk out of college. Unfortunately, the parents of these students frequently blame the college for the student's failure, criticizing the postsecondary institution for not doing enough to help. Instead, they should be upset both with the secondary institution for not preparing the child adequately for the tasks to come and with themselves for their own overprotection.

The Benefits of Demands

Many successful adults with disabilities sound common themes when asked about their ability to succeed in the face of a disability. Tom Gray, a Rhodes Scholar who has a severe learning disability, claims that having to deal with the hardest experiences gave him the greatest strength.[16] Stephen Cannell believes that, if he had known there was a reason beyond his control to explain his low achievement, he might not have worked as hard as he did. Today, he knows he has a learning disability, but he is also an Emmy Award–winning television writer and producer.[17] Paul Orlalea, the dyslexic founder of Kinko's, believes God gave him an advantage in the challenge presented by his disability and that others should work with their strengths. Charles Schwab, the learning-disabled founder of Charles Schwab, Inc., cites his ability to think differently and to make creative leaps that more sequential thinkers don't make as chief reasons for his success. Fannie Flagg, the learning-disabled author, concurs and insists that learning disabilities become a blessing *only if you can overcome them.*[18] Not every student with a disability can be a star performer, of course, but all should be expected to achieve all that they can.

Two decades ago, special educators thought it was their job to assess a student's achievement, to understand what the student wanted to do and what an average peer could do, and then to develop plans to bridge the gap, if possible. Most special educators wanted to see that each student had the tools and knowledge to succeed as independently as possible. Helping students enter the typical world was the mark of success for special educators.

The full-inclusion movement now insists that *every* student will benefit from placement in the mainstream. However, some of the modifications and accommodations now being demanded are so radical that we are doing an injustice to the entire education system.[19] Special education must not be associated in any way with "dumbing down" the curriculum for students presumed to be at a given grade level, whether disabled or not.

Counselors and administrators who want to enable students must focus the discussion on realistic goals and plans for each student. An objective, in-depth discussion and evaluation must take place to determine how far along the continuum of successfully completing these goals the student has moved. If the student is making adequate progress independently, or with minimal help, special education services might not be necessary. If assistance is required to make adequate progress on realistic goals, then special education may be needed. Every modification and every accommodation should be held to the same standard: whether it will help the student attain these goals—*not* whether it will make life easier for the student. Knowing where a student is aiming can help a team guide that student toward success.

And the student must be part of this planning. A student who claims to want to be a brain surgeon but refuses to take science courses needs a reality check. If a student is unwilling to attempt to reach intermediate goals or does not succeed in meeting them, then special education cannot "save" that student. At that point, the team must help the student revisit his or her goals. Goals should be explained in terms of the amount of work required to complete them, not whether or not the teacher or parent feels they are attainable. When goals are presented in this way, students can often make informed decisions regarding their attainability and desirability. Troy Brown, a university dean and politician who has both a doctorate and a learning disability, studied at home with his mother. He estimates that it took him more than twice as long as the average person to complete assignments. Every night, he would go to bed with stacks of books and read until he fell asleep, because he had a dream of attending college.[20]

General educators and special educators need to encourage all students to be responsible and independent and to set realistic expectations for themselves. Then teachers must help students to meet these expectations in a more and more independent manner. Special educators do not serve students well when they enable students with disabilities to become increasingly dependent on their parents, counselors, administrators, or teachers—or even when they fail to increase students' independence and competence.

Where We Stand

We want to make it clear that we think disabilities are real and that they make doing certain things either impossible or very difficult for the people who have them. We cannot expect people with disabilities to be "just like everyone else" in what they can do. The views of other writers differ:

> The human service practices that cause providers to believe that clients [students] have inadequacies, shortcomings, failures, or faults that must be corrected or controlled by specially trained professionals must be replaced by conceptions that people with disabilities are capable of setting their own goals and achieving or not. Watered-down curricula, alternative grading practices, special competency standards, and other "treat them differently" practices used with "special" students must be replaced with school experiences exactly like those used with "regular" students.[21]

We disagree. In our view, students with disabilities *do* have specific shortcomings and *do* need the services of specially trained professionals to achieve their potential. They *do* sometimes need altered curricula or adaptations to make their learning possible. If students with disabilities were just like "regular" students, then there would be no need whatever for special education. But the school experiences of students with disabilities obviously will not be—*cannot* be just like those of students without disabilities. We sell students with disabilities short when we pretend that they are no different from typical students. We make the same error when we pretend that they must *not* be expected to put forth extra effort if they are to learn to do some things—or learn to do something in a different way. We sell them short when we pretend that they have competencies that they do not have or pretend that the competencies we expect of most students are not important for them.

Like general education, special education must push students to become all they can be. Special education must countenance neither the pretense of learning nor the avoidance of reasonable demands.

Notes

1. James M. Kauffman and Daniel P. Hallahan, *Special Education: What It Is and Why We Need It* (Boston: Allyn & Bacon, 2004).
2. Doug Fuchs et al., "Toward a Responsible Reintegration of Behaviorally Disordered Students," *Behavioral Disorders,* February 1991, pp. 133–47.
3. Evelyn Deno, "Special Education as Developmental Capital," *Exceptional Children,* November 1970, pp. 229–37; and Dixie Snow Huefner, "The Mainstreaming Cases: Tensions and Trends for School Administrators," *Educational Administration Quarterly,* February 1994, pp. 27–55.
4. Robert B. Edgerton, *The Cloak of Competence: Stigma in the Lives of the Mentally Retarded* (Berkeley, CA.: University of California Press, 1967); idem., *The Cloak of Competence,* rev. ed. (Berkeley, CA.: University of California Press, 1993); and James M. Kauffman, "Appearances, Stigma, and Prevention," *Remedial and Special Education,* vol. 24, 2003, pp. 195–98.
5. See, for example, Scot Danforth and William C. Rhodes, "Deconstructing Disability: A Philosophy for Education," *Remedial and Special Education,* November/December 1997, pp. 357–66; and Phil Smith, "Drawing New Maps: A Radical Cartography of Developmental Disabilities," *Review of Educational Research,* Summer 1999, pp. 117–44.
6. James M. Kauffman, *Education Deform: Bright People Sometimes Say Stupid Things About Education* (Lanham, MD: Scarecrow Education, 2002).
7. Ibid.
8. James M. Kauffman, "Reflections on the Field," *Behavioral Disorders,* vol. 28, 2003, pp. 205–8.
9. See, for example, Clint Bolick, "A Bad IDEA Is Disabling Public Schools," *Education Week,* 5 September 2001, pp. 56, 63; and Michelle Cottle, "Jeffords Kills Special Ed. Reform School," *New Republic,* 18 June 2001, pp. 14–15.
10. See, for example, Dorothy K. Lipsky and Alan Gartner, "Equity Requires Inclusion: The Future for All Students with Disabilities," in Carol Christensen and Fazal Rizvi, eds., *Disability and the Dilemmas of Education and Justice* (Philadelphia: Open University Press, 1996), pp. 144–55; and William Stainback and Susan Stainback, "A Rationale for Integration and Restructuring: A Synopsis," in John W. Lloyd, Nirbhay N. Singh, and Alan C. Repp, eds., *The Regular Education Initiative: Alternative Perspectives on Concepts, Issues, and Models* (Sycamore, IL: Sycamore, 1991), pp. 225–39.
11. See, for example, Alan Gartner and Dorothy K. Lipsky, *The Yoke of Special Education: How to Break It* (Rochester, NY: National Center on Education and the Economy, 1989). For an alternative view, see James M. Kauffman and Daniel P. Hallahan, 'Toward a Comprehensive Delivery System for Special Education," in John I. Goodlad and Thomas C. Lovitt, eds., *Integrating General and Special Education* (Columbus, OH: Merrill, 1993), pp. 73–102.
12. Marc Fisher, "Students Still Taking the Fall for D.C. Schools," *Washington Post,* 13 December 2001, p. B-1.
13. Elizabeth Tener, "Blind, Deaf, and Very Successful," *McCall's,* December 1995, pp. 42–46.
14. Christina Cheakalos et al., "Heavy Mettle: They May Have Trouble Reading and Spelling, but Those with the Grit to Overcome Learning Disabilities Like Dyslexia Emerge Fortified for Life," *People,* 30 October 2001, pp. 18, 58.
15. Ibid.
16. Ibid.
17. Stephen Cannell, "How to Spell Success," *Reader's Digest,* August 2000, pp. 63–66.
18. Cheakalos et al., op. cit.
19. Anne Proffit Dupre, "Disability, Deference, and the Integrity of the Academic Enterprise," *Georgia Law Review,* Winter 1998, pp. 393–473.
20. Cheakalos et al., op. cit.
21. James E. Ysseldyke, Bob Algozzine, and Martha L. Thurlow, *Critical Issues in Special Education,* 3rd ed. (Boston: Houghton Mifflin, 2000), p. 67.

CHAPTER 27

Selling Out

Parenting, the Realities of Urban Education, and the Hidden Curriculum in Schools

Cara Kronen

This chapter describes my experiences with school choice. In addition to being a personal narrative, this chapter is a critical exploration of the nature of education in two schools: one in a high-poverty urban school system and one in an affluent suburb. Despite both schools being highly regarded and high achieving, it became apparent to me after experiencing both schools as a parent that they are preparing their students for very different places on the American socioeconomic spectrum.

This chapter draws from Jean Anyon's seminal article, "Social Class and the Hidden Curriculum of Work" (1980), which looks at curriculum and student-teacher interaction in elementary schools with disparate socioeconomic levels. The *hidden curriculum* can be described as the norms, values, beliefs, and behaviors that are taught and learned in school that are not explicitly part of the curriculum (Giroux & Penna, 1979). Anyon's theory of the hidden curriculum is that upper-middle-class and elite schools prepare their students to be executives, leaders, and policy makers, while the working-class schools prepare their students for jobs that require little ingenuity or problem solving. Anyon (1980) maintained that differences in educational methods help to reproduce inequality in society. As the children of the affluent and elite are afforded opportunities to learn, create, and express their needs and desires, children of families with less wealth and influence are instead taught to follow directions and procedures and are instilled with behavioral expectations that favor rules and obedience over creativity and self-regulation. Less affluent students are given little to no input regarding classroom activities or material, and memorization is valued over inquiry. Aside from type and quality of the curriculum found in each school, Anyon noted differences in interactions between students and teachers, as well as approaches to discipline. In the working-class schools, teachers issued more quick directives, had strict behavioral policies, and restrict student movement. In the elite schools, there were smaller classes and greater expectations regarding students' ability to regulate their own behavior. These students were given more freedom to move around the school and there was a more equal and respectful relationship between the teachers and their students. This may be in part because the students in upper echelon schools are wealthier and often in a higher socioeconomic bracket than their teachers.

It has been more than 35 years since Anyon conducted her study, and much has changed in the world of education. In 2001, Congress authorized No Child Left Behind (NCLB) which mandated yearly standardized testing and exposed achievement gaps among traditionally underserved students and their peers (U.S. Department of Education, 2014). All public schools were compelled to adopt rigorous standards-based instructional practices and meet annual benchmarks of success, known as Adequate Yearly Progress (AYP). Schools that fail to meet AYP for two consecutive years must construct school improvement plans. Schools known as Title I schools, those that serve high percentages of children from low-income families, face financial sanctions if they fail to make AYP.

In 2009, the Obama administration introduced the Race to the Top initiative, which focused on making all students college and career ready by raising educational standards, improving teacher effectiveness, and using data to drive instruction (U.S. Department of Education, 2015). Schools today are under increasing pressure to perform and to demonstrate their performance through the use of data and standardized testing. In an effort to prepare young people in the United States to compete with their peers in other countries for the limited number of high-skill jobs, 43 states have adopted the Common Core State Standards, a move that, among other things, has raised expectations of what students should know and be able to do when they graduate from high school (Common Core State Standards Initiative, 2012).

Much has also changed in the U.S. economy since Anyon's (1980) study. Thirty-five years ago, many of the parents of children who attended the working-class schools visited by Anyon worked in factories, storerooms, and warehouses, or as semi-skilled/unskilled laborers. Until the 1980s, these were often relatively well-paying union jobs that allowed families a certain level of economic stability, despite relatively low levels of education (Putnam, 2015; Wilson, 1996). A series of anti-union economic policies, deindustrialization, and more sophisticated telecommunication technology in the years since have made it easy for companies to send factory and customer service jobs overseas, leaving a wake of layoffs and economic devastation in working-class communities (Cowie & Heathcott, 2008; Friedman, 2005; Putnam; 2015; Wilson, 1996). Yet, much is unchanged in the approach to teaching young people in many working-class schools, and these schools are now preparing their students to work in low-skill jobs that simply no longer exist. If students leave school unprepared for today's jobs, they are more likely to fall prey to joblessness, economic instability, and what is commonly referred to as the school-to-prison pipeline (Wald & Losen, 2003).

Many of the differences between the pedagogy, curriculum, and discipline styles in the schools described by Anyon are based on the desires and demands of the children's parents. Parents of affluent children generally expect to raise children who are equally or more successful than themselves, and they expect the schools to which they send their children to equip them for this future (Lareau, 2003). Many lower-income parents have similar desires for their children, but are often unable to make the same demands as their affluent counterparts, and have different ideas about what successful teaching looks like (Jacob & Lefgen, 2007; Kalenberg, 2001; Posey-Maddox, 2014).

Annette Lareau (2003) studied child-rearing practices and found that children from different socioeconomic groups were being prepared differently for their lives as adults, both in their homes and in their schools. Lareau built on the work of Pierre Bourdieu (1986), who argued that families from upper-class groups socialize their children with a sense of "habitus," a cultural value system that determines for society as a whole what are the preferred foods, art, books, music, sports, and sources of entertainment. Much in the same way that parents pass down money and assets to their children (*economic capital*), they pass down cultural norms, known as *cultural capital*, and their access to social networks, known as *social capital*. Social class is therefore transmitted between generations (Putnam, 2015).

Lareau concluded that affluent children gain an emerging sense of entitlement from their parents and that parenting styles change with socioeconomic status. Middle-class and wealthier parents engage in "concerted cultivation," in which they use extracurricular classes, visits to museums, trips, and other activities as a means to impart specific knowledge and life skills to their children to prepare them for their future place in society. These parents rely on physical discipline less often and negotiate with their children more than working-class parents. Lareau contended that working-class families have a more natural approach to parenting, with less structured time and fewer activities. Similar to the schools to which they send their children, working-class parents stress discipline over negotiation and use short directives with fewer words to communicate with their children.

Method

In the subsequent sections, I discuss two public schools in two very different communities. All names of schools, communities, and people have been changed to maintain confidentiality. My daughter attended GEMS for nearly 3 years. Unfortunately, she was not thriving academically there and we chose to pay tuition for her to go to school in a different district. She is now completing her first year at Roaring Rock Elementary. The difference in the school communities was so striking, that I felt compelled to document these differences from the instant we first visited Roaring Rock.

I used direct observation and participant observation methods and took copious field notes to document what I saw and heard when attending public parent meetings, open houses, student parties, and other public events at both schools. As a mother and a part of these communities, I became what is known as a member-researcher (Adler & Adler, 1987). My presence is accepted as a part of the daily fabric of life and many of my observations were done while going through my daily parenting routines. Having been a member of both school communities gave me access to other parents. I formally interviewed 10 mothers: 5 from GEMS, 2 former GEMS mothers who have moved to wealthier and higher performing school districts, and 3 from Roaring Rock. All mothers considered themselves either somewhat or highly active members of the school communities. My insider status also allowed me to continue attending GEMS events without being seen or treated as an outsider. Since I am not at GEMS each day as I used to be, and since I did not do classroom observations in either school, I rely heavily on the experiences and words of other mothers to support my hypothesis.

I also employed autoethographic techniques to help explain my decision-making process for taking my daughter out GEMS and placing her at Roaring Rock, and to highlight our experience since the move. Autoethnography allows a scholar to systematically examine her ideas, beliefs, and behaviors while explaining her experiences. As I write this, I find myself at the intersection of scholar and mother. Autoethnography has allowed me to use my own experiences to explain broader cultural experiences and the structural factors that push parents to make school-choice decisions (Ellis, Adams, & Bochner, 2010).

This work has several limitations. First, though I have field notes from informal conversations with more than 15 GEMS and Roaring Rock parents, the sample of mothers formally interviewed was small. Since I was writing about my intersection of scholar and mother, I decided to only interview other mothers. Had I interviewed men, my findings may have been different. Also, all mothers formally interviewed, identify as middle or upper-middle class. None identify as working-class. I am relying on these subjects' interpretation of reality to help build my story. Also, I am admittedly biased as I have chosen one of these schools for my own child over the other. However, I argue that this does not make the story any less relevant; rather, it allows me to offer insight into the decision-making process surrounding school choice. The conclusions reached and the interpretations of my observations are my own. I have attempted to be as honest and objective as possible, but certainly my history as an educator and my status as a highly educated middle-class White woman shape my understanding of schools and societal structures.

Riverview and GEMS

Riverview is a medium-sized city in southern New York State. Like many other northeastern cities, Riverview has experienced deindustrialization, devastating mismanagement of city funds, and urban decay over the past 30 years. The city is ethnically and socially diverse. The demographics are as follows: 41% White, 19% African American 35%, Latino, and 9% Asian. Riverview's median household income is $59,195, just above that of New York State's $58,002 (U.S Census Bureau, 2015). In the city's more affluent neighborhoods, it is twice the state median, and in poorer parts of the city, families subsist on a third of the state median.

The Riverview City School District suffers from a reputation problem. This stems from a combination of factors, all of which keep many young middle-class families from wanting to buy a home in the city or send their children to schools in the district. Only about 16% of third- and eighth-grade students in Riverview read at or above grade level, and fewer than 14% graduate from high school prepared to enter college or the job market (New York State Education Department, 2014a, 2014c).

Many of the issues with Riverview's schools are a result of the high level of poverty in the district. High-poverty districts generally have lower rates of achievement than wealthier districts (Kahlenberg, 2001; Rumberger & Palardy, 2005). An achievement gap exists between poor and affluent students. Low-income students enter school less prepared than their affluent peers and are less likely to graduate from high school and attend college (Khalenberg, 2001). Riverview is a predominantly middle-class city, but more than three quarters of the students in the district qualify for free or reduced-price lunches (New York State Education Department, 2013).

It would be naïve to ignore the role of race in Riverview's school story. White families make up the largest share of Riverview's residents; however, Riverview's school system is only about 18% White (New York State Education Department 2015; U.S. Census, 2015). The district had been predominantly White until the mid-1980s, when a court ordered it to implement a desegregation plan. While the program alleviated the isolation of African-American children, it also drove the majority of White families from the city's schools. This phenomenon has often been referred to as "White flight," the large-scale exodus of White families from increasingly diverse urban centers to more homogenous suburbs (Massey & Denton, 1993; Wilson, 1993). Saporito (2003) described this in his outgroup avoidance theory, which maintains that White and other advantaged parents avoid schools and neighborhoods with high proportions of minorities or people whom they perceive to be of lower status. In Massey and Denton's seminal book *American Apartheid* (1993), the authors suggested that racial segregation is largely the result of White avoidance of areas populated by non-Whites.

GEMS (an acronym) is the crown jewel of the Riverview school system; it is highly regarded for academic achievement by students, best demonstrated by the fact that the school has the highest standardized test scores of all elementary/middle schools in the city (New York State Department of Education, 2014a). GEMS admission is based on verbally administered IQ tests in lower grades and a combination of IQ test, report card grades, and standardized test scores in the upper grades. Several GEMS mothers indicated that had their child not gained acceptance into GEMS, they would not have sent their child to public school in the district.

Programs for gifted and talented students are often criticized because they tend to enroll more White and Asian students and fewer Black and Latino students (U.S. Department of Education, 2012). This is not the case at GEMS. Enrollment in the school seems to be carefully balanced; more Black and Latino students attend than do White and Asian students, closely reflecting the demographics of the district as a whole (New York State Department of Education, 2014b). Also impressive is that GEMS caters to students of most socioeconomic backgrounds. GEMS is a Title I school, more than 45% of the students are economically disadvantaged (New York State Education Department, 2014b). The school has been recognized several times as a National Blue Ribbon School and has been cited by the U.S.

Department of Education as a school that successfully educates low-income students, when so many other schools fail to do so.

Diversity is one of the best things at GEMS, students' families come from all over the world and many are first-generation immigrants. Every GEMS parent interviewed spoke at length about the importance of the school's diversity. Diversity extends to the faculty and staff. While most of the teachers at GEMS would be considered middle class, are White, and identify as Italian, Irish, or Jewish American, there are several Black/African American and Hispanic teachers as well. The principal and one other building administrator are Black women, while the other two building administrators are White. Teachers are sensitive to diverse religious backgrounds of the students and an attempt is made to honor most of the students' traditions during holidays such as Diwali, Chanukah, and Lunar New Year. The curriculum is not truly multicultural, but it at least addresses the idea of multiculturalism.

GEMS is housed in a massive brick building in a mostly residential neighborhood in downtown Riverview and serves more than 1,000 students in the pre-K through eighth-grade school. The school building is 90 years old and in need of major repairs; none of the classrooms have air conditioning. Like many good schools located in urban centers, GEMS is overcrowded and has had several structural additions over the past few decades to serve its growing population. As a result, the school no longer has fields or large play areas for the students to congregate before or after school. There are two small, but relatively new playgrounds, one at the north and one at the south end of the building. Children are allowed to play on the play equipment during lunch, but because the playgrounds are too small for all children in one grade to play there simultaneously, the classes must alternate between using them and simply playing on the concrete.

The dropoff and pickup procedures for most schools is chaotic; at GEMS, it is particularly so. There are well over a thousand students converging each morning on a building with no driveway, roundabout, or visitor parking. The school is on a relatively busy city street, where cars drive too fast and a city bus stops right in front of the school every 20 minutes. More than 20 school buses line up on the street in front and to the side of the school each morning. Most parents wait in line to let their children jump out of the car and run across the busy street. Parents of smaller children who wish to walk their children inside have to fight for spots on one of the narrow residential blocks, which are generally filled with the cars of residents who have not yet left for work at 7:25 a.m. As the school buses pull away and leave spaces free in front of the school, parents use that opportunity to pull up in front of the school to let their children out or to walk them inside. A woman who is employed by the school has the responsibility to scream at parents who pull their cars up to the front of the school: "Hey! You can't park there. I'll have you towed if you leave that car there!"

Yelling seems to be a major component of the day at GEMS, especially among some of the school support staff. All the GEMS mothers interviewed mentioned incidents in the lunchroom or playground where yelling or screaming was employed as a means of crowd control. One mother reported that she had spoken to one of the assistant principals about the yelling in the lunchroom and was told that the problem would be addressed with the support staff, but little has changed since that conversation over a year ago. Another mother, who said she is thinking seriously about moving to another district in the near future, said that if she moves, the yelling would be one of the top three driving factors in her decision to do so.

To complement the yelling are a set of prescriptive rules for behavior. During lunch, children are not allowed to speak at the lunch table or get up from their tables to throw away garbage. Rules like this are meant to keep order, but even some prisons allow their inmates the opportunity to speak during meals and get up and walk around. Other rules include not being allowed to run in the school yard or in the gym or climb on the monkey bars in the playground. Again, these are meant to keep order and prevent injury, but why spend the effort and money building play equipment with monkey bars if children are not allowed to use them?

Parents interviewed complained about what several of them labeled as "harsh" punishments for small behavioral infractions. One reported her child being barred from recess for "talking back" to a school aide. Her child maintains that he was trying to explain to explain herself to the aide, but the aide would not listen. Another mentioned similar sanctions for talking while waiting on the lunch line. Still another said that her son had been punished during lunch or recess on more than one occasion without ever being told why he was being punished. When this parent complained to the school's administration about the second incident, she was assured that it would not happen again. And yet, she said, "about two months later, the whole class (her son's) was 'put on the fence' (as punishment) and none of the kids or mothers seemed to know why." Several mothers thought the school relied too quickly on suspension of students, especially for students of color. According to the New York State Department of Education (2014b), 52 GEMS students were suspended last year. No data was available regarding the race or ethnicity of those students.

The mothers interviewed had mixed feelings about the teachers at GEMS. Most of the mothers agreed that the teachers they have encountered at GEMS have been very good or excellent pedagogues and care about their profession. One mother said, "I think the GEMS teachers are amazing and really care about their jobs. They have to, since they have to do so much with so little." All agreed that the teachers in the lower grades are mostly warm and attentive to academic and social needs. According to the parents of middle school–age children, the yelling and punitive behavior that exists in the lunchroom and playground persists in many of the upper-grade classrooms.

Whatever their discipline approach, the teachers at GEMS strictly enforce rules to maintain order. Student mobility is strictly limited, students must ask to get out of their seats, use the pencil sharpener or the bathroom, and they must carry a bathroom pass. Some teachers limit how many trips students can make to the bathroom per month. Class sizes at GEMS are big, even in the early childhood and elementary settings, class sizes are 28–32 students. In pre-K and first grade, there are part-time school aides to assist teachers in the classroom; there are no aides or assistant teachers in the higher grades. In most classes, the teachers assign each student a number on the first day of school and that number is used to identify the work and belongings of each student for the rest of the academic year. On the GEMS parents' social media pages, several parents have expressed concern about the impersonality of their children being referred to as a number.

Neither the teachers nor the students at GEMS seem to have any real say in the material that is taught and learned. Curriculum is mandated by the school district and the state, and not much supplemental curriculum is offered. The new focus on the Common Core Standards means that little time is allocated for social studies or science instruction, and there is very little hands-on experimentation. One mother, who is also a high school science teacher, mentioned that her first grade daughter did not want to go to science camp last summer because she "thought that science meant reading out of text book and answering questions about animals and weather." She expressed concern about her children being able to compete for high-skill jobs in the science and technology fields if the school continued to put little emphasis on science instruction.

During the school day, students usually leave their classroom for "special" classes. This helps to complement the basic curriculum and is a scheduling tool to allow the classroom teacher contractual breaks from teaching. At GEMS, these include art, music theory, library, and physical education. The Great Recession forced the district to make austere budget cuts, which included cuts to the instrumental music program. It was eventually replaced, but only for students in the fifth grade and higher. In the seventh grade, students are offered Spanish class, but no other "special" classes are offered to younger students.

Once or twice a week, there is no "special" class for the children to attend. When this happens, a substitute teacher is brought into the classroom to watch the children while their teacher is taking a break. During this time, no instruction happens, and the students play games or do homework. Several mothers complained that this is a missed opportunity for students to be doing those science experiments or to introduce a foreign language, dance, or drama program. Unfortunately, these programs would require funds and faculty to which the school simply does not have access.

In the last round of budget cuts, the intra-district modified sports program for sixth through eighth graders was also discontinued. One mother suggested that without the modified sports programs at the middle school level, GEMS and other Riverview City students would be at a disadvantage in high school when playing teams from other districts in the county, who have sports programs that start in the fifth grade.

Students at GEMS do not take any classes that instruct them on computer science and there are no computer labs for students in the elementary grades. The classrooms at GEMS do have desktop computers in the classroom for student use, but the mothers report that these are often not functional. GEMS students mostly use the classroom computers for taking online reading or math assessments. Most schools in the county have had interactive whiteboards in all of their classes for several years; these have proven themselves to be invaluable interactive teaching tools. GEMS only has these interactive board in the middle-school grades.

Fortunately, the PTA at GEMS is very strong and the parents raise a great deal of money each year to supplement the school's limited resources. They provide money for an indoor recess program for when the weather is bad, bring in supplemental art programs, and have helped to start several lunchtime clubs. I asked an executive member of the PTA why they did not pay to supplement the technology at the school. She said that they had in fact bought computers and laptops once before, but that during a budget crisis the district appropriated the machines to other schools. After that, the PTA stayed with programs and activities that could not be taken away and given to students elsewhere.

In early October, GEMS parents are invited to an open house, where they meet teachers, and learn about expectations for their child's grade. I accompanied a mother acquaintance of mine to see what the expectations would be for third grade. Students are administered their first statewide standardized exams in the third grade, which makes this a benchmark grade for both students and schools. In the one-hour session, the teacher explained the daily routine, identified the class resources, and demonstrated a sample of model work. She was cordial and even a little funny, but kept stressing the importance of the third grade and the implications of the state exams on the child's future. She mentioned the words "Common Core" or "Common Core Standards" 18 times and referred to the "state test," "state assessment," or "third-grade test" 16 times.

Clearly, the teacher's intention was to stress the importance of this test for students and the school, and that message has been transmitted very clearly. All six GEMS mothers expressed concern about the new curriculum and what they called "teaching to the test." A mother of three who has had at least one child at GEMS for the last 13 years said,

> It didn't used to be like this, you know. It's changed, it's all test prep and standards and high-stakes stress. They treat the kids like robots. But, you know it wasn't like this before the Common Core. Madeline didn't spend all day doing math worksheets and reading passages, but Jessy does. They've taken a practice test for what feels like every week this month. ... And the work! The homework and the tests. She has a math and spelling test every week. Sometimes she has two tests in one day. I just think that's a lot for an 8 year old, don't you ... and they give homework on Fridays and over the break. ... Ms. Diani has become like a drill sergeant with them. It wasn't like this before, she wasn't like this before. It's all gotten so strict and so boring, and I think we all feel a little powerless to stop it.

The GEMS moms had split feelings regarding the amount of the work their children were doing for school. Some perceived the quantity of work positively and as one mother put it, "encouraged a strong work ethic." Others thought that in third grade and up, the students were given too much homework and too many projects. One mother reported that last year, her daughter's spring break packet was 90 pages of workbook sheets and she had a science fair project to complete as well. Another mother said her third-grade daughter was so overwhelmed that she started to cry because she had two hours of homework and two tests to study for in one night. The mother said, "I'm just not sure that's developmentally appropriate at this age." When asked how long it took for their younger GEMS student (fourth grade and below) to complete their homework each night, all said over two hours and two mothers said more than three hours.

Several of the mothers, both those still in GEMS and those that have moved, noted that the homework and classwork at GEMS was "tedious"; as one mother described it:

> It's always the same thing since first grade; a list of vocabulary words on Monday, write them three times. One Tuesday and Wednesday you use them in a sentence and on Thursday you alphabetize them. He's been doing that since pre-K, you'd think they'd come up with something else. Then in third grade, they added reading passages and threw in a couple of math sheets. It never changes.

Both mothers who have moved to higher performing districts told me that their children receive far less homework per night. More interesting was that both also said the type of work their children were doing in their new schools was more "meaningful" and one mother said, "It's like learning in context and so that makes it more fun." They also said that their children report feeling freer to move around their classrooms and hallways, speak up for themselves, disagree with adults, and engage in more meaningful classroom conversations.

All the mothers reported that, despite being somewhat or highly active within the school and district, they felt as if they had very little input in policy changes, curriculum, or discipline matters. When talking about school and district administration, one mother said, "they either ignore parents or they try to intimidate them and make them feel stupid, then they complain that parents aren't involved." In fact, the word "intimidation" was used by several of the mothers to describe the approach that teachers, school administrators, and district officials took with them and their children. When asked why they think the district believes they can treat parents and students like that, two mothers suggested it was because Riverview's Board of Education members are appointed by the mayor and not elected by the residents. When residents in smaller, wealthier districts complain about incidents or policies, they are addressed. GEMS mothers reported feeling ignored by school and city officials.

Roaring Rock

Roaring Rock is a small village with fewer than 10,000 residents. The median household income in nearly three times the state average and the median home sales price is more than $1 million (United States Census Bureau, 2015). The area is entirely suburban; there are no commercial centers or stores. Roaring Rock Elementary School is not a particularly fancy building; it looks like an elementary school that one would expect to see in television shows or movies. The elementary school sits on approximately 5 acres of land; there is a baseball diamond, a soccer field, and extra space for the students to run around or for the school to hold a field day. There is also a very large playground with several sets of apparatus on which students may play. As with GEMS, the population of the school must have grown in recent decades and a structural addition was built to accommodate that growth.

There is a large circular driveway to allow for movement of cars in the mornings and afternoons, a large parking area for teachers, and another for parents and visitors. In the driveway, three lanes are designated for traffic. One lane is specifically designated for parents dropping off their children each morning. As parents pull up to the door, a school aide walks up to the car, opens the door, and walks the child onto the sidewalk or into the building. When it is raining, he holds an umbrella over the child. The classrooms at Roaring Rock are not any larger than those at GEMS. However, they are air conditioned and each is equipped with several computers and an interactive whiteboard. Class sizes are considerably smaller, capped at 20 students, but usually with only 18 or 19.

Roaring Rock works on a six-day rotating schedule to accommodate the "special" classes offered to students. Students have physical education three times in the six-day rotation. In the physical education classes, there is a full curriculum which includes units on the circus arts, jump rope, riding scooters, basketball, etc. During those six days, students also take art, music, Spanish, computer, and a library skills class. In computer class, children learn file management, word processing, creating presentations, and coding. Additionally, each homeroom class does alternating units of social studies and science throughout the year.

Similar to the open house I attended at GEMS, I attended one at Roaring Rock where parents are invited to meet the teacher and talk about the curriculum. Until asked by a parent, the teacher never once mentioned the words "Common Core" or "state test." She acknowledged that the students will take the tests in the spring, but that they would not be doing anything in particular to prepare for it. She said that all of the material will be covered in the classwork during the year and told parents not to "worry too much." This is not to imply that the Roaring Rock administration and community is unconcerned or flippant about the implementation of the Common Core Standards and new statewide exams. In fact, the school has adopted new and much more rigorous math and reading programs to prepare students for the new exams. The Roaring Rock mothers interviewed expressed the same misgivings as GEMS mothers over the new demands placed on young children, the state's increasing reliance on test scores to assess students and teachers, and the increase in test preparation. However, they said that they did not feel that the school was putting any undue pressure on the students to succeed.

The new Common Core curriculum is implemented much differently at Roaring Rock. While the reading and math programs have changed, they have not supplanted the study of social studies, science, and other core subjects. When asked about increases in homework or classroom tests as a result of curriculum changes, one mother said,

> Oh, God no, are you kidding? These mothers were up in arms about the new math program. They went nuts. … They'd never stand for more homework and tests or vacation packets. Actually, I think there might be a school policy about not giving too much homework. They're angry enough about all the new test prep. But we don't do vacation packets or hours of homework a night. It's not fair to the parents. We're the ones who end up suffering for that. It becomes mommy work and it's so hard to get it all done between dinner and the after-school stuff or when you go on vacation.

Though I found no such formal homework policy, when asked how much homework their children receive each night, the mothers (of third graders) said 30–45 minutes per night.

Roaring Rock is absolutely lacking in racial and socioeconomic diversity. More than 90% of students are White, 5% are Asian, and only 2% are Hispanic (New York State Education Department, 2014b). Currently, there is not one single African American child enrolled in the school and only three of the more than 625 students are considered economically disadvantaged. This is almost unbelievable, considering the school's location in what is the nation's most diverse metropolitan area. The faculty and staff are also mostly homogenous; the administrators, most of the teachers, and the support staff are White and middle class. In fact, the only African American person with whom my daughter interacts during her entire school day is the school aide who opens her car door and walks her into the building each morning.

The Roaring Rock mothers interviewed all reported feeling some sense of empowerment in the district with regard to policies, rules, and discipline. They said they felt comfortable calling the principal, superintendent, and at least one school board member directly with issues and concerns regarding the school. However, they said they felt a decreasing sense that they had meaningful input in school curriculum and student assessment. All three mothers reported being comfortable with how the school handles matters of discipline. When asked about screaming or yelling in the lunchroom, classroom, or hallways, one mother shook her head said, "I've never heard anyone screaming here. Well, maybe the kids sometimes." In the 2014–2015 school year, Roaring Rock Elementary and Middle Schools suspended no students

A Mother-Scholar's Perspective

Through the research I do, I understand the devastating effects racial and economic segregation can have on all children (Massey & Denton, 1993; Khalenberg, 2001; Wilson, 1996). My husband and I chose Riverview to buy a home specifically for its diversity, as we did not want our children growing up in a homogenous suburb where they would never be confronted with people who did not look, think, sound, believe, and act as we do. Like the other mothers who contributed to this work, and those who choose urban public school systems, I was absolutely convinced of my own ability to supplement the lack of resources by making use of my own social, cultural, and political capital (Kimelberg, 2014).

Unfortunately, it became apparent that despite being highly intelligent, my daughter had a learning disability, and GEMS was ill-prepared to deal with her learning issues. After a long wait, she was given an Individualized Education Plan (IEP) and assigned to a resource room class where she got supplemental help in a small-group setting and was to see an occupational therapist weekly. Despite the efforts of the classroom and resource room teacher, there was little improvement during the first year of services. I asked several times what their plan was for my daughter and what additional services they planned to provide. The team kept insisting that I just needed to read to her more, but offered no additional services or action plan. My husband and I became frustrated with the school's inability to address her learning needs effectively or even efficiently and their insistence that the problem was that my husband and I were not fulfilling our duties as parents.

Eventually, we decided to move our daughter to Roaring Rock despite my misgivings about the schools lack of diversity. For the first time, my daughter is eager to learn and loves that she has yet to hear anyone yelling at students for what she calls "no big deal" infractions. She calls her new school "softer" and told me once that the new school makes it easier for her to breathe. While I am happy with our decision, I cannot help but wonder about her friends she left behind. When we met my daughter's new principal, she stressed wanting the children to be happy and love school, and she told my daughter how much she mattered. But what about all the other children? Why do they not get to love school and feel that they matter? Countless children attend schools where their needs are secondary to all other things in the municipality. We are sending those children the message that they do not matter.

Roaring Rock clearly provides services and courses that GEMS in Riverview does not and cannot provide. Roaring Rock is able to do this in part because their property tax revenue allows the school to spend nearly 25% more per child than does Riverview (New York State Education Department, 2014a). That money goes toward courses and activities that give Roaring Rock students basic essential skills, which they can build upon in high school and college. When Riverview students start college, they may be at a disadvantage if they are not well versed in modern technology, coding language, science, a foreign language, or even proficient in a sport. Unfortunately, parents in low-income schools such as GEMS do not have the ability to force their schools to provide top-quality services. As Rumberger and Palardy (2005) maintained, "Parents and students with the power to demand more challenging curriculum and command high expectations have schools with different 'school cultures' and 'academic pressures'" (p. 2022). In contrast, poor families feel less empowered and are less likely to make such demands.

Money is a powerful motivational tool in education. Both schools enjoy high test scores that keep the rhetoric and public impression surrounding them positive. However, GEMS' Title I status puts it at the mercy of those test scores. Roaring Rock's high test scores mean that, when middle-class parents in the area talk about which school districts are the best to move to, Roaring Rock is on the list. But as a Title I school, if GEMS fails to improve test scores year to year, they could face sanctions from the state and federal government and the possible loss of the ability to spend Title I money as they see fit (Braden & Schroeder, 2004). When a school has to be so narrowly focused on test scores, it cannot focus on much else and is therefore compelled to offer little other than test preparation to its students.

At our visit, Roaring Rock's principal asked my daughter whether she had any questions. My daughter thought for a long time and finally asked, "Yeah, are the kids here allowed to speak when they're eating lunch?" The principal looked at me in confusion, but I understood and my heart sank. Children are, in fact, allowed to speak during lunch in Roaring Rock. They are also allowed to leave their seats without asking permission, walk in the hallways without a bathroom pass, run in the playground, and climb on the monkey bars. I told the principal about the rules and yelling at my daughter's other school. She looked me in the eye and promised that would never be a problem if we decided to transfer my daughter. It has not been. The school functions well without strict social controls and punishment.

Roaring Rock seems to focus on what I can only refer to as "customer service." They want to keep the parents happy. They not only fulfill requests with expediency, but anticipate what requests will be made and try to fulfill them before the request is made. At GEMS, I felt that I was constantly asking for changes or complaining to the administration about something—the yelling, the lack of technology, the bland curriculum. I hated being *that* parent, and I am sure the administration grew tired of my requests. The other GEMS mothers, past and present agreed that GEMS is not focused on customer service and that the administration make parents feel that they are doing them a favor simply by allowing the child to attend the school.

I am still very troubled that my daughter is not exposed to people from diverse backgrounds and it makes me uncomfortable that one of the only people of color with whom she interacts is the school aide that opens the car door for her. When we are not confronted with people from other socioeconomic and ethnic/racial groups, it is easy for us to forget that they exist and that they often face structural and institutional barriers to their success. I also worry that my daughter will develop an unearned sense of entitlement and that she may get the wrong idea about which people in society can be the owners of capital and which are destined to merely serve the owners of capital.

I have spent my entire career as an urban educator and admittedly now feel like a sellout. I regret that I have turned my back on a system that I fought so hard to support. Unfortunately, the realities of education in urban locales mean that many parents, even the most well-intentioned ones, are not able to choose city public schools for their children. While I do not refute Saporito's outgroup avoidance theory or Massey and Denton's argument that White families generally avoid areas populated by non-Whites, I maintain that people and their situations are sometimes more complicated and nuanced than these scholars would lead us to believe.

It was immediately obvious to me that Roaring Rock had more physical resources, but what also became apparent was that the approach to teaching and learning was very different. The students in Roaring Rock were being prepared for a much different career path and future than the students at GEMS. Despite the changes that have occurred in this nation, the economy, and the schools during the past three decades, a hidden curriculum of work persists in the education system and schools are continuing to reproduce social stratification and therefore inequality. According to Robert Putnam (2015), inequality in the United States is widening and surmounting poverty to join the middle class is becoming increasingly hard for young people from working-class families. I maintain that the differences in the way we educate our young people is turning the gap between poverty and affluence into an insurmountable cavern. If low-income students start school at an academic disadvantage, it would make sense to offer these children access to more resources, not less. Furthermore, it is morally unacceptable that we allow whole communities of families to feel underpowered and disengaged from their schools.

References

Adler, P., & Adler, P. (1987). *Membership roles in field research.* Newbury Park, CA: Sage.

Anyon, J. (1980). Social class and the hidden curriculum of work. *Journal of Education, 162*(1), 64–96.

Bourdieu, P. (1986). The forms of capital. In J. Richardson (Ed.), *Handbook of theory and research for the sociology of education* (pp. 241–258). New York, NY: Greenwood.

Braden, J., & Schroeder, J. (2004). High-stakes testing and No Child Left Behind: Information and strategies for educators. In A. Cantor, S. Carroll, & L. Paige (Eds.), *Helping children at home and school II: Handouts for families and educators* (pp. 33–73). Washington, DC: National Association of School Psychologists.

Calarco, J. M. (2014) "Coached for the classroom: Parents' cultural transmission and children's reproduction of inequalities," *American Sociological Review, 79*(5), 1015–1037.

Common Core State Standards Initiative (2012). *Common core state standards for English language arts & literacy in history/ social studies, science, and technical subjects.* Washington, DC: National Governors Association Center for Best Practices and the Council of Chief State School Officers.

Condron, D. J. (2009). Social class, school and non-school environments, and Black/White inequalities in children's learning. *American Sociological Review, 94*, S683–S708. doi: 10.1177/000312240907400501

Cowie, J & Heathcott, J. (2008). The Meaning of Deindustrialization. In J. Cowie & J. Heathcott (Eds.), *Beyond the ruins: The meanings of deindustrialization* (pp. 1–18). Ithaca, NY: Cornell University Press.

Ellis, C., Adams, T., & Bochner, A. (2010). Autoethnography: An overview. *Forum Qualitative Sozialforschung/Forum: Qualitative Social Research, 12*(1). Retrieved from http://www.qualitative-research.net/index.php/fqs/article/view/1589/3095

Friedman, T. (2005). *The world is flat: A brief history of the twenty-first century.* New York, NY: Farrar, Strauss, & Giroux.

Giroux, H. A., & Penna, A. N. (1979). Social education in the classroom: The dynamics of the hidden curriculum. *Theory & Research in Social Education, 7*(1), 21–42.

Horvat, E, Weinberger, E., & Lareau, A. (2003). From social ties to social capital: Class differences in the relations between schools and parent. *American Educational Research Journal, 40*(2), 319–351.

Jacob, B. A., & Lefgren, L. (2007). What do parents value in education? An empirical investigation of parents revealed preferences for teachers. *Quarterly Journal of Economics, 122*(4), 1603–1637.

Kahlenberg, R. (2001). *All together now: Creating middle-class schools through public school choice.* New York, NY: Century Foundation.

Kimelberg, S. M. (2014). Beyond test scores: Middle-class mothers, cultural capital, and the evaluation of urban public schools. *Sociological Perspectives,* (57) 208–228.

Lareau, A. (2003). *Unequal childhoods: Class, race, and family life.* Berkeley, CA: University of California Press.

Massey, D., & Denton, N. (1993). *American apartheid: Segregation and the making of the under-class.* Cambridge, MA: Harvard University Press.

New York State Education Department. (2013a). *Examining individual school districts district wealth.* Retrieved from http://www.oms.nysed.gov/faru/Profiles/18th/wealt_indicators.htm

New York State Education Department. (2014a). *New York State 3–8 assessment data.* Retrieved from http://data.nysed.gov/assessment.php?year=2014&state=yes

New York State Education Department. (2014b). *New York State enrollment data.* Retrieved http://data.nysed.gov/enrollment.php?year=2014&state=yes

New York State Education Department. (2014c). *New York State gradaution rate data.* Retrieved from http://www.p12.nysed.gov/irs/pressRelease/20141218/home.html

Orfield, G., Frankenberg, E. J., & Kuscera, J. (2014). *Brown at 60: Great progress, a long retreat and an uncertain future.* Los Angeles, CA: University of California Los Angeles Civil Rights Project.

Possey-Maddox, L. (2014). *When middle-class parents choose urban public schools: Class, race & the challenge of equity in public education.* Chicago, IL: University of Chicago Press.

Putnam, R. D. (2015). *Our kids: The American Dream in crisis.* New York, NY: Simon & Schuster.

Rumberger, R., & Palardy, G. (2005). Does segregation still matter? The impact of student composition on academic achievement in high school. *Teacher's College Record, 107*, 1999–2045.

Saporito, S. (2003). Private choices, public consequences: Magnet school choice and segregation by race and poverty. *Social Problems, 50*(2), 181–203.

U.S. Census Bureau. (2015). *State & county Quickfacts: Westchester County, N.Y.* Retrieved from http://quickfacts.census.gov.

U.S. Department of Education. (2012). *Civil rights data collection.* Washington, DC: Author.

U.S. Department of Education (2014). No Child Left Behind. Washington, DC. Retrieved from http://www2.ed.gov/nclb/landing.jhtml

U.S. Department of Education (2015). Race to the Top Resources. Retrieved from http://www2.ed.gov/about/inits/ed/implementation-support-unit/tech-assist/resources.html

Wald, J., & Losen, D. J. (2003). Defining and redirecting a school-to-prison pipeline. *New Directions for Youth Development, 9*, 15.

Wilson, J.J. (1996) *When work disappears: The world of the new urban poor.* New York, NY: Random House.

CHAPTER 28

What Matthew Shepard Would Tell Us

Gay and Lesbian Issues in Education

Doug Risner

"We just don't have any gay kids in my school." —High School Principal

Of the many provocative topics in my undergraduate social foundations of education course, no discussion brings more anger, tears, confusion, and hostility than our readings and discussion about gay and lesbian issues. Within a spiraling curriculum that interrogates race, social class, gender and their myriad intersections, gay and lesbian issues in educational policy and practice remain the most volatile in this class. Knowing such, I continue to experiment with different pedagogical approaches that focus not only on the roots of sexism, discrimination, bigotry, and hate, but also on the ways in which these students as future educators are ethically obligated to confront their own attitudes and beliefs about gays and lesbians in schools—their students, their students' parents or family members, their fellow teachers and administrators.

Current teacher training programs in higher education in the U.S. focus upon discipline-specific competency classes and methods coursework, usually supplemented with one course in educational psychology and one in social/philosophical foundations of education. The vast majority of teacher preparation emphasizes *what* is to be taught and *how* (most efficiently) to teach it. Conversely, foundations courses emphasize for future teachers the *why* of democratic public education, for what purposes, in whose benefit, to what ends. And therefore, the course centralizes the aims of freedom, equality, human dignity, diversity, and social justice. Because students receive only one semester of such coursework, much needs to happen in a very short period of time.

For this reason, I use a multi-dimensional spiral progression, rather than a linear approach to social issues and their intersections with educational theory and practice. The helical structure of the spiral allows critical social problems of race, class, and gender to stand as a central pole, a cylinder around which the students' reflections and questions wind gradually, simultaneously receding from and drawing near, each time (hopefully) more informed. Advancing and retreating in a methodological coil enables students to see not only the interrelatedness and complexity of social constructions of privilege and marginality but also to reflect upon their own place within these hierarchical structures that inevitably dominant and oppress.

Confronting Difference and Hate

Having spent a good deal of class time on issues of sexism and gender inequity in education, we extrapolate more fully the prejudice and bias women experience in U.S. culture and the ways in which dominant patriarchal structures and sexism often lead to homophobia. In order to begin discussion about bigotry and hate directed toward gay, lesbian, and bisexual people, as well as their contemporary manifestations in schools, I turn to the senseless and brutal death of college student, Matthew Shepard. I do so, not so much for its horrific detail or its public notoriety, but because the tragedy moves us as educators to reconsider what our past educative efforts have accomplished and more importantly, where we might necessarily position our labors in the present.

In 1998, Shepard, who was gay, died after being tied to a fence outside Laramie, Wyoming, where he was pistol-whipped, beaten, and then left for dead in the freezing night by his killers. What we can learn from Shepard's highly publicized death, we could most likely learn from any number of others who suffered viciously horrific murders because they were gay: Brandon Teena, raped and shot to death in 1993; Billy Jack Gaither, beaten and set on fire in 1999; Danny Overstreet, gunned down in 2000; JR Warren, gang-beaten and run over with a car in 2000; or Army Pfc. Barry Winchell bludgeoned to death with a baseball bat while sleeping in 1999. I chose the Shepard case not because it was the most brutal or the most senseless, but rather because of its intense national reaction and what can be learned from such response.

I do not focus on the evil consciousness responsible for Shepard's murder, because frankly, that kind of wickedness is beyond my comprehension, and also because attending to such trivializes the significance and power of education. While I in no way wish to diminish the inhumanity of these violent acts of cruelty, I do not dwell on such evil that I simply cannot understand or explain. However, if we look at Shepard's death and all that surrounds it, as a symptom of our larger cultural and educative failures and accomplishments, we are moved to respond, rather than to fall into despair. The national response to this hate-motivated murder teaches us many things about understanding difference. At the same time, the tragedy encapsulates for students the confusion and frustration that accompany issues of sexual orientation in our culture and the divide this social dissonance deeply cuts in our society and schools.

Following Shepard's death, outrage was voiced throughout the United States Proclamations were made, petitions signed, vigils organized, memorials given, and hate crimes legislation demanded by those who found Shepard's death a needless and senseless atrocity: And at the same time, those in opposition to homosexuality responded with anti-gay protests—picketing rallies and memorial services across the country, posting Internet messages on websites such as, godhatesfags.com. Anti-gay protesters at Shepard's funeral shouted epithets at mourners and carried signs reading "Fags Deserve Death" and "Matthew Shepard Burns in Hell." Some conservative religious leaders offered sympathy, but also used Shepard's death to warn their congregations of the "dangers" of homosexuality.

The cultural divide widened as attorneys for the two defendants in the case sought to argue what has become known as the "gay panic" defense, in which straights fearing unsolicited homosexual advances act out of self-defense. This strategy, one not dissimilar from "she asked for it" type defense tactics employed for alleged rapists, portrays the victim as provoking and inciting, as in the Shepard case, his own violently fatal attack.

Public debate often revolved around notions that Shepard brought the attack on himself, or at best "should have known better." Conservative talk radio positioned Shepard's death to reaffirm gay rights as "special rights"—unnecessary and without merit. Although state lawmakers in Wyoming had rejected hate crime measures four previous times since 1995, four months after Shepard was beaten to death, an emotionally charged move to pass a hate crimes bill was thought to surely be ratified; however, the Wyoming State Legislature defeated the measure in early 1999.

The social dissonance in the national response to Matthew Shepard's murder resolves some of our questions, but also gives rise to new ones. As a culture we have an intense sense of justice and solidarity, one that shows both collective support and respect for human life, and the impulse for "the good." While at the same time, the impulse for hate, opportunism, division, self-preservation, and blame (not to mention evil) flourishes in reciprocal fashion. It is within this profound confusion that we must begin to imagine things otherwise, radically different. Because it should be abundantly clear that as a society we are highly adept at simultaneously holding two highly contradictory narratives in our collective heads and hearts.

In tandem, the Shepard tragedy allows students to see the unrelenting power of a society that focuses heavily on difference and the pejorative categorization of such. Discrimination, in a consumer capitalist culture, directed toward those who are different or perceived to be different, develops because the ethical vision of the culture socializes citizens to view difference as a fearful threat, a menace people are obliged to compete with, to commodify, to divide and conquer. Understanding homophobia in this context reveals that these fears may on one level be more about difference and competition in a generic sense, rather than specifically about sexuality, or challenges to heterosexuality. This view of difference, its discrimination and homophobic attitude, is the product of a "where's Waldo?" enculturation process rooted in rigid categorization, emphasizing dissimilarity and hierarchy. Although seemingly benign, this discriminatory vision of the world is pervasively potent from a very young age. Elmo and his *Sesame Street* cohorts have taught us well to discern "which of these things is not like the other?" Given that the voice of Elmo is in reality, that of a gay black male, this kind of socialization is especially incriminating.

Dominant Culture: Heterosexism and Homophobia

Though undergraduate students sometimes comprehend the racist and sexist systems operating in U.S. culture, they rarely, and I might add, then only reluctantly comprehend the heterosexist underpinnings and assumptions characteristic of the world in which they live. Although the murderers' motivation for Shepard's death facilitates deeper understanding of the ways in which anti-gay prejudice and heterosexist bias develop socially in the United States, I still find in necessary to engage the students on an even more profound level, their own sexuality. To achieve this kind of engagement, I ask students to complete the following survey that I adapted from Martin Rochlin (1985).

Heterosexual Questionnaire

I. When and how did you first decide you were heterosexual?

2. What do you think caused your heterosexuality?

3. Is it possible that your heterosexuality is just a phase you may grow out of?

4. Is it possible that your heterosexuality stems from a neurotic fear of members of the same sex?

5. To whom have you disclosed your heterosexuality? How did they react?

6. The great majority of child molesters are heterosexuals (95%). Do you really consider it safe to expose your children to heterosexual teachers?

7. Why do heterosexuals place so much emphasis on sex?

8. If you've never slept with a person of the same sex, how do you know you wouldn't prefer that?

9. Does your employer know you are heterosexual? Are you openly heterosexual when with your family members? roommates? co-workers? church members?

10. With 50% of first-time heterosexual marriages ending in divorce, and over 60% of second heterosexual marriages also ending in divorce, there seem to be very few happy heterosexuals. Techniques have been developed to change your sexual orientation; have you considered aversion therapy to treat your heterosexuality?

Although students have a fair amount of difficulty answering many of the survey questions, their understanding of heterosexual bias and heterocentric assumptions that characterize the culture in which they live greatly expands in attempting the exercise. In order for future educators to understand the nature of this kind of marginalization, and gay issues more specifically, I find it helpful to outline the manner in which the dominant culture not only organizes political, social, and economic privilege for some, but also separates, discredits and discriminates against others.

Simply put, when we refer to the dominant culture and its ideology we are referencing the assumptions, ideas, concepts, and values that prevail in the central ways in which we organize our lives. Although usually associated with the "taken-for-granted" socio-political realm, or more plainly, people and their relationship to power, dominant ideology powerfully colors societal opinion, behavior, and worldview. At the same time, the unquestioned nature of dominant culture allows a commanding control that unfortunately benefits some people at the expense of others, in this case at the cost of gays and lesbians.

Friend (1986) defines the systemic practice of valuing and privileging heterosexuality as superior over homosexuality as heterosexism. Heterosexist prejudice holds a bias in favor of heterosexual people and discrimination against bisexual and homosexual persons. Gay men and lesbians encounter discrimination, stigmatization, prejudice, and violence based upon their sexual orientation, or perceived sexual orientation. Oppressed segments of the population often serve as falsely depicted stereotypes, unjustly ridiculed scapegoats, and blameworthy villains solely by virtue of their perceived cultural and social dif ferences. As a system of domination and discrimination, pervasive heterosexism shapes the political, economic, social, religious, familial, and educational spheres in American culture. Jung and Smith (1993) contend that at the center of heterosexist prejudice is the organizing belief that heterosexuality is the normative form of human sexual relations. As such, the standard measurement used to evaluate and judge all other sexual orientations is defined as heterocentrism.

Homophobia, as first defined by sociologist Weinberg (1972), is the irrational fear and hatred of homosexuality, either in one's self, or in others. A more expansive understanding of homophobia advances the definition to include disgust, anxiety, and anger directed toward homosexuality (MacDonald, 1976). Herek (1984) asserts that homophobia is frequently considered appropriate and utilitarian by individuals who possess it, in as much as homophobia is frequently a primary defining characteristic of contemporary masculinity in our culture. Boys learn from a very young age that there is no worse slur or taunt than being called a sissy, fag, or queer. What's more, young children who use these epithets rarely know what the words actually mean, other than their expressly pejorative connotations.

Though often precipitated by heterosexism, homophobia does not fundamentally or logically indicate a relationship between the two. Whereas heterosexism is similar to racism and sexism, homophobia is analogous to racial bigotry and misogyny. Without critical examination, fear and hatred of homosexuality often reproduce exponentially. In addition, pervasive homophobic prejudice, customarily associated with heterosexuals, negatively affects all persons, institutions, and cultures.

More specifically, homophobia and homophobic discrimination often emerge from the dominant cultural construction of heterocentrism, and therefore all persons, heterosexuals, gay men, lesbians, bisexuals, and transgendered persons to some degree and in various contexts, experience the hegemony (or unquestioned ruling power) of the heterocentrist center. Because heterocentrism 1) defines the ways in which people regard homosexuality, 2) frames routinely performed heterosexist biases, and 3) maintains a myriad of disparaging moral judgments about gay men and lesbians, the underpinnings of heterocentrism and heterosexual hegemony situate gays in the marginalized fringe.

While forms of resistance have and continue to challenge preponderant controlling ideas, such as the civil and human rights movements, feminism, environmental groups, and the gay and lesbian movement, the prevailing influence in American culture remains largely based on "white" masculine, heterosexual values and practices. Furthermore, the nexus between gender, power, and authority gives rise to subsequent inequities manifested in sexism, racism, and heterosexism. As such, dominant culture normalizes this narrow perspective as a widely held worldview and thereby carves its socially accepted center, sub sequently situating or marginalizing "others" (women, racial minorities, gays) on the cultural fringe. Like sexism and racism, systems of heterosexism reinforce dominant ideological assumptions and messages that constitute the characterization of sexual minority groups.

A recent survey finds that nearly 70% of lesbian, gay and bisexual students face verbal, sexual, or physical harassment or physical assault while at school (Gay, Lesbian, Straight Education Network, 2001) and nearly half of all gay and lesbian youth suffer violence from their families, peers, and strangers (Edwards, 1997). Unfortunately, many gay and lesbian students, unable to escape the pervasive nature of heterocentrism and homophobic prejudice in American culture and schools, internalize negative feelings about themselves (Gonsiorek, 1987). In its most recent study, the *American Journal of Public Health* finds that teenagers with same-sex attractions are twice as likely as their heterosexual counterparts to attempt suicide. Massachusetts Safe Schools Program for Gay & Lesbian Students has shown important statistical links between levels of student harassment experienced and attempted student suicide. According to the Human Rights Watch, a non-profit advocacy and research organization, millions of gay teenagers may be subjected to such widespread harassment and teacher indifference in U.S. schools that they do not receive an adequate education.

Plotting the margin (gays, women, minorities) and center (straights, men, whites) in this manner allows students to address more thoroughly 1) the important links between socio-cultural attitudes about homosexuality/homophobia and recurrent manifestations in educational practice and policy, and 2) each student's own relationship to, and role in the dominant ideology of margin and center. Given the sobering assessment of current school climate, teacher indifference, and the tragic consequences that ensue for gay and lesbian youth, a fundamental shift in the way we view ourselves and our students, as difficult, controversial, and painful as it may be, is not only necessary, but obligatory given the highly problematic world in which we live and teach.

Gay and Lesbian Youth

Whether educators' work is rooted in K-12 instruction, school administration, higher education, research, counseling, or policy, it is absolutely crucial to realize that gay teens and young adults are in our schools and programs. As educators, our opportunities for making a better, more just world and eradicating hateful prejudice remain before us. To be sure, speaking openly with children about sexual orientation is perceived as problematic in the homophobic culture in which we find ourselves, although research shows that children and adolescents have far less difficulty accepting alternative family structures and sexual difference than might be supposed (Chasnoff and Cohen, 1996). A recent study of U.S. high school seniors finds that 85% of seniors believe that gay men and lesbians should be accepted by society (Gilbert, 2001). Despite the apparent support for gay students, however, the survey found that U.S. high schools remain a largely hostile environment for gay and lesbian youth. What is more, many parents, teachers, and administrators are frequently uncomfortable even in the limited discussions our culture currently presents. These obstacles, though certainly tangible and substantial, should not diminish or trivialize our deepest commitments and sincerest concerns for developing humanizing pedagogies that prioritize the safety and well-being of all students.

Regrettably, even when we are made aware of profound injustices and abuses, we frequently distance ourselves from the real dilemmas at hand—explaining away the necessary and ethically responsive action as someone else's problem—in someone else's classroom or school. For example, a high school principal, aware of my research interests, recently said to me, "we just don't have any gay kids in my school." Research, of course, strongly suggests that the principal's assessment of his student body is statistically impossible (Besner and Spungin, 1995). Common sense would indicate that although no students have publicly identified themselves as gay or lesbian, in all likelihood a school of 1000 pupils would have, by conservative estimates, a minimum of thirty non-heterosexual students. Other estimates might put the number of gay, lesbian, and bisexual teens in his school as high as 100. Unfortunately, this kind of dominant attitude assumes that discussion of sexual orientation has as its sole aim the support of gay and lesbian people only, without any benefit or of interest to, heterosexual persons. This perspective, which universalizes heterosexuality, or more simply, assumes that everyone is heterosexual, eliminates the need for discussion of gay issues, and in doing so also eliminates vast possibilities for greater understanding of sexuality and sexual difference, the reduction of prejudice, and the confrontation of bigotry and hate.

For those in K-12 environments, as well as those teaching and researching within academia, it is of utmost importance that we realize the significant impact that addressing sexual orientation issues in our own locales—our own classrooms, our faculty meetings, our communities, and through our authority positions as teachers and role models, can have. By not only acknowledging, but also acting upon the educative potential schools hold for reducing homophobia and anti-gay stigmatization, the profession has the ability to play a profoundly important leadership role in reshaping our culture's negative messages about difference and prejudice.

In particular, young boys' avoidance and denial of their homosexual orientation are facilitated by countless diversions perpetrated by a pervasively heterocentric culture, especially when considering the overwhelmingly ridiculed status of sissy boys in American society. While there is vast individual variation, young gay males tend to begin homosexual activity during early or mid-adolescence; similar feelings and activity for lesbian females does not begin until around age twenty (Lipkin, 1994). For male K-12 Educators—straight, gay, or bisexual—this profound opportunity for confronting homophobia in middle and high schools seems particularly cogent, especially when we take seriously the vulnerability of gay and bisexual male teens.

Because adolescents are only beginning to possess the capacity for abstract thought and formal reasoning skills to cognitively integrate their sexual experiences, educators must realize that gay male adolescents are extremely vulnerable to gendered criticism, homophobic attitudes, anti-gay slurs, and the absence of positive gay male role models. Young gay males may also suffer from internalized homophobia learned throughout childhood in which self-hate, low self-esteem, destructive behavior, and further confusion characterize their underlying attitudes and conduct. Moreover, gay adolescents and teens often have far fewer resources available to them for understanding homosexuality and same-sex attraction in a balanced and unbiased manner. Social support networks for the young gay male are rare. What is more, the embarrassment, humiliation, and contempt of being labeled the pansy, the fag, or the queer, demand that he actively "prove" his heterosexuality over and over again. This kind of environment is stressful and often threatening, particularly since these are young people struggling to claim and affirm their sexual orientation in a frequently hostile social atmosphere. Teachers, aware of it or not, have a profound impact on this environment.

Certainly these issues are in no way limited to the education profession. However, these concerns should compel each of us as teachers to ask ourselves about the choices we make consciously or unconsciously, the behaviors we tolerate or ignore, the [in]actions we take or avoid, and the world we create by doing so—for what purposes, for what ends? Not talking honestly and genuinely about sexual orientation, prejudice, and anti-gay violence not only nurtures a suspicious cultural perspective of sexual difference, but also makes matters worse by unnecessarily magnifying issues of sexual orientation more than is worthwhile or appropriate. Minimizing such in secrecy and denial energizes a deleterious and discriminatory homosexual mythology, one that is harmful to all in education. In order to make our schools and our teaching more humane, let us instead confront sexual orientation pedagogically, mine the larger social ramifications more candidly, and learn from our lessons more sincerely, as taught to us by Matthew Shepard's senseless death.

What Can Educators Do?

The approach I urge students to contemplate asks them not only to consider seriously their actions in the world, but also that they believe their actions do actually matter, and therefore, have the potential for making a more just and liberating world in the here and now. Although I in no way forecast a quick and painless end to our deeply rooted social problems, I attempt to communicate this approach with a fervent sense of support on one hand, but also with a profound sense of urgency on the other. From this renewed questioning and our response to such, we are compelled to commit ourselves to take action against these and other oppressive practices. There is much to be learned by questioning our own complicity with the domination and privilege of the white, middle-class inner circle. The internal contradictions and dissonances we harbor, when attended to and pestered further, may be in actuality our utmost source of energy and hope.

Unfortunately, the enormity of our social ills all too often paralyzes our daily capability for consider ing and creating a better world. In undergraduate teacher training programs, courses in social foundations are particularly at risk for producing socially conscious yet deeply discouraged pre-service teachers—more fully aware, but equally as numb. It is essential that cultural workers in educational foundations not only help their students "describe the world, but to take a stand in shaping its construction" (Hytten 1998, 253). Given the extent of continued discrimination, bigotry, hate, and its violence, as well as the difficult nature of contemplating the need for such vast cultural change, I offer students some insights on how this kind of approach might sensibly unfold for themselves and their schools.

Invariably, the frustration that many of these future teachers experience by the middle of the semester is accompanied by a desperate need to know what specifically can be done to help gay, lesbian, and bisexual students/colleagues as the course draws to a close. Before offering the students some particular suggestions for confronting anti-gay prejudice and harassment in schools, I attempt to make clear that this overarching framework emerges from identifying one's intimate connection to the whole of these critical issues in education. Exhuming one's "taken for granted" assumptions about the world is often characterized by intense struggle, sometimes-disheartening limitation, but always one of ethical obligation. Praxis—critical reflection and responsive action—requires that educators consider seriously their actions in the world and that they believe their actions in schools actually have the potential for making a more just and loving world, in the here and now. Having said that, I recommend some concrete suggestions in this arduous, yet compelling task. I briefly present them here for further contemplation and informed action (Griffin 1995, 61–63).

Teachers can:

- Evaluate and monitor their own attitudes and actions about homo/heterosexuality. Stop behaviors that either encourage a prejudiced or hostile environment for gay and lesbian students or condone any anti-gay actions by any student.

- Inventory their own heterosexist beliefs, assumptions, and actions that unnecessarily and unintentionally create an environment of shame, humiliation, or embarrassment for gay and lesbian students and teachers.

- Refrain from assuming that all students are heterosexual. Some probably are lesbian, gay, or bisexual. Others may be questioning their sexual identity.

- Realize the fact that learning about gays and lesbians does not cause young people to become gay, though it might encourage those who are struggling with their sexual identity to feel better about themselves. Present positive gay and lesbian role models.

- Use homophobic remarks in class and in after-school practices as "teachable moments."

- Understand the necessity of *age-appropriate approaches* to sexual orientation and alternative lifestyles. View the award-winning documentary film *It's Elementary* for guidance.

- Be available and prepared to talk with students or other teachers who are (1) questioning their sexual orientation, or (2) expressing homophobic beliefs. Many closeted gays use homophobic slurs and antigay epithets to buttress an outwardly heterosexual persona.

- Identify and readily make available pertinent resources for students and parents who need them, such as Parents and Friends of Lesbians & Gays (PFLAG, www.pflag.org); the Gay Straight Alliances (GSA), an extension of the Gay, Lesbian, Straight Education Network (GLSEN, www.glsen.org).

- Develop support networks with other teachers, parents, and administrators concerned about the well-being and safety of gay, lesbian, and bisexual students.

- Request that teacher's associations provide programs about homophobia and how to meet the needs of lesbian, gay, and bisexual students.

- Invite a guest, former students, counseling professional, or current faculty member who is gay or lesbian to speak about gay and lesbian issues for their students.

- Post informational items that address gay and lesbian issues in your classrooms. Display, in a place of visual prominence, the Pink Triangle—universally associated with safe zones for gay, lesbian, and bisexual people.

- Understand more fully your authority and power as a positive role model for students, and the respect you inherently garner from your students. Contemplate the fact that what you don't say is just as important as what you do.

- Challenge zero tolerance policies that do not address sexual orientation, anti-gay harassment and hate-based violence in schools.
- (For gay, lesbian, and bisexual educators.) Try to be as open and candid as you safely can about who you are. All youth need to know gay adults who are leading satisfying, productive, and meaningful lives.
- (For heterosexual educators.) Give unwavering support for your gay and lesbian colleagues by speaking out against antigay attitudes, actions, and policies.

Encourage administrators to:

- Establish non-discrimination and anti-harassment policies that include sexual orientation. Ensure that all teachers, parents, and students understand what actions are unacceptable, and what procedures are to be followed when the policies are violated.

- Establish non-discrimination and anti-harassment policies in the local, regional, state, and national education organizations that govern educational programs.

- Provide teachers with anti-homophobia education and gay and lesbian issues programmmg focused on the needs of gay, lesbian, and bisexual students.

- Initiate and develop strategies for addressing homophobia among parents.

- Be open and forthright in their attitudes, behavior, and conduct that openly address the physical, mental, and spiritual safety and well-being of gay/lesbian, and bisexual teachers, staff, and students.

Encourage parents to:

- Know their child's school or university program—its teachers, administrators, department head, and faculty. Inquire about its policies on discrimination, harassment, and sexual orientation. Talk to other parents.
- Challenge their own prejudices and biases about gay, lesbian, and bisexual people and evaluate how they condone or reaffirm anti-gay prejudice in their children.
- Understand that for adolescent boys and male teens, there is an especially great deal of social stigmatization and harassment for those who do not conform to cultural norms of masculinity. Explore the ways in which they support or discourage their son's interests and aptitudes, regardless of gender norms.
- Understand that a teacher's sexual orientation does not determine his or her ability to be an effective and respected professional.
- Contact a local chapter of Parents and Friends of Gays and Lesbians (PFLAG) if necessary for information and support.
- Contemplate the difficult and arduous struggle their child suffers and endures as a gay, lesbian, or bisexual person.
- Show sensitivity, caring, and support, regardless of their personal belief system, if their son or daughter comes out to them as a gay, lesbian, or bisexual. Remember that sexual orientation is a leading and contributing factor to teen depression, dropout rate, and suicide.

References

Besner, F., & Spungin, C. (1995). *Gay & Lesbian Students: Understanding Their Needs*. Philadelphia: Taylor & Francis.

Chasnoff, D., & Cohen, H. (1996). *It's Elementary: Talking About Gay Issues in Schools*. Ho-ho-kus, NJ: New Day Films.

Edwards, A. (1997). Let's stop ignoring our gay and lesbian youth. *Educational Leadership*, April.

Friend, R. (1986). The individual and social psychology of aging: Clinical implications for lesbians and gay men. *Journal of Homosexuality, 14*, 307–331.

Gay, Lesbian, Straight Education Network (GLSEN) (2001). Report of School Climate for Gays & Lesbians. www.glsen.org.

Gilbert, D. (2001). *High School Climate for Gay Youth Survey*. Clinton, NY: Zogby International/Hamilton College.

Gonsiorek, J. (1987). *Homosexuality and Psychotherapy: A Practitioner's Handbook of Affirmative Models*. New York: Haworth Press.

Griffin, P. (1995). Homophobia in sport: Addressing the needs of lesbian and gay high school athletes. In G. Unks (Ed.), *The Gay Teen: Educational Practice and Theory for Lesbian, Gay, and Bisexual Adolescents*, pp. 53–66. New York: Routledge.

Herek, G. (1984). Beyond "homophobia": A social psychological perspective on attitudes towards lesbians and gay men. *Journal of Homosexuality, 10*, 1–21.

Hytten, K. (1998). The ethics of cultural studies. *Educational Studies, 29*(3), 247–265.

Jung, P., & Smith, R. (1993). *Heterosexism: An Ethical Challenge*. Albany: State University of New York Press.

Lehne, G. (1976) Homophobia among men. In D. David & R. Brannon (Eds.), *The Forty-Nine Percent Majority: The Male Sex Role*, pp. 66–88. Reading, MA: Addison-Wesley.

Lipkin, A. (1994). The case for a gay and lesbian curriculum. *The High School Journal 77*, I.

MacDonald, A. (1976). Homophobia: Its roots and meanings. *Homosexual Counseling Journal, 3*(1), 23–33.

Rochlin, M. (1985). The heterosexual questionnaire. In G. Back (Ed.), *Are You Still My Mother?* West Hollywood, CA: Warner Books.

Reflection Questions

1. Identify key trends and issues that you believe will have an impact on 21st century schools and classrooms. Discuss how these trends and issues will influence schools and the changing roles and responsibilities of teachers.

2. Find an online philosophy of education inventory or ask your teacher for one. Take the inventory and find out which educational philosophy is most similar to your values and beliefs about education. Using your dominant philosophy as a guide, discuss how you will answer the questions presented in the introduction; specifically, discuss how you will address and accommodate individual differences. Remember, if there are discrepancies between your beliefs and your actions, you will need to provide a rationale for those shifts.

3. The curriculum typically reflects the values and beliefs of the dominant group in society. Is it possible to create a school environment that addresses the discrimination and bias that may be present in the curriculum? Defend your answer.

4. Research the changing demographics of 21st century America. Discuss the educational challenges presented by these changing demographics. What changes will have to occur in schools in order to successfully address the needs of families and children? What changes must be made in teacher preparation in order to prepare teachers to work with diverse groups of learners?

5. Do you have a personal story of how being different in any of the ways that one might be different has negatively impacted the educational experience of someone in school? The story can be your story or that of someone you know. Write up the story in a case study format and present it to the class for discussion.

Contributors

Angela Anselmo is a faculty member of the City University of New York. She received her PhD in bilingual developmental psychology from Yeshiva University. Dr. Anselmo is an ordained interfaith minister and Director of the SEEK (Search for Education, Elevation, and Knowledge) Program at Baruch College in New York. Her research interests include bilingualism, counseling, and spirituality. In addition to numerous articles in professional journals within the fields of sociology of language and multicultural education.

Eleanor J. Blair received her PhD from the University of Tennessee, Knoxville. She is an associate professor at Western Carolina University where she teaches foundations of education courses in curriculum, teacher leadership and history/philosophy of education at WCU and in Jamaica through the WCU-Jamaica program. She is a frequent presenter at regional, national, and international conferences, and she is the editor of two readers: *Thinking About Schools: A Foundations of Education Reader* (2011) and *Teacher Leadership: The "New" Foundation of Education* (2011). Her work utilizes qualitative methodologies and critical pedagogical frameworks to explore teaching, learning and leading in contemporary schools. References to her research on teacher moonlighting and the significance of place in the preparation of teacher leaders in rural communities occur in both popular and professional publications.

Michele Brigham taught high school special education and music at Albemarle County Public Schools, Charlottesville, Virginia.

Sandra A. Butvilofsky is a professional researcher associate at the BUENO Center at the University of Colorado-Boulder, teaches graduate-level courses, and is the director of the Colorado Literacy Squared® Research Project. Butvilofsky also has experience as a bilingual classroom teacher and a trained Descubrimiento a la Lectura/Reading Recovery teacher. Her research interests include classroom-based research in bilingual context with a focus on Spanish and English writing development of bilingual Latino elementary children.

Paul R. Carr is Associate Professor in the Departments of Sociology and Interdisciplinary Studies at Lakehead University, Orillia. His research focuses on democracy, critical pedagogy, media literacy, and peace studies, and he has some 50 articles and book chapters published in these areas. Recent books include *Doing Democracy: Striving for Political Literacy and Social Justice* (2008) (with Darren Lund) and the edited volume, *Pedagogies of Kindness and Respect: On the Lives and Education of Children* (2015) (with P. L. Thomas, Julie A. Gorlewski, and Brad J. Porfilio).

Michele Collay is Professor of Education at the University of New England in Maine where she oversees dissertation research in a fully online doctoral program in Educational Leadership. A former public school music teacher, she is a scholar practitioner who seeks to align teaching and scholarship in higher education and K–12 schools. Her research area is teacher professional socialization with attention to how race, class, and gender shape teachers' professional identities. Her 2011 book with Jossey-Bass, *Everyday Teacher Leadership: Taking Action Where You Are*, recognizes and celebrates the power of teacher leadership in schools. Other recent publications focus on transformational curriculum design that supports the development of leaders for social justice and equity.

Mary Cowhey has taught first and second grade at Jackson St. School in Northampton, MA, since 1997 and is the author of *Black Ants and Buddhists: Thinking Critically and Teaching Differently in the Primary Grades* (2006), winner of the 2008 National Association for Multicultural Education Philip C. Chinn Multicultural Book Award and the 2007 *Skipping Stones* magazine Multicultural Book Award. She is currently a Title I math teacher and math coach at Jackson St. School. She was a community organizer for fourteen years before becoming a teacher. She has received numerous awards for her teaching and activism, including the Milken National Educator Award and the Anti-Defamation League World of Difference Award.

Gregory J. Cramer, a bilingual social studies teacher, has been working in the Milwaukee Public School System for 11 years. He helped found and manage a small bilingual high school dedicated to promoting high levels of student achievement through bilingualism and biliteracy. Cramer has also taught English-as-a-second-language and literature, served as band and drama coach, and developed a school-wide sustained silent reading program. He received his PhD in Education from the University of Wisconsin, Milwaukee, in 2012.

Lisa Delpit attended the Harvard Graduate School of Education where she received her master's and doctoral degrees in Curriculum, Instruction, and Research. She was the recipient of the MacArthur "Genius" Fellowship in 1990. Currently, she is the Felton G. Clark Professor of Education at Southern University in Baton Rouge, Louisiana. She is best known for her essay, "The Silenced Dialogue: Power and Pedagogy in Educating Other People's Children" (1988) as well as for her books, *Other People's Children: Cultural Conflict in the Classroom* (1995) and *Multiplication Is for White People: Raising Expectations for Other People's Children* (2012).

John Dewey was the most significant educational thinker of his era and, many would argue, of the 20th century. As a philosopher, social reformer and educator, he changed fundamental approaches to teaching and learning. Dewey's *Democracy and Education: An Introduction to the Philosophy of Education* (1916) is a key text in most philosophy of education courses. His ideas about education sprang from a philosophy of pragmatism and were central to the Progressive Movement in schooling. In light of his importance, it is ironic that many of his theories have been relatively poorly understood and haphazardly applied over the past hundred years.

Robin DiAngelos is an assistant professor in the faculty of Education at Westfield State University in Massachusetts. Her research is in social justice education, Whiteness studies, and discourse analysis. She is concerned with the challenges of a predominantly White teaching force and an increasingly diverse student population. Her articles have appeared in journals including *Journal of Understanding and Dismantling Privilege*, *International Journal of Critical Pedagogy*, and *Equity & Excellence in Education*. She has twice been honored with the Student's Choice Award for Educators of the Year. She has provided diversity and antiracism training for a wide range of organizations, including the City of Seattle.

Patrick J. Finn is Associate Professor Emeritus of Education at the University at Buffalo, State University of New York. Finn was named the Robert F. and Augusta Finkelstein Memorial Lecturer for fall 2008 at Adelphi University. He is coeditor (with Mary E. Finn) of *Teacher Education with an Attitude: Preparing Teachers to Educate Working-Class Students in Their Collective Self-Interest*, published by SUNY Press.

Henry Giroux currently holds the Global TV Network Chair Professorship at McMaster University in the Department of English and Cultural Studies, and a Distinguished Visiting Professorship at Ryerson University. Giroux's work focuses on cultural studies, youth, democratic theory, public education, and the politics of higher education. Giroux has written over 55 books, including *On Critical Pedagogy* (2011), *Twilight of the Social: Resurgent Publics in the Age of Disposability* (2012), *Disposable Youth: Racialized Memories and the Culture of Cruelty* (2012), *Youth in Revolt: Reclaiming a Democratic Future* (2013), and *The Educational Deficit and the War on Youth* (2013). His two most recent books are *Neoliberalism's War on Higher Education* (2014) and *The Violence of Organized Forgetting: Thinking Beyond America's Disimagination Machine* (2014).

Julie A. Gorlewski is Assistant Professor of Secondary Education at the State University of New York at New Paltz. She earned a PhD in social foundations of education from the University of New York at Buffalo. She edits the column, "Research for the Classroom," in *English Journal*, has published numerous articles and chapters, and recently authored *Power, Resistance, and Literacy: Writing for Social Justice*, the recipient of the American Educational Studies Association's Critics Choice Award in 2011.

Aaron David Gresson III is Professor of Education and Human Development at The Pennsylvania State University. He writes on African American diaspora studies, psychology and communications, cultural studies, and pedagogy, and is the author of several books including the award-winning *The Recovery of Race in America* (1995) and *America's Atonement: Racial Pain, Recovery Rhetoric, and the Pedagogy of Healing* (2004).

Pat Hinchey holds an EdD from Teachers College, Columbia University, and is Professor of Education at Pennsylvania State University. Her research interests center on issues of equity and the undermining of education for democracy. Hinchey is the author of numerous articles and editorial pieces. Her popular introduction to critical theory, *Finding Freedom in the Classroom* (1998) published by Peter Lang, earned the 1998 American Educational Studies Association Critic's Choice Award. Having written extensively on the translation of critical theory to classroom practice, more recently she has turned her attention to teacher assessment and proposals for restructuring the teaching profession.

James M. Kauffman is Professor Emeritus of Education, Department of Curriculum, Instruction, and Special Education, University of Virginia, Charlottesville. His primary areas of interest are in special education generally, and more specifically, emotional and behavioral disorders and learning disabilities. Additionally, his work also focuses on the areas of policy and ethical issues in education and the history of special education.

Joe Kincheloe was a professor and Canada Research Chair at the Faculty of Education, McGill University in Montreal, Quebec, Canada. He wrote more than 45 books, numerous book chapters, and hundreds of journal articles on issues including critical pedagogy, educational research, urban studies, cognition, curriculum, and cultural studies. Kincheloe received his doctorate from the University of Tennessee.

Michelle G. Knight is an associate professor of Education at Teachers College, Columbia University, Curriculum and Teaching, New York, NY. Her scholarly interests include equity issues in urban education, teacher education, multicultural feminisms and feminist pedagogies, and African American teaching practices with diverse populations.

Cara Kronen was raised in New York City. She taught Social Studies and was a College Advisor in a South Bronx high school. She holds a PhD in Urban Systems with a concentration in Urban Education Policy from Rutgers University-Newark. She is currently an assistant professor of Education at the Borough of Manhattan Community College where she teaches Social and Psychological Foundations of Education. Her research includes work on postsecondary access and outcomes of low-income high school students as well as school choice in urban communities.

Gloria Ladson-Billings is the Kellner Family Professor of Urban Education at the University of Wisconsin. She is credited with coining the term "culturally responsive pedagogy," and is one of the leaders in the field of culturally relevant teaching. Her book *The Dreamkeepers: Successful Teachers of African American Children* (1994) offers a close look at the qualities to be found in teachers whose African American students achieve academic success. She is a past president of the American Educational Research Association (AERA). Among her accomplishments as AERA president was a presidential address that aimed to redefine the "achievement gap" as "educational debt"—highlighting the social, political, and economic factors that have disproportionately affected children of color in our schools. Ladson-Billings has been elected to membership in the National Academy of Education and has been a senior fellow in urban education of the Annenberg Institute for School Reform at Brown University.

Bettina L. Love is an award-winning author and associate professor of Educational Theory & Practice at the University of Georgia. Her research focuses on the ways in which urban youth negotiate Hip Hop music and culture to form social, cultural, and political identities to create new and sustaining ways of thinking about urban education and social justice. She also concentrates on transforming urban classrooms through the use of non-traditional educational curricula and classroom structures. Recently, Dr. Love was named the Nasir Jones Fellow at the W. E. B. Du Bois Research Center at Harvard University. She will begin her fellowship at Harvard in the spring of 2016, where she will develop a multimedia Hip Hop civics curriculum for middle to high school students.

Barbara Madeloni, currently the president of the 110,000-member Massachusetts Teachers Association, is a strong advocate for students and educators in the state's public schools and public higher education system. She is committed to growing an activist union that builds alliances with parents, students, and community members to give educators a strong voice in public education. Madeloni is on leave as a senior lecturer in the Labor Studies Department at the University of Massachusetts in Amherst. Beginning in 2004, she worked at the UMass School of Education, where among other responsibilities she coordinated the Secondary Teacher Education Program.

Kathleen McGee was a special education teacher at the high school level, Westerville Public Schools, Westerville, Ohio.

Yolanda (Jolie) Medina is Associate Professor of the Teacher Education Department at BMCC/CUNY where she teaches Social Foundations of Education and Art Education courses and is the coordinator of the Childhood and Bilingual Childhood Education Programs. She is the author of *Critical Aesthetic*

Pedagogy: Toward a Theory of Self and Social Empowerment (2012), *Latinos on the East Coast: A Critical Reader* (2015), and of several articles and book chapters on Critical Pedagogy, Cultural Studies, and Aesthetic Education. She is editor of the Critical Studies of Latinos/as in the Americas Book Series published by Peter Lang, President of the American Educational Studies Association (AESA), and the Vice President of the Maxine Greene Center for Aesthetic Education and Social Imagination.

Pedro Noguera is the Peter L. Agnew Professor of Education at New York University. He is a sociologist whose scholarship and research focuses on the ways in which schools are influenced by social and economic conditions, as well as by demographic trends in local, regional, and global contexts. Noguera holds faculty appointments in the departments of Teaching and Learning and Humanities and Social Sciences at the Steinhardt School of Culture, Education, and Development. He also serves as an affiliated faculty member in NYU's Department of Sociology. He is the executive director of the Metropolitan Center for Research on Equity and the Transformation of Schools. He has published over 200 research and scholarly articles, monographs, research reports, and editorials on topics such as urban school reform, education policy, conditions that promote student achievement, the role of education in community development, youth violence, and race and ethnic relations in American society.

Sandra Liliana Pucci is an associate professor of linguistics at the University of Wisconsin-Milwaukee, coordinates the Adult/University-Level TESOL Certificate Program at her institution, and teaches courses in bilingualism, second language acquisition, and sociolinguistics. She is the recipient of various bilingual teacher development grant from the U.S. Department of Education, as well as Refugee Teacher Training awards from the Department of Health and Human Services. Dr. Pucci currently serves on the executive board of directors of the Alliance for Multilingual and Multicultural Education (AMME). Her research interests are in the development of bilingualism and biliteracy in speakers of heritage language.

Diane Ravitch graduated from the Houston public schools, Wellesley College, and Columbia University. She is Research Professor of Education at New York University and a historian of education and a renowned author of books and articles on educational reform. From 1991 to 1993, she was Assistant Secretary of Education and Counselor to Secretary of Education Lamar Alexander in the administration of President George H.W. Bush. She was responsible for the Office of Educational Research and Improvement in the U.S. Department of Education. As Assistant Secretary, she led the federal effort to promote the creation of voluntary state and national academic standards. From 1995 until 2005, she held the Brown Chair in Education Studies at the Brookings Institution and edited the *Brookings Papers on Education Policy*. Before entering government service, she was Adjunct Professor of History and Education at Teachers College, Columbia University. Ravitch is the author or editor of over twenty books, including *Left Back: A Century of Failed School Reforms* (2000), *The Death and Life of the Great American School System: How Testing and Choice Are Undermining Education* (2010), and more recently, *Reign of Error: The Hoax of the Privatization Movement and the Danger to America's Public Schools* (2013). Her articles have appeared in numerous newspapers and magazines.

D. Kim Reid is a professor of Education at Teachers College, Columbia University, Curriculum and Teaching, New York, NY. Her scholarly interests embrace the sociopolitical construction of disability, particularly with respect to humor, as well as special education's role as an unintentional tool of institutional racism.

William Reynolds received his EdD in curriculum theory from the University of Rochester. Dr. Reynolds teaches in the Department of Curriculum, Foundations, and Reading at Georgia Southern University. He has authored, co-authored, edited, and co-edited numerous books including *Curriculum: A*

River Runs Through It (2013); *Expanding Curriculum Theory: Dispositions and Lines of Flight* (2004); *The Civic Gospel: A Political Cartography of Christianity* (2009); and *A Curriculum of Place: Understandings Emerging Through the Southern Mist* (2013). He has also published many articles and chapters on issues of curriculum and cultural studies.

Doug Risner, PhD, MFA, is Professor of Dance at Wayne State University, Detroit, Michigan, USA, and focuses his research on the sociology of dance training and education, curriculum theory and policy, social foundations of dance pedagogy, gender in dance, and online learning and web-based curriculum design. He is the author of *Stigma & Perseverance in the Lives of Boys Who Dance* (2009); *Hybrid Lives of Teaching Artists in Dance and Theatre Arts: A Critical Reader* (2014) with Dr. Mary Anderson; and *Gender, Sexuality and Identity: Critical Issues in Dance Education* (2015). Risner served as Editor-in-Chief of the *Journal of Dance Education* from 2006 to 2012 and is currently Associate Editor of the international journal *Research in Dance Education*.

Alma Rubal-Lopez is a faculty member of the City University of New York and Professor of Education at Brooklyn College. She received her PhD in bilingual developmental psychology from Yeshiva University. Dr. Rubal-Lopez co-edited *Post-Imperial English: Status Change in Former British and American Colonies 1940–1990*.

Ozlem Sensoy is an assistant professor in the Faculty of Education at Simon Frasier University in Vancouver, Canada. She conducts research in social justice education, critical media literacy, and cultural studies. Her research articles have appeared in journals including *Gender & Education, Discourse: Studies in the Cultural Politics*, and *Rethinking Schools*. She is the editor of *Muslim Voices in Schools: Narratives of Identity and Pluralism*, which in 2010 won the National Association for Multicultural Education Philip C. Chinn book award.

Joel Spring received his PhD in educational policy studies from the University of Wisconsin. He is currently a professor at Queens College and the Graduate Center of the City University of New York. Professor Spring's major research interests are history of education, globalization and education, multicultural education, Native American culture, the politics of education, and human rights education. He is the author of over twenty scholarly books that include some of his most important textbooks: *American Education* (now in its 16th edition); *The American School* (now in its 9th edition); *Conflict of Interests: The Politics of American Education* (now in its 5th edition), and *Deculturalization and the Struggle for Equality: A Brief History of Dominated Cultures in the United States* (now in its 7th edition).

Printed in Australia
AUHW011808170821
350528AU00006B/8

9 781433 129414